EARLY CHAUHĀN DYNASTIES

Sarasvatī, Goddess of Wisdom and Learning, from Pallu, Rajasthan.

Early Chauhān Dynasties

(*A Study of Chauhān Political History, Chauhān Political Institutions and life in the Chauhān Dominions From* 800 *to* 1316 A.D.)

DASHARATHA SHARMA, M.A., D. Litt.,
Professor of History (*Retd.*);
Director, Project of the History of Rājasthan
Jodhpur University, Jodhpur

With a Foreword By
SARDAR K.M. PANIKKAR

MOTILAL BANARSIDASS
Delhi :: Varanasi :: Patna

©MOTILAL BANARSIDASS
Indological Publishers & Booksellers
Head Office : BUNGALOW ROAD, JAWAHAR NAGAR, DELHI-7
Branches : 1. CHOWK, VARANASI-1 (U.P.)
2. ASHOK RAJPATH, PATNA-4 (BIHAR)

ISBN 0 8426 0618 1

First Edition : *Delhi*, 1959
Second Revised Edition : *Delhi*, 1975

Printed in India
BY SHANTILAL JAIN AT SHRI JAINENDRA PRESS, BUNGALOW ROAD, JAWAHAR NAGAR, DELHI-7 AND PUBLISHED BY SUNDARLAL JAIN, MOTILAL BANARSIDASS, BUNGALOW ROAD, JAWAHAR NAGAR, DELHI-7

To
Every Lover of the History
and
Culture of Rajasthan

तत्तत्पुरातननिबन्धविमर्शपूर्णं
श्रीचाहमानकुलवृत्तमिदं यशस्यम् ।
ऐतिह्यतत्त्वसुविकासनसद्गुणेन
संराध्नुयाद्बुधवरानितिहासविज्ञान् ॥

FOREWORD

The struggle of Hindu Kingdoms during the three centuries of Islam's fight for the political domination of North India is one of the least known chapters of India's mediaeval history. European historians, depending almost exclusively on the chronicles of Muslim court annalists, had familiarised us with the invaders' version of the conquest. But a little reflection would have shown that Hindu dynasties could not have survived in Rājasthān, Central India and Bundelkhaṇḍ, if the resistance of the people had not been determined, continuous and effective over large areas. It is in this important field that Dr. Dasharatha Sharma has long been known as a patient, competent and accurate worker; and his numerous contributions, published in Journals devoted to historical research, have helped to shed new light on this period of history.

In his present volume Dr. Sharma gives us, for the first time, a connected history of the Chauhāns, from their beginnings in Bhṛgukachchha in eighth century A.D. to the time of Alā-ud-dīn Khalji and Hammīra in the fourteenth. From the time of Mohammad Ghorī's invasion, the Chauhāns played a heroic role in the defence of freedom which ends only with the death in battle of Kānhaḍ Deva, defending his capital against the might of Alā-ud-dīn. Two of the greatest and famous Chauhān rulers whose achievements have been immortalised in literature Pṛthvīrāja III of Ajmer and Hammīra of Raṇthambhore, deserve to rank high in India's role of honour.

I have always held that works, like *Pṛthvīrāja-vijaya and Hammīra-mahākāvya*, are entitled to greater credence as historical sources than has so far been accorded to them. Their *kāvya* style and rhetorical exaggerations should not mislead the discriminatory student into the idea that the incidents around which they weave their narrative are not historically true. Even Bāṇa's *Harshacharita*, second only to *Kādambarī* as a prose-*kāvya*, has been found to be a store-house of historical information. Dr. Dasharatha Sharma, I am glad to see, has made a discriminatory use of literary material derived from different sources.

Dr. Sharma has, in fact, used every source available to a student of Indian history, inscriptions, bardic chronicles, *praśastikāvyas*. He has also laid under contributions body of Jaina literature which, so far, had not been greatly used by historians. The result has been not only an accurate and impartial history, fully documented in every sense, but a very readable book which could be appreciated by the general student.

The present volume should help to set at rest many favourite superstitions of foreign scholars. The foreign origin of Agnikula Rājpūts is one of the pet doctrines originated by Crooke and familiarised by Vincent Smith, that "the Agnikula myth represents a right of purgation by fire...whereby the impurity of the foreigners was removed and they became fitted to enter the Hindu caste system." Dr. Sharma has shown that the Agnikula myth goes back to the Rāmāyaṇa and is, in fact, traditional to Aryan Hindus. Dr. Sharma also establishes conclusively that contrary to the common belief that India fell an easy prey to Muslim invaders, and the resistance of the Hindu rulers broke down after the defeat of Pṛthvīrāja, the descendants of the Chauhān Emperor, even after they lost Ajmer, continued to fight with determination for two hundred years.

Considerable new light is also thrown on the relations between the Chaulukya Empire and the Chauhāns of Śākambharī, especially during the reigns of Siddharāja and Kumārapāla. Undoubtedly both these rulers exercised imperial sway, but how far the Chauhāns had been reduced to the position of feudatories, or had remained independent sovereigns accepting the suzerainty of the Gujarāt kings, had remained a doubtful question. Dr. Sharma traces these relations in some detail, and discusses the campaigns dealing with Arṇorāja's discomfiture at the hands of Kumārapāla.

A valuable portion of the book is devoted to the social and economic condition of the Chauhān territory during the eleventh, twelfth and thirteenth centuries. The enumeration and identification of the towns and villages in the country collected from the literature of the time is especially important. The names of the coins in use, the weights and measures will also be found very useful. The literary history of the period is also dealt with adequately. A period that produced Chand Bardāī, Jayānaka,

Nayachandra Sūri and saw the beginning of Ḍingal literature in Rājasthān and could count such names as Hema Chandra Sūri, Someśvara and Bālachandra in Gujarāt, must necessarily be considered an important one in the history of Indian literature. Dr. Sharma has only touched on the subject as his theme is not literary history. I can only express the hope that with his wide knowledge of Hindu and Jaina literature, of Sanskrit and of Ḍingal, Dr. Sharma will give us a companion volume, dealing with mediaeval literature in Rājasthān and Gujarāt. Dr. Sharma deserves the thanks of all lovers of Indian history for this competent and workman-like volume which, I trust, will be followed by many others of equal merit.

K.M. PANIKKAR

PREFACE TO THE FIRST EDITION

There is no better theme for history than the determined struggle of a brave people for the maintenance of its liberty, religion and culture. According to all our accounts, old as well as new, the eponymous hero, Chāhamāna or Chauhāna, was created to fight for and defend all that is best in the Indian values of life. His descendants, Arṇorāja, Vigraharāja IV, Pṛithvīrāja III, Kelhaṇa, Kīrtipāla, Hammīra, Sātala and, Kānhaḍadeva, to name only the best known among them, did much to fulfil this mission; and that their example remained neither unadmired nor unimitated can be seen from some thing akin to national resistance that Alā-ud-dīn Khaljī had to encounter in the desert State of Jālor.

A detailed history of the Chauhāns and the life in their dominions has long been overdue; and this thesis, which was approved for the award of the D.Litt. degree by the University of Agra and is published here in a slightly revised form[1] may in some measure supply this desideratum. I have utilised some newly discovered Chauhān inscriptions and old manuscripts, not available to Dr. J. Kielhorn, Dr. D.R. Bhandarkar, and Mahāmahopādhyāya Dr. G.H. Ojha, and reinterpreted some of the old records, literary as well as epigraphic, discarding even generally accepted interpretations, if they either went against Sanskrit grammar or well-known facts of history. Praise has been given where it is due; but I have not failed to point out also the political blunders of Chauhān leaders like Pṛthvīrāja III and Hammīra.

Part I (Chapters I-XX) deals with political history. Part II (Chapters XXI-XXVII), which occupies almost as much space as the first one, gives the first systematic account of the religious, social, economic, literary and educational conditions in the Chauhān dominions from c. 800 to 1300 A.D. In the last chapter I have discussed the causes of Chauhān failure in their fight against the Muslims. I hope to present this material

1. For some of the revised material see the *Addenda*.

more fully in my forthcoming work entitled, "Life in Rājasthān, 600-1400 A.D."

My grateful thanks are due to *kavi-vidvad-bāndhava*, the historian-statesman, Sardar K.M. Panikkar, at whose advice I took up this work. He has now obliged me still further by kindly contributing a very valuable and suggestive Foreword. To my examiners, Dr. Jadu Nath Sarkar and Dr. D.R. Bhandarkar, I am indebted for many valuable suggestions. Thanks are due to my elder brother, Vidyāvāchaspati Prof. Vidyadhar Shastri, M.A., and my wife, Malathi Sharma, M.A., for the ungrudging assistance rendered by them; to Sri U.C. Bhattacharya, Curator, Rajpūtānā Museum, for supplying estampages of some Chauhān inscriptions; to the Birla Educational Trust, Pilani, and Śārdūl Rājasthānī Institute, Bīkaner for the illustrations of Sarasvatī and the Jaina images of Neminātha and Śāntinātha; to my *dharma-bhrātā*, the renowned Hindi scholar, Dr. Dashrath Ojha, M.A., Ph.D., for his arranging the publication of the work; to Sri Brij Narain Sharma, for the help rendered in proof-reading; to Sri Brahma Nand Sharma for preparing the map; and to Messrs. S. Chand and Co., the publishers, and the Central Electric Press, the printers, for the care with which they have brought out the book. My only regret is that on account of various circumstances, it could not be published during the life time of my revered father, *Vidyāvāchaspati* Pandit Deviprasad Shastri (from whom comes my love of research work and Sanskrit literature) and *Guruvara* Mahāmahopādhyāya Dr. G.H. Ojha who readily put his valuable collection of inscriptions and books at my disposal. *Tebhyo Gurubhyaḥ satataṁ namaḥ.*

"Navin Vasant".
Krishnanagar, Delhi-6,
Ist March, 1959.

DASHARATHA SHARMA

PREFACE TO THE SECOND EDITION

There have been some changes in the second edition but ill health has prevented me from doing more. I thank M/s Motilal Banarsidas for bringing out this edition. They were also kind enough to arrange for the correction of proofs.

अङ्गं गलितं पलितं मुण्डं दशनविहीनं जातं तुण्डम् ।
वृद्धो याति गृहीत्वा दण्डं तदपि न मुञ्चत्याशापिण्डम् ॥
भज गोविन्दं० ॥

[*The body has become worn out, hairs have turned grey, the teeth have fallen, and the old man is walking supporting himself on a stick, yet desire leaves him not. Worship the Lord, etc.*]

Dasharatha Sharma

Delhi :
1st May, 1975.

DATES IN THE CHRISTIAN ERA

for

SOME CHAUHAN INSCRIPTIONS

(1)	V. 813, solar eclipse, Bhartṛvaḍḍha II's Hansot Plates. =	28th October, 756 A.D.
(2)	V. 898, Vaiśākha Śukla 2, Chaṇḍa-mahāsena's Dholpur inscription. =	16th April, 842 A.D.
(3)	Saṁvat 1147, Vaiśākha sudi 2, Jojala-deva's Nāḍol inscription. =	23 rd April, 1091 A.D.
(4)	V. 1176, Jyeṣṭha vadi 8, Thursday, Ratnapāla's Sevāḍī Plates. =	22nd April, 1120 A.D.
(5)	V. 1172, Sevāḍi inscription of the time of Kaṭukarāja. =	1115 A.D.
(6)	V. 1198, Śrāvaṇa vadi 8, Sunday, Nāḍol inscription of Rāyapāla's time. =	16th August, 1142 A.D.
(7)	V. 1200, Kārttika vadi 1, Sunday, Nādlāi Jaina inscription of Rāyapāla's reign. =	26th September, 1143 A.D.
(8)	V. 1200, Jyeṣṭha sudi, 5, Thursday, Nādlāi stone inscription of Rāyapāla's reign. =	20th May, 1143 A.D.
(9)	V. 1200, Bhādrapada 8, Wednesday, Nāḍol inscription of Rāyapāla's reign. =	23rd August, 1144 A.D.
(10)	V. 1209, Māgha vadi 14, Saturday, Kirāḍū inscription of Alhaṇa. =	24th January, 1153 A.D.
(11)	V. 1210, Mārga sudi 5, Sunday, *Harikeli* Ajmer inscription of Vigraharāja IV. =	22nd November, 1153 A.D.
(12)	V. 1210, Jyeṣṭha sudi 6, Thursday, Bhaṭūnd inscription of Sri Vaijāka. =	20th May, 1154 A.D.
(13)	V. 1213, Mārga vadi 10, Friday, Nāḍol plate of Kumārapāla's time. =	9th November, 1156 A.D.
(14)	V. 1213, Bhādrapada sudi, 14. Tuesday, Jaina inscription of Vaijalladeva's time. =	21st August, 1156 A.D.
(15)	V. 1216, Bālī inscription of Kumāra-pāla's time, Śrāvaṇa vadi, 1, Śukra. =	3rd July, 1159 A.D.

(16)	V. 1218, Śrāvaṇa vadi, 5, Monday, Nāḍol plates of Kīrtipāla. =	25th July, 1160 A.D.
(17)	V. 1218, Śrāvaṇa Sudi 14, Monday, Nāḍol plates of Ahaṇadeva. =	6th August, 1161 A.D.
(18)	V. 1220, Vaiśākha sudi, 15, Thursday, Delhi Pillar inscription of Vigraharāja IV. =	9th April, 1164 A.D.
(19)	V. 1220, Śrāvaṇa vadi 15, Wednesday, solar eclipse, Bāmnerā plate of M. Kelhaṇa (*vide*, however, the footnote). =	3rd July, 1163 A.D.
(20)	V. 1221, Māgha vadi 2, Friday, Sāṇḍerāv inscription of Kelhaṇa. =	Ist January 1165 A.D.
(21)	V. 1224, Phālguna sudi 2, Monday, Sādaḍī inscription of Kelhaṇa's reign. =	12th February, 1168 A.D.
(22)	V. 1230, Āṣāḍha sudi 9, Monday, Revāsā inscription of Someśvara's reign. =	10th June, 1174 A.D.
(23)	V. 1226, Phālguna vadi 3, Thursday, Bijoliā inscription of Someśvara's reign. =	5th February, 1170 A.D.
(24)	V. 1239, Vaiśākha sudi 5, Thursday, Jālor inscription of Mahārāja Samarasiṁhadeva. =	28 th April, 1183 A.D.
(25)	V. 1239, Āśvina vadi 10, Wednesday, Bhīnmāl inscription of Jayatsiṁha (*See* the footnote). =	21st August, 1182 A.D. or 12th Oct. 1183 A.D.
(26)	V. 1258, Chaitra vadi 3, Monday, Bāmnerā inscription of Mahārāja Sāmantasiṁha's time. (*See* the footnote). =	11th February 1202 A.D.
(27)	V. 1258, Māgha sudi 9, Friday, Bāmnerā inscription of Samantasiṁha's time. =	4th January 1202 A.D.
(28)	V. 1258, Chaitra sudi 13, Friday, Sāṇḍerāv inscription of Sāmantasiṁha's reign. =	8th March, 1202 A.D.

(29) V. 1258, Vaiśākha vadi 12, Sunday, = 5th May 1202 Bāmnerā inscription of Sāmantasiṁha's reign. A.D.[1]

1. I am indebted for the equation of the dates to Dr. D.R. Bhandarkar's *Inscriptions of Northern India*. I should like, however, to ascribe No. 19 to Alhaṇa instead of Kelhaṇa who is mentioned here only as a *kanwara*. The words *Mahārājādhirājāśrī-Alhaṇadeva-Kumara-Kelhaṇa-rājye* should be compared with *Mahārāja kula-śrī-Sāṁvatasiṁhadeva-Rājā-śrī-Kānhaḍadeva-rājye* of the Chohtan inscription (EI, XI, p. 60, note 10) where Kānhaḍadeva, though only an heir-apparent, is called a Rājā and made the joint ruler of the kingdom with his father. Kelhaṇa's position in V. 1220 might have been similar.

I do not regard 52 as a Chauhān inscription, because Chauhān rule had not till then extended as far west as Bhinmāl, and, even if it be admitted for the sake of argument that it did, it would be difficult to prove that the rulers of Nāḍol were ever the masters of Bhinmāl. It was probably some Sonigarā chief who first brought it under Chauhāns. On the other hand, I am tentatively putting Nos. 26-29 as Chauhān inscriptions. Dr D. R. Bhandarkar ascribes them to the Guhila ruler Sāmantasiṁha. The provenance of the inscriptions, however, indicates a Chauhān ruler.

ABBREVIATIONS

1. *ABORI*	*Annals of the Bhandarkar Oriental Research Institute.*
2. *ASI* or *ASIR*	*Archaeological Survey of India, Annual Report*
3. *ASR*	*Archaeological Survey Reports by Cunningham.*
4. *ASI, WC.*	*Archaeological Survey of India Reports, Western Circle.*
5. *BBRAS*	Bombay Branch of the Royal Asiatic Society.
6. *BSS*	Bombay Sanskrit Series.
7. *CCIM*	*Catalogue of the Coins in the Indian Museum, Calcutta, Vol. I, V.A. Smith.*
8. *CHI*	*Cambridge History of India.*
9. *CII*	*Corpus Inscriptionum Indicarum.*
10. *DHNI*	*Dynastic History of Northern India by* H.C. Ray, Vols. I and II.
11. *DK*	*Dvyāśrayamahākāvya* of Hemachandra.
12. *ED*	Elliot and Dowson's *History of India as told by its own historians.*
13. *EI*	*Epigraphia Indica.*
14. *G.O.S.*	Gaekwad Oriental Series.
15. *HK*	*History of Kanauj* by Rama Shankar Tripathi.
16. *HM* or *HMK.*	*Hammīramahākāvya* of Nayachandra Sūri, Rajasthan Purātattva Mandir, Jodhpur.
17. *IA.*	*Indian Antiquary.*
18. *JASB*	*Journal of the Asiatic Society of Bengal.*
19. *JASS*	Jaina Atmānanda Sabha Series, Bhavnagar.
20. *JBBRAS* or *JBRAS*	*Journal of the Bombay Branch of the Royal Asiatic Society.*
21. *JRAS*	*Journal of the Royal Asiatic Society.*
22. *KP,*	*Kharataragachchhapaṭṭāvali* of Jinapāla and his successors (also called *Kharataragachchhabṛhad-gurvāvali*).

23. *MER.*	*Madras Epigraphist's Report.*
24. *MT.*	*Muntakhab-ut-Tawārīkh* of Badaunī, English translation.
25. *NPS.*	Nāgarī Prachāriṇī Sabhā, Banaras.
26. *OUP or O.U.P.*	Oxford University Press Edition.
27. *PC.*	*Prabandhachintāmaṇi* of Merutuṅga, Singhī Jaina Granthamālā.
28. *PK.*	*Prabandhakośa* of Rājaśekhara, Singhī Jaina Granthamālā.
29. *PKG.*	Genealogy of the Chauhāns given at the end of the above edition of the *Prabandhakośa.*
30. *PV.*	*Pṛthvīrājavijaya* of Jayānaka, G.H. Ojha and Guleri's edition.
31. *RA.*	*Rāshṭrakūṭas and their Times*, A. S. Altekar.
32. *SC.*	*Surjanacharita* of Chandraśekhara.
33. *SII.*	*South Indian Inscriptions*, Hultzsch.
34. *SJG.*	Singhī Jaina Granthamālā.
35. *TF.*	*Tarikh-i-Firishtā,* Briggs' English translation, Vol. I.
36. *ZDMG.*	*Zeitschrift der Deutschen Morgenlandischen Gesellschaft.*
37. *TN.*	*Tabakat-i-Nāsirī*, Raverty's English translation.

CONTENTS

PART I

Political History

PART II

CHAUHAN ADMINISTRATION AND LIFE IN CHAUHĀN DOMINIONS

INTRODUCTION

The Arab invasion was no 'mere episode' in the history of our country. The Arabs conquered Sind and Multān; they overran Mārwār, Mālwā and Broach and threatened even the independence of Kashmir and Kanauj. And these raids contributed to a fairly permanent change in the political map of western India and the Deccan, for the powers which play the most prominent role in the history of these areas thereafter, almost up to the end of the tenth century, first come to the fore in this period of emergency. India needed people to fight for her culture and independence, and was lucky to have them in the Pratihāras, Rāṣṭrakūṭas and various other clans, now known to us by the generic name Rājpūt or Rājaputra. The Imperial Pratihāra, Nāgabhaṭa I, appeared like Nārāyaṇa to the people, because he "crushed the large armies of the powerful *Mlechchha* ruler, the destroyer of virtue".[1] Nāgabhaṭa II, who captured Turuṣka forts by force, was to them "the Primeval Man (the Supreme Puruṣa)[2] born again"; and his grandson, Mihira-Bhoja, assumed the significant title of *Ādi-varāha*, because he had come to believe that he was divinely commissioned to chastise the enemies of Indian culture and to rescue the people from their tyranny.[3] It was this dynasty, which in the years succeeding the Arab raids, established its supremacy in north India; and it lasted only as long as it remained a good bulwark against Muslim aggression. From the Deccan, the first independent Rāṣṭrakūṭa ruler, Dantidurga, led an attack on the Arabs with the co-operation of perhaps those very clans, the Saindhavas, the Kachchhelas, the Saurāṣṭras, the Chāvoṭakas, the Mauryas and the Gūrjaras who are mentioned in the Nausārī Grant of Pulakeśin Avanijanāśraya of Gujarāt as defeated by the Tājikas, *i.e.*, Arabs, when they tried to "enter the Deccan with a view to conquering all the southern kings." It was not

1. Gwālior inscription of Bhoja, verse 4
2. *Ibid*, verse 8.
3. See my paper, "Rāmabhadra and Bhoja, the Imperial Pratihāras," *IHQ* 1958, June issue.

Dantidurga alone, as generally but wrongly assumed, but probably all these *rājanyas* and perhaps a few more who performed the *hiraṇyagarbha-mahādāna* ceremony at Ujjayinī to celebrate their victory over the Muslim adversaries. For me this co-operative ceremony has no other meaning. The Rāṣṭrakūṭas later on reversed their policy, giving the Arabs various concessions and even appointing them to high official posts within their kingdom.[4] But this should not let us forget that the event which primarily raised high their military prestige and made them more liked by the people than the dynasty they had displaced was in all likelihood Dantidurga's victory over the Arabs.

In north India the Pratihāras were assisted in this fight against the Arabs as well as their schemes of imperial expansion by many clans, among whom the Chauhāns stand the foremost. In 756 A.D. the Chauhān chief, Bhartṛvaḍḍha II, was entrusted with the Government of the Pratihāra outpost of Broach. He probably occupied it, after assisting Nāgabhaṭa I in driving out the Arabs from that area. In 842 A.D. we find the Chauhān *mahāsāmanta*, Chaṇḍamahāsena, keeping the *Mlechchhas* of Dhavalapurī under his control. With their oft-avowed mission of protecting Hindu culture, of which the Agnikula myth may be a distant echo, the Chauhāns may be expected to have assisted the Pratihāras in their further fights also against the Arabs, though we have no record of this fact. Even about the Pratihāras' continued hostilities against these enemies of Indian culture, the only source of information is the account left not by Indians but by foreign travellers like Sulaimān and Al-Masūdī.

Of the Chauhāns' assistance in imperial expansion, again, the evidence is incomplete. When the Imperial Pratihāra, Vatsarāja, contended with Dharmapāla for supremacy in North India, Vatsarāja's trusted feudatory, the Chauhān chief Durlabharāja I of Śākambharī, led his army into Bengāl.[5] His son, Gūvaka I, achieved fame as a warrior at Nāgabhaṭa II's court; but we have no exact idea of the campaigns that brought him this fame. In the reign of Bhoja I, the Chauhāns' fame as

4. See *Indian Archaeology*, 1956-57. pp. 40-41.
5. See below p. 29 for the necessary evidence.
6. See below, p. 21.

doughty warriors remained undimmed; and their assistance was perhaps as eagerly sought for as before.

With the death of Mahīpāla (C.914-942 A.D.) the Pratihāra empire began to decline. Its hold on distant territories slackened, and the Pratihāra feudatories began fighting amongst themselves to gain their own private objectives and ambitions. This phase is represented in this book by the Chauhān-Tomara struggle which assumed serious proportions in the reign of Vākpatirāja I of Śākambharī and ended only with the capture of the Tomara capital of Delhi by Vigraharāja IV. During its course, one Tomara chief was slain, another was thrown into prison. The ambitious Chauhān chief, Siṁharāja, probably died in a battle in which his enemies were backed by his Pratihāra overlord, Vijayapāladeva. It is a pity that these two Rājput clans should have fought with each other and that the Tomaras should ultimately have been forced by circumstances to follow a policy which was obviously anti-national and which from the Chauhān point of view made their liquidation absolutely necessary.[7]

By 973 A.D. the Chauhāns had practically become independent. But with independence came new problems. Inter-statal rivalry became more bitter. The Chauhāns had now to provide also for their own defence against foreign aggression; the days when the Pratihāras could have rushed to their help were over. Inter-statal rivalry is represented mainly by the struggle for supremacy between the Chauhāns of Śākambharī and the Chaulukyas of Gujarāt. The Chauhāns of Nāḍol generally sided with the Chaulukyas. It was this banal rivalry which was largely responsible for the defeat of the Hindus at the hands of Muhammad Ghorī; Pṛthvīrāja III's bad relations with his two other strong neighbours, the Gāhaḍavālas of Kanauj and the Chandels of Khajurāho were, of course, contributory causes. With the Paramāras of Mālwā the Chauhān relations varied though they should generally have been friendly. As one reads the full story of these fateful years, one cannot help wondering why the Hindus did not learn to combine in the face of foreign danger.

Of this danger there had been enough since the accession of Sabuktigin in 977 A.D., and this increased further when

7. See our paper, "New Light on Tomara History," *PIHC.*, 1956.

Mahmūd Ghaznavī annexed the Punjāb. Durlabharāja III of Śākambharī lost his life in a battle with Ibrahim of Ghaznā. Pṛthvīrāja I had to fight against some *Hammīra.* The Ghaznavite general, Muhammad Bahlim, raided many kingdoms of India, including Ajayarāja Chauhān's kingdom of Sapādalakṣa. In the next reign the Muslims reached the walls of Ajmer. They were thrown back. But Kumārapāla of Gujarāt and Arṇorāja of Śākambharī instead of making the best of the weakness of the contemporary Ghaznavites, fought with each other. This unfortunate struggle continued in the reign of Vigraharāja IV, perhaps the most brilliant of the Śākambharī rulers. He beat back a Ghaznavite raid. By conquering Delhi he became the key figure in the struggle for Indian freedom. That he realised fully his responsibility is obvious from the Delhi-Siwālik inscription in which he boasts of having rendered Āryāvarta free from *Mlechchhas*, and also from his assertion that it would be disgraceful not to fight against the Muslims for the protection of Brāhmaṇas, *tīrthas*, temples and also his friends.[8] But with enemies like the Chaulukyas of Gujarāt threatening his rear, he had perforce to leave his mission unfulfilled, hoping however that his successors would go further than he had done. But his son died young, and in the reign of his successor, we find the Chauhāns on the defensive. Pṛthvirāja II merely strengthened the defences of Hānsī. A stronger ruler could at this time have attacked the Ghaznavites and ended their rule in the Punjab.

In 1175 A.D. Muhammad Ghorī began invading Indian territories. When he attacked the kingdom of Gujarāt in 1178 A.D., his army could have been annihilated, if Pṛthvīrāja III had not foolishly listened to the advice of his chief minister, Kadambavāsa, not to assist his neighbours and rivals, the Chaulukyas of Gujarāt. Not long after this we find him fighting against Bhīmadeva II. He looted the territories of Parmardin of Khajurāho, attacked the Paramāras of Ābū and probably came into conflict with the ruler of Kanauj. And all this internecine fighting went on, while Muhammad Ghorī was steadily building up his resources and increasing his territories. Nemesis was bound to overtake such folly.

8. See below p. 69.

With the second battle of Tarāīn, 1192 A.D., which might have been unnecessary if Pṛthvīrāja III had known to make good use of his success in the first, ended the independence of the Chauhāns of Śākambharī. These 'keepers of the gates of India' failed their Motherland at the time of her need, not on account of any lack of valour or generalship but of political sagacity. Over-confidence also perhaps proved their undoing. As rulers of Raṇthambhor, Pṛthvirāja III's descendants tried to keep up some of their old traditions. Hammīra proved no unworthy successor of Pṛthvīrāja; he was equally valiant but politically perhaps even more imprudent and improvident. Jayatsiṁha of Nāḍol fell fighting against Qutbuddīn Aibak; and Kānhaḍadeva and Sātaladeva of the Sonigarā family showed Alāuddīn Khaljī how Hindu rulers could, provided they had the backing of their people, withstand for years the immeasurably superior might and resources of the empire of Delhi. And the lesson which all these lovers of Hindu culture and traditions could teach, in spite of their defects, did not perhaps remain wholly unlearnt. Nor were their sacrifices in vain, for soon after we find the Hindus holding up their heads once again and solid blocs of Hindu resistance groups coming into existence in northern as well as southern India. The Chauhān kingdoms disappeared, but the Chauhān spirit lived on to instruct, to inspire and even to hold up a finger of warning; and with it lived on, with some changes brought on by the massive impact of Islām, the social system which had produced this spirit and largely conditioned its success as well as failure.

PART I

POLITICAL HISTORY

CHAPTER I

THE ORIGIN AND ORIGINAL HABITAT OF THE CHAUHĀNS

The opinions regarding the origin and original habitat of the valiant Chauhāns to whom, according to Tod, impartial opinion must assign "the van in the long career of arms" are almost as numerous as the authors who have thought it fit to deal with the subject. Bards and Rājasthānī chroniclers regard them as fire-born; their *gotrochchāra* makes them lunar Kṣatriyas; and Dr. G.H. Ojha, relying on a number of old *kāvyas* and other records, maintains that they are Rājpūts of the solar race. Ratnapāla's plates state that Chāhamāna was born from the eyes of the "lord of the eastern quarter."[1] Further, there are the views of many writers, Indian as well as European, who regard them as descendants of some foreign tribe or other. As, in the babel of these opinions, it is not easy to see where the truth lies, we shall, in the first instance, state a bit fully, wherever necessary, the arguments underlying the more prominent of the theories referred to above; then submit them to criticism; and finally give our own view, without in the least presuming, however, to assert that it would be the last word on the subject.

The Agnikula myth. Rājasthānī bards and chroniclers, of whom Chand Bardāī is the best known, regard the Chauhāns as fire-born. His account of the origin of the tribe can be thus summarised.

"Viśvāmitra, Gautama, Agastya and other sages began a great sacrifice on Mount Ābū. *Daityas* (demons), who always dislike such rites, rendered it impure by showering down flesh, blood, bones, urine and many other impure things. With a view to ridding the sages from this nuisance, Vasiṣṭha created, from the sacrificial pit three warriors, Parihāra, Chaulukya, and Paramāra, but none of these three succeeded in the work assigned to him. Vasiṣṭha, therefore, dug a new pit, and as a result

1. *EI*, XI, pp. 308 ff.

of the oblations poured into it, there issued forth a four-armed figure, of lofty stature, red-coloured, red-faced, and bearing weapons in all his hands. The sages named him Chahuvāna. With the assistance of Āsāpurī, whom he thereafter regarded as his family deity, this warrior defeated the *daityas* and drove them back to the nether regions of *Pātāla*."[2]

This story is repeated with a few alterations here and there by the Sisāṇā inscription of the Chauhāns of Bedlā,[3] Nainsī's *Khyāt*,[4] *Hammīrarāso* of Jodharāja,[5] *Vaṁśabhāskara* of Sūryamalla Miśraṇa,[6] and the *History of the Chauhāns of Mainpurī.*[7]

Criticism of the myth. No serious student of history can, of course, believe that fire actually produced warriors. But when one is ready to grant the existence of lunar and solar Kṣatriyas, the concept of an *Agnikula* race does not necessarily appear weird and extraordinary and we could easily put the Chauhāns among the fire-born septs, if there were any historical warrant for it. But research into their history shows that as far as the Chauhāns are concerned the Agnikula myth does not go beyond the end of the Christian era. In fact, it appears to be nothing more than the creation of the poetic or imitative brains of bards who, in their hunt for a fine pedigree for their patrons, happened to light on the story of the fire-origin of the Paramāras in some book like the *Navasāhasāṅkacharita*, and found that it could not only easily but also splendidly explain the origin of the Chauhāns too, if they (the bards) simply added the further detail that the Chauhāns, though coming from the same fire-pit as the Paramāras, the Pratihāras and the Chaulukyas,[8] were the last to be born and succeeded where their elder Agnikula brethren had failed. It really was a fine piece of work; but great indeed, would have been the astonishment of these bards who adapted it to their purpose, if they had

2. *Pṛthvīrājarāso*. Part I, pp. 45-51.
3. From Dr. G.H. Ojha's transcript.
4. I, p. 119, Nāgarī Prachāriṇī Sabhā edition.
5. pp. 7-14.
6. p. 515.
7. *Chauhān-chandrikā*, pp. 41-43.
8. It is to be noted that the Pratihāras and Chaulukyas too are not Agnikulas according to their early records. On the origin of the Pratihāras see my paper in *Poona Orientalist*, Vol. II.

known that the story of the Paramāras' origin was, in its turn, as shown elsewhere (*Rājasthān Bhāratī*, III, 2, 2ff.) by us, based on a similar legend in the *Rāmāyaṇa* regarding the Śakas, the Pahlavas, the Kāmbojas and some other non-Aryan tribes who are said to have been created by Vasiṣṭha to fight against Viśvāmitra, the snatcher of his cow, Kāmadhenu.[9] In the *Navasāhasāṅkacharita* the first Paramāra is said to have been created for the same purpose, i.e., for bringing back Vasiṣṭha's cow.[10]

Myths of origin from Indra, the Moon, and the Sun. The myth of origin from Indra is found only in the Sevāḍī Plates of Ratnapāla.[11] The descent from the Moon, besides being mentioned in their *gotrochchāra*, which speaks of the Chauhāns as *Somavaṁśins*, i.e., Kṣatriyas of the lunar family,[12] appears to have been accepted as true at one time by the Chauhān rulers of Chandrāvatī.[13] The *Pṛthvīrājavijaya*, a Chauhān *praśasti* (probably of Vigraharāja IV's reign), the *Hammīramahākāvya* and the *Surjandcharita* describe the Chauhāns as solar Kṣatriyas;[14] and of modern writers, Dr. G.H. Ojha has written much to support the Chauhāns' claim to solar origin.[15] The *Vaṁśabhāskara*, the authority of which is utilised by some writers of the traditional school, tries to strike a compromise between the theories of solar and fire origin by regarding the Sun and Fire as ultimately identical.[16]

Criticism of the above myths. The above myths go against and, in a way, refute each other. The theory of *Aindra* origin, as already stated, is supported by only one solitary epigraph; and even regarding that we are not sure whether the writer ever meant Indra by the word, *prāchīdikpati*. He might have mistakenly used it for the Sun, the actual lord of the eastern quarter for an unsophisticated mind. The theory of

9. *Bālakāṇḍa*, Cantos 54-55.
10. Canto XI, vv. 64-71.
11. See footnote 1.
12. *Annals and Antiquities of Rajasthan*, II, p. 357.
13. See verse 8 of Luṇṭigadeva's Ābū inscription, (v. 1377).
14. *PV.*, I and II; *praśasti*, vv. 35-37; *HM.*, I, 14-17; *SC.*, VIII, 151-62.
15. *History of Rājpūtānā*, I, pp. 72-74.
16. See for instance Pandit Jhabarmalla Sharma's paper in the *Rājasthānī*, Calcutta, III, Part 2, pp. 1-8.

lunar origin is never mentioned before V. 1377. The theory of solar origin cannot be traced earlier than the middle of the twelfth century. Thus, even this the earliest of these theories is not old enough to settle satisfactorily the question of the Chauhāns' real origin; it merely registers the Śākambharī Chauhāns' claim to solar descent, without providing even a single cogent argument to prove it. Even if we take all the statements in its support at their face value, they would not prove that the Chauhāns belonged to a pure Kṣatriya stock, because according to these the first Chauhān was born after Kaliyuga had set in, the Buddha had been an *avatāra* of Viṣṇu and the *Mlechchhas* had begun invading India.[17] To be a member of the solar family, he therefore should have been some very late descendant of Ikṣvāku, the first solar king of India. Curiously enough, however, he is described as such neither by the early *Pṛthvīrāja-vijaya*, nor the medieval *Hammīramahākāvya*; nor the comparatively late *Surjanacharita* of Chandraśekhara. He is mentioned instead as a son of the Sun-god, *i.e.*, as an uncle of Ikṣvāku, if we must decide at all the question of the exact relationship between Ikṣvāku and Chāhamāna; and that such uncles, when separated from each other not merely by some generations but aeons, actually had little connection with each other or with the epic solar Kṣatriyas needs perhaps no demonstration. We know that, like Chāhamāna, the monkey-king, Sugrīva, the divine twins Aśvins, the fiery Revanta, and Yama were reputedly the sons of *Sūrya*.[18] Yet does anyone maintain that they were solar Kṣatriyas (with their pedigrees running up to Rāma and Raghu) or even blood-relations in any recognised sense ?

The value of the myths. But, though individually indefensible, cumulatively the above myths are not without considerable value regarding the problem of the Chauhāns' origin. According to the Achaleśvara inscription of Luṇṭigadeva, the first Chauhān was created after the solar and lunar races had become extinct.[19] His services were needed to put down the *asuras* interfering with the sacrificial rites of the sage Vatsa. The

17. *PV.*, I, 36-74.
18. *Ibid.*, II, 31-84.
19. च्चितौ प्रशान्तौ किल सूर्यसोम-वंशौ विशालौ प्रवरौ हि पूर्वम्।

Agnikula myths centre round a similar core, though external details, no doubt, are quite different. The myths of solar origin regard Chāhamāna as a Kṣatriya created in Kaliyuga. He was produced, they say, to wipe out the *Mlechchhas*.[20] Thus these myths agree in pointing to two facts:—

1. That the Chauhāns were not tribally connected with the old lunar and solar Kṣatriyas.
2. That the Chauhāns probably gained recognition as Kṣatriyas rather late in history, and most probably by fighting for Hinduism against non-Hindus.

The views of Tod, V.A. Smith, and William Crooke. More than a century ago, Tod seems to have discovered these truths. But with the imperfect data at his disposal, he regarded the Chauhāns as descendants of the non-Aryan Takṣakas.[21] V.A. Smith believes them to be related to the three other Agnikula races, the Pratihāras, the Paramāras and the Solaṅkīs, and approvingly quotes William Crooke's remark that the Agnikula myth "represents a rite of purgation by fire, the scene of which was the southern Rājpūtānā whereby the impurity of the foreigners was removed and they became fitted to enter the Hindu caste system."[22]

Criticism of these views. Though not without a modicum of truth, the above views cannot be accepted, because while making too much of the Agnikula myth which, as shown above, is a fabrication of perhaps the fifteenth century, they wholly ignore the evidence of the inscriptions of the so-called Agnikula races according to which the Pratihāras of Maṇḍor were the descendants of a Brāhmaṇa, Hariśchandra, and his Kṣatriya wife, Bhadrā, the Paramāras perhaps of the Vasiṣṭha Brāhmaṇas of the Ābū area, and the Chauhāns of a Brāhmaṇa claiming Vatsa *gotra*.[23]

Dr. D.R. Bhandarkar's theory. Much more comprehensive, far better reasoned, and almost brilliant, though no less

20. *PV.*, II, 68.
21. *Annals and Antiquities of Rajasthan*, I, p. 80.
22. *Early History of India*, 3rd edition, p. 412.
23. For the Maṇḍor Pratihāras' origin see my paper in the *Birlā Vidyā Vihār Magazine*, Vols. II and III, pp. 11-20; for the Paramāras, the *Rājasthān Bhāratī* III, Pt. 2, pp. 2-8; and for the Chauhāns our view in this chapter.

boldly speculative than these is the theory of the Chauhāns' origin advanced by Dr. D.R. Bhandarkar who maintains that, most probably, the Chauhāns were Khazars and originally belonged to a priestly section of some foreign tribes.[24]

The first of Dr. Bhandarkar's theses, viz., that they were Khazars is based on a coin of Vāsudeva Vahman. On its obverse is a legend in Sassanian-Pahlavī which reads "Saf Varsu Tef-Sri Vāsudeva" in the inner circle to the right, and on the margin, "Saf Varsu Tef-Wahman Multān Malkā", meaning Śrī Vāsudeva Vahman, king of Multān. On the reverse we have Śrī Vāsudeva in Nāgarī characters and the Pahlavī legend, Tukan Zaulistān Sapardalakshan, i.e., Ṭakka, Zābulistān and Sapādalakṣa. As the letters *v* and *ch* were in old Indian scripts so similar to each other that one could easily be mistaken for the other, Dr. Bhandarkar concludes that "Vāsudeva Chahman", *i.e.*, Vāsudeva Chāhamāna is the right reading instead of "Vāsudeva Vahman" as read by Rapson, and that this Vāsudeva Chāhamāna, again, should be identified with Vāsudeva mentioned in the *Pṛthvīrājavijaya* and the *Prabandhakośa* as the founder of the Śākambharī line of the Chauhāns. The *Prabandhakośa* places him in V. 608, but according to Dr. Bhandarkar this dating is wrong, because the coin discussed above shows that he could not probably have flourished before 627 A.D. Vāsudeva of the coin probably was the chieftain of a foreign tribe called Khazar which later on came to be known as Gurjara. So Vāsudeva Chāhamāna of the *Pṛthvīrājavijaya* and the *Prabandhakośa*, with whom the Khazar Vāsudeva has been identified, and naturally also the tribe to which he belonged, must be regarded as of foreign extraction.

Criticism of the theory. It is not difficult to disprove the above view. It is undoubtedly easy to read Chahman for Vahman in the Nāgarī script of the seventh century, the two letters being similar as pointed out by Dr. Bhandarkar. But how does he explain its being read as Wahman when the legend is actually in Sassanian-Pahlavī script ? The coin under discussion has, according to Rapson,[25] the name Śrī Vāsudeva only in

24. Dr. Bhandarkar's article in *IA.*, XLI, pp. 25-29.
25. Rapson's *Indian Coins*, pp. 30-31.

Nāgarī characters and all the remaining portions in Sassanian-Pahlavī; and in this foreign script, in which alone, it might be noted, the name Vahman occurs, the letters *v* and *ch* are quite dissimilar. According to Dr. J.M. Unvala, with whom I had some correspondence on the subject, the forms of these two letters in Sassanian, invariably, are ¹(v) and '(ch) respectively in all the three positions, initial, medial and final. Only very rarely are archaic forms met with, viz., 2 and ꞩ or ꞩ. "In all the forms, however, *v* and *ch* are never ambiguous and *v* cannot be read *ch* or *vice versa*." As this similarity of the letters, however, forms the very foundation of Dr. Bhandarkar's theory of the Khazar origin of the Chauhāns, needing as it does as its first requisite the similarity of the words Vahman and Chahman, it loses all its force the moment we realise that the letters *v* and *ch* do not possess in Sassanian-Pahlavī the similarity that they have in the Nāgarī of the seventh century.

Priestly origin. In support of the second part of his theory, namely, that the Chauhāns "belonged to some priestly class of foreign tribes", Dr. Bhandarkar gives the following reasons :—

(1) Sāmanta, the earliest prince mentioned in records after Vāsudeva, has been called a Brāhmaṇa of the Vatsa *gotra* in the Bijoliā inscription.

(2) The poet Rājaśekhara's marriage with Avantisundarī, a Chauhān lady, can be explained only if we regard the Chauhāns as Brāhmaṇas.

Partial correctness of the view. We agree partially with this part of Dr. Bhandarkar's theory. That there is not much ground for assigning a foreign origin to the Chauhāns has been shown above. But that they were originally Brāhmaṇas has to be conceded, though not on the basis of Dr. Bhandarkar's second reason, the marriage of Avantisundarī with the Brāhmaṇa poet, Rājaśekhara, inasmuch as *anuloma* marriages were till then permitted both by canonical and customary law.[26] Personal examination of the cast of the Bijoliā

26. Ibn Khurdādbā mentions *anuloma* marriages as current in this time. The Brāhmaṇa Hariśchandra married the Kṣatriyā Bhadrā (*EI*, XVIII, p. 95). Saṅgamarāja of Kashmir gave his daughter in marriage to a Brāhmaṇa (*Rājataraṅgiṇī*, VII, 10-12).

inscription, kindly made over to me by the late Dr. G.H. Ojha, would convince others, as it has convinced me, that Dr. Bhandarkar is right in regarding "विप्रः श्रीवत्सगोत्रे भूत्" as the right reading instead of "विप्रश्रीवत्सगोत्रे भूत" of Kavirāja Shyamaldas's defective edition. This obviously is an unambiguous statement of the Brāhmaṇa origin of the Chauhāns; and in spite of all the attempts to explain it away,[27] we feel inclined to believe it, when we find it supported fully by the *Kyām Khān Rāso* of the Muslim Chauhān author, Jān,[28] and in a great measure by the Sūndhā inscription of the Chauhāns of Jālor and the Achaleśvara inscription of the Chauhāns of Chandrāvatī.[29] Jān makes Chahuvāna a descendant of Vatsa of the *Jāmadagnya* gotra; the inscriptions state that the first Chauhān was born from the eye and meditation of the sage Vatsa. The Chauhāns' *gotrochchāra* speaks of them as *vatsagotrins*, and though this by itself would be no strong argument, because the Rājpūts are known at times to have adopted the *gotras* of their *purohitas*,[30] the additional evidence supplied in this connection by the records just mentioned disposes one to treat this as an extra reason for regarding Sāmanta of Śākambharī and his ancestors as Brāhmaṇas who like the Pallavas, Kādambas, and the Guhilas were either forced or induced by the prevailing conditions to give up their priestly calling and enter the Kṣatriya fold.[31]

---

27. Mr. Akshaya Keerty Vyas equates *vipra* with *mahīdeva* and the latter term with Mahārāja, even though there is not a single instance in the vast range of Sanskrit literature and epigraphy where the word *vipra* can conclusively be shown to have been used for a Kṣatriya.

28. vv. 45-48 put as an appendix to this chapter. For a fuller discussion see my introduction to the Rāso (No. 13, राजस्थान पुरातत्त्व ग्रन्थमाला, जयपुर)

29. Sūndhā inscription, v. 4 and Achaleśvara inscription, v. 7.

30. For the controversy on the *gotras* of the Rājpūts see C.V. Vaidya's *History of Medieval India*, II, pp. 50ff. and Dr. G.H. Ojha's *History of Rājpūtānā*, I, pp. 347 ff. The matter can only be of secondary interest to a student of Chauhān history, because Sāmanta's *gotra* can only be his own and not his *purohita's*. He is mentioned by our authorities not only as a *Vatsagotrin* but also as a *vipra* or Brāhmaṇa; and a Brāhmaṇa is required by no authority, old or new, to take the *gotra* of a *purohita*.

31. For the Pallavas and Kādambas see Dr. D.C. Sircar's *Successors of the Sātavāhanas*, pp. 225ff. and Dr. K.P. Jayaswal's *History of India*, 150 *A.D.* to 350 *A.D.*, pp. 225ff. For the Guhilas read Dr. D.R. Bhandarkar's *Guhilots*, *JPASB*, 1909, pp. 167ff. and Mrs. M. Sharma's *Origin of the Guhilots*, *IHQ*.

The original habitat of the Chauhans. With our main problem thus settled, at least tentatively, we pass on to the next one most connected with it, namely, that of the original habitat of the Chauhāns. Negatively, we might, after our criticism of Dr. Bhandarkar's view and the Agnikula myth, state that it was neither Ābū nor probably a foreign country. On the positive side we have the following indications :—

(1) Inscriptions as well as old historical chronicles connect them with Jāṅgaladeśa and Sapādalakṣa.[32]

(2) Tradition maintains that they moved northwards and conquered Delhi from the Tomaras, which is a fact corroborated by epigraphic evidence.[33]

(3) The description in the *Pṛthvīrājavijaya* puts Vāsudeva's capital a little to the east of Sāmbhar.[34]

(4) The Harṣa inscription (V. 1030) shows that Ananta province (the tract situated near Sīkar in the Jaipur division of Rājasthān) was the Chauhāns' old seat of power. It was here that *tantrapāla* Kṣmāpāla tried to attack Vigraharāja II's grandfather Vākpati, and it was here that the Chauhāns had the temple of their family deity, Harṣadeva.

(5) The Bijoliā inscription regards Sāmanta as an *Ananta-sāmanta*, which in the light of the description in the

XXVIII, 83f. The progenitor of the Kādambas was, according to their earliest inscription, a Brāhmaṇa named Mayūraśarman. That the first Kādamba should have been, after the lapse of some time, regarded as a four-armed figure sprung from a drop of sweat that fell on the ground near a *kadamba* tree from the forehead of Śiva is an interesting fact showing how mythical accounts could be made up regarding the origin of important historical figures. Bappa, the founder of the Guhila dynasty of Mewār, is mentioned as a *vipra* up to Kumbhā's time.

32. See *IA*, 1912, p. 196 ; *ASR*, VI, Plate XXI ; *Surathotsava*, II, 46 ; *Sukṛtasaṅkīrtana*, II, 43 etc.

33. See *JPASB*, XLIII, p. 108 and my paper on the Tomaras of Delhi in the *Rājasthān Bhāratī*, III, parts 3-4. *Pṛthvīrājarāso* also speaks of the Chauhāns having reached Delhi from Ajmer.

34. Vāsudeva is made to start from the western extremity of the lake Sāmbhar, to have the town of Sāmbhar on the way, and to proceed from there to his capital, an anonymous city, which may have been in the Ananta district of Sapādalakṣa.

inscription can only mean that he was a *sāmanta* of the Ananta province.[35]

(6) The Bijoliā inscription mentions also his being originally at Ahichchhatrapura, a name not inappropriate for the capital of *Ananta-gochara*, *i.e.*, the land of Ananta, the lord of Nāgas.[36]

(7) The *Pṛthvīrājavijaya*, *Hammīramahākāvya* and the *Surjana-charita* give Pushkar as Chāhamāna's birth-place.

No part of this evidence will go against us, if we conclude that their cradle-land was in the tract extending approximately from Pushkar in the south to Harṣa in the north. It had every right to be called Jāṅgaladeśa on account of abounding in *pīlu*, *karīra*, and *śamī* trees, the characteristic vegetation of such a tract,[37] and was also included in the territory which, according to the *Skanda Purāṇa* was known as Śākambhara-*sapādalakṣa*[38] and has been mentioned as Siwālikh by Minhāj-us-Sirāj.[39]

---

35. The words of the Bijoliā inscription are : "सामन्तोनन्तसामन्त:"
These can be interpreted in two ways,
(1) Sāmanta, a *sāmanta* or chief of Ananta.
(2) Sāmanta who had *ananta* or innumerable *sāmantas*.
In view of the statements in the Harṣa inscription, we have adopted the first sense, though the second one is not impossible and the poet might have intended to convey that too in addition to its primary sense. A third interpretation, Sāmanta who was known as Ananta, suggested by Dr. H.C. Ray, can be regarded as incorrect.

36. For one more indication in the Bijoliā inscription see the last two sentences of the chapter.

37. आकाशशुभ्र उच्चश्च स्वल्पपानीयपादपः ।
शमीकरीरबिल्वार्कपीलूकर्कन्धुसंकुलः ॥
हरिणैणर्ष्यपृषदगोकर्णखरसंकुलः ।
सुस्वादुफलवान् देशो वातलः जाङ्गलः स्मृतः ॥
(*Śabdārthachintāmaṇi* p. 991)

38. See the Kumārīkhaṇḍa of the *Skanda Purāṇa* which mentions a few other *Sapādalakṣas*, *i.e.*, territorial units supposed to have $1\frac{1}{4}$ lac villages. The Chauhāns belonged to the Śākambhara-*sapādalakṣa* which probably is the territorial unit meant by Wassāf who writes that "Siwālik contains 125,000 towns and villages." (*ED.*, III, p. 31.)

39. Read for instance the following :—
(*a*) "Again, he (Muhammad Bahlim) rebelled, and founded the fortress of Nāghawr, in the territory of Siwālikh" (p. 110).
(*b*) "This Tāj-ud-dīn was in the service of Malik Karīm-ud-dīn hamzah at Nāghawr of Siwālikh." (p. 200).

The Harṣa inscription regards it as the Chauhāns' land; and it was so also according to the Bijoliā inscription, if my interpretation of the term, *Ananta-sāmanta* is correct. No Ahichchhatrapura is to be found there at present.[40] But that it could have existed in this tract alone can be inferred from the fact that Vāsudeva, the earliest Chauhān ruler known to us, is connected with the Sāmbhar lake, and another very early ruler, Nṛpa or Naradeva, the successor of Sāmanta of Ahichchhatrapura, is described as reigning at Pūrṇatalla or Pūntalā in the Jodhpur Division of Rājasthān.[41] Ahichchhatrapura may have been somewhere between Pūntalā and Sāmbhar; at least it could not have been very far from them, for we have no evidence whatsoever to put the early Chauhāns in any area except that indicated in the beginning of this paragraph.

(*c*) "The seat of territory, Ajmīr, with the whole of the Siwālikh (territory), such as Hānsi, Sirsutī, and other tracts were subjugated." (pp. 468-469).

(*d*) A year subsequent to this, in 624 A.D., he marched against the fort of Maṇḍāwar within the limits of the Siwālik territory (p. 11). Raverty's translation of the *Tabaqāt-i-Nāsiri*.

40. Dr. G.H. Ojha and Dewan Bahadur H.B. Sarda, however, think that Ahichchhatrapura still exists in the form of Nāgor, a town in the Jodhpur Division. Their chief arguments for identifying the towns are:—

(1) That the names Ahichchhatrapura and Nāgor are synonymous.

(2) That Nāgor was at a hard day's ride from Sāmbhar. The *Pṛthvīrājavijaya* puts Vāsudeva's capital, presumably Ahichchhatrapura, at the same distance from Sāmbhar.

The synonimity, however, is doubtful, because not only Ahichchhatrapura is not an exact equivalent of Nāgor or Nāgapura, the exact equivalent being Ahipura, but also because Nāgapura or Nāgor, in spite of being a well-known Jaina *tīrtha*, is never mentioned as Ahichchhatrapura in any Jain work. Even more unsound is the argument from the *Pṛthvīrājavijaya*. The description there shows that Vāsudeva passed the night in the temple of Śākambharī. (See the last verse of Canto IV.) Early in the morning, he started from there for his capital which he reached a little after sunrise. So naturally Vāsudeva's capital could not have been at a hard day's ride from Sāmbhar, at least according to the *Pṛthvīrājavijaya*.

41. See verses 11 and 12 of the Bijoliā inscription. Viṣṇu in verse 11 equals Vāsudeva.

APPENDIX A

An extract from the Kyām Khān Rāso regarding the origin of the Chauhāns

प्रगट्यो तिहि मारीच सुत···
वाकैं राजा जमदगिन, बिघु सुमिर्‌यो करि चाइ ।
परसराम तिहं सुत भयो, चार चक्कको राइ ।।४५।।
परसराम सुत सूर है, ताकैं बछ्छ बड़ जोत ।
चाहुवांन हैं जगत में, ते सब बछ्छ सगोत ।।४६।।
चाइ भयो सुत बछ को, बिघु सुमिर्यो करि चाइ ।
चाहुवांन तिहि सुत भयो, करता आयो भाइ ।।४८।।
चाहुवांन यातें कह्यो, चहूं कूट के आँन ।
सगरे जम्बू दीप में, समको गोत न आन ।।४९।।

(क्यामखां रासो, राजस्थान पुरातत्त्व मन्दिर संस्करण, पृष्ठ ४)

CHAPTER II

SOME EARLY CHAUHĀN DYNASTIES

The Chauhāns of Bhṛgukachchha (Broach)

To the Chauhāns of Broach belongs the earliest of the Chauhān inscriptions discovered so far, viz., the Hansot Plates of V. 813 = 756 A.D. which refer themselves to the reign of the illustrious Nāgāvaloka and record the gift of a village in the Akrūreśvaraviṣaya[1] (modern Ankaleśvar tālukā) by Bhartṛvaḍḍha II, the Chauhān chief of Bhṛgukachchha. The donor's genealogy has been given as follows:—

In the Chauhān family:—

Rājan **Maheśvaradāma**

|

Bhīmadāma

|

Bhartṛvaḍḍha (I)

|

Paramamāheśvara **Haradāma**

|

Dhrubhaṭadeva

Paramamāheśvara-samadhigatapañchamahāśabda-mahāsāmantādhipati
Bhartṛvaḍḍha (II)

It is obvious from the donor's titles that he was a feudatory of Nāgāvaloka (Nāgabhaṭa I of the Imperial Prathihāra dynasty[2]) to whose reign the grant has been referred. The five members of Bhartṛvaḍḍha II's family, who preceded him, have been given a good deal of conventional praise. But as the first of them bears merely the colourless title *rājan* and the others do not enjoy even this distinction, they probably were no more than petty chieftains. Broach, at least, could not have

---

1. Edited by Sten Konow, *EI*, pp. 197-204. The occasion of the grant was a solar eclipse.

2. That the termination *avaloka* was not confined to the Rāṣṭrakūṭas is shown by Nāgabhaṭa II of the Imperial Pratihāra dynasty being called Nāgāvaloka in the Patharī inscription of Parabala (*EI*, IX, pp. 252 ff.), the Harṣa inscription of Vigraharāja II of Śākambharī (*IA*, 1913, pp. 57 ff.) and in the *Prabhāvakacharita* (p. 109 of the Nirṇayasāgar Edition, Bombay).

been under them, for we find the Gurjara ruler Jayabhaṭa III ruling there up to 736 A.D.[3]

Bhartṛvaḍḍha II was, probably, the first Chauhān ruler of Lāṭa, and his rise to power was, in all likelihood, due to the incursions of Junaid, the Governor of Sind under Caliph Hishām (724-743 A.D.), whose armies are known to have raided Broach,[4] and advanced even further to the south towards Nausārī where their further progress was barred by strong Chalukya forces led by *Avanijanāśraya* Pulakeśin of Lāṭa.[5] The Arabs retired from there. But we hear no more after this of the Gurjara kingdom of Broach. Its place was taken, perhaps, immediately, or shortly after, by the principality founded by the Chauhān chief Bhartṛvaḍḍha II who is believed to have been related in some way or other to the rulers of Valabhī[6] and was, one might reasonably feel sure, helped in rising to this new dignity by his overlord Nāgabhaṭa I, the Gwālior inscription of whose descendant Mihira Bhoja[7] describes him (Nāgabhaṭa I) as a defeater of the big army of the lord of *Mlechchhas*.[8]

The destruction of the Gurjara kingdom of Broach took place somewhere between 736 A.D., the last date known for Jayabhaṭa III, and 738 A.D., the year of Pulakeśin's Nausārī grant mentioned above. Bhartṛvaḍḍha II's principality must, therefore, have come into existence between this slightly uncertain date and 756 A.D., the year of the Hansot Plates. Tammīm, the successor of Junaid, is known to have been a weak Governor during whose time the Arabs had to retire from many places that they had previously occupied.[9] Broach was obviously one of the places they had to be evacuated.

We have no information about the successors of Bhartṛvaḍḍha II. Probably the dynasty ended with him, because within one

3. See his *BBRAS* Plate of Āśvina, Chedi Samvat 486, published in the *Gujarāt-na-Aitihāsika-lekha*, II, pp. 53 ff.

4. Bilāduri, *E. & D.*, I, p. 126.

5. *Verhandlugen des VII internationalen orientalisten-congresses*, Vienna, 1888, arische Section, 231f.

6. Sten Konow reached this conclusion on the basis of Maitraka Dhruvabhaṭa Śilāditya VII having had the same name as Chauhān Dhrūbhaṭa, the father of Bhartṛvaḍḍha II. The reason is not very convincing.

7. *EI* XVIII, pp. 107ff.

8. *Ibid.* verse 4.

9. Bilāduri, *E. & D.* I, p. 126.

year of his Hansot Plates we find the Rāṣṭrakūṭa Governor Kakka II granting lands to a Brāhmaṇa from Jambūsar which is not more than 25 miles or so from Bhṛgukachchha.[10] The Ellorā Daśāvatāra inscription ascribes some victories in Lāṭa to Dantidurga, the founder of the Rāṣṭrakūta line of the Deccan.[11] As he was a contemporary of Bhartṛvaḍḍha II, both the establishment of the governorship of Kakka Rāṣṭrakūṭa in Gujarāt and the disappearance of the Lāṭa kingdom of the Chauhāns within the short period intervening between the Hansot and Āntrolī-Chhārolī grants may be ascribed to the brilliant military achievements of Dantidurga.

Later Chauhāns of Bhṛgukachha. Nearly four centuries later, we once more come across a Chauhān dynasty ruling in this tract with its headquarters at Broach. A little before V. 1279, the important port of Cambay also had belonged to it. It had been in the *bhukti* of the Sindhurāja, the younger brother of Siṁha, the Chauhān ruler of Broach, and had been captured by Lāvaṇyaprasāda Vāghelā of Dholkā as the result of a battle in which the Chauhān forces had been decisively beaten.[12] And then closely in the wake of this event had followed another defeat. Siṁhaṇa, the Yādava ruler of Devagiri, slew Sindhurāja on the banks of the Narmadā and put his son Śaṅkha[13] into captivity. But for the help of their erstwhile enemy Lāvaṇyaprasāda *who not liking any increase in the power of his rival Siṁhaṇa came to the Chauhans' rescue while their professed ally Devapāla of Mālwa hung back for sheer fear*, Bhṛgukachchha and its adjoining territories would have passed into the hands of the Yādavas.[14]

This act of political generosity turned Siṁha, the Chauhān ruler of Broach, into a friend of Lāvaṇyaprasāda.[15] But Siṁha does not appear to have lived long after this event. About V. 1280, he was succeeded by his nephew Śaṅkha who had been released from Yādava captivity with a view, perhaps, to

10. See Kakka II's Āntrolī-Chhārolī Grant, *JBBRAS* XVI, pp. 105 ff.
11. *Archaeological Survey of Western India*, V, P. 88.
12. *Kīrtikaumudī*, IV, 75 and 84-87.
13. *Ibid.*, IV, 82; *Vasantavilāsa*, V, 42-43; *Hammīramadamardana*, II, p. 17, Śaṅkha was known also as Saṅgrāmasiṁha.
14. *Hammīramadamardana*, I, 13, *Vasantavilāsa*, V, 29-30.
15. *Kīrtikaumudī*, IV, 71.

fomenting trouble against the Chaulukyas.[16] Śaṅkha was an ambitious chief eager to get back his patrimony of Cambay not only for sentimental but also monetary reasons, because Cambay, in this period, was one of the most flourishing ports of Western India. Moreover, the political situation was not, from his point of view, unfavourable. Siṁhaṇa of Devagiri was once again on the march, this time devastating Chaulukya territories; and the Mārwār princes had revolted against their Chaulukya overlord Bhīma II, probably on account of all political authority having passed away into the hands of the Dholkā Vāghelās, Lāvaṇyaprasāda and his son Vīradhavala.[17] Śaṅkha, accordingly, marched against Cambay, then held by Lāvaṇyaprasāda's Jain Governor Vastupāla, but after gaining some initial success, he was worsted in the battle that followed, most probably because his forces were numerically inferior to those of his adversary. He had to retire precipitately to Broach where, after some time, he succeeded in organising a strong anti-Chaulukya confederacy consisting of himself, the Yādava ruler Siṁhaṇa of Devagiri, and Devapāla, the ruler of Mālwā.[18]

This time the situation for Śaṅkha was better than even on the previous occasion, because Iltutmish, the Sultān of Delhi, had overrun the kingdom of Mewār, and was now advancing on Gujarāt with his mighty forces.[19] Had the allies now held together and struck, the Vāghelā forces would have been overpowered. But they let slip this golden opportunity, and Vastupāla, the Dholkā minister, making adroit use of the rivalry between the rulers of Devagiri and Mālwā and the fact that Śaṅkha's father had been slain in a battle by Siṁhaṇa of Devagiri, sowed so successfully the seeds of dissension among the allies that, instead of attacking the Vāghelā forces, they began fighting amongst themselves and Śaṅkha had once again to try single-handed his luck in an attack on Cambay.[20] He had apparently no success, because from V. 1279-1222 A.D. to at least V. 1288-1231 A.D. Cambay was being governed by Vastupāla's son

16. *Kīrtikaumudī*, IV, 89. See below also the account of Udayasiṁha of Jālor.

17. *Ibid.*, IV, 59, See below also the account of Udayasiṁha.

18. *Ibid.*, Canto V, *Vasantavilāsa*, Canto V, *Hammīramadamardana*, p. 6.

19. See below the chapter on Udayasiṁha of Jālor for references.

20. *Hammīramadamardana*, p. 20 f.

Jayatsiṁha.[21] Śaṅkha probably lost Broach soon after his second fight for we find it being ruled in V. 1298-1241 A.D. by Vastupāla's nephew Lāvaṇyasiṁha.[22] The Broach dynasty of the Chauhāns thus most probably ended with Śaṅkha.

Śaṅkha was a well-known warrior[23] and obviously a good diplomat. His attacks on the Vāghelās were well-timed, though they miscarried, because he had insufficient resources at his command and could not, with his position as a *mahāmaṇḍaleśvara*, direct the policy of stronger and more influential rulers like Devapāla. His was not, at least, an inglorious failure.

The relationship between the family of Śaṅkha and Bhartṛvaḍḍha II is unknown. But it is not unlikely, as surmised by Dr. H.C. Ray, that they might have been related, for both are known to have belonged to Broach.[24]

The Chauhāns of Dholpur.

The second oldest available inscription of the Chauhāns is that of Chaṇḍamahāsena of Dholpur[25] whose genealogy is given as follows :

In the Chauhāna family—

Īsuka
|
Mahisarāma = Kaṇhullā who became a *satī* on the death of her husband.
|
Chaṇḍamahāsena

The chief facts that we glean about Chaṇḍamahāsena from this inscription are that he ruled at Dhavalapurī (Dholpur) in V. 898 (A.D. 842), was extremely liberal to Brāhmaṇas whom he rewarded in various ways, and was probably a devotee of the Sun-god for whom he had a temple built in the forest adjoining Dholpur. The lords of the *Mlechchhas* settled on both sides of the river Chambal paid him homage, and chiefs

21. Jinavijaya, *Prāchīna-Jainalekha-saṅgraha*, II, p. 47.

22. *Catalogue of Mss. in the Pattan Bhaṇḍārs* (G. O. S.), p. 60.

23. Images of 12 chiefs defeated by him dangled, bound with a gold chain, from his left foot (*Vasantavilāsa*, V, 28). See also the *Hammīramadamardana* II, p. 21.

24. *Dynastic History of Northern India*, II, p. 1058.

25. Edited by Hultzsch, *ZDMG*, XL, pp. 38 ff.

like Anirjita, perhaps lords of small villages lying near Dholpur, moved about the town with downcast looks. Unfortunately, however, we know nothing about Anirjita and have no satisfactory means of identifying the *Mlechchhas* who served him. Dr. H.C. Ray throws out a suggestion that would identify them with the Arabs of Sindh.[26] But in view of the fact that there is no other evidence to prove that the Muslims were settled as far east as that before the time of Muhammad Ghorī, it is probably better to regard them as Bhīls who are even now found on both the banks of the Chambal and are expressly included by Hemachandra among the *Mlechchha* tribes of India.[27]

Chaṇḍamahāsena was probably a feudatory of Bhoja I, the Pratihāra ruler of Kanauj, whose Barāh grant was issued in V. 893. He may have reached the territory of Dholpur with the troops of Bhoja's grandfather Nagabhaṭa II, who conquered many strongholds on this side and died in V. 890.[28]

We know nothing about Chaṇḍamahāsena's successors.

The Chauhāns of Pratabgarh

For the Chauhāns of Pratābgarh we have two inscriptions, both of which were originally set up in the temples at Ghoṇṭāvārṣikā, modern Ghoṭārsī, a village seven miles to the east of Pratābgarh. The first of these, besides recording a grant of Mahendrapāla II of Kanauj, dated in the Vikrama year 1003 (A.D. 946), and of Bhartṛpaṭṭa, son of Khommāṇa, in V. 999, gives the following genealogy of Mahendrapāla II's Chauhān *mahāsāmanta* Indrarāja, the builder of the temple of the Sun-god Indrādityadeva where our inscription was originally set up.[29]

In the *Chāhamāna* family, the support of Bhoja—

Govindarāja
|
Durlabharāja
|
Indrarāja

26. *Dynastic History of Northern India*, II, p. 1059, n. 4.

27. मल्ल-भिल्ल-किरातश्च सर्वेपि म्लेच्छजातयः
(Quotation in the *Śabdārthachintāmaṇi*, III, p. 441)

28. See the Gwalior inscription of Bhoja, verses 8 and 11 (*EI.*, XVIII, p. 108).

29. Edited by Dr. G. H. Ojha, *EI.*, XIV, pp. 160 ff.

The temple must have been built before V. 999 (A.D. 942), the year of Bhartṛpaṭṭa's grant to the god Indrādityadeva.

From the Harṣa inscription we learn that Gūvaka I of Śākambharī held an honoured place at the court of Nāgabhaṭa II.[30] Gūvaka II gave his sister in marriage to the lord of Kanauj, most probably to Bhoja I.[31] So is it not likely that Indrarāja's ancestor who rendered conspicuous service to Bhoja might have been a member of the Śākambharī line ? The occurrence within three generations of the two names, Govindarāja and Durlabharāja (so common among Śākambharī rulers) suggests the same conclusion.

Indrarāja's grandfather bore the title *bhūpa* and is said to have helped the goddess of victory to cross the sea of battle with his powerful arms acting as oars. This might be mere conventional praise or refer to valuable help rendered by him to his overlord Mahīpāla against the Rāṣṭrakūṭas. Durlabharāja, the next ruler, appears to have been just an ordinary prince. Indrarāja has the title *mahāsāmanta*. As Mādhava, the Pratihāra Governor of Ujjain, was also nothing more than a *mahāsāmanta*, Indrarāja must have been a fairly powerful feudatory.

The second Ghoṭārsī inscription is unfortunately fragmentary.[32] The part containing the *Saṁvat* is gone but the name Durlabharāja is still there. So the Jaina temple in which the *praśasti* was set up may be assumed to have been built in the reign of Indrāditya's father Durlabharāja Chauhān mentioned above.

Nothing is known about Indrarāja's successors.

THE CHAUHĀNS OF CHĀNDWĀR AND RĀYABADDIYA

Chāndwār is known to most students of medieval history as the place where Jayachandra of Vārāṇasī and Kanauj fell fighting against Muhammad Ghori. It might then have been included in the extensive dominions of the Gāhaḍavālas. But later on we read of a Chauhān kingdom of Chāndwār which continued its existence there at least up to 1449 A.D.

30. Verse 13, *IA.*, XLII, pp. 66 ff.
31. *Pṛthvīrājavijaya*, V. 32.
32. Noticed by Dr. G. H. Ojha, *History of the Pratābgarh State*, p. 24.

We do not know when the Chauhāns first reached Chāndwār. But as the *Bhaviṣayatta-kahā* of Śrīdhara, written at Chāndwār in 1173 A.D., makes no mention of the Chauhāns as rulers of the locality, and Jayachandra fought his last battle there in 1193 A.D., it is likely that the Chauhān Kingdom of Chāndwār was founded after the fall of the Chauhān Kingdom of Ajmer and the Gahaḍavāla kingdom of Vārāṇasī and Kanauj. Its rulers are called Sambharīrāya or rulers of Śākambharī, an epithet perhaps indicating that they regarded themselves as descendants or relatives of Pṛithvīrāja III and came to Chāndwār after their paternal kingdom in Rājasthān had been overthrown by the armies of Muhammad Ghorī and Qutbuddīn Aibak. Thanks to the prevailing hatred of the Muslim conquerors among the Hindu populace, the new kingdom soon gathered strength enough to give trouble to the Sultans of Delhi and, in alliance with other Rājpūt Chiefships, to delay, not probably by decades but centuries, the complete subjugation of the present Uttar Pradesh.

We have the following genealogy of its rulers up to 1256 A.D. from the *Aṇuvrataratnapradīpa* of Śrīdhara:[33].

Bharatapāla of the Chauhān family
|
Jāhaḍa (either a younger brother or son of Bharatapāla)
|
Ballāla
|
Āhavamalla=Isarade. He might have been a younger brother of Ballāla who is mentioned as the first *nandana* or son of Jāhaḍa.

As Āhavamalla was on the Chauhān throne in 1256 A.D. it is easy to put Bharatapāla, the first member of the dynasty mentioned here, in the first quarter or so of the thirteenth century. He is referred to very briefly in the colophon of the *Aṇuvrataratnapradīpa* as a protector of his towns, villages, country and people, (not because he was unimportant but on account of the simple reason that the poet was interested mainly in eulogising his patron Kanhaḍa of the Lambakūrcha (Lemchū) family and his immediate ancestors, Soḍha, Abhayapāla and Hallaṇa. The details about the Chauhān rulers come in because the Lemchūs had been counsellors of these rulers.

33. See *Jaina-grantha-praśasti-saṅgraha*, II, pp. 30-31, edited by Paramanand Jain Shastri : Vir Sewa Mandir, Delhi 1963.

The most detailed account is that of Āhavamalla, the master of the Lemchū minister, Kanhaḍa.

This neglect of Bharatapāla's achievements, however, is nicely made up by what I regard as very pertinent, though extremely brief reference to him in the pages of the *Tabaqāt-i-Nāsirī.* This chronicle speaks of the great encouragement given to Timūr Khān by Sultān Iyāltimish, when the former presented himself at the court with Laddā (a son of the ruler of Chāndwār) who had been taken captive in the battle of Chāndwār.[34] There is no other direct reference to this important engagement. But we are told earlier in the account of Prince Nāsiruddīn that, on being appointed Governor of Oudh by Iyāltimish in 1226 A.D., he "sent to hell the accursed Bhartū under whose sword more than 1,20,000 Musalmāns had received martyrdom".[35] Sir Wolseley Haig thought that Bhartū was a ruler of Kāmarūpa.[36] Hodivala identified him with Pṛthu who, according to the tradition current in Rangpur, was a ruler of Bhītargarh in the Jalpaigurī district of Eastern Bengal. He 'drowned himself in a large tank in his capital to avoid pollution from the touch of the Kīchakas (Musalmāns) who invaded his country from the north.' But as pointed out already by Dr. Habibullah, this identification is untenable, because Bhartū is mentioned only in connection with Oudh.[37] It is better by far therefore to identify him with Bharat (भरत), Bhartū (भरतू) or Bharatapāla who belonged to the area referred to and could have been the natural leader of an anti-Delhi confederacy. It is easy also to think of him as having fought the battle of Chāndwār in which Laddā, the prince of Chāndwār, was taken captive by his enemies. It was probably again this reverse which was responsible for a temporary transfer of the Chauhān capital to Rāyabaddiya which was another of their strongholds on the river Yamunā.[38]

34. Rizvi—*Ādi-Turk-kālīna Bhārat*, p. 63.
35. *Ibid.*, p. 30.
36. *Cambridge History of India*, III, 54. See also Dr. Habibullah's *Foundation of Muslim Rule in India*, p, 103; for other references 24-26.
37. *Foundation of Muslim Rule in India*, p. 103.
38. *Rāyabaddiya* has not been satisfactorily identified so far. Dr. Hiralal regards it as Rāibhā on the Yamunā. Pandit Paramanand thinks that it is Rāprī.

From the description that we have in the *Aṇuvrataratnapradīpa* it appears that Āhavamalla, the fourth ruler of the Chāndwār line, used all expedients, force, intrigue as well as diplomacy to maintain his independence.[39] He is described also as "having rendered desolate the territories of his enemies, and carried out his duties as a Kṣatriya. He was the mighty wrestler in the arena of battle against the unapproachable *Mlechchha* Muslim ruler. He was like a spear in the heart of the valorous Hammīra"[40], i.e., the Muslim ruler of Delhi. As Āhavamalla was on the throne of Chāndwār in 1256 A.D., he can be presumed to have fought against Sultān Nāsir-uddīn (1246-1266 A.D.).

The next connected account of the Chauhāns of Chāndwār comes from the *Bāhubalicharita* of Dhanapāla which was written in V. 1454 (1399 A.D.) during the reign of the Chauhān ruler, Rāmachanda.[41] The genealogy given in it can be tabulated as follows:—

Yaśavanta Chāhūvāṇa[42]
|
Gaṇapati
|
Karṇadeva
|
Sāraṅga
|
Abhayachanda
|
Jayachanda — Rāmachanda

If we calculate backwards from the dates known to us, Yaśavanta could not have been separated by more than a generation or so from Āhavamalla of the *Aṇuvrataratnadīpa*; and as he (Yaśavanta) is mentioned as ruling at Chāndwār, which was the original capital of this line, perhaps either he or his father must have offered his allegiance to Balban or some one of his successors and agreed to rule as a tributary at Chāndwār.

39. *Jaina-praśasti-saṅgraha*. Part II, p. 28.

40. *Ibid.*, p. 28, column 2. *Hammīra* is a Sanskritised form of Amīr, a title used for Iyaltimish in *Hammīramadamardana* also.

41. *Ibid.*, p. 36.

42. The manuscript reads Asavanta.

The next link in the history of the line is supplied by the colophon to the *Puṇyāsravakathā* of Raidhū which speaks highly of Rāmachanda and mentions the fact that the ruler had himself passed on the work of administration to the *yuvarāja* Pratāparudra.[43] Both, father and son, are known also from an image inscription of V. 1506 (1449 A.D.) which speaks of the *rājya* of *rājādhirāja* Rāmchandradeva and *yuvarāja* Pratāpachandradeva.[44]

Gaṇapati, Karṇadeva and Sāraṅga probably ruled contemporaneously with the first three Tughlaq Sultāns, Ghiyāsuddīn, Muhammad bin Tughlaq and Firūz Shah. The death of the last Sultān was followed by various attempts at independence by local chiefs and provincial governors. The Chauhāns of Chāndwār with their traditions of resistance to Muslim supremacy were not the people to miss such an opportunity ; and in H. 795 (1392-1393 A.D.) we find Abhayachanda Chauhān leading a rebellious rising in which he was joined by Sumer Shāh of Eṭāwah, Sādhāraṇ, Jīt Singh Rāṭhore, Bīrbhān and many others.[45] The rebels probably had some success. Finding that he could not reduce Chāndwār by force, the Tughlaq general Mubarak Khān opened negotiations and by promises and engagements succeeded in persuading Abhayachand and his friends to cease hostilities and see him at Kannauj. Sumer (Shāh) of Eṭawah alone remained behind. The rest were treacherously put to death.[46] It was a good lesson in Turkish political morality.

This treachery, however, did not probably do the Tughlaqs much good. Guided by the old and experienced Minister, Vāsāhara, the Chauhāns appear to have continued their resistance and even to have become wholly independent of Delhi for the remaining duration of the Tughlaq dynasty.

In 1414 A.D., Delhi passed under the control of a new dynasty and its first member, Khizr Khān, tried to bring again

43. The reading by the Editor is 'Pahugaṇa pattihu' which obviously is wrong. Gaṇa and pattihu go together, so the right reading is 'pahu Gaṇapattihu'.

44. *Jainapraśastiśaṅgraha*, Pt. II. Introduction, p. 111, note 3.

45. *Tārīkh-i-Mubārakshāhī*, English translation, G.O.S., pp. 161-162.

46. *Tārīkh-i-Mubārakshāhī*, English translation, G.O.S., p. 162-3.

the whole of the Doāb and adjoining territories under the control of Delhi. His general Tāj-ul-Mulk succeeded not only in defeating the ruler of Chāndwār but in depriving him of the fort of Jalesar and reimposing Muslim supremacy over the area.[47] But the payment of tribute by the Chauhāns must have been very irregular, for in 1420 A.D. we find Tāj-ul-Mulk raiding and looting the area of Chāndwār and adjoining territories.[48]

Traditions speak of the Chauhāns of the Doāb having been left at peace by Bahlol Lodī. But with the reign of Sikandar Lodī, who transferred his capital to Agra, the days of their independence, complete or partial, were over. We learn that in 1480 A.D. Sikander Lodī attacked his uncle Ālam Khān who had been pretending to independence at Chāndwār and Raprī.[49] Obviously both these areas had by then passed out of Rājpūt hands; and the same inference can be drawn from another event of Sikandar's reign. Sikandar wanted to have Bayānā under imperial control. He, therefore, offered to give the fiefs of Chāndwār, Jalesar, Marabara and Saket to its governor Sharaf Jalwānī on the condition that he would surrender Bayānā.[50] This could have been possible only after the annexation of Chāndwār to the Lodī dominions.

Thus the Chauhān kingdom of Chāndwār appears to have lasted for a little more than two hundred and fifty years. During the course of this fairly long existence, its scions might have established quite a few chiefships in Uttar Pradesh and Madhya Pradesh. Their connection with Chāndwār should be an interesting subject of investigation for antiquarians and students of Rājpūt history. On my visit to Udaipur I found that Chandrabhān Chauhān from Mainpuri-Chāndwār had come to fight the Mughals in the battle of Khanwaha,[51] and was killed in action. His son Dalpat came to Mewār and was granted the Jāgīr of Bedlā. The present Rao, Manohar Singh of Bedlā, a Chāndwāri Chauhān and descendant of Dalpat, is a senior Umrāo of Mewār (Rajasthan).

47. *CHI*, III, p. 206.
48. *Tārīkh-i-Mubārakshāhī*, English Translation, G.O.S., 213.
49. *CHI*, III, p. 235.
50. *Ibid.*
51. See the *Veer Vinod* by Kaviraja Shyamal Das and *Rājpūtānā kā Itihāsa* by Mm. G.H.Ojha.

CHAPTER III

THE CHAUHĀNS OF SAPĀDALAKṢA OR JĀṄGALADEŚA VĀSUDEVA TO VIGRAHARĀJA II

Vāsudeva. The earliest ruler of the Sapādalakṣa line mentioned in our records is Vāsudeva. He was, in some way, connected with the Salt Lake of Sāmbhar. According to the mythical account in the fourth canto of the *Pṛthvīrājavijaya*, he received the gift of the Salt Lake of Sāmbhar from a *Vidyādhara* whom he had befriended. In the Bijoliā inscription, the lake is said to have been born of him.[1] The *Prabandhakośa* genealogy puts him in V. 608 or 551 A.D. As the number of generations, however, which separated him from Vigraharāja II (V. 1030), the first ruler of Sāmbhar with a definite date, is unknown, it is not easy to decide whether the date V. 608 for Vāsudeva's reign is right. Dr. D.R. Bhandarkar would, on the basis of a coin of Vāsudeva Bahman, identified by him with this ruler (Vāsudeva Chāhamāna), put him in V. 627 A.D. That the view is untenable has been shown above.[2]

Sāmanta. In Vāsudeva's family was born Sāmanta who is described in the Bijoliā inscription as a Brāhmaṇa noble of Ananta (the tract near Harṣa in Shekhāwāṭī) born in the Vatsa *gotra* at Ahichchhatrapura.[3] It is not now easy to identify the town. But, as already pointed out above, it might once have been the capital of the Ananta Province.[4] Sāmanta's exact date is uncertain. But as he preceded Gūvaka I, a contemporary of the Pratihāra ruler Nāgabhaṭa II (V. 872) by six generations, his reign might be assumed to have ended about V. 725. The same date will also be arrived at, if we assign twenty-five years for

1. शाकंभराजनि जनीव ततोपि विष्णोः Here Viṣṇu = Vāsudeva.
2. See above, Chapter I.
3. Verse 12. Dr. H.C. Ray's view that he was known as Ananta too is not correct (*DHNI II.* 1061).
4. See above, Chapter, I.

each reign and count backwards from Vigraharāja II (V. 1030).[5]

Naradeva. The next ruler was Naradeva who ruled at Pūrṇatalla, most probably the village Pūntalā in the Jodhpur State. He is mentioned by the name Nṛpa in the Bijoliā inscription and as Naradeva in the *Hammīramahākāvya*, the *Surjanacharita*, and the *Prabandhakośa* genealogy.[6]

Dr. D.R. Bhandarkar and Mr. Akshaya Keerty Vyas put one Pūrṇatalla as Sāmanta's successor.[7] But actually Pūrṇatalla of the Bijoliā inscription, wherein alone the name is mentioned, is the name not of a person but of a locality where Nṛpa or Naradeva flourished.[8] The real succession of the next four rulers after Naradeva, who are no more than mere names to us, can be tabulated as follows :—

Jayarāja, son of Sāmanta[9]
|
Vigraharāja (I)
|
Chandrarāja (I)
|
Gopendrarāja or Gopendraka.

Durlabharāja I. Gopendraka's son Durlabharāja I achieved greater fame than his immediate predecessors. According to the *Pṛthvīrājavijaya*, he bathed his sword at the confluence of the Gaṅgā and the ocean and enjoyed the Gauḍa land.[10] As his son Gūvaka I was an honoured courtier of the Imperial Pratihāra Nāgabhaṭa II, this should be taken as a reference to the success achieved by the Chauhāns in Bengal under the banner of their

5. Dr. H.C. Ray's date for this ruler in the middle of the seventh century is a bit early (*DHNI, II*, 1062).

6. Bijoliā inscription, v. 12; *Hammīramahākāvya*, III, 5; *Surjanacharita*, I, 20, *Prabandhakośa*, p. 133, line 6.

7. See *Inscriptions of Northern India*, No. 344, and *EI*, XXVI, p. 97.

8. *Pūrṇatalle Nṛpastataḥ*, v. 12 of the Bijoliā inscription. Mr. A. K. Vyas emends Pūrṇatalle into Pūrnatallo but without assigning any reason. We find the reading Pūrnatalle as clear as day in the cast of the inscription supplied to us by Dr. G.H. Ojha, and the words there mean that "there was then Nṛpa (Naradeva) at Pūrnatalla." The well-known Jain scholar Hemachandra belonged to the *Pūrṇatalla-gachchha*, *i. e.*, a branch which had its origin at Pūrnatalla or Pūntalā in the Jodhpur State.

9. *PV.*, v. 7.

10. V. verse 20.

overlord, Vatsarāja, the father of Nāgabhaṭa, who defeated Dharmapāla, capturing his two umbrellas of State and appropriating with ease the sovereignty of the Gauḍa kingdom".[11]

A different view, no doubt, can also be held. According to Dr. R.C. Majumdar, and others who think likewise, it is unsafe to rely on a verse of the *Pṛthvīrājavijaya*, 'composed about four centuries after the events described', and to conclude on its basis that Durlabharāja ever reached Bengal.[12] He discounts also the evidential value of the verse from the Rādhanpur Plates, which recounts Vatsarāja's success in Gauḍa, by interpreting it a bit differently and saying that there being no evidence of any extensive territorial conquests by Vatsarāja, we should place the encounter between Vatsarāja and the Gauḍa in "the Doāb or its neighbourhood in a territory far away from Bengal." We disagree with him, because he has brushed aside evidence that is sound enough. The verse from the Rādhanpur Plates[13] may not, as contended by Dr. Majumdar, necessarily mean that Vatsarāja advanced as far as Gauḍa. But that it means nothing else has to be conceded by every Sanskritist when he reads it along with the verse from the *Pṛthvīrājavijaya*, a *kāvya*, the comparison of which with old inscriptions proves without much possibility of cavil its immense value as a source of Chauhān history. So though it describes, as in the case of Durlabharāja I, events which happened four hundred years before its composition, it has every right to be believed, unless there is some good evidence to the contrary. And that no such evidence exists or has at least been discovered so far might be stated without much fear of contradiction. Nor can we think of any special difficulty which could have prevented Vatsarāja and the Chauhāns from reaching Bengal. Vatsarāja's conquests were exten-

11. हेलास्वीकृत-गौडराज्य-कमला-मत्तं प्रवेश्याचिराद्
दुर्मार्गं मरुमध्यमप्रतिव (ब) लैर्=यो वत्सराजं व (ब) लै [:] ।
गौडीयं शरदिन्दुपादधवलं च्छ (छ) त्रद्वयं केवल [ं]
तस्मान्नाहृत तद्यशोपि ककुभां प्रान्ते स्थितं तत्क्षणात् ॥
(*EI*. *XI*, pp. 196 ff.)

12. Dacca University, *History of Bengal*, 1, p. 105.

13. See footnote 6 p. 24 of this chapter.

sive enough. Dr. Majumdar would like us to believe that they were not so. According to the Gwālior inscription of Bhoja he forcibly carved out an empire (*sāmrājya*) for himself. The verse from the Rādhanpur Plates, the testimony of which Dr. Majumdar reinterprets in his own way, states actually that *he appropriated the fortune, not of the Gauḍa ruler, but the Gauḍa kingdom*; and this, we might remember, was nothing impossible, for once Vatsarāja overran the *Madhyadeśa*, as he actually did, no physical or political barrier barred his progress to Bengal. What Muhammad bin Bakhtyār achieved in 1197 and 1199 A.D., without any special backing and with ludicrous ease, could be achieved also by a ruler like Vatsarāja commanding the vast resources of Mālwā, Rājasthān and perhaps also the Uttar Pradesh.

As Dhruva Rāṣṭrakūṭa, who defeated both Vatsarāja and his Gauḍa rival, Dharmapāla, died about V. 850-793' A.D., the Chauhān campaign against the Pālas must naturally be placed before this date.[14]

Guvaka I, Chandrarāja II and Guvaka II. Durlabharāja's successor was his son, Gūvaka I or Govindarāja. He is said to have achieved fame as a warrior at Nāgabhaṭa II's court.[15] The actual fight, however, in which he took part has not been specified in any of our records. The temple of Harṣanātha, the family deity of the Śākambharī Chauhāns, was perhaps built by this ruler, though it was added to a good deal by his successors.[16]

Chandrarāja II, the next ruler, is a bare name in the Chauhān annals. His successor, Gūvaka II, however, is described in the Harṣa inscription as a warrior, as great as Gūvaka I.[17] According to the *Pṛthvīrājavijaya*, he gave his sister Kalāvatī in marriage to the "paramount" sovereign of Kānyakubja, even though she had twelve other suitors for her hand.[18] The

14. Dhruva was alive when the Daulatābād Plates were issued in 793 A. D. and dead when the Paithan Plates were issued by his successor in May, 794 A.D. See *RA*. p. 59, note 27.

15. Harṣa inscription, verse 13.

16. See the last two lines of verse 13 of the Harṣa inscription.

17. Verse 14.

18. Verse 32. Gūvaka II is said also to have defeated all these suitors and given away the booty thus gained as dowry to his sister.

Kānyakubja ruler thus referred to, probably, was Bhoja I (c. V. 893-950), who, in the Pratābgarh inscription of Indrarāja, is described as having attained to his high position with the help of the Chāhamāna family.[19]

Chandanarāja. The chief achievement of Gūvaka II's son and successor, Chandanarāja, was the slaying of the Tomara chief Rudra[20] who is regarded by some writers as a petty ruler of the tract now known as Taṁvaravāṭī. But in view of the fact that he is called *inabhūpa*, i.e., mighty monarch in the Harṣa inscription and also of the tradition ascribing the migration of the Tomaras to Taṁvaravāṭī to a period not earlier than V. 1200, it is better perhaps, as suggested by Dr. D.R. Bhandarkar, to regard him as a ruler of the Delhi area, the well-known seat of Tomara power in Northern India.

Chandana's queen was Rudrāṇī, known also as Ātmaprabhā on account of her Yogic powers.[21] She is said to have lighted 1,000 lamps daily before the *liṅgams* at Puṣkara.[22]

Vākpatirāja I. The next ruler Vākpatirāja I is credited with one hundred and eighty-eight victories by the *Pṛthvīrājavijaya.*[23] This is an exaggerated estimate. But, at least, a few great victories could not have been impossible in the unsettled political conditions of the period, when the Pratihāras, being under the necessity of marshalling all their forces against the Rāṣṭrakūṭas of the Deccan (whose raids reached as far as Prayāga or perhaps even further) had perforce to relax their hold on the outlying provinces and leave them to the tender mercies of ambitious rulers like Vākpatirāja Chauhān and Harṣa Chandel.[24] When the tide of the Rāṣṭrakūṭa invasion rolled back, the Pratihāras appear to have tried to reassert their autho-

19. येनोच्चैः सुखमासितं क्षितिभृता श्रीभोजदेवेन च. (verse 5)

20. Harṣa inscription, verse 14. Kielhorn takes the name of the ruler as Rudreṇa. But such a name being unusual in India, it is better to split it into Rudra and *ina* as done by Dr. D.R. Bhandarkar.

21. *PV.*, V., 31.

22. *Ibid.*, 37.

23. *Ibid.*, 37.

24. See *RA*, Indra III, pp. 102-104; *HK*, pp. 259 ff.; *Karṇāṭaka-bhāṣā-bhūṣaṇa*; Introduction; *DHNI*, II, 672 ff.

rity.[25] The attack of the *tantrapāla* (provincial Governor)[26] Kṣmāpāla on Vākpatirāja I, mentioned in the Harṣa inscription, represents one such abortive attempt. Proud of the authority he held from his master, this *tantrapāla* reached Ananta, the homeland of the Chauhāns. He was fully confident of success. But Vākpati with his fine cavalry proved more than a match for the elephant force of his adversary who, after trying fruitlessly to overtake him, had to retire from the field thoroughly humiliated and dejected. This victory over the Pratihāra arms must have greatly increased the prestige of the Chauhān ruler and strengthened his hold over his new conquests.[27]

25. According to Dr. R.S. Tripathi, Kanauj revived fully after the Rāṣṭrakūṭa raid was over (*HK*, pp. 264 ff.). We, however, believe the revival to have been only partial and are disposed to agree with the opposite view that "the prestige of the Pratihāras suffered a severe blow from which they never completely recovered."

26. For this sense of the word see the Pratābgarh inscription of Mahendrapāla II (*EI*, XIV, pp. 160-1) We have taken Kṣmāpāla as a proper name. Words like Kṣitipāla and Mahīpāla which are synonymous with it are known to us from Pratihāra history. Other alternative senses of the words *Kṣmāpālastantrapālaḥ* can be (1) the ruler Tantrapāla, (2) the ruler who was at the same time a provincial governor. There is nothing very decisive in favour of any of the three senses.

27. Verse 16 of the Harṣa inscription on which the above account is based runs as follows :—

येनादैन्यं स्वसैन्यं कथमपि दधता वाजि-वल्गा-मुमुक्षुः
प्रागेव त्रासितेभः सरसि करि-रटड्-डिण्डिमैर्-डिण्डु [-जे]।
वन्द्य-क्ष्माभर्तु राज्ञां समदमभिवहन्नागतोनन्तपार्श्वं
क्ष्मापालस्-तन्त्रपालो दिशि दिशि गमितो ह्रीविषण्णः प्रसन्नः ॥

Dr. D.R. Bhandarkar's interpretation of the verse is as below :—

"Vākpatirāja, at first, harassed the prince Tantrapāla, because he was coming haughtily towards the Ananta province, with the behests of his overlord. It appears that to check the haughtiness of Tantrapāla, Vākpatirāja did not first meet him. And Tantrapāla could not with his fagged elephants overtake Vākpati with his fleet horses, and so was struck with shame at not having been able to deliver his overlord's orders to him. But when Tantrapāla's haughtiness was curbed, Vākpatirāja met him and propitiated him".

Our interpretation is based on the following syntactical order of the verse :—

"येनादैन्यं स्वसैन्यं दधता सरसि करि-रटड्डिण्डिमैः प्रागेव त्रासितेभः वन्द्यक्ष्माभर्तु राज्ञां समदमभिवहन् अनन्तपार्श्वंमागतः प्रसन्नः तन्त्रपालः क्ष्मापालः दिशि दिशि ह्रीविषण्णः गमितः।

The Harṣa inscription calls Vākpatirāja a *mahārāja.* An undated inscription of Pushkar refers itself to the reign of Vākpatirāja.[28] It has, on paleographical grounds, been assigned to the tenth century and is, therefore, with reason, believed to be a record of the Chauhān ruler Vākpati's reign. Vākpatirāja was probably a Śaiva. He built at Pushkar a temple for the god Śiva which was in existence up to Pṛthvīrāja III's reign.[29]

The Bijoliā inscription puts one Viṁdhyanṛpati' (Vindhyarāja) after Vākpati.[30] He probably was an elder brother of Siṁharāja, the next ruler, whose other brothers were Lakṣmaṇa, the founder of the Nāḍol branch, and Vatsarāja, the donor of the village Kardamakhāta to Harṣanātha.[31] Dr H.C. Ray's suggestion that Viṁdhyarāja should be equated with Vākpati cannot be accepted, because the compound word "Vappairāja-Viṁdhyanṛpatī" has been put in the dual number. Vindhyarāja does not appear to have ruled long.

Siṁharāja. Nothing is known about the policy of Vindhyarāja. But his brother and successor, Siṁharāja, followed the aggressive policy of Vākpati I. He slew the Tomara chief Salavaṇa[32] putting his allies either to flight or into prison where they remained till the common overlord of Siṁharāja as well as his rivals came to secure their freedom.[33] This Salavaṇa might have been of the family of the Tomara chief, Rudra, slain thirty years earlier by Siṁharāja's grandfather Candana.[34] The overlord, mentioned in the

The last two words of the verse (see above) are interpreted as *prasannaḥ san āgataḥ hrīviṣaṇṇaḥ gamitaḥ.*

That the lord referred to was a Pratihāra ruler is generally acknowledged. Gūvaka I flourished at the Pratihāra court, Gūvaka II gave his sister in marriage to a Kānyakubja ruler, and Siṁharāja's overlord was *Raghukule bhūchakravartī.*

28. Noticed by Dr. G.H. Ojha in his *Three Lectures on Ajmer and one on Pushkar.*

29. PV, V, 43.

30. Verse 14.

31. See the prose portion of the Harṣa inscription.

32. Verse 19 of the Harṣa inscription.

33. *Ibid.*

34. See above the account of Chandana.

Harṣa inscription as *Raghukule bhūchakravartī* (the emperor belonging to the Raghu family) can be identified with *Paramabhaṭṭāraka-Mahārājādhirāja-Parameśvara* Vijayapāladeva of the Rājorgarh inscription (V. 1016), a weak Pratihāra ruler incapable of controlling the vast territories of the empire of Kanauj.[35]

For Siṁharāja's reign we have the Thāṁvalā inscription of V. 1013. Its transcript, as given by Mahāmahopādhyāya Bishweshwar Nath Reu, shows that Siṁharāja bore the title of *Mahārājādhirāja*. His father, Vākpati, had to remain content with the title Mahārāja, though he won 188 victories. Further, the inscription testifies to his mastery over the territory that included Merta and probably, also Pushkar. That Siṁharāja was a Śaiva is known from the Harṣa inscription of V. 1030/973 A.D. From this inscription, we further gather that he was a worshipper also of Āditya, i.e., the Sun.

Siṁharāja's son, Vigraharāja II, is described in the Harṣa inscription as "rescuing the fortune of his family and the Goddess of Victory from the distress that had befallen them."[36] Siṁharāja's end therefore might have been rather tragic. Perhaps he ultimately succumbed to a strong combination of his numerous enemies among whom might perhaps be included also the incensed Pratihāras of Kanauj.

Vigraharāja II. Siṁharāja was succeeded by his son Vigraharāja II, the greatest of the early Chauhāns of Śākambharī, for whom we have the Harṣa inscription of V. 1030 (973 A.D.). It is obvious from the description given therein that not only had the danger to his dynasty passed away by that time but that the new ruler had probably made some new conquests and was being served by feudatories.[37] The record, however, does not say anything about his most talked of achievement, the one that captured the imagination of all the Chauhān eulogists from Jayānaka to Chandraśekhara and has been recorded even by the chroniclers of Gujarāt. This great feat was the defeat of Mūlarāja Chaulukya. The omission is, perhaps, to be explained by its having occurred after V. 1030. and before V. 1055.

35. *EI*, III, pp. 266 ff.
36. Verse 21 of the Harṣa inscription.
37. See the glowing account in v. 24 of the Harṣa inscription.

According to the *Pṛthvīrājavijaya*, Vigraharāja forced the Gurjara ruler Mūlarāja to shut himself up in the Kanthā fort and carried his arms up to Bhṛgukachchha where he built a temple of the goddess Āśāpurī,[38] The *Hammīramahākāvya* goes further. It states that Vigraharāja killed Mūlarāja in battle and plundered the Gurjara country.[39] The *Surjanacharita* (VI, 3-14) also, though a fairly late production, knew well the story of the defeat of the Gurjaras by the Chauhān ruler. The account given by the pro-Chaulukya chronicler *Prabandhachintāmaṇi* can be thus summarised:—

Once the ruler of Sapādalakṣa and Bārapa, the General of the Tilinga monarch,[40] reached simultaneously the borders of Gujarāt. Mūlarāja (the ruler of Gujarāt) shut himself up in the Kanthā fort,[41] hoping that the Sapādalakṣa ruler would, at the time of *Navarātra*, return to Śākambharī to worship there his family goddess, Āśāpurī. On his not doing so, Mūlarāja had his levies secretly sent for. Then mounting on an elephant he reached the Sapādalakṣa camp just before dawn, and entered unannounced the tent of his adversary. Taken unawares the Sapādalakṣa ruler agreed to Mūlarāja's request, or rather demand, not to attack the Gurjara forces in the rear while they fought against Bārapa. Thereafter Mūlarāja easily defeated and slew the Tilinga general. The Sapādalakṣa ruler fled away as soon as he learnt the news from his spies.[42]

The statement of the *Hammīramahākāvya* regarding Mūlarāja's death at the hands of Vigraharāja II can, we believe, be rejected, inasmuch as it is not supported by our other sources. But that Mūlarāja did not have the upper hand in the encounter is sufficiently clear from the practical unanimity of the pro-Chauhān poems about the result of the war and from the fact that, even according to the pro-Chaulukya *Prabandhachintāmaṇi*, Mūlarāja had to sustain a siege in the fort of Kanthā to which

38. V. verses 50-53.
39. *HM.* II, 9.
40. Identified by common consent with the Western Chaulukya ruler Tailapa (c. 973-997 A.D.)
41. *PC* pp. 15-16.
42. *Ibid.*

the Chaulukya rulers are known to have retired only in case of grave emergency,[43] and also from the alleged going of Mūlarāja to the camp of his adversary with the request that he should not give him a side-blow.

The exact cause of the Gujarāt campaign is unknown. But it is not unlikely that it was connected in some way with Vigraharāja II's visit to Bhṛgukachchha, then the capital of the family of Bārapa.[44]

43. Bühler finds confirmation of Mūlarāja's siege in Kanthā in the line *Tryambaka iva vihitāchalāśraya* of the Kadi grant of Mūlarāja which he interprets as meaning that Mūlarāja resembled Tryambaka (Śiva) since he took up his residence on a mountain. As there is not a single hill within fifty miles of Aṇahillapaṭṭana, the poet is, according to him, referring to Mūlarāja's temporary stay on the Kanthā hill. Finding nothing better to compare him with Śiva, the writer of the grant is said to have boldly regarded this very fact as something comparable to Śiva's residence on Kailāsa. But it might be submitted that it is rather a far-fetched explanation of a fairly simple line. In view of the fact that no *praśastikāra* would mention a fact which, instead of redounding to his patron's credit, goes against it (and the siege of Kanthā by an enemy was nothing to crow over), we should interpret the words *Tryambaka iva vihitāchalāśraya*, when applied to Mūlarāja as meaning "he who had given refuge to the Achalā, *i.e.* earth". The words do not refer to any historical event; the comparison just stands on the same footing as Mūlarāja's comparison with Brahmā and Viṣṇu respectively in the lines *Kamalayoniriva vitatakamalāśrayaḥ* and "*Viṣṇuriva vikramākrāntabhūtalaḥ* of the very same Kadi grant. Mūlarāja was the *āśraya* of *Kamalā* like Brahmā who had *kamala* (*lotus*) as his *āśraya*. He was the *āśraya* of *achalā* like *Tryambaka* of whom the *āśraya* is an *achala* (Kailāsa mountain) (see also our paper, *Tryambaka iva vihitāchalāśraya*, published in the *JGNJRI*, I, pp. 479-80).

Bhīmadeva II shut himself in this fort when Mahmūd of Ghaznā captured Anhilwāṛā (Nazim, *Sultān Mahmūd*, p. 116). He thus managed to save himself from falling into the hands of the Muslims but the temple of his family deity Somanātha was destroyed and his kingdom pillaged by the ruthless Muslim invaders. The situation of Bhīmadeva's great-grandfather must have been equally serious to oblige him to leave unprotected the fertile plains of Gujarāt and betake himself to this waterless and inhospitable tract.

44. The *Pṛthvīrājavijaya* first mentions the collection of the *Bāṇaliṅgams* of the Narmadā by the Chauhān soldiers, next describes the driving of Mūlarāja into the fort of Kanthā, and finally reverts to the Narmadā, the waters of which are said to have been muddied by Chauhān horses and on the banks of which Vigraharāja II is said to have erected a temple of his family goddess Āśāpurā (V. 50-53). If this has any reference to the course of the Chauhān expedition, it would seem that Vigraharāja I first proceeded towards

Firishta, if believed in, would lead us to conclude that Vigraharāja II fought also against the Muslims; for, according to him, the *Rāy* of Ajmer sent a contingent to join the league organised by the ruler of Lahore against Subuktigin in the year 997 A.D.[45] But as Ajmer had not till then come into existence, and as no such league is mentioned by earlier and more reliable historians like Utbī, Ibn-ul-Athar and Nizāmuddīn, we are more than doubtful regarding the accuracy of Firishta's statement.

Vigraharāja II was, without question, the greatest of the early Chauhān rulers of Sapādalakṣa. He came to the throne when the Chauhān kingdom lay prostrate at the feet of his enemies. That he could within a few years restore his family not merely to its former glory but also add to its greatness by exacting tributes from many princes and humbling the pride of Mūlarāja, the strong ruler of Gujarāt, speaks volumes for his resourcefulness and excellent generalship. Like his grandfather Vākpati I, he was a great cavalry leader; the title *Khurarajondhakāra*[46] connotes well the great reputation that he must have enjoyed as a campaigner.

Lāṭa, probably allied himself with its Chaulukya ruler, as suggested by his later on building a temple of Āśāpurā at the Chalukya capital, and then, attacking Mūlarāja with this allied force compelled him to seek refuge in the fort of Kanthā.

The *Prabandhachintāmaṇi* speaks of Mūlarāja being attacked simultaneously by Bārapa and the Sapādalakṣa ruler. If our tentative reconstruction of the course of the struggle be right, this simultaneity would be explained by a previous understanding between these rulers. Instead of Bārapa, however, who, as pointed out by Hemachandra (*Dvyāśrayakāvya*, VI, 29-30) was rather the victim of aggression than an aggressor, we should like to put his son Goggirāja described in the Sūrat Grant of Trilochanapāla (S. 972) as "a greater Viṣṇu relieving the land seized upon by powerful enemies as demons." He probably achieved this liberation of his country with the help of his ally Vigraharāja II.

It must, however, be remembered that this is no more than a tentative suggestion.

45. *Tārikh-i-Firishta*, I, pp. 7 and 18.

46. *PV.* V 48.

CHAPTER IV

THE CHAUHĀNS OF SAPĀDALAKṢA (*continued*): DURLABHARĀJA II TO AJAYARĀJA

Durlabharāja II : The earliest reference to Durlabharāja II is in the Harṣa inscription wherein his elder brother Vigraharāja II is said to have been adorned by him as was Rāma by Lakṣmaṇa and Balarāma by Kṛṣṇa.[1] As his two other brothers Chandrarāja and Govindarāja do not find a place in the *praśasti* portion of the inscription, it might be assumed that, even as early as V. 1030, Durlabharāja held a higher position than his two other brothers and had perhaps been recognised as an heir-apparent. The other references to him are in Rāṣṭrakūṭa Dhavala's inscription of V. 1053 and the Kinsariyā and Sakrāi inscriptions of his own reign, both dated in V. 1056.[2] In the former of these, he is mentioned as holding undisputed sway over the earth and as attacking and over-powering Mahendra, who is rightly identified by Kielhorn with Mahendra Chauhān of Nāḍol. Dhavala is said to have used both diplomacy and force in relieving the beleaguered monarch[3]; but considering the strength of the kingdom of Śākambharī at the time and the terms in which Durlabharāja himself is referred to, there is greater possibility of Dhavala's having used more the former than the latter means against the aggressor. The reason for which Mahendra was attacked, in spite of being a Chauhān, was probably his alliance with Durlabharāja's rivals, the Chaulukyas of Aṇahillapattana, to whose ruler Durlabharāja II is known to have given his sister in marriage.[4] The Kinsariyā inscription states that Durlabharāja II was known also as *Durlaṅghyameru* on account of his orders being never transgressed by

1. Verse 26.
2. See respectively for these inscriptions *Prāchīnajainalekhasaṅgraha* of Muni Jinavijaya, pp. 175 ff.; *EI.*, XII, pp. 59 ff. and Dr. G.H. Ojha's transcript of the Sakrāi inscription.
3. *Senānīriva nītipauruṣaparonaiṣīt paraṁ nirvṛtim*, verse 11.
4. *Dvyāśrayamahākāvya*, VII, 66-108.

others.[5] The editor of the record sees in its verse twelve a reference to the conquest of a tract called the *maṇḍala* Asosittana or Rasosittana.[6] The Sakrāi inscription calls Durlabharāja a *Mahārājādhirāja*.

Govindarāja III : Durlabharāja II was succeeded by his son Govindarāja III, known also as Gandu. The *Pṛthvīrājavijaya* gives him the title *vairigharaṭṭa* or "a grinder of enemies."[7] The genealogy given at the end of the *Prabhandhakośa* mentions him as a defeater of Sultān Mahmūd,[8] meaning thereby perhaps Gandu's contemporary Mahmūd of Ghaznā. The lateness of the source, however, makes it difficult to decide whether the information is correct, even though it is, in some measure, supported by Firishta's statement that "Mahmūd had to return to Ghaznā by way of Sindh, because the route through Mārwār lay blocked by large forces under the ruler of Ajmer".[9] For Ajmer, of course, one should substitute Śākambharī, as there was no Ajmer in existence at the time.

Vākpatirāja II : The next ruler was Govindarāja's son Vākpatirāja II who slew, in battle, Ambāprasāda, the ruler of Āghāṭa (the then capital of Mewār.).[10] The *Surjanacharita*, which along with the *Hammīramahākāvya* and the *Prabandhakośa* genealogy, knows him as Vallabha, credits him with the defeat of Bhoja of Mālwā and a ruler of Chedi. Though here again there is no chronological difficulty, the lateness of the source and the fictitious details with which it embellishes the story make the information unreliable.[11]

Vīryarāma : Vākpati II was succeeded by his younger brother Vīryarāma.[12] He was slain in battle by Bhoja, the ruler of Avanti (c. 1010-1055 A.D.), [13] who, if the information supplied by the *Surjanacharita* be true, had already been fighting with

5. Verse 2.

6. The text being corrupt here, we are not sure whether the conquest of any tract is actually referred to.

7. Verse 57.

8. p. 133.

9. *TF*, I. p. 69.

10. *PV*. V. 55-60.

11. Canto V.

12. *PV* calls him Vākpati's son. We follow the Bijoliā inscription.

13. *Ibid.*, v. 66.

the Chauhāns in the previous reign. The Paramāra forces, perhaps occupied Śākambharī for a while as a result of this victory.[14]

Chāmuṇḍarāja and Siṁhaṭa : Vīryarāma's successor was his pious but brave brother Chāmuṇḍarāja who built a temple of Viṣṇu at Narapura.[15] His greatest achievement was the freeing of Śākambharī with the help of his clansman, Aṇahilla of Nāḍol.[16] The Bijoliā inscription puts one Siṁhaṭa between Chāmuṇḍarāja and his son, Dūsala or Durlabharāja.[17] He might have been Dūsala's elder brother.

Durlabharāja III : According to the *Pṛthvīrājavijaya*, Durlabharāja lost his life in a battle with the Mātaṅgas.[18] In the last verse of canto V of the *Pṛthvirājavijaya* the word Mātaṅga has been used for the Muslim invaders from the north-west. Jonarāja equates them with the *Mlechchhas*,[19] by which word we should, understand the Muslims who have been described as such in the Gwālior inscription of Bhoja Pratihāra and the Siwālik Pillar *praśasti* of Vigraharāja IV.[20] Nor is there any lack of evidence to prove that Muslim forces were at the time

14. See note 16.

15. *PV.*, V. 68.

16. This appears to be the right interpretation of the following verse of the Sūndhā inscription :—

दृष्टः कैनं चतुर्भुजः स समरे शाकम्भरीं यो बलाज्-
जग्राहानु जघान मालवपतेर्=भोजस्य साढाह्वयं
दंडाधीशमपार-सैन्य-विभवं......

Here the slaying of the Mālava commander is said to have followed immediately the capture of Śākambharī by Aṇahilla. This clearly indicates some connection between the two events. As Bhoja was an enemy of the Śākambharī Chauhāns too, what we naturally conclude from the almost simultaneous capture of Śākambharī and the slaying of Bhoja's General Sāḍha by Aṇahilla is that the latter came to the assistance of his clansmen, captured Śākambharī from the Paramāras, and soon after killed the Paramāra commander in the battle that followed as a result of Aṇahilla's *coup*.

17. He is given the title *rāṇakavara*. As the name however, does not find a place in the *PV*, cannot the words *Śrī-Siṁhaṭo Dūsalaḥ* mean ¡Dūsala who was known also as Siṁhaṭa ?

18. *PV*, V. 70.

19. Commentary on the above verse.

20. *EI.* XVIII, pp. 99 ff., *IA* XIX, p. 218.

actually operating in Rājasthān and fighting against the Chauhāns and their relatives. According to a Chauhān Grant discovered a few years ago by Dr. G.H. Ojha, Āsarāja rescued his brother Pṛthvipāla, (the ruler of Nāḍol and a contemporary of Durlabharāja III) from a Turuṣka attack.[21] Another grant discovered by the same savant describes Āsarāja's brother-in-law Haripāla as fighting a certain Hammīra who was not permitted by him to water his thirsty horses.[22] These two grants thus provide evidence enough to prove that Jonarāja was right in identifying the *Mātaṅgas* with Muslims, and to let us conclude that Durlabharāja III most probably fell at the hands of the Turuṣka Hammīra mentioned by them. As to who this Turuṣka ruler was and when exactly he invaded India, we find on turning to *Firishta's History* that in 1079 A.D. Ibrahīm of Ghaznā led a force into India which won many resounding victories, and succeeded in penetrating to the western coast of India.[23] He, obviously was the Mātaṅga or Muslim chief against whom Durlabharāja III, Pṛthvīpāla of Nāḍol, and the brother-in-law of Pṛthvīpāla's brother, Āsarāja, had to fight.

The *Hammīramahākāvya* and the *Prabandhakośa* genealogy speak also of Durlabharāja's fight against Karṇa Chaulukya of Gujarāt,[24] the former even stating that he killed the Gujarāt ruler in battle. The fight is likely enough. But that Karṇa did not get slain would be obvious from our account of Durlabharāja's successor Vigraharāja III.[25]

Dewan Bahadur H.B. Sarda and Dr. D.R. Bhandarkar regard Vīrasiṁha as another name of Durlabharāja III. The view is based on the misunderstanding of a verse from the *Pṛthvīrājavijaya*.[26]

21. See line 22 of the Grant in the Appendix H at the end of the book.
22. Lines 21-22 of the Grant.
23. *Tārīkh-i-Firishta*, I, p. 139, 23a.
24. II, 31 and p. 133 respectively.
25. See below.
26. The verse in question reads as follows :—

"मातङ्ग-सङ्गरे यस्मिन् वीरसिंहेऽस्तमागते ।
अपरागोऽनुतापश्च विधिना प्रापि ककंशः ।।"

Here *Vīrasiṁha*, when referred to Durlabharāja III, means nothing more than that he was a "lion among heroes."

Vigraharāja III : The successor of Durlabharāja III was his brother Vigraharāja III known also as Bīsala or Vīsala[27]. His queen's name was Rājadevī who, if the tradition preserved in the late *Bīsalderāso* be believed in, was the daughter of a ruler of Mālwā.[28] But whether such a matrimonial alliance was concluded or not, it is at least certain that the Paramāras and the Chauhāns were on the best of terms during this period. According to the *Pṛthvīrājavijaya*, *Vigraharāja* III helped Udayāditya of Mālwā in defeating Karṇa Chaulukya of Gujarāt.[29] The *Surjanacharita*,[30] a much later source, gives all this credit to the Chauhān ruler, though, no doubt, wrongly. As Udayāditya ruled up to V. 1143/1086 A.D. or so; and Vigraharāja III, most probably, ascended the throne about V. 1136, the defeat of Karṇa (c. V. 1120-1150) 1093 A.D. might tentatively be placed between these two dates.

According to the *Prabandhakośa* genealogy, Bīsala (Vigraharāja III) who was a libertine, died as a result of sores caused by the curse of a Brāhmaṇa woman whose chastity he had violated.[31] A similar story is repeated in the *Pṛthvīrājarāso* about Bīsala, the husband of a Paramāra princess of great beauty.[32] The lateness of the two sources, however, renders it impossible to assess the amount of truth in the tradition.

An old inscription at Sakrāi refers itself to the reign of the Chauhān king Vigraharāja and records that Dāyikā, queen of Vachchharāja, repaired the temple of Śankarādevī.[33] It bears the date Sam. 55, Māgha sudi 5. Regarding the hundreds as omitted, Dr. D.R. Bhandarkar assigned it to V. 1055 in the reign of Vigraharāja II. But as Vigraharāja II's successor Dur-

27. Bijoliā inscription, 14; *PKG*, 133, SC, VI, 45.

28. Bijoliā inscription, verse 14; *Bīsalde-rāso*, p. 13. In the latter of these sources, she is called Rājamatī, daughter of Bhoja. But as Bhoja was an old man when he died and Vigraharāja III ascended the throne nearly 25 years after his death, the Paramāra ruler in Mālwā, whose daughter she might have been, can be Bhoja's *bandhu* Udayāditya.

29. *PV*. 77-78. Vigraharāja III is described as having given Udayāditya an excellent horse named Sāraṅga riding on which he vanquished *Gūrjara* Karna.

30. VI. 47.

31. *PKG*, p. 133.

32. *Rāsosāra*, p. 12. See also p. 10.

33. *PRAS*, *WC*, 1909-10, p. 57.

labharāja II was on the throne of Śākambharī in V. 1053[34], Vigraharāja of the Sakrāi inscription must be identified with Vigraharāja III and the omitted figures regarded as 11 instead of 10. Vachchharāja, the husband of Dāyikā was, most probably, a feudatory of the Chauhāns of Śākambharī.

Pṛthvīrāja I : Pṛthvīrāja I, the next ruler, was the son of Vigraharāja III and husband of Rāsaladevī.[35] An inscription of the Vikrama year 1162, engraved on a pillar of the *sabhāmaṇḍapa of* Jiṇamātā in Shekhāwāṭī, calls him *Paramabhaṭṭāraka-Mahārājādhirāja-Parmeśvara*, showing thereby his independent position as a ruler of great power.[36] The *Upadeśamālāvṛtti* of Vijayasiṁha Sūri (V. 1191) and *Muni-Suvrata-charita* (V. 1193) of Chandra Sūri mention him as a contemporary of Jayasiṁha Siddharāja and state that he had golden cupolas put on the Jaina temples of Raṇthambhor.[37] This besides proving his mastery of Raṇthambhor testifies to his liberal views in matters of religion.

The fragmentary *praśasti* of the Chauhāns, now in the Ajmer Museum, refers to *Hammīra-surāri-chakra* in the fragmentary portion dealing with this ruler.[38] The traditional account preserved in the *Prabhandhakośa* genealogy speaks of his fight against Muslims.[39] Can this *Hammīra* of the *praśasti* not be his contemporary Masūd III Imād-ud-daulah (1099-1115 A.D.) one of whose commanders is known to have led an expedition into India ?[40]

Another exploit of Pṛthvīrāja I was the slaying of seven hundred Chaulukyas who had dispossessed Brāhmaṇas of their property.[41] As the *Pṛthvīrājavijaya*, however, gives no further

34. Durlabharāja II is referred to in Dhavala's inscription of V. 1053. See above the account of Durlabharāja II.

35. *PV.*, *V.* 79; Bijoliā inscription, verse 14.

36. *Catalogue of the MSS in the Pattan Bhaṇḍārs*, p. 312.

37. *Ibid*, p. 316.

पुरइराएण सयम्भरी-नरिंदेण जस्स लेहेण ।
रणखम्भउर-जिनहरे चडविया कनयकलसा ॥

38. Line 6.

39. *PKG*, p. 133.

40. *Tabaqāt-i-Nāsiri*, *ED*, II, p. 278.

41. *PV*, V, 81. For a similar story of Pṛthvīrāja III in the *Pṛthvīrājarāso*, see its 5th *samaya*.

details about this achievement, it is difficult to say who these Chaulukyas were, whether soldiers of Gujarāt raiding Sapādalakṣa or Chaulukyas already settled there.

Pṛthvīrāja I was probably a Śaiva. The Chauhān *praśasti* refers to Someśvara, meaning thereby Somanātha perhaps, as the *Pṛthvīrājavijaya* mentions his free distribution of food on the way leading to Somanātha.[42]

Ajayarāja : Pṛthvīrāja I was succeeded by his son Ajayarāja who is known also as Ajayadeva and Salhaṇa.[43] Ajayarāja defeated Naravarman Paramāra of Mālwā on the borders of Avanti[44] and captured alive his general Sollaṇa,[45] after slaying the three warriors Chachchiga, Śindhula and Yaśorāja[46] and storming perhaps the fort of Śrīmārgga.[47]

42. *Praśasti*, line 7; *PV*, V. 120.

43. *PV*, V. 83-84; Bijoliā inscription, verse 14; *PKG*, p. 133. Both *PKG* and *HM* know him as Alhaṇa which is probably a corrupt form of the Salhaṇa of the *Pṛthvīrājavijaya*.

44. अवन्ति-पर्यन्ते-विजित-नरवर्म्मं ।" Line 11 of the *Praśasti*.

45. ह (द) त्वा चच्चिग-सिन्धुलाभिध-यशोराजादि-वीरत्रयं ।
क्षिप्रं क्रूर-कृतांत-कुहरे श्रीमार्ग्ग-दुद्दी (र्ग्गा) न्वितम् ।
श्रीमत्-सोल्लण-दण्डनायकवरः संग्रामरंगांगणे
जीवन्नेव नियंत्रितः करभके. . . . . . .

(verse 15 of the Bijoliā inscription)

The *Pṛthvīrājavijaya* calls Sollaṇa the ruler of Mālwā (V. 85). The ruler of the kingdom, however, at the time was Naravarman (see note 42). Combining the evidence of the *Bij, I, PV,* the Chauhān *praśasti*, we can, hence, say that Sollaṇa was the *daṁḍanāyaka* of the king of Mālwā.

46. See *Bij. I*, 15.

47. In the present state of our knowledge, it is difficult to be quite sure of the meaning of the word *Srīmārggadurddānvitaṁ* of the second line of the verse quoted above. We consider *durdda* as a mistake for *durgga* and are inclined to regard *Śrīmārgga* as some fort of Mālwā with which the three warriors Chachchiga, Sindhula and Yaśorāja were associated, most probably as its defenders. Mr. A. K. Vyas, the editor of the Bijoliā inscription, on the other hand, splits *Śrīmārggadurdda* into two words, Śrīmārgga and Durdda, identifying them respectively with Śrīpatha or Bayānā and Duddahī of Central India. Our disagreement from Mr. Akṣaya Keerty Vyas is based on the following grounds :—

The *Pṛthvīrājavijaya* credits Ajayarāja also with a victory over the *Garjana Mātaṅgas*,[48] which term must mean the Ghaznavites, if on the authority of the *Pṛthvīrājavijaya* itself, we equate *Garjana* with Ghaznā[49] and the Mātaṅgas with Muslims. That he had to fight against the Ghaznavites is certain; but we have a right to be rather sceptical about the accuracy of the Chauhāns' claim to victory, for we learn from the *Tabaqāt-i-Nāsirī* and *Tārikh-i-Firishta* that Muhammad Bāhlīm, *whom Bahrām Shah of Ghaznī had appointed the Governor of his dominions in Hindustan in A.D.*,[50] captured and fortified the town of Nāgor, and bringing his army, dependants and treasure there made it a base for further depredations on the territories of

(*i*) That not only does the phonetic equation Durdda—Duddahī stand in need of explanation, but also there is not much justification for regarding Duddahī as having ever been conquered by Ajayarāja. Madanavarman Chandel granted it to a Brāhmaṇa in V. 1219 (vide the Semrā Grant of Paramardin, *EI*, IV, pp. 158-170). Even Pṛthvīrāja III, claims to have merely plundered and devastated the country thereabouts and not to have conquered it.

(*ii*) That the words *Śrīmārggadurddānvitam vīratrayaṁ* of the Bijoliā inscription indicate that the three warriors Chachchiga, Sindhula and Yaśorāja belonged most probably to one place and not to two as supposed by Mr. Vyas.

(*iii*) That the statement that Ajayarāja captured the Mālavā commander Sollaṇa, *after having slain these three* does not suggest their belonging to a kingdom very far removed from Mālwā.

(*iv*) That if Ajayarāja had actually conquered Bayānā and Jejākabhukti, the facts should, probably, have been mentioned either in the Chauhān *praśasti* or the *Pṛthvīrājavijaya*.

(*v*) That Bayāṇā was, even as late as 1196 A.D., outside the Chauhān empire. It was a possession of the ruler of Tribhuvanagiri from whom it was captured by Muhammad Ghorī (vide *ED*, II, p. 226 and *CHI*, III, p. 44.)

Of these points, we should stress most the first and the least the fourth, because silence by itself is not a very strong basis for reaching valid conclusions.

48. *PV*. V, 113.

49. X verse 40.

50. Raverty, *Tabaqāt-i-Nāsirī*, p. 110; Briggs, *Tārikh-i-Firishta*, p. 151 Vol. I.

native rulers.[51] As Nāgor had, according to the *Prabhāvakacharita*, been under Ajayarāja up to V. 1178,[52] he was probably the ruler who suffered most at the hands of this ambitious and unscrupulous marauder. On Muhammad Bāhlīm's death, Bahrām Shāh appointed Salār Hussain as Governor of his Indian territories.[53] Ajayarāja's victory over the *Garjana Mātaṅgas*, if any was actually secured, might have amounted to nothing more than the repulse of a strong raid either by Salār Hussain or his predecessor.

Ajayarāja was the founder of the stately city of Ajmer, known originally as Ajayameru after the name of this ruler. It was certainly a much better place of refuge against Muslim attacks than Sāmbhar and in some ways better placed for raids on kingdoms like Mālwā. It must have been founded before V. 1170, for it is mentioned in the *Paṭṭāvalī* of Palha copied by Jinarakṣita at Dhārā in that year. The name finds a place in a *sati* slab of r. 489 also.[54]

Another achievement which has given Ajayarāja abiding fame is the issue of coins for not merely himself but also his queen Somalladevī.[55] Ajayadeva's coins are found minted both in silver and copper and bear the effigy of a seated goddess on the obverse.[56] That they were in use in the Sapādalakṣa kingdom is obvious from their mention in the Menāl inscription of V. 1225 and the Dhod pillar inscription of V. 1228.[57] Somalladevī's

51. *Tārikh-i-Firīshta*, Vol. I. p. 151.

52. p. 182. The ruler's name is given as Ālhādana, which is a Sanskritised form for the alternative name Alhaṇa given to Ajayarāja by *PKG.* and *HM.* A very old *Devasūricharita* in the possession of my friend, Mr. Agarchand Nahata, also speaks of Nāgor being under the Chauhāns in the time of Devasūri, a contemporary of Ajayarāja.

53. Briggs, *Tārikh-i-Firīshta*, Vol. I. p. 151.

54. *Apabhraṁśakāvyatrayī* (G. O. S.), p. 112. Another copy of the *Paṭṭāvalī* is dated in V. 1171.

55. "He filled", states the *PV*, "the earth with silver *rūpakas* (rupees) and the poets filled it instead with *rūpakas* (dramas) bearing golden letters. He wrested the fame of present rulers by means of his soldiers *eager for victory* (*jayapriya*) and of those already past or to come with his Ajayapriya coins. His beloved queen Somalekhā too had not her hands sullied because she had new coins issued daily" (Canto V, verses 87-89.)

56. Dr. G.H. Ojha, *IA.*, 1912, pp. 209-211.

57. See our paper on the coins of Ajayadeva and Somalladevī in the *Nāgarī-prachāriṇī-patrikā*, XLV, pp. 357 ff.

copper coins bear the effigy of a horseman on the obverse and the queen's name on the reverse. Her silver coins are comparatively rarer and are of the type "king's head", popularly known as *Gadhaiyā kā paisā*.[58]

Ajayarāja was a devotee of Śiva.[59] But there does not seem to have been any rabidity about his views, for he is known to have paid due respect also to the followers of Vaiṣṇava and Jaina sects.[60] He permitted the Jainas to build temples in the newly founded city of Ajmer,[61] presented a golden *kalaśa* to the temple of Pārśvanātha,[62] and acted as a judge in the religious discussion between the *Śvetāmbara* teacher Dharmaghoṣa.sūri and his *Digambara* opponent Guṇachandra.[63]

According to the fragmentary Chauhān *praśasti* of the Rajpūtānā Museum, Ajayarāja put his son Arṇorāja on the throne and retired to the forest adjoining the sacred lake Puṣkara.[64] The event must have taken place before V. 1190, the probable year of the death of Naravarman of Mālwā, who was, according to the Bijoliā inscription, defeated by Ajayarāja's son and successor, Arṇorāja.

58. The chief reasons for assigning the coins to Ajayarāja's queen Somalladevī can be summarised as follows:—

1. The Bijoliā inscription gives the name of Ajayarāja's queen as Somalladevī.
2. These coins are generally found in places once ruled over by the Chauhāns.
3. The copper coins of Somalladevī bear, like many other Chauhān coins, the effigy of a horseman on the reverse.
4. The *Pṛthvīrājavijaya* mentions the issue of coins by Ajayarāja's queen Somalekhā who, as we know from the Bijoliā inscription, is identical with Somalladevī.
5. These have been found in close association with the coins of Ajayadeva as proved by the discovery by the Rāo of Parsolī in Mewār, of a pot containing copper coins of merely these two types.

For a more detailed treatment of the question see the two articles by Dr. G. H. Ojha and ourselves referred to in notes 57 and 58.

59. *PV*, V. 97.

60. See the Devasūricharita of the *Prabhāvakacharita*.

61. *Kharataragachchhapaṭṭāvalī* of Jinapāla MS. p. 16.

62. *Ibid.*

63. *Catalogue of Manuscripts in Pattaṇ Bhandars*, I, p. 369 verses 25 and 26 of the *Dharmagh oṣastuti* by Raviprabha Sūri.

64. Verse 21, See *Appendix* I for the text of the *praśasti*.

CHAPTER V

THE CHAUHĀNS OF SAPĀDALAKṢA (*Continued*)

ARṆORĀJA

Arṇorāja, known also as Analadeva. Ānaladeva, Anna and Ānāka was the son of Ajayarāja and Somalladevī.[1] He was born before V. 1170, because the "gaḍha Analliu", the fort of Ajmer, which bears his name is mentioned in the *Jinadatta-sūri-stuti*, of Palha, a manuscript of which was copied out in V. 1170.[2] As already shown, he ascended the throne of Ajmer a little before V. 1190, the probable date of the death of his rival Naravarman of Mālwā.[3]

The available dated references to Arṇorāja are in the following records:—

(1) Two stone inscriptions of Revāsā, dated in V. 1196 (1139 A.D.) which mention him as *Mahārājādhirāja-Parameśvara*-Śrī-Arṇorājadeva.[4]

(2) The *Śatakabṛhadbhāṣya* of Chakreśvara, dated in V. 1197, the colophon of which mentions him as *nṛpati* Analadeva the *pasāyameha* of Siddharāja.[5]

(3) The colophon of a manuscript of the *Āvaśyakaniryukti* (copied out at Pṛthvīpura, a suburb of Ajmer), which is dated in V. 1198 A.D. (1141 A.D.) and mentions him as *Paramabhaṭṭāraka-Mahārājādhirāja-parameśvara-śrīmad-*Arṇorājadeva.[6]

1. *PV.* V., 91.

2. *Apabhraṁśakāvyatrayī*, p. 110.

3. An Ujjain grant states that Yaśovarman performed the funeral ceremony of Mahārāja Naravarman on the 8th day of the bright half of Kārttika, V. 1191. See *IA*, XIX, p. 353, lines 6-8.

4. Noticed in *ASI, WC*, 1909-10, p. 52. Our reference is from the transcript by Dr. G.H. Ojha who visited the place himself.

5. *Catalogue of Mss in the Paṭṭana Bhandars*, p. 285. The *pasāyameha* looks like the Prakrita form of *prasādamegha*, the cloud in the form of the pleasure of Sidhharāja. The likelihood of this Arṇorāja being a different man, however, should be kept in view.

6. *Ibid*, p. 129.

Thus these dates for Arṇorāja range from V. 1196 to 1199. But he can be proved from other sources to have ruled much longer, say for about a period of eighteen years *i.e.* from V. 1190 to 1208[7]

The fragmentary Chauhān *praśasti* of Ajmer Museum makes special mention of the following achievements of Arṇorāja:[8]—

1. Slaughter of Turuṣkas near Ajmer.
2. Defeat of Naravarman of Mālwā.
3. Carrying of Chauhān arms up to the Sindhu and the Sarasvatī.
4. An expedition into the Haritānaka country.

We shall deal with these in the above order, supplementing the account of the *praśasti* by means of details from other sources.

The fight against the Turuṣkas, *i.e.* the Yāminis of Lahore and Ghaznā, was an inheritance from the reign of his father Ajayarāja who perhaps never succeeded in recovering Nāgor from the Muslims. Very early in Arṇorāja's reign, these foreign invaders reached as far as Ajmer and in the battle that followed on the plain outside the city, where the Ānāsāgara lake was later on excavated and filled with the waters of the river Chandrā to wash off the stains of Muslim blood, the Yāmini commander was decisively beaten and fled before the pursuing Chauhāns. Many Muslim soldiers died of the exhaustion caused by their heavy armour, and not a few perished of thirst in the waterless desert. Some found their graves in the shifting sands of Rajasthān, and the bodies of others lying in large numbers along the path leading away from Ajmer were burnt by the villagers who did not like their stinking smell. A large amount of booty, consisting mainly of horses, fell into the hands of the soldiers of Arṇorāja and for some days Ajmer became a scene of festivities held to celebrate this great victory.[9]

7. V. 1190, as noticed above, is the date of his rival Naravarman's death. Another rival of his, Kumārapāla Chaulukya, refers to his defeat in an inscription of V. 1207. Arṇorāja's son Vigraharāja IV was on the throne of Ajmer in V. 1210. Arṇorāja died somewhere between V. 1207 and V. 1210.

8. See the text of the *praśasti* in the Appendix.

9. *PV*, VI, 1-27. See also line 15 of the Chauhān *praśasti* which states, "The land of Ajmer, soaked with the blood of the Turuṣkas, looked as if it had dressed itself in a robe of deep-red colour to celebrate the victory of her lord."

Equally great was Arṇorāja's success in Mālwā. Using the well-known rhetorical figure *śleṣa*, the Bijoliā inscription refers to the defeat of Nirvāṇa-Nārāyaṇa *i.e.* Naravarman the ruler of Mālwā, in its 17th verse.[10] The fragmentary Chauhān *praśasti* too begins its account of Arṇorāja by mentioning Naravarmman.[11] But the rest of the verse after the words जयश्रियं नरवर्म्मं is unfortunately gone. After four lines, however, we find Arṇorāja's soldiers being described as taking away by force, on the battlefield, the elephants of the *Mālaveśa*.[12] This *Mālaveśa* obviously is the ruler Naravarmma of the earlier part of the *praśasti*.

The details of the expedition to the Sindhu and the Sarasvatī are not clear. "Rendered thirsty", says the Chauhān *praśasti*, "by having remained in the waterless desert and with his thirst unquenched by Prahlādakūpa (perhaps modern Pallū in the Bikāner State), Arṇorāja reached the Sindhu and Sarasvatī".[13] The *Dvyāśrayakāvya* of Hemachandra, a contemporary writer, speaks of Anna being helped by the rulers of Eastern Madra and the towns of the Vāhīkadeśa.[14] Should not this fact as well as Arṇorāja's designation *udīchyarāṭ* mentioned by the same author[15] lead us to conclude that Arṇorāja did, as the result of his expedition to the Sindhu and the Sarasvatī, bring some portions of the Eastern Punjab under his subjection?

The details of Arṇorāja's attack on the Haritānaka country can hardly be regarded as sufficient. All that we can learn from the fragments of the Chauhān *praśasti* available to us is that his soldiers' march rendered muddy the waters of the river

10. "We regard it", says the verse, "as strange that he, Arṇorāja a pious man, should have shown disrespect to the lord of gods by humiliating Nirvāṇa-Nārāyaṇa". This element of incongruity and wonder referred to by the poet can be removed if we know that Arṇorāja was actually humiliating not Nārāyaṇa, the lord of gods, but Nirvāṇa-Nārāyaṇa, the ruler of Mālwā.

Since the above was written Mr. A. K. Vyas has independently reached the same conclusion.

11. Verse 22, line 13.

12. यत्सैनिकैः समरमूर्धनि मालवेशादाच्छिद्य सान्द्र-मदमोदित-भृङ्गमाला आलानिता करटिनो....

13. मन्ये समाक्रान्त-मरु-पिपासुः संसारसिन्धुञ्च सरस्वतीञ्च line 14

14. XVI, 15.

15. *Ibid.* 8.

Kālindī (Jumnā) and the women of the Haritānaka country shed tears.[16] Now Haritānaka or Hariyānā is, according to the Pālam Bāolī inscription of V. 1337 and the Delhi Museum inscription of V. 1384, the country which was ruled over by the Tomaras before its conquest by the Chauhāns.[17] Delhi or Ḍhillikā was its capital and Kālindī or Yamunā, as all know, is the river on the right bank of which the city stands. The reference in the Chauhān *praśasti* is thus to a fight between Arṇorāja and the Tomaras of Delhi in which the latter were worsted, though not decisively because the struggle continued, as we shall see, at least up to the reign of Vigraharāja IV.

Close by Hariyānā lay the kingdom of Vāraṇa (modern Bulandshahr) then held by the Ḍoḍ Rajputs. That it did not escape the victorious arms of Arṇorāja might be seen from the first part of verse 17 of the Bijoliā inscription which states:[18]

16. Line 16.

वाष्प–वारिणि कालिन्दी हरितानक-योषिताम् ।
सत्त्वाक्रान्तस्य मिलिता यत्प्रमाणे रजस्वला ।।

17. D.R. Bhandarkar, *Inscriptions of Northern India*, Nos. 598 and 603 *JASB*, XLIII. p. 108; *EI*, I, pp. 98 ff.

18. यद्राज्यं कुशवारणं प्रतिकृतं राजांकुशेन स्वयं
येनात्रैव नु चित्रमेतत्पुनर्म्मन्यामहे तं प्रति ।
तच्चित्रं प्रतिभासते सुकृतिना निर्व्वाणनारायण-
न्यक्कारावरणेन भंगकरणं श्रीदेवराजं प्रति ।।१७।।

The Editor of the record, Mr. Aksaya Keerty Vyas, reads *prati* and *kṛtaṁ* of the first line of this verse as one word *pratikṛtam*. As it is however an insult or injury and not a kingdom that is avenged (pratikṛta), the right reading is *rājyaṁ prati kṛtam* instead of *rājyaṁ pratikṛtaṁ* of Mr. Vyasa's edition. That our view is the right one might be seen also by referring to the latter part of the verse which reads *bhaṁgakaraṇaṁ Śrī-Devarājam prati.*

Mr. Vyas further regards Kuśa and Vāraṇa as the names of two kingdoms. But as pointed out by the editor of the *Epigraphia Indica*, the context indicates one kingdom (XXVI, 94, note 1). In fact, Kuśavāraṇa has two meanings. When applied to a kingdom, itmeans the *kuśa* (sinful) kingdom of Vāraṇa (Bulandshahr). In the case of *Vāraṇas* or elephants, it means *kuśa* (rutting) elephants.

Mr. Vyas identifies Kuśa with Kuśasthalī or Kanauj which, according to him was fast fading in importance due to the increasing influence of the Chauhāns. As a matter of fact, however, the Gāhadvāla kingdom was at

"We do not regard as strange what he did against that sinful kingdom of Vāraṇa which resembled, as it were, a rutting elephant, for he was verily a goad for elephant-like rulers."

The ruler of Vāraṇa at the time was either Sahajāditya or Bhojadeva.[19]

Only on one side did the almost ever-victorious army of Arṇorāja suffer a serious check. In the south-west of Sapādalakṣa was the powerful and equally ambitious kingdom of Gujarāt, ruled successively by Jayasiṁha Siddharāja and Kumārapāla. They did not remain satisfied with their ancestral dominions; Siddharāja captured Nāgor in V. 1178 and Malwa in V. 1200.[20] Thus the struggle between the Chauhānas of Śākambharī and the Chaulukyas of Gujarāt appears to have begun some years earlier than Arṇorāja's accession to the throne. In his own reign, it perhaps entered a more bitter phase. According to the *Dvyāśrayamahākāvya* of Hemachandra, Arṇorāja was obliged to recognise the supremacy of Jayasiṁha Siddharāja,[21] and a similar statement is found in the *Surathotsava* of Someśvara. The latter writer's *Kīrtikaumudī* further states that Jayasiṁha gave Arṇorāja his daughter in marriage, though he (Jayasiṁha) had defeated him in battle.[22] From the *Pṛthvīrājavijaya*, we learn that this daughter was named Kāñchanadevī.[23] A Sāmbhar inscription giving the genealogy of the Chaulukyas from Mūlarāja to Jayasiṁha, and actually men-

the height of its glory in the reign of Arṇorāja's contemporary Govindachandra (c. V. 1171-1211).

Considering all these facts, Mr. Vyas's translation that he "revenged the kingdoms of Kuśa and Vāraṇa" and "the ocean...handed over the mad elephant to Indra" seems rather fanciful. (vide *EI* XXVI, P. 94).

19. In V. 1233, the ruler was Sahajāditya's son Anaṅga, (see D.R. Bhandarkar's *Inscriptions of Northern India*, No. 376).

20. *Devasūricharita*, vv. 70-80.

21. XVII, 84 and XVI, 19-21 : *Surathotsava*, XV, 22.

22. II. 27-28.

23. VI, 34. The verse itself is missing, but the commentary remains and gives this name.

tioning Sambhar even, suggests that Sāmbhar was occupied, for a while, by the Chaulukya forces of Jayasiṁha.[24]

It is impossible to give with any certainty the cause of this conflict. Ambition would perhaps explain much, and then there were the conflicting interests of the two in Mālwā, on which both the Chauhāns of Śākambharī and the Chaulukyas had, for some time past, been casting their greedy eyes.[25] We cannot say how long the war lasted. It was perhaps, finally ended by Jayasiṁha's desire to be given a free hand in Mālwā.[26] He won over Ārṇorāja to his side by giving him his daughter in marriage.

The peace thus established did not, however, outlast the reign of Jayasiṁha Siddharāja. In V. 1199, Kumārapāla ascended the throne of Gujarāt and once again the Chauhāns of Sapādalakṣa and the Chaulukyas of Gujarāt began fighting against each other.

The earliest writer to refer at any length to this renewed conflict is Hemachandra, (the author of the *Dvyāśrayamahākāvya*, and spiritual teacher of Kumārapāla Chaulukya), according to whom the war was caused by the ambition of Anna (Arṇorāja) of Śākambharī who allying himself with certain northern princes and a discontented Gujarāti noble Chāhaḍa, a relative of Kumārapāla, had proceeded against the Chaulukya kingdom. Ballāla, a friend of Anna, agreed to attack the Gujarātīs

24. *IA*, 1929, pp. 234-236. It cannot be a very sure indication though. It is fragmentary and could have been set up by any Chaulukya chief accompanying Kāñchanadevī or by this queen herself like the Nāgarī (Udaipur State) inscription of Sṛṅgāradevī, daughter of Jodhājī, who gives at length the exploits of her father's family.

25. See above for Ajayarāja's attack on Mālwā.

26. Arṇorāja's messenger while trying to have peace with Kumārapāla is made to utter this verse in the *Dvyāśrayamahākāvya*:—

रमणीयं यथासीत् प्राक् सिद्धेशे प्राग्गतागते ।
भृत्येनान्नेन देव त उपर्यपि तथास्तु ते ॥

It means that if he would have Anna as his subordinate, his position in Mālwā would be as secure as it had been in the time of Siddharāja when Anna was a Chaulukya feudatory. (See Abhayatilakagaṇi's commentary on the above verse). The verse is important as showing what Arṇorāja's hostility could and most probably did do in Mālwā before the conclusion of a treaty with him.

from the rear, when Kumārapāla marched out to meet the threat of the Chāhamāna invasion.[27]

Other writers regarding Anna as an aggressor are Abhayatilakagaṇi, a commentator of the *Dvyāśrayamahākāvya*, and Merutuṅga, the author of the *Prabandhachintāmaṇi*, who composed their works respectively in V. 1312 and 1361. According to the former of these, Anna attacked Gujarāt, because he believed that Kumārapāla was weaker than the predecessor Jayasiṁha Siddharāja and could easily be defeated.[28] Merutuṅga's account is more detailed.[29] He throws the responsibility of the war on Chāhaḍa, a prince who had been regarded as his son by Siddharāja. Having no mind to take orders from Kumārapāla, Chāhaḍa had taken refuge at the court of Ānāka, the ruler of Sapādalakṣa. In a few days he won over to his side most of the Gujarāti nobles and brought Ānāka with his large army to the borders of Gujarāt. The *Prabhāvakacharita*, composed in V. 1334, though silent about Ānāka's aggression states that Kumārapāla set out to fight against Arṇorāja who was intoxicated with pride.[30] This probably means that the Chāhamāna ruler had somehow tried to violate the integrity of the Chaulukya kingdom before Kumārapāla marched out against him with his big army.

Later writers, however, give us quite a different story regarding the origin of the war. According to the *Prvbhandhakośa* (V. 1405).[31] Kumārapāla had a sister who was married to Ānāka (Arṇorāja). Once while the husband and wife were playing chess, the former taking away one of the chessmen of the latter remarked (in jest), "Kill these *Muṇḍikas*. Kill these *Muṇḍikas*." This offended the queen, because the word *Muṇḍika* could refer to the Gujaratīs who generally wore no caps and also to their hairless *gurus*, the *Svetāmbara* Jainas. She accordingly asked Ānāka to keep his tongue under control, telling him that unless he did so he ran the risk of having it torn out from his mouth by her brother, the *Rājarākṣasa* Kumārapāla. Ānāka's only reply

27. *Dvyāśrayamahākāvya* XVI, 7, 14.
28. Abbayatilaka's commentary on the *Dvyāśrayamahākāvya* XVI, 7, 14.
29. *Prabandhachintāmaṇi*, p. 79, Singhī Granthamālā.
30. *Hemachandrasūri-prabandha*, vv. 416, 423 and 518.
31. P. 59 Singhī Jain Granthamālā.

to this threat was a kick. Thus insulted the queen at once left for Paṭṭana and reaching there told Kumārapāla of the way she had been treated by her husband. Kumārapāla determined to avenge the insult.

The story gets further amplified in the works of Jayasiṁha Sūri,[32] Jinamaṇḍana[33] and Charitrasundara.[34] They all refer to Kumārapāla's sister, Devaladevī, who was married to Ānāka, to her playing chess with her husband, and to the jesting remark which led to the war. Dissatisfied with earlier accounts, which probably appeared tame and rather secular to them, they went on developing the theme, first set forth by Rājaśekhara. This religious perversion of facts, we believe, is most manifest in Charitrasundara (c. V. 1507), according to whom the war was due to Ānāka's having talked of slaying a chessman. Such things, of course, were not even to be thought of, because they were not merely against the principles of Jainism, but also against Kumārapāla's express orders against slaughter.[35]

Diwān Bahādur Har Bilas Sarda knew of these two different accounts of the origin of the Chaulukya-Chāhamāna struggle. But instead of regarding the contemporary and earlier authorities as the only trustworthy sources of information and the latter as a monastic perversion of facts, he thinks that they refer to two distinct wars separated from each other by a number of years. "The first war evidently took place," writes the Diwān Bahādur, "because Arṇorāja...espoused the cause of Siddharāja's adopted son, Bāhaḍa and wished to place him on the throne in place of the usurper, Kumārapāla. The result of this war appears to have been unfavourable to Kumārapāla, as he hastened to make peace with Arṇorāja and gave the latter his sister to wife...The second war of Saṁvat 1207 appears to have taken place in consequence of Arṇorāja's ill-treatment of his queen Devaladevī, sister of Kumārapāla.[36]

32. *Kumārapālacharita* p. 199 (Jāmnagar edition).

33. *Ibid.*, pp. 40a-40b.

34. *Ibid.*, pp. 37a-38-a.

35. *Ibid.*

36. Har Bilas Sarda, *Speeches and Writings*, pp. 285-86.

We admit that there is some substance in the Diwan Bahādur's reconstruction of the story. The Chaulukya-Chāhamāna struggle actually took place in two stages. But in relying on Rājaśekhara and his successors and making Devaladevī the cause of the second phase he has certainly committed a mistake. Actually there was no Devaladevī in the affair, because no sister of Kumārpāla named Devaladevī can be proved to have existed. According to the *Pṛithvīrājavijaya*, the most authentic account of the Chāhamanas of Sapādalakṣa, Arṇorāja had two queens, Kāṅchanadevī, a daughter of Siddharāja Jayasiṁha, and Sudhavā of Mārwār.[37] The *Kīrtikaumudī*, a well-known old Gujarāti source, also speaks of only one Gujarātī queen of the Chāhamāna ruler, namely, the daughter of Jayasiṁha.[38] Had Kumārapāla too given one of his sisters in marriage to Arṇorāja after being defeated by him, as supposed by the Diwān Bahādur, there was nothing to deter the author of the *Pṛithvīrājavijaya* and the *Kīrtikaumudī* from noting down this important fact. But how could they do it, when Kumārapāla had actually no sister to offer in marriage to Arṇorāja ? According to the earliest biography of Kumārapāla at our disposal, Kumārapāla's only sister was Premaladevī, and she had been given in marriage to Kṛṣṇarāja, a Gujarātī noble, before the accession of Kumārapāla to the throne.[39] Somatilaka Sūri and the Purātanāchārya too knew of only one sister of Kumārapāla.[40] Devaladevī, who is believed to have quarrelled with her husband and thus brought about a war between him and her husband, may therefore safely be regarded as a creation of either Rājaśekhara (V. 1405) or some one of his immediate

37. VI, 29. Dr. G.H. Ojha's edition.
38. II. 28.
39. त्रिभुवनपालस्याभूत् सुतैका तनयास्त्रयः ।
आद्यः कुमारपालाख्यः राज्यलक्षण-लक्षितः ॥
मह्ीपालः कीर्तिपालस्तथा प्रेमलदेव्यभूत् ।
श्रीकृष्णभटदेवेन योदूढा मोढवासके ॥
(*Kumārapāladevacharita* p. 2; Muni Jinavijayaji's edition, Singhī Jain Granthamālā.)
40. *Kumārapāladevacharita*, p. 9, 11.15-18; edition as above.
Kumārapāladevaprabandha, p. 43, 11. 6-8; edition as above.

predecessors who had heard that a Chaulukya princess had been married to Arṇorāja but did not know that she was not Kumārapāla's sister but his aunt. And that this Kumārapāla's aunt too could not have brought about the war might be easily inferred from the fact that out of the four authors we have before V. 1445, not one refers to a Gujarāt princess as the cause of a war between the kingdoms of Śākambharī and Gujarāt. One cannot see really why it was left only for a late author like Rājaśekhara and his successors to make this discovery.

As a contemporary and *guru* of Kumārapāla, Hemachandra was in the best position to know about the real causes of the war ; and the account left by him as well as the three writers next to him in order of time, namely, Abhayatilakagaṇi, Prabhāchandra and Merutuṅga makes it sufficiently obvious that the reasons leading to the war were purely political. Jayasiṁha's death had not left any unanimously recognised successor. Chāhaḍa, an adopted son of the deceased ruler, was a candidate in the field, and Arṇorāja supported his claims perhaps hoping thereby to have on the throne of Gujarāt a ruler who would be less of a check on his ambition and more open to his influence than Kumārapāla could ever be expected to be. Kumārapāla's reign had just begun. If he was to be removed from the throne at all, it was, in Arṇorāja's opinion, the best time to begin hostilities against Gujarāt.

But who was this Chāhaḍa ? The *Rāsamālā* regards him as a brother of Kumārapāla's minister, Vāgbhaṭa.[41] Its authority for this assertion, most probably, is the *Prabandhachintāmaṇi* which once mentions Vāgbhaṭa's brother Chāhaḍa as the "king's son".[42] The *Prabandhakośa* mentions him as a prince of Mālwā who had on Jayasiṁha's death desired to be made the ruler of Gujarāt and had been refused the honour, because he did not belong to the Chaulukya clan.[43] Jayasiṁha Sūri and Prabhāchandra mention him as Jayasiṁha's adopted son but add no further details. The *Moharājaparājaya* of Yaśaḥpāla (c. V. 1230) speaks of him as the excellent prince Tyāgarāja

41. p. 177.
42. p. 94. Singhī Jain Granthamālā.
43. p. 52. *Ibid.*

who took refuge at Śākambharī and faced Kumārapāla in battle[44] but is as unhelpful as the above sources regarding his identity. The only author, in fact, who can be of some use on the point is Hemachandra. According to him Chāhaḍa was a relative of Kumārapāla and ruler of the village Kanthā (located by the commentator Abhayatilakagaṇi on the shore of the lake Varṇā) in the part of the country known as Śivirūpa.[45] Village Kanthā might be the same as Kanthā-durga to which Mūlarāja retired on being pressed hard by Vigraharāja II.[46] Chāhaḍa's being mentioned as a relative of Kumārapāla makes one think that he might have been either a Chaulukya or a Paramāra.[47] By all accounts he was a good controller of elephants.

Most of our authorities confine the war between Arṇorāja and Kumārapāla to one campaign. But keeping in view the statement of the *Prabhāvakacharita* that it lasted for twelve years and also considering the epigraphic evidence on the point, we might tentatively reconstruct its main events as follows:—

The war, probably, began early in the reign of Kumārapāla, with the disputed succession to the Chaulukya throne and the ambition of Arṇorāja as its chief causes. Arṇorāja advanced towards Gujarāt and was met and defeated somewhere near Mount Ābū by Kumārapāla's forces, though the defeat was by no means decisive. Vikramasiṁha, the Paramāra ruler of the place, was about this time detected conspiring against the Chaulukya monarch's life.[48] He was therefore deposed and replaced by Yaśodhavala for whom we have an inscription at Ajāri (V. 1202).[49] Another change introduced probably in the same year was at Nāḍol where the pro-Chaulukya ruler Ālhaṇa took the place of Rāyapāla whose last inscription is dated in the same year. The Chaulukya forces perhaps advanced even as far as Ajmer, but its fortifications, consisting

44. V. 36.

45. XVI, 14.

46. See *Pṛithvīrājavijaya* V. 51.

47. Rājaśekhara calls him a prince of Mālwā. From other sources we know that Kumārapāla's chief queen belonged to Mālwā.

48. See the *Hemachandrasūricharita*. The fact is mentioned also by Jinamaṇḍana and some other writers.

49. *IA*, LVI, p. 12.

chiefly of a 16 miles fence of acacia, *karīra*, *khadira*, *badarī* and other thorny trees kept them at bay and they had ultimately to retire baffled to Gujarāt.[50]

Arṇorāja was not a man to take all this lying down. Within three or four years he was once again in a position to try conclusions with his Chaulukya adversary. His first blow fell on his own neighbour and clansman Ālhaṇa whom he drove out of the kingdom of Nāḍol.[51] Next he fomented trouble in Mālwā where he instigated its ruler Ballāla to organise a rising against the Chaulukyas.[52] Like the good general that he was, Kumārapāla left the task of extirpating Ballāla to his feudatories and advanced personally with a large force against his chief enemy, the ruler of Ajmer. This time his preparations appear to have been very good. Advancing into the territory of Nāḍol which was now in hostile hands, he captured Pālī in V. 1207 and, out of anger, had ginger sown there, an operation which probably involved the sack of the town and destruction of some of its chief buildings.[53] Sthirachandragaṇi, a Jaina monk, who was copying the *Pañchāśaka-vṛtti* of Abhayadeva, had to leave it unfinished for the time being and to run away and complete it at Ajmer in V. 1207/1150 A.D.[54] Proceeding further Kumārapāla reached Ajmer and encamped outside its walls. Arṇorāja came out with his army, a few days later, letting the secret agents of Chāhaḍa utilise the interval to win over to his side the Chaulukya monarch's elephant-driver, Chauliga, and undermine the loyalty of feudatories like Kelhaṇa.[55] After thus fully preparing the ground for an action, likely to be successful, Arṇorāja attacked Kumārapāla's army. But as luck would have it, Kumārapāla's suspicions had been aroused and Chauliga, the ruler's elephant-driver, resigned almost on the eve of the battle. Ignorant of the fact the driver had been changed, Chāhaḍa tried to step from his own elephant to that of Kumāra-

50. *Hemachandrasūricharita*.
51. We have no inscriptions for Ālhaṇa between V. 1205 and 1218.
52. *Dvyāśrayamahākāvya* XVI, 8.
53. *Kumārapālacharita* of Jinamaṇḍana, p. 42b.
54. *Catalogue of Mss. in the Jaisalmer Bhandars*, G.O.S., p. 7.
55. *Prabandhakośa*, p. 51; *Kumārapālacharita* of Jinamaṇḍana, p. 41b; *Kumārapālacharita* of Jayasiṁha Sūri, p. 188.

pāla, and failing to do so fell down on the ground and was taken prisoner by Chaulukya foot-soldiers.[56] Next followed a duel between the two rulers in which Arṇorāja was wounded in the chest by Kumārapāla's arrows and fell unconscious on his elephant. Arṇorāja's individual defeat proved the defeat of his whole army; it precipitately left the field carrying away its unconscious leader.[57]

This time Arṇorāja's defeat was severe enough to make him buy peace by offering the old Chaulukya ruler the hand of his young daughter, Jalhaṇā, and along with her a large number of horses and elephants by way of dowry.[58] He had to suffer also the humiliation of not celebrating the marriage at Ajmer but at Aṇahillapaṭṭana where he sent his mother and *guru* to give away the princess in marriage.[59] Ballāla, the Mālava ally of Arṇorāja, was slain, somewhere about the same time, for the news of his death reached Kumārapāla almost immediately after the celebration of his nuptials.[60]

The defeat of both Arṇorāja and Ballāla is mentioned in the Vaḍnagar *praśasti*, dated Thursday, the 5th of the bright half of Āśvina, V. 1208,[61] and that of Arṇorāja alone in the Chitor inscription of V. 1207 which states that, after having defeated the ruler of Śākambharī, Kumārapāla reached Śālipura and fixing his camp there went to have the glorious view of the Mount Chitrakūṭa.[62] Thence he proceeded to Pālarī where, according to Tod, he placed an inscription in the month of Pauṣa, V. 1207.[63] As the slow march from Ajmer to Pālarī must have taken considerable time, Kumārapāla may be assumed to have started from his dominions early in the Indian campaigning season, which begins with *Vijayādaśamī*, and to

56. *Dvyāśrayamahākāvya*, XVIII, 108.

57. Vaḍnagar *praśasti*, 1, 21, *EI*, I, p. 266 ff. The story that Kumārapāla had Arṇorāja put in a wooden cage is a later invention. (See *Prabandhakośa*, p. 52) Charitrasundara, not content with Arṇorāja's defeat, makes his queen Devaladevī go to the field and beg for her husband's life.

58. *Dvyāśrayamahākāvya*, XIX, 21-4.

59. *Ibid.*, p. 507, Bombay Sanskrit Series.

60. *Ibid*, p. 530.

61. See note 55.

62. Lines 10-13; *EI*, II, p. 421 ff. Śālipura is modern Sālerā.

63. *Annals and Antiquities of Rājasthān*, III, p. 1651 (O. U. P. edition.)

have reached Ajmer, after some battles on the way, somewhere towards the end of Kārttika or the beginning of Mārgaśīrṣa and to have fought the decisive battle against Arṇorāja within a few days of his arrival there.

As regards the consequences of the war, the one who benefited most was, of course, the victor. It not merely increased Kumārapāla's reputation as a soldier, but also fixed firmly the Chaulukya supremacy in south-western Rājpūtānā and Mālwā. Arṇorāja lost much of his well-earned prestige and wealth, though his kingdom did not perhaps suffer any appreciable diminution in territory. The Chauhāns were not crushed, though they had to confess themselves beaten for the time being ; for in Vigraharāja IV's reign, they once more successfully measured their swords with Kumārapāla and his feudatories. Far more serious were its results for others who were, in some way or other, involved in it. Vikramasiṁha, who according to Hemachandra, did all that he could to entertain the Chaulukya soldiers on their way to Sapādalakṣa,[64] lost his kingdom because of being suspected of treason. Ballāla, the ally of Arṇorāja lost not merely the throne of Mālwa but also his life; and in the kingdom of Nāḍol not only were the changes equally important but also more frequent on account of its position as a buffer state between the Chauhān and Chaulukya dominions.[65]

Arṇorāja did not survive long his defeat. He was murdered by Jagaddeva, his eldest son by Sudhavā of Mārwār.[66] His other sons were Vigraharāja, Devadatta and Someśvara. The last one was born of the Chaulukya princess, Kāñchanadevī.[67]

Arṇorāja was a Śaiva. "But his relations with other sects also were cordial. He built a temple of Varāha at Pushkar[68] and gave the followers of the Kharatara-gachchha an extensive plot of land for the construction of a temple at Ajmer.[69] The *Bhāg-*

64. See above, p. 52.
65. See below the account of the Chauhāns of Nāḍol.
66. *PV*, VI, 32, VII, 12.
67. *Ibid*, VI, 34.
68. See G. H. Ojha's *Three lecturers on Ajmer and one on Pushkar*, p. 136.
69. *Gaṇadharasārdhaśatakabṛhadvṛtti*. (Introduction to the *Apabhraṁśakāvyatrayī*, p. 46.) The *vṛtti* mentions also the reception of the Kharatarāchārya Jinadatta Sūri at Arṇorāja's court.

vata teacher, Devabodha, had an honoured place at his court.[70] The *Śvetāmbara* scholar, Dharmaghoṣa Sūri, received a *jayapatra* from him by defeating his *Digambara* rival, Guṇachandra.[71]

Despite the defeat at the hands of Kumārapāla, Arṇorāja deserves to be regarded as one of the great rulers of his dynasty. He added to the glory of his people and the territory of his kingdom by his expedition to Mālwā, Hariyānā and other lands bordering his territories. But his greatest achievement was the decisive defeat of the Ghaznavites which kept them away from Sapādalakṣa for nearly twenty years and thus ensured the peace and prosperity not merely of Sapādalakṣa but also of Gujarāt and other kingdoms to which the way lay through Arṇorāja's dominions. "He enjoyed" writes Jayānaka, "the religious merit of building all temples of the present as well as future, for had he not defeated the Muslims, the temples would have passed into the sphere of non-existence,"[72] and there is not perhaps much exaggeration about this statement of the poet, provided we do not interpret it too literally.

70. *Prabhāvakacharita* (Nirṇayasāgara edition), pp. 282-3; *Catalogue of Palm-leaf Mss. in the Paṭṭan Bhandars*, p. 395.

71. *Catalogue of the Palm-leaf Mss. in the Paṭṭan Bhandars*, p. 395, v. 10.

72. *Pṛithvīrājavijaya* VI (p. 155 of Dr. G. H. Ojha's edition). The verse itself has disappeared, but Jonarāja's commentary gives us its import.

CHAPTER VI

THE CHAUHĀNS OF SAPĀDALAKṢA (*contd.*): *Jagaddeva to Pṛithvirāja II*

Jagaddeva. The parricide Jagaddeva did not rule long.[1] Revolted by his heinous deed, his younger brother, Vigraharāja, appears to have headed a rising and slain him in battle. "Having slain his affectionate father", states the *Pṛithvīrājavijaya*, "Jagaddeva himself perished, leaving behind himself a stinking name."[2] At another place too the *kāvya* describes him as the only one of the Chauhān rulers of Śākambharī who did not attain heaven.[3]

Vigraharāja IV. For Vigraharāja IV, known also as Bīsaladeva, we have eleven inscriptions ranging from V. 1210 to 1220.[4] As the earliest of them was incised in his magnificent *Sarasvatīmandira* of Ajayameru, later on converted by the Muslims into the present *Aḍhāī-din-kā jhoṁprā* mosque, which must have taken years and not months to build, Vigraharāja IV probably ascended the throne about V. 1208. The other limit of his reign is fixed by the births of Pṛthvīrāja III and Harirāja which, as shown later, took place, respectively in V. 1223 and 1224.[5]

Retaliation and revenge were perhaps the uppermost ideas in Vigraharāja IV's mind when he succeeded to his father's patrimony. Arṇorāja's death had already been avenged. He

1. That he actually ruled, however, is proved by *PV.*, *HM.*, *PKG.*, *SC* and the old bardic *bahī* in our possession. His mother, Sudhavā was not a princess of Avīchi, which means hell, as wrongly supposed by Drs. D.R. Bhandarkar and H.C. Ray, but of Marukoṭṭa or Marot. Her brother, Siṁhabala, the ruler of Marukoṭṭa from V. 1217 to 1232, was a Yaudheya Rājpūt and a trusted adviser and general of Vigraharāja IV.

2. VII, 13.

3. VII, 74.

4. Of these six come from Ajmer, one from Lohārī in the Jahāzpur district of Mewār, one from Narhaḍ in the Jaipur Division of Rājasthān, and three from the Śiwālik Pillar of Aśoka, now in Delhi.

5. See below the account of Pṛithvīrāja III, and our paper on the Date of Pṛithvīrāja III's birth published in the *Rājasthānī*, I, Part 2.

now proceeded also to avenge Arṇorāja's defeat and humiliation at the hands of Kumārapāla by leading a number of retaliatory expeditions against the Chaulukya empire; and if his achievements, mentioned in the Bijoliā inscription be regarded as arranged in a chronological order, he must have first proceeded against Sajjana, "the most wicked person of the land", whom he "despatched to the abode of Yama".[6] Sri Aksaya Keerty Vyas identifies this Sajjana with Sajjana, the *daṇḍādhipati* of Surāṣṭra, for whom we have an inscription dated V. 1176 at Girnār.[7] Actually, however, he is the pot-maker Sajjana who, in view of his past services, was made the governor of Chitor by Kumārapāla[8] and is mentioned in Kumārapāla's Chitor inscription of V. 1207 as *daṇḍādhīśa* Sajjana, a donor of one *ghāṇaka* of oil to the god, Samiddheśvara.[9] According to Somatilaka Sūri, Vigraharāja IV's armies reduced Chitor and captured Sajjana's elephant force.[10] Kumārapāla tried a diversion by besieging Nāgor, but raised the siege rather precipitately on hearing of Vigraharāja's success. The Sajjana, of V. 1176 an officer of Jayasiṁha Siddharāja, must have been in V. 1208 about eighty years old[11] and quite incapable of holding such a difficult post as the governorship of Surāṣṭra; and even if it be conceded that he did so he could not be Sajjana, the adversary of Vigraharāja IV, for we have not any evidence whatsoever for Vigraharāja's triumphal march to Surāṣṭra. Such a feat could have been possible only on his conquest of the greater part of the Chaulukya empire; Vigraharāja did nothing more than touch its eastern fringe.

The *kuntapāla*, Kuntapāla, attacked next by Vigraharāja and "reduced to lancelessness" is rather difficult to identify. He can either be the Nāḍulīya Chāhamāna Kuntapāla mentioned

6. *EI*, XXVI, p. 105; verse 20 of the epigraph. The *asajjanatā* of Sajjana may have a covert reference to his low birth also.

7. *EI*, XXXI, p. 105: verse 20 of the epigraph. The *asajjanatā* of Sajjana may have a covert reference to his low birth also.

8. *Kumārapāladevacharita* of Jayasiṁha Sūri, p. 165. See also our paper on the *daṇḍanāyakas* Sajjana and Bosari in the *Bhāratīya Vidyā* (English), 1943, pp. 221 ff.

9. *EI*, II, pp. 421 ff. See line 27 of the epigraph for Sajjana's name.

10. *Kumārapāladevacharita*, pp. 29-30.

11. He was appointed governor of Surāṣṭra early in Jayasiṁha's reign which began probably in V. 1150. If actually alive in V. 1208 he must surely have been a very old man.

in the Nanāṇā inscription of Kumārapāla[12] or Kuntapāla, the Paramāra ruler of Jālor who, according to Naiṇsī,[13] was defeated and dispossessed of Jālor by Kīrtipāla or Kītū, the younger brother of Kelhaṇa of Nāḍol. As the contemporaneousness of the Chāhamāna Kuntapāla with Vigraharāja is certain,[14] while that of the Paramāra Kuntapāla is doubtful,[15] and also because the title *kuntapāla*[16] appears more appropriate for a governor than a ruler, it is better to accept the first of the identifications suggested above.

During the course of these retaliatory expeditions, Naḍḍūla (Nāḍol) "was turned into a bed of reeds", Jālor into "a city of flames", and Pallikā or Pālī into "a small hamlet".[17] Vigraharāja's ire against these is easily understood, if we remember that they were all ruled by Chaulukya feudatories,[18] most of whom had actively participated in Kumārapāla's war with Vigraharāja's father, Arṇorāja. Being the part of the Chaulukya empire nearest to Sapādalakṣa, it naturally suffered the most; and perhaps none suffered more than Naḍḍūla (Nāḍol) which during the period of ten years or so, from V. 1208 to 1218, was governed successively by Ālhaṇa, the Nāḍūlīya Chāhamāna Kuntapāla, *daṇḍādhīśa* Vaijalladeva, and then by Ālhaṇa again.[19] Kumārapāla must have found it difficult to

12. *ABORI, Silver Jubilee Volume*, p. 317. His daughter set up the deity, Lakhaṇadeva, in the temple of Tripuruṣadeva and received for its worship, by Kumārapāla's orders, the sum of 1 *dramma daily* from the customs house of Nāḍol.

13. The suggestion is by Sri Aksaya Keerty Vyas. See *EI*, XXVI, p. 105.

14. See the next paragraph. He was the governor of Nāḍol about V. 1212.

15. Kīrtipāla, the dispossessor of Kuntapāla, Paramāra, was the youngest son of Ālhaṇa, a contemporary of Vigraharāja IV.

16. The title *Kuntapāla* is of the same type as *Khaḍgagrāha* and *Khaḍgapāla* found in some inscriptions. (Cf. the Grant of Īśvaraghoṣa, *Inscriptions of Bengal*, III, p. 149).

17. *EI*, XXVI, p. 150; verse 21 of the inscription.

18. According to Jayasiṁha Sūri, Jālor was the first kingdom to submit to Kumārapāla when he set out on *digvijaya*. (*Kumārapālacharita*, p. 175.) From an inscription at Jālor we learn that Kumārapāla built there a temple called Kuvaravihāra (*EI*, XI, p. 55). Pālī was a part of the Nāḍol kingdom then ruled over by Chaulukya feudatories, the Nāḍūlīya Chāhamānas.

19. For further details see below the account of the Chauhāns of Nāḍol.

find a governor capable enough to hold this outpost against his redoubtable enemy, Vigraharāja IV.

Kumārapāla could not have allowed the Chauhan ruler carry out these retaliatory expeditions without any counter-measures on his part. We have seen how he besieged Nāgor for a while. But on the whole the advantage in the struggle rested with Vigraharāja. In the Chauhān *praśasti* he is described as having reduced Kumārapāla to the position of a *karavālapālas*,[20] which perhaps means an officer of the same standing as *pratihāra* and *kuntapālas*. This is certainly exaggeration, pure and undiluted, but excusable when we remember that Vigraharāja's material gains were by no means inconsiderable. Large amounts of booty must have fallen into his hands during the course of his retaliatory campaigns and he annexed also the greater part of Mewār to his dominions. It is in Vigraharāja IV's reign that we find Chauhān records appearing for the first time in the area comprising Bijoliā, Maṇḍalgarh and Jahāzpur.[21]

Vigraharāja's defeat of the Bhādānakas, (a fact that has passed unnoticed on account of the *śleṣa* in verse 19 of the Bijoliā inscription)[22] was another great achievement. According to the *Kāvyamīmāṁsā* of Rājaśekhara, the Bhādānakas lived in the Maru and Ṭakka regions. They spoke Apabhraṁśa.[23] As

20. The only words decipherable in the line are

"कुमारपाल: करवालपाल:"

21. See the list of inscriptions given above. In V. 1207 Chitor and its adjacent territories probably recognised the supremacy of the Chaulukyas and Jahāzpur also might have been under them.

22. The verse reads as follows :—

"भादानत्वं चक्रे भादानपते: परस्य भादान: ।
यस्य दधत्करवाल: करालतां करतलाकलित:"

Sri Aksaya Keerty Vyas, the editor of the inscription in *EI*. XXVI, has the following note on the word "Bhādānapateḥ" of this verse :—

"This word is adjectival to *yasya* in the third quarter. It means of him who was *bhāpatiḥ* (the most illustrious) and *ādānapatiḥ* (all acquiring)".

This forced interpretation is due to his having missed the important fact that the Bhādānakas were a strong power of the period and continued to be so at least up to the reign of Pṛthvīrāja III.

23. p. 51.

Maru, most probably, means the Thār desert and Ṭakka, south-eastern Punjab, the Bhādānakas must naturally be looked for somewhere in tracts adjoining either one or both of these provinces. They can, we think, best be placed in that part of the country which adjoins northern Shekhāwāṭī and goes now by the name of Ahīravāṭī.[24] Its rulers were probably Ahīrs, who are known to have been intimately connected with Apabhraṁśa, and even now preserve the tradition of having fought against the Chauhān rulers Vīsaladeva and Pṛthvīrāja (III).

Another exploit of Vigraharāja IV mentioned in the Bijoliā inscription is the capture of Delhi and Hānsī. The former of these was, according to the Pālam Bāolī and Delhi Museum inscriptions of respectively V. 1337 and 1384[25] a possession of the Tomaras before its capture by the Chauhāns. Hānsī had been recaptured by the Tomaras from the Ghaznavites and most probably remained in their hands till its conquest by the Chauhāns.[26]

Tradition supports this inscriptional evidence. An old *Bahī* in our private Library speaks of a battle between the Chauhāns and the Taṁvars, in the Vikrama year 1209. The event is placed in the reign of Vīsaladeva, *i.e.* Vigraharāja IV. The Taṁvaras were defeated and lost Delhi.[27] The date does not seem unreasonable, though it is not possible to vouch for its absolute accuracy.

With the capture of Delhi and Hānsī by Vigraharāja, the long drawn out struggle between the Chauhāns and the Tomaras may be said to have ended. It began with Chandana. In Arṇorāja's reign the Chauhāns gained some notable successes; but it was Vigraharāja who dealt *coup de grace* to Tomara independence. Weakened by its continual fighting against the Muslims, the Gāhaḍavālas and the Chauhāns, the Tomara

24. For further proofs in this connection see the Appendix on the Bhādānakas.

25. For the inscriptions see respectively *JASB*, Part I, p. 108 and *EI*, I, p. 98 f.

26. It had been captured by Māsūd in 1038 A.D. and recaptured after some time by Mahīpāla (See Brigg's translation of *Tārikh-i-Firishta*, I, p. 106).

27. P. 40b.

kingdom thought it best to surrender its free existence and continue thereafter as a dependency of the Chauhāns of Śākambharī. In V. 1222 it was ruled by Madanapāla Tomara.[28] At the time of Muhammad Ghorī's invasion, it was under a feudatory prince who may be presumed to have been a descendant of this Madanapāla.[29]

The conquest of Delhi turned the Chauhāns of Śākambharī and Ajmer into an all-India power. From that time onward their independence became identified with the independence of Āryāvarta. Standing at the entrance of *Madhyadeśa,* they had per force to accept every challenge to Indian independence and culture and repel every enemy who attempted to destroy them. Vigraharāja IV performed this duty well enough; and it is with no little pride that he speaks of his having rendered Āryāvarta worthy of its name by the repeated extermination of the Mlechchas, *i.e.*, the Muslim invaders from the north-west.[30]

Vigraharāja IV's first war against the Muslims appears to have been fought in self-defence. Advancing as far as Vavverā,[31] now a small village about six miles from Khetṛī in the Jaipur division of Rājasthān, the *Hammīra* invited Vigraharāja to submit to his authority. Vigraharāja's Chief Minister, Śrīdhara, seems to have been for buying off the invader. Vigraharāja, however, regarded such a course as disgraceful. He had decided to protect his friends ; and he was determined also to protect Brāhmaṇas,

28. See the *Kharataragachchhapaṭṭāvalī* of Jinapāla for the date and his capital, Yoginīpura or Delhi. Thakkur Pherū mentions Anaṅgapalāhe and Madanapalāhe as coins of the Tomaras of Delhi and gives the proportion of silver in them.

29. See below the account of Pṛthvīrāja III.

30. See his Delhi-Siwālik inscription of V. 1220, Stanza I. Madanapāla's defeat is indicated also in the following verse:

तस्मिन्नुदग्ररिपुवर्गजये निसर्ग-
वैयग्रवानजनि विग्रहराजदेवः ।

31. Dr. Kielhorn identified the place tentatively with Bagherā. This being 47 miles to the south-west of Ajmer could not possibly have lain on *Hammīra's* way in his attack on Ajmer. This identification should therefore be rejected. Dr. D. R. Bhandarkar identifies Vavverā with Rūpnagar in Kishangarh, Rajasthān, but on very insufficient grounds. Actually it is, as pointed out in the text, now a small village a few miles from Khetri. The Gauḍa Brāhamaṇs of this place are found all over Rājpūtānā and are known as Babbervāls.

sacred places, and temples.[32] Though the *Lalitavigraharāja*, our only source of information regarding this Muslim invasion, breaks off at this point, it is reasonable to conclude that in the ensuing battle, the *Hammīra* was beaten and forced to retire to his own dominions. Of people who agreed with Vigraharāja's policy and co-operated fully with him special mention might be made of his maternal uncle, Siṁhabala, the Johiyā chief of Marukoṭṭa at least from V.1217 to V. 1232.[33] The *Hammīra* or Muslim leader vanquished by Vigraharāja probably was the Ghaznavite Amīr Khusrau Shāh (1153-1160 A.D.)[34]

Next must have followed offensive operations on the part of Vigraharāja IV. We have no details about them; but by V. 1220, the year of the incision of his Siwālik Pillar inscriptions, Vigraharāja had succeeded in freeing most Hindu territories from Ghaznavite domination. Only the Punjab remained under the Muslims after that year.

Vigraharāja probably conquered a few more territories. The *Pṛthvīrājavijaya* speaks of the large number of hill-forts that he captured.[35] The *Dharmaghoṣasūristuti* of Raviprabha shows the ruler of Mālwā and Arisīha assisting him in hoisting the flagstaff of the Jaina temple, Rajavihāra, at Ajmer.[36] Arisīha can, I think, be identified with Arisiṁha of Mewār whose brother-in-

32.

राजा—अकीर्तिः काप्युच्चैः सुहृदभयदानव्रतहति-
स्तथा ध्वंसस्तीर्थद्विजसुमनसां वीर्यविगमः ।
मर्मैतेषु व्यस्तेष्वपि भृशमसह्येषु सकला—
निमानङ्गीकर्तुः कथयत विधेयं किमसुभिः ॥"

(*Lalitavigraharāja-nāṭaka*)

33. In V. 1217 according to Jinapāla's *Kharataragachchhapaṭṭāvalī* and in V. 1232 according to the *Upakeśagachchhaprabandha* as well as the colophon of a Ms. of *Anekārthasaṅgraha* of Hemachandra, copied out in V. 1232. Of the authorities the first two are still unpublished. For a notice of the last see the *Jainapustakapraśastisaṅgraha*, Singhi Jaina Granthamālā p. 10).

34. The other contemporary Ghaznavite ruler was Khusrau Malik (1160-1186 A.D.). As the first Muslim invasion in Vigraharāja's reign was perhaps not long after his accession, Khusrau Shāh, who ruled up to V. 1217, may have been the *Hammīra* who reached Vavverā. Khusrau Malik, a "mild and voluptuous prince to whom authority was irksome" is not very likely to have undertaken an arduous campaign into the sandy tract of Rājasthān.

35. VIII, verse 64.

36. *Catalogue of Mss. in the Jaina Bhaṇḍārs of Paṭṭan*, G.O.S, p. 370.

law Gayākarṇa was on the throne of Tripurī in V. 1208.[37] The Mālava ruler may have been some claimant to the throne of Mālwā. If these two recognised the suzerainty of Vigraharājā, as seems likely enough by their presence in a foreign capital and their assisting the Chauhān monarch in offices like the hoisting of a flagstaff, there is enough of truth in Vigraharāja's bold claim that he had rendered tributary the lands lying between the Himālayas and the Vindhyas, and some point in the exhortation that his descendants should not be lax in exacting tribute from the rest of the country.[38] That in the north, his power extended up to the foot of the Himālayas is obvious enough from the original location of the Siwālik Pillar containing three of his most important inscriptions. In the south, the suzerainty over Mālwā, whether actual or merely claimed, could carry his empire up to the Vindhyas, at least in name. If, however, the words हिमवद्-विन्ध्यान्तरालं भुवः be taken to signify the whole of Āryāvarta, the claim certainly looks exaggerated, though here too we must not be oblivious of the fact that he may have actually received subsidies from the other powers of North India on account of his fighting incessantly and with success against the Muslims, and these free gifts may have been mentioned as tributes in the Chauhān eulogy.[39] At this distance of time, and in absence of other corroborative evidence, it is, in fact, difficult to be perfectly sure about the truth or falsehood of a claim, or even to say what the claim actually came to. Kumārapāla Vijayachandra, Yaśovarman, Madanavarman and Ballālasena were strong enough not to pay him any tribute, but some of them may have regarded their money as rightly invested, if it was paid to him and used for fighting against the Muslims. But this is, after all, no more than a plausible conjecture and should be regarded as such by our readers.

Vigraharāja's greatness is an undisputed fact, for besides being a first class general and a mighty conqueror he was a patron of literature, a good poet himself, and a builder with

37. *EI*, II, p. 12.

38. See his Delhi Siwālik inscription, No. 3 verse 2.

39. The Gāhaḍavāla inscriptions speak of a tax called *Turuṣkadaṇḍa* which may have been used for this purpose.

imagination and vision. To his contemporaries he was known as *kavibāndhava.* "When he died," states the *Pṛthvīrājavijya* "the term *kavibāndhava* became useless; there was none else to whom it could be applied with aptness".[40] The pro-Chaulukya source, the *Prabandhachintāmaṇi* of Merutuṅga, also has a good anecdote about Vigraharāja and Kumārapāla in which, after criticising the meanings of the Chauhān ruler's two other names, Vigraharāja and Viśvala (Bīsal), it states that he, afraid of having his name criticised any more, ultimately assumed the name *kavibāndhava.*[41] Vigraharāja's court-poet, Somadeva, wrote *Lalitavigraharāja* which might easily be classed as a first class historical drama. We have lost much by its being fragmentary. The Chauhān *praśasti*, to which we have referred more than once, is a good *kāvya* and so is the *stuti* of various gods of the Hindu pantheon, found inscribed on a slab in the *Aḍhāī-dinakā-jhoṁpaṛā* mosque.

Somadeva regarded Vigraharāja as the foremost not only of heroes but even the learned people of his time.[42] We are entitled to regard this as undue praise on the part of a court-poet. But that Vigraharāja IV was not without considerable distinction as a writer of Sanskrit might be seen from his drama *Harakeli.* With the subject matter of this work and other literary compositions of Vigraharāja's reign we shall deal at some length in a subsequent chapter. Kielhorn appears to have held Vigraharāja's poetic powers in high estimation; for according to him we find in *Harakeli* "actual and undoubted proof that Hindu rulers of the past were eager to compete with Bhavabhūti and Kālidāsa in poetic fame."

Of his taste in building, we have a fine example in the college built by him at Ajmer, on the model of Bhoja's *Sarasvatīkaṇṭhābharaṇavidyālaya* at Dhārā. Though converted into a mosque in the reign of Qutb-ud-din, it still retains all signs of having been originally a Hindu structure and is, according to Tod, "one of the most perfect, as well as the most ancient, monuments of

40. *PV*, VIII, 55.
41. *PC.*, p. 90.
42. "वीराणां च विपश्चितामाद्यस्त्वमेवाधुना ॥"

(*Lalitavigraharāja*)

Hindu architecture."[43] Equally unstinted is the praise of Cunningham in whose opinion this building may "for gorgeous prodigality of ornament, beautiful richness of tracery, delicate sharpness of finish, laborious accuracy of workmanship, endless variety of detail....justly vie with the noblest buildings which the world has yet produced".[44] Another memorial of his reign is the Vīsalsar lake now known as Visalyā. It is about 2½ miles in circumference. Temples and palaces must have at one time surrounded it, and in its middle were two islands with Vigraharāja's magnificent palaces. On its banks stood images which sent forth jets when the water rose to their lips.[45]

Vigraharāja founded a number of towns which he called Vīsalapura after his alternative name Vīsala. Of these one stands "at the mouth of the chasm-like gorge which runs through the Girwar mountain range in Mewār to Rājmahala. The pass is very narrow at each end with high precipitous cliffs approaching each other from the opposite sides, but it widens out into a great mountain-girded amphi-theatre in the centre, where the Banās river in the rainy season forms a great lake called Ānāsāgar after Vīsaladeva's father Ānāji"[46]

According to the *Pṛthvīrājavijaya* Vigraharāja IV erected as many buildings as the hill-forts that he captured. On account of the iconoclastic zeal of the Muslim conquerors, however, only a few of them have survived. Many were destroyed. Not a few perhaps, like his college were converted into Muslim structures.

Though an ardent worshipper of Śiva, as proved by the drama *Harakeli*,[47] as well as the *Pṛthvīrājavijaya*,[48] Vigraharāja followed in the footsteps of his father, grandfather and most great Indian rulers by being no less respectful towards other Hindu gods and goddesses. For Jainas he built *vihāras*, participated in their religious ceremonies, and on the representation of one of their religious teachers, Dharmaghoṣa Sūri, prohibited the slaughter of animals on the *Ekādaśī* day.[49] Few rulers have been more tolerant than Vigraharāja IV.

43. *Annals and Antiquities of Rājasthān*, I, p. 609.
44. *ASI*, II, p. 263.
45. *Ibid*, p. 261.
46. Sarda, *Writings and Speeches*, p. 255.
47. See the concluding portion of the drama.
48. VIII. 55.
49. *Catalogue of the Palm-leaf Mss. in the Paṭṭan Bhaṇḍārs*, p. 370.

Vigraharāja IV's reign is to be regarded as the golden age of Sapādalakṣa. In V. 1207, just a year or so before his accession to the throne, it lay defeated, humiliated and shorn of much of its wealth and prestige. By V. 1210, all these wrongs had been avenged. He had by his retaliatory expeditions punished all who had taken part in the war against his father, captured Chitor from the Chaulukyas, and annexed a part of Mewār to his territory. In the north he defeated the Bhādānakas, reduced the Tomaras to subjection and drove back the Muslims, conquering a part of the territory which had previously been occupied by them. Art and literature flourished under his enlightened patronage. Every sect enjoyed toleration. For a short period Sapādalakṣa had almost everything it needed. We have, elsewhere, called him Vigraharāja the Great. Perhaps, the title is not inappropriate.

Aparagāṅgeya or Amaragāṅgeya : Vigraharāja IV was succeeded by Aparagāṅgeya,[50] perhaps his son by Desaladevī, the heroine of the drama *Lalitavigraharāja*. Amaragāṅgeya was probably slain by his cousin Pṛthvīrāja. According to Jonarāja, he died unmarried.[51]

Pṛthvībhaṭa or Pṛthvīrāja II : The next ruler Pṛthvībhaṭa or Pṛthvīrāja II was the son of the parricide Jagaddeva. We have four inscriptions for this ruler, one at Hānsī dated the 7th of the bright half of Māgha, V. 1224, two at Menāl in the Maṇḍalgarh district in Mewār, dated in V. 1225 and 1226 and a fourth at Dhoḍ, a village 7 miles to the south-east of Jahāzpur in Mewār, dated the 13th of the dark half of Jyeṣṭha, V. 1225.[52]

From the Dhoḍ inscription, we learn that he defeated the ruler of Śākambharī in battle. This clearly means that he secured

50. Called Amaragāṅgeya in *PKG*, Gaṅgadeva in *HMV* and *SC*, and Amaragaṅgu in the *Āin-i-Akbarī*, (II. p. 298). The name does not occur in the Bijoliā inscription.

51. For his death see the account of Pṛthvīrāja II. We are not sure of the correctness of Jonarāja's assertion. He does not seem to have known that Vigraharāja's son's name was Aparagāṅgeya. He rather regards it as an adjective qualifying the word *suta* and so explains it off by saying—

"वीरत्वब्रह्मचारित्वाभ्यां द्वितीयो भीष्मो विग्रहराजस्य पुत्रो यमेन नीत: ।"

52. See respectively *IA*, XLI, p. 19; Dr. G. H. Ojha, *History of Udaipur*, I, pp. 60-61 and p. 57. We are indebted for the transcripts of the last three inscriptions to Dr. G. H. Ojha.

the throne of Ajmer by defeating Aparagāṅgeya, whom he, as the son of the eldest son of Arṇorāja, might have regarded as a usurper. The Hansi inscription states that he secured the elephant Manaḥsiddhikarī from the ruler Vastupāla whom we may identify with Vasantapāla, the grandfather of Aparagāṅgeya.[53] He, as a relative of Vigraharāja IV and the young ruler Aparagāṅgeya, could not have been regarded as friends by Pṛthvīrāja II. Another ruler defeated by him was the chief of Pañchpura, probably Panjaur, a very old town near Kālkā. He (the ruler of Pañchapura) saved his kingdom by surrendering a valuable pearl necklace,[54] and offering homage to the Chauhān ruler.

The struggle against the Muslims appears to have continued unabated in Pṛthvīrāja II's reign. With a view to checking their inroads, he had the important fort of Hānsī strengthened by his maternal uncle Kilhaṇa whom he appointed governor of the place.[55] Perhaps he had other forts too on the Punjab frontier to keep out the invaders.

Pṛthvīrāja's chief queen Suhavā was like her husband a devout Śaiva.[56] Pṛthvīrāja II granted villages, and precious metals like gold to the Brāhmaṇas, and though fully attached to his own form of religion, gave the village Morājhari to the Jaina temple of Pārśvanātha at Bijoliā.[57]

53. In the well-known *kāvya*, *Vasantavilāsa*, published in the Gaekwad Oriental Series, Vastupāla has been called Vasanta. So Vasantapāla and Vastupāla can rightly be regarded as variants of one name.

Since the above lines were first written Mr. A. K. Vyas too has suggested the above identification.

54. Identified by some writers with Pañchapaṭṭana on the Satlaj river. "If the identification of "Pañchapura" with Pañchapaṭṭana on the Satlaj is accepted", writes Dr. H.C. Ray, "he must have had some successes against the Yāminī prince Khusrau Malik Tāj-ud-Daulah". The inference is unjustified, because the Hānsī inscription, which mentions the submission of the ruler of Pañchapura, makes it clear at the same time that the Afghān Amīr was an inveterate enemy of Pṛthvīrāja II. He never submitted to the Chauhān ruler. It was, in fact, to keep off the Hammīra, "a great source of trouble to the world" that the fort was strengthened.

55. See his Hānsī inscription, verses 4-6, *IA* XLI, p. 19.

56. The Śiva-temple at Menāl bears the name Suhaveśvara and enjoyed from her the grant of 20 *drammas* a year.

57. vv. 24-25 of the Bijoliā inscription. *EI.*, XXVI, p. 105.

Pṛthvīrāja II died before the end of the Vikrama year 1226, probably without leaving any issue.[58] The ministers, therefore, offered the throne to his uncle Someśvara, the only surviving son of Arṇorāja, who was at the time in Gujarāt.[59] With Pṛthvīrāja II ended the line of the queen Sudhavā, after having been on the throne for nearly 19 years. This short period saw four rulers of whom two, owing to the guilt of the parricide Jagaddeva, were probably slain by their own kinsmen.

58. Pṛthvīrāja's last inscription is dated in the (V.) year 1226/1169 A.D. His successor Someśvara's Bijoli inscription is dated Thursday, the 3rd of the dark half of Phālguna V. 1226/5th February, 1169 A.D.

59. सपादलक्षमानिन्ये महामात्यैर् महीपतिः

PV, VIII, 57.

CHAPTER VII

THE CHAUHĀNS OF SAPĀDALAKṢA (*Contd.*) : SOMEŚVARA

Someśvara's early life was passed in Gujarāt where he had been carried away, probably, within a year or so of his birth, by his grandfather Jayasiṁha Siddharāja.[1] Kumārapāla, the next Chaulukya ruler was, in spite of his enmity with Someś-vara's father Arṇorāja, kindly disposed towards Someśvara and brought him up with care ;[2] and Someśvara, in his turn, more than repaid this affection and kindness by his valuable services to the Chaulukya throne. "Leaping from one mighty elephant to the other", states the *Pṛthvīrājavijaya*, "he snatched the small sword of the lord of Kuṅkuṇa and rendered him headless with it."[3] On turning to the *Prabandhachintāmaṇi*, we find that the lord of Koṇkaṇa, against whom Kumārapāla had to fight, was Mallikārjuna, known also as *rājapitāmaha* (grandfather of rulers).[4] As this ruler's latest inscription is dated in Śaka year 1082 (V. 1217),[5] and the earliest of his son Aparāditya in Śaka 1084 (V. 1219),[6] he must have been slain between these two years.

The Paramāra ruler Dhārāvarṣa also seems to have taken a prominent part in the Chaulukya campaign "when Dhārā-varṣa inflamed with anger, held his ground in the battle-field, the wives of the lord of Koṅkaṇa shed drops of tears from their lotus-like eyes."[7] The Jaina chroniclers of Gujarāt ignore alto-gether the services of Someśvara as well as Dhārāvarṣa giving all the credit of slaying as well as defeating Mallikārjuna to the Jaina general Ambaḍa, a brother of Kumārapāla's minister

1. *PV.* VII, 35 and commentary of Jonarāja on the verse preceding it.
2. *Ibid,* verse 11.
3. *Ibid,* verse 15.
4. pp. 80-81.
5. See the *Bombay Gazetteer,* I, Part I, p. 186 and Part II, p. 544.
6. *Ibid,* and *DHNI,* II, p. 992.
7. क्रोधाक्रान्त-प्रधन-वसुधा-निश्चले यत्र जाताः ।
   च्योतन्नेत्रोत्पल-जलकणाः कोङ्कणाधीशपत्न्यः ।।
   (*EI,* VIII, p. 216, verse 36).

Vāgbhaṭa.[8] In view, however, of not merely the early character but also the greater reliability of the *Pṛthvīrājavijaya* as compared with other sources, we must regard Someśvara as the actual slayer of Mallikārjuna, though it might be conceded that Ambaḍa was probably the chief commander of the army in which Someśvara served and achieved this enviable feat of arms.

Someśvara's marriage took place while he was in Gujarāt. He married Karpūradevī, daughter of one Achala who is described in the *Pṛthvirājavijaya* as the lord of Tripurī[9] and identified by Dr. D. C. Sircar with the Kalachuri ruler Gayā-Karṇa (c. 1125-1155 A.D.). But it would be better to identify him with Gayakarṇa's son Nṛsiṁha (K. I 07, K. 909, V. 1216),[10] during whose reign Karpūradevī was married, an event which, according to the *Pṛthvīrājavijaya*, took place after Someśvara's slaying of Mallikārjuna, *i. e.*, not before V. 1217.

Someśvara's two sons, Pṛthvīrāja and Harirāja, were both born in Gujarāt. They accompanied their parents to Sapādalakṣa when a new turn in the wheel of fortune put Someśvara on the throne of Ajmer and Śākambharī in the Vikrama year 1226.[11]

Someśvara assumed the title, *Pratāpalaṅkeśvara* (Bijoliā inscription verse 27). Of his five inscriptions discovered so far, one comes from Bijoliā, two from Dhoḍ, one from Revāsa, and one from Āṁvaldā.[12] Their dates range from V. 1226 to V. 1234, and give almost the exact period of his reign.

Someśvara built a town named after his father and erected five temples of which one was dedicated to Tripuruṣa and another to Vaidyanātha. He had two statues erected, one of his father riding a horse and the other of himself standing before it.[13]

8. See the *Prabandhachintāmaṇi*, pp. 80-81 and the *Prabhāvakacharita*, p. 339.

9. VIII. 18. Jonarāja gives the ruler's name as Tejala. It may be a scribal error, because the actual name Achala is to be found in *PV*, IX. 87.

10. *LNI*, p. 302.

11. This is the year of the last inscription of Pṛthvīrāja II and of the Bijoliā inscription of Someśvara.

12. For these inscriptions see respectively *EI*, XXVI, pp. 102 ff. *Annual Report of Rājpūtānā Museum*, 1892-93, p. 2, *PRAS*, WC, 1909-10, p. 52. *Annual Report of the Rājpūtānā Museum*, 1922-23, p. 8.

13. *PV*, VIII. 62-66.

By conviction he was a Śaiva, but in practice he was as tolerant and liberal towards other sects as his predecessors had been,[14] and is known to have granted the village Revnā to the temple of Pārśvanātha at Vindhyavallī or Bijoliā.[15]

Someśvara issued some coins of the "Bull and Horseman type". On their reverse is the figure of a humped bull and the legend "āsāvarī śrī-Sāma (ntadeva)" and on the obverse the figure of a horseman with the legend "Sri -Someśvaradeva".[16]

Of his ministers, we know two, Skanda and his son Soḍha. They were Gujarātī Nāgara Brāhmaṇas and probably came with him to Ajmer on his accession.[17] Kadambavāsa, the chief minister during Pṛthvīrāja III's minority, might also have been one of Someśvara's ministers.[18]

According to the *Pṛthvirājarāso*, Someśvara was slain in a battle with Bhīmadeva II of Gujarāt.[19] This no doubt, is pure fiction. But that he had to fight against the Chaulukyas and was defeated by them is now known from Bhīmadeva II's Pātan inscription of V. 1256 which mentions Ajayapāla as having exacted tribute from the ruler of Sapādalakṣa.[20] The same fact is referred to by Someśvara (a Gujarātī poet) in his *Kīrtikaumudī*, when he speaks of Ajayapāla Chaulukya having taken by force a gold *maṇḍapikā* and rutting elephants from the ruler of the Jāṅgala country.[21] As Ajayapāla ruled from V. 1229 to 1232, the Sapādalakṣa or Jāṅgala ruler defeated by him could only be Someśvara the Chauhān ruler of Ajmer.[22]

14. For the religious policy of his predecessors see the last chapter. That he was a Śaiva is obvious from his title *Pratāpa-laṅkeśvara* and his being described as having attained *sāyujya* with Śiva (*PV*, VIII, 93).

15. See the Bijoliā inscription, verse 28.

16. *CCIM*, pp. 257 and 261.

17. *Viruddhavidhi-vidhvaṁsa*, Catalogue of Sanskrit Mss. in the Library of the India Office, page 488 f. Part III.

18. See the next chapter.

19. 39th *samaya* Nāgarī-prachāriṇī-sabhā edition.

20. *Karadīkṛta-Sapādalakṣa-śrī-Ajayapāladevaḥ* (*IA*, XI, pp. 71 ff., lines 12-13 of the inscription).

21. II. 53. The fact is mentioned also by Arisiṁha in his *Sukṛtasaṅkīrtana*,

22. A war between the Chaulukyas and Chauhāns in Someśvara's reign in which the former were successful, is indicated also by lines 4-5 of the Kirāḍu inscription (V. 1235) of Madanabrahma, a tributary of Bhīmadeva.

According to the genealogy at the end of the *Prabandhakośa*, Pṛthvīrāja III ascended the throne in V. 1236.[23] So Someśvara should naturally be concluded to have died in that year. But as surmised by us long ago, this could not be the right date, because Pṛthvīrāja III was already on the throne of Ajmer in 1178 A.D. when Muhammad Ghori invaded India and captured Nāḍol.[24] We are now glad to have this surmise confirmed by the discovery of the Baḍlā inscription of Pṛthvīrāja III, dated in V. 1234.[25]

(*Continued from page* 78)
which reads as follows :

अनेक-समर-संघटट्-वैरि-करि-घटा-पीठ-दारुण-करवाल-(शा) कंभरी भूपा (ल)...महाराजपुत्र-श्रीमदनब्रह्मदेव etc.

The inscription does not, of course, clearly mention the defeat of the Śākambharī ruler. It is too fragmentary to do so. But the words, occurring, as they do, in the record of Chaulukya feudatory, can perhaps mean nothing else.

23. p. 134.

24. *PV* , X, 50.

25. Published below and first edited by Sri Brij Narain Sharma and present writer in the *Marubhāratī*, Vol. II, part 3, pp. 2-3.

CHAPTER VIII

THE CHAUHĀNS OF SAPĀDALAKṢA (*Continued*)

PṚTHVĪRĀJA III

Pṛthvīrāja III was born on the 12th of Jyeṣṭha.[1] He is said to have been conceived at a very auspicious moment when Mars was in Capricorn, Saturn in Aquarius, Venus in Pisces,[2] the Sun in Aries, the Moon in Taurus, and Mercury in Gemini. The positions of Jupiter and the Dragon's Head have been lost through damage to the manuscript of the *Pṛthvīrājavijaya*; but fortunately the author has stated that two of the planets occupied their own houses and five their houses of exaltation.[3] Hence we might conclude that Jupiter was in Cancer. These planetary positions indicate V. 1222 as the year of conception, giving V. 1223 as the year of birth.[4]

In V. 1234/1179 A.D. Pṛthvīrāja's father Someśvara died, leaving the young Pṛthvīrāja and his younger brother Harirāja to the care of their mother Queen Karpūradevī, who, according to the *Pṛthvīrājavijaya*, proved an excellent regent.[5] Kadambavāsa, known as Kaimāsa or Kaimbāsa in popular legends and mentioned as *maṇḍaleśvara* Kaimāsa in the *Kharataragachchhapaṭṭāvalī* of Jinapāla, was chief minister during the regency[6] and for some time thereafter. His presiding over a discussion between two Jaina scholars Padmaprabha and Jinapati Sūri,[7] during the temporary absence of his master from the court shows the high

1. PV, VII, 50. We have to be very near this date also because Karpūradevī's marriage took place after V. 1217 (See above, 10, 68-9)

2. Dewan Bahadur H. B. Sarda wrongly puts Jupiter in Pisces, and the mistake is copied by Dr. H. C. Ray. "Danujānāṁ guru" is not Jupiter. See also our paper, पृथ्वीराज तृतीय की जन्मतिथि, published in the *Rājasthānī* (Bikaner).. I, part 2.

3. See Jonarāja's commentary on PV, VII. 27.

4. We are indebted for the calculation of the planetary positions to the wellknown astronomer Jyotiṣāchārya Pandit Suryanarayan Vyas of Ujjain and Śrī B. K. Chaturvedi, the Suba of Ujjain.

5. *PV*, IX, 1.34. The last inscription of Someśvara and the first of Pṛthvīrāja III belong to V. 1234.

6. Ibid. 35-45.

7. *Kharataragachchhapaṭṭāvalī*, Mss, pp. 25-34

position that he held in the State. Traditional accounts describe him as a great soldier. The contemporary poem *Pṛthvīrājavijaya* speaks eloquently of his administration and devotion to Pṛthvīrāja and gives him all the credit for the early victories of his master's reign.[8] Another minister of this period of regency was Bhuvanaikamalla, a younger brother of Karpūradevī's father Achalarāja, who is described as a man of extremely charitable disposition, ready to give away all that he had and fully proficient in the art of subduing *nāgas*.[9]

Pṛthvīrāja assumed the reins of administration about V. 1237/1180 A.D. and soon found himself engaged in a number of wars. Of these the first may be regarded as one of the most serious, for it involved the question of succession. Pṛthvīrāja II had defeated and probably slain one of Vigraharāja's sons Aparagāṅgeya; but another named Nāgārjuna had survived and bided his time. Encouraged perhaps by the new king being young and inexperienced, he had the temerity to rise against him and capture the town of Guḍapura.[10] The success achieved

8. According to the *Pṛthvīrājarāso* as well as the *Pṛthvīrājaprabandha* published in the *Purātanaprabandhasaṅgraha* of the Singhī Jain Granthamālā, Kāimbāsa was later on slain by his master. According to the Rāso, he was shot down with an arrow, because, Pṛthvīrāja, on returning rather unexpectedly to his palace, found Kāimbāsa in the apartments of his favourite concubine Karnāṭī (57th *samaya*, Nāgari Prachāriṇī Sabhā Edition). The *Prabandha* ascribes the minister's death to the machinations of one Pratāpasiṁha who succeeded in poisoning the ears of Pṛthvīrāja and making him believe, though wrongly, that Kāimbāsa was responsible for the repeated attacks of the Muslims on India (*Purātanaprabandhasaṅgraha*, pp. 86-87). Both these accounts deserve to be rejected, because of being in conflict with the evidence of the *Pṛthvīrājavijaya* a book written most probably between 1191 and 1193 A.D. It compares Kadambavāsa with Hanumān and credits him, as pointed out above, with the early successes of Pṛthvīrāja III's reign. None suspected of treachery or even worse could, we believe, be described in this strain by a court-poet.

9. *PV*, IX, 67-86. Dewan Bahadur H. B. Sarda interprets the word *nāga* as the Nāga tribe and Jonarāja as elephant. In absence of any reference to fighting against the Nāga tribe it is better to agree with Jonarāja.

10. अथ कुविधि-यदृच्छयैव नागार्जुन इति निन्दित-भिक्षु-योग्यनामा ।
निगड-परिग्रहाय मातुर् ग्रह इव विग्रहराज-वल्लभायाः ॥६॥
पितुरखिल-नृपाविलङ्घ्य-भाग्याद्भुत-बल-निर्मथनैक-वीर-जन्मा ।
गुडपुरमिति दुर्गमध्यरोहन्मधु-रसाहृति-दोहदेन बालः ॥७॥.

(*Pṛthvīrājavijaya*, X)

The first line of the second verse quoted here would show that this

by Nāgārjuna seems not to have been negligible, because in some of our historical sources we even find him mentioned as one of the rulers of Ajmer.[11] Pṛthvīrāja marched against him with a large army consisting of horses, elephants, camels and infantry, and laid siege to Guḍapura. Nāgārjuna managed to escape from the beleaguered fort; but his wife, mother and followers fell into the hands of the victor along with a large amount of booty. The soldiers who continued fighting against Pṛthvīrāja under the leadership of Devabhaṭa, probably an officer of Nāgārjuna, were soon killed to the last man and a garland made of their heads was hung across the gate of the fort of Ajmer.[12]

Another early war of Pṛthvīrāja was against the Bhādānakas whose territory comprised the present Rewāri Tahsīl, Bhiwānī and its adjoining villages, and a part of the Alwar State. It must have occurred some time before V. 1239, when in the course of the discussion between Padmaprabha and Jinapati Sūri, the latter composed two verses in honour of Pṛthvīrāja's victory over the Bhādānakas.[13] The overthrow of the Bhādānakas seems to have been decisive, for we hear no more of them as a ruling power.

Such successes could easily have spurred the ambition of any ruler for *digvijaya*. We do not, therefore, wonder when we read

Vigraharāja "whose fortune could not be surpassed by any ruler" could be none but Vigraharāja IV. In XII, 58, of this *kāvya*, Vigraharāja IV, is mentioned merely as Vigraharāja. The way this ruler's reign is cursorily referred to in the *PV*, in spite of the splendid achievements to his credit, shows that Someśvara, and therefore naturally the rest of his family, had never been on very good terms with Vigraharāja IV.

11. *Āin-i-Akbari*, p. 298; Our bardic Bahī, P. 54 b. The name in these is not, however, Nāgārjuna. It is Nāgadamana in the *Bahī* and Nāgadeva in the *Āin-i-Akbari*

12. *PV*, XII, 8-38.

13. Translated into English, these verses would stand as follows:—

"How should we describe the incomparable lustre of the valour of Pṛthvīrāja whose armies fill the quarters in every direction, on whose entry attends the goddess of Victory, and struck by whose sharp missiles, *the elephants of the Bhādānakas* form indeed the figure of *svastika*, with the rows of pearls trickling down their temples."

"O Pṛthvīrāja, the gladdener of numerous subjects, where is the ground for competition between hostile rulers and thee who art verily the Sun on account of thy intense splendour, and who has, acting like a lion, with thy hand bearing a sword, *torn asunder even the irresistible force of the lord of the Bhādānaka land*".

in Jinapāla's *Kharataragachchhapaṭṭāvalī* that in V. 1239 Pṛthvīrāja had already started on his conquest of all the quarters and pitched his first camp at Narānayana.[14] The book does not mention the names of the territories he attacked. It would not, however, be altogether without justification to presume that the march was against Jejākabhukti, which according to Madanpur inscriptions, "was laid waste in V. 1239 by Pṛthvīrāja, the son of Someśvara and the grandson of Arṇorāja."[15] The *Pṛthvīrāja-rāso* and the *Ālhākhaṇḍa* would have us believe that the Chauhāns conquered Mahobā, the capital of the Chandel ruler Paramāla, after a stiff fight with the Banāfara heroes Ālhā and Ūdala who were aided also by an army from Kanauj.[16] Their free mixture of facts with fiction, however, makes it difficult to judge how far their statements may be regarded as true history. Of one thing, at least, we can be sure : Pṛthvīrāja decisively defeated Paramardin, the Chandel monarch in some action or other. This fact is not only indicated by the accounts of these books but also proved by the date of the Madanpur inscriptions just referred to above, and by stray verses in the *Śārṅgadharapaddhati* and the *Prabandhachintāmaṇi*,[17] according to which Parmardin saved himself by putting a piece of straw in his mouth when attacked by Pṛthvīrāja.[18] Help to the Chandelas from the side of the Gāhaḍavālas of Kanauj too does not seem impossible.[19] But as Pṛthvīrāja's inscriptions claim not the conquest but merely the devastation of Jejākbhukti, and as Parmardin's inscriptions

14. p. 25. Narānayana is modern Naranā, It is at the distance of 12 miles from Phulera station.

15. *ASIR*, X, p. 98, XXII, pp. 173f. *PRAS, EC*, 1903:-1904, p. 55. For text see below, p. 95.

16. See the *Mahobā-yuddha-samaya* of the *Rāso* and the account of the last battle of the Banāfara heroes in the Ālhākhanda.

17. In the *Prabhandhachintāmaṇi*, the verse is referred to Paramardin of Kuntala, even though his adversary is mentioned as Pṛthvīrāja of Sapādalakṣa. This Paramardin lived about V. 1143. So the actual Paramardin meant by the verse is Paramardin of Jejākabhukti, a contemporary of Pṛthvīrāja III.

18. *Śārṅgadharapaddhati*, verse 1254, *PC*. p. 116.

19. The Mau stone-inscription shows friendly relations between the Gāhādavālas and Madanavarman Chandel (V. 1186-1220 c.). These good relations probably continued in Parmardin's time.

are found both at Kāliñjara and Mahobā in V. 1240, nearly a year after the Chauhān invasion,[20] and as Parmardin is described as *Daśārṇādhipati* in one of his late Kāliñjara inscriptions,[21] we have to look askance at the story of the complete conquest of Bundelkhand as given in our later and less reliable sources.

We do not know against whom the *digvijayin* Pṛthvīrāja next turned his arms. The *Kharataragachchhapaṭṭāvalī* of Jinapāla tells us that he had been at war with Gujarāt before V. 1244, and its evidence is happily corroborated by that of the Verāval inscription according to which Jagaddeva Pratihāra, the Prime Minister of Bhīmadeva II of Gujarāt, was verily "the Moon to the lotus-like queens of Pṛthvīrāja".[22] It was probably during the course of this war that Pṛthvīrāja led the night attack on Dhārāvarṣa Paramāra of Ābū which we find described in the *Pārthaparākrama-vyāyoga* of Dhārāvarṣa's younger brother Prahlādana. The attack is said to have been a failure.[23]

The only work dealing in detail with this Chaulukya-Chauhān struggle is the late and unreliable *Pṛthvīrājarāso* according to which its main events were the capture of Nāgor by Bhīmadeva, its recapture by Pṛthvīrāja, the defeat and death of Someśvara at the hands of Bhīmadeva, and the latter's defeat and death at the hands of Pṛthvīrāja III, the successor of Someśvara.[24] Now, we have good reasons to believe that Someśvara was not slain by

20. See *EI*, V, Appendix, p. 26 and *ASR* XXI p. 72 : *PASB* 1879-pp. 143-44.

21. Dated in V. 1258 (*IA*. XIX, p. 254).

22. Line 38, *Historical Inscriptions of Gujarāt*, II, p. 218.

23. किं श्रङ्ग, भवान् जाङ्गलपतेः (Var पृथ्वीराजस्य) सौप्तिकप्रस्तावोपश्लोकनमाकर्णितवान् ?

यस्याद्यापि यशः शिलीमुखमुखोत्कीर्णप्रशस्त्यक्षरः
स्वःस्त्रीणां दिवि नाकनायकसभास्तम्भेन संस्मार्यते ।
सेहे सोऽपि न सौप्तिकं विनिपतद्-द्रौणेस्तदत्यर्जुनं
धारावर्ष, तवाद्य पौरुषमभूत् तीर्णोपमानं भुवि ॥

Pārthaparākramavyāyoga, p. 3.

24. See the 12th, 39th, and 44th *samayas* of the *Rāso* published by the Nāgari Prachāriṇī Sabhā, Benares. The account is found in all the recensions of the *Rāso*.

the Chaulukya monarch. He probably died before Bhīmadeva ascended the throne; but even if he did not, Bhīmadeva was in V. 1234 too young to have fought a personal duel with him.[25] The death of Bhīmadeva II at the hands of Pṛthvīrāja III is even more improbable, because the former is known to have survived the latter by nearly half a century.[26] But the fight between the Chaulukyas and Chauhāns at Nāgor, though undoubtedly not quite certain, is far from improbable. Two inscriptions found at Charlū, a village in the south-east of the Bīkāner State, commemorate the death of certain Mohila heroes in the battle of Nāgor in the Vikrama year 1241.[27] Is it not likely that this might actually be the battle of Nāgor referred to in the *Rāso*, the ground for such supposition being:—

1. That the Mohilas were themselves Chauhāns.
2. That the territory they lived in was a part of Pṛthvīrāja III's empire, fighting for whom was, hence, their bounden duty.
3. That the year V. 1241 precedes that of the treaty between the Chauhāns and Chaulukyas mentioned in the *Kharataragachchhapaṭṭāvalī* of Jinapāla.
4. That neither history nor tradition tells us of any other battle of Pṛthvīrāja III near Nāgor which was one of the strongest forts of the Sapādalakṣa empire.

Jagaddeva Pratihāra might have scored a few initial successes against the Chauhāns who as we have seen, failed also in their night-attack on Dhārāvarṣa. But the war seems, on the whole, to have gone in Pṛthvīrāja's favour, for the *Kharataragachchhapaṭṭāvalī* represents Jagaddeva Pratihāra as extremely anxious to preserve the treaty with the Chauhāns which he had concluded with great difficulty in or shortly before V. 1244.[28]

25. Someśvara died in V. 1234. Bhīmadeva II ruled, according to Dr. H. C. Ray, from V. 1235 to 1298. According to the *Kīrtikaumudī*, he was very young when he ascended the throne, and incapable of managing the affairs of the State.

26. Bhīmadeva II's last inscription is found in V. 1296, but he probably continued ruling for two or three years more.

27. See the *Rājasthān Bhāratī*, Vol. I for the text of these inscriptions. See *Infra* for ready reference).

28. The passage in the *Kharataragachchhapaṭṭāvalī* is as follows:—

"V. 1244... The messenger sent by the *daṇḍanāyaka* Abhayaḍa going to

Tradition speaks also of a war between Jayachandra of Kanauj and Pṛthvīrāja. That there should have been some rivalry between the two is but natural. Both were ambitious rulers aspiring to the first place in the Indian polity. "From his large army and grandeur," states the Tāju-l-Maasir, "the desire of something like the conquest of the world had raised a phantom in the (Pṛthvīrāja's) imagination."[29] Other authorities though a little later in date, ascribe the same ambition to Jayachandra,[30] who could never have been well pleased with Pṛthvīrāja's success against his neighbours, the Bhādānakas of Ahīravāṭī and the Chandels of Jejākbhukti. The immediate cause, however, of the outbreak of hostilities between the two is believed to have been the "daring abduction of the not unwilling daughter" of Jayachandra by the gallant Pṛthvīrāja. The story does not find a place in the *Pṛthvīrājaprabandha*, the *Prabandhachintāmaṇi*, the *Prabandhakośa*, and the *Hammiramahākāvya*, all of which have something to say about the Chauhān hero. Nevertheless we find it difficult to regard it as a mere romantic product of a bardic fancy because—

1. Silence on the point of the books just mentioned is no argument for the non-occurrence of the abduction : they are also silent on the four main exploits of Pṛthvīrāja, namely the capture of Guḍapura, the fight against the Bhādānakas, the attack on the kingdom of Dhārāvarṣa Paramāra of Chandrāvatī, and the war against Chauluk-yas.

the camp, put his master's application at the feet of Jagaddeva Pratihāra. By the latter's orders, a servant read this communication, "Many wealthy people of Sapādalakṣa have, at present, come here. If you order me, I shall manage to provide fodder for the royal horses." On hearing this, Jagaddeva got angry, and had, immediately the following order written by his clerk. "I have recently concluded a treaty with Pṛthvirāja after taking a lot of trouble. If you therefore lay your hands on the people of Sapādalakṣa, I shall have you sewn in the belly of donkey." Returning with speed with this order, the messenger handed it over to the *daṇḍanāyaka* who on reading it paid his respects to the *Saṅgha* and let it proceed on its way.

29. *ED*, II, p. 214.

30. See the *Pṛthvīrājaprabandha* and the *Pṛthvīrājarāso*. Accordin to the former of these (copied in V. 1528) Jayachandra had his capital illumined when he heard of the news of Pṛthvīrāja's death *Purātanaprabandhasaṅgraha*, pp. 86 and 89).

2. The incident is given by three fairly old authorities Abu Fazl, Chandraśekhara and Chand Bardāi., the first two of whom can, by no means, be accused of having been fond of inventing tales.[31]
3. There is, we believe, a reference to Saṁyogitā in the *Pṛthvīrājavijaya* also, the extant fragment of which mentions, towards its end, an *upaśruti* (a voice revealing the future) that Pṛthvīrāja would, if he tried hard, secure his desired object, *i.e.*, Tilottamā who had incarnated herself on the earth as a princess (XII, 38). It should be remembered that in the *Pṛthvīrājarāso* also Saṁyogitā has been mentioned as the incarnation of an *apsaras*."[32]
4. Like the *Pṛthvīrājarāso* the *Pṛthvīrājavijaya* also states that Pṛthvīrāja fell violently in love with this incarnation of an *apsaras*, even though he had been married more than once before and had never seen her in person.[33]

The story, as given by Chand Bardāi, Abul Fazl and Chandraśekhara, the author of the *Surjanacharita*, is too well known to be cited at length. Pṛthvīrāja, who loved the beautiful daughter of Jayachandra of Kanauj and had his passion fully reciprocated, succeeded in carrying her off from a *svayaṁvara* to which he had deliberately not been invited on account of his rivalry with her father for the overlordship of India. His *sāmantas* covered the eloping pair's flight, engaged the forces pursuing them and fell fighting to the last for their beloved master. Not many were the heroes who returned to the Chauhān capital where Pṛthvīrāja duly married the princess and thereafter spent most of his time in the company of the new queen.'[34]

No doubt it is very romantic ! But such things do sometimes happen in actual life. There is for instance, the well-known case of the Rāṣṭrakūṭa prince Indra, who though a feudatory of the

31. For the story see the *Āin-i-Akbarī* II, pp. 300ff., *SC.* X, 13-128, and the *Pṛthvīrājarāso*, XLV-L and LX-LXI *samayas* of the Nāgarī Prachāriṇī Sabhā edition.

32. See its 45th *Samaya*.

33. *PV*, X, 2, and XII, 1-38.

34. There are slight differences in the three versions, which cannot be noted in this summary account.

Chalukyas, succeeded in carrying off their princess Bhavanāgā by force from her marriage *paṇḍāl* at Kairā.[35] Besides, as pointed out elsewhere by us[36] much of the strangeness of this story would disappear, if we agree to regard Pṛthvīrāja's *sāmantas*, not as individual warriors like the knight-errants of European romances but as leaders of units or regiments of Pṛthvīrāja's cavalry which swooped almost unexpectedly on the Gāhaḍavāla capital while Jayachandra was engaged in certain religious rites and carried off the princess as desired by their master and commander Pṛthvīrāja of Delhi and Ajmer.[37] That Pṛthvīrāja was not incapable of such lightning strokes is obvious enough from his nocturnal attack on the Paramāra forces of Chandrāvatī and the devastation of the powerful kingdoms of Jejākbhukti within the short space of nearly three or four months.[38] At Kanauj, his tactics might well have been similar though carried out with a different object. The *coup* was undoubtedly more impolitic, if, as averred by tradition, it crippled his army and permanently estranged him from a neighbour of great strength and vindictive nature.

All authorities giving any account of the abduction of Jayachandra's daughter put it a little before Pṛthvīrāja's final fight with Muhammad Ghorī in 1193 A.D. The Chauhāns first came into contact with this foreign foe in 1178 A.D., but to avoid a break in our narrative we have not so far taken any notice of him. We now turn to his exploits on the Indian soil.

From the *Tabaqāt-i-Nāsirī* we learn that Muhammad Ghorī was appointed to the governorship of Ghaznā in 1173[39] A.D. by his elder brother Ghiyāsuddīn Muhammad and led his first expedition into India in 1175 A.D. *i.e.*, nearly two years before Pṛthvīrāja's accession. He captured Multān from the Karamitah and took Uchchhā from its Rājpūt ruler after having him poisoned

35. *Indrarājastatogṛhṇāt yaś-Chālukyanṛpātmajām, rākṣasena vivāhena raṇe Kheṭakamaṇḍape*/ (*EI.* XVIII. p. 243).

36. Introduction to the Bikāner recension of the *Pṛthvīrājarāso*.

37. Hammīra of Raṇthambhor was similarly attacked by Khaljī forces while he was performing a *yajña*.

38. Up to *Kārttika Suklā* 7, Prthvīrāja was not far away from Ajmer, though engaged in preparations for the *digvijaya*. So the time left at his disposal in the year V. 1239 when Jejākabhukti was devastated was only a few months.

39. Raverty's translation, p. 449.

by his queen.[40] Having thus secured a sort of bridgehead for further conquests, he advanced against Gujarāt in 1178 A.D.[41] Proceeding most probably by way of Kirāḍū, where the *Turuṣkas* are known to have destroyed the image of the deity Someśvara before Kārttika, V. 1235,[42] he reached Nāḍol and captured it more or less easily.[43] It was high time for Pṛthvīrāja to face this common danger threatening all the Indian kingdoms, for he too had already been approached by a messenger from Muhammad Ghorī who probably desired Pṛthvīrāja to pay tribute or otherwise render homage.[44] The proposal was scornfully turned out, as it should, of course, have been; but it is a pity that Pṛthvīrāja did not draw any lesson from it. The Gujarātīs needed help, but they had none from Pṛthvīrāja because of the advice of his Chief Minister Kadambavāsa.[45] Taking both the Gujarātīs and the Muslims alike as their enemies, the Chauhāns of Ajmer were rather glad to see that they were fighting against and destroying each other. Thanks to the serious reverse sustained by Muhammad Ghorī at the hands of the Gujarātīs in the battle of Kāsahrada, the Chauhāns were not called upon to taste immediately the bitter fruit of their policy; but the example thus set by them was followed by others when it was the Chauhāns' turn to struggle against the Muslims between 1191 and 1195 A.D. In fact, we cannot but deplore this attitude of the Chauhāns; for as subsequent events amply show, Kadambavāsa's or Pṛthvīrāja's failure to help the Gujarātīs proved in a few years detrimental not merely to the cause of the Chauhāns but also to that of the Hindu nation as a whole.

40. Raverty—*Tabaqāt-i-Nāsirī*, p. 449.
Briggs — *Tārikh-i-Firishta*, I, p. 169.

41. Raverty—*Tabaqāt-i-Nāsirī*, p. 451.

42. *PRAS*, *WC*, 1906-7, p. 42.

43. *PV*, X, 50.

44. According to Dr. H. C. Ray, the *PV* tells us that "hearing of the activities of Mlechchha Ghori, Pṛthvīrāja vowed to exterminate the Mlechchhas" and that the Muslims' chief hearing of this vow sent an ambassador to Ajmer (*DHNI*, II 1086). What the *PV* actually says, however, is as follows:

"What more should we say of him (Muhammad Ghorī). Not keeping in view even the fact that Pṛthvīrāja was initiated in the ceremony of destroying these devils in the shape of men, he sent a messenger to this lion residing in the cave of the Meru hill, generally known as Ajayameru" (X, 42).

45. XI, 2-4.

In 1181 A.D. Muhammad Ghori marched to Sialkot and built a fort there. Five years later, he made himself the master of the Punjab by treacherously seizing Khusrau Malik, the last Ghaznavite ruler of Lahore. From this new base, he proceeded to the conquest of further Indian territory and naturally soon came into conflict with Pṛthvīrāja who regarded the destruction of the Muslims as his special mission in this world.[46]

According to all the old Hindu writers on the subject, Pṛthvīrāja defeated Muhammad Ghorī at least seven times before he was himself vanquished, imprisoned and eventually slain after the second battle of Tarāin.[47] Muslim writers, on the other hand, mention only two battles between these rulers, one in 1191 A.D. and the other nearly a year later.[48] The discrepancy can, in the absence of any other independent evidence, be reconciled only by supposing that the Ghorī generals began raiding the Sapādalakṣa empire soon after their capture of Lahore but were beaten back by the Chauhān forces stationed on the frontier, and that while these frontier forays have been magnified into big battles by the Hindu chroniclers, the Muslims have gone to the other extreme and overlooked them altogether.

The campaign leading to Muhammad Ghorī's first great battle with Pṛthvirāja began in the winter of 1190-1191 A.D.[49] Advancing from either Ghaznā or his new base at Lahore,[50] Muhammad Ghorī captured Tabarhindah[51] in the dominions

46. See the verse translated in footnote 44.

47. The *Prithvīrāja-prabandha* and the *Hammīramahākāvya* give the number of Chauhān victories as seven, and the *Prabhandhachintāmaṇi*, the *Prabandhakośa* and the *Pṛthvīrājarāso* as twenty-one.

48. See the *Tabaqāt-i-Nāsirī*, the *Tārik-i-Jirishta*, and the *Tabaqāt-i-Akbarī*.

49. Almost all Muslim historians put the first battle of Tarāin in 587 H. (1191) A.D. But Raverty would put it in 586 H. We think that the operations began in the winter of 586 H., but the battle was actually fought in 587 H., as stated by most of our historians.

50. *MT*, I, p. 69.

51. All the Ms. of the *Tabaqāt-i-Nāsirī* collated by Raverty give either Tabarhindah or Tabarhindh. The *Tabaqāt-i-Akbarī*, *Mirāti-Jahān-Numā*, and *Khulāsāt-ut-Tawārīkh* have Sirhind. The *Tārikh-i-Alfi*, *Zubadat-ut-Tawārīkh* and *Mantakhab-ut-Tawārīkh* have *Tarahindah*. Firishta has either Paṭhindah or Bhaṭindah. The *Lubb-ut-Tawārīkh-i-Hind* speaks of it as Tabarhindah now known as Bhaṭindah. Sir Wolseley Haig, Dr. H. C. Ray, and some others

of Pṛthvīrāja and put it under the charge of Qāzi Ziyā-ud-dīn of Tulāk and a garrison of 1200 horseman, asking them to hold it until he returned there after a period of eight months.[52] But before he could himself leave the fortress, he received the disturbing news that Pṛthvīrāja was marching towards Tabarhindah with Govindarāja, the feudatory ruler of Delhi, some other princes, and a large force of elephants and horses.[53] He therefore set out to meet the Chauhān force and encountered it at Tarāīn,[54] a village in the Karnāl District—in that very field of Kurukṣetra where the Pāṇḍavas and Kauravas are said to have fought against each other and decided the fate of their country in days of yore.

The fight began with the Chauhān attack on the right and left flanks of the Muslim army which, finding it difficult to resist the Hindu onset, soon took to flight.[55] The Muslims vanguard consisting of the Khalj Amīrs followed a similar course. But even then the brave Sultān did not lose heart. Rallying round himself the remainder of his troops, he rushed on the Chauhān force, and seeing Govindarāja, the Rājā of Delhi, moving

identify it with Bhaṭindā, probably on the basis of the last two authorities. But, if we keep in view the fact that Pṛthvīrāja was marching from Ajmer to retake Tabarhindah and Muhammad Ghorī marched out against him to defeat his object, and then have a look at the map, we shall find that Sirhind, a town situated in the defunct Paṭiālā State, and actually mentioned instead of Tabarhindah by some of our authorities, has a much better claim than Bhaṭindā to be regarded as Tabarhindah or Tabarindh of the *Tabaqāt-i-Nāsirī*. If the place had been Bhaṭindā instead of Sirhind, the site of the battle between the Chauhāns and the Muslims would most probably have been to the south of Bhaṭindā, instead of being at Tarāorī which is one hundred miles directly to its east. That it would be just the right place for a battle, if the Chauhāns were proceeding to retake Sirhind and the Muslims or any other party to check them, needs perhaps no demonstration. A look at the map would be proof of the correctness of our view.

52. Raverty, *Tabaqāt-i-Nāsirī*, p. 455.

53. The numbers of the Hindu army given by Firishta are 200,000 horse and 3,000 elephants.

54. Tarāīn which Firishta and Badāūnī identify with Tarāorī must be the village of this name in the Karnāl District.

55. Translation from Firishta's History by Raverty in his footnote to the *Tabaqāt-i-Nāsirī*, p. 463. Briggs' translation of the relevant passage is very faulty.

in front of the Chauhān forces and directing them from the back of his elephant, he seized a spear and struck the Rājā with such effect that two of his teeth were knocked out.[56] But the Rājā, who seems to have been no less valiant and skilful in the use of arms than his adversary, launched a javelin which severely wounded the Sultān on his upper arm.[57] So great was the agony caused by the injury that the Sultān turned round his charger's head and receded, and might have fallen off his horse and perished in the general melee, had he not been recognised by a Khalj youth who, seeing the Sultān's danger, sprang up behind him, and, supporting him in his arms, carried him out of the field of battle.[58] The Muslim army had been in the meanwhile utterly routed. Flying headlong from the field the Muslim horsemen did not draw rein till they had reached a place where they considered themselves safe from pursuit, and loud were their lamentations when they found that the Sultān was not among them ; but this grief was soon after turned into relief, if not something like rejoicing, when they found the Sultān brought to the halting place in a litter improvised with broken spears. All the dispersed elements of the vanquished army united once again, when they heard of the providential escape of the Sultān, and returned after that in good order to their own dominions.[59]

It is obvious from the above account that the Hindus were so superior, well-led, and well-commanded that the Muslims

56. *Ibid.*

57. *Ibid.* p. 460.

58. Raverty, *Tabaqāt-i-Nāsirī*, p. 460. The corresponding passage from the *Muntakhab-ut-Tawārīkh* has been rendered by Ranking as follows:—

"The Sultān got off his horse and taking up his son Khaljī upon his horse and mounting behind him took him off the field."

Who is responsible for this howler, Budāūnī or his translator?

59. Raverty, *Tabaqāt-i-Nāsirī*, I, p. 464. The *Hammīramahākāvya* gives the account of two battles of Pṛthvīrāja against Muhammad Ghorī. Of these the first looks like a description of the causes and course of the first battle of Tarāīn. According to it the battle was due to the appeal of the western rulers who, headed by Chandrarāja, son of Gopālachandra, approached Pṛthvīrāja and requested to be protected from the attacks of Muhammad Ghori. Chandrarāja does not appear to be a fictitious person. But we have not unfortunately any means of identifying him. Can he be the original of Chandra Puṇḍīra of the *Pṛthvīrājarāso*, the head of the Puṇḍarīka clan whose home Puṇḍarī is not far away from Tarāorī?

could hardly have avoided the defeat, even if their leader had not been badly wounded. Pṛthvīrāja could now easily have consummated this victory by chasing and annihilating his routed enemy; but instead of doing this he allowed the scattered Muslim army to re-form itself at some distance from the field and retire almost unmolested. This sort of ideal magnanimity (if it was actually an act of magnanimity as represented by Hindu writers and not of sheer indolence), though in full accord with the humane dictums of Hindu *Śāstras*, which give the Kṣatriyas their high notions of chivalry in the treatment of a fallen or fleeing foe, was out of date and altogether unwarranted by the canons of prudence and warfare as understood now and as understood then by the Muslim adversaries of Pṛthvīrāja. It was indeed the second nail in the coffin of Hindu independence for which we have to hold Pṛthvīrāja responsible.

Traditional accounts state that the Chauhān Emperor passed the interval between this victory and his final defeat in fighting first against the Gāhaḍavālas and thereafter enjoying the company of his newly-wedded wife Saṁyogitā.[60] Muhammad Ghorī occupied himself differently. Muslim historians tell us that, after spending a few months with his brother at Firūzkuh, he returned to Ghaznā, and "having made sleep and rest unlawful to himself" devoted all his energies to the one task of revenging his defeat.[61] At length, having enlisted 1,20,000 select Turk, Tājik and Afghān horsemen, well-equipped with arms and armour, he started towards India, and passing through Multan and Lahore and receiving also some help from Pṛthvīrāja's enemies,[62] he once more reached the plains of Tarāin, though not soon enough to relieve the garrison of Tabarhindah which had, after undergoing a siege of nearly thirteen months, instead of the stipulated eight, surrendered on honourable terms to the Chauhān besiegers.[63] Pṛthvīrāja, who had haughtily rejected

60. See the 64th and 65th *samayas* (Nāgarī Prachāriṇī Sabhā edition).

61. *Tarīkh-i-Firishtā*. The translation by Briggs being wrong, we have followed the translation by Raverty in his English translation of the *Tabaqāt-i-Nāsirī*, p. 464. footnote 7.

62. In the *History of Jammū* of which a summary would be found in Raverty's translation of the *Tabaqāt-i-Nāsirī*, Vijayarāja of Jammū is said to have helped Muhammad Ghorī against the Chauhāns.

63. Raverty, *Tabaqāt-i-Nāsirī*, I, p. 464.

Muhammad Ghorī with his ultimatum to embrace Islam and recognise the Muslim sovereign as his overlord, was already on the battlefield with an army of 300,000 horses, 3,000 elephants and considerable infantry.[64] One hundred and fifty of the chiefs fighting under his banner swore by the water of the Ganges to conquer or die, and then wrote a letter to the Sultān offering to do him no harm, if he chose wisely to return to his country, but threatening him with complete destruction if he were determined to fight. Muhammad Ghorī, who was no stranger to the great bravery of the Rājpūts, preferred, according to his wont, to try strategem before force and wrote back saying, "I have marched into India at the command of my brother whose general I am. Both honour and duty bind me to exert myself to the utmost...., but I shall be glad to obtain a truce till he is informed of the situation and I have received his answer".[65] The ruse had the desired effect on the credulous and over-confident Hindus who, regardless of the past record of the Sultān, took him at his word, and falling into a holiday mood passed the night in merry-making. Early the next morning they had to taste the bitter fruit of this hasty and imprudent relaxation and dilly-dallying.[66]

According to Muhammad Utī, who wrote his *Jami'ul Hikāyāt* under Iltutmish and must therefore have known something of the actual events, the Ghorī invader, with a view to preventing any possible suspicion of movement, kept a number of fires burning all the night where his army had encamped during the day, and marched off himself in another direction with the rest of his forces.[67] Then leaving the centre of his army, luggage, paraphernalia, and elephants several miles away, he divided the remaining part into four divisions, each of 10,000 archers and ordered them to attack the Hindus, right and left, front and rear, and retire pretending flight.[68]

It was hardly daylight when these troops reached the Chauhān

64. Briggs, *Tārikh-i-Firishta*, I. p. 175. Firishta calls this the most authentic estimate.
65. *Ibid.*, p. 176
66. *Ibid.*
67. *ED.* II, p. 200.
68. Raverty, *Tabaqāt-i-Nāsirī*, I, p. 468.

camp and delivered their first attack. Pṛthvīrāja was asleep,[69] the Rājpūt soldiers were just moving out for their daily ablutions and other morning duties.[70] Having thus been taken by surprise, the Rājpūts could not have escaped considerable losses, but they could still have drawn themselves up into fighting order if the well-thought out strategy of Muhammad Ghorī had not lured and drawn them out into an unsystematic and ill-advised pursuit. About three in the afternoon, when the Hindus had become thoroughly wearied, Muhammad Ghorī led his final charge with the troops that he had hitherto held in reserve. The Hindus were completely routed, losing about 100,000 men according to Hasan Nizāmī.[71] Govindarāja, the Rājā of Delhi, was among the slain. The Sultān recognised his head by the absence of the teeth that he had himself knocked out. Pṛthvīrāja, who must have joined the battle only very late, tried to escape on a horse, but was recognised, pursued and overtaken in the neighbourhood of Sarasvatī.[72]

69. i गतेऽन्यसंगरे स्कन्दे निद्रा-व्यसन-सन्नधीः ।
व्यापादितस्तुरुष्कैस्सः जीवन्मृतो युधि ॥

विरुद्ध-विधि-विध्वंस of Lakṣmīdhara. (*Catalogue of Mss. in the Library of the India Office*, No. 1577.)

(*ii*) The account of the *Pṛthvīrāja-prabandha*, though highly exaggerated no doubt, leads to the same conclusion. It begins with the words "Pṛthvīrāja had been asleep ten days...In the meantime the Prime Minister had the Sultān sent for" (See the *Purātanaprabandhasaṅgraha*, p. 68).

(*iii*) According to the *Prabandhachintāmaṇi* Pṛthvīrāja was asleep at the time after breaking his *ekādaśī* fast.

(*iv*) Firishta says that the Rajpūts had passed the night in revelry. So Pṛthvīrāja's being asleep at the time of the attack need not be regarded as strange.

70. *Tabaqāt-i-Nāsirī*, I, p. 468, note I; *Tārikh-i-Firishta* I, p. 176; *Hammīra-mahākāvya*, III, 58.

71. *ED.* II, p. 215.

72. Sarasvatī can mean the neighbourhood of the Sarasvatī river as suggested by Raverty. But just two lines later the *Tabaqāt-i-Nāsirī* speaks of Sarasvatī as a fort that surrendered to the Muslims. Firishta too speaks of it as a fort captured by the Muslims soon after the battle of Tarāīn. Ibn Batūtā puts it down as a place on the route from Abohar to Delhi. So the place meant is most probably Sirsā of the Hissār District, Punjāb, which we found actually mentioned as Sarasvatī in the *Karmachandravaṁśotkīrtanakakāvya* of Jayasoma.

Pṛthvīrāja's life, however, was spared for a while, and he was carried, not to Ghaznā, as averred by some Hindu writers,[73] but to his own capital Ajmer which the Sultān captured after slaying thousands of its heroic defenders and reserving the rest for slavery.[74] "The pillars and foundations" of its temples were destroyed, and it was despoiled of the greater part of the wealth accumulated in the days of its prosperity.[75] Muhammad Ghorī was equally successful in other directions; for soon after the greater part of Sapādalakṣa, including the forts of Hānsī, Sarasvatī, Samānā and Kohrām fell into his hands with comparative ease.[76]

According to the *Prabandhachintāmaṇi*, Muhammad Ghorī had some intention of reinstating Pṛthvīrāja on the throne of Ajmer, but had him beheaded instead when it was found that his picture gallery contained paintings representing Muslim soldiers being killed by pigs.[77] The statement is, no doubt, not wholly true. But that the Sultān had some intention of retaining Pṛthvīrāja as a vassal chief can be seen from a unique coin, bearing the names of both Pṛthvīrāja and Muhammad bin Sām which was issued from Delhi mint and has been noticed by Thomas in his *Chronicle of the Pathān Kings of Delhi.*[78] Such an issue could be possible only after Pṛthvīrāja had been defeated by the Muslims and agreed to rule as their subordinate.[79] Pṛthvīrāja's "ancient hatred was", in the words of Hasan Nizāmī the author of *Tāju-ul-Ma- āsir*, "deeply rooted and concealed in the bottom of his heart."[80] He was detected in an intrigue, the nature of which Hasan Nizāmī does not make clear, and was beheaded by the orders of the Sultān.[81]

73. Cf. the *Pṛthvīrājarāso*, 66th *samaya*.
74. *Taju-i-Ma-āsir*, ED. II, p. 215; De, *Tabaqāt-i-Akbari*, I, p. 39.
75. *Ibid.*
76. Raverty, *Tabaqāt-i-Nāsirī*, I, p. 468; *Tārikh-i-Firishta*, I, p. 177.
77. pp. 117-118.
78. pp. 17-18.
79. That the Sultān was not then eager to take over the direct administration of Ajmer might be seen also from his making it over to Govinda on the death of his father Pṛthvīrāja. *See* also my paper on the joint coin of Muhammad-bin-Sām and Pṛthvīrāja. III in *JNSI*, XVI, p. 122.
80. *ED.* II, p. 215.
81. Could this intrigue have originated the story described as follows in the *Pṛthvīrāja-prabandha*, a manuscript of which was copied out in 1471 A.D.

Thus sadly ended the life and career of one of the strongest rulers of medieval India. The very city where he had reigned supreme, hailed by poets as a veritable incarnation of Rāma,[82] witnessed his fall and wept over it. That he had some excellent qualities is generally admitted. He was, by all accounts, handsome, brave, courageous, unequalled in the art of archery, and the very embodiment of chivalry. His victories over the Bhādānakas, the Chandelas, Nāgārjuna, Bhīmadeva II, and also over the Gāhaḍavālas conclusively prove his greatness as a general.[83] And then, Pṛthvīrāja was no mere soldier. He was, in his time, one of the foremost patrons of letters. His court was graced by the poet-historian Jayānaka, the writer of the *Pṛthvīrājavijaya*;[84] Vidyāpati Gauḍa;[85] *vāgīśvara* Janārdana;[86] Visvarūpa, a poet who befriended Jayānaka;[87] Pṛthvībhaṭa, the royal bard;[88] who was proficient in traditional lore and has been identified by some writers with Chand Bardāi, the author

but which, according to Muni Jinavijaya, was composed very much earlier:—

"The Sultān sat in the court in front of the place where they had housed Pṛthvīrāja (after his capture). This distressed him (the Rājā). The Rājā's Prime Minister, who was a traitor but unknown as such to him, approached him and said, "My lord, what can be done? It was so destined." The Rājā replied "If thou givest me my bow and arrows, I shall kill the Sultān." He assented and going to the Sultān asked him not to sit at his usual place. The Sultān had a metal statue of himself put there. Then going to the Rājā, the minister provided him with a bow. The Rājā shot the arrow and the statue fell divided into two pieces. The Rājā threw off the bow, saying 'My task has not been accomplished; somebody else has been killed'. Then the Sultān had the Rājā thrown into a pit and pelted with stones." (*Purātanaprabandhasaṅgraha*, p. 87.)

It is difficult to be sure about the amount of truth in this story of which versions even more exaggerated occur in the *Pṛthvīrājarāso*, the *Surjanacharita*, and the *Āin-i-Akbarī*.

82. Read the *Pṛthvīrājavijaya* for instance where he is depicted throughout as an incarnation of Rāma.

83. The second battle of Tarāin might be regarded as a blot on his generalship. But as he was asleep at the time (*see* note 68), it could be no good test. He could have taken part in the battle only towards the end when the situation had already got out of hand.

84. See *PV*, I, 31 and XII, 62 to the end.

85. *Kharataragachchhapaṭṭāvalī* of Jinapāla, p. 25.

86. *Ibid.*

87. *PV*, 129.

88. *Ibid*, XI, 13-17.

of the original *Pṛthvīrājarāso*;[89] and a host of lesser luminaries whose names have not come down to us but who received due recognition and were occasionally called into conference by Padmanābha, the minister in charge of *paṇḍits* and poets.[90]

But with all his virtues, Pṛthvīrāja had faults serious enough to deny him a place among the greatest rulers of India. He lacked foresight, he had not also statesmanship enough to see that the times had changed and old policies required to be either entirely discarded or to be adapted to the changing circumstances of the day. He seems to have prided himself on being a *dig-vijayin*, perhaps on having followed the instructions of his uncle Vigraharāja IV.[91] He never realised that with the Ghorī hamm-ering at the gates of his northern frontier, a thorough pursuit of this policy could not be anything but suicidal. Instead of making new friends and presenting a united front to the Muslim invaders by organising a friendly confederacy of which he could have been, by virtue of his position, one of the most prominent mem-bers, he made enemies on all sides by his raids on Jejākabhukti, Kanauj, and the empire of Gujarāt. The attacks brought him fame and wealth, but they also brought him the ill-will of his neighbours; consequently, when he was defeated in the second battle of Tarāīn, not a single ruler came forward to support the tottering empire of Sapādalakṣa. Even standing alone Bhīma-deva II of Gujarāt and Pṛthvīrāja III had, respectively, been

89. The first mention of Chand Bardāī, however, is found in the account o {*Pṛthvīrāja* in the *Purātanaprabandhasaṅgraha* (copied V. 1528).

90. *PV*, XII, 58. Badlā inscription was his composition.

Among occasional visitors to his court might be mentioned the learned Jinapati Sūri of the *Kharataragachccha*, who got a *jayapatra* from him by defeat-ing Padmaprabha of the *Upakeśagachchha* in discussion.

91. (a) अस्माभिः करदं व्यधायि हिमवद्-विन्ध्यान्तरालं भुवः।
शेष-स्वीकरणाय मास्तु भवतामुद्योगशून्यं मनः ॥
(Siwālik Pillar inscription, 3, v. 2)

(b) श्रीचाहुमान-वंश्येन पृथ्वीराजेन भूभुजा ।
परमर्दी-नरेन्द्रस्य देशोयमुदवास्यत ॥
अर्णोराजस्य पौत्रेण श्रीसोमेश्वर-सूनुना ।
जेजाकभुक्तिदेशोयं पृथ्वीराजेन लूनितः ॥

(c) See also the reference to Pṛthvirāja III in the Mahābhāratī, III, p. 885.

able to defeat Muhammad Ghorī on two different occasions, at the battle of Kāsahrada in 1178 A.D. and that of Tarāīn in 1191. United together, these could not have merely stemmed the tide of Muslim invasion, but also freed the Northern Punjāb from Muslim domination. But the policy of the *digvijayin* Pṛthvīrāja and the advice tendered to him by his counsellors when the Muslims invaded India in 1178 A.D., as pointed out already, so far estranged the Chaulukyas that, acting exactly as Pṛthvīrāja had done fifteen years earlier,[92] they did not make the slightest move against the Muslims until the power of the Chauhāns of Sapādalakṣa had been completely destroyed. If traditional accounts be believed, and there is no cogent reason for not doing so, Pṛthvīrāja's policy towards the Gāhaḍavālas had been equally bad, and Jayachandra, rejoiced instead of grieving when he heard of the Chauhān ruler's defeat and death at the hands of the Muslims.[93]

Pṛthvīrāja was not, we fear, also without a large share of good-natured indolence. He could be active when he chose, as active perhaps as the Mughal Emperor, Humāyūn, who within the course of a few months conquered the greater part of the empire of Gujarāt. But he could also be equally lazy. We have already criticised his conduct subsequent to the first battle of Tarāīn. His conduct in the second battle was even worse. He under-estimated the strength of his opponents, and believed, like a novice, the words of Muhammad Ghorī without keeping in view what the Sultān had done at Uchchha and Lahore.[94] He was not inexperienced in the line of night-attacks, for he had himself led one against Dhārāvarṣa Paramāra. So he should have remained on the look-out for some such action on the part of an enemy, ruthless and determined, and as skilful as himself. But he passed, instead, the whole night in revelry, and was fast asleep, perhaps sleeping off the effects of a night's orgy. For such conduct, especially on the eve of an important engagement, a general however strong or able he might be, deserved to lose

92. See *PV*, XI, 2-4.

93. See above footnote 30.

94. At Uchchha he had the ruler poisoned by his queen. He put the Ghaznavite Kursrav Malik in prison after promising him a safe conduct. (See the *Tabaqāt-i-Nāsirī*, I, pp. 455-7).

an empire and all the power that he had. "The earth is to be enjoyed by the heroic and the ever-wakeful", state the writer on Indian polity, and the king's behaviour just before the second battle of Tarāīn was neither that of a hero nor of a great general, awake to all the possibilities and probabilities of warfare, but that of a novice in the art of finesse and of a common reveller.[95]

95. "He with his intellectual faculties clouded with the vice of sleep was", states Lakṣmīdhara, "killed in the engagement because he was (as good as) dead though alive". See also above, footnote 69 in which we quote a few other authorities to support Lakṣmīdhara's view.

APPENDIX B

THE BHĀDĀNAKAS

The Bhādānakas or Bhayāṇayas, if we use the Apabhraṁśa equivalent of the term, are known to us from various sources. Rājaśekhara's *Kāvyamīmāṁsā* describes them as speakers of Apabhraṁśa and groups them as such with the people of Maru and Ṭakka *deśas*.[1] That their territory adjoined that of the Cāhamānas of Śākambharī can be inferred from the Bijoliā inscription of Someśvara's reign, V. 1226 (1169 A.D.), according to which the lord of the Bhadānaka land was deprived of his *bhā* (lustre) by the Cāhamāna ruler, Vigraharāja IV;[2] and the same inference can be drawn also from the *Kharataragacchapaṭṭāvalī* of Jinapāla, which states that Pṛthvīrāja III, the ruler of Sapādalakṣa, defeated the Bhādānakas somewhere between V. 1234 (1177 A.D.) and V. 1239 (1182 A.D.)[3]. As regards the political importance of the Bhādānakas, it is indicated not only by these references, according to the last one of which they fought against Pṛthvīrāja III with a mighty elephant force but also by the Bhādāna-*deśa* being described in the *Skandapurāṇa* as a kingdom with 1,25,000 villages.[4] The Cāhamānas of Sapādalakṣa, the rulers of which aspired to the position of *Cakravartins*[5] and claimed having subjected the whole of Āryāvarta[6] to their power, had traditionally no greater number of villages in their kingdom.

The *Sakalatīrtha-stotra* of Siddhasena Sūri puts the Bhadānaka-*deśa* between Kanauj and Harṣapura (Haras of Shekhāwāṭī, Rājasthān) and mentions Kammaga and Siroha as two of its

1. *Sāpabhraṁśa-prayogāḥ sokala-Marubhuvaṣ=Ṭakka-Bhādānakādyāḥ* (*Kāvyamīmāṁsā*, G.O.S., p. 51)

2. Verse 19.

3. p. 28, Singhī Jaina Granthamālā edition. As Pṛthvīrāja III ascended the throne in V. 1234 and his victory over the Bhādānakas was extolled in V. 1239 by Jinapati, the event has to be put between these two dates.

4. *Kumārikā-khaṇḍa*, Ch. XXXIX.

5. See *Pṛthvīrājavijaya*, XI. 8.

6. Delhi Siwālik Pillar Inscription of Vigraharāja IV.

Jaina sacred sites.[7] From the *Vividhatīrthakalpa* of Jinaprabha Sūri we find that Siroha was situated on the road connecting Daulatābād or Devagiri with Delhi[8] and was somewhere north of Alāpura,[9] which according to the *Āin-i-Akbarī* was a stronghold in the *Sarkār* of Gwālior. Kammaga, the Sanskrit equivalent of which is Kāmyaka, must be Kāmān which is about 40 miles west of Mathurā in the old Bharatpur State. In the middle of the town there is an old fort with fragments of Hindu sculptures and a mosque called *Chaurāsī Khambā* built out of the materials of Hindu temples wrecked most probably by Muslim iconoclastic fury. From here we have also two inscriptions of the Śūrasena family descended from a ruler named Phakka, one assigned to the middle of the eighth and the other to the middle of the tenth century.[10]

If we put together all this evidence, we have good reason to conclude that Bhadānaka was a *janapada* which included Kāmān, Bharatpur and some territory, south of these on the well-known and well-frequented Delhi-Daulatābād highway of that period; and we are now happy to have this information supplemented by the evidence of an old Apabhraṁśa manuscript, the *Sambhavanāthacarita* by Tejapāla, which, according to its *praśasti*,[11] was written at Siripaha (Śrīpatha or Bayānā) of the Bhayāṇaya-*deśa* when it was being ruled by Dāūd Shāh. As Tejapāla's time can be easily ascertained with the help of his two other works, the *Varāṅgacarita* and the *Pārśvanāthacarita*, written respectively in V. 1507 (1450 A.D.) and V. 1515 (1458 A.D.), there is no difficulty in identifying Dāūd Shāh of Śrīpatha or Bayānā in the Bhadānaka-*deśa* with Dāūd Shāh Auhadī, who was confirmed in 1454 A.D. in the government of Bayānā by Mahamūd Shāh Khaljī of Mālwā.[12] His father, Muhammad Khān Auhadī had been forced by Sultān Mubārak Shāh of Delhi to evacuate Bayānā, though only temporarily, for in 1446 A.D.

7. *Catalogue of MSS in Pāṭṭan Bhaṇḍāra*, I; G.O.S., p. 156, verse 22.
8. Singhi Jaina Granthamālā, edition, p. 95.
9. *Ibid.*, p. 96.
10. See *Bhandarkar's List of North Indian Inscriptions*, No. 71, 1849.
11. *Jaina-praśasti-saṅgraha*, II, Vīrasewā Mandir, Delhi edition and its English Introduction by the present writer (in the press).
12. *Cambridge History of India*, III, p. 356.

we find him ruling there once again. Obviously then, not only Kammaga and Siroha but also Śrīpatha was an important town of the Bhadānaka-*deśa*, perhaps even its capital from a very early period. Included within the Bhādānaka kingdom was the strong fort of Tahangarh which is barely 14 miles south of Bayānā. Adding the testimony of the works of Tejapāla, therefore, to the evidence already adduced in the preceding paragraphs, we might say that Bhadānaka-*deśa* comprised not only the old Bharatpur State but also Dholpur, Karaulī and parts of Mathurā and Alwar Districts; and that in c. V. 1239 (1182 A.D.) when Pṛthvīrāja III of Śākambharī attacked the Bhādānaka kingdom, it was probably bounded in the south-east by the Chambal river and the Gwālior principality of the Kacchapaghāṭas. In the north-east lay the Yamunā and the kingdom of the Gāhaḍvālas of Vārāṇasī and Kannauj. On the remaining sides was the Cāhamāna Empire of Sapādalakṣa.

Up to V. 1012 (955 A.D.) Śrīpatha or Bayānā appears to have remained under the Śūrasenas[13] and as tradition appears to state correctly that the Yādavas of Tribuvanagiri or Tahangarh and Karaulī originally ruled at Bayānā, either this very Śūrasena dynasty or one of its offshoots came to be designated as Yādava. Śūrasena was a Yādava.[14] One of his descendants could, therefore, call himself either a Yādava or a Śūrasena as he liked; and a new branch of the family might have preferred to call itself Yādava, just to distinguish itself from the older branch which had perhaps become either extinct or dispossessed of the Bhādānaka throne for reasons of which we have no knowledge.[15]

The ruler of Bhadānaka-*deśa* against whom Vigraharāja IV of Śākambharī had to fight probably was either Kumārapāla I who was instructed by the Kharatara *Ācārya* Jinadatta Sūri (1112-1154 A.D.)[16] or Kumārapāla's successor *Mahārājādhirāja*

13. See the Bayānā Inscription of the year, *PRAS. WC.*, 1918-19, pp. 43 ff. and 1919-20, p. 57.

14. He was Vasudeva's father and Kṛṣṇa's grand-father.

15. A parallel case is that of the Vaghelas of Dholkā who, though Chaulukyas like the members of the preceding line, are known as Vaghelas. This latter name has given rise even to the fanciful story of their origin from a tiger.

16. See the *Kharataragacchapaṭṭāvalī*, p. 19.

Ajayapāla who was ruling near Mathurā in V. 1207 (1150 A.D.)[17] He was succeeded by Haripāla whose rule is vouched for by tradition as well as an inscription of V. 1227 (1170 A.D.)[18] As to Pṛthvīrāja III's Bhādānaka rival, he should probably be Haripāla's successor, Sāhaṇapāla, for whom we have an image inscription from Āghāṭapura in the old Bharatpur State. In 1196 A.D., when Tribhuvanagiri was captured by Muhammad Ghorī, the ruler on the throne of Bayānā was Kumārapāla,[19] and he has to be called Kumārapāla II, as we know of another Kumārapāla of this line as Jinadatta Sūri's contemporary.[20] Further history of this line can be had from the *Vṛttavilāsa* of the poet Jadunātha who was patronised by Gopāl Singh of Karaulī, a direct descendant of Kumārapāla II.[21]

Incidentally, the location of the Bhādānaka kingdom helps us in solving some other problems. It clears up the mystery of the name Bayānā. No phonetic rule can change Śripatha into Bayānā. Nor is the place mentioned as Bayānā by any early non-Muslim writer. Obviously it is Bhadānaka then, the Apabhraṁśa form of which is Bhayāṇaya, that has turned into Bayāna or Bayānā of the Muslim writers. In a language and a script which makes no fine distinction between *ba* and *bha* such a change would be the easiest and the most natural thing to occur.[22] The other point on which the location of Bhadānaka-

17. See his Mahāban *praśasti* of the year, V. 1207, *EI*, I, pp. 289ff. and II, 276ff.

18. *EI*, II, p. 275.

19. *Tāj-ul-Ma'āsir*, *ED*, II, pp. 204-43.

20. See the first sentence of the paragraph.

21. See the *Ojhā-nibandha-saṅgraha*, Pt. 3, pp. 1-9.

22. Before we leave the subject of the location of the Bhādānakas, it might not be out of place to refer to some of the earlier attempts at the identification of the Bhadānaka deśa. N.L. Dey identified the *janapoda* with Bhadriā, 8 miles south of Bhāgalpur. Disagreeing with him, C.D. Dalal equated Bhadānaka with Bāṭadhāna (a country mentioned in the *Mahābhārata*) which he located between the Śatadru and Vināśana. Dr. B.N. Puri gives no reasons for disagreeing with Dalal but "propose(s) its identification with Bhadraunā in the Patiala State" as "this would meet the requirement of its contiguity with Ṭakka and Maru countries as suggested by Rājaśekhara" (*JIH*, 1962, p. 424). With the positive evidence on the subject placed before the readers of this paper, any elaborate discussion of these identifications becomes unnecessary. We modify also our view on the subject expressed earlier.

deśa throws light is the nature of the Apabhraṁśa from which Vraja-*bhāṣā* has originated. As Bhadānaka-*deśa* was almost conterminous with Śūrasena *janapada*, we may designate the Apabhraṁśa of the area as Śaurasenī Apabhraṁśa and regard it as the parent of the modern Vraja-*bhāṣā* and seek for the evolutionary history of the latter in the Apabhraṁśa literature which this area continued producing[23] almost up to the period when poets of Vraja-*bhāṣā* may be said to have assumed charge of the literary field.[23]

23. For the notice of these works see descriptive catalogues and lists published by the Digambar Jaina Atiśaya Kṣetra Mahāvīrajī, Jaipur.

APPENDIX C

SOME RECENTLY DISCOVERED INSCRIPTIONS OF PṚTHVĪRĀJA III

Fourteen inscriptions of Pṛthvīrāja III have been discovered so far. The earliest is an inscription found near Ajmer. It is dated V. 1234, and is given below on page 106. The next inscription, dated V. 1236, comes from Lohārī. Nearly of the same time is an inscription from Phalodī. The Madanpur inscriptions are dated V. 1239. The Charlū inscriptions published by me in *Rājasthāna Bhāratī*, Vol. I, are, in view of their historical importance, reproduced here. The Revāsā inscriptions referring to certain Chandels of Khaluvāṇā village in the Chandel *parganā* are published here for the first time. When and why these Chandels migrated from Bundelkhaṇḍa to Rājasthān is unknown.

Charlu Inscriptions

Inscription 1

(1 horseman, 1 *satī*)

Line 1. ओम् स्वस्ति ।. मा––
,, 2. ......
,, 3. ......
,, 4. द्रित ...रः पातु वः ॥ संवत् ॥ १२०० पौ[ष] वदि...
,, 5. [चा] हमानान्वय-विष्णुदत्त-सुत-देवसरा (?) दे...
,, 6. वलोके गतः ॥ सं० १२३४ फाल्गुन वदि २ सोमवा[रे]
,, 7. पौत्र-आहडेन कारापितमास्ते शिवमस्तु ॥

Inscription 2

(1 horseman, 1 man under the horse)

Line 1. [ओम्] स्वस्ति संवत् १२४१ मा—
,, 2. ग्रसि[र] सुदि १२ शुक्रवारे मोहिल

Line 3. आहडपुत्र अम्बरक श्रीनागपु-
,, 4. रे संग्रामे दे [वलो]के गतः ॥

Inscription 3

(1 horseman, 1 man under the horse)

Line 1. ओम् सम्वत् १२४१ मार्गसिर
,, 2. सुदि १२ [शुक्र] वारे मोहि-
,, 3. ल श्री [आह ?] सुत आहड श्री-
,, 4. नागपुर संग्रामे देवलोके
,, 5. गतः

Inscription 4

(1 horseman, 3 *satīs*)

Line 1. ओम् सम्वत् १२४४...वदि १५ शुक्रे
,, 2. ......श्री दु[र्यो]ध......
,, 3. ....
,, 4. ......

Revāsā Stone-inscription of Pṛthvīrāja III's reign

V. 1243

Line 1. ॥ओम्॥ स्वस्तिमदे (हे) व पृथ्वीपालदेव-राजेन्द्रः
,, 2. [चंदे] ल-प्रतिगणके खलुवाणाग्रामस्य शशिहरवंशे
,, 3. [चंदेल] सीघ (सिंह) राजसुत-चंदेलनान्नव
दे (दि) वं गतः।......कारा...
,, 4. पिता चंदेल जसराके (जे) न। संवत् १२४३ मार्ग० सदि
११ बुध
,, 5. मंगलं महाश्रीः ॥

Baḍlā Inscription of Pṛthvīrāja III

V. 1234[1]

1. सिद्धम् ओम् नमः शिवाय ॥ देवः सोव्याद् वरुणो[2] यदीया श्रीज्जं-
गमस्थावरजन्महे [तुः...]

1. The above transcript is based on Śrī U.C. Bhattacharya's photograph of the inscription published in the *Proceedings of the Indian History Congress*, 1951. The reading prepared by Sri Brij Narain Sharma was published with a historical note by me in the *Marubhāratī*, January 1955. A very much improved reading was published in the *Śodhapatrikā* by Sri Prithvi Singh Mehta. Some of Mr. Sharma's readings criticised by Mr. Mehta, however, are only printing mistakes.

2. Mr. Mehta's reading वरणो does not seem correct.

2. च(ह)व्यमपि प्रसूते ॥१॥ चाहमानाह्वयः कोपि पुरा वीरो विरो-
चनात् । प्रादुर्व्व(र्ब्व)भू[व...

3. मादिहोद्भूय चिराय भुक्त्वा कृत्स्नां महीं विग्रहराजदेवे । पृथ्वी-
भटे भ्रातृसुते च तस्य मा...

4, रदेवे क्षोणिपते (तौ)[4] त्रिदशपत्तनं प्राप्ते । पृथ्वीराजस्तनयस्तस्य
पदं भूषयामास ॥४॥ युग्मं......

5. नी सद्ब्राह्मणाः कौशिकवंशदीपाः । यन्निर्गमः स्फीतिमतोतिशाख
(:)[5] नाम्नोग्रहाराद...

6. खम्मदेवो देवविप्राद्यपासा[6] प्रसरदमलकीर्तिस्तत्कुले नीतिशाली
सकलगुणगरिष्ठ [:]...

7. भवदुचितज्ञः श्रीयशोराजसंज्ञः ॥ काश्यपान्वयसंभूत -सहदेवाग (ग्र)
जन्मनः । उदयस्तनूज...

8. तवान् । जयन्त इव पौलोमीपाकशासनयोरयं
तयोष्ठक्कुरप[7]—को दम्पत्योरभवत्सुतः ॥८॥ सत्वञ्च.....

9. द्रो[8] महत्त्वेन मरुद्गिरिः शौचेन यः शान्तनवः सत्येन च युधिष्ठिरः
॥९॥ वाणिज्योपार्जितं यस्य ध[न].....

10. रकं तथा ह्यनेन वापीयं निरमाप्यत शर्म्मकृत्[9] ॥१०॥ यद्वारि
शिशिरं स्वादु पायं पायमपक्लमाः.....

11. पांथास्तत्र सविस्मयं ॥११॥ पितृव्यराहडस्यापि निपानेस्मिन्
कियद्धनं । व्ययित्वानृण्यमग(म)त्ठक्कुरः.....

12. देदमा सलखू लक्ष्मीरुत्तमा चेति तस्य तु । धर्मपत्न्यः पितृव्यस्य चतस्रः
पतिदेवताः ॥१३॥ कृतिरियं श्रीमदाचार्य.....

3. There is no necessity of amending it as भुङ्क्त्वा as done in Mr Mehta's edition.

4. Considering the locative case of 'देवे' we should read क्षोणिपतो as क्षोणिपतौ and रदेवे should be read as सोमेश्वरदेवे

5. Meter needs ख as a long syllable.

6. Read पाता

7. (a) The letter intervening between प and क must be a conjunct long letter.

8. (इं) द्रो

9. Sri Mehta reads निर्माप्यत शर्म्मंकृत्

12. वेः श्री पद्मनाभस्य ॥ उत्कीर्णेयं पंडितयशोधरपुत्रेण जगतसिंहेन ॥ संवत् १२३४ चैत्र शुदि ४ ॥ श(शि)वमस्तु[10] । स्थेयाच्चे...

For a possible literary reference to Pṛthvīrāja III see also the *Marubhāratī*, III, p. 85.

Madanpur Inscriptions, V. 1239.

श्री चाहुमान-वंश्येन पृथ्वीराजेन भूभुजा ।
परमर्दी-नरेन्द्रस्य देशोयमुदवास्यत ॥
अर्णोराजस्य पौत्रेण श्रीसोमेश्वरसूनुना ।
जैजाकभुक्तिदेशोयं पृथ्वीराजेन लूनितः ॥
संवत् १२३९ ॥

10. Sri Mehta proposed reading शुभ, for शव but with a question mark.

APPENDIX D

HISTORICITY OF SAṀYOGITĀ, THE HEROINE OF THE PṚTHVĪRĀJA-RĀSO

The chief arguments advanced against the historicity of Saṁyogitā can, in brief, be given as follows:

1. Saṁyogitā is not mentioned in the *Rambhāmañjarī*, a play by Nayachandra Sūri (written c. 1403 A.D.) which has Jayachandra of Kannauj as its hero and describes his qualifications and achievements in nearly two pages.

2. Saṁyogitā is not mentioned also in Nayachandra Sūri's poem, the *Hammīramahākāvya*, which deals with the Chauhān hero Hammīra of Raṇthambhor and his ancestors.

3. The details of Saṁyogitā's *svayaṁvara* and marriage to Pṛthvīrāja III are too romantic to be true.[1]

But the writers who advance these arguments should first see whether their authorities are really reliable. They have to think also of the nature of the evidence they have. All that the *Rambhāmañjarī*, for instance, says about Jayachandra of Kannauj can be boiled down to this much:

(a) That he was a scion of the Ikṣvāku family.
(b) That his arms served as an elephant's post for Madanavarman's goddess of fortune.
(c) That he was a son of Malladeva and Chandralekhā.
(d) That he bore the designation *dalapaṅgula* on account of the immensity of his forces.

Of these the first three statements cannot be substantiated. The last one may be true, because he is given a similar designation in the *Pṛthvīrājarāso*. Gāhaḍavāla records do not describe Jayachandra and his ancestors as solar Kṣatriyas. The line actually is said to have come into existence when the solar line

1. The above arguments were advanced by Dr. G.H. Ojha (vide the *Ojhā-nibandha-saṅgraha*, II, pp. 78-112) and have been repeated, without any attempt at their critical assessment by most of the subsequent writers on the historicity of the *Pṛthvīrājarāso*.

had disappeared.[2] Their modern representatives in the Uttar Pradesh regard themselves as lunar Rājpūts.[3] Madanavarman, the Chandel ruler of Jijhotī, passed away before 1165 A.D. How could then Jayachandra, who succeeded to the throne of Banaras and Kannauj in 1170 A.D., be described as doing anything to buttress or destroy Madanavarman's prosperity? A way out of the difficulty would perhaps be to assume that the reference is to one of Jayachandra's exploits as a *yuvarāja*, but this too is ruled out by the fact that Jayachandra's installation as a *yuvarāja* took place on 16th June, 1168 A.D.,[4] *i.e.*, nearly three years after Madanavarman's death. Jayachandra's father is said to have been some Malladeva. Gāhaḍavāla records, however, state that Jayachandra was the son of Govindachandra's son, Vijayachandra. If it be assumed that Malladeva was one of Vijayachandra's titles, should not one enquire why the title was known only to Nayachandra Sūri, who wrote the *Rambhāmañjarī* nearly two hundred years after Jayachandra's death, and to none of the numerous Gāhaḍavāla inscriptions incised during the reigns of Vijayachandra and his successors?[5]

As regards the *Hammīramahākāvya*, it is silent not only about Saṁyogitā's *svayaṁvara* but also about Pṛthvīrāja's victories in his wars with Nāgārjuna, the Chandel ruler Paramardin, the Chaulukya king Bhīmadeva II and the Bhādānakas. It has nothing to say also about Pṛthvīrāja's many marriages, though they are mentioned even in the fragmentary *Pṛthvīrājavijaya*. If on the basis of its silence, we neither regard his wars and victories as unhistorical nor conclude that Pṛthvīrāja remained unmarried, what valid reason can we have to make that very silence the main reason to discredit an old tradition, found at least in three languages, Sanskrit, Persian and old Rājasthānī, and having, as we propose to show, its roots in the contemporary poem, *Pṛthvīrājavijaya*? No doubt the traditional story of Saṁyogitā is extremely romantic. But romance is a part of life and can therefore be equally true and real. That the story had a

2. *Āsīdaśītadyutivaṁśajātakṣmāpālamālāsu divaṁ gatāsu.*
3. *Mirzāpur Gazetteer*, p. 204.
4. R.S. Tripathi, *History of Kanauj*, p. 321.
5. Dr. R.S. Tripathi has listed 4 inscriptions of Vijayachandra, 16 of Jayachandra and 2 of Hariśchandra.

romantic setting from the beginning can be inferred from the *Pṛthvīrājavijaya*, which brings earth and heaven together, as it were, before describing the romance.[6]

Tradition is unanimous in recognising the existence of Saṁyogitā, though sometimes under names that differ from each other. The *Surjanacharita* of the Bengali poet Chandraśekhara, written to commemorate the achievements of Surjan Hāḍā, a scion of the Sapādalakṣa-Raṇthambhor line and a *mansabdār* of Akbar, has almost the same account of the *svayaṁvara* as the *Pṛthvīrājarāso*, though it gives the name of the heroine as Kāntimatī.[7] As early as the sixteenth century and probably earlier still—because the tradition could not have sprung into existence all of a sudden—the descendants of Pṛthvīrāja III and Hammīra must thus have regarded Kāntimatī—Saṁyogitā as one of their ancestresses. Similarly, Akbar's historian, minister and friend, Abul Fazl, recounts the whole story, mentioning Jayachandra's sacrifice, Saṁyogitā's *svayaṁvara*, the installation of Pṛthvīrāja's statue in the place of a gate-keeper, the carrying away of Saṁyogitā by her lover, and the bravery of his *sāmantas* who fought a rear-guard action to cover the escape of Pṛthvīrāja.[8] In its most popular form the story, as most historians and students of Hindī literature know, is found in the *Pṛthvīrājarāso*, which originally may have been an *Apabhraṁśa* work written in the thirteenth century of the Vikrama era.[9]

According to the *Pṛthvīrājavijaya*, Pṛthvīrāja III fell in love with the heavenly nymph, Tilottamā, even though he had many beautiful queens, the reason for this otherwise inexplicable behaviour being that in his previous life as Rāma, Tilottamā had won his favour by playing excellently the role of Sītā in a play staged by the gods. A little further, we are told that Tilottamā was born

6. See the next but one paragraph.
7. In this connection, the following papers of mine may be consulted:
(a) The historicity of the *Pṛthvīrājarāso*, *IHQ*, 1940.
(b) *Pṛthvīrājarāso kī kathāon kā aitihāsik ādhāra*, *Rājasthānī*, Calcutta, Vol. III, part 3.
(c) *Surjanacharita-mahākāvya*, *Nāgarī Prachāriṇī Patrikā*. 1929.
8. See the papers listed in the last footnote.
9. See our paper, "The original *Pṛthvīrājarāso*, an Apabhraṁśa work", in the *Rājasthān Bhāratī*, I, 1, pp. 93-103.

as a princess destined to marry Rāma's incarnation, Pṛthvīrāja III[10]. Can we identify her with Saṁyogitā of our tradition ? Though the printed editions of the poem do not help us in settling the issue, we are, thanks to further investigations into the manuscript material of the *Pṛthvīrājavijaya* by Dr. S.K. Belvalkar, now in a position to state that the lost verses referred to a *nāka-nadī*, *i.e.*, the Gaṅgā, to a palace or town situated on its bank (*nāka-nadī-taṭa-sthita*), and to certain circumstances in which the heroine with her heart set on her lover could be compared to a *kamalinī* (lotus-flower) thinking of the Sun alone, when faced by the Moon.[11] Should not we conclude from these references that she was probably the daughter of a ruler, whose capital was on the bank of the Gaṅgā and who had decided to give her in marriage to a prince who, whatever his other good qualifications may have been, did not enjoy the privilege of having the princess's love ?

The above account has obvious resemblances to the story of Saṁyogitā in the *Pṛthvīrājarāso*. In the *Rāso*, Saṁyogitā is regarded as an incarnation of the heavenly nymph Rambhā. The princess of the *Pṛthvīrājavijaya* is the *apsaras* Tilottamā born in this world. Both the princesses had their residence somewhere near the Gaṅgā, and both obviously had been promised to suitors they did not love. Other resemblances also exist. What is there after all then that makes Saṁyogitā's story incredible ? Her father, Jayachandra, is said to have been on bad terms with Pṛthvīrāja III. We know from history that it was actually so.[12] His putting up of Pṛthvīrāja III's statue at the gate reminds one of an old Rājpūt custom which was calculated to humiliate one's rivals. Dantidurga Rāṣṭrakūṭa, for instance, made his rivals, the Gurjara ruler and some others, his gate-keepers in the *hiraṇyagarbhamahādāna* at Ujjain.[13] Even *rākṣasa vivāhas* were not unknown to Indian history.[14] Pṛthvīrāja merely carried off a not very un-

10. See the last verse of canto XI and the whole of canto XII.

11. The verses are 74-78 of canto 12.

12. See our account of Pṛthvīrāja III, the last Hindu Emperor of Delhi, *Indian Culture*, 1944.

13. Sanjan Plates of Amoghavarṣa, *EI*, XVIII, pp. 235-57.

14. Rāṣṭrakūṭa Indra married the Chālukya princess Bhavanāga in this way. We are not quoting examples from the epics, for they may be dismissed as legendary and pre-historic.

willing princess. Even in this twentieth century, the present writer has seen a bride being carried away from a marriage *maṇḍapa*.

We, of course, have every right to examine the truth of an old tradition. But if the only arguments that can be advanced against it are those summed up above, the old tradition must be permitted to hold its ground. There is nothing illogical or irrational about it. Nor does it go against any known historical facts.

CHAPTER IX

GOVINDARĀJA AND HARIRĀJA

On the death of Pṛthvīrāja III, his son Govinda was made ruler of Ajmer on the payment of a heavy tribute.[1] But the Chauhāns had still some fight left in them; they were not disposed to submit so readily to the Muslim invader. Advancing from the hills of Alwar, where he had retired after the disastrous defeat of Tarāorī, Pṛthvīrāja's younger brother Harirāja drove out Govinda from Ajmer, and made himself the master of at least a fraction of his ancestral kingdom.[2] His friends in the other parts of the old Chauhān Empire tried their best to help him. A Chauhān chief rose against the Muslims near Hānsī. But he was defeated and slain on the borders of Bāgar by Qutb-ud-dīn, the representative of Muhammad Ghorī in India.[3] Delhi too, which had submitted to the Muslims soon after the fall of Ajmer, raised its head once again in insurrection. The city was captured after a long siege. The Rājā escaped, but only to be defeated and slain soon after in an action with Qutb-ud-dīn.[4] Harirāja on his side had not been quite idle. He attacked the

1. *Tāju-l-Ma-āsir, ED.*, II, p. 216. It may, however be noted that the exact relationship is uncertain.

2. TF. I, 179. For the further history of Govinda see the next chapter.

3. Elliot read Jatwān, instead of Chauhān and interpreted it as a leader of the Jāts. Firishta makes him a commander of Bhīmadeva II's forces and states that he was killed in 591 H. while trying to meet Qutb-ud-din's attack on Anhilwāḍā. This shows his ignorance of the actual facts, because we know from the *Tāju-l-Ma-āsir*, a contemporary source, that he was defeated and slain on the border of Bāgar in 588 H. Jatwān is, as pointed out by Prof. Hodivala, a mistranscription of the word Chauhān (See Prof. Hodivala's *Studies in Indo-Muslim History*, p. 179). By Bāgar, the tract where this Chauhān chief was slain, is meant the region stretching from the south and south-west of Fatiābād, Sirsā, Hissār and Bhiwāni (See the *Indian Gazetter*, XIII, p. 149). There is another Bāgar in the south including the Bānswārā and Dūngarpur States. The knowledge of this fact and the mention of Bāgar as the tract where "Jatwān" was slain perhaps led Firishta to conjecture that he was a relative of Bhīmadeva II whose kingdom included this tract.

4. *Tāju-l-Ma-āsir*, ED, II, p. 220.

Muslim nominee Govinda who had, after being driven from Ajmer, retired to Raṇthambhor. A better policy, would, perhaps, have been to attack the Muslims while they were besieging Delhi. Harirāja allowed, instead, his partisans to be defeated piece meal and then himself to be driven with ease from before the walls of Raṇthambhor by Muslim forces freed from their task elsewhere.[5]

All these events took place in 1192 A.D. The next two years were a period of almost unbroken success for the Muslims. In 1194 A.D. Muhammad Ghorī and his generals captured Kanauj, Banāras, Asnī and Kaul or Koil.[6] Harirāja tried his luck once more. He sent his general Jaitra towards Delhi while the Muslims were away on their eastern expeditions. "The people were", writes Hasan Nizāmī, "caught in the darkness of his oppression and turbulence, and the blood and property of the Musulmāns fell into danger and destruction."[7] But this state did not last long. The defeat of Jayachandra once again left the Muslims free to employ their full force against the Chauhāns. Realising the gravity of the new menace from their side Qutb-ud-dīn returned to Delhi, and marched against Jaitra, even though it was the middle of the hot season and the Turks and Afghāns of the army found it extremely inconvenient to wear their armour and ride against the enemy.[8] Jaitra fell back upon Ajmer. Here, according to Firishta, Jaitra and his master Harirāja gave battle to the Muslims and were defeated and slain.[9] According to the *Hammīramahākāvya*, however, Harirāja, despairing of putting up any effective resistance, consigned himself to flames, and thereafter the fort fell into the hands of the Muslim ruler.[10] That this is the right version may be seen from the *Taju-l-Ma-Āsir*, a contemporary source, according to which too Jaitra (and most probably also his master) "sacrificed himself in the flames of a fire" immediately before the fall of the fort.[11] Thus with Hari-

5. *Tāju-l-Ma-Āsir*
6. *Ibid.*, pp. 222-23.
7. *Ibid.*, p. 225.
8. *ED*, II, p. 225.
9. *TF*, p. 194. The name of the general is given as Jihtar in the *Tāju'l-M-āsir* and as Chutrarāy in *TF*. The actual name appeared to be Jaitra or Jaitrarāja.
10. Canto IV, verses 18-19.
11. *Annual Report of the Rajputānā Museum*, 1911-12, p. 2. Tuntoṭī (mentioned as Taṁtuṭhī in the inscription) is nearly 20 miles from Ajmer.

rāja, who had been on the throne of Ajmer at least up to the 8th day of the dark of Vaiśākha, V. 1251,[12] ended the kingdom of Sapādalakṣa after a continued existence of nearly five centuries. It had on the whole, a glorious history, and the Indian bard still gets eloquent and rhapsodical, as he sings of the brave deeds of the mighty Bīsala and the gallant Pṛthvīrāja.

12 *ED*, II, p. 220.

CHAPTER X

THE CHAUHĀNS OF RAṆTHAMBHOR; GOVINDA TO JAITRASIṀHA

The founder of the line of the Chauhāns of Raṇthambhor was Pṛthvīrāja III's son Govinda. When the Chauhāns got decisively beaten in the second battle of Tarāīn, he or his ministers saw no further use in resisting the Muslims, and he was, on the payment of a heavy tribute, allowed to retain the possession of Ajmer.[1] To give his country peace, he gave Qutb-ud-dīn rich presents, and dissuaded him from attacking Delhi which, as shown in the last chapter, was at the time under a Chauhān feudatory.[2] But his policy, however expedient it might have been under the circumstances, was naturally, in many quarters regarded as cowardly, unpatriotic and disgraceful. These dissentient elements found, as already recorded, a leader in Pṛthvīrāja's younger brother Harirāja who first drove out Govinda from Ajmer and then tried to deprive him also of Raṇthambhor. How Harirāja was driven away has been stated above. Govinda was favoured with a robe of honour. He gave, in return, large sums of money to his Muslim benefactor together with three gold kettledrums, the price fetched by one of which sufficed to build a big mosque at Herāt.[3]

In due course, Govinda was succeeded in the kingdom of Raṇthambhor by his son Vālhaṇa.[4] That, like his father, he continued to recognise the supremacy of the Delhi Sultanate is obvious from the Manglānā stone inscription which refers itself to

1. *Tāju'l Ma-āsir*, *ED*, II, p. 216. Hasan Nizāmī merely calls him the son of Pṛthvīrājā. The name is given as Gola by Firishta. As we know from the *Hammīramahākāvya* that his name was actually Govīnda, it is perhaps better to regard Golā as a mistranscription for GUVA a well-known contraction of the word Govinda, and not to interpret it as "a natural son". As Pṛthvīrāja, however, died at the age of 27 or so, the relationship between him and Govinda remains a bit uncertain.

2. *TF*, p. 178.

3. *Tārīkh-i-Fakhruddīn Mubārakshāhī*, p. 23.

4. *HM*, IV, 32.

the victorious reign of Shamsuddīn, the lord of Ghor and Ghaznā and the *gaḍhapati* Vālhaṇadeva ruling at Raṇthambhor. It is dated Sunday, the 11th of the dark half of Jyeṣṭha, V. 1272-[1215 A.D.], and records the construction of a step-well by Vālhaṇa's feudatory Jaitrasiṁha, son of *Mahāmaṇḍaleśvara* Padmasiṁhadeva of the Dadhīchaka family.[5]

Vālhaṇa's son and successor Prahlādana did not rule long. He died of injuries sustained in a lion-hunt. Vīranārāyaṇa was the next ruler, with his uncle Vāgbhaṭa as his regent.[6]

Vīranārāyaṇa had, early in his reign, to face the armies of Shamsuddīn Iltutmish of Delhi. While proceeding to Āmer to marry the daughter of its Kachhwāhā chief, he was attacked by the Muslims and had some difficulty in getting back to Raṇthambhor. Here, however, he successfully withstood the Muslim onslaughts. Finding mere force useless, Iltutmish, therefore, next tried diplomacy. He assured Vīranārāyaṇa of his friendship, promising to do him no harm, if he came over to Delhi. Vīranārāyaṇa who wished to have Muslim help against Vigraha of Vakṣasthalapura proved foolish enough to believe the Sultān's word and was poisoned to death. Thereafter it was easy to capture Raṇthambhor.[7] The *Tabaqāt-i-Nāsirī* puts the event in 633 H. (1226 A.D.).[8]

Vīranārāyaṇa's uncle Vāgbhaṭa had advised his nephew not to accept Sultān's invitation and left for Mālwā on his advice being angrily and disrespectfully rejected. Here he slew the Mālava king on learning that he was conspiring against his life with the Muslims and carved out a small principality for himself.[9]

Vāgbhaṭa got the desired chance of regaining Raṇthambhor in the year 1236. Iltutmish died. The weak Ruknuddīn Firoz Shāh succeeded him. There were revolts on all sides.[10] It was too good an opportunity to be missed. Vāgbhaṭa, therefore, soon assembled a big force and reaching Raṇthambhor invested

5. *IA*, XLI, p. 87 f.
6. *HM*. IV, 41-75.
7. *Ibid.*, verses 82-106. Can this Vigraha be the same as Vigraha, the father of Malayavarman of Gopagiri ?
8. *ED*, II, pp. 324-325.
9. For Vāgbhaṭa's career see *HM*. IV, 107-123. The Mālava ruler slain by him perhaps was Devapāla (died V. 1292). The *PKG* also mentions Vāgbhaṭa as conqueror of Mālwā.
10. See *ED*, pp. 330-331.

it closely. After some time, water and food in the fort became scarce,[11] and all that Raziyā, the successor of Sultān Ruknuddīn, could do was to get out the half-starved garrison by sending Malik Qutb-ud-dīn Husain to its assistance.[12]

Vāgbhaṭa had to fight twice again against the Muslims. In 646 H. (1248 A.D.) Nāsiruddīn sent against him a large force under Ulūgh Khān, who later on became Sultān Balban of Delhi. Vāgbhaṭa must have, by that time, become very powerful, because Minhāj calls him the greatest of the Rāis of Hindustān. Ulūgh Khān ravaged Vāgbhaṭa's territory. But his military success was practically nil. His assistant Bahāuddīn Aibak was slain while trying to attack Raṇthambhor, and the Muslim army had to retire discomfited, and not probably without some loss, to Delhi.[13] The second fight was in A.D. 1253. Ulūgh Khān had, in that year, prepared a large force to attack Raṇthambhor and other important Hindu strongholds. Vāgbhaṭa met him with a well-equipped army, and though the Muslims claim to have scored some sort of success, it could not have been very great, because instead of proceeding any further, Ulūgh Khān returned thereafter to Nāgor, the base from where he had started. The Muslims just captured some horses and prisoners and "returned safe" with their booty.[14]

The Rataul plate mentions one Mahākumāra Chāhaḍadeva in the family of Arṇorāja and Pṛthvīrāja.[15] As the letters *v* and *ch* were very much alike each other in the 13th century, it is not unlikely that this ruler might actually be Vāgbhaṭa of Raṇthambhor. Mr. Dayaram Sahni's suggestion, however, that the Raṇthambhor prince should be identified also with Chāhaḍadeva of Narwar is unacceptable, because the latter belonged not to the Chauhān but to the Yajvapāla family.[16]

11. *HM*, IV, 122-123.
12. *Tabaqāt-i-Nāsirī*, *ED*, II, p. 334.
13. *Ibid.*, p. 367.
14. *Ibid.*, pp. 370-371.
15. *EI*, XII, p. 224.
16. See the inscriptions of Āsaladeva (V. 1319) and Gopāla (V. 1339) quoted in *JASB*, XVI, No. 3, p. 81. Further, as remarked by Mr. Garde, had the Jājapellas been a branch of the great. Chauhān clan, the *praśasti* writers would certainly have mentioned the fact. Vāgbhaṭa ruled probably only up to 1253 A.D. Chāhaḍadeva's coins go up to 1259 A.D.

According to the *Hammīramahākāvya*, Vāgbhaṭa ruled at Raṇthambhor for twelve years.[17] If this be regarded as an approximately correct period, Vāgbhaṭa must have died a little after Ulūgh Khān's second attack in 1253 A.D. His greatness was recognised in every quarter. Even his enemies called him "the greatest of the Rāis, and the most noble and illustrious of all the princes of Hindustan",[18] and that their estimate was perfectly justified might be seen from his achievements detailed above.

Vāgbhaṭa was succeeded by his son Jaitrasiṁha. According to the Balvan inscription, he, acting as some new Sun, scorched Jayasiṁha, even though he was seated in Maṇḍapa, sharpened the edge of his axe on the throat of the Kūrma ruler, looked glorious with his sword playing on the skull of the ruler of Karkarālagiri and captured at Jhaṁphāithaghaṭṭa hundreds of the soldiers of the ruler of Mālwā who were thereafter thrown into prison at Raṇastambhapura and enslaved.[19]

The *Mālaveśa*, who is mentioned here as Jayasiṁha of Maṇḍapa, is apparently Jayasiṁha II for whom we have an inscription in the Vikrama year 1326. The fight between him and Jaitrasiṁha looks like a continuation of the Chauhān-Paramāra struggle begun in Vāgbhaṭa's time. The victory of Jhaṁphāithaghaṭṭa,[20] however, does not seem to have been decisive; the Paramāras remained strong enough to fight against the Chauhāns of Raṇthambhor a few years later. The *Kūrma* ruler was probably the successor of the Kachhwāhā prince of Āmrapurī whose daughter was to have been married to Jaitrasiṁha's cousin Vīranārāyaṇa.[21] Karkarālagiri looks like Karkarālā of the *Hammīramahākāvya*. As the ruler of Tribhuvanagiri (modern Tahangarh and Tahankir of the *Tārīkh-i-Mubārakshāhi*) is said to have rendered homage to Hammīra at Karkarāla, the place could not probably have been far away from Tahangarh.[22]

17. IV, 120.

18. See the *Tabaqāt-i-Nāsiri*, *ED*, II, p. 370.

19. *EI*, XIX, pp. 49-50.

20. Jhaṁphāitha-ghaṭṭa, stands for Jhapait-ghāṭ on the Chambal river ten miles due south of the Railway Station of Lākherī in Koṭā-Būndi. Balvan is 7 miles north east of Lākherī.

I am indebted for these topographical details to Dr. Jadunath Sarkar.

21. See above, p. 119.

22. For reasons regarding the identification of Tahangarh with Tribhuvanagiri, see the *Bhāratīya Vidyā*, II, 63 ff. Karkarāla too might have been

Jaitrasiṁha also had to fight against the Muslims. After having failed twice in Vāgbhaṭa's reign, they tried their luck again in that of Jaitrasiṁha. Nāsiruddīn sent Malik-un-Nawwāb who proceeded with a force against Raṇthambhor on the 18th February 1259, but as the *Tabaqāt-i-Nāsiri*, the source of our information on this point, does not say a single word more about the expedition, it might be assumed that it was unsuccessful.[23]

Jaitrasiṁha had three sons, Suratrāṇa, Vīrama and Hammīra.[24] Of these the last was annointed the ruler of Raṇthambhor with his father's own hands on Sunday, the 15th of the bright half of Māgha in the Vikrama year, 1339, even though he was not the eldest of the three brothers.[25] The genealogy at the end of the *Prabandhakośa* gives V. 1342 as the year of Hammīra's accession.[26] As both the *HM* and *PKG* are almost equally reliable for the reign, this difference in dates can, I believe, be reconciled by supposing that Jaitrasiṁha lived on for three years more before starting for Paṭṭana on the river Chambal and expiring on the way to it at the village of Pallī.[27]

like Tahangarh once in possession of the line later on known as the Yādavas of Karaulī

23. Raverty, *Tabaqāt-i-Nāsirī*, I, 713.

24. *HM*, IV, 150.

25. *Ibid.*, VII, 53-56.

26. p. 134.

27. *HM*, VIII, 106-115. Kirtane, the editor of the *HM*, regards Śrī *Āśrama* as the destination of Jaitrasiṁha in this journey. We have, it on the basis of the *Hammīra-mahākāvya* and the *Surajanacharita*, specially the latter identified it with the Keśorāya-paṭṭana on the Chambal (For detailed arguments see the "Chhotelal Smṛt numberi of the *Anekānta*, pp. 70-73). It seems to have been a fairly important *tīrtha*. It contained the temple of Mahādeva mentioned as *Jambupatha-sārthavāhī* in *HM* and as *Jambūmārga Mṛtyuñjaya* in *SC*, XI, 35-42.

CHAPTER XI

HAMMĪRA CHAUHĀN OF RAṆTHAMBHOR

There is no lack of historical information regarding Hammīra, the last and most famous of the Chauhāns of Raṇthambhor. Besides the Balvan and Gaḍha inscriptions,[1] we have the *Hammīra-mahākāvya* of Nayachandra Sūri which, though not a contemporary work, has been found generally correct in its account of Hammīra and his immediate predecessors. Muslim writers like Amīr Khusrau and Ziā-ud-dīn Baranī give details of his fight with Alā-ud-dīn Khaljī. The account in the *Surjanacharita* can be used with some caution. The *Prākṛtapiṅgala* and *Śārṅgadharapaddhati* give a few verses about him; and then there are late Hindi works like the *Hammīrāyaṇa* of Bhāṇḍan Vyās, *Hammīra-prabandha* of Amṛtakalaśa, *Hammīrarāso* of Jodharāja and *Hammīrahaṭha* of Chandraśekhara which, though not entirely historical are useful as evidence of the great reputation that Hammīra enjoyed for his chivalry, gallantry and bravery in war.

Hammīra had, as we have seen, ascended the throne in V. 1339. Not very long after this, he started, according to the *Hammīra-mahākāvya*, on a *digvijaya* or conquest of all the quarters. He first defeated Arjuna, the ruler of Bhīmarasa, and then exacted tribute from the fort of Maṇḍalakṛta or Māṇḍalgarh.[2] Striking southwards from here, he reached Ujjayinī and Dhārā and defeated the Paramāra ruler Bhoja. From here he turned northwards, and reached home passing through Chitor, Ābu, Vardhanapura, Chaṅgā, Pushkar, Mahārāṣṭra, Śākambharī, Khaṇḍilla, Champā, and Karkarālā, at the last of which places he received the homage of the ruler of Tribhuvanagiri.[3] There-

1. See respectively *EI*, XIX, pp. 49 ff. and *ASI*, 1916-17, I, p. 20.

2. Kirtane identifies it with Gaḍhamaṇḍala. Actually it is Māṇḍalgarh (See the Sṛṅga-ṛṣi inscription, V. 1485, verse 7, quoted by Dr. G. H. Ojha in his *History of Udaipur*, I, p. 56).

3. Keeping the route in view, I am inclined to identify Mahārāṣṭra with Maroṭ, Khaṇḍilla with Khaṇḍelā. Tribhuvanagiri is Tahangarh, once the capital of the Yādavas of Karauli. Karkarālā is Karkarālagiri of the Balvan inscription, Vardhanapura is Badnore. Changa, a fortress of the Mers, still retains its old name. Śākambharī is Sāmbhar. Champā is Chāksū.

after came a *Koṭi-yajña* which was very much like the *aśvamedha* of Samudragupta. It was under the direction of his *purohita* Viśvarūpa.[4]

This *digvijaya*, or rather a number of raids from time to time magnified into one systematic *digvijaya*[5] by Nayachandra, took place before V. 1345 (c. 1288 A.D.). The Balvan inscription of the year mentions the performance of not only one but two *Koṭi-yajñas* by Hammīra and describes the capture of the elephant force of Arjuna, the ruler of Mālwā, a kingdom the condition of which was indeed bad enough to invite interference from all sides. On the death of its ruler about V. 1300, dissensions had broken out between his son and minister, and after long hostilities and much bloodshed each had made himself master of a part of the country, but without giving the kingdom any peace. Rulers from many parts of India, of whom Hammīra was only one, raided it every year and carried away much property and wealth, and captives and fine linen.[6]

The ruler Arjuna of Mālwā, mentioned in the Balvan inscription, as defeated by Hammīra, was probably the successor of Jaitrasiṁha's rival, Jayasiṁha II, mentioned above. It is difficult to say how he was related to Bhoja, the other Paramāra ruler described by Nayachandra as defeated by Hammīra at Dhārā. Was he a rival ruler stationed there, or a nominee of the minister who had made himself the master of a part of Mālwā ?[7] We, personally, have no opinion to offer.

But Hammīra was not the only *digvijayin* of the period. The Sultāns of Delhi had similar ideals. If Raṇthambhor had been for a time, left to itself it was due to the fact that the Sultāns

4. *HM. IX*, 90.

5. I say "magnified into one systematic *digvijaya*", because the contemporary Balvan inscription, (*EI*, XIX, pp. 49. ff) written at the instance of one minister of Hammīra and composed by another, does not, while recounting almost the same events, *viz.*, the performance of *koṭi-yajña* and the attack on Mālwā, speak of any *digvijaya* by Hammīra. The *digvijaya*, according to Nayachandra, preceded the *koṭi-yajña*. The Balvan inscription describes the *koṭi-yajña* well enough, but has not a single word about Hammīra's *digvijaya*. All that it speaks of is the attack on Mālwā, which may, hence, be the only true detail in the fictitious account of the *digvijaya*.

6. *ED*, III, p. 31.

7. See Footnote on the next page.

were engaged elsewhere or were too weak to interfere. In 1290 A.D. there was a change in the dynasty at Delhi and with that also a change in the attitude of the Sultanate. The first Khaljī Sultān Jalāl-ud-dīn led in that year an army to Jhāīn which he captured after a stiff fight with Hammīra's forces led by one Gurdās Sainī who was slain in the action. From Jhāīn the Khaljī forces advanced to Raṇthambhor. The Sultān ordered *manjaniks* to be erected, *sabāts* to be built, and the siege to be pressed with vigour; but as the task was far from easy, he retired soon after to Delhi without accomplishing his design.[8] Jhāīn was recovered soon after by Hammīra, for we find Jalāl-ud-din leading his army once again against this fort in 1292 A.D., and this time without gaining any appreciable success.[9]

In 1296 A.D. the weak Sultān Jalāl-ud-dīn had to make way for his nephew and murderer Alā-ud-din Khaljī. Intoxicated by his success on every side, he conceived about 1298 A.D. the design of founding a new religion like Muhammad and conquering the whole world like a second Alexander.[10] He gave up the first design, after some time, as impious; the second he modified

7. The event is described thus in the *Hammīramahākavya*. Ulūgh Khan, who commanded the army sent by Alā-ud-din, encamped on the banks of the river Banas, began plundering and burning the countryside. As Hammīra was under a vow of silence at the time, his general, Bhīmasiṁha, acting on the orders of the chief minister Dharmasiṁha, attacked the Muslim army and marched towards Raṇthambhor on defeating it. As he entered the pass leading to Jhāīn, he was imprudent enough to sound the drums he had captured from the Muslims. The latter thinking that it was a signal for their rendezvous rushed to the pass and Bhīmasiṁha was caught almost unawares and died fighting along with the few soldiers left with him. The *Śakendra* (lord of the Muslims) returned to his camp and afraid of Kṣatriya vengeance returned to his own city.

When we compare this account with that of Amīr Khusrau's *Miftah--ul-Futūh* it becomes absolutely clear that the events mentioned in the paragraph should be placed in the reign of Jalāl-ud-dīn Khaljī. According to the *Tughlaqnāmā* as well as the *Tārikh-i-Firuzshāhī*, Jalāluddīn was happy to get back to Delhi without sustaining any loss. (See the writer's *Rājasthān through the Ages*, pp. 624-25).

8. *Ghurratu-l-kamāl* of Amīr Khusrau, *ED*, III, pp, 540. 42. *Tārīkh-i-Firoz Shāhī, ED*, III, pp. 146-147.

9. *Tārīkh-i-Firoz Shāhī, ED*, III, p. 148.

10. *Ibid.*, pp. 169 ff. Alā-ud-dīn's coins too describe him as a second Alexander.

by first concentrating his attention on the conquest of Raṇthambhor, Chanderī, Dhār and Ujjain.[11] And of these strongholds again, Raṇthambhor received the earliest attention, partly on account of its pre-eminence as the seat of one of the strongest Hindu rulers, a descendant of the mighty Pṛthvīrāja III, and partly also on account of an incident which highly incensed the Sultān. Alā-ud-dīn's generals Ulūgh Khān and Nasrat Khān had, while returning to Delhi after their conquest and plunder of Gujarāt, provoked a mutiny near Jālor by demanding from the soldiery one-fifth of their spoil and by instituting inquisitorial enquiries about it. Muhammad Shāh, a neo-Muslim leader of these rebels had, along with his brother and other followers, found refuge at Raṇthambhor, and had not been, in spite of the Sultān's demand, surrendered to his tender mercies.[12]

These events took place in the winter of 1299-1300 A.D.; a little later followed the retribution in the form of a Khaljī attack on Raṇthambhor. Both the *Hammīramahākāvya* and the *Surjana-charita* state that Hammīra was at the time engaged in certain religious rites.[13] The Khaljī general Ulūgh Khān marched unopposed up to the river Banās; here, however, his further progress was barred by the Chauhān forces led by Hammīra's general Bhīmasiṁha. Had these kept themselves at the top of the pass leading to Raṇthambhor, the Muslim forces might have been forced to retire baffled to Delhi. But Bhīmasiṁha attacked them headlong, underestimating their strength. He gained some initial advantage too or at least thought that he had done so and was returning to the capital under the illusion that he had thoroughly beaten the Muslims, when his enemies, hearing the sound of their kettledrum, re-assembled and surrounded the Chauhān force, Bhīmasiṁha fought bravely. But being out-numbered and out-generalled he was soon overpowered and slain.[14]

11. *Tārīkh-i-Firoz Shāhī*, *ED*, III, pp. 169 ff.

12. *Tārīkh-i-Firoz Shāhī*, *ED*, III, p. 169. As to how the relatives of the rebels were treated, one has just to read the relevant portions of Baranī's *Tārīkh-i-Firoz Shāhī*.

13. *HM*, X, 104; *SC*. XI, 63-64.

14. *HM*, IX, 108-150. According to Nayachandra, Bhīmasiṁha was slain by the Muslim troops which re-assembled on hearing the sound of their

This defeat and death of Bhīmasiṁha had some unforeseen consequences. As it was under the advice of the minister Dharmasiṁha that Bhīmasiṁha had left his strong position on the hills, Hammīra not merely rated the minister severely but had him castrated and blinded, saying that he was blind not to have seen the strength of the Muslim position and impotent as he had allowed Bhīmasiṁha to die unaided. Hammīra's natural brother *khaḍgavāhika* Bhoja now became the chief counsellor.[15]

But Bhoja was no great financier. The wars against the Muslims had been extremely expensive. A big army was needed. Mālwā could have provided some money. But with the Khaljīs threatening Raṇthambhor, it was not possible to move out and plunder other countries especially Mālwā, parts of which had perhaps by that time passed under other powers. Bhoja's failure to provide financial means for a new army, which was, under the circumstances, urgently needed proved his undoing. Dharmasiṁha, the blind and dismissed minister, who had been biding his time, offered through Dhārā, the court-dancer, to raise as many horses as Hammīra needed.[16] Hammīra accepted his offer, but in doing so signed his own death-warrant.

Dharmasiṁha kept his promise of finding money for the king's army. But the taxes that he laid on the people were so heavy and unfair that Hammīra became unpopular.[16a] Acting under the blind minister's advice, again, he asked Bhoja to render a full account of his period of ministry. In other ways too Hammīra made Bhoja's position so intolerable that the latter had with his brother Pīthasiṁha to leave Raṇthambhor. Hammīra, instead of being sorry, was glad that the brothers had gone away and gave Bhoja's post of *daṇḍanāyaka* to a general named Ratipāla.[17]

own drums which had been captured earlier in the day by the Hindu army and sounded at the time in the pride of their victory. Actually the Muslim soldiers seem to have intentionally dispersed after their traditional manner with a view to depriving the Hindus of their advantage of preparedness, and then to have attacked them at a given signal and overpowered them with comparative ease. That the Hindu defeat was due to some tactical blunder of theirs is shown by the words used by Hammīra in reproving Dharmasiṁha.

15. *HM*, IX, 153-55.
16. *Ibid.*, 150-160.
16a. See the *Hammīrāyaṇa*.
17. *Ibid.*, 171-188.

Burning to avenge the insults that had been, repeatedly, heaped upon him, Bhoja repaired to the court of Sultān Alā-ud-dīn Khaljī where he was received with honour and given the jāgīr of Jagarā which had formerly been a possession of the neo-Muslim leader Muhammad Shāh. Bhoja advised Alā-ud-dīn to attack Raṇthambhor before the crops were garnered. The advice was accepted, and very soon a big army, estimated at one lac by Nayachandra, marched upon Raṇthambhor, devastating and subjugating all the Hindu territories lying on the way. So the Muslim forces proceeded up to the Hinduvāṭa pass where they were unexpectedly attacked by Hammīra's army directed by Hammīra's brother Vīrama, the generals Ratipāla, Jājadeva and Raṇamalla, and the neo-Muslim leaders Muhammad Shāh, his brother Garbharūka, and two others called Tichara and Vaichara.[18] The Khaljīs sustained a heavy defeat. Much of their equipment fell into the Hindu hands. A number of Muslim women were captured and forced to sell sour butter-milk in the villages of the Raṇthambhor kingdom to make known everywhere the great victory gained by the Chauhāns.[19]

The neo-Muslims followed up this success with an attack on Jagarā, the jāgīr of Bhoja whose family was captured and brought to Raṇthambhor, though Bhoja himself escaped this fate on account of being at Delhi at the time.[20] Great was the anger of the Sultān when he heard the news. He sent for military levies, states Nayachandra, from all parts of India and put them under the command of Ullū Khān (Ulūgh Khān) and Nisurata Khan (Nasrat Khān).[21] Barāni, who begins his account of Alā-ud-dīn's Raṇthambhor campaigns with this one, has practically the same thing to say, for, according to him, "Ulūgh Khān, who held the territory of Biānā, was sent against the fort and Nasrat Khān, who was governor of Karrā that year, was ordered to march to his assistance with the army of Karrā and other provinces of Hindustān."[22]

18. *The Hammīrāyaṇa X* 35-61. The names Tichara, Vāichara, and Garbharūka are as given by Nayachandra. Their real Muslim equivalents were Yalchak, Barq, Qamizi and Kāmnu.

19. *Ibid.*,

20. *Hammīramahākāvya*, X, 68, XI, 2.

21. *Ibid.*

22. *Tarikh-i-Firoz Shāhī*, p. *ED*, III, p. 172.

This time the Muslims easily crossed the difficult pass of Hinduvāṭa, captured Jhāīn, and encamped near the walls of the fort of Raṇthambhor. This difficult task was, according to Nayachandra, accomplished by Ulūgh Khān's pretending tha he was coming to negotiate a peace with Hammīra.[23] The messenger offered two alternatives. Hammīra could either offer four lacs of *mohurs*, present four elephants, and give his daughter in marriage to Alā-ud-dīn; or he could surrender the four Mongol chieftains who had flouted the authority of Alā-ud-dīn and taken refuge at Raṇthambhor.[24] Hammīra scornfully rejected these offers, saying that Alā-ud-dīn could have from him as many swordcuts as the number of the gold *mohurs*, elephants and horses that he had demanded.[25]

The Muslims tried to capture the fort by carrying mines to the foot of the fort and scaling its walls. It was while engaged in the construction of a *pāshib* and the raising of a *gargaj* that Nasrat Khān was struck by a ball shot from a *maghrabi* in the fort and died in three or four days.[26] According to Firishta, Hammīra took advantage of this fact, and marching out of the fort gave battle to the Muslims who were defeated in the engagement and forced to fall back on Jhāīn with great loss to their army.[27]

Now Alā-ud-dīn himself assumed the command of the army, and reaching Raṇthambhor after barely escaping assasination near Tilpat pressed the siege with great vigour.[28] Hammīra led out two sorties.[29] But this time his success does not seem to have been very great. Alā-ud-dīn had ropes woven into sacks which were filled with sand and thrown into the moat of the fort.[29a] Piling one sand-bag on another, the Muslims constructed a *pāshib*, and when it had reached high enough to touch the western tower of the fort, put *maghribis* on it and shot large earthen balls from

23. *HM*, *XI*, 23.
24. *Ibid.*, 54-72.
25. *Ibid.*
26. *Ibid.*, 100; *Tārikh-i-Firoz Shāhī*, *ED*, III, p. 172.
27. Briggs, *Tārikh-i-Firishtā*, p. 337.
28. *Tarikh-i-Firoz shahī*, *ED*, III, pp. 172-4.
29. *HM*, XII.
29a. Barani's *Tarikh-i-Firazshahi*, English translation by Prof. M. Habib in his edition of the *Khazainu-l Futuh*, p. 42.

them.[30] A mine was constructed at the same time. The Chauhāns destroyed the *pāshīb* with stones from their own *maghribis* and killed the soldiers engaged in the construction of the mine by throwing on them oil mixed with resin.[31]

Alā-ud-dīn's big army was now getting tired. Continuous failure and news of revolts in Delhi and Oudh had dispirited the soldiers. But such was the dread of the Sultān that none dared to set off for Delhi or any other place.[32] The rainy season increased still further the difficulties of the besiegers, and it seemed that Alā-ud-dīn was making a genuine offer of peace when he wished Hammīra's general Ratipāla to be sent for preliminary negotiations to the Muslim camp. Ratipāla was received with every mark of honour, regaled with the choicest of food and drink, and sent back fully convinced that if the Muslims ever captured the fort, it would be made over to him. Ratipāla, therefore, returned a determined and dangerous traitor who, instead of reporting the real state of affairs in the Muslim camp, told Hammīra that Alā-ud-dīn cared little for the losses that he had suffered and demanded the hand of the Rājā's daughter.[33] By a ruse, the details of which can be read in the *Hammīramahākāvya*, he also succeeded in turning, another commander named Raṇamalla against Hammīra. A little after sunset, both these traitors got out of the fort and joined the enemy.

There was now little hope of Alā-ud-dīn's raising the siege. The Muslims' condition was bad enough. But they now knew that the condition of the besieged was even worse. Hammīra had till then put up a brave show. But with traitors from Raṇthambhor in the hostile camp, it was not easy to keep up false appearances.[34] With starvation, therefore, staring him in the face, deserted by those who had once been his most trusted servants, and surrounded by people in whom he saw potential traitors and

30. Habib, *Khazāin-ul Futūh*, p. 39.
31. *HM*, XIII, 42-47: *Tārīkh-i-Firūzshāhī*, *ED*, III, pp. 174-75.
32. *Tārīkh-i-Firūzshāhī*, *ED*, III, p. 177.
33. *Hammīramahākāvya*, XIII, 71-86.
34. "Yes," writes Amir Khusrau, "their provisions became finished, they ate stones. Famine prevailed to such an extent in the fort that they would have purchased a grain of rice for two grains of gold but could not get it." (Habib, *Khazāin-ulFutūh*, p. 40)

enemies, Hammīra at length decided to perform the dreadful rite of *jauhar*, though not before offering to escort the Mongol leaders to a safe place.[35] Hammīra's queens and his daughter Devalladevī ascended the funeral pyre. The Muslim army saw these fires and knew what they meant.[36]

Next Hammīra had all his valuables thrown into the Padmasara, and crowning the Chauhān Jājā as his successor[37] (for his own brother Vīrama refused to stay behind) he advanced to the head of the *pāshīb* with some of his followers.[38] Vīrama died fighting bravely. Hammīra killed himself, on being in danger of falling into the hands of his enemies. Muhammad Shāh, the neo-Muslim chief, lay faint with wounds received in the cause of his friend when he was accidently seen by Alā-ud-dīn who thus accosted him, "What wouldst thou do, if I order thy wounds to be attended to, and save thee from this imminent danger; and after this how wouldst thou behave?" "If I recover," replied the heroic Muhammad Shāh, "I would have thee slain and raise the son of Hammīradeva to the throne." Angered by this retort, the Sultān had him placed under the foot of a rampant elephant and crushed to death. But he had him decently buried, because, at heart, he appreciated loyalty.[39] Ratipāla, Raṇamalla, and other traitors received their true deserts. Ratipāla was flayed alive.[40] Raṇamalla was put to death with all his followers, for, said Alā-ud-dīn, "those who have betrayed their natural sovereign will never be loyal to another."[41]

35. *Hammīramahākāvya*, XIII, 139-66. The same book tells us that instead of accepting the offer, Muhammad Shāh killed his wife and children and followed Hammīra in his last fight.

36. *Ibid.*, 173-81; *Khazāīn-ul Futūh*, p. 40f.

37. He was known also as Jājala. The *Prākṛtapiṅgala*, a work on Prākṛta prosody, has two verses about him. See also Appendix E.

38. Nayachandra gives the number of his followers as nine, the *Khazāīn-ul Futūh* as one or two unbelievers (p. 41). The rest perhaps thought it best either to escape by the *dharmadvāra* or thought it politic to stay behind.

39. *HM*, XIII, 198-225; De's translation of the *Tabaqāt-i-Akbarī*, p. 167 f. Firishta gives the same story.

40. *HM*, XIV, 21.

41. Briggs, *Tārīkh-i-Firishta*, I, p. 343 f.

The Chauhān Jājā who stayed behind in the fort is said to have continued the resistance for two days more.[42] Amīr Khusrau gives the date of the fall of the fort as Tuesday, the 3rd Zil Qa'd. 700 A.H. corresponding to July 10, 1301 A.D.[43] Nayachandra's date is two days later than this.[44] This discrepancy can be removed, if we assume that Nayachandra's date is not of the death of Hammīra but of the final evacuation of the fort by Jājā, which as noted already took place two days later.

The city of Raṇthambhor was, after its capture, sacked by the Muslim victors. The splendid temple of Bāhar Deo (Vāgbhaṭa) was razed to the ground along with many other splendid buildings.[45] Ulūgh Khān was put in charge of the fort, but such was the deep hatred aroused by his cruelty, that he thought it best to stay in the suburbs.

Nayachandra extols Hammīra for his generosity to Brāhmaṇas and respect for all schools of Indian philosophy including Jainism.[46] Both the Balvan Inscription and the *Hammīramahākāvya* show that he patronised the poet Bījāditya.[47] The *Śārṅgadharapaddhati* mentions Hammīra as a pupil of the great scholar and poet Rāghavadeva, the grandfather of the well-known anthologist Śārṅgadhara.

With Hammīra ended the Chauhān kingdom of Raṇthambhor. He was not a man without some serious faults; he had an ungovernable temper and his choice of servants was, to say the least, not good. We cannot also commend his wars with his neighbours with the Muslim danger ever present in the background. Towards the end of his reign, he was rendered unpopular by the heavy taxes laid on the people owing to the exigencies of war with the Khaljīs. But the admiration for the gallant fight that he put up in the defence of his kingdom, the honour of his family, and the protection of the neo-Muslim chiefs who had taken refuge with him generally puts all these faults into the background, and one finds almost every lover of Rājasthānī

42. *HM*, XIV, 15. For a short account of Jāja see Appendix E.
43. *Khazāīn-ul Futūh*, p. 41.
44. See *H.M.* XIII, 196.
45. Habib, *Khazāīn-ul Futūh*, p. 41.
46. *HM*, XIV, 3.
47. *Ibid.*, VIII, 124; *EI*, XIX, p. 52.

culture quoting, with readiness and some pride, the famous couplet,

> सिंह-सवन सत्पुरुष-वचन कदलन फलत इक बार ।
> तिरिया-तेल हम्मीर-हठ चढ़े न दूजी बार ।।[48]

As a warrior-king, Hammīra perhaps could have desired no higher tribute than this.

48. The English translation of the couplet would be something as follows:

"A lioness gives birth to a cub only once; once alone is the word of a good man given; once only does a plantain bear fruit; a woman is anointed only once with oil for marriage; and once alone did Hammīra give his irrevocable promise.

APPENDIX E

JĀJA, JĀJĀ, JĀJADEVA, OR JAJJALA, A MINISTER AND COMMANDER OF HAMMĪRA OF RAṆTHAMBHOR

In the annals of Rājpūt chivalry, there is scarcely a name better known than that of Hammīra the *haṭhī*[1] ruler of Raṇthambhor. The fight put up by him against Alā-ud-dīn Khaljī, the tyrannical Sultān of Delhi, with a view to protecting the neo-Muslim leaders, Muhammad Shāh and his brothers, who had taken refuge at the Raṇthambhor court, has inspired many a poet of Sanskrit, Prākṛta, Hindī as well as Rājasthānī to sing his glory and offer the incense of admiration at the shrine of his memory. Of people, whom he had favoured, many deserted him. His chief general, Ratipāla, and the finance minister Dharmasiṁha, proved traitors. In his last fight, Hammīra was accompanied by only nine warriors, of whom four were not even his co-religionists. But besides these he had at least one more follower of undoubted loyalty, the Chāhamāna Jāja, Jājā, Jājadeva or Jajjala who was left behind to put up a last ditch fight for Raṇthambhor.

The material for Jāja's life is extremely scanty. The *Prākṛtapaiṅgalam*, a book on Prākṛta prosody written some time in the fourteenth century, quotes five verses from some Apabhraṁśa poem dealing with Hammīra's achievements. Of these two refer to Jājadeva; none, it might be noted, mentions even by name, the other ministers and generals of Hammīra. This fact in itself should be testimony enough for Jājadeva's pre-eminent position in Hammīra's kingdom. Had this Apabhraṁśa poem drawn upon by the *Prākṛtapaiṅgalam* come down to us, we might have received a full account of the great hero, Jāja. In its absence, all that we can present to our readers is an incomplete, though by no means incorrect sketch of his achievements, based on two

1. Of dogged resolution; one who sticks to his word even against the dictates of common sense.

extant Apabhraṁśa verses and a few stray references from the *Hammīramahākāvya* of Nayachandra Sūri.

According to the *Hammīramahākāvya*, Jājadeva was one of the eight members of Hammīra's (*mantri*) *pariṣad.*[2] The *Prākṛtapaiṅgalam* mentions him as Hammīra's *mantrivara, i.e.*, excellent minister.[3] But it is not as a *mantrin* but as Hammīra's brave general that he lives on in the minds of the people. When Alā-ud-dīn, egged on by the traitor Bhoja, a natural brother of Hammīra, sent Ulūgh Khān against the kingdom of Raṇthambhor, Jājadeva was one of the eight generals who attacked and defeated the Khaljī army in the Hinduvāṭ Pass. It was a well-executed piece of strategy. The Rājpūts waited for the coming of darkness, and then fell on the Muslims from all directions, causing the greatest confusion in their camp. Hammīra's brother, Vīrama, came from the east, Muhammad Shāh from the west, Jājadeva from the south, and Garbharūka from the north. From the south-east, north-east, south-west, and north-west, the attack was, respectively, directed by Ratipāla, Raṇamalla, Tichara, and Vaichara.[4] Whoever the conceiver of the plan may have been, perhaps it was Hammīra himself, it was thoroughly successful. With the cry of "Hammīra", "Hammīra", the Rājpūts filled the ditch surrounding the camp, burnt the stockades, cut down the ropes of the tents, and caused such havoc that Ulūgh Khān's army was soon on the run, leaving behind all its war material, camp equipage and even women.[5]

Immediately after this victory the neo-Muslim leader, Muhammad Shāh, sacked Jagarā, the jāgīr given to the traitor, Bhoja, by Alā-ud-dīn Khaljī. And about the same time perhaps Hammīra and Jājadeva raided Delhi. The Chāhamāna warriors must have by then become well-known in the Khaljī dominions. They had defeated even Ulūgh Khān, the most skilful of Alā-ud-dīn's generals; they had made the captured Muslim women sell butter-milk in the countryside of Raṇthambhor. Is it therefore to be wondered at that the *Prākṛtapaiṅgalam* should state

2. X, 33-34.
3. P. 249. For the verse *see* footnote 6.
4. *Hammīramahākāvya*, *X*, 35-39.
5. *Ibid.*, 40-62.

that when Hammīra marched forth with his "excellent minister", Jajjala, in the van, the hearts of the Muslim populace of Delhi sank with fear; many even fainted when the city-drum announced the dreadful news to them.[6]

We have no information from the *Prākṛtapaiṅgalam* regarding the results of the raid. Nor does Nayachandra, intent on belauding Hammīra and depicting in lurid colours the seditious activities of a group of Hammīra's officers, say anything about Jājadeva till we reach the last two cantos of the *Hammīramahākāvya*. Jāja, may however, be expected to have efficiently discharged his duties as a defender of the beleagured fort. His counsel too could never have been one of craven despair and flight.[7] Even when all hope had been lost, he is represented as saying, "Putting on firmly my armour and covering my horse with armoured trappings, I shall bid farewell to my relatives, and with the permission of Hammīra, my lord, enter the battlefield. Brandishing my sword through the air, I shall strike it on the enemy's head, and, breaking the armours of others with mine own, turn aside even mountains (from my path). For Hammīra's sake I shall burn myself in the fire of the Sultān's anger and striking my sword on his head go to heaven, leaving behind this body."[8]

Jāja might have made this proposal when Hammīra, himself, was thinking of opening the front gate of the fort and rushing down on the enemy with a handful of his followers. He had the fullest faith in Jāja; he knew that death held no terror for this brave warrior. But where was, he might have thought, the need of sending Jāja to his sure destruction when he had for him work

6. *Dhollā māria Ḍhilli maha, muchchhiya Mechchha-sarīra*
pura Jajjalā mantivara cholia vīra Hammīra (page 249)

7. See footnote 10.

8. *Pindhau diḍha sanāha vāha uppara pakkhara dai*
bandhu samadi raṇa dhasau sāmi Hammīra baaṇa laī /
uḍḍata ṇahapaha bhamau khagga riu sīsahi ḍārau
pakkhara pakkhara ṭhelli pelli pabbaa a phālau //
Hammīra kajju Jajjala bhaṇaha
kohāṇala muha maha jalau /
Sulatāṇa-sīsa karavāla dai
tajjikalevara dia chalau //

(*Prākṛtapaiṅgalam*, p. 180)

which made the doughtiest warriors' blood run cold. He put Jāja in charge of the *jauhar* of the fair ladies of his harem, his queens, his daughters, and other female relatives. When this part of his duties had been accomplished, Jajjala came back to his master and presented him with nine heads of elephants, saying, "I worship thee, as Rāvaṇa worshipped Śiva. I, however, having only one head, offer these nine as substitutes. The tenth head offered would be mine."[9]

Another duty also remained to be performed. Even when Hammīra fell, the fort must not pass into the hands of the enemy without a bitter struggle. Hammīra appointed therefore Jāja as his successor, after having vainly requested him to leave the fort and save his life. "Hammīra had," says Nayachandra, "asked Jāja twice to go away. Therefore deliberately concluding that two negatives made one affirmative, he decided to stay behind in the fort."[10] How well Jāja discharged his duty as the last defender of the fallen fort may be seen from the following tribute paid by Nayachandra:

"In this world, really to be congratulated is Jaja alone, the upholder of that affection and loyalty which came naturally to him, for he defended the fort for two days, even after the death of the ruler (Hammīra)."[11]

A devoted and loyal warrior or statesman, perhaps, needs no better epitaph.[12]

9. *Hammīramahākāvya*, XIII 187-89. This is rather a free rendering of the verses.

10. *dvau nañau prastutārthaṁ pravadata itivata kṣmābhṛtā dviḥ prayukatā-mauchityādyāhi yāhīti vacanarachanāṁ svārthasaṁsthāṁ vīdhāya/ yaṣtiṣṭhannapyalumpanna khalu nijavibhoḥ śāsanaṁ svāmibhaktaḥ / khyātastenaiva namnāpi sa jayatu chiraṁ Chāhamānaḥ sa Jājā //*
(*Hammīramahākāvya* XIV, 18)

11. *Hammīramahākāvya*, XIV, 16.

12. *Cf.* Bismarck's epitaph, "A faithful servant of Emperor William I."

CHAPTER XII

THE CHAUHĀNS OF NĀḌOL; LAKṢMAṆA TO AHILA

Another important dynasty of the Chauhāns was that of Nāḍol, now a small town in the Goḍwāḍ region of Mārwar. Its founder was Rāval Lākhā, Lākhaṇa, or Lakṣmaṇa. According to *Naiṇsī's Khyāt* as well as the *Purātanaprabandhasaṅgraha*, a collection of historical and semi-historical tales compiled before V. 1528, his father's name was Siṁharā or Siṁharāva.[1] The name appears as Sindhurāja in the Achaleśvara inscription of Luṇtigadeva.[2] Kīrtipāla's Nāḍol Plates (V. 1218) and the still earlier fragmentary inscription of Sahajapāla, however, mention Vākpati of Śākambharī as Lakṣmaṇa's father;[3] and as these happen to be our earliest records on the point, their testimony must be accepted in preference to that of the others.[4]

Fully reliable details regarding Lakṣmaṇa are scanty. Tod claims having discovered two inscriptions of this ruler, bearing the dates V. 1024 and V. 1039, according to the former of which he was a contemporary of Guhila Śaktikumāra of Āṭpur.[5] An inscription of his descendant Kelhaṇa, dated V. 1233, incidentally speaks of Lākhaṇa and his date V. 1039.[6] Then there is an inscription in the temple of Nīlakaṇṭha Mahādeva at Nāḍol which refers itself to Lākhaṇa and is dated the 5th of the bright half of Phālguna, V. 1125, the year here probably being the scribe's mistake for V. 1025, the real date of Lākhaṇa.[7] According to Ojha Grant 4, he built a temple of Viṣṇu at Nāḍol

1. *Naiṇsī's Khyāt* I, p. 123; *Purātanaprabandhasaṅgraha*, p. 102.
2. *EI*, IX, p. 79.
3. Kīrtipāla's Plates, verse 2; Sahajapāla's Maṇḍore fragmentary inscription, line 6.
4. Siṁharāja is found (on inscriptional evidence) not to be Lakṣmaṇa's father but his brother.
5. *Annals and Antiquities of Rājasthān*, (O.U.P.) II, pp. 807-8.
6. *EI*, XI, p. 67.
7. Dr. G.H. Ojha's transcript.

and named it after himself.[8] This may be the temple of Lakṣmaṇasvāmin mentioned in Jojaladeva's Sādaḍi and Nāḍol inscriptions of V. 1147. The fort at Nāḍol is also believed to have been built by him. It is "on the declivity of a low ridge to the west-ward of the town, with square towers of ancient form and built of a very curious conglomerate of granite and gneiss of which the rock on which it stands is composed."

The *Purātanaprabandhasaṅgraha* and *Naiṇsī's Khyāt* profess to give a few more details about Lakṣmaṇa's life.[9] According to the *Saṅgraha,* Lakṣmaṇa started from Śākambharī with two companions only, his wife and a *Harijan,* and at night took shelter in a temple outside Nāḍol. His fighting, almost singlehanded, against the Medas, who had been terrorising the country all around with their freebooting raids, so pleased the Brāhmaṇa masters of Nāḍol, that they gave him the job of guarding the town. Gradually Lakṣmaṇa built up a small band of troopers and so intensively harried the Medas in their own territory that they agreed to keep off from villages paying tribute to Lakṣmaṇa. But once Lakṣmaṇa ventured out too far into Medapaṭa. He was seriously wounded and barely escaped being caught by Medas. Lakṣmaṇa naturally felt despondent; but his tutelary goddess appeared to him and said, "Grieve not, O Lakṣmaṇa. I shall make thee great. Driven helter skelter by a storm, a convoy of horses belonging to the ruler of Mālwā will come riderless to your town and enter it. You have only to sprinkle them with saffron-water. It will change permanently their colour." The next day every thing turned out as predicted by the goddess. So perfect was the transformation that even the masters of the horses failed to recognise them as their own. Master of 12,000 horses now, Lakṣmaṇa extended his dominions with ease. Outside Nāḍol he built a great palace, with the temple of his family goddess at its entrance. Of his numerous sons, some were by a Vaiśya wife. They were put in charge of royal stores and became known as *Bhāṇḍāgārikas*. The account found in the *Khyāt* is materially the same. It puts the number of horses secured by Lakṣmaṇa as 13,000.

8. Line 7, For the text see Appendix G (iv).

9. *Naiṇsī's Khyāt* I, p. 152; *Purātanaprabandhasaṅgraha,* pp. 101-2.

If we disregard the supernatural element in these accounts, they would be found credible enough. It is, in fact, the tale of the rise of all soldiers of fortune. Haidar Alī, Shivājī and Rāva Sīho had similar careers; they began with practically nothing excepting their unflinching determination to carve out a new kingdom for themselves, and succeeded in enterprises wherein others with better material means had failed. Lakṣmaṇa may have started similarly with only a few followers. We need not necessarily assume that he had only one. The protection that he afforded the people against the depredations of the Medas made his rule welcome to the people of Godvāḍ; and he probably did rob some caravan of all its horses, because this is the only meaning that we can assign to the story of thousands of horses coming to him of their own accord. His looting expeditions, whose field probably included the confines of Mewār as well as Gujarāt, appear to have been glorified into the bardic story given by Tod that Lākhā "collected the transit duties at the further barrier of Pāṭṭan and levied tribute from the prince of Cheetore." Lākhā may have been a great figure in the history of Nāḍol, brave, adventurous and perhaps also chivalrous, but we cannot believe that he was strong enough to exact tribute from his powerful neighbours of Gujarāt and Mewār.

Śobhita. Lakṣmaṇa was succeeded by his son Śobhita, Sohita, or Sohiya. The Sūndhā inscription states that he took away the glory of the lord of Mount Ābū.[10] The Sevāḍi Plates of Ratnapāla (V. 1176) call him the lord of Dhārā.[11] He must, therefore, have fought against the Paramāra rulers of both Mālwā and Ābū. Rājpūtānā, Mālwā, and Gujarāt formed at this time the scene of a triangular fight among the Chauhāns, the Chaulukyas and the Paramāras. The Chauhāns of Nāḍol, who were behind none in this race for power, appear for the first thirty years or so, to have sided with the Chaulukyas of Gujarāt. Mūlarāja I of Gujarāt attacked and uprooted Dharaṇīvarāha of Ābū.[12] Śobhita took away his glory.[13] Mūlarāja fought

10. *EI*, IX, p. 75.
11. *Ibid.*, XI, pp. 308 ff.
12. यं मूलादुन्मूलयद-गुरुबलः श्रीमूलराजो नृपो दर्पान्धो धरणीवराह-नृपतिं...।

(*EI*, X, p. 21)

13. The Ābū ruler whose glory Śobhita took away was this very Dharaṇī-varāha.

against the Paramāras of Mālwā; Śobhita occupied their capital Dhārā.

Balirāja. The struggle continued unabated in the reign of Balirāja, the son and successor of Śobhita. Though he claims to have defeated the army of Muñja,[14] the ruler of Dhārā, success seems to have, on the whole, lain with the Paramāras, for it is not only Parimala, the Paramāra court-poet, who states that the people of Mārwār trembled at the approach of Muñja, but also the Kauthem Grant of Vikramāditya VI of Kalyāṇī which as the verdict of a third party has every right to be trusted in this matter.[15] The plight of Balirāja's ally Mūlarāja was even worse. He was decisively defeated by Muñja near Āghāṭa and barely escaped with his life from the battle-field.[16] His armies found shelter at Hastikuṇḍī,[17] but he personally appears to have sought refuge at the court of his ally, the Mārwār ruler, Balirāja. "The Gurjara ruler," says Parimala, "neither took food nor drank water. He did not enjoy the company of women. Giving up all sensual pleasures, he slept on the sand, and bore the hottest sunshine. He underwent this austere penance in Mārwār, as it were, with a view to obtaining even the smallest part of the favour of thy lotus-like feet, O Lion of Mālwā."[18] Here Maru or Mārwār might stand for any of the three Mārwār kingdoms, Sāmbhar, Hastikuṇḍī and Nāḍol. Sāmbhar, however, is obviously impossible because of the deadly feud between Vigraharāja II of Śākambharī and Mūlarāja Chaulukya.[19] Hastikuṇḍī merely gave shelter to the Chaulukya army; its leader is said to have fled away.[20] So the only place left for him in Mārwār to run to was Nāḍol, the rulers of which had more than once held their own against the rulers of Mālwā.

14. Sūndhā Inscription, verse 7, *EI*, IX, p. 75.
15. For the Kauthem Grant see *IA*, XVI, p. 23, lines 41-42. For Parimala's verse see *JBBRAS*, XVI, p. 173.
16. Bījāpur Inscription of the Rāṣṭrakūṭa rulers Dhavala and Bālāprasāda, verse 10 (Jinavijaya, *Prāchīna-Jainalekhasaṅgraha*, p. 176).
17. *Ibid.*
18. *JBBRAS*, XVI, p. 174.
19. See above Chapter III.
20. हरिणइव भिया गूर्जरेशो विनष्टे (v. 10 of the Bījāpur Inscription of

Vigrahapāla. Balirāja's successor was his uncle Vigrahapāla. His name does not occur in Ojha Grant 2 and the Sūndhā Hill inscription. He is, however, described as a ruler in the Moṇḍor inscription of Sahajapāla,[21] the Nāḍol Plates of Kīrtipāla,[22] the Nāḍol Grant of Ālhaṇadeva[23] and line 10 of Ojha Grant 4.[24]

Mahendra. Vigrahapāla was succeeded by his son Mahendra.[25] He must have ascended the throne of Nāḍol before V. 1053, the date of Rāṣṭrakūṭa Dhavala's Bījāpur inscription where he is referred to.[26]

In Mahendra's time the danger from the Paramāras receded into the background on account of the crushing defeat suffered by the Mālwā army at the hands of Chālukya Tailapa II of Kalyāṇī. The history of the Chaulukya dynasty of Gujarāt too, after the death of Mūlarāja I, was comparatively inglorious for nearly one quarter of a century. The real menace to the independence of the Chauhāns of Nāḍol now was from their own ambitious brethren of Śākambharī who in the reign of Vigraharāja II had carried their victorious arms as far as Bhṛgukachchha on the mouth of the river Narmadā.[27] According to the Bījāpur inscription of Rāṣṭrakūṭa Dhavala of Hastikuṇḍī, Mahendra was over-powered by the powerful armies of Durlabharāja (the younger brother and successor of Vigraharāja II).[28] Dhavala

Dhavala Rāṣṭrakūṭa). The root "naś" in the sense of running away is common enough in Jaina Sanskrit literature.

21. *ASIR*, 1909-10, Part II, pp. 102 f.

22. *IA*, XL, pp. 146 ff.

23. *EI*, IX, pp. 64 ff.

24. For the text of the Grant see Appendix G (iv).

25. See Ratnapāla's Sevāḍī Plates, verse 7, Kīrtipāla's Nāḍol Plates, verse 4. Alhaṇadeva's Nāḍol Plates, verse 4.

26. As Lakṣmaṇa, the founder of the line was alive in V. 1039, we must put three rulers Śobhita, Balirāja and Vigrahapāla within the short space of 14 years.

27. See above Chapter III.

28. The identification of this Durlabharāja with Durlabharāja Chaulukya suggested by Dr. H.C. Ray cannot be accepted for the simple reason that the inscription of Rāṣṭrakūṭa Dhavala was incised in V. 1053. Durlabharāja Chaulukya did not, on the other hand, ascend the throne of Gujarāt before V. 1066 or so.

gladdened Mahendra's heart by helping him out of the trouble. In the inscription of Dadhīchaka Chachchha, Durlabharāja is said to have conquered a country called Assossitana. As the only war that he is known to have engaged in was that against Mahendra, could not Assossitana have been some part of the Nāḍol territory conquered by the Chauhāns of Śākambharī ?[29]

Another important event of Mahendra's reign was the marriage of Mahendra's sisters Durlabhadevī and Lakṣmī, respectively, with Durlabharāja, the Chaulukya ruler of Gujarāt and his younger brother Nāgarāja.[30] Both Śobhita and Balirāja had, as we have seen, been on very good terms with the rulers of Gujarāt. This friendship was cemented still further by this new matrimonial alliance.[31]

The date of Mahendra's death is not known with any exactness but he could not have died earlier than V. 1067, the date of the accession of Durlabharāja Chaulukya to whom his sister Durlabhadevī was married.[31a]

Aśvapāla and Ahila. Mahendra's successor was his son Aśvapāla. The idol of god Āsaleśvara might have been, as surmised by Dr. D.R. Bhandarkar, named after this ruler. In the reign of his son Ahila there was a change in the foreign policy of Nāḍol, owing to the ambitious nature of Bhīmadeva I (V. 1078-1120c.) of Gujarāt who, caring little for the ties of relationship, had attacked Nāḍol. Ahila, perhaps, proved a match for him, for he is said to have defeated in battle the forces of Bhīmadeva.[32]

29. See, however, Chapter IV above where we have doubted the reading Assossitana.

30. *Dvyāśrayakāvya* of Hemachandra, VII. That by Mahendra is meant Mahendra of Nāḍol is obvious from Abhayatilaka's commentary on verses 66, 73, and 74 of the canto. The princesses are said to have chosen their husbands in a *svayaṁvara* of which the details, at least, seem to be fictitious.

31. Dr. H.C. Ray's suggestion (*DHNI*, II, p. 1106) that the alliance was meant to end the hostilities between the Nāḍol Chauhāns and the Chaulukyas has to be rejected on account of being based on the mistaken identity of Durlabharāja of Dhavala Rāṣṭrakūta's inscription with Durlabharāja Chaulukya of Gujarāt. (See footnote 28 of this Chapter regarding the mistake made by Dr. Ray).

31a. Durlabharāja Chaulukya's inscription of V. 1067, has been published by the author in the *Marubhāratī*, *XIII*, Part 2, pp. 50-1. It names the donee as Nannuka, a Brāhmaṇa of the Lāṭyāyana *gotra*, who resided at Bhillamāla.

32. गुर्जराधिपति-भीम-भूभुजः सैन्यपूरमजयद् रणेषु यः ।

(*Sūndhā Inscription*, *v.* 13, *EI*, *IX*, *p.* 57)

CHAPTER XIII

THE CHAUHANS OF NĀḌOL (*Continued*); AṆAHILLA TO JOJALADEVA

Aṇahilla. Ahila was succeeded by his uncle Aṇahilla[1], one of the most successful and energetic rulers of the Nāḍol line. He successfully continued the war against Bhīmadeva II of Gujarāt whom he defeated at Pratiṣṭhāna.[2] Three other achievements to his credit are the capture of Śākambharī, the slaying of Bhoja Paramāra's general Sāḍha, and the defeat of a certain terrible Turuṣka.[3] Of these, two exploits have been dealt with in our account of Chāmuṇḍarāja of Śākambharī.[4] Bhoja was one of the strongest rulers of Northern India. Defeating his general Sāḍha and liberating Śākambharī must have greatly added to Aṇahilla's fame as a brave leader. The Turuṣka might be either some general of Mahmūd or Mahmūd of Ghaznā himself who left his capital on the 18th of October, 1025, with 30,000 regular horsemen and many thousands of volunteers to destroy the temple of Somanātha and passed through Multān, Lodravā in the Jaisalmer State and Aṇahillapaṭṭana, the capital of Gujarāt.[5] It was probably on the way to the last of these towns that Mahmūd passed through the territory of Nāḍol "whose prince", in the words of Tod, "hesitated not to measure his sword with Mahmūd". The fighting was perhaps severe enough for Mahmūd to make him determine not to return by this way to Ghaznā.

According to the Ojha Grant 4. Aṇahilla's kingdom comprised merely seven hundred villages when he ascended the throne;

1. Ratnapāla's Sevāḍī Plates, v. 8; Kīrtipāla's Nāḍol Plates, v. 4; Alhaṇadeva's Nāḍol Plates, v. 4 etc.

2. "He defeated at Pratiṣṭhāna," says the Ojha Grant 4, "the elephant force used by Bhīma, killed the drivers, and cut off the tails of the elephants out of mere fun." See Appendix G (iv) for the text of the Grant.

3. Sūndhā Inscription, verse 17.

4. See above Chapter IV, footnote 16.

5. See Farrukhi's Ode, Dr. Nāzim's *Sultan Mahmūd*, p. 217.

these he turned into 7,000 by killing in battle the rulers of adjoining kingdoms[6]. Even if this be regarded as an exaggeration, Aṇahilla must be regarded as one of the most successful rulers of Nāḍol who raised high its inter-state position and held his own against the strongest rulers of the time, Indian as well as foreign.

Bālaprasāda. Aṇahilla's successor was his eldest son Bālaprasāda. As he is said to have defeated other rulers even while he was a mere boy, he must have been very young when he ascended the throne.[7] It was probably this fact which made him submit to Bhīmadeva I of Gujarāt who acceding to his request released Kṛṣṇarāja II, the Paramāra ruler of Ābū, from captivity.[8]

Bālaprasāda pre-deceased Bhīma I of Gujarāt. He must, therefore, have died before V. 1120, the year of Bhīma's death.[9] If V. 1117 might be regarded as the first year of his contemporary and friend Kṛṣṇarāja Paramāra's reign, Bālaprasāda must have been alive up to V. 1117.[10]

Jendurāja. Bālaprasāda's submission to Bhīma perhaps never found favour with the old warriors of the Nāḍol court who had seen service under Ahila and Aṇahilla. Hence we find almost an immediate orientation in the attitude towards Gujarāt on the death of Bālaprasāda and the accession of his younger brother Jendurāja, also known as Jesaladeva, Jendrarāja and perhaps Jendrapāla too. "He burst through the multitude of his enemies at Sāṇḍerā", states the Sūndhā Inscription, "as the Sun does through darkness".[11] From the Ojha Grant 4, we find that the leader of this hostile force was none else than Bhīma, the old enemy of the Nāḍol Chauhāns.[12]

6. हत्वा सीमाधिपान् संख्ये तेषां ग्रामान् प्रगृह्य च ।
देशः सप्तशतो येन सप्तसाहस्त्रिकः कृतः ॥
7. Line 15 of Ojha Grant 4. See Appendix G (iv) for the text.
8. भीम-क्ष्माभृच्चरणयुगली-मर्दन-व्याजतो यः
कुर्वन् पीड़ामतिबलतया मोचयामास कारा-
गाराद् भूमिपतिमपि कृष्णदेवाभिधानम् ।

Sūndhā Insrciption, v. 18.

9. Bālaprasāda's successor Jendrarāja fought against Bhīma.
10. We have two inscriptions for this ruler dated in V. 1117 and V. 1123.
11. Verse 20, *EI*, IX, p. 76.
12. संप्राप्ते भीमसैन्यजलधौ ग्रामेत्र संडेरके ।

In the Sevādi Copper Plates of Ratnapāla, Jendrarāja is extolled as a giver of horses and gold.[13] He built perhaps the temple known as Jendrarājeśvara. The Āuwā Inscription of Khindrapāla, dated in the Vikrama year 1132, is generally believed to be of this ruler, but without much reason.[14]

Pṛthvīpāla. Jendrarāja's eldest son and successor Pṛthvīpāla continued his father's policy of hostility towards Gujarāt. According to the Sūndhā Inscription, he destroyed an army of Karṇa, the lord of Gurjaras.[15] This Karṇa is certainly Karṇa Trailokyamalla, son of Chaulukya Bhīma I. Pṛthvīpāla attacked also a ruler named Māṇḍalika. "In the battle of Rohaḍavāpika," says Ojha Grant 4, "the subjects of Māṇḍalika, struck with spearheads by Pṛthvīpāla's troopers, left far away their shame, sons, wives as well as property, and fled away in all directions."[16] This Māṇḍalika obviously is Māṇḍalika Paramāra of Vāgaḍa for whom we have two inscriptions of V. 1116 and 1136. The locality Rohaḍavāpika may have lain somewhere in Māṇḍalika's dominions.

According to the Ojha Grant 4, Pṛthvīpāla's younger brother Āsarāja, "even when he was a small boy and the commander of a very small force, rescued Pṛthvīpāla when he, left without his people, was surrounded by a Turuṣka host".[17] The encounter probably took place before V. 1136. We have seen already how Durlabharāja Chauhān of Śākambharī lost his life in a battle with the Mātaṅgas whom I have tentatively identified with Muslims.[18] Pṛthvīpāla seems to have suffered at the hands of these

13. Verse 10.

14. The name in the inscription (*PRAS*, *WC*, 1908-1909. p. 50) is Khindrapāla, not Jindrapāla, son of Aṇahilla, without any royal titles for either the father or the son. The temple from which the inscription comes contains also some other inscriptions by people whose fathers' names ended in "pāla". Neither Khindrapāla nor these others have been called Chauhāns.

19. पृथ्वीपाल इति ध्रुवं क्षितिपतिस्-तस्यांगजन्माभवत्
प्रत्यक्षोरुनिधिः स गूर्जरपतेः कर्णस्य सैन्यापहः

(*EI*, IX, p. 76)

16. See Appendix G (iv) for the text.

17. *Ibid.*, line 22.

18. See above the account of Durlabharāja III and our paper, "Ibrāhim of Ghaznā, the Mātaṅga slayer of Durlabharāja III of Śākambharī" published in *JBORS*, 1944 (March issue).

very raiders whose leader, Ibrāhim of Ghanzā, crossed the southern border of the Punjāb in 1079 A.D. and conquered Pākpaṭṭan, Rudpāl and some places on the western coast of India.[19] Pṛthvīpāla could have come into conflict with Ibrāhim while he was proceeding westwards. We know of no other Turuṣka force which penetrated into the country so far in the thirties of the twelfth century of the Vikrama era.

Pṛthvīpāla abolished certain taxes laid on farmers.[20] He may have installed the deity Pṛthvīpāleśvara.

Jojaladeva. Pṛthvīpāla was succeeded not by his son Ratnapāla but his younger brother Yojaka, Jojaka or Jojaladeva who is described in the Sūndhā Inscription as having "by force, enjoyed himself in Aṇahillapura, with the white umbrella adding to his splendour."[21] If it is not mere exaggeration, it means that he succeeded for a while in making himself master of the capital of Gujarāt. The Gurjara ruler at the time might have been either the unfortunate Karṇa who had been defeated by one enemy after the other, or perhaps his minor son Jayasiṁha who could not have been, for the first few years of his reign, the powerful ruler that he later on proved himself to be.

We have two inscriptions for Jojaladeva both of them dated in V. 1147/1090 A.D. and having practically identical contents. Jojaladeva must have been very conservative in character, for he let courtesans take part in the festivals of gods like Lakṣmaṇasvāmin, even though a section of people was bitterly opposed to this old practice.[22]

19. Briggs, *Tārīkh-i-Firishta*, I, p. 137. De, *Tabaqāt-i-Akbarī* p. 33.
20. Verse 22, *EI*, IX, p. 76.
21. *Ibid.*, verse 24.
22. For the text of the inscriptions, see *EI*, XI, pp. 26ff. Their object is to record *Mahārājādhirāja* Jojaladeva's order that on the day of the festival or procession of any god, such as Lakṣmaṇasvāmin, the courtesans attached to the other gods were to put on their best clothes and attend it along with their managers, artists and musical instruments. *If any ascetic, old or learned person stood against the practice he was to be punished by the ruler.* The *vidhichaitya* movement, of which some account will be found in a later chapter, was opposed to the dancing of courtesans in Jaina temples and so were most of the Brāhmaṇas if we may apply Alberunī's testimony to Rājasthān also.

CHAPTER XIV

THE CHAUHĀNS OF NĀḌOL (*Continued*): ĀSARĀJA TO ALHAṆADEVA

Āsarāja. Jojaladeva was succeeded by his younger brother Āsarāja, known also as Aśvarāja. Of his inscriptions, two, dated respectively in V. 1167 and 1172, have been found at Sevāḍī.[1] I have the transcript of a third which I have termed Ojha Grant 4.[2] None of these records refers to Jayasiṁha Siddharāja of Gujarāt. It may, therefore, be assumed that during the earlier part of his reign Āsarāja was an independent prince. This period of independence ended before V. 1176. On the third of the dark half of Kārttika V. 1173, Āsarāja made a gift to the god Tripuruṣa.[3] In Jyeṣṭha, V. 1176, we find his nephew Ratnapāla, the rightful claimant to the throne after Pṛthvīpāla, making a grant from his camp at Nahurā in the kingdom of Nāḍol.[4] As all the inscriptions in this kingdom for the next quarter of a century belong to Ratnapāla's line, Āsarāja must have been driven out from there somewhere between 1173 and 1176 V.E.

The rest of Āsarāja's life was probably passed in the service of Siddharāja Jayasiṁha. Obeying his orders,[5] he went to Dhārā, forced its master Naravarman to shut himself in the fort, and so distinguished himself during the siege that Jayasiṁha granted him the high honour of using a golden *kalaśa* on his tent (*gupyad-guru*).[6] Āsarāja's queen Delhaṇadevī, mother of Alhaṇa, was a daughter of Rudrapāla who is described in Ojha Grant 2 as ruler of the sacred Sārasvata land.[7] Another queen Chāndalādevī is mentioned in Ojha Grant3.[8]

1. *EI*, XI, p. 29 f. and *EI*, XI, p. 31 f.
2. See Appendix G (iv) for the text of the Grant.
3. Ojha Grant 3, line 9. See Appendix G (iii) for the text.
4. *EI*, XI, pp. 308ff.
5. संप्राप प्रभु-सिद्धराज-वचसा युद्धाय धारानले ।

   Ojha Grant 2, lines 13-4.
6. Verse 26, *EI*, IX, p. 76.
7. Line 23.
8. Line 10 of the Grant; see Appendix G (iii) for the text.

Āsarāja built the shrine of Chāndaleśvara,[9] granted the village Piñchchhavallī to the Tripuruṣa temple,[10] and built hundreds of free kitchens, tanks, gardens, temples dedicated to Śiva, step-wells, wells, *prapās*, and religious houses.[11] That his relations with the Jainas were cordial might be seen from the benefaction granted by his son Kaṭukarāja to the temple of Vīranātha at Sevāḍī.[12]

Ratnapāla. Ratnapāla was perhaps above thirty when he recovered his patrimony of Nāḍol in V. 1176. Before this too he had probably made an attempt to reconquer the kingdom, for the Ojha Grant 4 speaks of the recapture of Maṇḍor by Āsarāja from a relative who had made himself its master.[13] He restored from his camp at Nahurā in the kingdom of Nāḍol a grant previously made by Mahārāja Jendurāja.[14] The Ojha Grant 3 styles him as *Mahārājādhirāja* and states that he granted the village Riyasakudapa to the temple of Tripuruṣadeva.[15]

Rāyapāla. For Rāyapāla, the son and successor of Ratnapāla, we have seven inscriptions ranging from V. 1189 to 1202. Of these five belong to Nāḍlāi and two to Nāḍol.[16] His independent position seems to be indicated not only by the absence of the name of Jayasiṁha Siddharāja from his inscriptions[17] but also

9. *Ibid.*
10. Lines 12-13 of the Ojha Grant 3.
11. Sūndhā inscription, verse 29, *EI*, IX, p. 77.
12. See the Sevāḍī inscription (V. 1172) of Āsarāja's reign; *EI*, XI, P. 31 f.
13. Lines 23-24. See Appendix H for the text.
14. See *EI*, XI, pp. 308 ff.
15. Line 18.
16. For these inscriptions see *EI*, XI, pp. 35f., 38f., 39,. 41f.; P.C. Nahar *Jaina Inscriptions*, I. p. 213f. *EI*, XI, 43f., and Bhandarkar's *List of Inscriptions of Northern India*, No. 250.
17. I mean as overlord, for the *Jayasiṁha-jagati* or the temple of Jayasiṁha in the Nāḍol inscription of V. 1198 may refer to this ruler as one who paid for its building.

The Ratanpur inscription of Kumārapāla Chaulukya and his feudatory Punapākṣadeva who received the *mahāsana* from Rāyapāla might lead to the impression that Rāyapāla was like Punapākṣa, a feudatory of the Chaulukyas. But the fact that Rāyapāla's rule never extended as far as Ratanpur in the Jaswantpurā District, which first came into Chauhān possession in the reign fo Udayasiṁha of Jālor, proves such an impression to be wrong. Either the Rāyapāla of the Ratanpur District is a different person altogether or it may be that Punapākṣa received from Rāyapāla of Nāḍol the honour of having a seat at his court. That such an honour was regarded highly can be seen from the concluding verse of every canto of the *Naiṣadhacharita* of Harṣa.

by his high sounding title *Mahārājādhirāja-Parameśvara*[18]. His administrative talent is testified to by the Nāḍol inscription of V. 1198 according to which he exacted, from the Brāhmaṇas assembled at Dhālop, a promise to find out, through the *chaukaḍikā*[19] or the police system of *chaukīs*, the things lost (on the road) by pilgrims, traders, and sons of state-servants. If the thing was lost within their village or jurisdiction, they were required to restore it. The villagers supplied the police, and the king, the weapons.[20]

Somewhere between V. 1198 and 1200, the line of Āsarāja made itself once again master of Nāḍol, probably with the help of the Chaulukya ruler Jayasiṁha Siddharāja. An inscription of (Siṁha) *Saṁvat*, 31, *i.e.*, V. 1200 shows Āsarāja's eldest son *Mahārājādhirāja* Kaṭudeva issuing a grant from Nāḍol and his son Jayatasīha enjoying the *bhukti* of Sevāḍī.[21] Kaṭudeva perhaps died the same year, because the Bālī Stone Inscription of V. 1200 speaks of the *mahāmātya* Āśvaka "subsisting on the lotus-like feet of *mahārājādhirāja* Śrī-Jayatasīhadeva,"[22] who is obviously Kaṭudeva's son and successor. Jayatasīha's queen was named Tihuṇakā.[23] Rāyapāla was not, however, a man to give in so easily. Profiting by the death of Jayasiṁha Siddharāja, a friend of the rival line, he recovered at least a part of his patrimony, for this alone could have enabled him to issue his grant of V. 1202 from Nāḍlāi in the kingdom of Nāḍol.[24]

18. See the inscription referred to in the last footnote, *EI*, XI, p. 39f.

19. Dr. D.R. Bhandarkar interprets *chaukaḍikā* as *panchāyat*. But it is better to regard it as a *chauki* or police post. Police warders are even now known as *chaukidārs*.

20. See his Nāḍol inscription of V. 1198, *EI*, XI, pp. 39-40. This very system of local responsibility for crimes was introduced in a modified form nearly four hundred years later by Sher Shāh and has won golden opinions from historians (see for instance the view of Abbās in *ED*, IV, p. 421).

21. *EI*, XI, pp. 33-34.

22. *EI*, XI, p. 33. See also No. 261 of Bhandarkar's *Inscriptions of Northern India*. That the ruler whom Āśvaka is said to have served cannot be Jayasiṁha Chaulukya, though such is the view of Dr. D.R. Bhandarkar, is obvious from the date of the record. It is dated in V. 1200. But we find from the colophon of the *Supārśvanāthacharita*, a contemporary work, that in Māgha, V. 1199, Kumārapāla the successor of Jayasiṁha, was already on the throne.

23. See the above record. We do not know of any Tihuṇakā as the queen of Jayasiṁha Chaulukya.

24. *EI*, XI, p. 43. To be a little more accurate one should state. "This alone should have enabled the *baṇjārakas* to issue a grant in his reign in V. 1202". Dr. D.R. Bhandarkar, the editor of the record, ascribes the grant to Rājadeva, but it is clearly one by the *baṇajārās* as shown by the words. बणजारकैः प्रदत्तम् ।

Rāyapāla had two queens Padmalādevī, mother of Sahajapāla and Sāhaṇapāla, and Mānaladevī, the mother of Rudrapāla and Amṛtapāla.[25] The deities Padmaleśvara, Sāhaṇapāleśvara, and Sahajapāleśvara were named after Queen Padmalā and her two sons, and were installed before V. 1192. In this year *mahārājaputra kumvara* Śāhaṇapāladeva made a grant to them.[62]

Sahajapāla. Rāyapāla was succeeded by his son Sahajapāla for whom we have a fragmentary inscription from Maṇḍor.[27] He probably lost his throne as a result of the Chaulukya success in the first round of the war between Arṇorāja of Śākambharī and Kumārapāla of Gujarāt, to which we have referred at some length in a previous chapter.[28] He was replaced by Āsarāja's son Ālhaṇa somewhere between V. 1202 and 1205. In the latter of these years Ālhaṇa is mentioned as *Mahārājādhirāja* in a benefaction that he made to the temple of Tripuruṣa at Nāḍol.[29]

Ālhaṇa. For Ālhaṇa we have six inscriptions ranging from V. 1209 to 1220.[30] These combined with other contemporary records, specially those discovered by Dr. G.H. Ojha, give us a good idea of his chequered history. In or before V. 1205 he had, as we have seen, made himself, somehow, master of Nāḍol.[31] But in V. 1209 we find him ruling not at Nāḍol but over the three towns of Kirāṭakūpa, Rāṭahrada and Śivā granted to him by

25. For Rudrapāla and Amṛtapāla and their mother Mānaladevī see the Nāḍlāi stone-inscription of V. 1189 (*EI*, XI, p. 35f.). For the two other princes and their mother see Ojhā Grant 3. Sāhanapāla made a grant in Kārttika, V. 1192.

26. See Ojhā Grant 3, lines 20-22.

27. *ASIR*, 1909-1910, Pt. II, p. 102 ff.

28. See chapter V.

29. Ojha Grant 3, line 23. See Appendix G (iii) for the text.

30. Kirāḍū stone-inscription, V. 1209 (*EI*, XI, pp. 43-46), Nāḍol Grant I, V. 1218 (*EI.*, IX, pp. 63-66). Nāḍol Grant 2 (*EI*, IX, pp. 66-70). Jhamverā inscription (*JPASB*, XII, pp. 102 ff.), Ojhā Grant 2 (see Appendix F for its text), and the Bāmnerā Grant of V. 1220, *EI*, XIII, pp. 208 ff.). Of these the last has been wrongly ascribed by the editor to Kelhaṇa. The mistake has been copied by Drs. D.R. Bhandarkar and H.C. Ray. Kelhaṇa is mentioned merely as a *Kumvara* there. The *rājya* was that of his father Ālhaṇa.

31. See the last paragraph and footnote 29.

Kumārapāla Chaulukya.[32] As the Chaulukyas had, while advancing against Ajmer, in V. 1207 to capture Palli, one of the strongest forts in the principality of Nāḍol,[33] it might be assumed that Arṇorāja had in V. 1206 or so driven out the Chaulukya feudatory Ālhaṇa from his ancestral possession. Arṇorāja's defeat at the hands of Kumārapāla freed Nāḍol from the hands of the Chauhāns of Śākambharī. Kumārapāla could have now, if he so desired, restored Ālhaṇa to his throne at Nāḍol. But instead of doing so, he gave him the three towns in Mārwār named above, keeping Nāḍol under his direct control for a while.[34] A little later he put it under his *daṇḍādhīśa* Vaijalladeva Chauhān, his reason for this perhaps being the desire to have it under someone who could withstand the mighty Vigraharāja IV of Śākambharī.[35]

But Ālhaṇa himself would not have been a bad choice for the job. He participated in many Chaulukya campaigns.[36] In Saurāṣṭra where Kumārapāla's army found itself in sore straits on being surrounded by the hostile Ābhīras on all sides,[37] Ālhaṇa

32. See his Kirāḍū inscription. Kirāṭakūpa is Kirāḍū, Rāṭahrada is modern Rāddharā, and Śiva is Sivā. All the three are in the western part of the modern Jodhpur division of Rājasthān.

33. सप्तोत्तर-सूर्य-शते विक्रमसंवत्सरे त्वजयमेरौ
दुर्गे पल्लीभंगे त्रुटितं पुस्तकमग्रहीत्तदनु ।
अलिखत् स्वयमत्रगतं श्रीमज्-जिनदत्त-सूरि-शिष्यलव:
स्थिरचंद्राख्यो गणिरिह कर्मक्षयहेतुमात्मन: ।।

(*Catalogue of MSS in the Jaisalmer Jain Bhaṇḍārs*, p. 7)

34. See Ojhā Grant I, now published in the *Silver Jubilee Volume* of the *ABOR*, pp. 314ff. wherein Nāḍol is mentioned as *svabhujyamānamaṇḍala* of Kumārapāla.

35. We have the following inscriptions for Vaijalladeva:—

(i) a stone inscription at Sevāḍī, V. 1213.
(ii) ,, ,, ,, ,, Ghānerāv. ,,
(iii) ,, ,, ,, ,, Bālī, V., 1216.
(iv) an inscription of the reign of the Chaulukya ruler, Ajayapāla, dated in the Vikrama year 1231, mentioning Vaijalladeva as a *mahāmaṇḍaleśvara* and *Chauhuyāna*, *i.e.* a Chauhān.

36-37. The Ojha Grant 2 reads,

...भीरधाराधिपान् हत्वा
रक्षितमेव गूर्ज्जरपतेर्ग्रस्तं महान्तं बलम् ।।

The word "dhārā" here can refer to Dhārā, the capital of the Paramāras of

gained a splendid victory[38] by slaying the Ābhīra leader Saumsara.[39] Such a success, indeed, was badly needed, for Saumsara had slain the Chaulukya general, Udayana; and Kumārapāla's army, unless immediately relieved, ran the risk of annihilation. Dr. Bhagwanlal Indraji puts the event in V. 1205. But it would be better to date it somewhere between V. 1209 and 1211. Had it occurred earlier than V. 1209, it would have been referred to in Ālhaṇa's inscription of that year. Its occurrence after V. 1211, of course, is impossible, because by that time Udayana, the general to whose help Ālhaṇa had rushed, was no more. Udayana's son, Vāgbhaṭa, not merely occupied his position as a minister in V. 1211 but had completed also the repairs vowed by Udayana a few days before his death.

In due course these meritorious services must have put Ālhaṇa in the good books of Kumārapāla.[40] Vaijalladeva Chauhān, the *daṇḍādhiśa* of Nāḍol, had not been very successful against Vigraharāja IV of Śākambharī who "reduced Pālī to the condition of a small hamlet and Nāḍol to that of a bed of reeds".[41] Equally unsuccessful perhaps had been another Chaulukya officer, the Nāḍūlīya Chāhamāna Kuntapāla. Vaijalladeva was therefore transferred to some other district, probably to Gambhutā-*viṣaya*, and Ālhaṇa, the successful warrior and unfailing ally of the Chaulukyas, was rewarded with the restoration of his hereditary principality of Nāḍol.[42] Rightly therefore, could

Mālwā. But the context favours the equation of "dhārā" with the van or front line of an army (See Apte's *Practical Sanskrit English Dictionary*). Had the reference been to *Dhārādhipa* Ballāla, the grant would have used the singular number, instead of the plural number actually used by it.

As regards his participation in many Chaulukya campaigns, it can be inferred from the statement.

यत्साहाय्यं प्रतिपदमहो गूर्जरेशश्चकांक्ष ।

(Sūndhā Inscription, v. 32)

38. Kīrtipāla's Plates, *EI*, IX, p. 69. Ojha Grant 2 Lines 15-16. See Appendix G (ii) for the text.

39. The *Prabandhachintāmaṇi*, p. 86. The chief is called Saṁvara also.

40. See the quarter of v. 32 of the Sūndhā inscription quoted in footnote 36-7.

41. See above Chapter VI.

42. In Śrāvaṇa, V. 1218, we find Ālhaṇa issuing a grant from Nāḍol. Up to V. 1216 at least, Vaijalladeva had been in charge there (See footnote 35 iii).

his son, Kīrtipāla, claim that Ālhaṇa secured the glory of *mahārājya* through his own valour.[43] The *jāgīr* of Kirāṭakūpa, Lāṭahrada and Śivā, which he had hitherto enjoyed, was now transferred to its hereditary owner, Someśvara Paramāra, who also had rendered good service to Kumārapāla in more than one campaign.[44]

Ālhaṇa built a temple of Śiva at Nāḍol[45] and granted valuable benefactions to the gods Chandaleśvara and Tripuruṣa and to the goddess Gaurī installed by his queen Śaṅkarādevī.[46] Nor was his charity merely confined to the orthodox Hindus. He gave a monthly grant to the Mahāvīra temple at Nāḍol[47] and his proclamation of the non-slaughter of animals shows that he knew how to respect the religious sentiments of his Jaina subjects.[48]

Ānallādevī, a daughter of Sahula was mother of his three sons Kelhaṇa, Gajasiṁha, and Kīrtipāla.[49] Naiṇsī makes him the father of one more son, Vijayasiṁha, who founded the Satyapura line of Chauhāns.[50] The Bāmnerā Grant mentions one *Mahārājaputra* Kumārasiṁha who held the village of Koretā in *jāgir*.[51] Kelhaṇa's Osiā inscription of V. 1235 shows that he was Kelhaṇa's son, and was known also by his title as *Siṁhavikrama*.

Ālhaṇa gave his two sons Kelhaṇa and Gajasiṁha a share in government as early as V. 1209.[52] Gajasiṁha was later on transferred to the government of Maṇḍor[53] which Ālhaṇa captured from his relative Sahajapāla. He wanted it to be in the safe and strong hands of his son. Kelhaṇa remained with his father and

43. Verse 5 (*EI*, IX, p. 69).
44. He subjugated for Kumārapāla the kingdom of Uchchha. (See Someśvara's inscription of V. 1218, P. C. Nāhar, *Jaina Inscriptions*, I, p. 251 ff).
45. Sūndhā inscription, verse 32, *EI*, IX, p. 77.
46. Ojhā Grant 3.
47. *EI*, IX, p. 64 f.
48. See his Kirāḍū Inscription, *EI*, XI, p. 44 ff. See also the chapter on Religion.
49. Ojhā Grant 3, *EI*, IX, p. 69.
50. *Khyāt*, I, p. 172.
51. *EI*, XIII, p. 208. In the inscription of Kelhaṇa he is a *Rājā*.
52. See Kirāḍu inscription, V. 1209.
53. *JPASB*, XII, p. 102 ff.

was appointed *yuvarāja*.[45] Kīrtipāla, the third son, was granted twelve villages, including Naḍḍulāi.[55] Towards the end of Ālhaṇa's reign he seems to have shared with his father and *yuvarāja* Kelhaṇa the government of Nāḍol, as evidenced by the Bāmnerā Grant of V. 1220 of which he was an approver.[56] In VI 1225 (?) he helped Kumārasiṁha in administering Maṇḍor and enjoyed himself a jāgīr which included Osia.[56a].

Ālhaṇa died somewhere between Śrāvaṇa, V. 1202 and Māgha, V. 1221.[57]

54. See Kīrtipāla's Nāḍol Plates, *EI*, IX, pp. 68 ff.

55. *Ibid.*

56. *EI*, XIII, p. 208. Wrongly ascribed to the reign of Kelhaṇa by the editor.

56a. (Osia inscription, unpublished).

57. Ālhaṇa's Bāmnerā inscription is dated 15th of the dark half of Srāvaṇa, V. 1220. Kelhaṇa's first inscription bears the date, the 2nd of the dark half of Māgha, V. 1221.

CHAPTER XV

THE CHAUHĀNS OF NĀḌOL: KELHAṆA AND HIS SUCCESSORS

For Ālhaṇa's eldest son and successor Kelhaṇa, we have sixteen inscriptions ranging from V. 1221 to 1250.[1] That he was associated with his father in the work of government as early as V. 1209 has been shown above. In V. 1218 he had been recognised as heir-apparent, and in V. 1220 we find the Bāmnerā inscription issued in his name and his father Ālhaṇa. This clearly shows the prominent position that he had in the administration of the kingdom. According to Jinamaṇḍana, he was one of the chiefs opposed to Arṇorāja but rather indifferently loyal to Kumārapāla.[2] This would indicate that he had come to the fore even earlier than V. 1209 *i.e.* about V. 1207, the probable year of the second fight between Arṇorāja of Śākambharī and Kumārapāla Chaulukya of Gujarāt.

It is not very often that Kelhaṇa's inscriptions mention his overlord. The Jhaṁverā record gives him even the title *Mahārājādhirāja-Parameśvara* borne generally by independent sovereigns.[3] He must therefore have been a very strong ruler. But that he continued to recognise Chaulukya supremacy, at least up to V. 1228, is clear from the Nāḍlāi Stone inscription of the year which refers itself to "the victorious reign of Kumārapāla when Kelhaṇa was ruling at Nāḍol."[4] In V. 1235 also, he acknowledged fealty to the Chaulukyas, because Nāḍol was, at the time of Muhammad Ghori's invasion of Gujarāt, regarded as a Gurjara

1. Sānḍerāv inscription (V. 1221). Bāmnerā Grant 1 (V. 1223), Bāmnerā Grant 2 (undated), Nāḍol inscription (V. 1223), Sādaḍī inscription (V. 1224), Jhraṁverā inscription (V. 1227), Hādlāi inscription (V. 1228), Pañchadevalī (Sirohī) inscription (V. 1231), Lālrāi inscription 1 (V. 1233), Lālrāi inscription 2 (V. 1233). Osiā inscription (V. 1236), Sānḍerā inscription (V. 1236), Pāla inscription (V. 1241), Pālaḍī inscription (V. 1249), Pāl inscription 2 (V. 1250), Osia (V. 125).

2. *Kumārapāladevaprabandha*, p. 41b.

3. *JASB*, 1916, pp. 103-104.

4. *EI*, XI, pp. 47-48.

fort captured by the Muslims.[5] Whether he did so later on in the reign of the weak Bhīmadeva II is a bit doubtful.[6]

We can have some idea of the extent of Kelhaṇa's kingdom and the system of his administration from his numerous inscriptions. In the south his dominions extended at least as far as Pālaḍī, a village in the Sirohī State which he put under his son Jayatasiṁha.[7] Māṇḍavyapura, the northern outpost of the kingdom, which had been in Ālhaṇa's reign under Kelhaṇa's younger brother Gajasiṁha, was respectively in V. 1241 and 1250 under Kelhaṇa's sons Kumārasiṁha Siṁhavikrama and Soḍhaladeva.[8] Saṇḍeraka, the western outpost was in the *bhukti* of Queen Jālhaṇadevī, and Goḍvāḍ was directly administered by Kelhaṇa himself. Pālaḍī and Māṇḍavypura seem to have been regular centres of provincial government, as evidenced by the stationing of a *mahāmātya* in the former place with a view to assisting the *kunwara* in the administration of the division[9]

The chief events of Kelhaṇa's reign were his battles with the Yādava Bhillima, the ruler of Devagiri, and Muhammad Ghorī, the well-known Muslim conqueror of northern India. In both of these actions he probably fought as a subordinate of the Gujarāt rulers. Bhillima invaded the Gurjara dominions before 1189 A.D.[10], say, somewhere between 1187, the year of his succession, and 1189 A.D., the year of his Mutugī inscriptions. As both the sides claim a victory, the fight may not have been very decisive in its character.[11] The fight with Muhammad Ghorī took place in 1178 A.D. when the Muslims, advancing by way of Multān

5. *PV*, X, 50.

6. Bhīmadeva II was a weak ruler. Many feudatory chiefs became independent during his reign. Kelhaṇa, however, may have recognised him as his overlord to the end.

7. See Kelhaṇa's Pālaḍī inscription (P.C. Nahar, *Jaina inscriptions*, I, p. 255 f.)

8. See Kelhaṇa's Pāla inscriptions, *JASB*, X, p. 407ff.

9. The name of the minister mentioned in the Pālḍī inscription is Vilhaṇa.

10. Bhillima was the Yādava ruler of Devagiri (c. 1187-1191 A.D.).

11. Sūndhā inscription, verse 34, mentions Kelhaṇa as having defeated Bhillima, the lord of the southern quarter. The Mutgi inscription, on the other hand, mentions Bhillima as "the dread roar of cloud to the flocks of those swans, the Gurjaras", under whose standard alone Kelhaṇa could have fought against the Yādavas. His own dominions never touched theirs.

Uchchha[21] and Kirāḍū[13] captured Nāḍol, the capital of Kelhaṇa. On reaching near Ābū the Muslims found themselves opposed by the combined forces of Kelhaṇa, his younger brother Kīrtipāla, Dhārāvarṣa, the Paramāra ruler of Ābū, and their overlord Bhīmadeva II. The Sūndhā Inscription puts the scene of battle at Kāsahrada, modern Kāyadrān of the Sirohī State,[14] a village about four miles from the Kīvarlī station on the Western Railway. The Gurjara army stationed itself at the mouth of the pass, and on being attacked, defeated the Muslim army and wounded their leader Muhammad Ghorī.[15] It was a decisive victory, for it kept away the Muslims from Hindustan for nearly thirteen years.

Kelhaṇa died before V.1251.[16] We know of his two daughters, one Śṛṅgāradevī who was married to Dhārāvarṣa, the Paramāra ruler of Mount Abu, and the other, Alhaṇadevī, a queen of the Pratihāra chief, Vigraha, of Gwālior.[17] The Lālrāi Inscription mentions Kelhaṇa's queen, Mahībaladevī (*EI*, XI, p. 49 f) and Jālhaṇadevī is known from Sāṇḍerāv Inscription. (*EI*, XI, p. 52). We have mentioned above some of his sons.[18] Another son, *Mahārājaputra* Chāmuṇḍarāya ruled at Maṇḍor in V. 1227. Of Kelhaṇa's grandsons Ajayasiṁha, son of Kuṁvarasiṁha, enjoyed a *jāgīr* at Bāmnerā, and Lakhanapāla and Sonapāla, sons of Kīrtipāla, were *jāgīrdārs* of Sonānā.[19]

Jayatasiṁha. Kelhaṇa was succeeded by his son Jayatasiṁha. In the Sādaḍī inscription of V. 1251, he is mentioned as

12. *Tabaqāt-i-Akbarī*, I, p. 36.

13. *PV*, p. 256 (Dr. G.H. Ojha's edition).

14. Sūndhā inscription. verse 36, *EI*, IX, p. 77. The place was identified with Kāyadrān by Dr. G.H. Ojha in his "History of Sirohī".

15. Briggs, *Tārikh-i-Firishta*, I, p. 170. Other writers also refer to the battle but give no details. Some idea of the actual events can, however, be had from the *Prabandhakośa* the account of which regarding the fight between Vīradhavala and the Muslims has been, I believe, based on the events as they actually occurred in 1178 A.D. Dhārāvarṣa, the ruler of Ābū, let the Muslims advance unmolested into the pass and then closed in upon them from the rear. In the front the Muslims were attacked by the Gurjaras. (See *PK*. p.117.)

16. In this year we get an inscription for his son and successor Jayatasiṁhadeva.

17. See respectively *Prāchīnajainalekhasaṅgraha* of Muni Jinavijaya and *PRAS*, *WC*, 1915-16, p. 59.

18. See above p. 157.

19. See below, Kīrtipāla's account.

Mahārājādhirāja Jayatasiṁha, son of Kelhaṇa.[20] We cannot agree with Dr. D.R. Bhandarkar's identification of this Jayatasiṁha with the Jayatasiṁha of the Bhīnmāl inscription of V. 1239,[21] because the Nāḍol kingdom never included Bhīnmāl. On the west it extended as far as Sāṇḍerāv, after which began the kingdom of Jālor; and even Jālor did not include Bhīnmāl before Udayasiṁha's reign.

In 1196 A.D. the Mers tried to expel the Muslims from Ajmer. Qutbuddīn Aibak, who rushed to the help of the beleaguered garrison, was himself defeated by the combined force of the Mers and the Chaulukyas of Gujarāt and forced to shut himself up in the fort and sustain a siege.[22] Timely arrival of reinforcements from Ghaznā saved the situation, and enabled the Muslims in their turn to assume the offensive. The Chaulukya feudatory, Jayatasiṁha vacated his forts of Pālī and Nāḍol and joining hands with Dhārāvarṣa Paramāra of Ābū and his equally renowned brother, Pālhaṇa or Prahlādana, faced the Muslim army in a pass near Ābū.[23]

Had the Hindu army stayed there, the Muslims might have retired without striking a blow. It was here that Muhammad Ghorī had been defeated and wounded eighteen years back; the Muslims had no desire to see the same fate befalling their commander, Qutbuddīn Aibak.[24] But mistaking this natural disinclination of the Muslims to advance for weakness, Jayatsiṁha and his friends abandoned their advantageous position and moved on to the plains where they were defeated after a fight lasting from early dawn till midday. Many Hindu leaders

20. Noticed by Dr. D.R. Bhandarkar, *EI*, XI, p. 73.

21. *Ibid.*

22. *Tāju-l Ma-āsīr*, *ED*, II, pp, 228-231.

23. *Ibid.* The names of the Hindu leaders have been given as Darabaras and Karaṇ by Hasan Nizāmī. Firishta calls them Darabaraz and Wallin (*TF*, I, p, 196). The identity of Darabaraz and Dhārāvarṣa is obvious enough. Karaṇ or Wallin is generally identified with Kelhaṇa of Nāḍol, which however must be regarded as a mistake, because Kelhaṇa had died either in or before V. 1251 (1194-95 A.D.). *i.e.*, one year before this battle of Ābū. It i s better to identify Wāllin, as done by us, with Pālhaṇa or Prahlādana, the heir apparent and younger brother of Dhārāvarṣa.

24. See *Taju-l Ma-āsīr*, *ED*, II, p. 230.

were slain or taken prisoners.[25] Jayatasiṁha might have been one of them.[26]

Sāmantasiṁha. For the years V. 1256-1258, we have five inscriptions of *Mahārāja* Sāmantasiṁha, three at Bāmnerā (Jodhpur Division), one at Uthmān (Sirohī), and one at Sāṇḍerāv (Jodhpur).[27] Considering their dates, as well as their provenance, *i.e.*, the principality of Nāḍol, we prefer ascribing them to Sāmantasiṁha of Nāḍol, a probable successor of Jayatasiṁha, than to Guhila Sāmantasiṁha of Mewāṛ-Dūngarpur[28] for whom we have two inscriptions, both of them near the Dūngarpur-Mewāṛ border and dated in the Vikrama years 1228 and 1236.[29]

In V. 1283, the territory near Nānā was under one Chahamā (Chāhamāna) Dhāṁḍhaladeva, son of Visadhavala, a feudatory of Bhīmadeva II.[30] His relationship to Jayatasiṁha and Sāmantasiṁha is unknown. Somewhere between V. 1262 and V. 1314, probably before V. 1288, Nāḍol passed into the hands of Udayasiṁha of Jālor.[31]

25. See *Tālju-l Ma-āsir*, *ED*, II, p. 230.
26. At least we hear no more of him after 1196 A.D.
27. See Dr. D.R. Bhandarkar's *Inscriptions of Northern India*, p. 64.
28. *Ibid.* Dr. D.R. Bhandarkar's suggestion regarding the ascription of the records to Guhila Sāmantasiṁha is accepted by Dr. H.C. Ray.
29. See the *Annual Report of the Rājputānā Museum, Ajmer*, 1914-1915.
30. Noticed by D.R. Bhandarkar, *PRAS, WC*, 1907-1908, p. 49.
31. See below.

CHAPTER XVI

THE CHAUHĀNS OF JĀLOR : KĪRTIPĀLA AND SAMARASIṀHA

Kīrtipāla. The founder of the Jālor line of the Chauhāns was Kīrtipāla, the youngest of the three sons of Ālhaṇa and Ānnalladevī. The heir-apparent Kelhaṇa and the ruler Ālhaṇa had either in V. 1218 or earlier granted him twelve villages of which Naḍḍulāī was the chief.[1] In the year V. 1220 he seems to have been given also some share in the government of the Nāḍol kingdom, for we find him countersigning and approving a grant made by Ajayasī, son of *Mahārājaputra* Kumarasī.[2] The same participation is proved by the Osian inscription of V. 1235 which mentions Kīrtipāla as *Najyavāhaka* while Kelhaṇa's son, Kumārasiṁha Siṁhavikrama ruled over Māṇḍavyapura and Kīrtipāla had Osian as his *bhukti.* In the Sūndhā inscription he is called the lord of Nāḍol.[3] This besides implying that he was a prince of the Nāḍol branch, perhaps points also to the share he had once in the government of his father. But he no longer countersigns or approves, nor is he found in charge of any post in the kingdom. In V. 1235, as shown above, he helped Kumārasiṁha in bearing the burden of government. Further as we find that even Sonānā, one of the twelve villages of Kuṅralars *jāgīr* in V. 1218 and the possession of his sons Abhayapāla and Lākhaṇapāla in V. 1233, had been assigned to a Thākura named Anasīha[4], who perhaps had no connection whatsoever with Kīrtipāla, it would perhaps not be wrong to conclude that the ruler could transfer a prince from one jagir to another. The two brothers do not seem after all to have been very cordial. Though the system left all the power to Kīrtipāla, it did not satisfy him a man of ambitious and adventurous nature, to seek his fortunes elsewhere.

1. *EI.*, Vol. IX, pp. 68 ff.

2. *EI.*, Vol. XIII, p. 208. The grant is, as shown above, not one of Kalhaṇa, but of Ālhaṇa.

3. श्रीजाबालिपुरे स्थितिं व्यरचयन्नड्डूल-राजेश्वरः ।

EI, IX, p. 77.

4. *EI*, XI, p. 48.

In Mewār of those days he found a ready field for the full exercise of his superabundant energy and intellect. Its ruler Sāmantasiṁha, though extremely brave as well as handsome,[5] had created enemies for himself both inside and outside his kingdom. He turned the nobles against himself by forfeiting their *jāgirs*,[6] and rendered the Chaulukyas of Gujarāt hostile to himself by wounding their ruler Ajayapāla in a battle fought about V. 1232.[7] Kīrtipāla realised fully the advantages offered by such a situation for an invader. Discontented perhaps with his lot at Nāḍol and also egged on and partly helped by the Chaulukyas who were eager to see Sāmantasiṁha punished for the insult to their arms, he attacked Mewār and drove out Sāmantasiṁha from there before V. 1236.[8] But however discontented the nobles of Mewār might have been, they do not appear to have liked the idea of being ruled by a rank outsider like Kīrtipāla. So, coming together, they offered the throne to Sāmantasiṁha's younger brother Kumārasiṁha[9] who proved himself

5. सामन्तसिंह-नामा कामाधिकसुन्दर-शरीरः ।
भूपालोऽजनि तस्मादपहृत-सामन्त-सर्वस्वः ॥
EI, XVI, p. 349.

6. *Ibid*, line 2.

7. Dr. G. H. Ojha cites the following two verses in support of his view that Ajayapāla was wounded by Sāmantasiṁha of Mewār :—

(i) सामन्तसिंह-समिति-क्षत-विक्षतौजाः
श्री-गूर्ज्जर-क्षितिपरक्षण-दक्षिणासिः ।
प्रह्लादनस्तदनुजो दनुजोत्तमारिः
चारित्रमत्र पुनरुज्ज्वलयांचकार
Mount Ābū, Lūṇigavasahīpraśasti, verse 38.

(ii) यः शौचसंयमपटुः कटुकेश्वराख्य-
माराध्य भूधरसुताघटितार्धदेहम् ।
तां दारुणामपि रणांगणजातघात-
व्रातव्यथामजयपालनृपादपास्थत् ॥

The view has found general acceptance with historians.

8. See the words, "Saṁvat 1236......Sāṁvatasiṁhadevarājye" from a Ḍūngarpur State inscription. (G. H. Ojha, *History of Dungarpur*, p. 35.)

9. This is how I interpret the story of Naiṇsī that Sāmantasiṁha getting pleased with the services of his younger brother Kumārasiṁha offered to him the throne of Mewār, and he, after remaining unwilling for a while, accepted it on the condition that the nobles of Mewār approved of the transfer. (See Naiṇsī's *Khyāt*, I, p. 78).

not merely a good leader but also an astute politician, for he won over to his side his old enemies, the Chaulukyas, and succeeded with their help in ousting Kīrtipāla from the territory of Mewār.[10]

Kīrtipāla could have hardly relished this sort of behaviour on the part of the Chaulukya ruler whom till then, perhaps, he had been regarding as his best supporter and whom he had helped in routing the forces of Muhammad Ghorī in the stiffly fought battle of Kāsahrada (V. 1235). What he naturally expected was gratitude and the recognition of his title to the new conquest. But the Chaulukyas had not, in all likelihood, after the first flush of joy at the defeat of their enemy Sāmanatasiṁha, ever liked the idea of Mewār being in the hands of an ambitious and energetic Prince like Kīrtipāla and hence recognised instead the claims of Kumārasiṁha. Highly incensed by this ingratitude and partiality for his enemy, Kīrtipāla seems to have disowned the allegiance to the Chaulukya throne in the latter part of his reign. On the basis of this supposition alone can we explain his attacks on territories included at the time in the Chaulukya empire and also the complete absence of the names of the rulers of Gujarāt in the records of the rulers of Jālor. Kīrtipāla was the first Jālor ruler to initiate an anti-Chaulukya policy. His successors merely followed in his footsteps. Kirāḍu or Kirātakūṭa whose ruler Āsala is mentioned in the Sūṇdhā inscription as wounded by Kirtipala's arrows[11] was a Chaulukya dependency. In V. 1209 and 1218, its rulers are mentioned as recognising the suzerainty

10. (a) सामन्तसिंहनामा भूपतिर्भूतले जातः ॥१४१॥
भ्राता कुमारसिंहोऽभूत् स्वराज्यग्राहिणं परं
देशान्निष्कासयामास कीर्तिसंज्ञं नृपं तु यः ॥१५०॥
स्वीकृतमाघाटपुरं नृपति प्रसाद्य
(Kumbhalgarh *Praśasti*)

(b) खोम्माणसंतति-वियोगविलक्ष्मलक्ष्मी-
मेनामदृष्टविरहां गुहिलान्वयस्य ।
राजन्वतीं वसुमतीमकरोत् कुमार-
सिंहस्ततो रिपुगतामपहृत्य भूयः ॥
(*EI.*, XVI, p. 349)

11. यो दुर्द्दान्त-किरात-कूटनृपतिं भित्त्वा शरैरासलम् ।
v. 36, *EI.*, IX, p. 77.

of Kumārapāla.[12] In V. 1235, it was ruled by Madanabrahmadeva, a feudatory of Bhīmadeva II.[13] Āsala was probably Madanabrahma's successor. Similarly Jāvālipura or Jālor which Kīrtipāla attacked and conquered and which became the capital of his new kingdom was a Paramāra dependency in Kumārapāla's reign. Kumārapāla built there a temple called Kuvaravihāra,[14] and Vigraharāja IV of Sapādalakṣa burnt it (Jālor) while fighting a war of vengeance against the Chaulukyas[15]. It continued in the hands of the Chaulukyan feudatories approximately up to V. 1238 when Kīrtipāla captured it.

According to Naiṇsī, Jālor and Siwāṇā, ruled respectively by the Paramāras Kuntapāla and Vīranārāyaṇa, were betrayed into Kīrtipāla's hands by their own servants the Dahiyās[16]; and epigraphic evidence supports Naiṇsī as regards the name of the dynasty which held sway at Jālor at the time of its capture by the Chāhamānas. Vīsala Paramāra's inscription[17] found in the *topkhānā* at Jālor gives the names of six Paramāra rulers, of whom the last, Vīsala, was ruling there in V. 1174. Kuntapāla was probably a descendant of this Vīsala. That he was most probably a feudatory of the Chaulukyas can be assumed on the basis of the evidence adduced in the last paragraph.

As the first record of the successor of Kīrtipāla belongs to V. 1239, Kīrtipāla must have died in this year or thereabouts. He was an ambitious, energetic and extremely resourceful person. It was no mean achievement for a younger scion of a feudatory family to have carved out for himself a kingdom in that hilly tract of Mewār which in future resisted for years even the great might of the Mughals of Delhi; and the achievement was still greater when, on being compelled by circumstances to evacuate it, he had resource and courage enough to lay the foundations of another kingdom almost equal in strength to that ruled over by his elder brother Kelhaṇa; and that too most

12. P.C. Nahar—*Jain inscriptions*, I, pp. 251 ff.

13. See Madanabrahma's inscription noticed by Dr. D.R. Bhandarkar, *PRAS*, *WC* 1906-7, p. 42, and edited by Bishveshwarnāth Reu, *IA.*, 1933.

14. See *EI.*, XI, p. 55f.

15. See above the account of Vigraharāja IV.

16. *Khyāt*, I, p. 152.

17. The six rulers named are Vākpatirāja, Chandana, Devarāja, Vijjala, Dhārāvarṣa and Vīsala.

probably by acting against the mighty Chaulukya power which had shown its strength not merely by evicting Kīrtipāla from Mewār but also measured swords successfully with the redoubtable to Muhammad Ghorī. That Kīrtipāla was one of the best generals of his time would be obvious enough if we consider his achievements even cursorily. That he was a good orthodox Hindu and at the same time a tolerant ruler is shown by his grant of V. 1218[18] where he is represented as worshipping the well-known Hindu deities Sūrya and Maheśvara, offering oblations to the sacred fire and then granting a benefaction to the Jain temple of Mahāvīra. His fame outlived his times. The well-known chronicler Naiṇsī says that "Kītū was a great Rājpūt". This is the highest form of praise that he gives to any ruler.[19]

Samarasiṁha. For Kīrtipāla's son and successor Samarasiṁha, we have two inscriptions at Jālor, dated respectively in the Vikrama years 1239 and 1256. The first refers to the *rājya-chintaka Rājaputra* Jojala, the maternal uncle of Samarasiṁha, who had put down the disturbances caused by the bandits of Pīlvāhikā.[20] These marauders are identified by Dr. D.R. Bhandarkar with the *bāvrīs* of Pīlvā, a village of the Parbatsar district of the Jodhpur State.[21] The second inscription, besides supplying two important dates, V. 1242 and 1256, for Samarasiṁha's reign,[22] shows that the *vidhichaitya* movement which illiberal rulers like Jojaladeva of Nāḍol had tried to strangle, had since then grown greatly in strength and was sponsored by strong rulers like Kumārapāla and Samarasiṁha.

The Sūndhā Inscription describes Samarasiṁha as fond of building, friendly towards the learned, and very charitable. He gave many *tulādānas*[23] and built extensive ramparts on the Kanakāchala or Suvarṇagiri at Jālor, equipping them with machines of many kinds, storehouses and battlements of the Vidyādharī

18. See *EI*, IX, p. 66 ff.
19. *Khyāt*, I, p. 152.
20. See *EI*, XI, pp. 53-54.
21. *Ibid.* The identification is probably right though Pīlvā does not seem at the time to have been included in the kingdom of Jālor.
22. *Ibid.*, p. 55. The date, V. 1242, would refer to Samarasiṁha, if we do not interpret the word *rājakula* in the inscription as the "royal family", as done by Dr. D.R. Bhandarkar, but regard it as the Sanskrit form of "Rāwal". Alhaṇa is called "Rājakula" in Kīrtipāla's plates of V. 1218 (*EI*, IX, p. 69) and the *Prabandhakośa*, p. 125.
23. Sūndhā inscription, verse 40.

type.[24] He built also a town named Samarapura which he beautified with[25] gardens. His sister Rūdaladevī built at Jālor two temples dedicated to Śiva.[26] Bhaṇḍārī Yaśovīra, repaired the temple called Kunvara vihāra by his orders.[27]

Samarasiṁha must have died before V. 1262, the date of the first inscription of his son and successor Udayasiṁha. He had also an elder son named Mānavasiṁha whose descendants were founders of the Chauhān kingdom of Chandrāvatī and Mount Ābū.[28] Samarasiṁha's daughter, Līlādevī, was married to Bhīmadeva II of Gujarāt.[29]

24. Sūndhā inscription, verse 38. Hasan Nizāmī, the author of the *Tājul Ma-āsir* calls Jālor that "exceedingly strong fortress, the gates of which had never before been opened by any conqueror" (*ED*, II, p. 238.)

25. Sūndhā inscription, verse 40.

26. *Ibid.*, verse 41.

27. See the Jālor inscription, No. 2 edited by Dr. D.R. Bhandarkar, *EI*, XI, 55.

28. See the Achalgarh inscription of Luṇṭigadeva, v. 20. See also our paper on the Devaḍā Chauhāns of Chandrāvatī and Ābū in the *Rājasthān Bhāratī*, I, Part 4, pp. 1-9.

29. *IA*, pp. 194 ff.

CHAPTER XVI

THE CHAUHĀNS OF JĀLOR (*continued*) : UDAYASIṀHA

For Udayasiṁha, the successor of Samarasiṁha, we have four Bhīnmāl inscriptions,[1] dated respectively in the Vikrama years 1262, 1274, 1305, and 1306.[1] Dated in the last of these years is also a manuscript of the *Nirbhayabhīmavyāyoga* of Rāmachandra.[2] It was long believed on the basis of these references that the latest date of Udayasiṁha was approximately V. 1306. But recently the discovery of the *Kharataragachchhapaṭṭāvali* begun by Jinapāla and continued by his successors enables us to push forward the date by nearly eight years. The book contains two notices of this important ruler, dated respectively in the Vikrama years 1310 and 1314.[3] In all, Udayasiṁha might thus be taken to have ruled for nearly 52 years.

From the Sūndhā Inscription we learn that Udayasiṁha was the lord of the districts of Naḍḍula, Jābālipura, Māṇḍavyapura, Vāgbhaṭameru, Sūrāchanda, Rāṭahrada, Kheḍa, Rāmasainya, Śrīmāla, Ratnapura, Satyapura, etc.[4] Of these Jābālipura or Jālor had been the capital of Udayasiṁha's ancestors since the days of Kīrtipāla. Naḍḍula was probably conquered from the Muslims during the rule of the weak Ārām Shāh.[5] Māṇḍavyapura or Maṇḍor had been, as already shown, once the outpost of the kingdom of Nāḍol. Udayasiṁha probably conquered it at the same time as Nāḍol. Iltutmish recaptured it in 1226 A.D.[6] After remaining in the hands of the Muslims at least upto 1242 A.D. it passed once again into Chauhān possession, for it had to be reconquered in 1294 A.D. by Jalāluddīn Khaljī.[7]

1. For the first three inscriptions see the *Bombay Gazetteer*, I, Pt. 1, pp. 474-476. For the fourth inscription See *EI*, XI, pp. 56-57.
2. Quoted by Dr. D.R. Bhandarkar, *EI*, XI, p. 76.
3. See pp. 50-51.
4. *EI*, IX, p. 73.
5. It had been captured by the Muslims in 1197 A.D. See *Tāju'l-Maāsir*, *ED* II, p. 229.
6. *Tabaqāt-i-Nāsirī*, I, p. 611.
7. *ED*, III,p. 148.

Vāgbhaṭameru or Bāhaḍmer was, according to Naiṇsī, once the seat of a Paramāra principality.[8] Kirāḍū, which is only a few miles from it, was in V. 1218 under Someśvara Paramāra, in V. 1235 under *Mahārājaputra* Madanabrahmadeva, and thereafter under Āsala.[9] Is it not likely that Bāhaḍmer too might have been under this Paramāra principality of Kirāḍū before its capture by the Chauhāns ? Satyapura was, according to Naiṇsī, captured from the Dahiyā Rājpūts by Vijayasiṁha Chauhān, son of Ālhaṇa[10]. As Sālha, a great-grandson of Vijayasiṁha, was a contemporary and *sāmanta* of Udayasiṁha's great-grandson Kānhaḍadeva,[11] Vijayasiṁha may have been Udayasiṁha's feudatory and the son of an Ālhaṇa different from Ālhaṇa, the ruler of Nāḍol. Rāṭahrada, later on known as Rāḍadharā, was situated in the same tract as the other Paramāra principalities mentioned above.[12] Kheḍa is the well known town of this name situated near the bend of the river Lūnī. Rāmasainya is the modern Rāmsen. Ratnapura was under a chief named Pūnapākṣadeva in the reign of Kumārapāla Chaulukya[13]. It must have been conquered from some one of his successors by the Chauhāns.

All these places had once been in the empire of the Chaulukyas of Gujarāt. How they actually passed out of their hands is not clear. But some of these, perhaps, were surrendered about V. 1278[14] when Lavaṇaprasāda the all-powerful minister of Gujarāt, and his son Vīradhavala had to fight against the Yādava ruler Siṁhana who had crossed the river Tāptī and was laying waste the Gurjara lands near Broach.[15] Udayasiṁha formed a powerful confederacy consisting of the Guhilas of Mewār, the Paramāras of Chandrāvatī, the rulers of Godrahā and Lāṭa, and four important Mārwār rulers including himself

8. *Khyāt*, I, p. 233.
9. See above the account of Kīrtipāla.
10. See below the account of the Chauhāns of Satyapura.
11. Ibid.
12. *Khayāt* II, p. 341.
13. *Bhāvnagar Inscriptions*, p. 206.
14. Most probably the western districts of the dominions described in the Sūndhā Inscription passed into his hands as a result of the revolt in V. 1278.
15. *Kīrtikaumudī*, IV, 59.

and attacked Lavaṇaprasāda's territory from the rear.[16] Lavaṇaprasāda tried to save the situation by concluding treaties with Siṁha of Broach and Siṁhana Yādava of Devagiri and turning almost immediately northwards to fight against the Mārwār confederacy.[17] In the fight that followed Udayasiṁha was wounded on the head by Lavaṇaprasāda.[18] The victory however remained with Udayasiṁha and his allies. "Lāvaṇyaprasāda, though still sore and hostile at heart," says the pro-Chaulukya chronicle *Kīrtikaumudī* "had to return to his capital, concluding a treaty with these heroic rulers on account of the trouble caused to his relatives and the public."[19]

Lavaṇaprasāda's son Vīradhavala fully honoured the treaty thus concluded. Udayasiṁha also, laying aside all feelings of rancour, gave his daughter in marriage to Vīrama, the eldest son of Vīradhavala. When the forces of Iltutmish tried to march into Gujarāt after burning and sacking parts of Mewār, Udyasiṁha and his allies helped Vīradhavala.[20]

For nearly sixteen years these cordial relations were maintained without any deceitful movement on either side. But in V. 1295, Vīradhavala died, leaving behind him two sons, Vīrama and Vīsala, to fight for the throne. Udayasiṁha should, as the father-in-law of the elder brother Vīrama, have sided with him. But strangely enough he had him assassinated,[21] most probably by his own son Chāchigadeva who, in his Sūndhā Inscription, prides himself on the destruction "of the roaring Gurjara lord Vīrama." The *Prabandhakośa* ascribes this rather inexplicable action to the influence of Vīsala's partisan, the powerful minister, Vastupāla; but it does so wrongly, for

16. According to the *Sukṛtakīrtikallolinī* (v. 75), Lavaṇaprasāda was on hostile terms with the rulers of Mewār and Chandrāvatī. The *Kīrtikaumudī* (II, 69) speaks of his wounding the ruler of Nāḍol in battle. So the four Mārwār princes who according to the *Kīrtikaumudī*, opposed Lavaṇaprasāda and Vīradhavala must have naturally included these three. See also the *Hammīramadamardana*, p. 11.

17. See the *Kīrtikaumudī*, IV, for the fight with the Mārwār rulers. For the draft of the treaty with Siṁhana see the *Lekhapaddhati* (G.O.S.) p. 52.

18. The *Kīrtikaumudī*, II, 69 and IV, 61.

19. *Ibid*, IV, 67.

20. *Hammīramadamardana* pr. II.

21. *PK.*, p. 125.

Vīrama instead of dying in Vastupāla's time survived him by three years or so. Vastupāla died in V. 1296.[22] Vīrama was on the throne of Dholkā up to V. 1299.[23]

There was also some fighting of an indecisive character between Udayasiṁha and Vīrama's successful rival and brother, Vīsala. If the *Purātanaprabandhasaṅgraha* be believed, Udayasiṁha had towards the end of his reign grown so proud of his might that he twice dared to ask Vīsala for tribute. Vīsala replied by sending punitive expeditions to Jālor, which however did not accomplish much.[24] To the last, Udayasiṁha remained, as aptly put by the Sūndhā Inscription, "invincible for the lords of the Gurjara kingdom."[25]

Udayasiṁha is said to have curbed the pride of the Turuṣkas.[26] The claim is in some sense true, for early in his reign he extended his territories at the cost of the rulers of Delhi, most probably of Ārām Shāh and perhaps even of Iltutmish. The capture of Nāḍol and Maṇḍor were notable feats,[27] and so was also the defeat of the Muslims near Jālor which is mentioned in an old *apabhraṁśa* verse (quoted by both the *Purātanaprabandhasaṅgraha* and *Naiṇsī's Khyāt*) which states that "the water which the *asuras* (the Muslims) had drunk from lake Sundara with their mouths was taken by the ruler Udaya out of the eyes of their (grief-stricken) wives."[28] But once Iltutmish had firmly secured his hold on the throne of Delhi, he tried to pay off the old scores. "The evil deeds and improprieties of the Chauhāns" had to be avenged some day.[29] The expedition against Jālor was by no means easy.[30] The army suffered for

22. See *Vasantavilāsa* (G.O.S.) , XIV, 37.
23. *Catalogue of the MSS. in Paṭṭan Bhaṇḍārs*, (G.O.S.)
24. p. 50.
25. verse 46 (*EI.*, IX, p. 78)
26. *Ibid.*
27. See above.
28. *Purātanaprabandhasaṅgraha*, p. 50; *Naiṇsī's Khyāt*, I, p. 153.
29. *Tāju-l Ma-āsir, ED*, II, p. 238, states for instance,
"After some time they represented to his Majesty that the inhabitants of the fort of Jalewar (Jālor) had determined to revenge the blood which had been shed and once or twice mention of the evil deeds and improprieties of that people was made before the sublime throne."
30. *Ibid. Tāju-l Ma-āsir* writes of the country of Udayasiṁha. "One might have thought that nothing but the faces of demons and sprites could be seen and the means of escape were not on the tablet of even providential design.

lack of food as well as water. But Iltutmish pushed on, and managed to reach Udayasiṁha's desert capital. Udayasiṁha opened negotiations ; and the Sultān though he could hardly have been satisfied with the token tribute of a hundred camels and two hundred horses offered by Udayasiṁha, accepted it and confirmed Udayasiṁha in his possessions.[31]

Nearly five years later, perhaps in V. 1278 when Iltutmish once again assumed the offensive against Rājasthān,[32] and after sacking Nāgdā advanced even upon Gujarāt, Udayasiṁha joined as already stated above, the league organised by Vīradhavala Vāghelā of Dholkā and his minister Vastupāla.[33] Iltutmish withdrew without fighting. He must have realised the difficulty,

31. *Ibid.* According to the *Purātanaprabandhasaṅgraha*, which tries to belittle Udayasiṁha's achievements on account of its pro-Gujarāt bias, the achievement of Iltutmish was a little more substantial. Fearing that his fort would fall as a result of the Sultān's mining operations, Udayasiṁha is said to have given 36 lacs of *pārutthaka drammas* by way of tribute and the son of his minister Yaśovīra as a hostage. On the withdrawal of the Sultān he raised money from Brāhmaṇas and temples and rebuilt the undermined walls of *Suvarṇagiri*. (*Purātanaprabandhasaṅgraha*, pp. 50-51).

32. The drama gives the name of the Muslim invader as *Mīlachchhrīkāra*, which Dr. G.H. Ojha equates with *Amīr-i-shikār*, a title once borne by Iltutmish. Drs. D.R. Barnett and H.C. Ray object to the identification, saying that *Mīlachchhrīkāra* cannot phonetically be the Sanskritised form of *Amīr-i-shikār*. It is no doubt so; but it can be easily the Paiśāchī form of *Mīr-i-shikār*. The Muslim ruler and his minister talk with each other in Paiśāchī; so it is only natural that he should have a Paiśāchī name. The dramatist changes *Mir* into *Mīla* and *shikār* into *chhrīkāra*, through the intermediate Sanskritised form Śrīkāra. The usual *sandhi* rules thereafter give us the *Mīlachchhrīkāra*, actually used in the drama.

As regards the date of this expedition we put it about V. 1278 (1221 A.D.) on the following grounds :—

(a) As the *MS.* of the drama, in which it is mentioned, is dated V. 1286, this would be the last date possible for it.

(b) Vastupāla, the chief organiser of the anti-Muslim Confederacy, was at the time Governor of Cambay. As he was appointed to the post in V. 1276, the expedition must have been launched between V. 1276 and 1286.

(c) As Vastupāla was transferred from his Cambay post in V. 1279, the limits can further be reduced to V. 1276-1279.

(d) Jalāluddin Manghabarnī appeared on the Indian scene in 1221 A.D. (V. 1278). If he be the Khapparakhāna of the *Hammīramadamardana*, the exact date of Iltutmish's raid may be put down as V. 1278.

33. See the *Hammīramadamardana*, pages 11 and 21-24.

if not folly, of facing the combined forces of Gujarāt and of the Mārwār princes, Udayasiṁha, Somasiṁha, and Dhārāvarṣa. And then there was another reason. His own frontiers were being threatened by Khapparakhāna whom we may, with some plausibility, identify with the dispossessed Khwārizmī prince, Jalāluddīn Manghbarnī.[34] In 1226 Iltutmish recaptured Māṇḍor.[35] As it is however listed in V. 1319 as one of Udayasiṁha's possessions, he must have recaptured it during the period V. 1283-1314.

Of other fights, Udayasiṁha must have had many during that period of political instability when everyone fought either in self-defence or for self-aggrandizement. The Sūndhā Inscription mentions Udayasiṁha's slaughter of one Sindhurāja,[36] whom Dr. D.R. Bhandarkar identifies on rather weak grounds with Sindhurājā Chāhamāna of Broach.[37] Actually he might have been some petty ruler of Sind.[38] Another rival and enemy of Udayasiṁha was Jaitrasiṁha of Mewār. According to the Ghāgsā inscription (V. 1332) of Mahārāval Tejasiṁha, the pride of Jaitrasiṁha (c. V. 1270-1309) was never brought low by the lord of Śākambharī.[39] The Chirwā Inscription of Mahārāval Samarasiṁha repeats the same statement in almost identical terms, substituting the word *Māraveśa* for "Śākambharīśvara";[40]

34. Iltutmish's invasion of Mewār and Gujarāt can, as shown in this chapter, be placed between the narrow limits V. 1276-1279; and V. 1278, when Jalāluddīn Manghbarnī reached India, would not at all be an unreasonable date, if we remember that Iltutmish's expedition synchronised with Śaṅkha's second attempt to capture Broach. His first attempt had been in V. 1277, shortly after Vastupāla's appointment as governor of Cambay.

35. *Tabaqāt-i-Nāsirī*, I, p. 611.

36. Verse 46, *EI*, X, p. 78.

37. *EI*, XI, p. 75. We prefer Dr. Kielhorn's interpretation of the term Sindhurāja as a ruler of Sindh.

38. A ruler of Sindh probably, because Sindhurāja of Broach, is known to have been slain not by Udayasiṁha but the Yādava ruler Siṁhana of Devagirī. (See above, Chapter II).

39. श्रीमद्गूर्ज्जरमालवतुरुष्कशाकम्भरीश्वरैर्यस्य
चक्रे न मानभङ्गो स स्वस्थो जयतु जैत्रसिंहनृपः ।
(G. H. Ojha, *History of Udaipur* I, p. 156)

40. न मालवीयेन न गौर्जरेण न मारवेशेन न जाङ्गलेन ।
म्लेच्छाधिनाथेन कदापि मानो ग्लानिं न निन्येवनिपस्य तस्य ॥
(Verse 6, Dr. G.H. Ojha's transcription)

and what this record meant by *Māraveśa* can be seen from his Ābū Inscription which states that Jaitrasiṁha destroyed Naḍūla.[41] The fort is known to us from the Sūndhā Inscription as one of Udayasiṁha's most important conquests.[42] Finally, however, even in this fight, the advantage rested with Udayasiṁha. Mostly the Mewār inscriptions do not say that Jaitrasiṁha defeated Udayasiṁha ; they put forward only the negative claim that the ruler of Maru or *Śākambharīśvara* did not succeed in breaking Jaitrasiṁha's pride. All claims of Guhila success are belied by the fact that in V. 1326 we find Chauhāns ruling not only over Goḍvāḍ but also a part of Medapāṭa.[43]

Udayasiṁha died somewhere between Māgha, V. 1314 and Māgha, V. 1316.[44] He had, at the least, two queens, Prahlādanadevī, the mother of Chāchigadeva and Chāmuṇḍarāja[45] and another, unknown to us by her name, the mother of Prince Vāhaḍasiṁha.[46] Of his daughters, one, as already mentioned,[47] was married to Vīrama, the eldest son of Vīradhavala Vāghelā of Dholkā; and of his brothers, Mānavasiṁha, who though older than Udayasiṁha had for some reason resigned his claim to Jālor and become the founder of a family from which are descended the present Mahārājas of Sirohī.[48]

Udayasiṁha was lucky in having a very good minister in Yaśovīra, a son of Dusāja Udaya. He began serving Jālor as early as V. 1245,[49] if not earlier still, and was at the helm of its affairs at least up to V. 1278,[50] when along with another Jaina minister, Vastupāla, he was responsible for an alliance

41. नडूलकूलंकख(ष)बाहुयोर्नि: · · ·

(*EI*, XVI, p. 349)

42. See above p. 143.

43. See the Karaheṭaka inscription of Chāchigadeva (*Jainasatyaprakāśa*, I, p. 10). Karaheṭaka is in Medapāṭa.

44. The *Kharataragachchhapaṭṭāvalī* gives Māgha V. 1314 for Udayasiṁha and Māgha, V. 1316 for his son, Chāchigadeva.

45. Sūndhā inscription, verse 45, *EI*, X, p. 78.

46. *Bombay Gazetteer*, I, Part I, p. 476.

47. See above, p. 145.

48. For a detailed account of the Devarās of Chandrāvatī and Ābū see my paper on the subject in the *Rājasthāna Bhāratī*, II. See also below.

49. See the *Arbudalekhasandoha*, Inscription Nos. 150-151.

50. See the *Hammīramadamardana*, p. 11.

between Udayasiṁha and Vīradhavala Vāghelā of Dholkā. If we place reliance on the account of the *Purātanaprabandhasaṅgraha*, he must have occupied this post even in V. 1300 or so.[51] His must have been always a moderating influence on the ambitious and aggressive policy of his master. Cultured and learned, he was an ornament of the court of Jālor. Someśvara describes him as a great poet surpassing in poetic excellence even Abhinanda, Māgha and Kālidāsa.[52] Others speak of him as *Sarasvatīkaṇṭhābharaṇa* and *Kavīndrabandhu*, showing thereby that he was an excellent poet as well as a patron of poets and *paṇḍits*.[53]

Udayasiṁha was the greatest of the Chauhān rulers of Jālor. He ascended the throne at a time when Hindu kingdoms were falling like ninepins before the terrible onset of Ghorīs and their lieutenants. The Chauhān empire of Sapādalakṣa and the kingdom of Nāḍol, from which Jālor had branched off nearly a quarter of a century back, had disappeared ; the power of Bhīmadeva II of Gujarāt had been crippled for the time being as a result of Qutbuddīn's invasion and sack of the wealthiest cities of the Gurjara empire. A person of lesser calibre than Udayasiṁha might have been borne down by the sheer weight of such adverse conditions. To Udayasiṁha the circumstances came as an incentive to hard solid work; and combined with caution and prudence, which some of his Chauhān predecessors had lacked, these opened the way to his future prosperity. Probably within a short time of Qutbuddīn's death he swooped down on the Muslim garrisons in eastern and northern Mārwār and made himself master of the greater part of the territory once comprised in the kingdom of Nāḍol. To Muslims he appeared as an avenging spirit, an embodiment of retribution for the blood that they had shed.[54] Even Iltutmish, the greatest

51. See p. 50. According to it, Yaśovīra was Udayasiṁha's minister when *amātya* Nāgaḍa besieged Jālor at the orders of his master, Vīsaladeva. As Vīsaladeva ascended the throne of Aṇahillapāṭaka in V. 1300, according to Merutuṅga's Therāvalī, some year thereabouts might have been chosen by Udayasiṁha for his alleged demand of tribute from Gujarāt. Nāgaḍa, though first mentioned as a *mahāmātya* in an inscription of V. 1317 had probably been appointed to that post even before V. 1300.

52. *Kīrtikaumudī*, I, 26.

53. See below the chapter on Literature.

54. See footnotes 28 and 29 of this chapter. Special attention is invited to footnote 29.

of the Slave rulers of Delhi, did not finally succeed in breaking the power of this Chāhamāna ruler of Rājasthān. The Gurjara lords found their interests best served by an alliance with him, even at the cost of some territory ; and Mewār must have realised, though rather late, the mistake of fighting against him. Perhaps Northern India had not then any ruler mightier than Udayasiṁha.

Nor was Udayasiṁha a mere soldier. With Yaśovīra as his chief minister, his court was bound to be a great intellectual centre, a centre however which might have remained second-rate, if Udayasiṁha himself had not been highly proficient in Metaphysics, Logic, and encyclopaedic works like the Mahābhārata.[55] Indra might not have actually become thousand-eyed to see and Śeṣa two-thousand-tongued to sing the praises of Udayasiṁha's glory,[56] but this at least can be said that during his reign Jālor reached the apex of its power, and many besides his own subjects, were impressed by his great prowess and his long, intensive and by no means unsuccessful fight for Hindu India.

55. प्रोद्दाम-न्याय-हेतु-भंरतमुख-महाग्रन्थ-तत्त्वार्थवेत्ता

(verse 46)

I translate the word *Bharata* of this line as *Mahābhārata*, on the ground that it is mentioned here as a *Mahāgrantha*. Kielhorn has taken it to mean *Nāṭyaśāstra* of Bharata (*EI*, IX, p. 73, footnote 5), which meaning too is not unlikely.

56. See verse 44 of the Sūndhā inscription.

CHAPTER XVIII

THE CHAUHĀNS OF JĀLOR (*continued*): CHĀCHIGADEVA

We have eight inscriptions for Chāchigadeva, the son and successor of Udayasiṁha.[1] Some three years earlier however than the earliest of these (which belongs to V. 1319) is the record of a *pratiṣṭhā* at Jālor, dated the 6th of the bright half of Māgha (V.) 1316. It states that Padru and Mūliga put a gold cupola and gold *dhvaja* on the temple of Śāntinātha at Suvarṇagiri in the reign of Chāchigadeva[2].

"Hating his enemies as thorns" states the Sūndhā Inscription, "he destroyed the roaring Gūrjjara lord Vīrama," enjoyed the fall of the tremulous (or leaping) Pātuka, deprived Saṅga of his colour, and acted as a thunderbolt for the mountain, the furious Nāhara"[3]. The roaring Gūrjjara lord Vīrama of this extract is Vīramadeva of Dholkā. His death at the hands of Chāchigadeva has been mentioned in the last chapter. Pātuka is more difficult to identify. Dr. D.R. Bhandarkar is inclined to regard him as Chāchigadeva's cousin Pratāpa, the son of Udayasiṁha's elder brother Mānavasiṁha[4]. But as none of the inscriptions of the Chandrāvatī Chauhāns indicates fighting or even ill-will between the Devaḍās and the Sonigaras, we must look upon this identification with suspicion. There

1. These range from V. 1319 to 1333. The earliest is the Sūndhā Inscription of V. 1319 edited by Dr. Kielhorn in *EI*, IX. pp. 74ff.

2. *Kharataragachchhapaṭṭāvalī*. p. 51.

3. स्फूर्जद्-वीरम-गूर्जरेश-दलनो यः शत्रु-शल्यं द्विषंश्-
चञ्चत्-पातुक-पातनैकरसिकः संगस्य रंगापहः
उन्माद्यन्-नहराचलस्य कुलिशाकारः···(V. 50)

Dr. Kielhorn regards the word "Śalya" in the first line of the above verse as standing for Śalya mentioned in the Dabhoī Inscription of Lavaṇaprasāda. But the use of the "*Śatṛ* suffix with Salya" and the regular noun-forms with others make me doubt the correctness of his interpretation. I am doubtful also of Śalya meaning anything more than a thorn in the Dabhoī Inscription.

4. *EI*, XI, p. 76.

were two other Pratāpamallas at the time, Pratāpamalla, the younger brother of Vīsaladeva Vāghelā of Gujarāt and Pratāpamalla, the Paramāra ruler of Ābū. Of these, history practically knows nothing about the Vāghelā Pratāpamalla excepting his relationship with the rulers of Gujarāt. The other Pratāpasiṁha was a more important figure[5]. As two of Chāchigadeva's inscriptions, namely, those at Sūndhā hill and Sonpur[6] lie only at a short distance from Ābū, it is not impossible that Pratāpasiṁha might have lost them to the Chauhān ruler. Saṅga, the third adversary of Chāchigadeva mentioned by the Sūndhā Inscription has not been satisfactorily identified till now. Dr. D.R. Bhandarkar's suggestion that he might be regarded as Saṅgana,[7] a ruler of Vanathalī near Jūnāgarh, who was a brother-in-law of Vīradhavala and is said to have been slain by him is unacceptable, because both the *Prabandhakośa* and the *Vastupālacharita* of Jinaharṣa make it clear that this Saṅgana died very early in the ministry of Vastupāla and probably before he (Vastupāla) gave up his duties as the Governor of Cambay. Even if we put the age of Chāchigadeva at 50 at the time of his accession, he (Chāchigadeva) could not have been more than a mere child in V. 1279 or so when the war against Saṅgana had been fought. Similar considerations bar the possibility of Saṅgana's identity with Saṅgrāmasiṁha of Broach. The "furious Nahara" of the inscription, again, is equally unidentifiable. Could he have been some Muslim general defeated either in Chāchigadeva's own reign or that of his father[8].

Chāchigadeva's inscriptions come from Sirohī, Mewār, as well as the western-most parts of the kingdom conquered during Udayasiṁha's reign[9]. So he appears to have preserved not merely intact but also added to the dominions left to him by

5. Pratāpasiṁha was the ruler of Ābū up to V. 1344.

6. For the texts of these inscriptions see respectively *EI*, IX, pp. 74 ff. and the *Annual Report of the Rājpūtānā Museum*, 1910-11.

7. See *PK*. p. 103, *Vastupālacharita*, pp. 116-117.

8. Nāhar Khān was not an uncommon name amongst Muslims.

9. Bhinmāl and Ratanpur inscriptions are from the western parts, the Sonpur and Sūndhā inscriptions from Sirohī and the Karheda inscription from Mewār.

his illustrious father. He was a contemporary of the Sultāns Nāsiruddīn Mahmūd and Balban, both of whom found it best to leave him undisturbed in the enjoyment of his dominions. Gūrjaras appear to have respected his independent status. No inscription of Chāchigadeva refers to them as his overlords. The Ratanpur Inscription of V. 1333 calls him *Mahāmaṇḍaleśvararāja*, but his usual titles are *Mahārājādhirāja* and *Mahārājakula*[10]. A stone inscription of V. 1333 for Chāchigadeva is found also in a Hanuman temple of Sonpur (*RHC.*, V. 29).

Chāchigadeva's queen was Lakṣmīdevī. His daughter by her was married to "the highly famed ruler Tejasiṁha", most probably Mahārāval Tejasiṁha of Mewār.[11] According to Naiṇśī, Chāchigadeva had three sons, Sāmantasiṁha, Chāhaḍadeva and Chāndra[12]. His Prime Minister in V. 1323 was Jakṣadeva[13]. The *mahāmātya* Jāravā mentioned in the Ratanpur Inscription of V. 1333 might be a misreading for Jākha, the Prakritised form of Jakṣa[14].

According to the Sūndhā Inscription, Chāchigadeva was a religious-minded and charitable ruler. At Śrīmāla he remitted the taxes levied from Brāhmaṇas, at Rāmasainya he granted money for the perpetual worship of Vigrahāditya and furnished a golden cupola and flag-staff for the temple of Aparājiteśa with several other things. At Sugandhādri (Sūndhā) he worshipped the goddess Aghaṭeśvarī and had a *maṇḍapa* constructed and consecrated for her.[15] Nor was he unmindful of his duty towards sects other than his own. At Karaheḍa he granted a

10. For the Ratanpur Inscription see P.C. Nahar's *Jaina Inscriptions*. Pt. 1. pp. 248 f. For the title *Mahārājakula* see his Karaheṭaka and Bhīnmāl inscriptions. In the Bhīnmāl inscription of V. 1334 he is termed *Mahārājādhirāja*.

11. See the Burtrā inscription of Sāmantasiṁha, edited by Kielhorn, *EI*, IV. pp. 313 f. We have inscriptions for Mahārāval Tejasiṁha in the Vikrama years 1317 and 1314.

12. *Khyāt* : I, p. 183.

13. See the Jālor inscription, Muni Jinavijaya's, *Prāchīna-Jaina-lekha-saṅgraha*, pp. 2, No. 563. For the Ratanpur inscription see P.C. Nahar's *Jaina Inscriptions*, Pt. 1, pp. 248 f.

14. See the last note.

15. vv. 51-57.

village to the god Pārśvanātha and at Sūndhā employed a Jaina *yati* to compose the *praśasti* of his family.[16]

Chāchigadeva must have died before V. 1339, the date of the first known inscription of his successor Sāmantasiṁha[17].

16. See the 59th verse of the Sūndhā inscription. The *yati's* name was Jayamaṅgala. His *guru* Rāmachandra was a disciple of the great Jaina āchārya Vādideva.

For the Karheḍa inscription see the *Jaina-satya-prakāśa*, I, 1;

17. I, p. 10.

See Sāmantasiṁha's Bhīnmāl inscription of V. 1339, *Bombay Gazetteer*, Pt. I, pp. 483 f., Inscription No. XIV.

CHAPTER XIX

THE CHAUHĀNS OF JĀLOR (*continued*) : SĀMANTASIṀHA AND KĀNHAḌADEVA

The inscriptions of Sāmantasiṁha range from V. 1339 to 1362 and show Sāmantasiṁha ruling over almost the same territories as his father, Chāchigadeva.[1] About V. 1353, he associated his son, Kānhaḍadeva, with himself in the government of Jālor[2]; and this was high time too, for Rājpūt culture and independence perhaps never stood in greater peril than during the years, 1296-1316 A.D. Five years earlier, in V. 1348, even the weak-kneed Fīrūz Khaljī had advanced as far as Sāñchor, an important city of the kingdom of Jālor, and retired only on Sāraṅgadeva Vāghelā's rushing to the aid of his neighbour[3]. In V. 1353 the ruler on the throne of Delhi was Fīrūz's nephew and assassinator, Alā-ud-dīn Khaljī, perhaps the greatest of Sultāns of Delhi, whose avowed ambition was to end all Hindu principalities and kingdoms, and who had been advised by his trusted counsellors to treat the Hindus as no better than slaves[4]. Sāmantasiṁha of Jālor does not appear to

1. Of Sāmantasiṁha's 16 inscriptions, four come from Bhīnmāl, three from the state of Sirohī, and the rest from various parts of the Jodhpur division of Rājasthān.

2. The Jālor inscription of Sāmantasiṁha, V. 1353, refers itself to the reign of *Mahārājakula* Śrī-Sāṁvatasiṁha, while Kānhaḍadeva was subsisting on his lotus like feet and bearing the burden of administration (*EI*, XI, pp. 61f.). Similarly the Chohṭan inscription V. 1356, for a transcript of which I am indebted to Mahāmahopādhyāya Bisheshar Nāth Reū, speaks of Mahārājakula Śrī-Sāṁvatasiṁhadeva and Rājan Kānhaḍadeva.

3. *Vividhatīrthakalpa* of Jinaprabha Sūri, Singhi Jaina Granthamālā, p. 30. In coming to Sāmantasiṁha's help, Sārañgadeva Vāghelā, the ruler of Gujarāt, must have looked to his own interests also. From Sāñchor the victorious Muslims could have marched on into Gūrjara territory.

4. Barni, *Tārīkh-i-Fīrūz Shāhi*, *ED.*, III, pp. 82-3. Alāuddīn had some idea of conquering even the whole world, a project from which he is said to have been dissuaded by Alā-ul-Mulk who advised him first to conquer Raṇthambhor, Jālor, Chanderī; and Chitor. As regards the persecution of the Hindus, Qāzī Mughisuddīn of Bayānā regarded it not only as lawful but less rigorous than it should have been. They were to open wide their mouths to receive even their Muslim masters' spittle (*ED*, III, p. 104).

have been a man gifted or capable enough to fight against such a redoubtable adversary. It was good that he realised the need of some assistance, and acting probably on the advice of his people[5] put the real direction of the affairs of the state into the hands of Kānhaḍadeva, then perhaps a young man of twenty-five years or so.

Kānhaḍadeva had not to wait long for a chance to prove his mettle. In the third year of his joint reign, *i.e.*, 1298 A.D., Alāuddīn decided to conquer Gujarāt and destroy the temple of Somanātha[6]. As the best route for his army lay through Mārwār, he despatched a robe of honour to Kānhaḍadeva and desired that he should permit the Khaljī forces to pass through his territory. Worldly wisdom should have dictated instant submission to the imperial orders. But to the brave Kānhaḍadeva *svadharma* mattered more than worldly pleasures, or a kingdom or even his life. He therefore sent back Alāuddīn's messenger with the blunt answer, "Your army would, on its way, sack villages, take prisoners, molest women, oppress Brāhmaṇas and slay cows. This being against our *dharma*, we cannot accede to your request."[7]

Though the refusal must naturally have angered Alāuddīn, he took no immediate steps against Jālor. The Khaljī army, commanded by Ulūgh Khān and Nusrat Khān, marched instead through Mewār.[8] Like a storm of extreme fury, it laid low every state, every chiefship, every principality that lay across its path, conquered very soon the whole of Gujarāt and Kaṭhiāwār, and destroyed the temple of Somanātha, in spite of the gallant opposition offered by the Jeṭhava, Valā, Bājā and Chūḍāsāmā Rājpūt.[9] And then on its way back to Delhi, Ulūgh Khān, either on his own initiative or acting on instruc-

5. It appears from *Kānhaḍadeprabandha* that the important decisions of the Jālor rulers were invariably taken with the full concurrence of their counsellors. See below the chapter on administration.

6. See the *Khazāin-ul Futūh*, *Journal of Indian History*, 1929, pp. 357-358.

7. *Kānhaḍadeprabandha*, I, vv. 32-33.

8. *Ibid.*, vv. 32-33; *Vividhatīrthakalpa*, p. 30.

9. For a full and spirited description of the Khaljī conquests read the *Kānhaḍadeprabandha*, Ist Khaṇḍa. According to the *Vividhatīrthakalpa*, the Khaljī army passed by way of Bāgaḍa, Moḍāsa, and Asāvalli, in its march on Somanātha.

tions given beforehand by Alāuddīn, decided to punish Kānhaḍadeva for the affront to Khaljī authority. Victorious everywhere, he saw no need of taking the Mewār route; unpermitted and unasked he marched through the Jālor territory, daring Kānhaḍadeva to do what he could.[10] Kānhaḍadeva had only one answer, to accept the challenge and to fight for his prestige and honour.

Nor was it an inopportune moment to defy the invader, for the Khaljī army was seething with discontent and almost on the point of mutinying. Not satisfied with the returns of the loot made by the soldiers, the Khaljī commanders had, in their attempt to recover the one-fifth of the booty due to the State, employed brutally inquisitorial methods, spurning not even the use of blows, kicks, and various forms of torture. They were determined also to deprive the soldiers of gold, jewels and other valuables. This drove them to desperation; and specially angry were the neo-Moslems, who were bound to the throne of Delhi neither by hereditary loyalty nor hereditary religion.[11] They were mercenaries in a sense, but mercenaries with a sense of honour perhaps not possessed at least in the same degree by their Khaljī compeers and masters.[12]

When the Khaljī army reached Sakrāṇā, a village nearly eighteen miles from Jālor, Kānhaḍadeva's chief minister, Jaita Devaḍā, conveyed his master's message to Ulūgh.[13] "You have,"

10. *Kānhaḍadeprabandha*, I, v. 112. The event is not referred to by Muslim historians; but that does not detract from its historicity. For an evaluation of the evidence of the *Kānhaḍadeprabandha* see my paper in the *Śodhapatrikā* III, Pt. I.

11. Neither by hereditary religion, because they were recent converts to Islām. For the details of the munity see the *Tārikh-i-Firūz shāhī*, *ED.*, III, p. 163 ff. Amīr Khusrau has nothing to say about it, most probably because it was nothing creditable to Alāuddin or his generals.

12. Muhammad Shāh's conduct at Raṇthambhor has something romantic about it. He was as great a man as Hammīra who gave him shelter and refused to hand him over to Alāuddīn.

13. The name of the village is given as Sirāṇa by the *Kānhaḍadeprabandha* (I, 194) and as Sakrāṇā by Naiṇsī (*Khyāt*. I, p. 158). Sakrāṇā still exists as a village near Jālor. Sirāṇā may be a misreading for Sakrāṇā. The *Kānhaḍadeprabandha* gives correctly the name of the Khaljī general as Alū Khān (Ulūgh Khān). Naiṇsī is mistaken in regarding Alāuddīn himself as the commander of the force which invaded Gujarāt.

it stated, "not done well in encamping at the foot of my fort, after slaying so many Hindus and with Somanātha as your captive. Do you not know that I am a Rājpūt?"[14] Jaita, who was received with all courtesy due to an envoy, utilised the opportunity to reconnoitre the Muslim camp, and on his way back got into touch with the disaffected neo-Moslem leaders, Muhammad Shāh and his brothers. Two days later, followed on one side a well-planned raid led by Jaita Devaḍā, and on the other a rising fomented and headed by the neo-Moslems. Nusrat Khān's brother, Malik Aizuddīn and a nephew of Alāuddīn were slain.[15] Ulūgh Khān barely escaped with his life. Probably some of the Gujarāt spoils also fell into the hands of Kānhaḍadeva's Rājpūts. But what they themselves valued most was the liberation of thousands of Hindu prisoners and the rescue of an idol of Somanātha which was being carried to Delhi "to be trodden under the feet of the faithful".[16]

14. *Naiṇsī's Khyāt*, I, p. 158.

15. *Tārikhi-i-Firūz shāhī* of Barnī, *ED*, III, p. 164, gives details of the neo-Moslem mutiny. It has nothing to say about the Hindus' share in it. The *Kānhaḍadeprabandha*, on the other hand, speaks only of the Rājpūt raid, its writer's natural desire being to give all the glory of the Muslim debacle to Kānhadade. Naiṇsī alone speaks of the co-operation between the Rājpūts and neo-Moslems. I believe him not only on account of his impartiality, a little coloured though it may be at times by pro-Rājpūt bias, but also because the time and location of the neo-Moslem mutiny and the Rājput raid coincide, a fact which can satisfactorily be explained only by assuming some connection between the two. If we read between the lines, we can draw also a similar conclusion from the account of Barnī (*ED.*, III, p. 164), according to whom the neo-Moslems when they dispersed took refuge with Rāis and rebels. The *Rāi*, that he could have most prominently in his mind was Kānhaḍadeva of Jālor, with whom the neo-Moslem leaders, Muhammad Shāh and his brothers actually stayed immediately after the mutiny (Naiṇsī's *Khyāt*, I, p. 160).

16. *Kānhaḍadeprabandha*, I, 220-1, *Raṇamalla-chhanda* (composed about 1390 A.D.) and *Naiṇsī's Khyāt* mention the rescue of Somanātha by Kānhaḍadeva. The *Khazāinul Futuh* of Amīr Khusrau, *Tārikh-i-Firuz shāhī* of Barnī and the *Vividhatīrthakalpa* of Jinaprabha speak of the idol being despatched to Delhi. This being so we must either regard the story of the rescue of Somanātha by Kānhaḍadeva as a late fabrication, though not very late for it was current as early as 1390 A.D., or suppose that it was some other idol of Somanātha, and such idols are even now not unknown, which was rescued by Kānhadadeva. Later generations may have mistaken this rescue for that of Somanātha of Prabhāsa-paṭṭana. I have tentatively adopted the second of these alternatives.

Kānhaḍadeva had its five fragments installed respectively at Prabhāsa, Bāgaḍa, Ābū, Jālor and his own garden. This rescue of Somanātha forms in the popular mind Kānhaḍadeva's best and greatest title to greatness.[17]

For nearly five years Alāuddīn slept over this insult to his authority, as far as Kānhaḍadeva was concerned.[18] Perhaps he had other affairs more urgent and weighty to attend to. But after the reduction of Raṇthambhor (1301 A.D.) (where the neo-Moslem leaders, Muhammad Shāh and his brothers, sold their lives dearly), of Chitor made famous by the *jauhar* of Padminī, and of the forts of Ujjain, Māṇḍū, Dhārā and Chanderī, the Khaljīs appeared once again, in 1305 A.D., before the walls of Jālor. Sāmantasiṁha was perhaps no more by this time,[19] and Kānhaḍadeva who now alone directed the affairs of the State had to think twice before taking any decision. The question was decided for him by the Khaljī commander Ainul Mulk Multānī, a man not only of the sword but also of great learning and tact. His conciliatory attitude induced Kānhaḍadeva to visit Delhi and enrol himself among its allies.[20] Like Shivājī who repaired to Delhi under similar circumstances, perhaps he wished to see whether he could have peace with honour; and like Shivājī he soon realised the impossibility of such a peace. Continued success had turned Alā-ud-dīn's head. On his coins he described himself as a second Alexander, and in his own assembly of "Yes-men" he probably boasted often of there being no Indian ruler who could withstand his forces.

17. See the Rājpūt sources mentioned in the last note.

18. For the neo-Moslems the punishment was not only terrible but extremely inhuman. Alāuddīn put their wives and children into prison. Nusrat Khān ordered the wives of the assassins of his brother to be dishonoured and exposed to most cruel treatment (*ED.*, III, pp. 164-5).

19. His latest inscription is of V. 1362.

20. *Tārīkh-i-Firishta*, English translation by Prof. Muhammad Habib (*Journal of Indian History*, 1929, p. 369, footnote 4). For Ainul Mulk's learning see the Dawāl Rānī.

Kānhaḍadeprabandha does not mention Kānhaḍadeva's submission to Alāuddīn. But *Naiṇsi's Khyāt* speaks of Kānhaḍadeva's having sent his son to Delhi, because his (son's) presence there had been demanded by Allāuddīn. This betokens submission, even though it may have been a very temporary thing.

But to do so in a *majlis*, where Kānhaḍadeva was present was to throw out a challenge to his proud Rājpūt spirit. He immediately left for Jālor, declaring that if he challenged and did not prevail, he would know how to die.[21]

Thus began the second round of the struggle between Alāuddīn and Kānhaḍadeva. The Khaljīs marched first against Siwānā, a strong fortress at the distance of nearly thirty miles from Jālor. Its governor, Sātaladeva, a nephew of Kānhaḍadeva was a warrior of the first rank whose sword had rendered many a chief subject to the authority of Jālor.[22] The Khaljīs first saw him in action at Maṇḍore perhaps, where his raid inflicted damage on the advancing Muslim forces. Next he drove them back pell-mell from before the walls of Siwānā itself by acting in concert with a large Chauhān force sent by Kānhaḍadeva from Jālor. Taken between two fires, as it were, the Khaljīs lost not only their camp equipage but also their commanders, Nahar Malik and Khānḍādhara Bhoja.[23]

This was no small reverse for the Muslim arms. But thanks to the iron will of Alāuddīn, Muslim forces still poured in, from month to month and year to year, "without being able to injure half a brick of the fort"[24] till at last in June, 1310, Alāuddīn himself marched against Siwānā, with one of the biggest armies that he had mustered so far.[25]

Sātaladeva faced him with his wonted vigour and courage. He sent out frequent sorties, bombed the Khaljī army with stones from the machines in the fort, and threw down the ladders whenever the Khalji troopers tried to escalade the fort. Other generals might have given up the task as hopeless. But once Alāuddīn personally began a siege, he rarely raised it;[26] by force or fraud he generally captured the fort. To capture Siwānā he constructed a *pāshīb* reaching up to its highest

21. *Tārikh-i-Ferishta*, English translation by Prof. M. Habib, *JIH*, 1929, p. 378.

22. *Dawāl Rānī*. English translation by Prof. M. Habib, *Ibid*, p. 377.

23. *Kānhaḍadeprabandha*,, II, 49-57.

24. *Dawāl Rānī*, English translation by Prof. Habib, *JIH*; 1929, p. 377.

25. See the *Kānhaḍadeprabandha*, II, vv. 80-95 and the *Khazāinul Futūh*, p. 53. (English translation by Habib).

26. *Khazāinul Futūh*, *JIH*., 1929, p. 375, last three lines.

point;[27] and, probably, guided from there by a traitor named Bhāyalā, he defiled the main tank of Siwānā with cows' blood.[28] Thus deprived of their main source of water supply, Rājpūt women performed the dreadful rite of *jauhar*, and the Rājpūt soldiers, now caring little for their lives, let the Khaljīs swarm in; determined only to kill and to be killed, they smeared their foreheads with sandal paste, put *tulasī* rosaries round their necks, and after offering *pūjā* to their tutelary dieties sallied forth for their last fight. Even Amīr Khusrau, a panegyrist of the Sultān, admits that "the besieged were brave and haughty", and "did not fly even when their heads were cut into pieces".[29] One party from Siwānā tried to get away to Jālor, but was ambushed and slain. On the morning of Tuesday, the 23rd Rabiul Awwal, Khaljī soldiers took the dead body of Sātaladeva to Alāuddīn. Everyone praised Kamāluddīn for having slain him. Perhaps he was the Muslim general who led the final Khaljī assault on the fort, which was after its capture officially given the name of Khairābād.[30]

From Siwānā Alāuddīn returned to Delhi, leaving however instructions to his generals to devastate and subjugate the country of Mārwār,[31] instructions which they tried to carry out not only dutifully but most thoroughly. One force striking westwards captured and sacked Bāhaḍmer,[32] and then turning southwards destroyed the great temple of Mahāvīra at Satyapura or Sāñchor.[33] In its fanatical fury it next burnt Bhīnmāl, a great centre

27. *Ibid.*, p. 376.
28. *Kānhaḍadeprabandha* II, 156.
29. *Ibid.* II. 148-167; *Khazāinul Futūh, JIH.*, 1929, p. 376.
30. *Khazāinul Futūh, JIH.*, 1929, p. 375 and 377.

Firishta's account makes Sātaladeva send a silver effigy of himself, to the Sultān, with gold cords round its neck and various other costly presents, Sātaladeva is said to have been restored also to his lordship of the fort, after the Sultān had divested it of all its riches. The account, as pointed out by Prof. M. Habib in his notes to the *Khazāinul Futūh* is wrong; Ferishta has wrongly applied to Sātaladeva the verses of the Khazāniul Futuh describing actually the fate of the *Rāi* of Wārangal.

31. *Khazāinul Futūh, JIH.* 1929, p. 377.
32. *Kānhaḍadeprabandha*, III, 29.
33. *Vividhatīrthakalpa*, p. 30. The event has been omitted by *Kānhaḍadeprabandha*. As the date given by the *kalpa* for the destruction of the temple is V. 1367, it must have occurred not long after the capture of Siwānā in August 1313 (V. 1367) and can be included among the list of ravages committed by the Khaljī army.

of Vedic learning and culture, the *Brahmapurī* of the Chauhāns of Mārwār as Padmanābha calls it, and carried away thousands of Brāhmaṇas as captives. A wave of horror and resentment must have passed through every Hindu heart, as the fleeing populace carried, far and wide, the tale of these Muslim atrocities. Kānhaḍadeva's sorrow was, naturally, greater than that of others ; but other Rājasthānīs also must have felt that their hearths and homes, nay even their religion, lives and culture were in danger, if the Muslims were permitted to run amok like this and ravage the countryside at their sweet will. Consequently warriors of all clans from Rājasthān,[34] and perhaps even outside it, readily responded to Kānhaḍadeva's call to arms ; with their horses, equipment and arms they flocked on to Jālor, eager to fight against the enemies of their country and their culture. And soon enough, with Kānhaḍadeva's orders to destroy the Muslim troops, wherever they found them, they galloped on by way of Revantī and Dhāṇasā and contacted the enemy at Khuḍālā.[35]

In its success as well as failure this feudal array typified most Rājpūt levies of the period. Composed of Rājpūt nobles and their hard-riding retainers, used to warfare on their own as well as others' account, they had not much difficulty in attaining their immediate objective. They went straight at their quarry, and within a few hours the Muslim army was a fleeing horde, shorn of all its camp equipage, elephants, and also of the men captured at Bhīnmāl, Satyapura, and other places.[36] A few hours pursuit might have completed the Rājpūt victory ; a little more of discipline and cohesion might perhaps have finished off also the detachment under Malik Nāib which had not till then come into action, on account of having been out for a hunt with its leader. But it was destined to be otherwise. While the two Devaḍā chiefs, Jaita and Mahīpa, who had been appointed

34. The clans mentioned are,
1. Vāghelās, 2. Solaṅkīs, 3. Rāṭhors, 4. Paramāras, 5. Bāraḍs, 6. Hūṇas, 7. Chāvaḍās, 8. Hariyaḍs, 9. Ḍoḍiyās, 10. Yādavas, 11. Nikumbhas, 12. Gohilas, 13. Devaḍās.
But in a general all the 36 Rājpūt clans are referred to.

35. *Kānhaḍadeprabandha*, III, 69-71.

36. *Ibid.*, III. 73-88.

to the chief command by Kānhaḍadeva,[37] raced back to Jālor with their booty and followers, eager perhaps only to be the first to congratulate their master on his brilliant success, three other nobles, almost equally prominent in Kānhaḍadeva's counsels, Śobhita's son, Sālha, Lākhaṇa Sevaṭā, and Ajayasī Molhaṇa elected to remain on the battlefield with nearly four thousand Rājpūts. Elated by their easy victory and finding that it was an *amāvasyā* day, they took off their armour and bathed in a tank nearby ; and someone in his over-confidence, or should we say folly, sounded even a drum captured from the Muslims.[38] Little could he have known or even dreamt of the consequences of this action. Malik Nāib, who was on the way back to the camp from his hunt, took the sound as summons for himself. Imagine therefore his surprise, when on rushing back he found that the Muslim camp had disappeared, in its place being only dead bodies of Muslim soldiers, and that at a short distance from there were thousands of the enemy, not only very much alive but enjoying a glorious bath.[39] What followed thereafter was more of a massacre than a real fight. None fled from the field ; none was given any quarter. Of the splendid Rājpūt array that had marched out from Jālor that morning, four thousand, with their leaders, lay dead on the field ; not one even was left to carry the news to Kānhaḍadeva.[40]

Next followed the siege of Jālor. For seven nights in succession Vīramadeva[41] and Māladeva[42] led out sorties, filling in ditches and destroying stockades surrounding the Muslim camp. On the eighth, there was a great conflagration, caused perhaps by a violent thunderstorm ; and the Khaljīs, finding the position

37. *Kānhaḍadeprabandha*, III, 36 and 89.

38. *Ibid.*, III, 94. For a similar incident elsewhere in Rājpūt or rather Chauhān history see above the account of Hammīra of Raṇthambhor.

39. *Ibid.*, 98.

40. *Kānhaḍadeprabandha*, III, 105. Sālha's death in this engagement can be inferred also from the Sāñchor inscription, V. 1444, of his great-grandson, Pratāpasiṁha. It states that Sālha liberated the people taken captive by the Turuṣkas at Śrimāla (तुरुष्क-बन्दीकृतविश्वलोकं श्रीमालतो मोचयति स्म धीरः *EI.* IX, p. 66) meaning surely the Khaljīs by the word *Turuṣka*.

41. Kānhaḍadeva's eldest son.

42. Kānhaḍadeva's younger brother.

untenable, retired towards Delhi.[43] At Moklāṇā, a village not far from Meṛtā, Kānhaḍadeva's Rājpūts delivered an eight-pronged attack on one of its detachments and captured its commander, Shams Khān along with his wife, a daughter perhaps of the Sultān himself.[44] This was success indeed, but it was indeed also the surest means to recall Alāuddin's forces to Jālor. Alāuddīn never failed to pay off old scores ; and the score of Jālor had by the end of 1310 A.D. surely mounted very high.

An army, more numerous and better equipped than the last one now marched on against Jālor. Kānhaḍadeva sent two Rājpūt forces to arrest its progress. One, commanded by Māladeva, operated from Vāḍī ; the other, led by Vīramadeva, had Bhādrājan as its headquarters.[45] But the Khaljīs, this time commanded by Kamāluddīn Gurg, one of the best generals of the empire,[46] moved on, though at a very slow pace, reducing thoroughly the territory they passed through and safeguarding also their long line of communications. They now understood Rājpūt tactics and knew how to meet them. They suffered losses no doubt ; but after a time the Rājpūt losses also were by no means inconsiderable.[47]

43. *Kānhaḍadeprabandha*; III, 170.

44. *Ibid.*, 177-185. I have given in the text the version of the *Kānhaḍadeprabandha* about the first Khaljī siege. Firishta also knew that the first Khaljī siege was unsuccessful. He says, "Alāuddīn ordered a slave-girl, named Gul-i-Bihisht, to march against Jālor and reduce it by force. Gul-i-Bihishth reached her destination, besieged the fort and displayed such wonderful courage that it never occurred to Kānaṛ Deo to come out and offer battle. The besieged were reduced to straits and the fort was about to fall when Gul-i-Bihisht suddenly fell ill and died. Her son, Shāhīn, took the army in hand and tried to overpower the besieged like his mother. But Kānaṛ Deo now saw that the Emperor's anger was inevitable and determined to make a desperate struggle. He collected all his men, came out of the fort and gave battle. As chance would have it, Shāhīn and Kānaṛ Deo came face to face and Shāhīn was killed. The other *amirs*, unable to continue the struggle, retreated a few stages."

The main facts, the raising of the siege and the retreat of the *amīrs*, are thus the same in the two books. As for the story of Gul-i-Bihisht, it must be, as suggested by Dr. Hodivala (*Studies in Indo-Moslem History*, p. 52), regarded as a late invention, designed to cover up the disgrace of Alāuddīn's army in retiring discomfited from before the walls of Jālor. It is first found in *Tārīkh-i-Alfī*, a history composed as late as 1585 A.D.

45. *Kānhaḍadeprabandha*, IV, 106-109.

46. He was the reducer of both Jaisalmer and Siwānā. For his appointment to the post see *Firishta's History* as well as the *Kānhaḍadeprabandha*, IV, 45.

47. *Kānhaḍadeprabandha*, IV; 115-121.

Kānhaḍadeva recalled Māladeva and Vīramadeva to Jālor. The former was sent out again to operate against the Khaljīs; but Vīramadeva stayed on to assist his father.[48] Kamāluddīn also duly reached the walls of the fort and began its siege in right earnest. He neither permitted anything to be moved into the fort, nor anything to be moved out of it, hoping thereby to starve the garrison into surrender[49]. New reinforcements also continued to pour in from Delhi, in spite of Māladeva's harassing tactics, which Kamāluddīn just disregarded[50] and Alāuddīn stopped after a while by moving against him with an army from Delhi, and forcing him to retreat to Vanādrā.[51] The only success that Kānhaḍadeva could claim during this phase of the siege was the destruction of a Khaljī outpost at Uddalapura, a suburb of Jālor.[52]

For some time the conditions inside the fort were pretty bad. The water in its tanks was drying up; the stock of fresh provisions also was running low. Timely rains and the *mahājanas*' offer to replenish any stores that might go bad averted the danger[53] and once more the surrender of the fort seemed as far as ever.

But where force failed, treachery succeeded. Lured on by the rosy dreams of being made the ruler of Jālor on its reduction by the Khaljīs, Bīkā, a Dahiyā Rājpūt, took the Muslims in by an unfrequented and difficult path which the defenders, believing that the enemy would never know about it, had left undefended and unmanned. The traitor did not indeed live on to profit by his treachery; he was slain by his own wife, Hīradevī, who lost no time in reporting the matter to Kānhaḍadeva.[54] But the fate of the fort was now sealed; it was no longer the impregnable fortress that had baffled so far all the ingenuity of Alāuddīn's commanders.

Kānhaḍadeva's *sāmantas*, Kāndhal, Jait Ulīchā, Jait Devaḍā,

48. *Kānhaḍadeprabandha*, IV, 121, 142-3.
49. *Ibid.*, 149.
50. *Ibid.*, IV, 45.
51. *Ibid.*, 165-170.
52. *Ibid.*, 152-162.
53. *Ibid.*, 122-140.
54. *Ibid.*, 181-206.

Lūṇ Karaṇ Molhaṇ, Arjun Baḍavāl, and many others equally devoted and brave, though perhaps a little less prominent, sacrificed their lives in a vain effort to dislodge the enemy.[55] On the fifth day the Muslims reached the temple of Kānhasvāmī, and the rumour went about that they wanted to destroy it. Kānhaḍadeva's brave queens had already consigned themselves to the flames of *jauhar* ;[56] now Kānhaḍadeva himself, along with his brave chiefs, prepared himself for the last fight in the right royal Rājpūt fashion. Fifty of them fell fighting round their master ; and last of all fell the brave Kānhaḍadeva, still believed by many merely to have disappeared and not to have died in his last battle against the Khaljīs.[57]

Thus ended in V. 1371 the Sonigarā dynasty and the career of the last of its independent representatives,[58] Kānhaḍadeva Chauhān. He was a man of character. On questions of principle he yielded to none. He must have been endowed also with sterling qualities of leadership to have retained to the last, in spite of the privations brought on by a protracted siege, the loyalty of not only his own clansmen and Rājpūts who had flocked to his standards but also of the civilians of his kingdoms. During the last phase of the siege, they offered him unstintingly all they had ; and when all defence was known to be hopeless 1584 fires were lit in a single day, in which died women of all castes.[59] As a general Kānhaḍadeva was not probably inferior to his Hindu contemporaries. To have kept fighting against Alāuddīn almost throughout his reign, in spite of his (Alāuddīn's) immense resources, was in itself a feat. None else equalled or surpassed it. Brave, intrepid to a degree, and sincerely religious, Kānhaḍadeva represented Rājpūt chivalry at its best ; and it is no wonder that not long after his death he was deified and regarded as an *avatāra* of Viṣṇu, the destroyer of the wicked and preserver of moral order. His failure was more of a society than an individual, of a society the members of which, with all

55. *Kānhaḍadeprabandha*, 207-250.

56. *Ibid.*, 228-249.

57. See *Naiṇsī's Khyāt*, I, 153.

58. If we except Kānhaḍadeva's son, Vīramadeva, who also is said to have ruled for 2½ days. For the date of the fall of Jālor, see footnote 60.

59. *Kānhaḍadeprabandha*, IV, 231-233 and 242.

their personal virtues, had not the political sagacity to combine and defeat the designs of a power which was swallowing up piecemeal the whole of independent India. Kānhaḍadeva had not that rare statesmanship which enables one to rise above the weaknesses and prejudices of one's age, and become the founder of a new and better order. He was a great man in his own way; but we should have regarded him as much greater had he combined with Raṇthambhor, Mālwā or Gujarāt and saved thereby his own independence and that of the rest of Hindu India.[60]

60. *Date of the fall of Jālor* :—

Firishta does not give any date, and Amīr Khusrau omits even any mention of the fall of Jālor. According to the *Kānhaḍadeprabandha*, the date of Kānhaḍadeva's death was Wednesday, the 5th of the bright half of *Vaiśākha*, V. 1368. Naiṇsī gives the same date. The actual date, however, was somewhere in V. 1371, some time after the 10th of the dark half of *Jyeṣṭha*, as proved by the following extract from the *Kharataragachchhapaṭṭāvalī* :—

श्री जाबालिपुरसमुदायगाढाभ्यर्थनया श्रीजाबालिपुरे बिहृताः । तत्र च संवत् १३७१ ज्येष्ठ बदि दशम्यां म० देवसिंह-प्रमुख-सकल-जाबालिपुर-समुदाय-कृत-सकल-स्वपक्षपरपक्ष-चेतश्चमत्कारी समस्तजनमनोहारी दीक्षामालारोपण-महोत्सवः श्रीपूज्यैः कृतः ।

ततो म्लेच्छकृतो भंगो जातः ।

For the reliability of the *Kharataragachchhapaṭṭāvalī* see my papers on the subject in *IHQ.*, XI, p. 779 f. and XXVI, 223-231.

The above extract shows also that the fall of the fort came rather unexpectedly. Till then life inside it was almost normal.

APPENDIX F

THE FEUDATORY CHAUHĀNS OF SATYAPURA (SĀÑCHOR)

Naiṇsī gives the following account of the conquest of Sāñchor by the Chauhāns :—[1]

"Sāñchor was originally under the Dahiyā Rājpūts. In the time of Vijayarāja Dahiyā, Vijayasiṁha, son of Ālhaṇa, ruled over Siṁhavāḍa. For some reason or other Vijayarāja Dahiyā's nephew Mahīrāvaṇa Vāghelā turned against his uncle and going to Vijayasiṁha Chauhān proposed the capture and equal division of Sāñchor between themselves. Vijayasiṁha agreed, and reaching Sāñchor, on being invited by the Vāghelā, killed the Dahiyās and had himself proclaimed the ruler of the place on the 11th of the dark half of Phālguna, Saṁvat 1141. The Vāghelā Mahīrāvaṇa also was put to death".

Thereafter is given the following genealogy :—

Ālhaṇa[2]
|
Vijayasī
|
Padamsī
|
Sobhrama
|
Sālo[3] — Vikamsī — Hāpo
|
(Vikamsī)
|
Patto
|
Vajrāṅga[4]

Naiṇsī's account cannot obviously be accepted in its entirety. If Vijayasiṁha was the great-grandfather of Sālo, a con-

1. *Khyāt*, p. 172, Vol. I.

2. *Ibid*. p. 173. The Mārwārī MS. of the *Khyāt* with me gives the following additional names before Vijayasiṁha, (1) Lākhaṇa, (2) Sohiya, (3) Mahiṁddarāva, (4) Aṇahala.

3. He died fighting for Kānhaḍadeva at the time of the siege of Jālor by Alāuddīn Khaljī (Naiṇsī's note).

4. He died fighting against Malik Mīr who captured Sāñchor. He wa a great Rājpūt (Naiṇsī's note).

temporary of Kānhaḍadeva, he could not possibly have been a son of Ālhaṇa of Nāḍol (c. 1205-1211), nor could he have captured Satyapura from the Dahiyās in V. 1141. Naiṇsī's mistake, or rather of the bard who informed him, was perhaps due to his confusing Vijayasiṁha's father Ālhaṇa, likely enough no more than a common Sonigarā Rājpūt, with Ālhaṇa, the ruler of Nāḍol. In V. 1051 Satyapura was under the Chaulukyas and there it seems to have remained till its capture by the Chauhāns in Udayasiṁha's reign.[5] Vijayasiṁha was probably the leader of Udayasiṁha's army which accomplished this feat.

Pratāpasiṁha's Sāñchor Inscription of V. 1444 helps us in adding a few more details. According to it the order of succession was :—

Śobhita[6]
|
Sālha[7]
|
Vikramasiṁha
|
Saṅgrāmasiṁha — Bhīmasiṁha (elder brother)
| |
Pratāpasiṁha = Kāmalladevī[8]

Śobhita of the above inscription is obviously identical with Sobhrama of the *Khyāt*. Sālha is the same as Sālo. He was a valiant fighter, and was, as noted in the last chapter, killed fighting against the Khaljī army after he had liberated the people taken captive at Śrīmāla. A little before his gallant fight and death, the Muslims had sacked Satyapura and destroyed its temples.[9] Vikramasiṁha, the next ruler, finds a place in both the genealogies,[10] though he is mentioned as

5. See above, p. 167.
6. According to the inscription, he was in the family of Lakṣmaṇa of Naddūla.
7. According to the inscription he liberated the residents of Śrimāla from the captivity of the Turuṣkas.
8. *EI*, XI, pp. 65-67.
9. *Vividhatīrthakalpa*, p. 30.
10. Naiṇsī's *Khyāt* I, p. 174. The account of the inscription is certainly the more reliable of the two. But the words "tasyātmajo" are a restoration by the editor. We do not know whether they could have been read also as "tasyānujo" in which case the account would agree with that of the *Khyāt*.

Sālha's son in the inscription[10a] and as his brother in the *Khyāt.* The inscription omits Hāpo probably because he was not in the direct line of succession. But that he did rule at Satyapura might be seen from the *Kharataragachchhapaṭṭāvali* which refers to his sway there in V. 1391.[11] His descendants were the masters of Sūrāchand in Naiṇsī's time.[12] Bhīma mentioned in the inscription as the elder brother of Saṅgrāmsiṁha was perhaps the next ruler[13]. His nephew Pratāpasiṁha ruled at Sāñchor in V. 1444 and was married to Kāmalladevī, a Paramāra lady of the Umaṭa section, who renovated the temple of Vāgīśvara at Sāñchor and granted for its worship one field and two *pāilās* from every maund of commodity reaching Sāñchor.[14] Pratāpasiṁha's successor Vajrāṅga is said to have lost Sāñchor in V. 1378. Malik Mīr who captured it and slew Vajrāṅga[15] cannot be identified. But Vajrāṅga might itself have been a title of Arjuna known from a Dhamdhupura inscription of V. 1347.

10a. In an inscription found at Dhandhupura (Sisrolu).

11. p. 86. Called *Rāṇaka* Haripāla there.

12. I, p. 173.

13. The words of the inscription are भीमाग्रजन्मा·····संग्रामसिंहो । This can mean either that he was the younger or the elder brother of Saṅgrāmasiṁha according to the way we analyse the compound. That the writer should go out of his way to mention a brother might mean that he was an elder brother, though not necessarily.

14. See the donative portion of Pratāpasiṁha's inscription.

15. *Khyāt*, I, p. 174.

CHAPTER XX

DEOṚĀ CHAUHĀNS OF CHANDRĀVATĪ AND ĀBŪ*

The founder of the Devaḍā line was Mānavasiṁha, the elder son of Samarasiṁha of Jālor.[1] Udayasiṁha, as the abler of the two brothers succeeded to the throne, but Mānavasiṁha appears to have been treated well and might have been assigned a small *jāgir* by way of compensation.[2] His son, Pratāpamalla, is described as "respected in the assemblies of rulers"[3], probably because he served well either his uncle Udayasiṁha, who lived on up to V. 1316, or his son and successor, Chāchigadeva, whose last date is about V. 1339.

According to the Sūndhā Inscription of V. 1319, Chāchigadeva delighted himself in felling the trembling Pātuka.[4] This has been interpreted by Dr. D.R. Bhandarkar to mean that Chāchigadeva defeated his cousin Pratāpamalla. But considering the fact that the relations between the Deoṛā and Sonigarā lines were, as indicated by the inscriptions of the former, cordial enough, it would be as already pointed out[5], better to identify the "trembling Pātuka" with the Paramāra ruler, Pratāpamalla of Chandrāvatī and Ābū during whose reign, Chāchigadeva's forces penetrated into the Ābū territory up to Sūndhā and Sonepur.[6]

Pratāpamalla's son, Vījaḍa, known also as Daśasyandana or Daśaratha, probably laid the foundations of the Deoṛā kingdom of the Ābū area, first by operating as a captain of Chāchigadeva's forces and later on by making new conquests on his own account. In the Dīlwāṛā inscription of V. 1377, he is described as the lord of Marumaṇḍala.[7] Shorn of its exaggera-

*Included here to complete the account of the Early Chauhān Dynasties.

1. See above, p. 166.
2. The Deoṛā inscriptions at Achaleśvar and Vimala-vasahī.
3. *Bhūpāla-sadassu mānyaḥ*, verse 19 of the Vimal-vasahī inscription of v. 1378.
4. *Chañchat-Pātuka-pātanaika-rasikāḥ*, verse 50.
5. See above, p. 176.
6. See above, p. 177.
7. *Marusthalī-maṇḍalabhūmibhartā*.

tion, the epithet indicates, we think, the assumption of an independent position by Vījaḍa. From Tonkṛā village of the old Sirohī State we have an inscription of a certain Vījaḍa, dated in the (Vikrama) year 1232. He must obviously be different from Vijaḍa Deoṛā[8], who came to the throne not earlier than V. 1340.

By his queen, Nāmalladevī, Vījaḍa had four sons, Lāvaṇyakarṇa, Lunḍha, Lakṣmaṇa and Lūṇavarman.[9] Of these Lāvaṇyakarṇa succeeded his father.[10]

During the life time of Lāvaṇyakarṇa, the Chauhāns were passing through one of the worst periods of their political existence. In V. 1367, the armies of Alāuddīn Khaljī captured the Chauhān strongholds of Siwānā and Sāñchor.[11] Four years later, Jālor also passed into Muslim hands, in spite of the gallant resistance put up by Kānhaḍadeva and his feudatories.[12] Thousands of Chauhāns must have as a result of these reverses sought refuge with Lāvaṇyakarṇa, his small principality being the only island of safety in the sea of troubles that seemed to be engulfing the Chauhāns everywhere. As the Achaleśvara Inscription of V. 1377 states, "when the *Asuras*, *i.e.*, the Muslims had destroyed the Kṣatriyas, he devoted himself to the protection of his clansmen and their lands."[13]

And this influx of the Chauhāns from elsewhere was not without some good effects as far as the Devaḍās were concerned. It made them numerically strong enough to expand further; and expansion was absolutely necessary, for the small principality of Lāvaṇyakarṇa could hardly be expected to contain and support the daily swelling numbers of the Chauhān refugees, who, uprooted from their lands in Rājasthān, naturally

8. Dr. Ojha regarded it as an inscription of Vījaḍa. But not only is the date inaccurate, there is no mention also of Vījaḍa's clan.

9. Verses 22-23 of the Achaleśvar Inscription of V. 1377.

10. Dr. G.H. Ojha thought that Lāvaṇyakarṇa pre-deceased his father. But this goes against the testimony of Luṇḍha's Achaleśvar Inscription of V. 1377, according to which Luṇḍha was preceded on the throne by Lāvaṇyakarṇa (see verses 24 and 26).

11. See above pp. 185 and 194.

12. See above p. 191.

13. *Nīte kṣayaṁ kṣatravare'surairyaḥ svagotragopālaparāyaṇobhūt*, verse 25 of the Achaleśvar inscription of V. 1377.

moved towards the fastnesses of the Arāvalli hills and soon overwhelmed the Paramāra principality of Chandrāvatī and Ābū, parts of which had been occupied by the Chauhāns even as early as V. 1319. Pratāpamalla Paramāra ruled at Chandrāvatī up to V. 1344.[14] For his successor, Vikramasiṁha, however, we have a solitary inscription at Barmān[15] in the old Sirohī State dated in V. 1356. So the Ābū area might have been conquered by the Chauhāns somewhere between this year and V. 1372, the year of Lumbhā's Vimalvasahī inscriptions No. 1 and 2 ; and this period can be narrowed further by regarding the Chauhān influx, that followed the reverses of V. 1367—1371, as the main cause of Chauhān expansionist activities.

Naiṇsī gives the following account of the Chauhān infiltration and conquest :—[16]

"Formerly the Paramāras ruled at Ābū. Rāwal Kānhaḍadeva was then the ruler of Jālor. It was then that Devaḍā Vījaḍa's sons, Jaswant, Samarā, Lūṇa, Lumbha, Lākhā, and Tejsī settled down near the Siraṇwā hill, which is not far from Sirohī. They possessed no land. So they decided to capture Ābū somehow. At that time a bard of the Paramāras came to them. They entertained him well, and he carried to the Paramāra ruler of Ābū the proposal that the Paramāras should marry the twenty-five daughters of the Chauhāns. They agreed but desired one of the Chauhān brothers as a surety. Lūṇa accompanied the bard in that capacity. He stayed with the Paramāra chief and twenty-five Paramāra bridegrooms set out to marry the Chauhān maidens with a small entourage. Twenty-five Chauhān youths disguised themselves as brides, and on receiving a set signal killed the twenty-five Paramāra bridegrooms. The rest of the Paramāras, who were by that time under the influence of strong drinks, were easily done to death, and news was sent to Lūṇa through a bard. As soon as he heard it, he told the Paramāra chief that Ābū belonged to the Chauhāns and that he would kill him as his brothers

14. See the Pātnārāyaṇa inscription of Pratāpamalla.
15. *ASI, WC.*, 1917, p. 72.
16. *Naiṇsī's Khyāt*, Hindi translation, I, pp. 120-123.

had killed the other Paramāras. This led to a fight in which both of them died. In the meanwhile the Chauhāns reached Ābū and captured it."

In spite of its many inaccuracies, this account probably points to the following true facts :—

1. That the Chauhāns conquered Ābū from the Paramāras. No Chauhān inscription states this fact explicitly.

2. That the conquest probably took place at a period not very far removed from Kāṇhaḍadeva's death in V. 1371.

3. That Devaḍās were at that time almost landless, and it was absolutely necessary that they should conquer some territory and live on the income accruing from it.

4. That though Vījaḍa's son Lāvaṇyakarṇa died without conquering Ābū, his had most probably been the master mind that conceived the plan. It is also likely that both valour and stratagem played a part in the conquest of Ābū.

For Lāvaṇyakarṇa's younger brother and successor, Lumbhā,[17] we have the following inscriptions:—

1. Vimal Vasahī Inscription No. 1 :—This is almost gone. Its date is the second day of the bright half of Jyeṣṭha, V. *Saṁvat* 1372. For the spiritual welfare of his parents, Vījaḍa and Nāmalladevī, he passed on to the temple all the corn, clothes and money that he received from the shrines of Ādinātha and Neminātha.[18]

2. Vimal Vasahī Inscription No. 2 :—This inscription also is in good condition. It is dated the 8th day of the dark half of V. *Saṁvat* 1372. It states that in the victorious reign of Luṇḍhaka, *Selahatha* Lūṇamaka decided from that very day

17. He was known also as Luṇḍha, Luṇṭiga, Luṇṭāgāra, Luṇṭigadeva, Luṇṭākara and Lūṇiga. Dr. F. Kielhorn and Dr. D.R. Bhandarkar are wrong in regarding Lūṇiga as a name of Lāvaṇyakarṇa, and Lumbhā as a name of Lūnavarman. The Achaleśvara Inscription states that Ābū and Chandrāvatī were conquered by Luṇḍha or Luṇṭiga. The Dilwārā Inscription has the same thing to say about Lumbha, proving thereby that Lumbha and Luṇḍha were identical. Still more specific is the assertion of the Dilwārā Inscription to the effect that Lūṇiga was known as Luṇḍha on account of destroying his enemies and as Lumbha by reason of watering the creeper of his fame with the tears of his enemies' wives.

18. Dr. D.R. Bhandarkar is mistaken in putting the inscription in V. 1373.

not to have any corn, money, cloth etc. from the gods Ādinātha and Neminātha.[19]

3. Vimal Vasahī Inscription No. 3:—This record is dated, the 1st day of the dark half of Chaitra V. *Saṁvat* 1373, and records the decision of the *grāmikas* of Dīlvāḍā not to have the tax of 24 *drammas* from the priests of Ādinātha and Neminātha.[20]

4. Achaleśvara (Ābū) Inscription:—Its verses 3-19 deal with the Chauhāns of Nāḍol and Jālor from whom the Deoṛās of Ābū were descended. Five verses have been devoted to the Deoṛā line from Mānavasiṁha to Luṇḍha. The five verses that follow tell us of the repair of the *sabhāmaṇḍapa* of Achaleśvara by Luṇḍha, the setting up the statues of himself and his queen in front of Achaleśvara and the grant of the village, Hethumjī, to the temple. The date of the inscription is the 8th day of the bright half of Vaiśākha, V. *Saṁvat* 1377, in the victorious reign of *Mahārājakula* Luṇḍhāgara.[21]

These inscriptions give us a fairly good idea of the character and policy of Lumbhā. He obviously was no mere conqueror. He knew also the princely art of winning the hearts of his newly conquered subjects and conciliating every section of society. Under the Paramāras, the Jains most probably had to pay a number of vexatious pilgrim taxes. By foregoing them he won over the extremely influential Jain community to his side. He spent also money on the temple of Achaleśvara, being most probably a Śaiva by religious conviction. He could thus claim, if he desired, to be a defender of the two great religions of India, then reeling under the terrible blows dealt by Alāuddīn Khaljī. He may have been famous also for his justice, for this alone justifies his being called "the spring season to that mountain called the way of justice."[22]

For Lumbhā's successor, Tejasiṁha, we have three inscriptions. Of these the first, dated in V. 1378, shows that Tejasiṁha had been associated with his father's administrative

19. Bhandarkar's *List of North Indian Inscriptions*, No. 669, wrongly puts it as an Achaleśvar Inscription.
20. Published in the *Prāchīna-Jaina-lekha-sandoha*.
21. Summarised here from Dr. G.H. Ojha's transcript.
22. न्यायमार्ग-शिखरि-मधुमासः

work along with his brother Tihuṇaka.[23] The third inscription dated in V. 1393 gives his last date. Like Lumbhā, Tejasiṁha may have been a Śaiva. But he made over to the temple of Vasiṣṭha the three villages of Jhābaṭū, Jyāluli and Tejalapura,[24] and thus probably won over for his dynasty the support of not only the Jainas and Śaivas but also the Vaiṣṇavas.[25]

Tejasiṁha was succeeded by Kānhaḍadeva either late in V. 1393 or V. 1394. We have at the Vasiṣṭha temple, Ābū, an inscription of his reign, dated in V. 1394, recording the grant of the village Vīravāḍā by the Deoṛā Tihuṇaka.[26] The second inscription is on the statue of Kānhaḍadeva in the Achaleśvara temple and is dated in (*Vikrama*) *Saṁvat* 1400.[27] Kānhaḍadeva was thus probably a Śaiva, though he may have patronised other sects also.

Sāmantasiṁha may have been the next ruler. From the Vasiṣṭha temple inscription we learn that he granted the villages of Luhuli, Chhāpuli and Kiraṇathalā to the Vasiṣṭha temple.[28] Tradition, as recorded by Forbes, makes him Kānhaḍadeva's successor, though he is mentioned neither by Naiṇsī nor the *Baḍavās* of Sirohī.

Sāmantasiṁha was succeeded by Raṇamalla whose son and successor, Śivabhāṇa, founded the town of Śivapurī in V. 1462.[29] It now lies in ruins.[30]

The reign of Śivabhāṇa's successor, Sahasramalla or Saisamala, saw many ups and downs. His energetic policy led to the extension of the Deoṛā dominions in the western direction, and like a true *vijigīṣu*, he went on from the annexation of one small territory to the other. But very soon he had to contend with rulers, equally able and ambitious and with much greater resources. Gujarāt, Mālwā and Mewār were at the time the three great states contending for supremacy in Western and

23. Published in the *Jaina-śilālekha-sandoha*.
24. *EI*, IX, p. 82.
25. On the basis of Dr. G.H. Ojha's transcript.
26. On the basis of Dr. G.H. Ojha's transcript. This Tihunāka may be Tejasiṁha's brother.
27. From Dr. Ojha's transcript.
28. *Ibid.*
29. Dr. G.H. Ojha's *History of Sirohī*.
30. Two miles from the town of Sirohī.

Central India, and the Deoṛās, even if they wished, could not have remained out of the orbit of their ambition. At some time before V. 1509, Mahārāṇā Kumbhā of Mewār made himself master of Ābū, and Chandrāvatī also became so indefensible that Sahasmal transferred his capital to Sirohī, which he founded on the 2nd day of the bright half of Vaiśākha, V. 1482 (1425 A.D.). Thus towards the end of the fifteenth century of the Vikrama era, the Deoṛā kingdom of Chandrāvatī and Ābū became transformed into the kingdom of Sirohī and the Deoṛās continued to rule there up to the time their State was amalgamated in Rājasthān in the middle of the present century.[31]

31. For a little more detailed account of the Deoṛās see my paper, *Chandrāvatī evam Ābū ke Devaḍe Chauhān* published in the *Rājasthāna Bhāratī*, I, Part 4, pp. 1-9.

APPENDIX G

SOME CHAUHĀN INSCRIPTIONS

(i) *Narhad Inscription of Vigraharāja IV's Reign* : 1215

1. श्रोम् संवत् १२१५ मार्ग्ग वदि १५
2. शनौ नैगमान्वय-कायस्थ-ठकुर—
3. श्री श्रीचन्द्रसुत-विल्हण-पुत्र—
4. ताल्हण (:) स्वर्ग्गलोके गतः ॥
5. परमभट्टारक-महाराजाधिराज-प-
6. रमेश्वर-श्रीमद् विग्रहराजदेवराज्ये ठ.
7. श्रीसोमदे(वे)न निजस्य भ्र(ा)तृ पुत्रार्थे
8. [देहा] कारापिता ।······

(ii) *A praśasti of the Sapādalakṣa line*

1. ······
2. प्रशास्तिम् ॥१॥ पञ्चैव यानि भुवनत्रय-कारणानि त्रेधा स्थितं नमह्-
3. ···कन्यकायाः । पुष्पेषुदत्तपुरशासन-ताम्रपट्टे रोमांच-वर्ण्णरुचिरौनि-
4. ···नागाः कति नाभवन् । समस्तार्थिकृतार्थत्वक्रियायां कल्पपादपाः ।
5. ···(पुरभि?)द्धरिप्रतापः पृथिवीप्रियः । यो न वर्ण्णविकारेण कदाचिल्लघुः
6. ···[पा]दपीठः[1] श्रीचाहमान इति भूमिपतिः क्रमेण । किं वर्ण्यतेन्यदिह त-
7. ...वृत्तौ यः साधुवृत्तः पृथुश्रीः ॥ निहत्य सुरारि-चक्रं यस्या-
8. ···त्तिम् । सोमेश्वरः सुरवरः पृथुमंडपांतः प्रोन्मीलितः प्रतिरवैः प्रददा-
9. ...[से?] वापदं सुरपदं प्रिययासुरसौ नृपः ॥ श्र···मथात्मजमात्मना
10. केसरी···पालिक[2] व्रतमिवात्युपगच्छति स्म ॥१५॥ व [···सिंधु] पतिग्र-
11. ···दिननाथो मत्कुलस्यैष वृद्धः···व[3]चिंतां तस्य विश्रामहेतोरसृजदजयमेरुं य···हि-

---

1. पादपीठः was most probably preceded by रंजित.
2. The word obviously is कापालिक.
3. द precedes व. But its मात्रा is gone.

12. ···॥१८॥ अवंतीपर्यन्ते विजितनरवर्म्म-तिनुतां मुदं नीत्वा येन प्रतिभटचमू मांसरुधिरै···प्रिय सह-
13. ···क[4] कूटशतैः समुपार्जितैः । अजयमेरुरनीयत येन तां कनकशैल-तुलां किल जिष्णुना ॥ र···थांतरं रि-
14. ···जं विन्यस्य सिंहासने पुण्ये पुष्करतीर्थराजविपिने प्राप्ता परा नि[वृं] तिः ॥२१॥ जयश्रियं श्री नरवर्म्मं च (?) रैः कुमार-
15. ...कूपे प्रह्लादकूपेप्यनिवृततृष्णः । मन्ये समाक्रांतमरुः पिपासुः संसार-सिंधुं च सरस्वतीं च ॥२३॥ पुरे[प]रेषामनि-
16. ···पिता[5] येन तुरुष्करक्तैर्विराजति स्माजयमेरुभूमिः । जयोत्सवे जीवित-वल्लभस्य वासो वसानेव कुसुम्भरक्तम्-
17. ···कटम् ॥२६॥ वाष्पवारिणि कालिन्दीहरितानकयोषिताम् । सत्वा-क्रांतस्य मिलिता यत्प्रयाणे रजस्वला ॥२७॥ विच···
18. ···२८॥ यत्सैनिकैः समरमूर्धनि मालवेशादाच्छिद्य सान्द्रमदमोदित-भृङ्गमाला आलानिताः करटिनो···
19. ···स्वल्पेनापि निपीडितः···ष्यमाणैरिव तुल्यभावः परेषु नाम्नापि नि···रस्य । यत्सौ स[म]···
20. तीं तन...हैव ॥३२॥ अभूत्ततोलंकरणं धरित्र्यास्तदी-
21. ···कुमारपालः करवालपालः ॥३४॥ आदाय यः प्रथ···
22. [रा]गिनीभिरभिनंदितभावनाभिः । सैवाफलत्सकलमंग···
23. ...न जनितं जगन्नेत्रं नीत्वा निजकुलगुरुं साक्षिपदवीम्
24. ...रमिपि व्यक्तीचकार क्षितौ ॥३८॥···
25. ···यो जिष्णुभावे प्रभुतां···
26. ···धानीग्रहणाति [शंका?]···
27. ···र्णस्य स्थावरीं वृत्ति [स्थापयामास यो] क्षितौ ॥४४॥
28. ···सकलासु दिक्षु···नीचो स्थितिं मा···
29. ···रक श्रीर[6]···

4. The word is कनक.
5. The word is संतर्पिता.
6. The line is largely illegible. It may have contained the name of the author of the प्रशस्ति. रक may be a part of काश्मीरक.

(iii) *A Nanāṇā Copper-plate registering the grants of Āsārāja (v. 1173, 1171), Ratnapāla, Sāhaṇapāla (v. 1192) and Ālhaṇa (v. 1205) (2nd Plate Only)*

पंक्ति १ विलासिनी प[द्मा]वती सुता-वीजलाया अपराभिः समं षोडशमं [प]दं तथा प्रदत्तम् । वंशिक-ल्हौडियाकस्त्रिपुरुषाणां···प्रदत्तः । मेहरी सी—

„ २ निकायाः वर्षं प्रति देवकीय[ा] दानमध्यात् गोधूमानां द्रोणाः पंच नंदानाग्रामीयभोगात् दातव्याः । गणिका गोछिणी सुतायाः···

„ ३ नं अपराभिः सप्तदशमं···पदँ प्रदत्तम् । तथा अत्रैव भीटलवाड़ा-ग्रामः श्रीचंदलेश्वरदेवा[थँ] त्रिपुरुषाणां प्रदत्तः ॥

„ ४ अस्माद् ग्रामादुत्प [त्ति] स्त्रिपुरुषाणां···सत्कवारिकैः समादाय स्वीयादानस्यैकत्वं च विधाय श्री चंदलेश्वरीय-विलासिनीनां विधा-

„ ५ य भक्तकादिकं अपरमपि यत्किंचिद्दे वस्य क्रियते भट्टारक-पुरः-सरं [वा] रि [कैः] स्त्रिपुरुषाणां । स्वकीयादानेन च कारयितव्यस् त्रिपुरुषाणाम् चतुर्थं

„ ६ स्थायी भट्टारकेण वारिकैश्च सर्वदा दृ(द्र)ष्टव्यः ॥ तथा श्री चंदले-श्वर-पूजनार्थं त्रिपुरुषाणां सत्कमठपतेः देव-नंदितग्रामे [व] खट्टक-नामा

„ ७ अरघट्टस्तत्र पति-श्रीपाल-समन्वितः प्रदत्तः स्थायी भट्टारकेण ॥ अत्र मेहरी विगडा-सीतडी-प्रेगली-रतना-श्रीयादेवी-आसदेवी । सू(ल?)वाल जसरा । पाणविक श्रीपाल (दो) ।

„ ८ यरक-वडियाकः । मार्दंगिक महीपतियाकः वांशिक गोविन्द-सुत-रिसिया [कः] भिटलवाडा-ग्रामीय-अरघट्टे कुमरद्रोणानां मध्या-दादाय द्रो५ प्रदातव्याः

„ ९ श्री-जसोधवलेन आहुमले शतपत्रभारः १ शतमेकं १०० प्रदत्तं । संवत् ११७३ कार्तिक वदि त्रि [तृ]तीयायां महाराजाधिराज-श्री आसरा-

„ १० जेन क···लोलियमठस्य प्रदत्ताः ॥ महाराज्ञी-श्रीचंदलादेव्या श्री चंदलेश्वरमध्यकारितगो (गौ) र्याः राजकुलेन प्रतिपादितपत्रा-

„ ११ णां शतं १ शतमेकं ॥ गु ंदकर्वायतवढातामोत्तामोवहंगत । टुलिया । ठहलहरा वालहरा । वीसल । वासलादि षड्भिः जनैः सर्वदा व॰ प्रति द्रम्मा-

„ १२ णां शतमेकं ददद्भिरंकितो द्र १०० तत्पत्रगोधूमानां त्रि(तृ)तीय-

पंक्ति भागं वर्मभिर्दातुकामैः कर्तव्यः ॥ अन्यदा संवत् ११७१ पौष वदि १० दश-

,, १३ म्यां महाराजाधिराज श्रीआसराजेन महरि सो[मि]काया गृहनिरीक्षणा-यागतेनास्याः पिच्छवल्लीग्रामः स्वसीमा-

,, १४ पर्यंतो ज्ञातमर्यादः प्रसादीकृतोस्या वुं(भुं) जयन्त्याः भुंजापयन्त्याः केनापि क्षितिक्षितिधरकालं यावत् परिपंथना न कार्या ॥

,, १५ अपरमग्रे मेहरी सोभिकायाः दीयमान-कुमर-द्रोणीय गोधूता (मा) नां पञ्चद्रोणी यावदेषां ग्रामं भुंजयति तावत् त्रिपुरुषैर्-

,, १६ भोक्तव्याः । अथ कदाचिद्-विधिवशाद् 'ग्राममेनं कोपि न पालयति तदा भूयोपि युज्यमाना कुमरद्रोणा महरिणा भोक्तव्याः ॥

,, १७ उपरिशासनमध्ये खर्वादायसहितः साऽलयी ग्रामो मठस्थायत्तः कृतस्तन्मध्यात् द्वौ भागौ मठस्य तृतीयांशस्त्रिपुरुषाणां प्रदत्तो अनया स्थित्या-

,, १८ भट्टारकेण वर्तनीयम् ॥ पुनर्महाराजाधिराज-श्री-रत्नपालेन नोरियाकः सकुटुम्बः प्रदत्तः श्री नड्डूलीयमंडपिकायां श्री आहव-

,, १९ म[ल्ले]न···मासं प्रति द्रो ६षट् आदातव्या अमीषां परिपंथना क्वापि न कार्या ॥ सम्वत् ११९२ कार्तिक वदि ५ शनावद्येह श्री-न

,, २० डूले महाराजपुत्र कुँवर श्री साहणपालदेवः शासनं प्रयच्छति यथा ॥ अग्रे नंदानाग्रामे वसमान-कुटुम्बिक सोहिय आसाइ [चौ]स पुत्रपौत्रादिको यावतजीजौ तावत् शासनस्थित्या श्री त्रिपुरुष-देवाय प्रद-

,, २१ त्तौ केनापि न लोपनीयः ॥ श्री त्रिपुरुषीयरथः श्री पद्मलेश्वर-साहण-पालेश्वर-सहजपालेश्वरादिदेवानां साध्यः सर्वदा ॥

,, २२ संवत् १२०५ भाद्र वदि शुद्रे (क्रे) महाराज-श्री आल्हणदेवेन प्राक् नंदानाग्रामीय-कुंटुकीकौ ॥ मदनपाल । महणसीहाः । अद्यैव श्री तृ (त्रि)पुरुषाणां शासनेन ।

,, २३ दत्ताः केनापि कदाचिद् न लोपनीयाः। तथानेन सालैपत्रा...सिंदासुताः प्रदत्ताः । तथा गोस्थलोभौ सडेन प्रदत्तौ । केनापि न लोपनीयं इति ॥

(*iv*) *The Nanāṇā Grant of Ālhaṇa, A Feudatory of Kumārapāla Chaulukya V.* 1219 *and* 1220

The copper plate grant published here was discovered in 1936. When I went to Ajmer the same year in connection with the present thesis the late Mahāmahopādhyāya Dr. Gaurishankar Hirachand Ojha was kind enough not only to show it to me but also to help me in deciphering it. He had discovered the grant at a village named Naṇāṇā,[1] about three miles from Bhagwānpur Railway Station on the Western Railway, which passes through Gujrāt and Rājasthān and links the two. This village was the findspot of another copper plate grant of Kumārapāla, published by Dr. Ojha in *ABORI*, XXIII

The script used is Nāgarī. Excepting the prose portion giving the date, the name of the Chaulukya overlord, Kumārapāla, his capital Aṇahilapāṭaka, details about donations, and a few words more, the record is in good Sanskrit verse. As regards orthography, the sign of *anusvāra* is mostly used, though at places, the nasal is also employed. A consonant following *r* is not unoften doubled. *Pṛiṣṭhamātrās* have been used.

The grant is issued from Aṇahilapāṭaka and is dated Monday, the 3rd day of the dark half of Pauṣa V. 1219 (26th November, 1162. A.D.) in the *Rāmarājya of Mahārājādhirāja* Kumārapāla, the vanquisher of the ruler of Śākambharī, while Yaśodhavala was in charge of the affairs of the State, secular as well as religious.

The genealogy of the donor, the Chāhamāna ruler, Ālhaṇa, begins with line five of plate I and can be tabulated as follows:—

1. Lakṣmaṇa in the Chāhamāna family ;
2. Sohi (Śobhita);
3. Balirāja at Naḍḍūla;
4. Mahīndra;
5. Aṇahila, who destroyed many rulers;
6. (Jendu) rāja (?) in the Saptaśata kingdom, the "mine of horses";
7. Āśārāja, who by the orders of his overlord, Siddharāja went to fight at Dhārā. Its ruler, Naravarman, shut himself behind the walls of his fort as soon as he saw Āśārāja;

1. *Rājasthān Museum Report*, 1937, Sri Om Prakash M.A., drew my attention to the notice of this grant in the report.

8. Ālhaṇa, son of Āśārāja and Delhaṇadevī, who saved the big army of the Gurjara King from extermination by slaying the Abhīra (?) chiefs, and also the ruler of Dhārā;

9. Prince Kelhaṇa.

Lines 16—23 of Plate I give the following genealogy of Ālhaṇa's maternal grandfather:—

1. Dhūhaḍa;
2. Haradatta, the ruler of Vishṇudvāra;
3. Kumārapāla;
4. Kīrtipāla at Devavardhanapura;
5. Haripāla, the brother of No. 4, of whom even the Hammīra was afraid. Out of his fear the Turuṣka horses, even though afflicted with thirst, did not dare to drink water.

A brother of Kumārapāla, No. 3 above, was the *nṛipati* Rudrapāla, the lord of Sārasvata *bhūtala*, whose daughter, Delhaṇadevikā, was the mother of Ālhaṇa Chāhamāna.

The details of donations begin with line 9 of Plate II. Ālhaṇa granted to the god Tṛipuruṣadeva the *balādhipābhāvya* (the cess due to the *balādhipa*) of the village Nandāṇā. This had so far been appropriated by 'merciless' rulers every year, even though the village revenues were being enjoyed by Tṛipuruṣadeva. Similarly he granted the *balādhipābhāvya* of the village Bhīṭalavāṭaka, then being enjoyed by Chaṇḍāleśvara, to that very god. To the image of Gaurī set up in the *garbhagṛha* of Chaṇḍāleśvara by Queen Śaṅkaradevī, he assigned 4 *drammas* from the customs house for her daily offerings.

The record up to this point was written by Kheläditya. To it there is an addendum in smaller letters, written by Ṭha (kkura) Śrīdhara, specifying the grant of three 'ploughs' of land by Ālhaṇa to Tṛipuruṣadeva from the village Chāmuṇḍī. This grant is dated Thursday, the 11th day of the bright half of Āṣāḍha, V. 1220.

Of the places mentioned in the grant Aṇahilapāṭaka is the present Pātaṇ, 25N. 70E. Naḍḍūla is Nāḍol of Western Rājasthān, 25 N. 72E. Saptaśata was the term used for the Chāhamāna kingdom of which Nāḍol was the capital. Dhārā (present Dhāra) was capital of the Paramāras of Mālwā. Sārasvatabhūtala may be some territory lying on the banks of the river Sarasvatī of Northern Gujarāt. Viṣṇudvāra looks like Haridwār, though it is difficult to be sure on this point; other geographical names in the record are Devavardhanapura, Nandāṇā, Bhīṭalavāṭaka and Caṁvoḍī. As the last three of these were obviously under Ālhaṇa who had been restored to the kingdom of Nāḍol sometime between V. 1216 and 1218, it may be assumed that they were in the modern Jodhpur division of Rājasthān which includes all the territory once ruled over by the Chāhamānas of Nāḍol. I am not sure of the location of Devavardhanapura.

The record is of considerable historical interest. So far the last known date for Ālhaṇa was V. 1218. The present record takes his reign upto V. 1220 in which year he was succeeded by Kelhaṇa. From Kīrtipāla's grant of V. 1218, Ālhaṇa is known to have defeated the Saurāṣṭrikas. The present record supplies the additional information that he slew the ruler of Dhārā, an adversary of the Gurjara ruler. We have perhaps to identify this ruler with Ballāla, though the credit of slaying him has been assigned also to Yaśodhavala Paramāra of Ābū by the *Tejaḥpālapraśasti* and to some Brāhmaṇa soldiers by the *Dvyāśrayakāvya* of Hemachandra.

We know from the Śūndhā Inscription that Ālhaṇa's father, Āśārāja rendered meritorious service in Jayasiṁha Siddharāja's Mālwā campaign. From the present record, it appears that Naravarman Paramāra, though defeated, did not lose Mālwā. Driven into the fort of Dhārā by the combined forces of Jayasiṁha Siddharāja and his feudatories, he stood the siege with success, for otherwise the record would have claimed that Āśārāja captured the Paramāra capital.

Interesting also is the reference to Haripāla, a cousin of Ālhaṇa's mother, Delhaṇadevī, as *Hammīraśaṅkākaraḥ*, *i.e.* as one who inspired terror in the heart of the Hammīra. That 'Hammīra' here stands for the word 'Amīr' is made obvious by the further statement that due to Haripāla's fear the Turuṣka horses did not drink water in spite of being extremely thirsty. I have identified elsewhere this Hammīra with Ibrāhim of Ghaznā who, according to Firishta, raided India and reached the western coast of the country.

Of the words used in the record, *baladhipābhāvya* needs some explanation. It appears from inscriptions of Western Rājasthān and Gujarāt that rulers and feudal chiefs regarded themselves as entitled to a number of minor cesses, besides their share in the land produce and customs duties. These cesses, called *ābhāvyas*, accrued to them on account of their real or supposed services as *balādhipas* and *talāras* etc. and could be realised even from villages given away in charity.

TEXT

Plate 1

Line 1. [ओ संवत्] १२१६···वर्षेषु एकोनविंशत्यधिकेषु च पौषवदि ३ सोमे । अ-

,, 2. द्येह श्रीमदणहिल [पाटके। महाराजाधिराजस्य जितशाकंभरीपतेः] श्रीमत्कुमारपालस्य रामराज्ये ज-

,, 3. ···।। श्री-यशोधवल···श्रीकरणमुद्रे व स्वामिधर्म्मार्थकारिणि ।। प्रसादा-

,, 4. [द्भू] भुजो मुख्यश्रीमदल्हणभूपतेः । सर्वभूभागे भुज्यमानक्रमागते ।। जाते एवंविधे काले शासनं

,, 5. लिख्यते यथा ।। कृत्वा शासन···पूर्वजवर्णनं ।। क्षोणीमंडनचाहमान-विमले वंशे विशालाचले

,, 6. श्रीमल्लक्ष्मणनामभूपति[रभू]त्सँग्रामरामोपमः ।। तत्पुत्रोथ बभूव सोहि···। नडडूले ब-

,, 7. लिराजभूपतिरतो जातो महीन्द्रो नृपः ।। सँजातोथ महीपतिरण-हिलः [श्रीमान्महीन्द्रा]त्मजो हत्वा येन न-

,, 8. रेन्द्रवृन्दमखिलं ···। यद्द्वारे रिपुसुन्दरीनिजधव [प्रध्वंसभीता सदा···नयनांबुना प्रति-

,, 9. दिनं तिष्ठन्ति तेज···।···यो बहुभूपदर्प्पदलनप्रोद्भूतभूपार्ज्जकस्तुं-गाश्वस्थितमत्तकुञ्जरमुखप्रक्षि-

,, 10. प्तकुन्ताहवः ।[1] तेजस्वी···[राज] तनयः पश्चादभूद् भूषणं राज्ये सप्तशताख्यदुर्लभतरे नानातुरँगाकरे ।

,, 11. तस्यानन्तर···भूपतिलकः काले [अ] दूरात्कले । पुत्रोभूत्कल (लि) कालकल्मषबहिःप्रोत्तुगंतेजाः स हि । आशा-

1. The compound is obscure. Does it mean तुंगाश्वस्थितेन मत्त-कुञ्जरमुखे क्षिप्तः कुन्त आहवे येन सः ।

,, 12. राजमहीपतिर्गुणगणालँकारभूमँडनो विख्यातो यशसा सुविक्रम··· कँदर्परूपाकृतिः । य[श्छ[त्रो-

,, 13. त्तानमेघडँबर [निभ] श्चँडप्रतापान्वितः सँप्राप प्रभुसिद्धराजवचसा युद्धाय धारानले (तले) । दृ[ष्ट्वा] मुँजगती-

,, 14. ···नड्लनाथाकृतिं तद्भीत्या नरवर्म्मभूपतिरभूत्प्राकारदुर्ग्गाश्रयः ।। तत्पुत्रोथकुलप्रदीपक[···]

,, 15. ···दभूदल्हणः क्षोणीपाल इलातलक्षितिभुजामुत्पा [ट] रक्षाक्षमः । येनैतान् गिरिगह्वरान्त-

,, 16. ···भीरधाराधिपान् रक्षितमे[व]गूर्ज्जरपतेर्ग्ग्रस्तं [म] हान्तं दलं । यन्मातामहपूर्वजः क्षितिभु-

,, 17. जां जेता च दातार्थिनां श्रीमद् घूहडनृपो बभूव सुकृती[2] । तस्याथ स्थिरचँडभास्करसमः

,, 18. ख्यातप्रतापो ह्यभूद् विष्णुद्वारनरेश्वरो रिपुवधूवैधव्यदानप्रदः । पश्चात्तत्र विचित्रविक्रमगुण-

,, 19. ···भूमीश्वरो जातः श्रीहरदत्तनामनृपतिस्तेजोधराभास्करः[3] ।। सूनुस्तस्य कुमारपालनृपतिस्त्या-

,, 20. गी वि··· [युद्ध] मु [च्छि] तमहीविन्यस्तकीर्तिक्रमः । त[त्सूनु-स्त्वथ देववर्द्धनपुरे] श्रीकीर्ति-

,, 21. पालाभिधो जा [तः···] पतेस्तुरँगमनृणां सँहारकर्ता रणे । तद्भ्राता हरिपालनाम विदितो हम्मीरशँका-

,, 22. करो य[द्भीत्या न जलँ] तुरुष्कतुरगैः पीतँ तृषार्तैरपि ।। भ्राता त] स्य कुमारपालनृपतेः···धरित्रीयशो-

,, 23. विख्यातस्त्विह रुद्रपालनृपतिः सद्वँद्यकर्म्मक्रमः ।। तत्सारस्वत-पुण्यभूतलपतेः प्राणप्रिया गुन्हिका । सँ-

,, 24. जाता हि महासती प्रतिदिनँ गंगेव वंद्या सतां ।। नाम्ना देल्हण-देविकेति जगति प्रख्यातशीलामला । सा-

,, 25. भूदल्हणभूपतेर्विजयिनो मातातिपुत्रप्रिया ।। तत्पुत्रस्य बृहस्पतेरिव गुणा बुद्धिश्च वि[ष्णो]र्यथा तेज-

,, 26. [स्तस्य] रवेरिव क्षितितले सौम्यत्वमिंदोरिव । रामस्येव जनानु-रागविभवः श्रीअल्हणक्ष्माप-

2. Some words are omitted here.

3. The text seems to be defective. Perhaps we may read तेजोधरो भास्करः ।

„ 27. तेः सौ [शौ] र्यं तस्य बलेरिवास्ति विदितं गांभीर्यमब्धेरिव ।। सांभोधि-
क्षितिखंडमंडनम-

28. हे दीनार्थिकल्पद्रुमो जातो भूपकुमारविक्रमयशोविख्यात-

Plate 2

Line 1. चूडामणिः । श्रीमत्केल्हण आत्मवँशकमलप्रद्योतनार्थो रविर्भक्तो
रामवदल्हणस्य नृपतेः पुत्रः प-

„ 2. वित्रो भुवि ।। ईदृग्वँशगुणाधारः श्रीमदल्हणभूपतिः । विचिन्तयति
सँसारमसारा [का] रदुस्तरम् ।।

„ 3. सँसारे दशदुःखभीतमनसा गत्वाथ ती[र्थो]दकैः स्नात्वा निर्मल-
धौतपोतयुगलँ विन्यस्य चांगे निजे ।

„ 4. पश्चात्तँ जगतां पतिं त्रिपुरुषं संतर्प्य (र्प्य) पंचामृतैः कर्पूरोदक-
चारुचन्दनरसैर्लिप्त्वा समग्रं ततः सद्यश्चँप-

„ 5. कमालतीशतदल-व्याकोषपुष्पांबुजैः सँपूज्याथ यथोचितँ सुमनसा
स्तुत्वा च नत्वा चिरँ । नैवेद्यं सरसं

„ 6. प्रदाय बहुधा पुण्यप्रदारात्रकँ[4] पश्चात्प्रेक्षणकँ मनोधृतिकरँ तौर्यं
त्रिकालँ कृतँ ।। कृत्वैतद्द्विजदेवता-[5]

„ 7. स गुरूनभ्यर्च्य नानाधनैः पित्रोः स्वस्य च धर्मकीर्तियशसां सँवृद्धये
श्रद्धया । अथानन्तरँ च । अनल्पचेतसा

„ 8. स्वर्गापवर्गमार्गाप्रयासप्रकाशकफलप्रदँ । धर्मस्थानकं तदुपद्रवश्च
क्षितितलमहीपालतिलको महीपतिरसौ प-

„ 9. रिभावयति । परिभाव्य च भगवतः सकलसुरासुरगुरोः श्रीमत्रि(त्त्रि)
पुरुषदेवस्य प्रभुज्यमाननँदाणग्रामस्य । ग्राम-

„ 10. स्यास्य परत्र भीरुमनसा दृष्ट्वा गृहीतँ तदा प्रत्यब्दँ हि बलाधिय-
(प)क्रमपदाभाव्यँ नृपैर्निष्क्रपैः । पश्चादल्हणदेवभूतल-

„ 11. भुजा चन्द्रार्क्ककालावधि कृत्वास्मै तिलदर्भतोयविधिना संकल्पदत्तँ
सदा ।। राजभिः कृतधर्माणां जन्मकल्याणकारि-

„ 12. णां । लुप्तिः केनापि नो कार्या स्वर्ग्गसौख्यप्रदायिना । एतदेव मया
दत्तँ लोभाद् गृह्णाति यो नरः । मातुस्तस्य चरत्येव रासभः प्र-

„ 13. तिवासरँ ।। तथा च श्रीमच्नँदलेश्वरदेवस्य प्रभुज्यमानभीटलवाटक-
ग्रामस्य बलाधिपाभा-

4. आरात्रक is the same as आरात्रिकं 'waving a light before a dīvine image'.

5. The text here is defective.

" 14. व्यँ श्रद्धानुविद्धया भक्त्या श्रीमच्चँदलेश्वरदेवाय प्रदत्तमिति ।।
" 15. अपरँ च महाराजाधिराजश्रीमदल्हणदेवेन चँदलेश्वरदेवकीयगर्भगृह-
मध्ये
" 16. राज्ञी श्रीशँकरदेव्या कारापितगौर्यै प्रतिदिनभोगनिमित्तं शुल्क-
मँडपिकायां
" 17. प्रतिमासँ प्रदत्ता द्रम्भाश्चत्वारः । ते च चन्द्रार्ककालं यावत् परिपा-
लनीयाः । लुप्ति यो-
" 18. स्य विधास्यति प्रगतधीः पंचातिपापालयो यो वा शासनलोपहेतुवचसां
वक्ता भविष्य-
" 19. त्यपि । स्वर्ग···कृष्टसप्तपितरस्तस्यैव पापात्मनः कुंभीपाकनिरंत-
घोरनरके
" 20. यास्यंति तेधोमुखाः ।। ममास्ते शासनारूढः श्रीमदल्हणभूपतेः ।
दानांबुनिर्मली-
" 21. भूतः स्वहस्तो दक्षिणो ह्ययं ।। महाराजाधिराजस्य श्रीमदल्हणभूभुजः ।
पुरतो लि-
" 22. खितं चेदं खेलादित्यने (त्येन) शासनं[6] ।। इति संवत्[7] १२२० आषाढ़
शुदि ११ गुरुदिने देवस्य प्र[ति]
" 23. एकादशीपर्वणि त्रित्रिपुरुषदेवाय चांवोडीग्रामभूमिमध्यात (त्) वी
[भ्र] हाइडुंगर-पश्चिम-दिग्भागे महाराजाधिरा-
" 24. ज-श्रीअल्हणदेवेन हलत्रयभूमी स्वसीमापर्यंता शासनेन प्रदत्ता ।
लिखितमिदं ठ० श्रीधरे ए (ण) प्रभुराज्ञतः ।। ओम् ।।

(v) *A Fragmentary Nāḍol Family Grant*

नाडौल के चौहानों का एक खण्डित ताम्राभिलेख

केवल पहला ताम्रपत्र (दूसरा प्राप्त नहीं है)

पंक्ति १ ॐ स्वस्ति ।। ॐ नमो विघ्नेश्वराय ।···
वंदित त्रिपथगास्रोत पवित्रीकृत...
प्रालेयांशुकला [सु] कंदलवती स्कंधे फणींद्रं सदा ।
निःशेषीकृत सारिद-
" २ पंदलनं पाणौ पिनाकं धनुः
······ध्रियुगलो देवो हरः श्रेयसे ।।
ब्रह्मा ब्रह्मज्ञानं भवतां भगवान् सर्गकृद्राट् ।
यस्य चतुराननेभ्यश्चत्वा-

6. From तथा च (p. 212) the letters are bold and in a different hand. From संवत् to the end of the epigraph, letters are again small.

पंक्ति ३ रो······[4]ता वेदाः ॥
हरिर्हरतु······यस्य स्मरण······
·········भास्पदं भवति ॥
वंशेस्त्यत्र धरातलस्य सकलस्यास्य परो-

,, ४ क्षालयः
पत्रालीभिरवेष्टितः कलरवः पर्वप्रधानो महान् ।
अ[- -] सरलो द्विजैः परिवृतो यश्चोन्नतः सर्वदा
श्रीमाणिक्य-सुचाहमानजनकोना···

,, ५ —आसी—गुणान्वितः सुचरितः सत्यप्रधानः शुचिः
शांतः शंभुरतः शशांकसदृशः श्रीश्लिष्टदेशेश्वरः
विख्यातो वसुधातलैकवसुदो वि [ज्ञा]·····

,, ६ ······श्री लक्ष्मणोस्यां क्षितौ ।
स्थानेस्मिन् प्रवरे कलांकविकलश्रीबालखिल्यात्मके
नाडूले द्विजपुंगवैः श्रुतिपरैः संसे-

,, ७ वितः सर्वतः ।
येनेदं चित···लोपलमलं नाम्ना निजेनांकितं
नानारूपकरूपरंजितजनं हर्म्यं हरेः कारितम् ॥
तस्मादाविरभूदनंतमहिमा प्राज्यप्रतापान्वितः

,, ८ पुत्रः शोभितसंज्ञितः शुभमतिः संशोभितः सद्गुणैः ।
संख्येसंख्यपराक्रमरतो वैरीभपंचाननो
नानानागमदप्रवाहसलिलैः संसिक्तभू-

,, ९ मण्डलः ॥
तस्माद् बभूव नृपतिर्बलिराजसंज्ञः
भूरिप्रभावसहितो रणकृत्यविज्ञः ।
यस्यारिभिः प्रियतमैरपि पीलुसेवा-
सुश्रीफलादनपरैर्विहिता सदै-

,, १० व ॥
तस्माद्विग्रहपालसंज्ञ-नृपतिर्जज्ञे जनेस्मिन् जयी
नानाविग्रहकर्मलब्धमहिमा त्यागैकधाराधरः ।
यातैर्यस्य समुत्थितेन रजसा तन्मण्डलं भास्यते

4. त्रुटित स्थान पर "निःसृ" रखा जा सकता है ।

पंक्ति ११ मेघेनैव जलान्वितेन पिहिते न ज्ञायते कुत्रचित् ।।
योो नित्यं विवु(बु) धाश्रितो गुरुरतो नागेन्द्रगामी च यः
,, १२ प्राप्तं येन महास्पदं सुरभवं मुख्यैर्मखैर्निर्मितैः ।
सो···त्र महेन्द्रतुल्यनृपतिर्नाम्ना महेन्द्रोभवत्
तस्याभूदणहिल्लदेवनृपतिः क्षत्र······ण्णवैः ।।
,, १३ ल··························
संग्रामांगणमंडनो निजकुलव्योमार्क वि(बि) म्वो (म्बो) दयः
भीमा भीमनियोजिता गजवरा येन प्रतिष्ठानके
हत्वा तद्रथिकान् कुतूहलवशाद् भग्ना विपुच्छाः
,, १४ कृताः ।
हत्वा सीमाधिपान् संख्ये तेषां ग्रामान् प्रगृह्य च
देशः सप्तशतो येन सप्तसाहस्रिकः कृतः ।।
बालप्रसाद इत्युक्तो बालार्काभोत्र तत्सुतः
ह्यभूद् वा (बा) ल्ये-
,, १५ पि भूपाला
येन ·········विनिर्जिताः ।।
तस्यानुजो जने जेता जेंद्रराजो यतोभवत् ।।
जगत्यां जगतीपालः पालिताशेषमण्डलः ।।
संप्राप्ते भीम-सैन्य-जलधौ ग्रा-
,, १६ मेत्र संडेरके
नानावाद्य-राश्वस···निस्त्रिंशमालाकुले ।
प्रो [न्मत्त] द्विप [रोधि] वीर्यसहिते प्रासोर्मिमालाधरे
कोपाग्रेण विचित्रशस्त्रनि [क] रे······
,, १७ पृथुवत् पृथिवीपालस्तत्पुत्रः पृथुलोचनः पृथिव्यां
पार्थिवो जज्ञे पार्थतुल्यपराक्रमः ।।
त्यक्त्वा पुत्रकलत्रमातृविभवान् लज्जां तथा दूरतो
नष्टा मंडलिक [प्र] जा
,, १८ प्रति दिशं काम्मेण संप्रेषिताः ।
तस्मिन् रोहडवापिको [त्थ] समरे यत्प्रासपृष्ठाहताः
सर्वे रक्तपरिप्लुता भयपराः प्रापुः स्थितिं न क्वचित् ।।
तस्यानुजो जयी जज्ञे रा-
,, १९ जा राजीवलोचनः ।
जोजकाख्यो महाभिख्यस्ततो विनततथ्यभाक् ।।

पंक्ति आसाराजो महाराजस्तस्यानुजोऽभवत् ।
भवभूधरशंभूनां भूरिशक्तिसमन्वितः ॥
पराः पर-
,, २० मदुः······गाः प्रमदोत्कटा यस्य
द्वारे प्रदृश्यंते शृंखला [स्ख] लिता हयाः ॥
शौचं पाशुपतं दयां जि [नवरां] दानं सदा यज्विनः
भक्ति भागवतां ······
,, २१ मताः कौलाः गौरवम् ।
एवं दर्शनषट्कजव्रतधरा एतान् गुणान् कृत्स्नशः
मन्ये यस्य महात्मनः क्षितिभृतः···सदा शिक्षिताः ॥
बालेनापि सतात्र येन-
,, २२ समरे········· ॥
पृथ्वीपालमहीपतिर्गजगतौ रुद्धः परैः स्वैर्विना
स्तोकेनापि बलेन शक्तिवशतो हत्वा तुरुष्कोत्करान् ।
स्कँदेनेव गणेश्वरो दनु -
,, २३ जैः सँवेष्टितः सर्वतः ॥
दायादापहृतँ च दुर्गमतुलँ माण्डव्यसँज्ञँ पुरँ
यः श्रुत्वा बलसंयुतः प्रकुपितः गत्वा·········च ।
नाना-शस्त्रधरैः नरैः परितँ
,, २४ ·····························
-त्प्राकारमुपेत्य योधनिकरान् हत्वा तु चक्रे वसे (शे) ॥
लोकाज्ञाततलँ सनिर्मलजलँ कल्लोलमालाकुलँ
नाना प [क्षि]-
,, २५ धरँ प्रभूत सह···मँडूककर्माकरँ ।
वृक्षालिसदनँ स्वनामकथनँ तृष्णार्तिनिर्णाशिनँ
येनास्मिन् विततँ तडागमुचितँ पाश्चात्यभागे कृतम् ॥

PART II

CHAUHĀN ADMINISTRATION AND LIFE IN THE CHAUHĀN DOMINIONS

CHAPTER XXI

CHAUHAN INSTITUTIONS : CIVIL AND MILITARY

We have no books like the *Kauṭilīya Arthaśāstra*, *Śukranītisāra*, or the *Āin-i-Akbarī* dealing specifically or in general with the administration and administrative problems of the Chauhān kingdoms and their neighbours. Consequently we have to glean the necessary details from Chauhān inscriptions and literary sources like the *Kharataragachchhapaṭṭāvalī*, the *Lalita-Vigraharāja-nāṭaka*, the *Kānhaḍadeprabandha*, and the *Lekhapaddhati*,[1] all of them good enough in their own way no doubt, but none of them sufficient to give us the complete picture that we should like to have.

The ruler. In the Chauhān dominions, as elsewhere in the Indian kingdoms of the period, the ruler formed the keystone of the administrative arch. Legally he was an absolute monarch, the head of the civil as well as military administration, with his powers circumscribed, indeed by the will of the overlord, if he had any. Poets and scholars described him as divine, sometimes even identifying him either with Viṣṇu himself or one of his famous *avatāras*. The Śiwālik Pillar Inscription (V. 1220) hints at Vigraharāja IV's identity with Viṣṇu;[2] the *Pṛthvīrājavijaya* calls him an *aṁśa*[3] of *Madhudviṣa*.[4] To the writer of the Hānsī Inscription (V. 1226) Pṛthvīrāja II is, undoubtedly, Rāma[5]; the *Pṛthvīrājavijaya* gives the same honour to his cousin, Pṛth-

1. The *paddhati* deals in the main with the institutions of the empire of Gujarāt which included at times the Chauhān kingdoms of Nāḍol and Jālor and was almost throughout in relations of enmity or friendship with the Chauhān empire of Śākambharī.

२. शङ्का वा पुरुषोत्तमस्य भवतः नास्त्येव वारांनिधे-
न्निर्म्मथ्यापहृतश्रियः किमु भवान् क्रोडे न निद्रायितः

(2nd inscription, verse 2)

3. VI, 33. *Aṁśa*=a secondary incarnation.

4. "Enemy of Madhu", a name of Viṣṇu.

५. पृथ्वीराजो महाराजो रामोसौ संशयं विना

(line 14)

vīrāja III.[6] Both, *Naiṇsī's Khyāt* and the *Kānhaḍadeprabandha*, regard Kānhaḍadeva of Jālor as an *avatāra* of Kṛṣṇa or Gokulanātha ; and his enemy, Alāuddīn Khaljī as some demon reborn to avenge his previous discomfitures.[7] A natural corollary of such suppositions, that on their death the rulers got merged into the divinities they represented, was also not unknown.[8]

But this ascription of divine character to the rulers did not mean that they were to rule arbitrarily. They were divine, if their conduct was above reproach; they were *avatāras* of Viṣṇu, if they upheld the established moral and social order and fought against its enemies. Vigraharāja IV tried to turn Northern India into a real Āryāvarta;[9] he could not tolerate any insult to Indian sacred places, gods and Brāhmaṇas.[10] Similar was also the role played by the other rulers regarded as divine in some way or other. They were divine because of their divine function. When one overstepped *dharma*, Indian writers consigned the ruler to hell, in spite of his royalty.[11]

Another check on the autocratic tendencies of a ruler was supplied by the established usage that a ruler should consult his ministers on all important matters of policy, internal as well as external. The *Lalita-Vigraharāja* shows Vigraharāja IV taking counsel with the *mantrin*, Śrīdhara, and the *Senāpati* (?) Siṁhabala before proceeding against the Hammīra. Pṛthvīrāja III's decisions were influenced by Kadamabavāsa; Kānhaḍadeva's were mostly those of the King-in-Council.[12] A third check, that of local usage and local government, also operated as strongly in Rājasthān as in other parts of India. "The self-governing groups", as remarked by Dr. R.K. Mookerji, "upon

6. I, 33; VI, 35 and 47; VII, 5; VIII, 10; IX, 32-3 etc.

7. *See* above the account of Kānhaḍadeva and *Kānhaḍadeprabandha*, III v.v. 215-220 and IV, 219-220.

8. *See PV*. VIII, 77-78; *Kānhaḍadeprabandha*, IV, 293.

9. *See* above, p. 70; footnote 38.

10. *See* above, p. 69; footnote 32.

11. *See* for instance,

तेषामेकतमं मध्ये नापश्यत् पितृवैरिणम् ।
क्वचिदप्यन्धतामिस्रे मग्नं व्रीडावशादिव ॥

(*PV*., VIII, 741)

12. *Kānhaḍadeprabandha*, I, 32; III, 131; IV, 55, etc.

which the State was founded formed a vast subterranean democracy limiting the absolutism of the sovereign at the top."[13]

When a ruler overrode any of these salutary checks, as was for instance done by Hammīra towards the end of his reign, there was serious disaffection. Jagaddeva, the parricide, could not rule long, because his heinous crime shocked public conscience. On the other hand, Kānhaḍadeva retained to the last the affections of his people, on account of his being one with them in their prejudices as well as aspirations.

The early rulers of Śākambharī called themselves *bhūpas*, *nṛpas*, and *mahārājas*.[14] But from the time of Pṛthvīrāja I onwards, they are styled *Paramabhaṭṭāraka-Mahārājādhirāja-Parameśvara*. This new title reflects a great increase in their power. Pṛthvīrāja III had the additional title, *Bhārateśvara*, because he aspired to the overlordship of the whole of Northern India.[15] Bālaṇa deva of Raṇthambhor was a mere *gaḍhapati i.e.*, the owner of a fort,[16] and Hammīra, though described as a *digvijayin* by Naya chandra Sūri, did not claim any title higher than *nṛpa*,[17] rather a non-commital appellation used also by the Chauhān rulers of Dholpur and Rāyabaddiya. Bhartṛvaḍḍha II of Broach must have been a little higher in the feudal scale. He was a *Parama māheśvara-samadhigatapañchamahāśabda-mahāsāmantādhipa ti i.e.*, a feudatory chief of the first order entitled to the five *mahāśabdas*.[18] The highest title of the rulers of Nāḍol and Jālor was *Mahārājādhirāja*.[19] Indrarāja of the Pratāpgarh branch was a mere *mahāsāmanta*, and Saṅgrāmasiṁha of Broach remained a *mahāmaṇḍaleśvara*, even though he claimed to be independent of the Yādavas of Devagiri as well as the Chaulukyas of Gujarāt), probably, because his immediate predecessors had recognised the Paramāras of Mālwa as their overlords.

The Yuvaraja and other members of the royal family.

13. Chandragupta, Maurya, 1st edition , p. 84.
14. See the Harṣa inscription of v. 1030.
15. PV, XI,8.
16. See his Manglānā inscription, IA., 1912, pp. 85-88.
17. See his Balvan inscription as well as the Hammīramahākāvya.
18. See above the account of the Chauhāns of Bhṛgukachchha.
19. Kelhaṇa is once called also Mahārājādhirāja Parameśvara Jhaṁvera inscription, JASB., 1916, pp. 103-4. But he does not have the imperial title Paramabhaṭṭāraka even in this record.

Next in importance to the ruler stood the *Yuvarāja*. He was mostly but not always the king's eldest son.[20] Many Chauhān inscriptions combine the name of the *Yuvarāja* with that of the ruler, showing thereby the high estimation in which the public held the heir-apparent's office.[21] *Yuvarāja* Kelhaṇa shared with his father the privilege of granting and confirming *jāgīrs*.[22] Kānhaḍadeva, though merely a *Yuvarāja* up to V. 1262, so far overhadowed his father in ability and influence, that even the achievements of his father's reign were ascribed to him by later generations.[23] If the ruler considered himself unfit or was, for any reason, disinclined to carry on the work of government, he could abdicate in favour of the *Yuvarāja*. Ajayarāja of Śakambharī, for instance, retired to the Puṣkara forest after putting Arṇorāja on the throne.[24] The motive might have been to have on the throne someone energetic enough to deal with the increasing frequency and ferocity of Ghaznavite raids. Jaitrasiṁha of Raṇthambhor, similarly, went away to a hermitage on the Chambal. An incurable disease, perhaps leprosy, rendered the abdication necessary.

The inscriptions of Āsarāja and Kelhaṇa show their younger sons taking an important part in administration.[25] But it is difficult to generalise from these particular instances. And equally difficult it is to speak of the power wielded by the Chauhān queens in general. Some of them were influential enough. Ajayarāja's queen, Somalladevī, had coins of her own.[26] Chandana's queen, Rudrāṇī, was a person of some consequence.[27] But mostly we hear of queens only in connection with donations and charities or *jauhar* fires.

Regents. Minor kings had not any great chance in that

20. Hammīra, for instance, was not the eldest son of Jaitrasiṁha. In the neighbouring kingdom of Chandrāvatī, Prahlādana was the *Yuvarāja*, even though his brother Dhārāvarṣa had a son named Somasiṁha.

21. See for instance the Sevāḍi stone-inscription of Aśvarāja, the Sevāḍi inscription of Kaṭudeva, and the Jālor inscription of Sāmantasiṁha (*EI*, XI, pp. 29, 31 and 61 respectively).

22. *See* the Nāḍol plates of *Rājaputra* Kīrtipāla (*EI*, IX, p. 66 f.)

23. *See* above, p. 180.

24. *See* above, p. 47.

25. *See* above, p. 154, 157.

26. *See* above, p. 46.

27. *See* above, p. 31.

turbulent age. Generally they were passed over in favour of someone better qualified to rule. But in a few cases there were regencies. Jojalla, the *rājyachintaka*, a maternal uncle of Samarasiṁha, may have been a regent.[28] Vāgbhaṭa, the younger brother of Prahlādana of Raṇthambhor, supervised the kingdom for his nephew, Vīranārāyaṇa, during his minority.[29] The administration of the regent, Karpūradevī, won the deserved encomium of Jayānaka.[30]

The royal court. A splendid court generally surrounded the ruler. On being divested of its exaggerations and verbosity, the contemporary account of Pṛthvīrāja III's court in the *Kharataragachchhapaṭṭāvali* shows that it was mainly composed of ministers, *mahāmaṇḍaleśvaras*, *sāmantas*, warriors of well-recognised merit, pandits, poets, bards, musicians and courtesans.[31] The Hall of Audience was paved with stone of high quality, strewn with fragrant flowers, and overspread by a rich canopy of blue cloth, with pendants ending in strings of pearls. Here the ruler took counsel on public matters; and here were judged not merely the claims of ordinary litigants but also of religious and literary disputants, the ruler in the latter case being largely guided by the advice of his court *pandits* and poets. The entrance to it was regulated by *pratihāras*; and everyone, whatever his caste or religion, could have access to the ruler.[32]

Ministry. In his transaction of the business of the State, the ruler naturally had to seek the assistance of a number of ministers whose number and importance might have differed according to the size of the State and the ruler they advised. On the basis of available evidence, we have the following list of Chauhān ministers.

28. *See* above, p. 165, 166

29. *See* above, p. 119.

30. *See* above, p. 80, footnote 5.

31. *See* p. 28.

32. *Lalita-Vigraharāja*, line 32 of the inscription, *IA*, XX, p. 201 ff. *PV.*, XI, 6-7.

Another good description of a Chauhān ruler's *darbār* is to be found in Padmanābha's *Kānhaḍadeprabandha*, which in spite of the comparative lateness of its composition, appears in this case to have given a true picture of the Jālor court. Perhaps the successors of Kāṇhaḍadeva, at the court of one of whom

(1) *Mahāmantrin or Mahāmātya.* The *Mahāmantrin* was in charge of the royal seals, exercised general supervision over all departments, specially revenue, and generally was the most trusted and influential member of the ministry.[33] Of Vigraharāja's *Mahāmantrins* we know two, Śrīdhara and *rājaputra* Sallakṣaṇapāla[34]. Pṛthvirāja III's chief adviser, Kadambavāsa, held the title *Maṇḍaleśvara*, which fact indicates perhaps the assignment of some territories to him either by way of salary or to support his dignity[35]. Of the *Mahāmātyas* of Nāḍol, Lakṣmīdhara held the post in V. 1218 in the reign of Ālhaṇa. Bālhaṇa was a *Mahāmātya* in V. 1249, in Kelhaṇa's reign. Yaśovīra and Jaita Devaḍā are names famous in the history of Jālor; and the career of the notorious Dharmasiṁha shows that the Chief Minister, though a creature of his master's will, could by his policy and cunning encompass the ruin of a State.[36]

Padmanābha flourished, kept up the old state, in spite of the decline of their power.

The description is as follows:—

शतभूमिका सहस्रभूमिका सभानी रचना। सिंहासन परठु छइ। मेघवना ऊलेच बांध्या छइ। परियचि ढली छइ। महाराजाधिराज कान्हडदे सभा पूरी बइठु छइ। केतकी ना गंध गहगहिया छइ। सोरभ ना सोड आवर्या छइ। सभा मांहि सेरी मेल्हाणि छइ। जाइ, वेल, वालु, कंद, मचकंद, दमणु, मरुउ, पाडलना परिमल। पंचवर्ण पुष्पजातिना प्रकर पाथर्या छइ। गुलालना गन्धराग गहिगह्या छइ। पडियां कपूर पगि चांपीय छइ। घोडा विहालइ घाला छइ। हाथीयानी सारसी आगलि कांनि पडिउ कांइ नथी सांभलीत। पतिलहरना मादलनो धौंकार बाजि छइ। नृत्यकी नृत्य करि छइ। तत वितत आनन्द घन शुषिर पंचशब्द वाजि बाजइ छइ। पंचवर्ण छत्र धरियां छइ। चामर व्यजन विहु पासि हुइ छइ। अमात्य मंडल प्रधान, सामन्त, माण्डलिक, श्रीगरणा, वयगरणा, मुकुटबर्द्धन, अङ्गलेह मसाहणी, टावरी, वारहीया एवंवधि पुरुषि बइठु छइ।

(*Kānhaḍadeprabandha, Bhaṭāulī, Pariśiṣṭa*)

33. The chief departments were *Śrīkaraṇa*, *Vyayakaraṇa*, *maṇḍapikā-karaṇa*, and *Koṣṭhika* (*See* the *Lekhapaddhati*, G.O.S. for further details).

34. *See* respectively the *Lalita-Vigraharāja-nāṭaka* and the Śiwālik Pillar Inscription of V. 1220.

35. Or it may be that he was a *Maṇḍaleśvara* in his own right as a hereditary ruler of certain territories.

36. *See* above, pp. 127 ff.

(2) *Senāpati or Daṇḍanāyaka.* Next in importance to the Chief Minister was the *Senāpati* or *Daṇḍanāyaka.* We have already mentioned Vigraharāja IV's Commander-in-chief, Siṁhabala.[37] During Pṛthvīrāja III's minority, the post was probably held by Bhuvanaikamalla Chedi.[38] Later on perhaps the *Senāpati* was Skanda.[39] Directly under the *Senāpati* were *Sādhanikas* and *Dussādhyas* or *Dussādhasādhanikas* or cavalry commanders[40] and *balādhipas* or officers in charge of the military stationed in outposts and towns;[41] and the whole administration was controlled by a department, the *balādhikaraṇa,* stationed at the capital and supervised not only perhaps by the *Senāpati* alone but also the ruler.

(3) *Sāndhivigrahika.* He was, as the word signifies, a Minister for Peace and War. But in addition to this, his chief function, he was required to draft royal charters and despatches.[42] *Sāndhivigrahika* Khelāditya is mentioned in the Kirāḍū Inscription of Ālhaṇa[43] and Ojha Grant 2.[44]

(4) *Minister in charge of Poets and Paṇḍits.* The *Pṛthvīrājavijaya*

37. *See* above, p. 69.

38. *See PV,* IX, 86-88.

39. Mentioned as *Daṇḍanāyaka* and *Senādhipati* in the *Viruddhavidhividhvaṁsa* of Lakṣmīdhara.

40. The word, *Sādhanika,* is the same as modern *Sāhni.* For *Dussādhya* and *Dussādhasādhanika see* respectively the Harṣa inscription (V. 1030), and the Sevāḍi Plates of Ratnapāla.

41. *See* Kaṭukarāja's inscription (*EI,* XI, p. 30 ff.) and Jhaṁvrā inscription of *Mahārājaputra* Gajasiṁha (*JPASB,* XII, p. 102 f.)

42. This is the role assigned to him also by the *Mitākṣarā* on the *Yājñavalkyasmṛti,* I, 319:—

सन्धिविग्रहकारी तु भवेद्यस्तस्य लेखकः ।
स्वयं राज्ञा समादिष्टस्स लिखेद् राजशासनम् ॥

Generally good scholars were appointed to this post. Viśvanātha, the writer of the *Sāhityadarpaṇa,* for instance, was a *Sāndhivigrahika.* The *Prabandhachintāmaṇi* mentions a good grammarian as a *sāndhivigrahika* of Vigraharāja IV. The great Bengālī scholar, Bhavadeva, and his grandfather, Ādideva, similarly were *sāndhivigrahikas.* Much earlier we find Hariṣeṇa, the composer of the Allahabad *praśasti* of Samudragupta as a *sāndhivigrahika,* a fact proving that the appointment of good scholars as *sāndhivigrahikas* is a well-established tradition of the Indian people.

43. *EI,* XII, pp. 44 ff.

44. For the Grant *see* Appendix, pp. 210-213

mentions one Padmanābha as a minister whose duty consisted in calling conferences of learned people and who was also in charge of their reception.[45] This new post, a unique one in Indian history, might have been created in the reign of the *Kavibāndhava* Vigraharāja IV, though later it fell in some abeyance.

(5) *Paurāṇika.* Under Hammīra of Raṇthambhor we find also an *amātya* called, *Paurāṇika*,[46] who like the *Purohita* of an earlier period may mainly have been in charge of religious affairs. We do not know the designation given to this officer in our other Chauhān kingdoms. Maybe it kept up the old designation.

The ministry's function was largely advisory; the last word always lay with the King. Vigraharāja IV, for instance, rejected the advice of Śrīdhara, and Arṇorāja that of his old and experienced ministers. But during emergencies, the ministers could and did exercise a good deal of authority. When Pṛthvīrāja II died without leaving any son, the ministers brought over Someśvara from Gujarāt and put him on the throne of Ajmer. On his death, they made the widowed queen, Karpūradevī, the regent for her minor son, Pṛithvīrāja III, and helped her to administer successfully the affairs of the kingdom, in spite of hostile neighbours on almost every side.[47]

Other Central Officials. The other central officials mentioned in the Chauhān inscriptions are :—

(1) *Dūtaka.* He conveyed the ruler's sanction of a charter to local officials who then had the charter drawn up and delivered.[48]

(2) *Purohita and Vyāsa.* Either a *Purohita* or a *Vyāsa* generally was a ruler's adviser in religious matters. Hammīra's *Purohita* was one Viśvarūpa.[49] At Jālor Somachandra Vyāsa occupied almost the position of a minister.[50]

(3) *Pratihāra.* The *Pratihāra* (literally a door-keeper)

45. *PV.*, XII, 58.
46. *EI*, XIX, p. 52. Line 29 of the inscription.
47. *See* above, p. 80.
48. *See CII. III, p.* 100, footnote 3.
49. *Hammīramahākāvya*, IX, 76.
50. *See* the *Kānhaḍadeprabandha*. In almost every emergency, especially in those having even the slightest religious character, Somachandra Vyāsa is mentioned as Kānhaḍadeva's adviser.

regulated the people's entrance to the King's presence.[51]

(4) *Bhāṇḍāgārika.* A *Bhāṇḍāgārika* had, during our period, come to occupy almost the position of the Kauṭilyan *Sannidhātā.* Hammīra's *Bhāṇḍāgārika*, Jāhaḍa, was in charge of provisions as well as Hammīra's treasure.[52]

(5) *Khaḍgagrāha.* A *Khaḍgagrāha* was perhaps a body-guard or an *Āntarvaṁśika*, the officer in charge of the Royal Household. Hammīra's natural brother, Bhoja, was a *khaḍga-grāha.*[53]

Chauhān inscriptions mention also the usual *chāṭa-bhaṭas* (regular and irregular soldiers)[54] and the *ratha-hastyādi-niyogins* (servants employed for elephants and chariots etc.). Accounts were maintained by an officer called *Bahikādhikṛta*;[55] and though the name *Akṣapaṭalika* (a head-keeper of accounts) is absent from the Chauhān records available to us, his presence in Chauhān dominions may be inferred from the records of the neighbouring kingdoms of Mewār and Gujarāt. *Bahikādhikṛtaṣ* might have, like the Kauṭilyan *Gāṇanikyas*, worked under the *Akṣapaṭalika.*[56] And then the Court may not have been also without its usual *Rāja-vallabhas*, or favourites. Tradition ascribes Chand Bardāī a very high place in the counsels of Pṛthvīrāja III. The *Pṛthvīrājavijaya* assigns a similar role to a bard named *Pṛthvībhaṭa.*[57]

Territorial administration. In Vigraharāja II's reign, the kingdom of Śākambharī was divided into a number of *viṣayas*, of which the Harṣa Inscription mentions the following :—

1. Paṭṭabaddhaka (modern Paṭauda in Sīkar estate)

51. Mentioned in the *PV.* as well as the drama, *Lalitavigraharāja.*
52. *Hammīramahākāvya*, XIII, 194 and 136-138.
53. *Ibid.*, IX, 154. The title is found also in Rāmganj copper-plate inscription of Īśvaraghoṣa.
54. The word *Chāṭa* is interpreted by some writers also as "the head of a *parganā* responsible for the internal management of a district, for the collection of revenues and the apprehension of criminals. *Bhaṭas*, in that case, might be regarded as his employees.
55. Chāchigadeva's Bhīnmāl inscription of V. 1333.
56. *See* the *Arthaśāstra*, Book II, Chapter 7.
57. *See PV.* XII. He is extolled specially for his knowledge of *Itihāsa.* For other officers probably included in the Chauhān courts *see* footnote 32 p. 223.

2. Sarahakoṭṭa (modern Sargot in the Maroṭ Division of the former Jodhpur State).

3. Darbhakakṣa (modern Ḍhākās in Sīkar estate).

4. Khaṭṭakūpa (modern Khāṭu in the Sāmbhar Nizāmat of the former Jodhpur State)

5. Jayapura.

These *viṣayas* were further subdivided into smaller groups, each one named after its chief village. One such group, for instance, was Tūṇakūpaka-*dvādaśaka*, *i.e.*, a unit of which the chief village was Tūṇu or Tūṇakūpaka. Bigger divisions like those of 84 villages also probably existed in Sapādalakṣa.[58]

With the expansion of the Sapādalakṣa kingdom, there were some changes in the territorial set up. Besides the old territorial divisions, it now included subordinate States like Delhi and Marukoṭṭa, *maṇḍalas* or units ruled over by *Maṇḍaleśvaras*, (who perhaps were descendants of the rulers subjugated by the Chauhāns),[59] and important frontier forts like Hānsī, Samānā, Kohrām, Sarasvatī and Tabarhindah. The forts had to be carefully manned and now and then further strengthened on account of the ever-present menace of Muslim invasions from the north-west. Not unoften we find them put under the ruler's most trusted relations; Hānsī, for instance, was under Pṛthvīrāja II's uncle, Kelhaṇa, in V. 1224[60], and a few years later under Harirāja, the younger brother of Pṛthvīraja III.[61] Village Unions continued, but we hear now also of *pratijāgaraṇakas*[62], which like the *parganās* of the Mughal period must have been important administrative units, standing somewhere between the *Viṣaya* and the Village Union.[63]

Epigraphs give us some insight also into the divisional administration of Nāḍol. We cannot say what it was in the

58. Punapākṣadeva ruled over Ratnapur 84. This group unit exists even now and may be presumed to have existed in Rājasthān before Punapākṣa also.

59. Kaimāsa, for instance, was a *Maṇḍaleśvara*. So was *Rāṇaka* Tiāka at Vikramapura (V. 1236).

60. *See* above, p. 74.

61. Called *Kumārabhukti* of Harirāja (*Purātanaprabandhasaṅgraha*) p. 86.

62. *See* Appendix C, p. 107.

63. For *parganā* as a unit of administration, *see* Dr. P. Saran's *Provincial Government of the Mughals*, p. 207.

earlier period of its history. But in the reign of Kelhaṇa, we find the outposts of his kingdom governed by his sons and near relatives. Pālaḍī was entrusted to his eldest son, Jayatsīha, Bāmnerā to Kumarasīha, Māṇḍavyapura first to Siṁhavikrama (V. 1241) and then to Soḍhaladeva (V. 1250), and Saṇḍeraka to his queen, Jalhaṇadevī, who might have governed it through a deputy.[64] Perhaps only the central portion of the State was directly administered by Kelhaṇa himself. Such decentralisation, even in a small State like Nāḍol, could be held justified on account of the unsettled conditions of the period. It made every *sāmanta* and governor interested in the defence of the State; as a long-range policy it was certainly wrong, for it rendered the central government weak and encouraged fissiparous tendencies.[65]

Feudal Proprietors. No small portion of the State, specially in Nāḍol and Jālor, was held by *jāgīrdārs*, known variously as *Ṭhākuras*, *Rāṇakas*, and *Bhoktās*, on the condition that they supplied either a certain quota of soldiers, mounted and unmounted, whenever required, or paid annually the sum fixed by the State.[66] Non-fulfilment of the conditions entailed the confiscation of the estate which could take either the form of its inclusion thereafter in the State territory or general orders to the tenants not to respect the *Rāṇaka's* authority.[67]

The *jāgīrdārs* or *bhoktās*, as we might preferably call them, had definite rights and duties. They were entitled to the taxes, usually paid to the State,[68] they were in a restricted sense also the masters of the land. They could not however interfere with properties donated to Brāhmaṇas and temples; nor

64. *See* above the account of Kelhaṇa, p. 157.

65. It was, it might be noted, during the reign of Kelhaṇa that his younger brother, Kīrtipāla, established the new kingdom of Jālor, instead of looking after the interests of the parent kingdom of Nāḍol and increasing its power.

66. *See* the *Lekhapaddhati*, pp. 7 and 9. The account of the *jāgīrdārī* system is based mainly on the *Lekhapaddhati*, partly because the feudal conditions in a neighbouring kingdom would have been not very dissimilar and partly also because they must have been practically identical in the Mārwār area which for a considerable period was under Chaulukya suzerainty.

67. *Lekhapaddhati*, pp. 22-24.

68. For the taxes *see* below, pages 235 ff.

could they, without the previous sanction of the States, grant any new lands to them. In some of these *jāgīrs* there were perhaps also peasants who had direct relations with the State.[69] Doing military service was the *jāgīrdār's* main duty. But they were required besides to put down minor disturbances, to safeguard the highways passing through their territory, and to recover and return any articles that might be lost in the villages under their jurisdiction.[70] During the period of frequent warfare that followed the Muslim occupation of a great part of Northern India by Muslims, central control must have lessened and the powers of the *jāgīrdārs* increased a good deal; even so much in some cases that chiefs like Sātaladeva of Siwānā may practically be regarded as independent princes.

Local Self-government. In villages, village unions, and towns, whether they were directly under a ruler or a feudal chief, considerable power lay in the hands of the people. They had a General Assembly, called the *Mahājana*, which sanctioned new imposts, policed its charge,[71] evidenced grants and held general discussions regarding local affairs and sometimes even state policies. *Thākura* Rājadeva of Naḍūlaḍāgikā, for instance, was permitted by the local *Mahājana* assembly to collect certain cesses for the temple of the Jaina Tīrthoṅkara, Mahāvīra.[72] It bore witness also to Rājadeva's grant of 1 *viṁśopaka* and two *palikās* to the temple of Ādinātha in the same year (V. 1200).[73] The *Baṇajārās* of the village, who as members of a floating population could not naturally participate in the proceedings of the *Mahājana*, met separately to give a donation.[74] In V. 1352, the *adhikārins* of Sāmantasiṁha at Bāhaḍmer acted in the same way as *Thākura* Rājadeva. They requested the sanction of the *Mahājana* assembly, before levying for the gods, Vighnamardana-Kṣetrapāla and Chāmuṇḍarāja, either a *pāilā* or 10 Bhīmapriya *viṁśopakas* from every incoming or outgoing caravan

69. *See* the *Lekhapaddhati*, p. 7, line 26.
70. *Ibid.*, p. 7. Village *pañchāyats* also had similar duties. *See* below.
71. *See* below.
72. P.C. Nahar, *Jaina Inscriptions*, Part I, p. 213 ff.
73. *EI*, XI, p. 41 f.
74. *Ibid.*, p. 43.

exceeding 10 camels and 20 bullocks.[75] Nearly 19 years later, in V. 1371, when the Jālor garrison faced starvation on account of the shortage of provisions in the royal stores and granaries, the *Mahājanas* proposed to supply the daily necessaries and advised Kānhaḍadeva to continue the struggle against Alāuddīn Khaljī.[76] Kings respected the representative character of the *Mahājanas*;[77] influential people felt that it was an honour to be its leaders.[78]

As an assembly consisting of all the adult members or even heads of families might have been too unwieldy for deliberative and specially executive work, the *Mahājanas* probably delegated their functions either to their representatives or to *Pañchakulas* or Committees of Five, an institution which has come down to us from Mauryan or perhaps even pre-Mauryan times.[79] An example of the first type is to be found in the Nāḍol Inscription of *Mahārājādhirāja* Rāyapāla's reign (V. 1200), according to which the 8 wards of Dhālop village,[80] sent two representatives each and appointed one of them as *Madhyaka*, *i.e.*, their chief.[81] The signatures of these 16, who undertook to police the territory within their jurisdiction, were to be regarded as the signatures of *sarvaloka* (all the residents of Dhālop). But the summoning of such a representative body was perhaps necessary only when one needed the community's sanction either to some new decree or some new impost, the usual village and town work being carried on by the other body we have referred to, i.e. the *Pañchakula* or Committee of Five. Its members were no mere village leaders recognised as such by the village

75. *Ibid.*, pp. 59 ff.

76. *Kānhaḍadeprabandha*, IV, verses 125-135.

77. *See* the respectful terms used by Kumārapāla Chaulukya for the *Mahājana* of Aṇahillapaṭṭana:—

अथ क इदानीमस्मासु महाजनस्य नियोगः

(*Moharājaparājaya*, p. 51, last line).

78. *Balādhipa* Yaśodeva describes himself as

राज्ञां महाजनस्यापि सभायामग्रणीः स्थितः

(*EI*, XI, page 31).

79. According to Megasthenes the city of Pāṭaliputra was administered by a Board of 30 divided into six Committees of Five Members each.

80. *See EI*, XI, pp. 39-41.

81. This seems to be the meaning suggested by the context.

alone. They had a definite standing and it is not unlikely that the State might have had some share in the final constitution of the Committee.[82]

Chauhān inscriptions show the *Pañchakulas* taking cognisance only of grants to temples. That their activities actually might have been of a character, much more varied and extensive, can however be seen from contemporary records of the neighbouring kingdoms as well the *Lekhapaddhati* which describes them as arbitrating between disputing parties, granting certificates of sale and concessions to traders; farming out villages, collecting the State's share of the revenue, and taking cognisance not merely of religious but also of secular grants, if made by private individuals.[83] With such important duties assigned to the *Pañchakulas* in Gujarāt, it would perhaps be wrong to assume that the jurisdiction and powers of their friends in the Chauhān dominions were far more limited. Those days it was custom that reigned supreme; and customs did not change from village to village or merely because of one village being in Sapādalakṣa and the other, a neighbouring one, being in the empire or kingdom of Gujarāt.

Official element in the countryside and towns was represented by *Paṭṭakilas*, *Balādhipas*, *Talāras*, *Selahathas*, *Rakṣākaras*, *Vahikādhikṛtas* and *Parigrahins*, besides perhaps some other minor officers, whose names have not come down to us. *Paṭṭakila's* duties might have been similar to those of the modern Paṭel, a village official entrusted with the realization of the village revenue.[84] *Balādhipa* probably was a miltary officer put in charge of the Customs House or *Maṇḍapikā* and entitled to a certain share in its revenue known as the *Balādhipābhāvya*.[85] The *Maṇḍapikā* being one of the best sources of revenue, it

82. Mostly the *Pañchakulas* are mentioned as *tanniyukta*, i.e., appointed by the ruler whose name precedes the word, *tanniyukta*.

83. *See* the *Lekhapaddhati*, pp. 8-9, 10, 12, 19, 33, 50, 57 and *JBBRAS*, XV, p. 324.

84. For *Paṭṭakila see* Ratnapāla's Plates of V. 1176.

85. The name *Balādhipa* occurs mostly in relation to the *Maṇḍapikā*. *See* the Jhāṁvarā Inscription of Kelhaṇa's reign, V. 1210. *JPASB*, XII. p. 104. *Lekhapaddhati*, p. 14, gives four instances of a *Balādhipa* with the *Pañchakula* in charge of a *maṇḍapikā*.

must have been necessary to provide it with a *posse* of soldiers to prevent smuggling and enforce the various customs regulations which could not then have been more popular than they are now. The *Talāra* was a *purādhyakṣa* or *Nagararakṣaka*.[86] It is obvious from the *Pṛthvīchandracharita* of Māṇikya Sūri that he acted as a police officer going about the city at night and arresting thieves.[87] Like the *Baladhipa* he had his share of revenue from the Customs House.[88] *Selahatha* or *Śalyahasta* was mainly concerned with the countryside,[89] and perhaps was a high executive and revenue officer put in charge of a *Mahāsthāna* or administrative centre.[90] *Vahikādhikṛta* was the village or town accountant,[91] and the *Rakṣākara*, the village or town watchman.[92] *Parigrahin*[93] may have been a *Peshkār*.[94]

Police System. The Police System was in a large measure a part of the feudal and village administration. As already mentioned above, both *jāgīrdārs* and village councils were required to detect crimes committed within their jurisdiction. The towns had their *Talāras*. For villages the State sometimes

86. This is the explanation given by Trivikrama and Hemachandra. (*See EI*, XI, p. 47). Dr. D.R. Bhandarkar's explanation of it as an officer in charge of the suburbs of a town (*tala*) does not seem to be right in view of the clear evidence of the *Pṛthvīchandracharita* (*Prāchīna-Gūrjarakāvya-saṅgraha*, G.O.S., p. 105) The *Kānhadadeprabandha* mentions *Talāras* as *Nagara-talāras*.

87. *Amhe Talāra, karaum nagara-taṇi sārā*, p. 105.

88. *See EI*, XI, p. 46 f. It is also likely that the State might have levied *talārabhāvya* as a general tax and the *talāra* may have been paid a certain fixed sum whatever its proceeds may have been (*See* the Mangrol Inscription, *Historical Inscriptions of Gujarāt*, Vol. II, p. 31, lines 11 & 20).

89. *Nagara Talāra deśa Selahuta* (*Kānhadadeprabandha*. IV. 40)

90. *See* the Sānchor inscription of Sāmantasiṁha, V. 1345 (*EI*, XI, p. 59). The *Purātanaprabandhasaṅgraha* mentions *Salyahasta*, Pratāpasiṁha, who went to collect the tribute due to Pṛthvīrāja Chauhān (p. 86). The *Pṛthvīchandracharita* (p. 128) puts the *Selahatha* immediately after the *Māṇḍalika* in its list of officers. When posted away from the capital, he stayed in *Mahāsthānas* like Nuddula, Satyapura etc., the term *Mahāsthāna* having here perhaps approximately the same sense as in the Kauṭilīya *Arthaśāstra*.

91. See Chāchigadeva's Bhīnmāl inscription of V. 1333.

92. *See* Rāyapāla's inscription of V. 1198 (*EI*, XI, p. 40).

93. Mentioned in the Bijoliā inscription of V. 1226. Śrī A. K. Vyas, the editor of the record, translates the word as a "revenue collector". But the *KP* (p. 46) suggests a sense similar to that of the modern *peshkār*.

94. See the last footnote.

appo nted *Rakṣākaras*; but not unoften the duty of policing them was left to the villagers themselves, provided they agreed solemnly, like the villeges of Dhālop,[95] to rovide their own watchmen and to find out, in accordance with established customs and the *Chaukaḍikā* system, the things that might be lo t by door-keepers, ascetics,[96] Vaṇajārakas, and soldiers[97] passing through their territory. If the articles were lost in the village itself, there could be no question of resorting to the *Chaukaḍikā* system; they had to be found by the villagers thems lves. The state expected them to do this duty; none was to be freed from it, even if he offe ed *satyāgraha*.[98] In return, no doubt the State allowed them one important concession; it did not ask them to supply weapons or money for policing the highways.[99]

This type of policing, the basic principle of which was local responsibility, was nothing new to India. It appears to have succeeded well in the Kauṭilyan State which required the lost goods to be restored by the *Grāmasvāmin*, the *Vivītādhyakṣa*, the *Chorarajjuka* or the *Sīmāsvāmin* (*Arthaśāstra*, IV. 13) ; and is known to have succeeded equally well under Sher Shāh and the Great Mughals. It succeeded, we might presume, no less in the Chauhān dominions. The *Chaukaḍikāpravāha*, interpreted by Dr. D.R. Bhandarkar, as the *Pañchāyat* System, may actually have been the relay of the Ḍāk Chowkī runners,[100] the first institution of which is wrongly ascribed to Alāuddīn Khaljī.[101] With the help of such a relay alone the police could hope to capture a criminal who passed beyond the limits of a village or *jāgīr* after committing a crime.

95. *EI.* XI, p. 49.

96. *Kārpaṭikas*. Apte's translation of the term as "a caravan of pilgrims" would suit the context better.

97. *Bhaṭṭaputras*. Dr. D. R. Bhandarkar translates the word as "bards". I prefer translating it as "soldiers", a use which is fairly well known.

98. According to the inscription, one who committed suicide by starvation because of being opposed to these regulations died a donkey's death.

99. *See* lines 15-17 of the inscription.

100. Police warders are even now known as Chowkidāras. The context in which the word has been used in the inscription clearly suggests the meaning. "a relay of Dāk Chowkī runners".

101. *See* Elliot. III. p. 203 ; Barni's *Tārīkh-i-Firūzshāhī*.

Revenue. Chauhān inscriptions mention the following terms connected with the revenue system of the period :—

1. *Talārābhāvya.* This, as already mentioned above, was the *Talāra's* share of the revenue from the Customs House or *Maṇḍapikā.* It perhaps either came directly to him or was collected by the State as an additional impost only a part of which was paid over to him. As the ultimate guardian of the lives and property of townsmen, the State could, if it so desired, claim *Talārābhāvya* for itself and pay a part of it as salary to the actual *Talāra.*[10]

2. *Selahathābhāvya.* Like the *Talāra*, the *Selahatha* or *Śalyahasta*[103] had his share of revenue from the Customs House. This was known as *Selahathābhāvya* and might have been collected and paid like *Talārābhāvya.*

3. *Balādhipābhāvya.* The *Balādhipābhāvya* was the share of the Customs revenue payable to the *Balādhipa.*[104]

4. *Dāna or Customs Tax. Dāna*, a shortened form perhaps of *ādāna*, is almost the equivilent of the Kauṭalyan *Śulka*, and forms one of the most important sources of the Chauhān States' revenue.[105]The *ābhāvyas* or additional taxes for various services rendered by the State to the community were all collected through the *Dānamaṇḍapikā* ; and then the *Maṇḍapikā* was also the means through which the ruler or the community itself provided for religious benefactions, benefactions sometimes comprehensive enough to include every economic good and to provide for even the costliest ceremonies.[106]

102. The Sāṇḍerāv stone inscription of Kelhaṇa reign suggests the first course (*EI*, XI, p. 46). The Māngrol inscription of V. 1202 from the neighbouring kingdom of Gujarāt shows that the second was the normal system in a State with a strong centre.

103. For the meaning of the word *see* above, p. 233.

104. *Ibid. See* also *JPASB.*, XII, p. 102ff.

105. *See JPASB.*, X, p. 407. The term, *dāna*, occurs frequently in the *Lekhapaddhati.* For the collection of the *ābhāvyas see specially* the *Lekhapaddhati*, pp. 8 and 14.

106. Two examples, though not from the Chauhān dominions, may be cited, one from Hastikuṇḍī in Mārwār and the other from Māngrol in Kāṭhiāwār. According to the first of these Vidagdha of Hastkuṇḍī granted (1) one rupee for each twenty loads carried for sale, (2) one rupee on each cart filled, (3) one *karṣa* for a *ghaṭa* at each oil-mill, (4) 13 *chollikas* of betel-leaves

5. *Ādāna.* This looks like a variant of *dāna.* But while *dāna* had come to mean customs-tax, *ādāna* still had its old meaning, due. The *Bhoktā*, Rājadeva of Naḍdulāi, for instance, had a certain sum due (*ādāna*) on all the baskets coming on oxen to that town, and could transfer a share of it to others.[107]

6. *Lāga.*[108] The word might be translated as impost. It is still in common use in Rājasthān, and is contrasted with *Bhāga*, *i.e.*, regular land-tax.[109]

7. *Ātmapāilā.* The word occurs in the Nāḍlāi Stone Inscription of Rāyapāla's reign (*EI*, XI, p. 37). It means the *pāilā*[110] due to the *Bhoktā* or *jāgīrdār.*[111] The articles on which the *pāila* was due have not been specified.

8. *Talapada.* The word is found in Alhaṇadeva's Nāḍol Inscription of V. 1218[112] and Chāchigadeva's Bhīnmāl Inscription of V. 1332. Regarding it as synonymous with *Svatala* of the Valabhī inscriptions, Kielhorn renders the term as "grounds." Dr. U.N. Ghoshal's meaning for it is "land fully assessed for revenue."[113] As this latter meaning agrees with that given later on to it in Gujarāt, it may be accepted.

9. *Halasadī.* This probably was a tax calculated per plough

by the *Bhaṭṭas*, (5) *Rellakoṭelloka* by the gamblers, (6) one *āḍhaka* of wheat and barley from each *oraghaṭṭā*, (7) five *palas* for *peḍḍo*, (8) one *viṁśopaka* for each *bhāra*, (9) ten *palas* from each *bhāra* of articles such as cotton, copper, saffron, gum-resin, madder and so forth; and (10) one *māṇaka* from each *droṇa* of wheat, *mūng*, barley, salt, *rāla*, and such other objects as can be measured.

Most of these imposts could obviously have been collected only through the *Dāna-Maṇḍapikā*.

The Mangrol inscription (*Historical Inscriptions of Gujarāt*, II, No. 145) states expressly that the dues granted were to be collected through the *Śulka-maṇḍapikā*. For details which are similar to those of Vidagdha's inscription just cited, *see* the inscription itself.

107. *EI.*, XI, p. 37.

108. *Ibid.*, pp. 59 f.

109. cf. *the Lekhapaddhati*, p. 3.

110. A certain weight. See below, Chapter XXVI.

111. Literally it means the *pāilā* due to oneself. As it refers in the context to a *Bhoktā*, I have adopted the meaning given above. In case of a *Rājā* it would similarly mean the *pāilā* due to the *Rājā*.

112. *EI*, IX, p. 63.

113. *Hindu Revenue System*, p. 298.

and paid over like various *ābhāvyas* to the *Vahikādhikṛta* and the *Cheṭaka* stationed in a *ta'apada-maṇḍapikā*.[114] A tax per plough was known in Mughal India as an *ābwāb* and evidently comes down from [15] the pre-Muslim period of our history.

10. *Daśabandha*. *Daśabandha*, a tax of one-tenth (tithe), was universal throughout Asia from the Jewish tithe to the *dahiek* (one in ten) of Persia, Central Asia and Muslim India.[116] The *Daśabandha*, (mentioned in a Nāḍol Inscription of V.1200), from which Bhūtala, a Kārṇāṭa *rāṇaka*, is said to have freed the dancing girls of Usapapattana served as an income-tax.[117]

11. *Devadāya*. It is money or property donated for religious purposes.

12. *Dohalikā*.[118] It is a rent-free benefaction of land.

13. *Nidhāna*. Dr. U.N. Ghoshal translates the term as "a kind of cess imposed on agricultural land." But the Bāmnerā Grant of Kelhaṇadeva (V. 1223)[119] suggests articles like treasuretrove. Numerous epigraphs and also drafts in the *Lekhapaddhati* mention नवनिधान,[1 0] meaning thereby perhaps nine types of treasure to be found underground.

14. *Ābhyantarasiddhi*.[121] It is the right to the mineral wealth in the interior of the earth. It was usual to pass it on to the donee along with the donated land.

15. *Rājakīya-bhoga*.[122] Dr. D.R. Bhandarkar translates the term as "the king's personal property."[123] According to Dr. U.N. Ghoshal, *Bhoga* means "periodical supplies of fruits, firewood,

114. See Chāchigadeva's Bhinmāl inscription of V. 1332.
115. I am indebted for the information to Dr. J. N. Sarkar.
116. For this information also I am indebted to Dr. Sarkar.
117. The word *Daśabandha* is used also in the *Manusmṛti*, VIII, 107. It is also of frequent occurrence in the *Arthaśāstra* in the sense of one-tenth. A very good example is the following from the *Lekhapaddhati*:

हेडाउनागडेन क्रीतं श्रीषण्डघोडु १ मूल्ये द्रम्मा पञ्चसहस्र द्रम्मा: घोडकस्यास्य दानसम्बन्धे दत्ता: बन्धे देयद्रम्म ५०० पञ्चशतानि द्रम्मा: श्रीकरणे प्रवेशिता: ।

118. Bāmnerā Plate of Kelhaṇa's reign. *EI*. XIII.p. 208.
119. *EI*, XIII, p. 210.
120. p. 6. खनि, आकर, निधि, निक्षेप, etc. are perhaps some of these.
121. See the Hansot Plates of Bhartṛvaḍḍha II.
122. See the Sāṇḍerāv stone inscription of Kelhaṇadeva's reign, *EI*, XI, p. 47.
123. *Ibid*.

flowers and the like which the villagers had to furnish to the king."[124] As the Chauhān inscription, however, in which the term occurs, mentions one *hāel* of *yugandharī*, *i.e.*, as much *jwār* as could be produced in land tilled by one plough, as a part of the *rājakīyabhoga* due from Sāṇḍerāv, we might, while rejecting Dr. D.R. Bhandarkar's interpretation, amend also Dr. Ghoshal's by saying that whatever the original nature of this impost might have been, the Chauhāns included also cereals under it. Nor was *bhoga* used merely to give perquisites to local officers, as Dr. A.S. Altekar suggests,[125] for the illustration before us shows a part of it being passed on to the temple of Mahāvīra. From a draft of the *Lekhapaddhati* which mentions 40 *kalasīs* and 4 *mūṭakas* of peas as *bhoga*, but provides sureties only for the payment of other *i.e.*, non-*bhoga* dues from the village, the total of which came to 4,244 *drammas*,[126] it may further be inferred that *bhoga* was paid in kind and used locally. Its proceeds did not find a way to the royal treasury, even though its appropriation could be according to royal orders.[127]

16. *Udraṅga.* The word occurs rarely in Chauhān inscriptions ; its only use that I have been able to trace is in the Hānsot Plates of Bhartṛvaḍḍha II. Dr. Fleet and Dr. U.N. Ghoshal give it the meaning of "revenue imposed upon permanent tenants".[128] But its actual meaning, as suggested by Dr. A.S. Altekar, may be land-tax and it may be synonymous with *bhāga* or land-tax with which it is never used in inscriptions.[129]

17. *Uparikara.* This word generally goes with *Udraṅga.* Dr. Fleet and Dr. U.N. Ghoshal regard it as an impost levied on temporary tenants.[130] Dr. A.S. Altekar equates it with *Bhoga.* But both *Uparikara* and *Bhoga* are used together, in Kar-

124. *Hindu Revenue System*, p. 200.

125. *The Rāshṭrakūṭas and their Times*, p. 215.

126. p. 9.

127. Kauṭilya also mentions *Bhoga* very often. If the character of the cess was the same under the Chauhāns as in Kauṭilya's time, it may have been assessed from house to house. (*Arthaśāstra* II, 35. Gaṇapati Śāstrī's edition, I, p. 347, lines 2-3.)

128. *Hindu Revenue System*, p. 299.

129. *The Rāshṭrakūṭas and their Times*, p. 216.

130. *Ibid.*

ṇadeva's Nausārī Plates of S. 996,[131] a fact which goes against their identity. We would rather equate *sodraṅgaḥ soparikaraḥ* with *bhāga-lāga*[132], so well known to us even now. *Uparikara* was an additional impost, if the word be interpreted literally, and thus included *Bhoga* also. Its sphere was much more comprehensive than that of *Bhoga*.

18. *Daṇḍa*. Of *Daṇḍa* or fines there could be many varieties. But in Chauhān inscriptions we find the mention of only a fine for the slaughter of animals on certain days of the month.[133] When farming out a village, it was usual for the overlord to reserve to himself the income from fines, even though the actual realization of the money was left to the farmer.[134]

Obviously, we cannot have a systematic or satisfactory knowledge of the actual system of revenue and taxation in the Chauhān dominions on the basis of this imperfect and fragmentary information. All that we can say is that the people paid :—

(*i*) a land-tax, called variously *udraṅga*, *bhāga* and *dānī*, to the ruler or to whomsoever he thought it fit to assign it;[135]

(*ii*) customs tax or *dāna* to the ruler or the *bhoktā*;

(*iii*) various imposts, to be realised through the customs house or *Śulka-maṇḍapikā* to *Talāras*, *Śelahathas*, *Balādhipas* and the like either directly or through the State ;

(*iv*) customary presents to either the master of the land or his official, with a view to being used locally ;

(*v*) cesses for temples ;

131. सहिरण्य-भा[गभो] गः सवृक्षमालाकुलः सदंडदशापराधः सोपरिकरः सर्वदायसमेतः

(*Historical Inscriptions of Gujarāt*, Chaulukya Inscriptions, p. 23)

132. For *bhāga-lāga*, see above, p. 236. For reasons against accepting Dr. Ghoshal's position see Dr. Altekar's *The Rāshṭrakūṭas and their Times*, pp. 214-216.

133. See the Kirāḍū inscription (V. 1209) of Alhaṇadeva and the Ratanpur inscription of Pūnapākṣadeva.

134. See the *Lekhapaddhati*, pp. 12 and 16.

135. *Bhāga* and *dānī* are used in Chaulukya inscriptions and the *Lekhapaddhati*. It is very likely that these terms were in use in the Chauhān dominions also. It is only the paucity of Chauhān village grants that prevents us from being certain on such points.

(*vi*) fines for contravening the orders of the State ;
(*vii*) a part of their income in some cases.[136]

Another source of revenue for the Chauhāns of Śākambharī was the Sāmbhar Lake.[137] Mines and quarries also, of which there are many in Rājpūtānā, must have yielded some revenue to the State, if not already made over along with the land to some donee or *jāgīrdār*. Nor should we regard as inconsiderable the revenue derived from the *digvijayas* of rulers like Vigraharāja II, Vigraharāja IV and Pṛthvīrāja III.[138] It was perhaps the money derived from them that went to the beautification of Ajmer and the construction of grand Chauhān public works.

A far more satisfactory account of the contemporary sources of revenue can be had on the basis of Chaulukya inscriptions and the *Lekhapaddhati*, the system described in which was probably current, at least in part, in the Chauhān principalities of Mārwār. These bordered Gujarāt and were for a long period subordinate to it. A few details from the *Lekhapaddhati* would be found in an Appendix to this chapter.

Judiciary. As regards the Chauhān judiciary, again, the details from our sources are meagre in the extreme. In the first instance the cases probably went to the Village Councils, which are probably the popular courts mentioned by the Arab traveller, Sulaimān.[139] The highest tribunal of justice, however, was the ruler who heard plaints of every type, original as well as appellate. This evidence at our disposal prevents us from agreeing with Dr. Altekar's conclusion that the "King's Courts did not entertain any cases at first instance,"[140] for the only instances of royal justice that we have from the *Kharataragachchhapaṭṭāvalī* of Jinapāla and the *Lekhapaddhati* are of the people going direct to the *Rājakula* and requesting justice.[141] The ruler gave no arbit-

136. See for instance *daśabonaha* or 1/10 of the income realised from prostitutes. similarly *aroghaṭṭas*, *ghāṇakos* and barns had to pay a certain percentage to the royal treasury.

137. *PV*. IV. 85.

138. Vigraharāja's *digvijaya* is said to have rendered *karada* the land between the Vindhyas and the Himālayas. Pṛthvīrāja III looted the territories of the Chandellas in V. 1239.

139. *Sulaimān Saudāgar*, p. 81 (Quoted by Dr. A.S. Altekar in *RA*.)

140. *The Rashṭrakūṭas and their Times*, p. 210.

141. *Kharataragachchhapaṭṭāvalī*.
Lekhapaddhati, pp. 15, 16-18, 49-50.

rary judgment. He generally referred the matter to the *Paṇḍitas* in the *Dharmādhikaraṇa*, who then called for documentary evidence and witnesses and, in the absence of these two, perhaps resorted also to ordeals.[142] From these, however, they exempted women, children, and weak, old and sickly persons.[143] A Brāhmaṇa accused was required to submit a *gardabhapatra*, i.e., a declaration to the effect that if he committed suicide on account of his dislike of the judge's verdict, he died the death of a donkey or a *chāṇḍāla*. No blame was laid on the judges (*Paṇḍitas* of the *Dharmādhikaraṇa*) or the ruler.[144] Of the Chauhān records, Rāyapāla's Nāḍol Inscription of V. 1198 provides the best instance of such a *gardabhapatra*.

Military System. That our rulers largely depended on irregular forces must have become obvious from our account of *jāgīrs*, the holders of which were almost invariably required to serve the ruler at the capital with a number of footmen and horses and could be punished with the deprival of the *jāgīr* in case they did not render the stipulated service.[145] Traditions give Pṛthvīrāja III a hundred *sāmantas* or feudal lords; Firishta mentions one hundred and fifty rulers who fought under his banner.[146]

At the time of Vigraharāja IV's advance against the *Hammīra*, the Chauhān army is said to have consisted of 1,000 elephants, 100,000 horsemen and 1,000,000 infantry.[147] Firishta's most "authentic estimate" of Pṛthvīrāja III's army puts its strength at 300,000 horses and 3,000 elephants.[148]

Elephants formed the most valued section of the army. Generals directed the battle from their backs and used them, as in the Mauryan and Mughal periods, to batter down the gates of forts. Like Kauṭilya, the Chauhān rulers and their

142. विवादेन्विष्यते पत्रं तदभावे तु साक्षिणः ।
साक्ष्यभावे ततो दिव्यं प्रवदन्ति मनीषिणः ॥
(*Ibid.*, p. 18)

143. *Ibid.*, p. 23, verses 1-4.

144. *Ibid.*, pp. 49-50.

145. See above, p. 229.

146. *T.F.*, I, p. 175.

147. *Lalita-Vigraharāja* inscription, lines 16-17; *IA.*, XX, p. 201 ff.

148. *Tārikh-i-Firishta*, I, p. 17.

advisers probably, again, believed that the victory of Kings and destruction of an enemy's army depended on elephants.[149]

Cavalry, the next important arm of the army, appears to have received adequate attention from the Chauhāns. Pṛthvīrāja III was a good cavalry leader. In a Chauhān inscription the *Saptaśatabhūmi*, i.e., the kingdom of Nāḍol, is extolled as a mine of horses.[150] Kānhaḍadeva's raids on the Khaljī army were, without any exception, carried out by his horsemen. In the second battle of Tarāīn, the use of cavalry gave some respite to the sore pressed Chauhān force.[151] Numerically, infantry perhaps exceeded all the other arms. But from the slight mention it receives in most of our records, it appears to have sunk to an insignificant position. Chariots are there, but more as an ornamental feature than an essential part of the army.[152] Even nobles of Kānhaḍadeva Chauhān perhaps used them.[153]

The sandy nature of the country favoured camels as animals of transport.[154] The *Pṛthvīrājavijaya* describes them also as carrying Chauhān colours in the march against Guḍapura.[155] The Pratihāras of Kanauj,[156] from whom perhaps the Chauhāns inherited the usage, are known to have had a camel corps in their army. But as regards the system of fighting from their backs, it was an innovation due to the Persians and Durrānīs in the 18th century.[157]

On the northern frontier of the Empire of Sapādalakṣa as well as inside it and their other kingdoms, the Chauhāns had a number of strong forts like Hānsī, Tabarhindah, Samānā, Nāgor, Maṇḍor, Siwānā, Jālor, Ajmer, Delhi, Nāḍol, Kohrām, and Sirsā. Of these some fell easily into the hands of the Muslims, thanks to the demoralisation following the defeat of

149. See the *Arthaśāstra*, II, 2, VII, II, X, 4.
150. See Ojha Grant, Appendix G (iv), p. 186.
151. *Tārikh-i-Firishtā*, I. p. 176.
152. See *PV*, X, 19.
153. *Kānhaḍadeprabandha*, p. 116.
154. Even Kauṭilya recommends their use in such tracts, *Arthaśāstra* IX, I.
155. X, X, 20.
156. *ED.*, I, pp. 4 and 25.
157. I am indebted for the information to Dr. Jadu Nath Sarkar.

Pṛthvīrāja III in the second battle of Tarāīn. But the others were defended with the greatest skill and determination against the invaders' onslaughts. The besieged led out frequent sorties, threw hot oil on the besiegers, and tried to set fire to the enemy's towers by means of burning arrows.[158] They used also machines to bombard the enemy with stones.[159] The thought of surrender was anathema to these brave Chauhān defenders; if fate went against them they would rather open the gates with their own hands, perform the dreadful rite of *jauhar*, and rush out to kill and be killed.[160] It is, however, doubtful whether the Chauhāns were equally good in their offensive action against forts. Muhammad Ghorī captured Tabarhindah within a few days. Pṛthvīrāja III spent thirteen months before it.

The higher ranks of the army led a comfortable life. Umbrellas overspread the heads of officers; attendants waved *chāmaras*, as their masters proceeded on their leisurely march against the enemy.[161] Of barbarity, too, there was enough. Jayānaka describes in glowing term how Pṛthvīrāja III had the heads of his enemies strung into a garland to be hung across the gate of his capital, Ajmer; and of these enemies not a few were perhaps[162] his own relatives. The Bijoliā Inscription, though the composition of Jaina *yati*, praises not merely Vigraharāja IV's victories but also his burning and devastation of hostile capitals.[163]

In the Maurya period the Indian army was noted for its discipline. In Harṣa's reign we find the conditions very much different. The people knew that an army's march through their territory meant destruction of their crops and property;[164] and the conditions thereafter do not seem to have improved in any appreciable degree. Even the most well-laid plans of the

158. See the *Hammīramahākāvya*, XIII, 42-47.
159. Called *ḍhīnklīs* in the *Kānhaḍadeprabandha*.
160. Read the accounts of the fall of Raṇthambhor, Siwānā, Jālor etc.
161. *PV.*, X, 15-17. Luxury in the Chauhān army was probably less after the fall of the Empire of Sapādalakṣa.
162. The ruler of Guḍapura was Pṛthvīrāja III's cousin, *PV.*, X, 38.
163. Verse 21.
164. *Harśacharita*, Nirnayasāgar edition, p. 208.

Chauhāns sometimes miscarried, because feudal levies were after all feudal levies, quick to muster, quick at times also to strike,[165] but incapable of sustained and concerted action for any long period.

The defects of the Chauhān military machine are obvious enough. It was too loosely built to stand any heavy and unexpected strain. The Chauhān camp life, up to the fall of Pṛthvīrāja III, was too luxurious to be consistent with military efficiency; and the Chauhāns relied too much on elephants, with the result that the other arms were comparatively neglected. Though it is a bit doubtful whether any better system could have been devised in those days of continual fighting on the borders, which by itself gives rise to small chieftainships in a widely flung and loosely organised kingdom, one cannot help wishing that things had been otherwise, for undoubtedly it was the feudal character and weak structure of the Indian military system that was largely responsible for the downfall of the Chauhān monarchies of Rājasthān.

165. Especially true of the post-Pṛthvīrāja period.

APPENDIX H

COURT OFFICIALS ACCORDING TO THE KANHADADEPRABANDHA

The *Kānhaḍadeprabandha* mentions the following court officials :—

(1) *Amātyas.*

(2) *Pradhāna, i.e.*, the Chief Minister.

(3) *Sāmanta i.e.*, nobles in attendance at the Court.

(4) *Māṇḍalikas*, rulers of *Maṇḍalas* or feudatory principalities.

(5) *Śrī-garaṇās i.e.*,members of the Department of Income.

(6) *Vaya-garaṇas* (*Vyaya-karaṇikas*), *i.e.*, members of the Department in charge of Expenditure.

(7) *Mukuṭa-vardhanas.*

(8) *Aṅgalehas*, perhaps attendants who massaged and put scents etc. on the ruler's body.

(9) *Masāhaṇī.* Perhaps he is identical with *Sādhanika* or *Sāhaṇī.*

(10) *Tāvarī.* The meaning is not clear to me.

(11) *Bhaṇḍārīs i.e.*, Bhāṇḍāgārikas. These two are said to

(12) *Koṭhārīs* provide the means for the *Rāula's* expenses.

(13) *Sāṇahitas.* The meaning of the word is not clear to me.

(14) *Mehtās.*

(15) *Talāras, i.e.*, Kotwals.

(16) *Selahutas* (*Śalyahastas*).

(17) *Purohita.*

(18) *Dehrāsaris*, priests in charge of the royal temples.

(19) *Avadhānias i.e.*, attendants in general.

Though the *Kānhaḍadeprabandha* was written more than a hundred years after the death of Kānhaḍadeva, the list of officials may be regarded as trustworthy, because his descendant, Akhayarāja, at whose court Padmanābha flourished, may have tried to keep up the old Chauhān state and style.

A much longer list than this is to be found in the *Pṛthvīchandracharita* or *Vāgvilāsa* (p. 97). Some of the additional members of a court that it mentions are (1) *Gaṇanāyaka*, (2) *Daṇḍanāyaka*, (3) *Vahīvāhaka*, (4) *Vṛttināyaka*, (5) *Māṇḍavika*, (6) *Indrajāli*, (7) *Aṅgarakṣaka*, (8) *Tantrapāla*, (9) *Talavarga*, (10) *Chaurāsiyā*, (11) *Dharmādhigarṇā*, (12) *Senādhipati*, (13) *Khaḍgadhara*, *kuntadhara*, *dhanurdhara*, (14) *Vāra-vadhū*, (15) *Paṇḍitas*, poets and writers, (16) *Sejapāla*, (17) *Śreṣṭhins* and *Sārthavāhas*.

The *Charita* is a Gujarāti composition of V. 1478 (A.D. 1421) and reflects in a general way the conditions obtaining in Gurjaratrā. Therefore it is quite likely that of the officers bearing these titles many were to be found in the Chauhān courts also. Its author, Māṇikyachandra Sūri, though professing to write an old Jaina story, has largely utilised the material as it was before him *i.e.*, in his own times and in the territory he generally resided in.

APPENDIX I

ADMINISTRATIVE DETAILS FROM THE LEKHAPADDHATI

According to the *Lekhapaddhati*, the chief sources of revenue were the taxes called *siddha, dāna, dāya, dānī* and *bhoga*. The meaning of the first of these may be a tax on manufactured articles. In the 12th century we find it levied also at Bādāmi.[1] *Dāna* meant customs duty. *Dāya* was a religious cess. The meaning of *Bhoga* has been discussed above.[2] *Dānī* meant land-tax. According to one of the drafts in the *Paddhati*[3], it varied, as follows, according to the fertility of the land :—

(1)	One *viśopaka*	of	*samakara-bhūmi*	24	*drammas*
(2)	,,	,,	,, *pechila-bhūmi*	20	,,
(3)	,,	,,	,, *uddhakhila-bhūmi*	16	,,
(4)	,,	,,	,, No. 3 given to new settlers	10	,,
(5)	,,	,,	,, *naḍīyaka-bhūmi*	10	,,
(6)	,,	,,	,, *mahiṣa-gochara*	2	,,
(7)	,,	,,	,, *balivardagochara*	1	,,
(8)	,,	,,	,, *bālodhiyā-chhāliya-gochara.*	½	,,

The editor of the *Paddhati* explains *Viśopaka* as a *bighā*. The terms *samakara* etc. have, respectively, been explained as the land whose rental value has been permanently fixed, soft land, uncultivated table-land, the lands where the carts stand to dispose of their goods, pastures for buffaloes, pastures for oxen, and pastures for rams and sheep. Even though a *Viśopaka* may not really be a *bighā* and *naḍīyaka-bhūmi* is perhaps land covered with reeds, the table is useful in many ways. It shows that the survey of lands according to their fertility was already there when the Muslims began taking over and adapting old institutions to their own use. Secondly, it gives also some idea of the basis of the classification, whether a land was cultivated or

1. *S.I.I.*, III, p. 391. See also *RA.*, p. 230.
2. See above, p. 238.
3. p. 16.

uncultivated, pasture ground or good land merely needing the use of the spade and pickaxe.

From another draft in the *Lekhapaddhati*, we learn that farmers deposited $\frac{1}{3}$ of their produce in the *Jāgīrdār's* barn and paid besides a barn-tax and certain other cesses.[4]

Of fines, the *Paddhati* mentions the following:—

(1) For stealing hides ...25 *drammas*.
(2) „ *mastakasphoṭana* (breaking heads) ...6 „
(3) „ *bhāgakarṣaṇa*(appropriating the share due to another) ...5 „
(4) „ disobedience ...5 „
(5) „ sakanakanam va (cha) rake ...1 „

Of the exact percentage of *dāna* we cannot perhaps have any exact idea. In the case of the sale of a horse it was 1/10.[5] Perhaps the percentage varied from article to article and place to place.

4. p. 19.
5. See footnote 117 of this Chapter.

CHAPTER XXII

RELIGION

Of religions, the chief ones now represented in Rājasthān are Jainism and various systems of orthodox Hinduism; and this seems to have been the case in our period also. Buddhism, which had flourished here in the first few centuries preceding and succeeding the birth of Christ,[1] had died out almost wholly by the time the Chauhāns established their kingdom in Rājasthān.

Jainism. At the time our period begins, Jainism had gone far enough on the road to decadence; but it was saved from sharing the fate of Buddhism by a number of brilliant teachers of whom Haribhadra Sūri of Chitor (6.700-770 A.D.)[2] was the foremost. A learned Brāhmaṇa of well-recognised erudition, who had accepted Jainism merely because it appeared to him as more rational than other systems of thought,[3] Haribhadra, followed the teachings of his new creed to the fullest, in letter as well as spirit, without caring in the least about popular prejudices and patronage.

1. Eight inscriptions at Sānchi record gifts of certain inhabitants from Puṣkar (G.H. Ojha, *Three Lectures on Ajmer and one on Pushkar*, p. 33).

2. The traditional date, V. 585, for Haribhadra Sūri's death is in conflict with the internal evidence of his books. I follow the date suggested by Muni Jinavijayajī.

3 बन्धुर्न नः स भगवानरयोऽपि नान्ये
साक्षान्न दृष्टतर एकतमोऽपि चैषाम् ।
श्रुत्वा वचः सुचरितं च पृथग् विशेषं
वीरं गुणातिशयलोलतया श्रिताः स्मः ॥
नास्माकं सुगतः पिता न रिपवस्तीर्थ्या धनं नैवतै-
र्दत्तं नैव तथा जिनेन न हृतं किञ्चित्कणादादिभिः ।
किन्त्वेकान्तजगद्धितः स भगवान् वीरो यतश्चामलं
वाक्यं सर्वमलोपहर्तृ च यतस्तद्भक्तिमन्तो वयम् ॥
(लोकतत्त्वनिर्णय, Verses. 32-33)

The situation that Haribhadra Sūri found was bad enough. As *Nirgranthas*, the Jaina *sādhus* were expected to move about almost continuously, without being bound down to any place or people by the ties of kind, kinship and property. Theirs was to be a rational religion, without any mysteries of super abundant ritual and ceremonies, a religion the message of which was to reach everyone without any distinction of caste and class, wealth or poverty. Asceticism, self-abnegation, self-control and chastity were to be the characteristics of a true follower of Jina, for thus alone could one disassociate oneself from the impure *kārmika* material which holds down a soul. Yet Haribhadra Sūri found many Jaina *sādhus* (now known as *Chaityavāsins*) living in *chaityas* and *maṭhas*, building Jina temples, putting to personal use money collected for religious purposes, wearing scented and coloured clothes, singing in the presence of women, paying court to the rich, using *tāmbūla*, *lavaṅga* and flowers, taking rich food, selling images of Jina, practising astrology, reading omens, quarrelling with each other to have disciples, putting off religious discussion by telling people that abstruse matters could not be discussed with them—in short doing practically everything which a Jaina *sādhu* should not do.[4]

Haribhadra Sūri raised his powerful voice against all these corrupt practices. As a rationalist to the core, he wanted others also to be rationalists, to exercise their own individual judgment and reach their own conclusions, instead of taking anything on mere authority. As a sincerely religious spirit, he wished all to be sincerely religious and not to have mere lip-sympathy with the religion they professed. Though the attribution of 1400 books to his authorship may be an exaggeration, it is certain that both by the word of his mouth and his pen he did more than any other Jaina teacher to meet the arguments of the Buddhists as well as Hindu revivalists and to purify the Jaina Church of many evils that were steadily dragging it down.[5]

4. See Haribhadra Sūri's *Sambodhaprakaraṇa*, verses 27, 34, 46-49, 61, 63, 68 etc.

5. Of his works the best-known are :—

The great work thus begun did not stop with Haribhadra. He succeeded in influencing at least thought, if not the actual practice, of the entire Jaina world. Uddyotana Sūri, pupil of the great *āchārya* himself, and Siddharṣi Sūri,[6] the writer of that supremely beautiful and inimitable allegory, the *Upamiti-bhavaprapañcha-kathā*, tried in their own way to carry his message to the people. But the *āchāryas* who succeeded most in popularising it in Rājasthān were probably of the Gachha known as Kharatara. No passive believers in Haribhadra's teachings, they actually made them into a living force by their continuous preaching, discussions and personal example.

Jīneśvara Sūri, in whose time his followers received the designation of *Kharatara* on account of their following the strict and true path laid down in the Jaina scriptures,[7] defeated the *chaityavāsins* in a religious discussion at the court of Durlabha-rāja Chaulukya (c. 1010-22 A.D.) of Gujarāt. Abhayadeva Sūri wrote his commentaries on the Jaina *aṅgas* from 1063 to 1071 A.D., and by his teachings as well as personal example won over numerous people to the new path, the most important of them being his great disciple Jinavallabha who, leaving all his proprietary rights in the *maṭha*, garden and temple at Āsikā (Hānsī), dedicated his life to the work so dear to his master. Gujarāt had perhaps already made some progress towards the right path, the *vidhi-mārga*, as the *Kharataras* called it; so he chose Rājasthān as the sphere of his missionary activity. In spite of the great Haribhadra and his followers having worked

---

समराइच्च-कहा, घूर्तारूयान, द्विजवदनचपेटा, स्वोपज्ञवृत्तिसहिता अनेकान्तजयपताका, अनेकान्तवादप्रवेश, आवश्यकसूत्रबृहद्‌वृत्ति, दशवैकालिक-सूत्रवृत्ति, नन्दीसूत्रवृत्ति, अनुयोगद्वारसूत्रवृत्ति, अष्टकप्रकरण, उपदेशप्रकरण, पंचांशकप्रकरण, पंचसूत्रप्रकरणटीका, लोकतत्त्वनिर्णय, शास्त्रवार्तासमुच्चय, सम्बोधप्रकरण, योगविन्द, योगदृष्टिसमुच्चय, षड्‌दर्शनसमुच्चय, न्यायप्रवेशसूत्र-वृत्ति, घर्मविन्दु, घर्मसंग्रहणी ।

6. Author of the *Kuvalayamāla-kathā*

7. Of the various explanations of the term, this perhaps is the most acceptable and true also.

here for generations, it was still full of *chaityavāsins* and their followers.[8]

The task before Jinavallabha was not easy. People preferred to stick to their old dogmas and teachers.[9] They tried to find fault with his life as well as methods.[10] If he succeeded in establishing a *vidhichaitya*[11], they tried to capture it, sometimes using the influence of local rulers to achieve their mean ends.[12] Now and then blood even flowed, as Jinavallabha's followers tried to defend their rights.[13]

Undaunted by these difficulties, Jinavallabha made Chitra-Kūṭa his headquarters and, by his complete mastery of the different Indian systems of Indian philosophic thought, astrology, astronomy and poetics, and even more by a life of absolute simplicity, sincerity and complete adherence to the words of the Jina, won over to his way of thinking many followers, lay as well as clerical, who soon made his teachings well known in Rājasthān and Mālwā, especially in that part of the former of these which is known as Bāgaḍ.[14] Reformed temples (*vidhichaityas*) were established at Marukoṭṭa, Narwar, Nāgor and Chitor, and perhaps at other places also,and each one of these bore the following inscription :—

8. जिनवल्लभगणि-वाचनाचार्योपि कतिचिद्दिनानि पत्तनभूमौ विहृत्य न तादृशो विशेषेण बोधः कस्याप्यत्र गूर्जरत्रामण्डले विधातुं शक्यते, येन समाधानमुत्पद्यते मनसीति मनसिकृत्यात्म तृ (द्वि) तीय आगम-विधिना सुशकुनेन भव्यजनमनःसुक्षेत्रभूमिकासु भगवद्भणित-विधिधर्मबीजनिक्षेपणार्थं श्रीमेदपाटदेशादिषु विहारं चकार। ते च देशाः सर्वेपि प्रायेण चैत्यनिवासाचार्यैर्व्याप्ताः, सर्वोपि लोकस्तद्विवासितो वर्तते।

गणधरसार्धशतकबृहद्वृत्ति, अपभ्रंशकाव्यत्रयी-भूमिका, १-१५

9. *Upadeśarasāyana* of Jinadatta Sūri, verse 52.
10. *Ibid.*
11. For the definition of विधिचैत्य see below.
12. *Upadeśarasāyana*, verses 23-24.
13. *Ibid.*, verse 26.
14. *Gaṇadharasārdhaśataka-bṛhadvṛtti* of Sumatigaṇi (G.O.S.) No. XXXVII. Introduction, pp. 20-24.

"अत्रोत्सूत्रक्रमो न च न च स्नानं रजन्यां सदा
साधूनां ममताश्रथो न च न च स्त्रीणां प्रवेशो निशि ।
जाति-ज्ञातिकदाग्रहो न च न च श्राद्धेषु ताम्बूलमि-
त्याज्ञात्रेयमुनिश्रिते विधिकृते श्रीजैनचैत्यालये ॥[15]

And Jinavallabha's influence, already by no means negligible, must have grown still greater when Naravarman of Mālwā, at the time the overlord also of Chitor, sent for him to Dhārā and in recognition of his poetic talent and selfless life granted him two *Pāruttha drammas* daily from the customs house of Chitor for the maintenance of its two *vidhichaityas*.[16]

Besides, Jinavallabha left behind himself literature enough to serve as a sound basis of anti-*chaityavāsa* propaganda.[17] His style was perhaps a bit polemic, and the language sometimes even vitriolic. Yet this, in his view, was necessary.[18] No reformer can afford to mince matters when dealing with religious, social or moral corruption.

A good specimen of his writings is the *Saṅghapaṭṭaka*. There was not, he said, a greater enemy of the Jaina religion than these so-called *sādhus* who donned the monastic garb and yet yearned for pleasures and enjoyments. No Jaina *sādhu* is permitted by his scriptures to take food specially prepared for him ; he is only a recipient of what is superfluous and can easily be spared by the house-holder for others' use. Yet these so-called *sādhus* took greedily what their disciples prepared for them. They made Jaina temples their homes, in spite of the fact that their religious life in them was bound to be interfered with by the singing of musicians, dancing of courtesans,[19]

15. *Ibid.*, p. 18. A free translation of the verse would be something like this, "Here are followed no rites of those who go against the *Sūtras*. None ever bathes here at night. It is no property of the *sādhus*. Women do not get admission here at night. There is no insistence on the privileges of castes and sub-castes. The worshippers here are given no *tāmbūla* (betel leaves). Such are the rules of a *vidhichaitya*."

16. *IHQ.*, XXVI, p. 224.

17. The *Sārdhaśataka-bṛhadvṛtti* of Sumatigaṇi notes the following as his chief works :—

सूक्ष्मार्थसिद्धान्तविचारसारषडशीति, सार्धशतक, पिण्डविशुद्धि, पौषधविधि, प्रतिक्रमणसमाचारी, सङ्घपट्टक, धर्मशिक्षा, द्वादशकुलक, प्रश्नोत्तरशतक, शृङ्गारशतक

18. See *Saṅghapaṭṭaka*, verses 24, 28.

19. Required to dance before the idols, a common practice of the times.

sounding of drums, and crowding in of spectators wearing costly garlands.[20] For a real *sādhu* a layman's house was a far better habitation ; in fact this had been the practice of the great Jaina *tīrthaṁkaras* and teachers. Jaina canonic law condemns acceptance of money and property, undertaking of worldly projects and the un-Jaina practice of eating many times a day. They do not allow also the use of padded and comfortable seats, such use being indicative of lack of self-control and desire for enjoyment, both of them ridiculous in a *bhikṣhu.*[21] But the *chaityavāsins* taught something different. They told the people to adhere to their own *gachchha*, saying that a man's *gachchha* was fixed for ever. When questioned about property, they told their disciples that a *yati* had the right to possess a temple and that it was a layman's duty to look after all his requirements.[22] Even if a *Kharatara*[23] taught something prescribed by the scriptures, a *chaityavāsin's* follower had directions not to accept such a teaching.[24] What could it be, thought Jinavallabha, but the bad influence of the times that the country was passing through which made these so-called *sādhus* influential and persuaded sometimes sincerely religious people even to follow the lead of brats, picked from the streets and made into *āchāryas*, who defying all religious injunctions and enjoying the best of life courted popularity by organizing religious processions, bathing ceremonies of gods, spectacles and the like,[25] and acted almost as ordinary householders, regarding the *gachchha* as their household and the temples as their property.[26] Such *sādhus* were bound to invite the ridicule of the populace and make them feel that there were not any greater hyprocrites than the Jaina *sādhus* who were thought to be practising penance even when they had property, comfortable houses to live in, luxurious beds to lie on and almost every vice and weakness of the common herd.[27].

20. *Saṅghapaṭṭaka*, verse 7.
21. *Ibid.*, verse II.
22. *Ibid.*, verse 12.
23. A follower of Jinavallabha.
24. *Ibid.*, verse 12.
25. *Saṅghapaṭṭaka*, verse 21.
26. *Ibid.*, verse 15.
27. *Ibid.*, verses 24-25.

When Jinavallabha died in V. 1167, the *vidhichaitya* movement had received a good start and his work was carried on by his distinguished pupil, Jinadatta Sūri, popularly known as Dādājī, who perhaps won over more adherents to the *Kharatara* fold than any *āchārya* that preceded or followed him. He was a powerful preacher and a fearless critic.[28] But no small part of his success probably was due to his adopting *Apabhraṁśa*, in preference to Sanskrit and Prākrit, as a mode of popularising his ideas.[29] His *Charcharī Upadeśarasāyana* and *Kālasvarūpa-kulaka* convey in simple yet poetic language the ideas of his masters ; the first two could even be set to music and sung while dancing.[30] Chitrakūṭa (Mewār), Nāgor (Mārwār), Narabhaṭa[31] and Kanyānayana (Northern *Bāgaḍ*), Ajmer, Vikramapura (Jaisalmer), Tribhuvanagiri (modern Tahangarh, 24 miles north of Karauli), Vyāghrapura (Southern Bāgaḍ) Rudrapallī, Ujjayinī and Dhārā (Mālwā), and even the distant Uchcha (Sind) were among the various cities visited by this untiring reformer and his disciples.[32] At Ajmer, he met the Chauhān

28. See *Saṅghapaṭṭaka*, verses 33-34.

29. This should not however be taken to mean that he did not write any books in Prākrit and Sanskrit. These too had their readers, and the Sūri's objective was to reach one and all, the learned as well as the illiterate.

30. See the *G.O.S.*, No. XXXVI. See specially p. 1, the commentary of Jinapāla on the *Charcharī*.

31. For Jainism at Narabhaṭa read my paper on Narhaḍ in the *Marubhāratī*, VI, October issue. From here come two very beautiful images of Neminātha and Śāntinātha (8th-9th century).

32. Jinadatta Sūri must have been also a good organiser. The following are according to Jinapāla the rules of discipline laid down by him :—

When the chief *āchārya* entered a city he was to be received with the sounding of the five instrumentsic, of music, the *pañchaśabda*. The *nichchhāvara* ceremony was to be performed and an auspicious pitcher full of water was to be brought before him. There was to be no waving of lamps and *pañchakottāraṇa*. When the lecture for the day was over, female followers of the *āchārya* were to sing songs. This, in brief, is the way in which respect was to be shown to the chief *āchārya* (*yugapradhānāchārya*).

When an *āchārya* of the second rank entered a town, the Saṅgha, comprising the four classes received him. A conch was sounded. Women sang. But the drums were not beaten and the *nichchhāvara* ceremony was not performed. When he entered a house, there was no spreading of silken clothes.

An *upādhyāya* was received by laymen and *sādhus*. There was no sounding of the conch, no *nichchhāvara*, no singing at the time of his entering a temple. There was no *maṅgalakalaśa* or sounding of drums for him. But women sang at his lecture.

A *vāchanāchārya* was not received by *sādhvīs* and laywomen. There was no singing of songs at the end of his lecture. If there was any *sādhu* senior to him, that *sādhu* enjoyed the privilege of precedence.

In a *chaitya* a conch was sounded in the traditional manner for the *āchārya*, *upādhyāya*, and *vāchanāchārya*. An *āchārya* received three blankets'

ruler Arṇorāja, who was pleased to donate a good site for the construction of some new temples, in which worship was to be performed in accordance with Jinavallabha's teachings. At Tribhuvanagiri he preached to its ruler Kumārapāla and made the city into a good centre of Jaina worship.

The next *āchārya*, Jinachandra Sūri, did not live long. But in the long ministry of Jinapati Sūri, the reformist message of the *vidhichaitya* school made further progress. In fact, by the time of his death the need of reform had become fully recognised, and many other *āchāryas* too, not belonging to the *Kharataragachchha*, had denounced *chaityavāsa* and rid their *gachchhas* of later excrescences and corruption. And some among them, notably Hemachandra Sūri of the Pūrṇatalla *gachchha*, wielded religious and even political influence enough to shape the events of the times and give them a trend that persisted and had the greatest influence on the cultural history of Rājasthān.

Largely due to this great influence of the Jaina *āchāryas* of the period, Jainism had either the favour or the active and steady support of a number of Chauhān rulers and their ministers. Pṛthvīrāja I had a golden cupola put on the Jaina temple at Raṇthambhor.[33] Ajayarāja presented a golden *kalaśa* to the Pārśvanātha temple at Ajmer.[34] Arṇorāja patronised the Jaina scholar Dharmaghoṣa Sūri,[35] and Vigraharāja IV not merely built a Jaina *vihāra* at his capital but also prohibited the slaughter of animals on certain days in a month throughout

an *upādhyāya* two, and a *vāchanāchārya* one. This was the way they were seated.

When a *mahattarā* entered a city she was received by laywomen only. A conch was not sounded. No laymen came. Laywomen sang no songs. There was no *maṅgalakalaśa*, and when she entered a temple there was no singing, no sounding of the conch and *nichchhāvara*. *Karpūra* was put on her forehead. No blanket was put at her back, but she had two blankets to sit on.

In the case of a *Pravartinī*, there was no *karpūrakṣepa*, and she had only one blanket to sit on.

For the Sanskrit original *see* Sri Agar Chand Nāhta's *Jinadatta Sūri*, pp. 94-96.

33. See above, p. 43.

34. See above, p. 47.

35. See above p. 62.

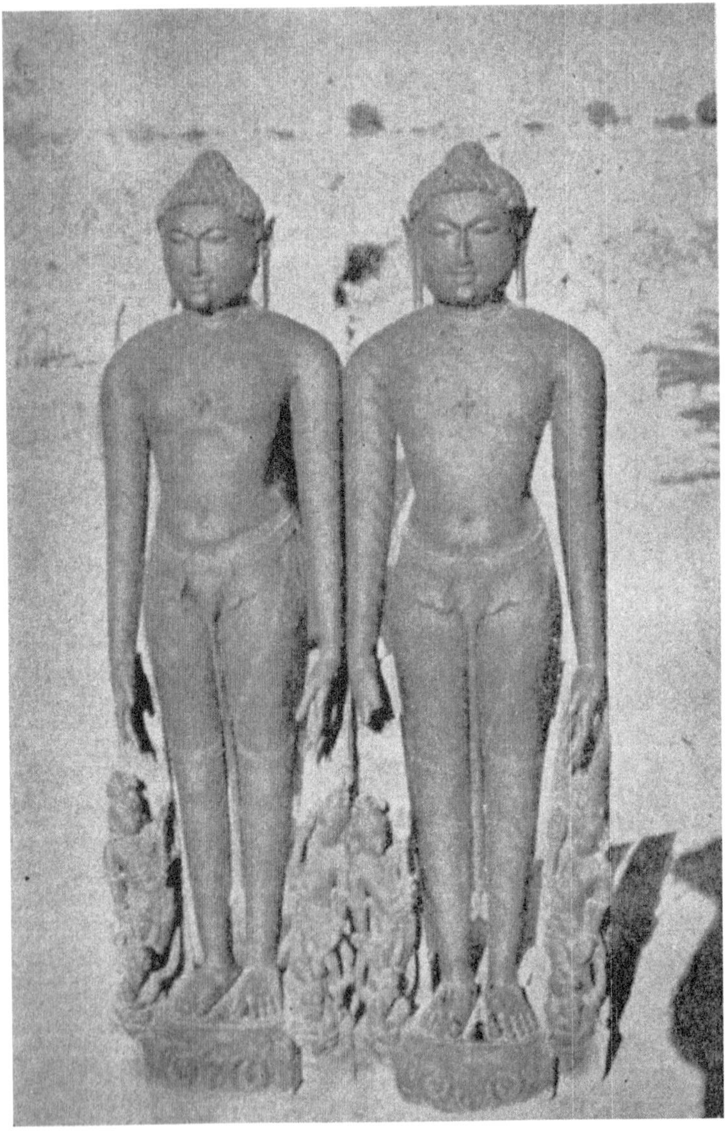

Tirthaṅkaras, Neminātha and Śāntinātha from Narhad, Pilani.

his extensive dominions.[36] Someśvara granted a village to the Jaina temple of Bijoliā,[37] and Pṛthvīrāja III employed Jainas in his service and granted a *jayapatra* to Jinapati Sūri in V. 1239.[38] Kaṭukarāja of Nāḍol granted in V. 1172 the sum of *drammas* for the worship of Śāntinātha. Rāyapāla's sons, Rudrapāla and Amṛtapāla, made with their mother a donation to the Jaina temple at Nāḍlāi; and the number of such donations in the Nāḍol kingdom increased appreciably with the accession of the Jaina emperor, Kumārapāla, the overlord of Nāḍol. The *amāri-ghoṣaṇas* (proclamations of non-slaughter) issued by Alhaṇa of Nāḍol and Punapākṣa-deva of Ratanpur are also good indications of this growing Jaina influence. Similar proofs of the good position that the Jainas of the 12th, 13th and 14th centuries had built up for themselves can be had from the kingdom of Jālor.[39] Udayasiṁha Sonigarā's chief minister, Yaśovīra, was as prominent a figure in Rājasthān as Vastupāla in Gujarāt.[40]

To the end of our period, Jainism was a proselytising religion, and among its members are to be found members of all castes, though the Vaiśya caste perhaps preponderated. The Bhaṇḍārīs or Bhāṇḍāgārikas trace their descent to Lakṣamaṇa, the founder of the kingdom of Nāḍol.[41] Sonīs appear to have been Rājpūts at one time.[42] Haribhadra, the great Jaina reformer, was a Brāhmaṇa.[43] Many Gūrjaras also professed Jainism.

Nor was the influence of Jainism confined to its professors. Many Rājasthāni Brāhmaṇas of the twelfth century appear to have been non-vegetarians.[44] Their descendants of today, how-

36. See above, pp. 72-73.

37. See above, pp. 80-82.

38. See above, p. 149.

39. See above, the account of the dynasty.

40. See above, p. 174.

41. *Purātanaprabandhasaṅgraha*, p. 102.

42. "Of the Māheśvarī Sonīs it is stated that their *nokh* or original clan was Sonigarā. What is true of Māheśvarī Sonīs is, in all probability, true of other Sonīs also" (Dr. D. R. Bhandarkar's comment on the Jālor inscription of Sāmantasiṁhadeva, *EI*, XI, p. 61).

43. *Prabhāvakacharita*, p.62.

44. Kirāḍū inscription of Alhaṇa, V. 1209, relaxes the *amāri* order as far as the *purohitas* were concerned. See also the *praśasti* of Ratnaśekhara's commentary on the *Prākṛta-dvyāśraya*.

ever, are vegetarians, most probably due to the humanising influence of Jainism. It offset not merely the influence of their meat-eating patrons, the Rājpūt princes and chiefs, but made them, in due course, the staunchest advocates of *ahiṁsā*.

Orthodox sects. Of the other religious sects, now generally grouped under the head Hinduism, there were many. They had their own rituals and systems of thought, the only marked characteristic indicating their unity and differentiation from Buddhism and Jainism being their professed belief in the Vedas, a belief however which allowed them the widest latitude of thought and let them differ from each other almost as much as from the heterodox systems.

Worship of Brahmā. We have no idea of the philosophical tenets of Brahmāism. But Brahmā, though no longer a popular god elsewhere, had his temples in Rājasthān. Pushkar, which is believed to represent the site of Brahmā's sacrifice, had then and has even now a great temple dedicated to Brahmā. There is an old temple of Brahmā at Kheḍ and another of Sāvitrī and Brahmā at Bīṭhū. The Brahmā temple of Vasantagarh (Sirohī) had a two-armed and three-faced figure of the god. His other images have been found at Sevāḍi (Jodhpur), Basad (Pratābgarh), Sirod (Kotāh), Kirāḍū (Jodhpur), Bijoliā (Mewāṛ), and Osiā (Jodhpur). At Rāṇapur (Jodhpur) is an image of which the upper part represents Brahmā, Viṣṇu and Śiva and the lower one, the Sun. A similar image was found at Rāmgarh (Koṭāh). Osiā and Kirāḍū have images representing this *chaturdeva* conception, though a conception far more popular was that of the Tripuruṣa, *i.e.*, Brahmā as one of the Hindu Trinity, Brahmā, Viṣṇu and Śiva. Rāyapāla's inscription of V. 1198 mentions the temple of Tripuruṣadeva, and so do the Ojha Grants and the *Pṛthvīrājavijaya.*[45] From the *Kānhaḍadeprabandha* we learn of the existence of the temple of Brahmā at Jālor.

Vaiṣṇavism. Viṣṇu perhaps had a greater number of worshippers than Brahmā, a fact evidenced by a fairly large number of old Viṣṇu images that now grace Rājasthānī museums. Lakṣmaṇa of Nāḍol and Chāmuṇḍarāja of Śākambharī built temples

45. IX, 68. Rājputānā Museum, No. 286, perhaps shows the way these three gods were worshipped collectively.

dedicated to this deity. Pṛthvīrāja II and Pṛthvīrāja III took pride in being regarded as incarnations of Rāma. Arṇorāja and Ajayarāja patronised the Vaiṣṇava teacher Devabodhi, whose invariable mention as a Bhāgavata probably indicates the prevalence of the Bhāgavata form of worship[46] in Rājasthān.

Śaivism. But the sect that found the greatest acceptance throughout the Chauhān dominions was Śaivism in some form or other. The Hansot Plates of Bhartṛvaḍḍha II of Broach (V. 813) show that he was a *Paramamāheśvara*, i.e. one intensely devoted to Śiva[47]. Harṣanātha was the family deity of the Chauhāns of Śākambharī[48] Vākpati and Siṁharāja built temples of Śiva on the Puṣkara lake[49] and Vākpati's mother, Rudrāṇī, lit daily a thousand lamps before the *liṅgas* installed there.[50] Pṛthvīrāja I established a continuous *annasatra* for the pilgrims proceeding to Somanātha.[51] Ajayarāja was a Śaiva; so also was his son Arṇorāja who built a temple named after his father on the lake Ānāsāgara.[52] The *Harakeli* drama was probably written to give the world a concrete proof of Vigraharāja IV's devotion to Śiva, with whose help, like Arjuna of old, he had succeeded in beating his enemies.[53] Pṛthvīrāja II's queen, Sudhavā, built the Sudhaveśvara temple at Menāl in Mewār.[54] Someśvara bore the unusual title of *Pratāpalaṅkeśvara*, probably on account of being not only as powerful but also as devoted to Śiva as the *Laṅkeśvara*, Rāvaṇa. On his death he is said to have gone to Kailāsa and become merged in Īśvara.[55]

That like their brethren of Śākambharī, the Nāḍol Chauhāns were Śaivas can be seen from the names of their deities,

46. It regards Vāsudeva as the supreme manifestation of God. The chief means to reach Him are going to temples (*abhigamana*), collecting materials for His worship (*upādāna*), worship (*ijyā*), study (*svādhyāya*) and *yoga*.

47. See above, page 15.

48. See verse 27 of the Harṣa inscription (V. 1030).

49. *PV*, C, 43 and 45.

50. See above, p. 31.

51. See above, p. 44.

52. *PV.*, V, 193.

53. At the end of the drama Śiva is represented as appearing in person and blessing Vigraharāja IV.

54. *PRAS.*, *WC.*, 1905-6, p. 58.

55. See above p. 220, note 8.

Anahileśvara, Aṇupameśvara, Pṛthvīpāleśvara, Āsaleśvara, Padmaleśvara, Sāhaṇapāleśvara and the like mentioned in their inscriptions and obviouly named after the kings and queens of Nāḍol. Alhaṇa and Kīrtipāla first pay obeisance to Śiva, even while making grants to Jaina temples. Kelhaṇa erected a *toraṇa* "like a diadem for the holy Someśa".[56]

Of the Jālor line, Kīrtipāla's daughter, Rūdaladevī, and Udayasiṁha built temples of Śiva at Jālor; Kānhaḍadeva is said to have rescued the fragments of the Somanātha idol from Alāuddīn's army, even at the risk of his life and independence. Their brethern, the Chauhāns of Chandrāvatī (and later on of Sirohī) still have Śiva as their tutelary deity, the only exception being the late ruler of Sirohī who developed Muslim leaning towards the latter part of his life.

Śiva figures mostly in the form of the *liṅgam*. Sometimes it would be a *Mukhaliṅgam*. Its upper part being indicative of *Brahmāṇḍa* would be round; the eastern side bore the figure of the Sun, the northern that of Brahmā, the western of Viṣṇu and the southern that of Rudra. Thus the whole image was a result of the highly philosophic Śaiva conception that Rudra, Sūrya, Viṣṇu and Brahmā were only manifestations of one and the same deity, the great Śiva, who ultimately was without any form and any attributes and could therefore be represented best in the almost shapeless form of *liṅgam*, which, whatever its original significance might have been, had come to mean the Supreme Being in which everything recedes in the end.[57] In the form of Trimūrti, of which we have a good example at Chitor, Śiva's image had practically the same meaning; it is, however, less indicative of his *nirguṇa* character.

Of the four well-known Śaiva schools, *Śaiva*, *Māheśvara*, *Kāpālika* and *Pāśupata*, we find references only to the latter two in Chauhān inscriptions. The temple of Nityapramodita at Dhoḍ gave shelter to *Kāpālikas*.[58] The Siddheśvara temple at Lohārī, the monastery at Menālgarh and the temple of Harṣanātha were *Pāśupata* institutions.

56. Verse 34 of the Sūndhā inscription, V. 1319.

57. *yasmin sarvaṁ layaṁ gachchhati talliṅgam*.

58. It was probably also in *Kāpālika* possession. See the words, *Mama pṛṣṭhe yadi kopi Kāpālikabhaṭṭārakaḥ sthānaṁ pālayati ye kechit Kāpillātapasvino deśāṁtarādāgachchhanti tatraiva pratiśrayām......* (Dhoḍ inscription).

The details of *Kāpālika* worship and ways of life can be gathered from Hieun Tsang's *Records of the Western World*, Mahendravarman's *Mattavilāsa*, Bhavabhūti's *Mālatīmādhava*, Soḍḍhala's *Udayasundarīkathā* and the *Mohaparājaya* of Yaśaḥpāla.[59] If its express teachings have not been deliberately covered up with foul verbiage,[60] it must have been a horrid sect, worthy of nothing but the speediest extermination.

Far better, much more philosophic and hence also naturally more popular was the *Pañchārthāmnāya*[61] or *Pāśupata* school, professed by great teachers like Viśvarūpa, the head of the Harṣa monastery. Its final objective being *Mahaiśvarya*, mere cessation of pain was not deemed enough; the *Pāśupata* devotee concentrated more on the attainment of omniscience, omnipotence, freedom from *saṁsāra*, and control over souls in bondage, these being the attributes of Maheśvara with whom they tried to be at one by means of *yoga*. This positive ideal must have appealed to many, though the discipline prescribed for the *pāśupata* ascetic was far from easy. One required knowledge, the strictest adherence to the prescribed ritual, and the guidance of an expert *guru* to reach the destination. For the layman the conditions were easier. He earned merit enough to push him forward on the path, if he served the *Pāśupata* church and had full faith in the grace of Maheśvara[62].

Early *Pāśupata* monks appear to have been free from undue attachment to worldly things. Allaṭa of Harṣanātha, for instance, went without any clothes, was a *brahmachārin* from his birth, and devoted all his time to the worship of Śiva. His pupil Bhāvadyota's worldly belongings are similarly summed up as "matted locks, *bhasma*, the earth as a bed, the four quarters as his garments, begging as a means of livelihood, and a bowl to bring it."[63] But it is doubtful whether this austere way of life was followed consistently to the end of our

59. Beal, *Records of the Western World*, pp. 55 and 76 (Vol. I), *Mālatīmādhava*, Act V., *Udayasundarīkathā*, p. 61., *Moharājaparājaya*, IV. 23.

60. Even the *Pāśupata* system had a stage, the *avyakta*, when the devotee deliberately tried to give the people a wrong idea about himself.

61. So called on account of the doctrines of "Groups of Five" taught by it. For details see the *Gaṇakārikā* (G.O.S.)

62. The account given here is based on Bhā-Sarvajña's *Gaṇakārikā*.

63. See the Harṣa inscription of Vigraharāja II, V. 1030.

period. From the ridicule poured on them in some Jaina books it would rather appear that they were here and there falling away from their pristine standards of morality and sincere religious piety.[64]

The *Kāpālikas* used human skulls as their bowls and bones as ornaments.[65] They went about naked. As against this, the *Pāśupata* ascetics generally covered their private parts with pieces of thick cloth. They bore staves, smeared their bodies with ashes, ate insipid food, and carried *Śivaliṅga* either in their hands or in their matted hair. Instead of *kapālas*, they used gourds like many other religious sects of India.[66] The *Pāśupatas*, further, were believers in eighteen incarnations of Śiva, of whom the chief was Lakulīśa, the founder of the sect, who according to Dr. D.R. Bhandarkar's calculations flourished about 150 A.D.[67] A good many images of Lakulīśa have been found in Rājasthān, and of these most can be referred to our period. In these he is represented as a two-armed, *ūrdhvameḍhra*[68] deity with matted hair, carrying a citron in one hand and a *lakula* or staff in the other.

Neither the *Kāpālikas* nor the *Pāśupatas* appear to have cared for the caste system in admitting people to their ascetic orders.[69] For the latter every soul in bondage was a *paśu*;[70] it mattered little whether he was a Brāhmaṇa, Kṣatriya, Vaiśya or Śūdra.

Śaktism. Only a little, if at all, less wide-spread than the worship of Śiva, was the worship of Śakti in the Chauhān dominions. The porch of the famous temple of Sakarāi or Saṅkarā Mātā, now a place of pilgrimage for thousands of people from Rājasthān and elsewhere, was built by the local

64. See, for instance, the *Dhūrtākhyāna*.
65. See footnote 57 of this chapter.
66. See the *ṣaḍdarśanosamuchchaya* of Haribhadra.
67. The 18 incarnations were Nakulīśa, Kauśika, Gārgya, Maitreya Kauruṣa, Īśāna, Paragārgya, Kuṣmāṇḍa, Manuṣyaka, Aparakuśika, Atri, Piṅgalākṣa, Puṣpaka, Bṛhadāchārya, Agasti, Sanātana, Rāśikara and Vidyāguru.

For Dr. D. R. Bhandarkar's views see *EI*, XXI, p. 8, f.

68. Indicative of his absolute continence according to Dr. G. H. Ojha (*Madhyakālīna Bhāratīya Saṁskṛti*).
69. See Haribhadra's *Ṣaḍdarśanasamuchchaya*.
70. See the *Gaṇokārikā*.

goṣṭhikas, in V. 749.[71] Goddess Āśāpurī was the tutelary goddess of the Śākambharī line;[72] Vigraharāja II had her temple built even in the distant Broach.[73] The coins of Someśvara, Pṛthvīrāja III, Picchhimbadeva, Pipalarājadeva and Chāhaḍedeva bear the legend, "Āsāvarī Śrī Sāmantadeva", wherein the word Āsāvarī obviously stands for Āśāpurī.[74] Śākambharī was the chief goddess of Sāmbhar.[75] The Sūndhā Inscription of V. 1319 records the construction of a *maṇḍapa* of *Aghaṭeśvarī* by Chāchigadeva.[76] The Kinsariyā Inscription of Dādhīchaka Chachcha mentions the building of Śākta temple in the reign of Durlabharāja II of Śākambharī.[77] For Jīṇamātā at Revāsā we have an inscription of V. 1162; for Bahughṛṇā at Bālī an inscription of V. 1200, and for Arbudeśvarī an old reference showing that her temple was regarded, of old, as a *pīṭha* of the *Kaula* sect.[78] We know also of the shrine of Śrī Mātā being regarded as almost the proprietor of the whole of Mount Ābū. To its shrine were passed over the dues payable by the managers of the Jaina temple of Dilwārā.[79] At Maṇḍor and Kekind we have the images of *Aṣṭamātṛkā i.e.* Durgā and her *Śaktis*, Brahmāṇī, Kumārī, Vaiṣṇavī, Indrāṇī, Māheśvarī, Vārāhī, and Nārasiṁhī.[80] Indrarāja Chāhamāna was a worshipper of Vaṭayakṣiṇī.[81] From Narabhaṭa we have an image of Mahiṣamardinī (8th century).

Nor was Śakti worship confined to the orthodox sects, and that is no wonder too, for *Mā* or *Durgā* belongs to a period when these sects had not come into existence : and her wor-

71. *Varadā* II, 64.
72. See *PV.*, *IV*, 84.
73. See above, p. 35.
74. See Thomas, *Chronicles of the Pathan Kings of Delhi*, pp. 59, 63, 64, 70.
75. See *PV.*, *IV.*, 63-4.
76. See above p. 178.
77. *EI*, XII, pp. 59 ff.
78. *Kaulajñānavinirṇaya*, VIII, 22.
79. Jayantavijaya, *Śrī-Arbudalekha-sandoha.*
80. For iconographical details about these see the *Bṛhatsaṁhitā* of Varāhamihira and the *Mānasāra.*
81. *EI.*, XIV, pp. 184.

ship has more of Dravidian and even Proto-Australoid than Aryan elements in it.[82] So popular has she been all along in the various strata of society, the upper as well as the lower, that the only way to have their willing adhesion was to accept the goddess as one of their own deities, even though she might be relegated to the second place in a pantheon which naturally assigned the first place to the chief deity of the proselytising sect. It was probably thus that the worship of Chaṇḍikā was taken over by the Brāhmaṇas who, as the circumstances demanded, identified her with Gaurī, Brahmāṇī, Lakṣmī, and the like.[83] They continued also her worship in her original form of Chaṇḍikā or Chāmuṇḍā with all the bloody ritual of the Proto-Australoids. The Jainas too could not do without her. In the cities where Chaṇḍikā worship prevailed, they adopted her as the tutelary goddess of their *gachchha*, turning her however into a vegetarian who had to be satisfied with sweets and flowers. Sachchikā, Ambikā and Chaṇḍikā thus came into the Jaina fold sometimes along with their own *Kṣetrapālas* and other attendants,[84] and Jainism spread without any further serious objection on the part of the Chaṇḍikā worshippers.

Minor Śaiva and Śakti sects. Closely connected with the worship of Śiva and Śakti was that of Gaṇapati, the elephant-headed god, who is believed to remove all obstacles and give success. Of the numerous Gaṇesa images of our period, we might specially mention those found at Ghaṭiyālā Buchkalā, Maṇḍor and Biṭhū, all of them in the present Jodhpur division of Rājasthān. We have the images of *dikpālas* at Kekind and Kheḍ, of Bhairava at Kirāḍū, of Kubera at Bhīnmāl and Bīṭhū, and Kārttikeya at Buchkalā. Sarasvatī, the goddess of learning, naturally received the homage of all sects, orthodox as well as heterodox. The image of Jaina Sarasvatī from Pallū, an old town in the Chauhān dominions, is hard to beat for its beauty.

The Saura sect. The worship of the Sun-god has come down to us from the Vedic period; but the way we find him worshipped in Rājasthān during the Chauhān period shows unmistakable

82. See Dr. S.K. Chatterjee's chapter on 'Race Movements and Pre-Historic Culture'. (Bhāratīya Vidyā Bhavan Series, Vol. I).

83. See the *Durgā-saptaśatī*, specially Chapter XI, verses 37-51.

84. See for instance the account in Jinapāla's *Kharataragachchhapaṭṭāvalī* and the *Ukeśagachchhapaṭṭāvali*.

signs of foreign influence.[85] Bhīnmāl was a great centre of Sun-worship, with its famous Sun-icon called Jagatsvāmin. At Osiā we have an image of the Sun dressed in a tight-fitting long coat reaching up to the ankles, with his waists tied with a scarf and the legs covered in long boot. We find there also the images of his two sons, Revanta and Saturn. The seated figure of the god at Maṇḍor is believed to have been carved in the eighth century or so. Other well-known images of the Sun-god are those of Beḍā, Pokaraṇ, Kirāḍū, Bīṭhū and Pālī. In fact, the whole of Rājasthān was studded with Sun-temples of great splendour the remains of which serve to remind us of the great vogue that *Saura* worship once had in western India.

That the Sun-god sometimes combined with Viṣṇu, Śiva, Brahmā etc. to form a *Trideva* or *Chaturdeva* has been pointed out already; and the increased popularity of Sun-worship that resulted consequently was probably increased still further by his worship by even non-Brahmanical sects like the Jainas.[86].

Of Chauhān rulers, Chaṇḍamahāsena was a Sun-worshipper.[87] Indrarāja of Pratābgarh built the splendid temple of Indrādityadeva.[88] Alhaṇa and Kīrtipāla were worshippers of the Sun as well as Śiva.[89] The Sonigarā Chauhāns of Jālor made several benefactions to the temple of the god Jagatsvāmin,[90] whose shrine at Bhīnmāl was visited by numerous devotees from various parts of India.

Two Common Elements. We close the chapter with a few remarks regarding the elements common to most people in India, whatever their religion, namely, superstition, which found a place even in the best educated minds of the period, and toleration, born not of indifference but true appreciation of the great principles underlying all Indian thought.[91]

85. Spread in Rājasthān most probably by *Śākadvīpī Brāhmaṇas.*

86. See *Prabandhachintāmani*. p. 82, It may interest us to remember that Akbar was taught Sun-worship by Jainas, a fact indicating the continuity of this worship upto the 16th century.

87. See above, the account of Chaṇḍamahāsena.

88. See the account of the Chauhāns of Pratābgarh above, pp. 20-21

89. See above, p. 154, and *EI*, IX, 65, 69.

90. For details see above.

91. This spirit of toleration goes as far back as the Vedic Period when various gods were regarded as manifestations of one Supreme Spirit. Aśoka saw truth in every religion. In the period we deal with, we find this spirit of toleration expressing itself in various ways, in theory as well as practice. For an instance of *samanvaya*, one might read the following:—

"Superstition," writes Joseph Hall, "is devout impiety. The superstitious man dares not stir forth, till his breast be crossed and face sprinkled. If but a hare crosses his way, he returns, or if his journey began unawares on the dismal day...In the morning he listens whether the crow crieth even or odd... There is no dream without an interpretation. This man is strangely credulous and calls impossible things miraculous." This description can almost literally be applied to the people in the Chauhān dominions. Śārṇgadhara, the grandson of Rāghavadeva, a renowned scholar of Hammīra's court, speaks highly of omens, declaring that through them one could know of the past and future, tell the period of men's lives, and predict profit and loss, victory and defeat, success and failure. His *kṣetraja, āgantuka,* and *jānghika* omens, dealt with in about five hundred verses of the *Śārṅgadharapaddhati* include all the types of superstition mentioned above. Nor was superstition confined to Rājasthān. Its all-India character is shown by books on omens composed in most parts of India during the period, 800-1400 A.D.[92] Excessive belief in astrology, predictions and alchemy may also be ascribed to the credulous nature of the common man,[93] and characterised equally the people everywhere in India.

Not merely toleration but genuine respect for the beliefs of others was another equally common characteristic. Brāhmaṇas regarded Ṛṣabha as an *avatāra* of Viṣṇu; Vāsudeva Kṛṣṇa and Rāma were *śalākāpuruṣas* of the Jainas.[94] An epigraph of V. 1218 goes even so far as to mention Brahmā, Viṣṇu and Śiva as Jinas.[95] They were worshipped also as Tripuruṣa, *i.e.* as three different aspects of one and the same Divinity which

---

श्रोतव्यः सौगतो धर्मः' कर्तव्यः पुनरार्हतः ।
वैदिको व्यवहर्तव्यो ध्यातव्यः परमः शिवः ।।
(पुरातनप्रबन्धसंग्रह, पृ २०)

92. Perhaps the most comprehensive treatment of the subject is to be found in the *Adbhutasāgara* of Ballālasena.

93. Read the *Kharataragachchhapaṭṭāvalī* of Jinapāla and the *Upamitibhavaprapañcha Kathā* of Siddharṣi Sūri, both of which represent social conditions of Rājasthān.

94. See the *Triṣaṣṭiśalākāpuruṣacharita* of Hemachandra Sūri.

95. *EI.*, IX, pp. 67-8.

combined at times with Sūrya to form *Chaturmūrti* or *Chaturdeva*. The Pratihāras of Jālor and Kanauj paid equal respect to Maheśvara, Bhagavatī and Āditya and changed their *iṣṭadevatā* from almost reign to reign.[96] Their feudatories, the Chauhāns of Śākambharī, though not so quick in changing their tutelary gods and goddesses, were not behind them in their liberal attitude towards the different sects of their kingdom. From the evidence already recorded, it is clear that their relations with the Jainas were extremely cordial. They honoured Jaina teachers, granted lands to Jaina temples, and took part in their religious ceremonies. And we can say this not only of the Chauhāns of Śākambharī and Ajmer, but also of the Chauhāns of Nāḍol, Jālor, Raṇthambhor and Rāyabaddīya. Hammīra worshipped the images of Jaina *Tīrthaṅkaras* at Mount Ābū.[97] The fact that he is enthusiastically praised by a Jaina writer and selected as the hero of his historical poem is also indicative of his excellent relations with the Jaina community. The followers of the various *darśanas* entered into discussions with each other, but this led to no ugly incidents. Each had liberty to follow the way he thought best, without any compulsion on the part of the ruler. With *mokṣa* as their goal, self-control as the chief *sādhanā*, and their belief in *karma*, it was not difficult for Indian sects to find a common platform. Outsiders generally wondered at the absence of religious acrimony in India.[98] The case of Islam was different. But even that they were ready to tolerate and leave to itself. The Rāṣṭrakūṭas permitted the Muslims to build mosques within their dominions;[99] Siddharāja Jayasiṁha of Gujarāt punished the Hindus who damaged Muslim property at Cambay.[100] While we read often of the desecration by Muslims of Hindu temples in the Chauhān dominions, we read not even once of the desecration of mosques though this could have been no difficult task on part of people like Hammīra and Kānhaḍadeva.

96. See Bhoja's Barāh Plate, *EI*, XIX, pp. 17-18.

97. *Hammīramahākāvya*, IX, 34.

98. See *Alberunī's Indian*, I. p. 19.

99. See *ED.*, I, p. 27 and 38. Epigraphic evidence of this can be seen in *India. Archaeology, a Review*, 1956-7. pt. 4c-1.

100. *Ibid.*, II, pp. 163-164.

CHAPTER XXIII

SOCIAL CONDITION

Section I

(i) *Caste System*

The Hindu Caste System is the result of two widely different and not unoften antagonistic ideals expressed by the words, *varṇa* and *jāti*, the first laying stress on culture, character, profession, social duties, and the organic nature of human society; and the other on birth, heredity and hereditary privileges. To these two idealistic tendencies, neither of which can be regarded as wholly inoperative even during our period, further complications had been added by the influx of foreigners, inter-caste marriages, Aryanising of people on the frontiers, and growth of occupational groups, with the result that the Hindu Society consisted no longer of the four original *varṇas*, based on *guṇa* and *karma*[1] or even *janma*,[2] but of numerous castes and sub-castes in the differentiation of which so many factors had a share.

The Brāhmaṇas of our period were not so much a class as a hereditary caste divided into a number of sub-sections. We find the mention of the Śrīmālīs and Visalnagarā Brāhmaṇas in the *Kānhaḍadeprabandha*,[3] of the Nāgaras in the *Viruddhavidhi-viddhvaṁsa* of Lakṣmīdhara,[4] of the Pañcha-Gauḍas and Pañcha-Draviḍas in the *Skanda-Purāṇa*,[5] of the Rāyakavālas in the Pāṭan Inscription of Bhīmadeva II,[6] of the Dadhyā or Dāhimā Brāhmaṇas in the Sakrāi Mātā Inscription,[7] of the Puṣkara community, most probably the Pushkaraṇās, in a Pushkar

1. This is the *Bhagavadgītā* idea (IV. 13) which in the formative period of the caste system must have been an actual fact.
2. See Manu, IX, 317, for the heredity idea, though he also insists on their receiving due education and behaving properly.
3. III, 22-28, IV, 370.
4. See above, p. 78.
5. Sahyādrikhaṇḍa, X, vv. 2-3.
6. *IA.*, XI, pp. 71 ff.
7. From Dr. G. H. Ojha's transcript.

Inscription of V. 982,[8] and of the Āvasathikas, Purohitas, Dvivedins, Trivedins, Chaturvedins, Miśras, Dīkṣitas, and Tripāṭhins in the provinces adjoining Rājasthān.[9]

It is difficult to say when these sub-divisions began; their germs at least can be detected as far back as the Sūtra period, when the Brāhmaṇas of the north and the south began to mark the differences in their social customs and condemn what they disliked.[10] In the early Smṛti period, the Brāhmaṇas of Brahmāvarta were regarded as superior to those settled elsewhere. Vaṅga, Aṅga and Oḍra being almost regarded as *Mlechchha* countries.[11] Later we find the same sense of cultural superiority among the Brāhmaṇas of Antarvedī in Northern India, of Śrīmāla in Rājasthān, and of Ānandanagara or Nagara in Gujarāt. Many Brāhmaṇa families of Bengāl trace their descent from the Brāhmaṇas of Kanauj,[12] and learned Brāhmaṇas from Ahichchhatra figure prominently among Brāhmaṇa donees even outside Madhyadeśa. Śrīmālīs might have come into prominence on account of Śrīmala or Bhīnmal being a great cultural and religious centre,[13] and the same may perhaps be said of the Nāgaras or Brāhmaṇas from Nagar.

When the Muslims reached India, the Brāhmaṇas as the recognised custodians of Hindu culture tried to protect it not by liberalising its tenets and improving it spiritually, but by emphasising its physical content, *i.e.*, laying stress on *jāti-śuddhi* (purity of birth) and non-contamination with foreign blood. Ours was the age of the *kalivarjyas*, of taboos and

8. *PRAS, WC*, 1909-10. Dr. Bhandarkar may be wrong in regarding them as Pārāśara Brāhmaṇas.

9. *JAOS.*, VII, p. 25; *EI.*, XIV, p. 207, 205, 204, 208, and *EI.*, IV. p. 98 etc.

10. See for instance the *Baudhāyana-Dharmasūtra*, I. 1.42.

11. *Manu, II*, 17-18. For the prejudice against outlying areas see also *Manu*, X, 43-44, *Devalasmṛti*, 4-5, 16, *Baudhāyanasmṛti*, I, 1, 31-34.

12. I am not concerned with the truth or otherwise of the tradition. What is emphasised is merely the fact that Madhyadeśa was at one time regarded as a great cultural centre, the Brāhmaṇas of which were superior to the Brāhmaṇas, at least according to some, to the Brāhmaṇas already settled in Bengal.

13. Padmanābha, the author of the *Kānhaḍadeprabandha*, though himself a Visalanagarā Brāhmaṇa, speaks very highly of the Brāhmaṇas of Śrīmāla, the "Brahmapurī of the Chauhāns."

prohibitions that mark the end of the liberal era of Hinduism. Inter-caste marriages were disallowed ; a Brāhmaṇa undertaking a sea voyage was excommunicated and not taken back into the community even after performing the prescribed penances; he could not have food even at the houses of his slave, his cowherd, a hereditary Śūdra family friend and a Śūdra who cultivated his fields, even though earlier texts had allowed him this concession; and he was not to have food cooked by Śūdras, even though they observed rules of cleanliness and worked under a Brāhmaṇa's supervision.[14]

Under such conditions the sub-divisions of the Brāhmaṇas were bound to multiply. A Brāhmaṇa coming into habitual contact with Muslims, either on account of changed political conditions or on account of his professional duties, was regarded as inferior to the one who could keep himself aloof and go on as before, maintaining his cultural as well as ceremonial purity. In Rājasthān, the Brāhmaṇas gave up eating meat, and found it difficult to keep up their social contacts with the Brāhmaṇas using a nonvegetarian diet. Migration to distant parts of the country, adoption of professions regarded as ceremonially impure, differences on philosophic and religious grounds and quarrels on grounds of social behaviour among different sections of one and the same community may also have been some among the many other likely causes adding to these divisions.

That the ancient cultural idea of *varṇa*, the emphasis of which was mainly on *guṇa* and *karma*, could sometimes assert itself even when these fissiparous tendencies were at their full swing can be seen from the case of the Magas or Bhojakas who, though certainly outsiders,[15] were on account of the similarity of their work to that of Brāhmaṇas permitted to enter the Brāhmaṇic fold, and have actually been mentioned as

14. For a very good and authoritative account of the *kalivarjyas*, *i.e.*, practices disallowed in *kaliyuga*, see P. V. Kane's *History of Dharmaśāstra*, III, pp. 926-968.

15. Varāhamihira, the author of the *Bṛihatsaṁhitā* was probably a Maga Brāhmaṇa. The *Harṣacharita* speaks of the Bhojaka. *i.e.*, Maga, Tāraka as an astronomer, thoroughly proficient in all the *grahasaṁhitās i.e.*, astronomical works, and having knowledge of all the three times, past, present, as well as future. (p. 128, Nirṇayasāgara Edition).

The following arguments can be advanced to prove the original foreign character of the Magas :—

Brāhmaṇas in the *Bṛhaddharma Purāṇa*, and the Govindapura Inscription of S. 1059 or 1137 A.D. Their chief profession probably was astrology.[16] Sun-worship was their monopoly,[17] and we find many of them associated even with the worship of Jaina gods and goddesses,[18] which probably again indicates their original non-Brahmin character.[19]

The Rājpūts were the ruling class. The *Kānhaḍadeprabandha* speaks of 36 Rājpūt clans, though actually it enumerates only the Chauhāns, the Vāghelās, the Devaḍās, the Solaṅkīs the Rāṭhoḍs, the Paramāras, the Bāraḍas, the Hūṇas, the Hariyaḍas the Chāvaḍās, the Ḍoḍias, the Jādavas, the Hūlas, the

(*a*) They admit having come from Śakadvīpa, *i.e.*, Scythia.
(*b*) Originally they were followers of Zarasasta, which looks like a Sanskritised form of Zarathustra.
(*c*) The *avyaṅga*, a sort of girdle prescribed for their constant use, has its counter-part in the Avestan Avyaonghen.
(*d*) Their four Vedas, mentioned in the *Bhaviṣya Purāṇa* have nothing Aryan about them.
(*e*) Alberunī, who knew a good deal about them, identifies them with the Persian Magīs.
(*f*) They are worshippers not of the Vedic Sūrya but of a Sun icon imported from outside India which shows him wearing long boots.

For further discussion of the question, see R. G. Bhandarkar's *Vaiṣṇavism, Saivism and Minor Religious Systems*, pp. 218-222, and the *Bhaviṣya Purāṇa*, Chapter 139.

16. See note 15.

17. *Viṣṇor-Bhāgavatān Magāṁścha Savituḥ* (*Bṛhatsaṁhitā*, 60. 19.)

18. See the Sachiyāya Mātā Inscription of Osiā, (P.C. Nahar, *Jaina Inscriptions*, Part 1, p. 198). Even now they perform this duty in most Jaina temples of Bīkāner.

19. We have left out topics like the usual duties of a Brāhmaṇa, his duties in times of emergency and the like, because there is nothing new about them. To the end of the period, they continued *Svādhyāya i.e.*, the study of the Vedas, performance of *Agnihotra* and sacrifices, and *adhyāpana* or teaching (see the account of Śrīmāla in the *Kānhaḍadeprabandha* and of Ajmer in the *Pṛthvīrājavijaya*). The popular idea that the coming in of Pauraṇic deities and Paurāṇic worship led to the discontinuance of Vedic rites, ceremonies and worship has to be given up as mistaken, inasmuch as the Brāhmaṇas neither liked to officiate as permanent priests nor held the temple priests in any high estimation. In this connection the following extracts are worth studying:—

(a) न द्विजाः परिगृह्णन्ति देवस्य स्वीकृतं धनम् ।।४।।
देवचर्यागतैर्धर्मैः क्रिया ब्राह्मी न विद्यते ।।५।।
(भविष्यपुराण, ब्रह्मचर्य अध्याय १३६)

(b) श्येनगर्दभचाण्डालमद्यमांसरजस्वलाः
स्पृष्ट्वा देवलकं चैव सचैलस्नानमाचरेत् ।।
(कुमारपालदेवचरित, पृ० ४)

In the *Manusmṛti* (III, 152) a Devalaka is counted among Brāhmaṇas who do not deserve being invited to a Śrāddha ceremoney; and the reason for this seems to be that given by Devala

Nikumbhas and the Guhilas.[20] On the basis of contemporary literature and inscriptions we can add to these the Bhāṭīs, the Yaudheyas, the Varāhas or Birāhās, Pratihāras or Paḍihāras, Tomaras, Kachchhapaghātas or Kachhawāhās, Balās, Jeṭhwās, Dāhīmās, Dahiyās and Chandels.

Towards the end of our period all these clans regarded themselves as Kṣatriyas, though earlier there were some among them who had not forgotten their non-Kṣatriya origin. We have indicated above the Brāhmaṇa origin of the Chauhāns. The Guhilas were originally Brāhmaṇas, and mention this Brāhmaṇa descent of theirs up to the time of Mahārāṇā Kumbhā.[21] The Kṣatriya Pratihāras of Maṇḍor had a Brāhmaṇa as their ancestor and recognised their relationship with the Brāhmaṇa Pratihāras, the progeny of Hariśchandra by a Brāhmaṇa wife.[22] The Hūṇas, mentioned both in the *Kumārapālacharita*[23] and the *Kānhaḍadeprabandha* as one of the thirty-six ruling families,[24] were actually foreign immigrants into India from Central Asia. The Paramāras, who trace their descent from the fire-pit of Vasiṣṭha at Ābū and regard their *gotra* as *Vāsiṣṭha*, have more reason to be regarded originally as Brāhmaṇas than Gūrjaras.[25] So, though not many Kṣatriyas may have become Brāhmaṇas during our period, owing to the increasing exclusiveness and vigilance of that class, it is certain that many Brāhmaṇas became the founders of Rājpūt families, a tendency which was neither new nor confined merely to Rājasthān or even Northern India.[26]

देवार्चनपरो विप्रवित्तार्थी वत्सरत्रयम् ।
असौ देवलको नाम हव्यकव्येषु गर्हितः ॥
देवकोशोपजीवी च नाम्ना देवलको भवेत् ।
अपांक्तेयः स विज्ञेयः सर्वकर्मसु सर्वदा ॥

(Quotation in स्मृतिचन्द्रिका, II, p. 396)

20. Canto 3, vv. 38 ff.

21. On the origin of the Guhilas of Mewār see D.R. Bhandarkar, *JPASB*, 1909, G.H. Ojha, History of Udaipur, I; and Mrs. Malati Sharma, IHQ., XXVIII, 83ff.

22. See the Jodhpur inscription of Bāuka, *EI*, XVIII, pp. 99 ff. and my paper on the Pratihāras of Maṇḍor in the *Pilāni Vidyā-vihāra-rajata-jayantī* number.

23. For the list from the *Kumārapālacharita*, see Tod's *Annals and Antiquities of Rājasthān*, O.U.P. edition I, the table facing p. 96.

24. See footnote 20.

25. See my paper on the *Origin of the Paramāras*, *Rājasthāna Bhāratī*, Vol. III, part 2, pp. 2-8.

26. See the relevant references in the chapter on the "Origin and original habitat of the Chauhāns", pp. 1-13.

The assimilation of Brāhmaṇas into the Kṣatriya fold did not prove difficult, because the two castes were the inheritors of one and the same culture, and there was not much to distinguish between a Kṣatriya and a Brāhmaṇa, the moment the latter adopted a military career, either for monetary reasons[27] or for defending Hindu *dharma* which could not have been less dear to him than to a Kṣatriya.[28] To some Brāhmaṇas, specially to those born of a Brāhmaṇa's Kṣatriya wives, military profession may have been more congenial than the priestly; and it is probably an actual fact which the later *Smṛtis* recognised, when contradicting the dictates of Manu and other early lawgivers, they laid down the new rule that a Brāhmaṇa's sons by a Kṣatriya wife should be recognised not as Brāhmaṇas but as Kṣatriyas.[29]

Nor did the assimilation of foreign fighting tribes into the Kṣatriya fold prove impossible, even though this must have taken more time than the assimilation of Brāhmaṇas. Unconsciously or consciously the people realised that every fighter was inherently a Kṣatriya and thus entitled to become a Hindu, provided he changed his barbaric ways and shared with the indigenous Kṣatriyas the great task of defending Indian culture. Even the orthodox lawgiver, Manu, stated, "In the beginning Pauṇḍras, Draviḍas, Cholas, Kāmbojas, Yavanas, Śakas, Pāradas, Pahlavas, Chīnas, Kirātas, Daradas, and Khasas were Kṣatriya people. Gradually they became *Vṛṣalas* as a result of losing contact with Brāhmaṇas giving up their (Vedic)

27. Profession of arms is an *āpaddharma* for Brāhmaṇas. Baudhāyana (I. 1. 20) notes, though with disapprobation, that many Brāhmaṇas of the north earned their living by fighting. Actual instances of Brāhmaṇas serving in armies in the post-Harṣa Hindu period are by no means rare. Ballāla of Mālwā was killed by Kumārapāla's Brāhmaṇa soldiers. Skanda, commandant of Pṛthvīraja III, was a Brhāmaṇa.

28. As good instances we can have Puṣyamitra Śuṅga, identified with Kalkī by Dr. Jayaswal; Mayūraśarman, the founder of the Kādamba dynasty; Bappā Rāwal of Mewār; and perhaps also Kallar, the founder of the Brāhmaṇa Shāhiyā dynasty of Udbhāṇḍapura.

29. (a) यत्तु ब्राह्मणेन क्षत्रियायामुत्पादितः क्षत्रिय एव भवति, क्षत्रियेण वैश्यायामुत्पादितो वैश्य एव भवति, वैश्येन शूद्रायामुत्पादितः शूद्र एव भवतीति शंखस्मरणम्। (मिताक्षरा on याज्ञवल्क्यस्मृति, आचाराध्याय, श्लोक ९१)

(b) नृपायां विधिना विप्राज्जातो नृप इति स्मृतः
औशनस-स्मृति (स्मृतिसमुच्चय), Verse 28

rites"[30] The *Purāṇas* took up the cue and provided as it were an explanatory note. According to them, when Sagara wanted to avenge the death of his father by punishing the Śakas, Yavanas, Pahlavas and Kāmbojas, these people sought refuge with Sagara's *guru*, Vasiṣṭha, who protected them from Sagara's ire by telling him that his enemies could be regarded as dead, for he had deprived them of what is as good as life, *i.e.*, their *dharma* and the company of Brāhmaṇas. Thus deprived of the privilege of Vedic studies, Vedic rites and Vedic teachers, these Kṣatriyas became *Mlechchas.*[31]

As the Aryans probably entered India by way of the north-western passes and were, therefore, racially and to a good extent culturally[32] not very different from the later invaders from the northwest, such views, however inaccurate historically must have, on account of their being in consonance with the ancient theory of the classification of *varṇas* according to *guṇa* and *karma*, helped in the incorporation of the new-comers into the Kṣatriya caste. The only thing necessary was that these new people should follow Vedic rites and traditions; and this they appear to have done early enough. Rudradāman I was a Sanskrit scholar,[33] Nahapāna's son-in-law, Uṣavadāta, went to Puṣkara for a bath and granted liberal donations in most of the Hindu sacred places,[34] the *Yavana* Heliodorus was a *Bhāgavata,*[35] Kaniṣka a Buddhist,[36] and Mihirakula a Śaiva.[37]

30. X, 43-44. Remarkable also is X, 42 :—

तपोबीजप्रभावैस्तु ते गच्छन्ति युगे युगे ।
उत्कर्षं चापकर्षं च मनुष्येष्विह जन्मतः ॥

31. *Viṣṇu Purāṇa*. Book IV, Chapter 3. Sagara is said also to have ordained that the Yavanas should completely shave off their heads, the Śakas shave half their head, that the Paradas should have long hair and the Pahlavas, beards.

32. Some of these similarities have been noted by Tod. (see Chapter VI, of his *Annals and Antiquities of Rājasthān*, I, pp. 68-97), but wrongly attributed to the Rājpūts' supposed decent from Scythians. Many of the customs were to be found in India before the Śakas reached this country.

33. See his Jūnāgarh Inscription, *SI*, pp. 172-74.

34. See his Nāsik Cave Inscription, *SI*, pp. 160-2, wherein he is described as having visited Bārāṇasī, Bhṛgukachchha, Daśapura, Govardhana, Sorpāraka, Prabhāsa, Suvarṇamukha, Rāmatīrtha etc. A brief account is to be found also in his Kārle Cave Inscription, *SI*, 165.

35. See his Besnagar Garuḍa Pillar Inscription, *SI*, pp. 90-91.

36. H.C. Raychaudhuri, *Political History of Ancient India*, fifth edition, pp. 475 ff.

37. Verse 6 of the undated Mandsaur inscription of Yaśodharman describes Mihirakula as *Sthāṇoranyatra yena praṇatikṛpaṇatām prāpitaṁ nottamāṅgam*, *SI*, p. 394.

Another step towards incorporation in orthodox Aryan society may have been intermarriage. Rudradāman gave his daughter in marriage to a Sātavāhana prince of the Deccan,[38] Samudragupta had in his harem ladies from the Kuṣāṇa, Śaka and Siṁhala royal families.[39] Yaśaḥkarṇa Chedi was the son of a Hūṇa princess.[40]

When this assimilative tendency came to an end is difficult to determine. But it certainly slackened with the advent of the Muslims into India. Islam knew no compromise. It was out to convert, not to be converted to any non-Quranic religious attitude or position, however rational it might be. For the first time in its history, Hinduism faced a rival which it could not conquer and with which there could not be even easy peace. Under the circumstances, Hinduism like Roman Catholicism in the sixteenth century was forced to redefine its dogmas and institutions, and the caste system as the most obvious of these received in the succeeding centuries an exactitude, rigidity and definition that it probably had never possessed before. Tribes which had already become Hinduised and almost forgotten that their ancestors had once been non-Hindus began now to connect themselves with the Sun, the Moon, or even the Fire and the Sea in their search of pedigrees to prove that only the bluest of Kṣatriya blood coursed through their veins. The Rāṣṭrakūṭas now described themselves as Yādavas of the Lunar family of Kṣatriyas, though their earlier records had nothing to say on this point[41]. The Pratihāras became *Raghuvaṁśins*,[42] and the Paramāras, not to be outdone by their rivals, adapted a myth from the *Rāmāyaṇa*. Thus was laid the basis of the Agnikula myth so well known to students of Rājpūt history.[43] The Pālas

38. H.C. Raychaudhuri, *Political History of Ancient India*, 5th edition, p. 496.

39. See lines 23-24 of Samudragupta's Allāhabād Inscription, *SI.*, p. 258.

40. *EI.*, XII, p. 212, verse 15. The Guhila ruler, Allaṭa of Mewār, had a queen belonging to the family of "Hūṇakṣoṇīśa" (a Hūṇa ruler), *IA.*, xxxix p. 191.

41. See *RA*, pp. 15-16.

42. First described as Lakṣmaṇa's descendants in the Sāgartāl inscription of Bhoja I.

43. See my paper, Origin of the Paramāras, *Rājasthāna Bhārati*, Vol. III, part 2, pp. 2-8.

are described by two writers belonging to the twelfth century as descendants of Samudra and Sūrya respectively, which can only indicate that the Pālas' origin was very doubtful.[44] Of the Chauhāns we have said a good deal already.

By the time of the *Kumārapālacharita* and *Kānhaḍadeprabandha*, 36 clans had become recognised as Rājpūt Kṣatriyas, though of the 36 there probably were some whose recognition as Kṣatriyas was purely local or at the most provincial.[45] All these clans interdined and intermarried, whether settled in Gujarāt or Madhyadeśa and had thus much less of exclusiveness than the various sub-divisions of the Brāhmaṇas. It may be that some of them had forgotten their *gotra and pravaras*, but a good many perhaps never had any. We are therefore not surprised to find either Medhātithi stating in his comment on the *Manusmṛti*, III, 5 that distinction of *gotra* and *pravara* applied only to Brāhmaṇas, or *Mitākṣarā* laying down that the Kṣatriyas and Vaiśyas should adopt the *gotra* and *pravaras* of their *purohitas*, inasmuch as they (the Kṣatriyas and Vaiśyas) had no *gotras* of their own.[46] The only rules of exogamy and endogamy observed were that a Kṣatriya generally married Kṣatriya, and did not marry within his own clan.

Among the Vaiśyas again we find the same influence of the two ideals of *varṇa* and *jāti*. The doors of the *varṇa* itself were open to every new comer who took up the profession of trading, even though the incomers generally fell into a sub-caste of their own, quite distinct from those already in existence. The Agrawālas, the Māheśvarīs and Oswāls, the three important divisions of *vaṇiks* in Rājasthān, all claim a Kṣatriya origin. They ascribe their present position as Vaiśyas to their eschewing of meat-eating and the profession of fighting under the influence of humanitarian movements like Jainism; and a certain amount of epigraphic support for their contention has been found in the Jālor Stone-Inscription of Śāmantasiṁha (V.

44. *Rāmacharita*, Canto I, verse 4; Kamaulī Grant of Vaidyadeva.

45. See the lists given by Tod, *Annals and Antiquities of Rājasthān* I, Table facing page 98 (O.U.P.), for the local and provincial differences. No two lists agree fully.

46. राजन्यविशां प्रातिस्विकगोत्राभावात् प्रवराभावस्तथापि पुरोहितगोत्रप्रवरौ वेदितव्यौ। (Comment on याज्ञवल्क्यस्मृति I, 53.)

1353), which, while describing the donor, Narapati, his brothers and father, as Sonīs, *i.e.*, as Oswāls of the sub-section bearing this name, mentions his grandfather and great-grandfather as Ṭhākuras. Narapati's ancestors, according to Dr. D. R. Bhandarkar, probably were originally Sonigarā Rājpūts. It was the grandfather, Mahaṇasiṁha, who seems to have become a Jaina and dropped the Rājpūt title Ṭhākura.[47]

The *Smṛtis* prescribe four means of livelihood for a Vaiśya, agriculture, cattle-rearing, trade and money-lending. Of these the first two gradually passed into the hands of the Śūdras, probably on account of Vaiśyas' growing distaste for professions involving *hiṁsā*.[48] Hieun Tsang mentions Vaiśyas as a class that engaged in commercial exchange and followed profit at home and abroad.[49] Jaina books generally describe them as traders, money-lenders and financiers. The *Kavikalpalatā* recommends their appointment as ministers; and the maxim had certainly the approval of many states in Rājasthān and Gujarāt. Vastupāla was a Vaiśya and so were Yaśovīra, the chief counsellor of Udayasiṁha of Jālor, and the *Balādhipa* Yaśodeva who served Kaṭukadeva of Nāḍol. Though bravery in the battlefield was not their forte, we now and then find a few good generals among them. Rāmadeva, a courtier of Pṛthvīrāja III, was a good wrestler.[50]

Various divisions of Vaiśyas find a mention in our records specially towards the end of our period. We hear for instance of the Prāgvāṭas, Ukeśavaṁśa, Śrīmālas, Moḍhs, Humbaḍs, Dharkaṭas[51] and Lemchūs, to name only a few out of the many who had a share in the literary and religious life of the period. About the Vaiśyas belonging to orthodox Hinduism we may refer to the Ḍhūsaras, Māheśvarīs, Daās, and Bīsās.[52]

47. *EI.*, XI. p. 61. The argument, however, is of doubtful value.

48. Jainism especially did not encourage the pursuit of agriculture.

49. Beal, *Buddhist Records of the Western World*, I, 64.

50. See my paper on the *Kharataragachchhapaṭṭāvalī* of Jinapāla in *IHQ.*, 1950, pp. 223 ff.

51. Dhanapāla, the writer of *Bhaviṣyattakathā*, was a Dharkaṭa.

52. See Sakrāi (Rājasthān) inscription of V. 879, *Kānhaḍadeprabandha*, IV, 12-13. We are not sure, however, of the existence of Dasās and Bīsās in our period. Such a grading may have been a late manifestation of the growing caste-spirit.

Though the *Smṛtis* have many hard things to say about the Śūdras, their position appears to have improved steadily; and this had to be for various reasons. When Śūdras became rulers at times, some of them attaining even the imperial position,[53] they could not obviously be treated as mere hewers of wood and drawers of water in their relation to the higher castes. They had to be treated better also because they were the real Vaiśyas of our period. With agriculture, handicrafts and cattle rearing as their virtual monopoly, they formed the backbone of the Indian society, at least in Northern India, and had to be given in some way the respect due to their economic position. Medhātithi's commentary on the *Manusmṛti* reflects this change. He concedes the Śūdra's right to private property, and to freedom from attending on the three other castes, unless he did so with a view to earning spiritual merit.[54] He could have his *saṁskāras*, though without the use of Vedic *mantras*; and participated in many religious activities of the community. He shared in the management and maintenance of temples and was a member of the watch and ward committees of villages and towns.[55] That sometimes a Śūdra could rise to a very high position in the service of the State is shown by the example of the potter Sajjana who was made the Governor of Chitor by Kumārapāla Chaulukya.[56]

Like the three other castes, the Śūdras had their subdivisions. We find the Mehrās mentioned in some Chauhān inscriptions.[57] In the list of the various professional people who are said to have accompanied Alāuddīn in his march against Kānhaḍadeva of Jālor,[58] we find the Bhoīs, Kahārs, Suthārs, Mālīs, Kumhārs, Lohārs, Silāwaṭs, Tambolīs, Darjīs, Ghānchīs,

53. Yuan Chwang mentions Śūdra rulers in North India. Nandas, the Imperial rulers of Magadha, were also of Śūdra extraction.

54. III, 156; VIII, 415.

55. See the Pāl inscription of V. 1250 for the Mehrā's donation to the local temple. Another inscription of the same locality gives them a place in the local assembly.

56. See above p. 64 and also my paper on Sajjana and Bosari in the *Bhāratīya Vidyā*, English Edition, 1944, p. 221.

57. *JPASB*, X, p. 409.

58. *Kānhaḍadeprabandha*, II, vv. 87-92.

Tunāras, Bhaṭīyāras and *Baghanighaḍas* who, probably as now, were ranked as Śūdras.

Of classes whose exact position in the caste system is rather uncertain Rājasthān must have had many. Ahīrs probably occupied the area to the south of Delhi. The *Mahābhārata* regards them as a Kṣatriya tribe reduced to the status of Śūdras on account of the non-contact of its members with Brāhmaṇas.[59] The *Mahābhāṣya* does not include them among Śūdras,[60] and some of our lists of Rājpūts put them among the 36 Rājpūt royal families of Rājasthān and Gujarāt.[61] If the *Kāmasūtra* and Aparārka's commentary on the *Yājña-valkya Smṛti* be believed, their code of social behaviour was in some ways different from that of most Kṣatriya families.[62] The Ahīrs of the Gurgāon district now call themselves Yādavas.

The Kāyasthas, who at one time were only a professional class, had in our period hardened into a caste divided into many subdivisions. Some *Smṛtis* mention them as Śūdras.[63] In the *Udayasundarīkathā* of Soḍḍhala, they are assigned a Kṣatriya origin.[64] It is impossible to state what their exact position was in the Chauhān dominions. Their castes mentioned in our inscriptions are Naigama, Gauḍa and Kaṭāriyā Māthur.[65]

The Khatrīs probably were a *pratiloma* class, born of a Kṣatriya father and a Brāhmaṇa mother. At least that is the tradition now current in Rājasthān, though some of them maintain that they are full-blooded Kṣatriyas who have gone

59. *Āśvamedhikaparva*, 29, 15-16. The *Sabhāparva* 51. 12 mentions them along with *Pāradas*.

60. See Pāṇini I, 2, 72. The difference in the status does not seem, however, to have been very great.

61. See the lists facing page 98 of the *Annals and Antiquities of Rajasthan*. O.U.P. edition.

62. *Kāmasūtra*, p. 294; *Aparārka's Commentary* on *Yājñavalkya*, II, 17.

63. *e.g.* Uśanas and Vedavyāsa (35 and I. 10-11 respectively). The account of the *Śukranītisāra*, the date of which is uncertain, also proves that they had become a caste.

64. Read the introductory portion.

65. *EI.*, XIX, p. 45; *EI*, XI, pp. 39 ff., *Prāchīnajainalekhasaṅgraha*, II No. 402.

down in the social scale on account of their taking to trading, commerce and money-lending.

The residence of the Jāṭs was in the northern part of the Chauhān dominions, and they appear to have had a share in the struggle for independence waged by the Chauhāns after the defeat and death of Pṛthvīrāja III. It is not unlikely that many of the early republican people might have contributed to the formation of the present Jāṭ caste, some becoming Rājpūts and the others remaining Jāṭs according to their circumstances and predilections.[66] The Jāṭs of the Rohtak District of the Punjab regard themselves as Kṣatriyas, though in some parts of Rājasthān they are classed as Śūdras. By temperament they are unorthodox; and this more than anything else marks them out from the Rājpūts.

The Gūrjaras formed another important element of the population, in fact, one so important that the western part of Rājasthān received the name, Gurjaratrā, and was so known for centuries. According to a number of scholars, the Agnikula clans were originally Gūrjaras.[67] One Mathanadeva is mentioned as a Gūrjara Pratihāra in the Rājorgarh inscriptions of V. 1016.[68] The Chauhāns are said to have originally been Khazarṣ. Though we need not, as shown elsewhere,[69] believe these theories *in toto*, it is not unlikely that some of the Gurjars were actually regarded as Kṣatriyas. The Baḍ-Gūjars, who obviously are Gurjaras, are reckoned among the 36 Rājput clans and inter-marry with them. There is, however, not much ground, as shown by K.M. Munshi,[70] to believe that Gūjars were a foreign tribe.

66. Many Jāts have the same *gotras*, as the Rājpūts, *e.g.*, Gahlot, Dāhimā, Panwār, Mor, Solankī, Yādava and Tanwar. I regard the Dhāraṇas as belonging to the *gotra* of the Imperial Guptas.

67. Notably Dr. D.R. Bhandarkar, and A.M.T. Jackson. Dr. R.C. Majumdar identifies the Gūrjaras with Pratihāras and Dr. D.C. Ganguly with the Guhilas of Chāṭsū. For the criticism of these views see my papers, the Origin of the Pratihāras (P.O., Vol. II), The terms Gurjara and Gurjareśvara, (*IHQ*. 1937), and the Pratihāras of Maṇḍor *Pilānī Vidyā Vihār Journal*, Vols. II and III.

68. *EI.*, III. p. 266.

69. See Chapter I and also my paper on the "Origin of the Chauhāns" in the Jadunath Sarkar Commemoration Volume, Punjab University.

70. *The Glory that was Gūrjaradeśa*, Part I, Book University Series.

Last in the social scale stood the *Antyajas*. But even their social status showed variety according to the occupations they followed and the amount of independence they enjoyed. The Medas formed an important section of the population and were in their forest and mountain haunts as influential as any other caste. Another *Antyaja* class, the Bhīls, lived in various parts of the Arāvalli hills and adjoining areas. An allied tribe was that of the Mīṇas who lived in and at times terrorised parts of south east Rājasthān by their predatory activities. The Bāvarīs, according to Dr. D.R. Bhandarkar, are perhaps referred to in the Jālor Inscription of V. 1239.[71] The *Antyaja* who helped Lakṣmaṇa in the foundation of his kingdom[72] may have been a Mīṇa or Bhīl or perhaps even a Bāvarī.

The *Upamitibhavaprapañchakathā* speaks here and there of these depressed classes. The quarters the Mātaṅgas lived in must have been extremely unhygienic.[73] There could be in life no station higher than that of a *Mahārāja* and none lower than that of a Chāṇḍāla.[74] The Ḍoms were so poor that they formed the subject of a saying, "These two can never co-exist, the Ḍom and an *āḍhaka* of gingelly seeds."[75] One of the characters of the *kathā* is a ruler called Adhamarāja. He was looked down with contempt by his subjects on account of his relations with a Mātaṅga woman. Coming together the people declared the king's course of action to be highly improper and drove him out of his kingdom.[76] It was a sin to drink water touched by the *Antyajas*.[77] Even while taking a bath in a jungle tank, the *Antyaja* would think, "Here is a "touchable" (*spṛsya puruṣa*). He would take me to task for bathing here. So let me hide somewhere."[78]

The *kathā* does not give exact indications about the various professions followed by the *Antyajas*. It states in a general way

71. *EI*, XI, pp. 53-54.
72. See above, Chapter XII.
73. *Upamitibhavaprapañchakathā*, p. 36.
74. *Ibid.*, p. 98, p. 230.
75. *Ibid.*, p. 221. An *āḍhaka* equals four *prasthas* or 64 *palas*, or 4096 *māṣakas* (*Yogachintāmaṇi*, I, 6-13).
76. *Upamitibhavaprapañchakathā*, p. 502.
77. *Ibid.*, p. 764.
78. *Ibid.*, p. 212.

that Mātaṅgas and Ḍombs were "miserable sinners who followed callings entailing cruelty."[79] A specific instance is that of a Chāṇḍāla whose profession is that of a fowler and who is proficient in the use of his bow and arrows.[80] Among the people following low callings, the *kathā* includes agricultural labourers (*talakheṭakas*), cutters of grass and fuel, runners carrying messages, and huntsmen.[81] Slightly higher than them were the *Śailūṣas* or actors.[82]

More detailed, with regard to the professions of the Depressed Classes, is the account of Alberunī who enumerates the following twelve classes of the *Antyajas*[83] :—

(1) Juggler (the *naṭa* of the *Smṛtis*),
(2) Basket and shield maker (*buruḍa*),
(3) Sailor (*kaivarta*),
(4) Fisherman (*Jālopajīvī*),
(5) The hunter of wild birds and animals (*vyādha*),
(6) Weaver (*tantuvāya*),
(7) Fuller (*rajaka*),
(8) Shoemaker (*charmakāra*),
(9) Hāḍī,
(10) Ḍoma (Domba),
(11) Chāṇḍāla, and
(12) Badhatau.

Of these the first five were higher in status than the next three, *i.e.*, the weaver, the fuller and the shoemaker and intermarried. The last four, the Hāḍīs, the Doṁs, the Chāṇḍālas and Badhataus constituted what the Smṛtis would call the *antyāvasāyin* class, the members of which were excluded from social contact even by the other depressed classes.[84] Actually they constituted, according to Alberunī, one class the members of which were distinguished from each other only by their occupations. This perhaps signifies intermarriage and

79. *Ibid.*, p. 588.
80. *Ibid.*, p. 212
81. *Ibid.*, p. 588.
82. *Ibid.*, 591.
83. *Alberuni's India*, I, p. 101 ff.
84. For the word, *antyāvasāyī*, see *Manu*. X. 39 and the *Mitākṣarā* on the *Yājñavalkya-smṛti*, III, 260.

also change of profession at will within the ambit permitted to them.

The Hāḍī may be identical with the Ḍhāḍī whose occupation at present is not very different from that of a Domba. Or is he to be regarded as Hālī, an agricultural labourer or *talakheṭaka* ?[85] The Ḍomba is identified with *śvapacha* by Kṣīrasvāmin and the *Rājataraṅgiṇī*, the latter of which mentions them also as professional singers.[86] Manu puts the houses of Chāṇḍālas outside a village.[87] Uśanas assigns to them the duty of cleaning a village in the first part of the day. They acted as hangmen; and their chief wealth was their asses and dogs.[88] Fahien describes how they had to give notice of their approach by striking a piece of wood, a fact confirmed also by Bāṇa who describes a *Mātaṅga kanyā* as striking the pavement of Śūdraka's court with a spilt piece of wood.[89] The Badhatau can perhaps be identified with the Bādhī, a depressed class of S.E. Punjab and U.P.

The *Kānhaḍadeprabandha* mentions eighteen *varṇas* or castes,[90] the *Rājataraṅgiṇī*, sixty-four; Uśanas forty; and the number goes on differing from *Smṛti* to *Smṛti*.[91] From the description in the *Kānhaḍadeprabandha* it is obvious that its eighteen *varṇas* are merely guilds of craftsmen and workers mentioned as *Śreṇīs* in early Buddhist literature and as *prakṛtis* in the *Skandapurāṇa*. As for the castes, dubbed as *Saṅkīrṇa* or "mixed" by the lawbooks, their number obviously had no fixity. It could be more or less according to the basis of classification adopted by a writer, e.g., either birth or profession or both. Profession was a relatively fixed feature; heredity could vary

85. For *Talakheṭaka* see above the account from the *Upamitibhavaprapañchakathā*.

86. *Rājataraṅgiṇī*, V, 354, 389-94, and VI, 182, 192. In Rājasthān both Ḍomas and Hāḍīs are included among professional singers. From them come also many dancing girls. A Rājasthānī proverb says, *Dūmaṇī rai rovaṇ meṁ hī rāg*.

87. X. 51-6.

88. *Ibid*, IV, 79; X, 39.

89. *Kādambarī*, p. 68 (Jībānanda's edition)

90. Canto I, verse 238.

91. See P.V. Kane's *History of Dharmaśāstra Literature*, II, Part I, p. 50.

according to a writer's information about a caste tradition, and sometimes perhaps even according to his predilection.

Like all human institutions, the caste system, as it developed during our period, had its virtues and vices. Earlier, when the *varṇa* conception was more operative than later on, it had helped Hinduism in assimilating new blood and given it a constitution, flexible yet strong enough to withstand barbaric influences. For every one prepared to pass a period of novitiate, there could be a place in Hinduism. But with the coming of Islam to India things began to change. Hinduism could not respond to the challenge of Islam in the same way as to that of the early invaders. It was so different, so unassimilable, so contemptuous at times of the Hindu view of life, that something had to be done to counteract its disintegrating influence. But, as pointed out in the beginning of this chapter, our religious leaders, instead of internally strengthening Hinduism by the removal of its chief defects — of which untouchability and the low position assigned to certain classes were the worst—began erecting defences in the form of rigid class rules and taboos, *e.g.*, not crossing the seas, not interdining with one's workers even, not having *anuloma* marriages and not permitting widow-marriages under any circumstances. In their immediate objective these religious leaders had success. Hinduism did not disappear from the land of its birth.[92] But these very defences have at times been like bars of prison protecting the inmates from outside intrusion but denying them at the same time that free atmosphere of thought and action without which no culture can progress. Hinduism towards the end of our period presents a picture of arrested growth The castle of the caste system was its asylum as well as prison.[93]

92. But for this good effect the good features of Hinduism may really be responsible, though credit is generally given to the caste system.

93. For the disastrous political effects of the system see the last chapter also.

SECTION II

Women

Indian women have perhaps never enjoyed the same amount of freedom as their modern sisters in Europe.[94] From ancient times the management of the household and looking after her children and husband have been an Indian woman's main concern, whatever else she might or might not have done.[95] Girls have not always been unwelcome; but the birth of sons has generally been preferred, on religious as well as economic grounds.[96] The girl is like a pledge that has to be made over to its owner (the bridegroom) in due course;[97] looking after her till then is to the Indian mind no light responsibility.[98] For ages people have agreed with Bāṇa's statement, "As soon as a girl attains her youth, her parents begin getting consumed by that fire called agony. As the coming up of *payodharas* (clouds) darkens the day, so does the coming up of her *payodharas* (breasts) darken their minds. By whomsoever it might have been laid down, I do not like the religious injunction that one's own children, born from one's own limbs, brought up in one's own lap and wholly unforesakable should, all of a sudden, be carried away by strangers. The worst of this fire of grief is that though both son and daughter are equally one's offspring, people get grief-stricken the moment a daughter is born and give her water with their tears.[99] The Rājasthānī writer, Siddharṣi Sūri, goes a step further when he declares, "The birth of a daughter causes grief. She increases anxiety, and reduces *dharma*. In poverty she causes the greatest distress. It is only when she is given to a bridegroom with a good character

94. We deliberately put the word 'modern', for in Europe also the amount of female freedom has varied from period to period and country to country.

95. For very early conditions read the *gāthā* of Isidāsī in the *Therīgāthā*.

96. A son has generally been supposed to save his parents from the hell called *pum*. In a moderately populated country, male hands were needed also to produce food and to protect the country against invasions and hostile inroads.

97. *Arthastu kanyā parakīya eva* (Kālidāsa).

98. *Putrīti jātā mahatīha chintā, kasmai pradeyeti mahān vitarkaḥ.*

99. *Harṣacharita*, Nīrṇayasagar edition, pp. 140-1,

and riches and also suitable in other ways that one feels satisfied."[100]

It is not unusual also to find tirades against women in religious books. They are said to be as fickle as the wind, deceitful in their ways and an impediment in the road to spiritual progress.[101] But such have been the views everywhere in the monkish world, whether in India or Europe. Far more representative of the people's view is the opinion of the great *Āvantika* scholar, Varāhamihira, who backed the cause of women by writing, "Brahmā created woman as the best of jewels to bring happiness to man. It is for her that he earns money. She is instrumental in promoting his *dharma*. From her he gets pleasures like having sons etc. She is the goddess of prosperity in the house; one should (accordingly) honour her by giving all respect and wealth. Let us say truly which fault of women is not to be found in men too ? It is sheer impudence that men should speak ill of women. They are superior to men in virtues." Even Manu has said, "Soma has given them purity, Gandharva speech and Fire the power to consume everything (without defiling themselves). Women are like the *niṣka* ornament.........They are clean through and through." In the case of a moral transgression, the scriptures blame both women and men. If it is the women who mostly observe rules of morality and men, who is to be adjudged as the better of the two ?.........Just see the impudence of those scoundrels who speak ill of a woman. Is it not like a thief caught red-handed and bawling out, "Stop O, Thief ! Stop !" ? Men speak words of love only in private. But women are so grateful that even when a man dies, they enter the fire embracing him.[102] Our poets also speak highly of women,[103] and as literature has always been nearer to life than monkish diatribes, we can dismiss the idea that the Indians in general thought ill of women.

The early life of a girl passed under the tender care of her

100. *Upamitibhavaprapañcha Kathā*, p. 698.

101. *Ibid.*, pp. 331 and 643.

102. *Bṛhatsaṁhitā*, *Strīpraśaṁsādhyāya*.

103. Reference may be made to Kālidāsa, Bhavabhūti, and Rājaśekhara among others.

parents.[104] That this care, however, did not always include literary education may be inferred even from the remarks of a singularly sympathetic writer, the poet Rājaśekhara, who states, "Women also can be poet like men, for *saṁskāra* inheres in the soul, irrespective of a person's sex. We have heard and seen too that many princesses, daughters of *mahāmātras*, courtesans, and actresses have been proficient in poetics and good poets."[105] He has by way of illustration given the names of Śīlā-bhaṭṭā-rikā, Vikaṭa-nitambā, Vijayāṅkā, Prabhudevī and Subhadrā. His own wife, Avatisundarī, a Chāhamāna on her father's side, was a good poet and her husband quotes appreciatively many of her opinions on poetic subjects.[106] It may be that Chāha-mānas had in their circle created an atmosphere where female education could flourish. Rudrāṇī, the queen of Chandana of Śākambharī, was proficient in Yoga.[107] Gūvaka II's sister, Kalāvatī, is described as proficient in sixty-four *kalās*.[108] On the whole, however, the examples are too few to reach any definite conclusions.

The next stage in a woman's life was her marriage. From the descriptions that we have it appears that princesses in India, as in mediaeval Europe, could be pawns in political games played on the chess-board of dynastic ambition and desire for glory. Jalhaṇā, the daughter of Arṇorāja of Śākambharī, could hardly have been more than eighteen years old, when she was given in marriage to Kumārapāla Chaulukya of Gujarāt, a man nearly 57 years old.[109] If even rulers who receive in history high praise for their self-control, could behave like this, the general conditions must have been bad enough. We read now and then of *svayaṁvaras*. Gūvaka II's sister, Kalāvatī, had twelve other suitors, besides the ruler of Kanauj to whom she

104. *Pitā rakṣati kaumare*, (Manu).
105. *Kāvyamīmāṁsā*, G.O.S., p. 53.
106. Introduction to the *Karpūramañjarī*, and the *Kāvyamīmāṁsā*, G.O.S., pp. 20, 46, 57.
107. Read above Chandana's account.
108. *Pṛthvīrājavijaya*, V, 38,
109. Hemachandra's *Dvyāśrayamahākāvya*, XIX, vv. 21-35. The *Prabandhachintāmaṇi* tells us that he was *pañchāśadvarṣadeśīya* at the time of his coronation. The marriage took place not less than seven years after that.

was eventually married.[110] Durlabhadevī, the sister of Mahendra of Nāḍol, chose her husband in a *svayaṁvara,* and even more famous is the story of Saṁyogitā's elopement with Pṛthvīrāja.[111]

Anuloma marriages were, as already pointed out, not unknown in our period. We have just spoken of the Chāhamāna Avantisundarī's marriage to the Brāhmaṇa poet, Rājaśekhara. The Jaina Bhaṇḍārīs of Mārwār regard themselves as the descendants of Lakṣmaṇa of Nāḍol and one of his Vaiśya queens.[112] *Khaḍgadhara* Bhoja of Raṇthambhor is said to have been related in the same way to Hammīra as Vidura to Pāṇḍu.[113] The Rājpūt Pratihāras of Maṇḍor are the descendants of Hariśchandra and his Kṣatriya wife, Bhadrā.

One of the best descriptions of marriage is to be found the *Samarāichcha-kahā,* a work by the Rājasthāni poet and philosopher, Haribhadra Sūri. Many of the rites and customs described by him still live on in Rājasthān. The auspicious time for marriage was, as almost everywhere in orthodox circles in India, determined by astrologers, and the ceremonies began with charities, the extent of which must naturally have been determined by a person's station in life. The courtyard was beautified with *raṅgavallī* patterns. The bride sat facing eastwards on a *vedikā* covered with a nice white sheet, wearing red silk and surrounded by youthful *saubhāgyavatī* women who used *dūrvā* blades to sprinkle her with a mixture of curds and unbroken rice. After that followed the bath from a *kalaśa,* in the water of which were put flowers, tender sprouts and leaves. The elders in the family put *akṣatas* on her head, as they blessed her. Her feet were dyed red with *alaktaka.* On her thighs they put saffron, on her breasts a *patralekhā,* and collyrium in her eyes. The face was cleaned with saffron mixed with sandal-water. Lips were dyed, perhaps red, and covered with wax. On her forehead was put a *tilaka.* Hair was nicely dressed. On her feet were put jewelled *nūpuras,* on her fingers rings set with jewels, and on her waist

110. *Pṛthvirājavijaya,* V, 31.

111. See above the account of Mahendra of Nāḍol and the Appendix on the historicity of Saṁyogitā.

112. *Purātanaprabandhasaṅgraha,* p. 102.

113. *Hammīramahākāvya,* IX, verses 153-55.

a girdle. Near her arm-pits hung *bāhu-mālās*, a *plavaṅgabandha* adorned her breasts, and a pearl-necklace reaching her hips encircled her neck. Ears were also dyed with saffron, and decked with a circular ornament called the *chakralatā*. On her head was put a *chuḍāmaṇi* and a *dusurullaka* of pearls round her neck.[114]

When the time of the *pāṇigrahaṇa* drew near, the parties were informed accordingly by astrologers.[115] The bridegroom reached the marriage pavilion, and the brideswomen after usual jokes and pranks asked for costly presents, before giving him his first view of the bride's face. The ceremony was given the significantly pretty name, *mukhachhavisphoṭanikā*.[116] The members of the bridegroom's party were entertained on a lavish scale; and while the entertainment went on, other essential marriage ceremonies like *lājāhoma* also continued, and when the couple circumambulated the holy fire, the bride's father gave as dowry costly metals like gold, valuable ornaments and dresses, and vessels that could be useful to the married couple.[117]

With the marriage began the second stage in the woman's life, for after that the husband was expected to be every thing to her. He was her god;[118] theoretically at least she was inferior to him, whatever her actual position may have been. If the husband slaved, while she sat idle, it was regarded as something queer.[119] So great was the stress placed on chastity and almost blind devotion to the husband[120] that the *satī* system, *jauhar* and *purdā* appeared something natural in the atmosphere it created. With some sections of Indian society, though happily not with all, burning oneself with the dead body of the husband became common enough, and we read of *satīs* not only in literature but also in the following epigraphs of Rājasthān :—

1. *Satī* Sāṁvaladevī, wife of Rāṇuka (V. 947, Ghaṭiyālā inscription, *Inscriptions of Northern India*, No. 107).

114. For the ornaments see below, pp. 294ff.

115. The time is said to have been found by means of *śaṅkuchchhāyā*.

116. "Revealer of the beauty of the face."

117. Second *prastāva* of the *Samarāichchakahā*. The *Upamitibhavaprapañchakathā* also contains some good descriptions of marriage ceremonies.

118. *Bhartṛdevatā nārī* (*Upamitibhavaprapañchakathā*, p. 129), *patirhi devo nārīṇām*, *Mahābhārata*, Anuśāsanaparva, 46, 55.

119. *Upamitibhavaprapañchakathā*, p. 128.

120. Cf. *Manusmṛti*, pp. 154-55, *Śārṅgadharapaddhati*, v. 606.

2. *Satī*... ... ..., wife of Ṭhākura Guhila (Puṣkar Inscription, *Ibid*., No. 407).

3. *Satī* Kaṇahullā, mother of Chaṇḍamahāsena of Dholpur (*ZDMG*, XL, p. 39).

4. *Satī*... ... ..., Pāl Inscription of V. 1244, *Inscriptions of Northern India*, No. 423.

5. *Satī* Mohilī Rāji, wife of Rāṇā Motīśvara (Unstrā Inscription of V. 1248, *ibid*., No. 423).

6. *Satī* Hammīradevī, wife of Māṅgaliyā Rāva Sīho.

It is clear from the above inscriptions that the popularity of the *satī* system was the greatest among the warrior clans of India; and as this conclusion tallies also with the injunctions of the *Dharmaśāstras*, we may accept it without any great hesitation. According to Aṅgiras, for instance, if a Brāhmaṇa widow became a *satī*, her death was to be regarded as suicide. Her inconsiderate action neither took her nor her husband to heaven.[121] It was far better that she should lead an ascetic life, after the husband's death, abjuring all earthly pleasures.[122]

Very much different from this was the custom of *jauhar*. When it became almost certain that a fort would fall into the enemy's hands, Rājpūts donned saffron clothes, put *tulasī* necklaces round their necks and rushed down on the enemy, determined to kill and to be killed, and their wives, as brave as they and determined not to fall into the hands of the Muslim conqueror, entered the *Yamagṛha* (Jamghar-Jauhar). Many have been the occasions, when Chauhān ladies thus sacrificed their lives at the call of honour. At Raṇthambhor the queens bathed and decked themselves with all the ornaments that *saubhāgyavatīs* should put on. Hammīra gave them a braid of his hair, and when they entered the fire offered the usual funeral oblations of water.[123] Similar was the procedure at Śiwānā with the queens of Sātaladeva. When Alāuddīn captured Jālor, there were 1584 *jamagharas* (*jauhars*)[124] and the Muslim soldiers saw from a great distance these fires which betokened the imminent fall of the fort. When Ajmer could

121. See P.V. Kane's *History of Dharmaśāstra*, II, part 1, page 627, footnote 1468.

122. *Ibid.*

123. *Hammīramahākāvya*, Canto XIII.

124. *Kānhaḍadeprabandha*, IV, 243.

not be defended successfully Harirāja burnt himself along with his queens.[125] This also may be regarded as some sort of a *jauhar*.

Of women some claimed to be even *asūryampaśyas*, *i.e.*, so devoted to their husband that they would not look even at the Sun, regarding him as a *parapuruṣa*.[126] The existence of the *purdā* system in Rājasthān is proved by the *Śiśupālavadha* of Māgha.[127] In palaces eunuchs guarded the women's apartments. But here again, as in the case of the *satī* system, the custom was probably confined to Rājpūt clans and that too not universally.[128] Neither the *Upamitibhavaprapañchakathā*, which is a fairly voluminous work, nor any other work of this period proves the existence of this custom among the people in general.

Another evil from which women suffered was the institution of polygamy. Of Arṇorāja's two queens, one came from Maroṭ and the other from Gujarāt. Pṛthvirāja III had many queens. Polygamy was not uncommon also among nobles and rich people, to whichever caste or class they belonged. We hear also of keeps or *saṅgrahaṇīs* whose issues did not have the same rights as sons and daughters of wedded wives,[129] even though the evils of polygamy were not unknown. Various are the tales of the jealousy of co-wives. The *Atharvaveda* knew of black magic to destroy a co-wive's influence, and the *Purāṇas* describe how queens sometimes conspired to poison the son of a co-wife, merely because his existence increased the co-wive's influence with the King. If the stories found in our period have any basis in fact, these evils persisted in our period, and polygamy was as ever a source of conflicts and heart-burning.[130]

125. *Hammīramahākāvya*, IV, 18-19.

126. See my paper, "Gleanings from the works of Vāchaspati Miśra", *Indian Antiquary*, 1933.

127. Canto V, verse 17, See also *Śāntiparva*, 91, 4; *Moharājoparājaya*, G.O.S., p. 59; *Vikramāṅkadevacharita*, p. 97; *Daśakumāracharita*, p. 149; *Satyahariśchandra*, p. 23, and *Harṣacharita*, pp. 96-8.

128. See *Upamitibhavaprapañchakathā*, p. 687 for *sauvidallas*. Sulaiman states that Indian princes allowed their woman to be seen by those who attended the *Darbār* (*ED*, I, p. 11).

129. *Purātanaprabandhasaṅgraha*, p. 89; *Upamiti*, p. 332.

130. For our period see *Upamiti*, p. 540.

With the pronounced insistence on chastity which was so characteristic of India, widow-marriage can be expected to have been almost non-existent among the higher castes of India, though not always with good effects. Siddharṣi Sūri, for instance, mentions young widows, wives of people away in other parts of the country, *raṇḍās* and *vratinīs*,[131] as women who could be seduced easily.

Rājasthān had plenty also of women of easy virtue. Cities appear to have been proud of their beautiful courtesans. A poet describing a capital city could and did omit many details which we now regard as important; but he rarely omitted a colourful description of the courtesans' quarters and their seductive inmates. Nŏ big temple probably was without them. Many maidens had been presented to the Harṣanātha temple.[132] The Kārṇāta chief, Bhūtala, freed courtesans from the *daśabandha* cess, *i.e.*, the tithe they had to pay on their earnings.[133] Rājā Jojalladeva of Nāḍol did not merely order courtesans to join the processions of all the temples of Nāḍol, but even directed his descendants to punish (even) learned people, old men and others who tried to interfere with this time-honoured custom.[134] The fragmentary copper-plate inscription of Alhaṇa (V. 1205) is mainly a record of the arrangements made by various rulers for courtesans and musicians attached to the temples of Chandaleśvara and Tripuruṣadeva.[135] Towards the middle of our period and even a little earlier there must have been puritanic agitation against the practice to make rulers like Jojalladeva issue their edicts. Haribhadra Sūri raised his powerful voice against it, the *Kharataras* were as a general rule opposed to it, and there may have been a few others who thought alike. But as the people were not ready to forego the entertainment provided by courtesans (and to the rulers they were not only a means of exhibiting their magnificence but also a source of income), they continued to flourish; and we find in the fairly late Bhīnmāl inscriptions of V. 1306, V. 1334

131. *Ibid.*, pp. 572-3.
132. See the Harṣanātha Inscription of Vigraharāja II (V. 1030).
133. *Inscriptions of Northern India*, Nos. 259-260.
134. *EI.*, XI, p. 28.
135. See the inscription, Appendix G (iii).

and V. 1345 elaborate arrangements for the *pramadā-kula* of the Sun temple of Jagat-svāmin.[136] The *Kharataras* probably finding their voice going unheeded, permitted young dancers to entertain the audience in the *vidhichaityas*.[137] Even Kumārapāla Chaulukya who tried to eradicate many social evils from his dominions had to say about prostitutes, "I have already banished theft and adultery from my dominions. As for prostitution, it is something insignificant. Nothing is lost or gained by its removal or continuance."[138]

Unless Kumārapāla rose much above his times, and this he does not seem to have done, he was bound to argue as above and let the institution of courtesans remain, for who in that period could have thought of a *darbār* without courtesans.[139] They bathed the ruler,[140] performed his *nīrājanā* by waiving lights in front of him, accompanied him to the temple and danced in front of his favourite deity.[141] Feudatories tried to please their overlords by presenting beautiful *gaṇikās*.[142] The *Kharataragachchhapaṭṭāvalī* of Jinapāla describes their presence in Pṛthvīrāja III's court. The courtesan Dhārā of Hammīra's court was so influential that she had his blinded minister, Dharmasiṁha, restored to favour, with consequences to the Chauhān State that we have detailed above.[143] Naiṇsī regards some *gaṇikās* as the cause of ill-feeling between Kānhaḍadeva and the Mughal leader, Muhammad Shāh.[144] Harirāja's downfall may have been partly due to his fondness for *gaṇikās*.[145]

On the other side of the social scale were women who took holy orders, leaving behind everything of the world. Haribhadra

136. *Bombay Gazetteer*, Vol. I, Part I, pp. 469 ff.
137. For the *Kharataras* see our account above, pp. 249. ff.
138. *Moharājoparājaya*, p. 83.
139. *Kāvyakalpalatāvṛtti*, a Jaina work of the thirteenth century for instance lays down the general rule that the description of a royal court should describe the courtesans attending on the ruler.
140. Read Śūdraka's description in *Kadambarī*; *Priyadarśikā*, I, II.
141. *Kumārapālacharita*, VI, 32; I, 66-67.
142. See verse 24 of the Harṣanātha Inscription of Vigraharāja II.
143. See the account of Hammīra, pp. 123 ff.
144. See above the account of Kānhadadeva, pp. 182-183
145. See above the account of Hariraja, pp. 115 ff.

Sūri is said to have first realised his lack of full knowledge when he could not interpret a *gāthā* recited by the female Jaina ascetic, Yākinī *mahattarā*.[146] The Śvetāmbara Jaina sect not merely permitted women to take to ascetic life but regarded them as entitled also to *kaivalya* or complete emancipation.[147] The *Digambara* attitude was less liberal.[148] Among the *Śāktas* there was a *Yoginī Sampradāya*, and we know of some *siddhas* who received instruction in the highest knowledge from women ascetics.[149] Other Hindu *parivrājikās* are also known.

If a man died without leaving any male issue, his property probably lapsed to the State. The widow could keep to herself only ornaments and a few other things to which we might apply the name, *strīdhana*. In Gujarāt, the Chaulukya ruler, Kumārapāla stopped the confiscation of a sonless man's property.[150] It is likely that his example may have been followed by his Chauhān feudatories in Rājasthān.

Section III

Dress, Ornaments, Food and Drink, Fasts, Festivals, and Pilgrimages

Our best purely Rājasthānī account of ornaments and dress is supplied by the comparatively late *Hammīramahākāvya*[151] which describes Hammīra's queens as decked with *kuṇḍalas* in their ears, *kastūritilakas*[152] on their foreheads, hanging pearl-drops in their noses, pearl necklaces on their breasts, *nūpuras*[153]

146. *Prabandhakośa*, p. 24.
147. *Prabandhachintāmaṇi*, p. 67.
148. *Ibid.*,
149. See see lists of the 84 *siddhas*. Rudrāṇī of Śākambharī was also a *yoginī* and her *sampradāya* name was Ātmaprabhā.
159. *Moharājaparājaya*, pp. 52, 65-66.
151. *HM*, XIII, 173-80.
152. *Tamālapatrākṛitiḥ kastūryādinā lalāṭe tamālapatram, tilakākṛtiḥ tilakaṁ chitrakaṁ nānāvarṇam, viśinaṣṭi viśeṣakam, itthaṁ tilakaparyāyāḥ.*"
(*Ṭīkāsarvasva on Amarakośa*, II, 123).
Lanman translates *tilaka* as a sectarial mark in the *Karpūramañjarī* most probably because of this being its modern meaning.
153. Called *nevarī* now in Rājasthān.

for their ankles, *champaka* buds for their *dhamillas*,[154] rings for the fingers of both the hands, *alaktaka*[155] for the feet and blue *dukūla*[156] dress on their hips. But this list is by no means exhaustive. It omits the jingling girdle (*kāñchī*) and the ivory *valayas* which were in common use in Rājasthān and are referred to not merely in the Rājasthānī literature of the period[157] but also depicted in sculptures at Kirāḍū, Ābū and Pallū. The *Samarādītyakathā* supplies further the names of *bāhusārikā*, an ornament for the *bāhumūla* or arm-pits, a pearl *dusurullaka* for the neck, a *plavaṅgabandha* for the breasts, *ratnachakralatā* for the ears, and a *chūḍāratna* for the forehead.[158] The differences between the two lists, of which the latter has been described here partially, may have been partly due to local variations and partly to the distance of time that separated Haribhadra and Nayachandra Sūri.

For dress and ornaments in the northernmost part of the Chauhān dominions, specially for the earlier part of our period, we can utilise Bāṇa's account of the women of Sthāṇvīśvara.[159] Aids to beauty were many. Māgha speaks of the use of the unguents of saffron, musk and sandal for the body in general, of *lodhra* and *kuṅkuma* for the complexion and of a certain resin for the lips;[160] and Haribhadra of *kuṅkumarāga* for

154. Hair done into a top-knot and decked with flowers : *Kusumagarbheṣu bahirmauktikalatikādinā saṁyateṣu keśeṣu dhammillaḥ*." (*Ṭīkāsarvasva* on the *Amarakośa*, VI, 97).

155. red lac.

156. The *Amarakośa* gives *kṣauma*, i.e. linen as a synonym of *dukūla*. For the meaning of *kṣauma* see my note in the *Marubhāratī*, V, 1, 84.

157. Cf. *Karṇasundarī*, p. 7, *Śiśupālavadha*, VI, 14, VII, 5, X, 43 and *Pārthavijaya*, verse 38.

158. *Bhāva* II, pp. 93-101, *Bibliotheca Indica* edition. We have a good list of ornaments also in the *Bhāvaprakāśa* of Śāradātanaya, the *Mānasāra*, the *Mānasollāsa* and the *Ṭīkāsarvasva* which should be consulted by students of social history.

159. Women of the place are described as decked with *muṇḍamālās* (a garland put over hair) made of the leaves of blue lotus, wearing *kuṇḍalas* in their ears, necklaces on their breasts, veils on their faces, *kañchukas* on their bodies, *nūpuras* on their feet, and using camphor powder for their faces and saffron to beautify their skin.

160. *Śiśupālavadha*, IX, 7, VI, 24, XVI, 84.

the thighs, *patralekhā*[161] for the breasts, collyrium for the eyes, and also of *alakāvali.*[162] Flowers were used in *muṇḍamālās*,[163] stuck in the *dhammilla*, the ears and *kabarīs*[164] and made into garlands. Use of *agaru* for scenting the hair was almost universal. Good accounts of how the toilet was actually performed can be had from the *Samarādityakathā*, partially summarised in our account of marriages, and the *Karpūramañjarī of Rājaśekhara.*[165]

Men were not behind women in the use of ornaments. Chāhamāna, according to the *Pṛthvīrājavijaya*, had a *kirīṭa* set with gems, a pearl necklace, *kuṇḍalas* with pearls and pairs of *keyūras* and *aṅgadas*;[166] and that this abundance of ornaments was nothing unusual can be seen from the accounts left by Alberunī and Abu Zaid.[167]

Regarding clothes used and worn in Rājasthān our information is rather scanty. The usual dress must have been, as in most parts of India, the *adhovasana* and an *uttarīya.*[168] Men in Sapādalakṣa perhaps used besides head-covers with *jihvās* at the back.[169] Women wore *sārīs*,[170] and perhaps *kūrpāsakas* also[171] Of soft clothes the *Upamitibavaprapañchakathā*

161. See *Samarāichchakahā*, *Bhāva* II, pp. 93-101, for a general account of ornaments. *Patrāvalīs* are mentioned also by the *Sarasvatīkaṇṭhābharaṇa*, pp. 510 and 570 and *Naranārāyaṇānanda*, X, 58 showing that this ornament was common to the greater part of Āryāvarta.

162. See footnote 161.

163. See footnote 159.

164. braids.

165. *Samarādityakathā*, *Bhāva* II, pp. 93-101. For the account from the *Karpūramañjarī*, see my paper, "Gleanings from Sanskrit Literature, the Works of Rājaśekhara," *JIH*, 1930.

166. II, 17-30.

167. Sachau, *Alberunī's India*, p. 181; *ED*, I, p. 11. See also the *Kuṭṭanīmatam*, p. 38, Kāvyamālā Series.

168. The common dress of our country is described also by Yuan Chwang.

169. See the *Kumārapālaprabodhaprabandha* of a Purātanāchārya, p. 99.

170. See the description from *HM* quoted above. Siddharṣi Sūri describes *bhavitavyatā* as a *sāṭikābaddha subhaṭa* (p. 127).

171. A sort of bodice. Kṣīrasvāmin explains it as *kūrpare asyate kūrpāsaḥ strīṇāṁ kañchulikākhyaḥ*, *Amarakośa*, VI, 118. This would make *kūrpāsaka* a purely female dress. But the *Tilakamañjarī* represents a 15 years old painter also as wearing a *netra-kūrpāsaka* (p. 134, Nirṇayasāgar edition).

mentions *bṛhatikā*, *pravāra*, *rallaka*, *devāṁśuka*, *chīnāṁśuka*, and *paṭṭāṁśuka*.[172] Luxurious beds, with pillows full of soft cotton, and seats filled with the soft feathers of swans are also described very often.[173] The *Pravārī* is mentioned as a costly woollen cloth by the *Kalpadrukośa*.[174] *Rallaka* may have been prepared from the hair of Kāshmir goats.[175] *Chīnāṁśuka* looks like China silk. *Paṭṭāṁśuka* and *devāṁśuka* may have been prepared from Indian silk and the latter of these may have been a finer and softer variety.

Food and Drink. Wheat, rice, pulses, barley, *jwār* millet, oil, *ghī*, spices and meat are among the articles of food mentioned in Chauhān inscriptions. Under the growing influence of Jainism, specially towards the end of our period, vegetarianism was becoming popular. But that Brāhmaṇas had not up to the beginning of the thirteenth century of the Vikrama era given up meat wholly can be seen from the *amārīghoṣaṇā* of Alhaṇa, which while threatening the *mahājanas* and *tāmbolikas* with capital punishment, if they slaughtered animals on certain days specified in the inscription, laid on the *purohitas* a fine of merely five *drammas* for the same offence.[176] Among Kṣatriyas, who stuck to the fighting profession, the success of vegetarianism was even less. They liked the pleasures of chase, as before, and mostly continued to be meat-eaters,[177] and drinkers of wine.[178] No festive occasion of theirs went without meat and drink, if we are to believe the detailed and extremely life-like descriptions in the *Upamitibhavaprañchakathā*.[179] Among

172. p. 154. For a fuller discussion of the topics covered in this chapter see my paper *Dasavīṁ Śatābdī meṁ Ānandavilāsasukhādi kī Sāmagrī* published in the *Rājasthāna-Bhāratī*, V.

173. *Ibid.*

174. *Pravara* is known also to the *Pravachanasāroddhāra*.

175. Amara regards it as a synonym of *Kambala*. But see Watter's *On Yuan Chwang*.

176. *EI*, XI.

177. Kṣatriyas, who changed over to Jainism, generally took up trade as their profession.

178. Harichandra's Kṣatriya sons are simply described as *madhupāyinaḥ*. See also *PV.*, I, 1-27; IX, 20.

179. See my paper from the *Rājasthāna-Bhāratī* cited above.

vegetarians we find the use of milk, milk-products, sweets and numerous vegetarian dishes.[180]

Fasts, Festivals, and Pilgrimages Ekādaśī, Mahāchaturdaśī of Śrāvaṇa and *Sivarātri* are the only fasts mentioned in Chauhān inscriptions.[181] Of festivals *Akṣaya-tṛtīyā* finds a mention in the Sūndhā Inscription.[182] Eclipses, lunar as well as solar, were occasions for making gifts, and so were many sacred days of the year. The festival of the Sun-god, Jagat-svāmin of Bhīnmāl, began in Āśvina and lasted the whole month.[183] *Yātrās* or processions in honour of gods, Jaina as well as Hindu, were a common feature of our socio-religious life. Jains had their *yātras* mostly on the *kalyāṇaka* days of their Tīrthaṅkaras.[184] A Gūjarī *yātrā* of Śāntinātha is mentioned more than once.

Most big temples were centres of pilgrimage. The sacred lake of Puṣkar drew pilgrims from every part of India. Mount Ābu or Nandivardhana was full of Hindu and Jaina shrines. Sāñchor had a famous image of Mahāvīra which was destroyed in V. 1367 by Alāuddīn Khalji.[185] Other important centres of Jaina pilgrimage in Rājasthān were Phalavardhikā, Narabhaṭa, Nānā, Kanyānayana, Śuddhadanti, Chandrāvatī, Osiā, Karaheṭaka, Rāmsen, and Kāsahrada.[186] The temples of Ekaliṅga, Sakrāi and Harṣanātha may also have drawn big crowds every year. Pṛthvīrāja I had an *annasatra* instituted for pilgrims visiting Somanātha in Saurāṣṭra.[187] The *Lalitavigraha-rāja-nāṭaka* represents a Muslim spy disguising himself as a

180. *Ibid.*

181. Sevāḍī stone-inscription of V. 1172; Ālhaṇa's inscription of V. 1209, *EI*, XI, p. 65. See also the *Kānhaḍadeprabandha*, I, 159.

182. *EI*, IX, p. 79, verse 57.

183. See the Bhīnmāl inscription of Udayasiṁha, V. 1306, *EI*, XI, p. 57.

184. The five *kalyāṇakas* are *chyavana* (conception), *janma* (birth), *dīkṣā* (initiation), *kevalajñana* (perfect knowledge), and *nirvāṇa* (death and mokṣa). For the *kalyāṇakas* of all the Tīrthaṁkaras see the *Vividhatīrthakalpa*, pp. 100-101.

185. *Vividhatīrthakalpa*, p. 30.

186. The list is based on the *Vividhatīrthakalpa* and the *Kharataragach-chha-bṛhadgurvāvalī*.

187. See above, p. 38.

pilgrim to Somnātha.[188] Narapati, a minister of Hammīra, visited Siṁhapurī, Kurukṣetra and the Godāvarī.[189] The Jainas formed themselves into *saṅghas*, drawn from people from all parts of Rājasthān and adjoining territories, and went on pilgrimage to great *tīrthas* like Ujjayanta, Śatruñjaya, Tāraṅgā hill, Rājagṛha, Champāpurī, and Stambhanakapura.[190]

Of festive occasions there were many every year. The birth of a son was celebrated grandly whether a man was rich or poor. *Nāmakaraṇa* also was an expensive ceremony. We find the day of going to the *guru* for the first day made the occasion of some festivity. But far grander than it was the wedding, of which some account has been given above. Among seasonal festivals the most important was the *vasantotsava*, the presiding deity of which was Madana or Cupid. People went out in big crowds and processions to worship Kāmadeva and Rati, turned parks into big swing-houses and taverns, danced, sang, cracked jokes and threw coloured water with syringes on each other. The modern Holī even would look like a pale version of this wonderful *utsava*. Of the autumnal festive days, Siddharṣi Sūri mentions *Śakrotsava*, *Dīpamālikā* and *Kaumudīmahotsava*.[191] *Rāsa-nṛtyas* of herdsmen were a common feature of the country-side; but strangely enough there is no mention of Daśaharā and *Durgāpūjana* in Āśvina, though the worship of this goddess was by no means unknown to Siddharṣi Sūri and is mentioned by him in connection with *Vasantotsava*. Of summer, rainy season and winter festivals he has nothing to say, even though the rainy season is regarded by the Rājasthānīs as the best part of the year and is now crowded with festive days. In an appendix to this chapter, we reproduce a list of fasts and festivals mentioned by Alberunī, which on account of being current even now in Rājasthān, have every likelihood of having been observed also during our period. This list thus usefully fills in a gap in our knowledge.

Lastly we may mention the festivals held by the Jainas on the days of the *dīkṣā* or initiation, promotion to higher grades

188. Act IV, line 16.

189. *EI, XIX*, p. 52.

190. See the accounts in the *Kharataragachchha-bṛhad-gurvāvalī* and *Nābhinanadanajinoddhāraprabandha*.

191. See my paper referred to above in footnote 22.

in the spiritual line, and succession to the *āchāryapada*. The *Upamitibhavaprapañchakathā* has many beautiful accounts of *dīkṣā*.[192] For an account of festivities in connection with *pratiṣṭhā* and *dhvajāropaṇa* one should consult the *Kharataragachchha-bṛhad-gurvāvali*. The descriptions in both these books are rich in details.

192. *Ibid.*

APPENDIX J

A list of fasts and festivals mentioned by Alberunī (II, 175-184) and still current in the Bikaner Division:—

Fasts

1. *Devaśayanī ekādaśi* in (the bright half of) Āṣāḍha.
2. The 8th of the same month, a fast day holy to Bhagavatī.
3. *Janmāṣṭamī.*
4. *Devotthānī* and *Bhīṣma-pañcharātri.*
5. The sixth day of Pauṣa, a fast in honour of the Sun.
6. *Gaurī-tṛtīyā* on the 3rd of Māgha.

Festivals

1. The 11th of the month of Chaitra, a day on which the image of Vāsudeva was swung to and fro.
2. The 22nd day, a day of merriment holy to Bhagavatī.
3. *Gaurī-tṛtīyā*, on the 3rd of Vaiśākha, when women worshipped Gaurī, washed and dressed gaily, abstained from eating, and played with swings.
4. All the days of Āśāḍha. These were devoted to alms-giving.
5. Full moon day of Śrāvaṇa.
6. *Mahānavamī*, in Āśvayuja.
7. 23rd of Āśvayuja called *Ahoī*, a day of merriment and wrangling.
8. Bhādrapada new moon was the first day of the fortnight devoted to the distribution of food in the name of the Fathers.*
9. A festival to celebrate the birth of Vāsudeva, when the Moon stood in Rohiṇī.
10. 1st Kārttika or Diwālī, called also *Balirājya.*
11. *Śivarātri*, the 16th Phalguna they worshipped Mahādeva keeping a vigil at night.**

*It is Bhādrapada full moon that is at present the first day of the श्राद्धपक्ष.

**We have the शिवरात्रि on चतुर्दशी now.

CHAPTER XXIV

LITERATURE

Works of Chauhan Kings and their ministers. Ajayarāja, Arṇorāja, Vigraharāja IV and Pṛthvīraja III were not merely great conquerors and builders but also lovers of good literature.[1] The distinction, however, of being an author belongs only to one, the illustrious Vigraharāja IV, known by unanimous consent as *kavi-bāndhava* or friend of poets. He composed the drama, *Harakeli*, the theme of which was the penance of Arjuna and his fight with Śiva. Of its original five acts, only one, the *Krauñchavijaya*, survives now in the form of an inscription, dated Mārga Sudi 5, Saṁvat 1210.[2] Dr. Kielhorn's remark that "actual and undoubted proof is here afforded of the fact that Hindu rulers of the past were eager to compete with Kālidāsa and Bhavabhūti for poetical fame" indicates that he regarded the *Harakeli* as a work of real merit. Of the rulers of Jālor, Udayasiṁha was a good scholar. But we have no evidence of his having been also a writer of any distinction.

Padmanābha, the minister charged with the duty of holding conferences of poets and *paṇḍitas* may have been the writer of the Pṛthvīrāja III's Baḍlā Inscription of V. 1234.[3] Udayasiṁha Sonigarā's chief minister, Yaśovira, had the title, *Sarasvatīkaṇthābharaṇa*. Someśvara regarded him as superior even to the great poets, Kālidāsa, Māgha and Abhinanda.[4] But perhaps all that has survived of his poetry are a few verses in praise of Vastupāla, the friend and minister of Vīradhavala of Dholkā[5]. Vaijāditya, the *paurāṇika* and *amātya* of Hammīra,

1. See above for details.
2. Edited by Kielhorn, *IA.*, XX, p. 210 ff.
3. For the text of the inscription, see *Marubhāratī*, II, part 3, p. 3 and Appendix C, p. 94.
4. *Kīrtikaumudī*, I, vv. 27-30.
5. श्रीमत्कर्णपरम्परागतभवत्कल्याणकीर्तिश्रुतेः
प्रीतानां भवदीयदर्शनविधौ नास्माकमुत्कं मनः ।

(*Contd. on next page*)

composed in verse the Balvan Inscription of V. 1343.

Poets patronised by Chauhan rulers. Somadeva, a court poet of Vigraharāja IV, dealt with the love-story of Vigraharāja and Desaladevī, a princess of Indrapura, and also with Vigraharāja's defeat of a certain Hammīra of Ghaznā.[6] It is this double theme, coupled with the name of his patron, which probably suggested the name *Lalitavigraharāja* for his play. Of this only a fragment has been recovered so far.[7] Somadeva is good at characterization. But the play lacks movement. It is primarily valuable as a good source of Chauhān history.

The *Pṛthvirājavijaya* of Jayānaka, a Kāshmīrī poet partronised by Pṛthvīrāja III, must have primarily dealt with the loves and exploits of Pṛthvīrāja, especially his great victory over Muhammad Ghorī in 1191 A.D. But what we have now is only a fragment, a little more than eleven cantos in all, of which the first eight are devoted to Pṛthvīrāja III's predecessors. The language of the poem is elegant, though at times not as simple as modern taste would have it. In the fifth canto, the poet exemplifies various figures of speech, but without disregarding his main object of narrating the history of the Chauhāns of Sapādalakṣa.[8] The poem may have gained fame in the

(*Contd. from page* 302)

श्रुत्वा प्रत्ययिनी सदा ऋजुतया स्वालोकविस्रम्भिणी
दाक्षिण्यैकविघानकेवलमियं दृष्टिः समुत्कण्ठते ॥ १ ॥
लक्ष्मीं नन्दयता रतिं कलयता विश्वं वशीकुर्वता
त्र्यक्षं तोषयता मुनीन्मुदयता चित्ते सतां जाग्रता ।
संख्येऽसंख्यशरावलिं विकिरता रूपश्रियं पुष्णता
नैकट्यं मकरध्वजस्य विहितो येनेह दर्प्पव्ययः ॥ २ ॥
हंसैर्लब्धप्रशंसैस्तरलितकमलप्रत्तरङ्गैस्तरङ्गै-
र्नीरैरन्तर्गभीरैर्वकचटुलकुलग्रास [लीनै] श्च मीनैः ।
पालीरूढद्रुमालितलशयितस्त्रीप्रणीतैश्च गीतै-
र्भाति प्रक्रीडदातिस्तव सचिव! चलच्चक्रवाकस्तटाकः ॥

Purātanaprabandhasangraha, pp. 70, 72.

6. Edited by Kielhorn, *IA.*, XX, pp. 201 ff. Edited by the same in *Gottinger Festschrift*, 1901, pp. 1-15.

7. Surviving portions are the beginning of the second act, the end of the third act, and a large portion of the fourth act.

8. Some of these are very good and could have been illustrated but for exigencies of space.

author's life time, for it is quoted by Jayaratha, a Kashmirian author of about 1200 A.D.

Jayamaṅgala, the writer of the Sūndhā Inscription, uses with ease long metres like the Śārdūlavikrīḍita, Sragdharā, Mandākrāntā, Mālinī, Rathoddhatā, Śikhariṇī and Hariṇī. His *rūpakas* are excellent. He wrote also a book on *Kaviśikṣā*, i.e. instructions for a would-be-poet.[9] His *Mahāvīra-janmābhiṣeka* is a work in Apabhraṁśa.[10]

Tradition makes Chand Bardāī a writer of Pṛthvīraja III's reign. He may have written in Apabhraṁśa, the *Rāso* or heroic poem about the exploits of his master, which has formed the nucleus of the present *Pṛthvīrājarāso*, a work of composite authorship and doubtful historicity.[11]

Other works. We have already spoken of the *vidhichaitya* movement. Its great advocate Jinavallabha (died V. 1169) was a prolific writer.[12] He had his *Aṣṭasaptaṭīkā*, *Saṅghapaṭṭaka* and *Dharmaśikṣā* inscribed in the *vidhichaitya* temples at Chitrakūṭa, Mārwār, Nāgor and Maroṭ. His pupil, Jinadatta Sūri (died V. 1211) was highly respected by Arṇorāja of Ajmer, for his learning and character. He wrote in Sanskrit, Prākrit and Apabhraṁśa.[13] The three short Apabhraṁśa works, the *Upadeśarasāyana-rāsa*, the *Charchari*, and *Kālasvarūpakulaka*, published in Gaekwad Oriental Series, show that he was a writer of great vigour, with full command over the popular medium of expression needed to reach the masses. Jinapati Sūri (died V. 1277) wrote commentaries on the *Saṅghapaṭṭaka* and *Pañchaliṅgī*. He wrote also an original work, the

9. Desāi, *Jaina Sāhitya no Itihāsa*, p. 412.
10. *Ibid.*, p. 608.
11. See the bibliography.
12. Sri M. D. Desai mentions सूक्ष्मार्थसिद्धान्तविचारसार, आगामिकवस्तुविचार, पिंडविशुद्धिप्रकरण, पौषधविधिप्रकरण, संघपट्टक, प्रतिक्रमणसमाचारी, धर्मशिक्षा, द्वादशकुलक, प्रश्नोत्तरशतक, शृंगारशतक, स्वप्राष्टकविचार, अजितशांतिस्तव, भावारिवारस्तोत्र, जिनकल्याणकस्तोत्र, and वीरस्तव as some of his works (जैन साहित्य नो इतिहास, पृ० २३१-२)।
13. Some sixteen of his works have been listed in the introduction to the *Apabhraṁśakāvyatrayī*.

Prabodhavādasthala advocating the *vidhichaitya* point of view regarding temples and Jaina ceremonies. It elaborated mainly the arguments he advanced in his discussion with Pradyumnāchārya of Āśāpallī. His pupil, Jinapāla Upādhyāya, wrote the *Satsthāpaka vṛtti* and the *Sanatkumāracharita* in V. 1262, the *Upadeśarasāyana-vivaraṇa* in 1292, the *Dvādaśakulakavivaraṇa* and the *Pañchaliṅgī-vṛttī* in V. 1293, and the commentary on the *Charcharī* in V. 1294. We have to be grateful to him also for the *Kharataragachchha-paṭṭāvalī* in which he describes the lives of the *Kharataragachchha āchāryas*, carefully mentioning with dates the contacts they had with various rulers.[14] Jinapāla's friend, Sumatigaṇi, composed the *Gaṇadharasārdhaśataka-bṛhad-vṛtti* in V. 1295. Chandratilaka began writing the *Abhaya-kumāracharita* at Bāhaḍmer in V. 1312.[15] Palha wrote the *Jinadattasūri-stuti* before or in V. 1170. It is the earliest available account of the *Kharatara ācharyas* up to Jinadatta.[16] Dharmaghoṣa Sūri, the great Jaina teacher, honoured by Ajayarāja, Arṇorāja and Vigraharāja IV, wrote the *Dharma-kalpadruma*. His pupil, Yaśobhadra, was the author of the *Gadyagodāvarī* and a commentary on the *Āgamikavastuvichārasāra* of Jinavallabha.[17]

Meritorious from both the historical and poetical points of view is the Harṣa Inscription composed by Dhīranāga, son of the *karaṇika* Thīruka. Guṇabhadra, the writer of Bijoliā Inscription, was just as learned but inferior to Dhīranāga as a poet. He is overfond of *anuprāsa*, *śleṣa* and *virodha*, with the result that what was clear to the poet himself and his

14. See the bibliography and my paper, *Gleanings from the Kharatara-gachchhapaṭṭāvalī* published in *IHQ*, XXVI, pp. 223-32.

15. Desai, *Jaina Sāhitya no Itihāsa*, I, p. 411. *Catalogue of Palm-leaf MSS. in the Paṭṭana Bhāṇḍāras*, p. 394. Other well-known *Kharataragachchha* writers of our period were Padmānanda, the author of *Vairāgya-śataka* (*Kāvya-mālā*, VII) Devabhadra Sūri (whose literary activity was largely limited to Gujarāt), Jinamata, Nemichandra Bhāṇḍāgārika, the writer of *Satthisaya*, Pūrṇabhadra Sūri, the reviser of the *Pañchatantra*, Kumārakavi, Purṇakala-śagaṇi (V. 1307), Abhayatilakagaṇi (V. 1312), Dharmatilaka (V. 1322), Prabodhamūrti, Prabhānanda, Taruṇaprabha Sūri (V. 1411) and Pūrṇa-bhadragaṇi (V. 1285).

16. Published as an Appendix to the अपभ्रंशकाव्यत्रयी, G.O.S.

17. *Catalogue of the Palm-leaf MSS in the Paṭṭan Bhaṇḍāras*, p. 394. M. D. Desai, *Jaina Sāhitya no Itihāsa*, I, p. 411.

generation has become obscure to later students of history and literature. An excellent piece of poetry is the fragmentary Chauhān *praśasti*. Its author may have been a Kashmirian.

Āśādhara, the great Digambara scholar, was a native of Maṇḍalgarh in Sapādalakṣa.[18] The Lemchū ministers of the Chauhāns of Chandwār, Rāybaddīya, and Dattapalli also helped in the production of good literature. We have already referred to *Aṇuratnapradīpa* written in V. 1313 by Lakkhaṇa. The Apabhraṁśa poet, Dharmadhara, flourished under the Chandwār Chauhāns a little later than our period and produced works of great poetic merit.[19] Mention might be made also of the *Pārśvanāthacharita* of Śrīdhara written at Delhi nearly nineteen years before it passed into the hands of the Chauhāns.[20]

A general review of the facts given above shows that the period witnessed literary activity in all the three languages, Sanskrit, Prakrit and Apabhraṁśa. But Prakrit, being no longer the spoken language of the people, had lost its old advantage over Sanskrit and was being gradually displaced either by the latter i.e. Apabhraṁśa, the vernacular of the people. This Apabhraṁśa literature, at first small and perhaps largely oral, continued increasing in volume, till it finally merged itself into old Mārwārī *rāsos*, *ākhyānas*, *charitas* and *prabandhas*. The earliest specimens of old Hindi belong to this period. The number of non-Jaina works that we have been able to list is not large, not because none or very few were written, but because they did not receive the same private care in *bhaṇḍāras* as the writings of Jaina scholars, poets and *āchāryas*. It is only those works of outstanding merit which the Jainas themselves either studied or commented on that have come down to us. The rest of the non-Jaina works have perished. Books in the royal libraries of the Chauhān princes might have been mostly burnt in the holocausts that generally followed the capture of Hindu towns and forts by iconoclastic Muslims.

18. See the *Dharmāmṛta-praśasti*, verse 1.

19. See the *Anekānta*, March 1955, pp. 227 ff. and the *Praśasti-saṅgraha* published by the Managing Committee of the Digambara Jaina Atiśaya Kṣetra Mahāvīrajī, Jaipur.

20. The *Praśasti-saṅgraha* published by the Managing Committee of the Digambara Jaina Atiśaya Kṣetra Mahāvīrajī, Jaipur, p. 129.

CHAPTER XXV

EDUCATION

SECTION I

Authors and Subjects Studied[1]

Our information about the subjects and authors studied in Rājasthān, and specially the Chauhān dominions, cannot be regarded as exhaustive. We have no Brāhmaṇic sources worth mentioning except the *Śārṅgadharapaddhati* which falls a little outside our period, being the work of the grandson of Rāghavadeva, a court-poet and Paṇḍit of Hammīra of Raṇthambhor. Yet the position is not so unsatisfactory, as it appears to be at first sight, for the Jainas while devoting the greatest attention to their own system, studied the philosophic works of others, and tried also to vie with non-Jainas in the knowledge of secular subjects like poetics and drama, with the result that their *Bhaṇḍāras* have preserved invaluable books and their commentaries which, but for their care, would have been lost to posterity. In India few have served the cause of Sarasvatī so well as the Jaina custodians of the big *bhāṇḍāras* at Paṭṭan, Jaisalmer and Bīkāner.

Subjects Studied. From the *Gaṇadharasārdhaśatakabṛhadvṛtti*, we learn that a good Jaina scholar was expected to master his own *siddhānta* along with the philosophic systems of the Buddhists and Brāhmaṇas. He read also classical poetry, prose and drama, astronomy and astrology, poetics, prosody and grammar; and had specially to be an adept in propounding his own theories and refuting the views of rival schools.[2]

(*a*) *Jaina āgama.* Of the Jaina *siddhānta* works generally 84 are enumerated[3]; and these had many commentaries and sub-

1. For full references read our paper on the subject in the *Rājendra Sūri Memorial Volume*, pp. 841-866.
2. See the *Apabhraṁśakāvyatrayī*, p. 20.
3. The *siddhānta* included ११ अङ्ग, १२ उपाङ्ग, ६ छेदसूत्र, ४ मूलसूत्र, १० प्रकीर्णक, अनुयोगद्वारसूत्र, नन्दीसूत्र, १२ निर्युक्ति, विशेषावश्यकभाष्य, २० अन्यप्रकीर्णक, पर्यूषणकल्प, जितकल्पसूत्र, श्राद्धजितकल्प, पाक्षिकसूत्र, वन्दित्तुसूत्र, क्षामणासूत्र, यतिजितकल्प, and ऋषिभाषित.

commentaries by authors, of whom some were Rājasthānīs. The first great Jaina commentator of Rājasthān was Haribhadra Sūri of Chitor (700-800 A.D.) who in his works[4] utilised the labours of many earlier writers.[5] Obviously Jaina scriptures were being intensively studied at Chitor in the eighth century.

Many other Jaina scholars carried further Haribhadra's work.[6] Specially notable was the work of the great Kharataragachchha scholar, Abhayadeva Sūrī, who in spite of his ill-health wrote wonderfully lucid and learned commentaries on many Jaina scriptural works.[7] These were studied not only in Kharataragachchha circles but also by others in Rājasthān, nay in fact, in every part of India where the Śvetāmbara Jainism flourished. And almost equally popular in Rājasthān were the works of Malayagiri Sūri,[8] a younger contemporary of Kumārapāla's *guru*, Hemachandra Sūri.[9]

(*b*) *Philosophy and Logic.* The exegetical work on the *āgamas* was important. But in an age of religious controversy, where one system had to contend against the other, it was obviously equally necessary to give a systematic presentation of the Jaina system, specially its fundamental principles. To our period

4. He commented on the अनुयोगद्वारसूत्र, आवश्यकसूत्र, दशवैकालिकसूत्र, नन्दीसूत्र, and प्रज्ञापनासूत्र.

5. He mentions जिनदास महत्तर, जिनभद्रक्षमाश्रमण, देववाचक, भद्रबाहु and संघदासगणि.

6. सिद्धर्षिसूरि and वर्धमान सूरि commented on the उपदेशमाला and शीलाङ्कसूरि on the आचाराङ्गसूत्र.

7. अभयदेव is known as the नवाङ्गवृत्तिकार, *i.e.*, commentator on the nine *aṅgas* to distinguish him from other Abhayadevas. Though he passed most of his life in Gujarāt, his disciple, Jinavallabha and his successors had Rājasthān as the main centre of their activity.

8. His पिण्डनिर्युक्तिवृत्ति was copied at Chitrakūṭa and the व्यवहारसूत्रटीका at सिंहपुरी in Śākambharī respectively in the Vikrama years 1289 and 1344 (जैनपुस्तक प्रशस्तिसंग्रह, pp. 118 and 133).

9. Other writers on *āgama* subjects like मलधारी Hemachandra, Droṇāchārya who revised the commentaries of नवाङ्गवृत्तिकार Abhayadeva, Nemichandra Yaśodeva whose पाक्षिकसूत्रवृत्ति was copied at Āghāṭa in V. 1309, क्षेमकीर्ति, Koṭyāchārya, Devendra Sūri and Śānti Sūri were also well known in Rājasthān. For fuller references see the *Rājendra Sūri Memorial Volume*, pp. 841-866.

belongs the credit of having accomplished this work not only with success but great distinction.

Besides his commentaries on the *āgamas*,[10] already referred to, Haribhadra wrote the *Anekāntajayapatākā* and *Anekāntavāda-praveśa*, in which he not merely expounded the Jaina philosophy of *Anekānta* but also reviewed critically other current philosophic systems.[11] How popular the study of his latter work was can be seen not only by the laudatory references to it in Jaina literature but also by the pride eminent Jaina teachers had in studying and teaching it. The *Gaṇadharasārdha-śatakabṛhadvṛtti* speaks of Jinavallabha's proficiency in the treatise. Jinapati Sūri sent his students to study it at the feet of Yaśobhadrāchārya. Jinapati's rival, Pradyumna Sūri, boasted of having read it. Of his other philosophic works, we should like to mention the *Yogabindu* and the *Yogadṛṣṭisamuchchaya*, both of which present a valuable synthesis of old Jaina and Pātañjala Yogic systems. Haribhadra's commentary on the *Nyāyapraveśa* of Diṅnāga introduced the Jaina world to Buddhist logic; and from his reference to the Jaina teachers Kukkā-chārya, Divākara (probably Divākaramitra of the *Harṣacharita*), Dharmapāla (the great Buddhist teacher mentioned also by Yuan Chwang), Dharmakīrti (c. 635.50), Dharmottara, Vasu-bandhu, Śāntirakṣita and Śubhagupta, it may not be even too much to presume that Buddhist philosophy had many students in Rājasthān, in the beginning of our period, and to a certain extent influenced Jaina logic. Jaina scholars inside as well as outside Rājasthān, commented on Buddhist books.[12] Jinavalla-

10. As supplementary to the work on the *āgama* texts, Haribhadra had his religious compositions, the *Dharmasaṅgrahaṇī*, *Kṣetrasamāsaṭīkā*, *Pañchavastu*, *Dharmabindu*, *Aṣṭaka*, *Soḍaśaka*, *Panchāśaka*, and *Sambodhaprakaraṇa*. In some of these he not merely expounded Jaina principles but sounded a clarion call for all-sided reform, doctrinal as well as social.

11. (1) जिनेन्द्रमतव्यवस्थापक···अनेकान्तजयपताकादि(गणधरसार्धशतक-बृहद्वृत्ति)

(2) जुगपवरागमु मन्निउ सिरिहरिभद्दपहु,
पडिहयकुमयसमूहु पयासिहमुत्तिपहु। (चर्चरी, १४, अपभ्रंश-काव्यत्रयी)

See also अनेकान्तविजयपताकावृत्तिटिप्पणक of Munichandra.

12. Rabhasanandi wrote a commentary on Dharmakirti's *Sambandha-parīkṣā*. Kalyāṇachandra commented on Dharmakirti's *Pramāṇavārttika*.

bha Sūri studied Kamalaśīla's commentary on the *Tattvasaṅgraha*[13] and so did many of his disciples.

Umāsvatī, Mallavādin, Samantabhadra, and Siddhasena Divākara were the Jaina philosophers studied most in Rājasthān in Haribhadra's time.[14] The Brāhmaṇa philosophers known to him were Avadhūtāchārya, Īśvarakṛṣṇa, Āsuri, Kumārila, Patañjali, Kālātīta and Bhgavad Gopendra. If we identify Avadhūtāchārya with Advayavajra or Avadhūtipāda, he has to be regarded as a Buddhist writer. But Dattātreya also, for whom there is a shrine at Ābū, had this designation.[15] Āsuri, a great Sāṅkhya teacher, preceded Īśvarakṛṣṇa, the writer of the *Sāṅkhyasaptati*.[16] Kumārila is a well-known *Pūrvamimāṁsā* philosopher. Patañjali's *Yogasūtras* supplied the basic material for Haribhadra's works on Yoga and were later on utilised also by Hemachandra in his work, the *Yogaśāstra*. Bhagavad Gopendra and Kālātīta were Yogins.[17]

The *Sanmatitarka* of Siddhasena Divākara was commented on by the *Tarkapañchānana* Abhayadeva Sūri in his great work, the *Vādamahārṇava*. The book presents not only the Jaina point of view but also the theories of others to show how the Jaina view was superior to theirs, and should like the *Tattvasaṅgraha* of Śāntirakṣita and the *Pañjikā* of Kamalaśīla be regarded as an encyclopaedia of Indian Philosophy. It richly deserves the title *Jinendramatavyavasthāpaka* given to it by Sumatigaṇi.

13. See the *Gaṇadharasārdhaśatakabṛhadvṛtti*, Introduction to the *Apabhraṁśakāvyatrayī*, p. 20.

14. Umāsvāti, known also as Vāchakaśramaṇa, is the famous author of the *Tattvārthādhigama-sūtra* which is accepted as an authoritative exposition of Jaina philosophy by both the *Digambaras* and *Śvetāmbaras*. Siddhasena wrote two important works on logic, the *Nyāyāvatāra* and the *Sanmatitarka*. Jinapati Sūri's disciples studied the *Nyāyāvatāra* with Yaśobhadrāchārya. It was commented on by Siddharṣi Sūri (10th century). Samantabhadra is the great *Digambara* scholar, the author of a commentary on the *Tattvārthādhigamasūtra*, called the *Gandhahastimahābhāṣya* Its introductory portion is known as the *Āptamīmāṁsā*. Mallavādin is the author of the *Nayachakra*, a book on *Anekānta* philosophy. The *Dharmottaraṭippaṇaka*, a commentary on the Buddhist logical treatise, *Nyāyabinduṭīkā*, is also ascribed to him.

15. The *avadhūtas* were known as such, either because they tried to get the knowledge of the नाडी called अवधूति or because they followed the धूत discipline in which there is no place for the recognition of वर्णाश्रमधर्म.

16. The popularity of the सप्तति can be gauged by the presence of its copy at Jaisalmer with the commentary of Gauḍapāda.

17. *Yogabindu*, verses 200 and 300. The *Yogadṛṣṭisamuchchaya* refers to Patañjali, Bhagvaddattavādī, and Bhadanta Bhāskarabandhu, the last one of whom may have been a Buddhist writer on Yoga.

The Kharataragachchha *āchārya*, Jineśvara Sūri wrote the *Pramāṇalakṣaṇa*, along with a commentary. "to take away from his seet the blot that it had no *tarka* work of its own"; and the trail he blazed was followed by many others. The great debater Devasūri, who is generally known as Vādi-Devasūri, wrote the *Pramāṇatattvālaṅkāra* and furnished it with a commentary of his own, the *Syādvādaratnākura*. Next followed the works of Hemachandra, a younger contemporary of Devasūṛi and *guru* of Kumārapāla, and of his pupils, Rāmachandra and Guṇachandra.[18] Towards the end of our period, Mallīṣeṇa Sūri wrote the *Syādvādamañjarī*, though we cannot be sure that it reached Rājasthān during our period. And the same may be said of the works of some other Jaina logicians.[19] But we speak of them here, because most of the good literature produced in Gujarāt of those days reached Rājasthān. The *vihāra* of Jaina *sādhus* from Gujarāt to Rājasthān and back was a frequent affair and so were the pilgrimages to religious places in Rājasthān and Gujarāt; and this intercommunication was rendered all the easier by the fact that the inhabitants of these provinces spoke a common language, now generally termed Western Rājasthānī.

It was really magnificent work that these Jaina savants accomplished for Indian philosophy. Their peculiar mode of thinking inclined them towards toleration and let them appreciate truth wherever they found it. For truth, according to the *Anekāntavādin*, is manysided. What is true under a ccrtain set of conditions need not necessarily be true under others; and truth may sometimes be where we least expect it.

18. प्रमाणमीमांसा of Hemachandra and द्रव्यालङ्कारवृत्ति of Rāmachandra and Guṇachandra.

19. Of these writers Nemichandra is said to have refuted the views of Kanāda. चन्द्रप्रभ was the author of दर्शनशुद्धिप्रमेयरत्नकोश and न्यायावतारविवृत्ति. पार्श्वदेवगणि wrote the न्यायावतारप्रवेशपञ्जिका. Ānanda Sūriand Amarchandra may have written the book known to गङ्गेश उपाध्याय as सिंहव्याघ्री. श्रीचन्द्र wrote the न्यायप्रवेश-टिप्पण. Devabhadra's न्यायावतारटिप्पण is a commentary on the न्यायावतारविवृत्ति. Ratnaprabha had a commentary on the प्रमाणनयतत्त्वालोकालंकार called the स्याद्वादरत्नाकरवार्त्तिक. राजशेखर wrote the रत्नावतारिकापञ्जिका and the स्याद्वादकलिका.

(*c*) *Brāhmaṇa philosophers.* We have mentioned above the names of some Brāhmaṇa philosophers. For the post-Haribhadra period, we have to add the names of Śaṅkaranandana, Kaṇāda, Akṣapāda, Vātsyāyana, Bhāradvāja, Uddyotakara, Vāchaspati, Vyomaśiva, Aniruddha, Śrīdhara, Vatsāchārya, Udayana, Jayanta and Harṣa. Śaṅkaranandana is perhaps the great *Advaitic* philosopher, Śaṅkara. From the rare references to him and his system of thought in Jaina literature, it appears that *Advaita* was not a popular subject with the Jainas, though in some ways it is nearer to the Jaina system of philosophy than even Buddhism. Their favourite subject of study was *Tarkaśāstra* or *Hetuvidyā.* In this field Devasūri criticized Udayana, who in his *Kusumāñjali* maintained a theory of creation radically opposed to that of the Jainas.[20] Udayana's *Kiraṇāvalī* was studied by the Kharatara *āchārya* Jinavallabha as well as Pradyumna Sūri of the line of Vādideva Sūri. Jayanta's *Nyāyamañjarī*, an independent commentary on the *Nyāyasūtras* of Akṣapāda shares with Udayana's works the honour of being attacked by Vādī Deva Sūri. Kaṇāda was criticised by Nemichandra. Śrīkaṇṭha's *Nyāyakandalī* was commented on by Abhayatilakagaṇi (1257 A.D.) and Ratnaśekhara. The latter in his *Nyāyakandalīpañjikā* describes the views of Kaṇāda, Praśastakaradeva, Vyomaśivāchārya, Udayana and Vatsāchārya. The *Kharataragachchhapaṭṭāvalī* refers to Śrīdhara's view on the nature of darkness. The young Kharatara *āchārya*, Jinachandra, had studied this subject and defeated Padmachandrāchārya of Rudrapallī in a debate about it. Copies of the *Nyāyakandalī* have been found in many Jaina *Bhaṇḍāras.* Vāmeśvaradhvaja's *Nyāyakusumāñjalisaṅketa*, though now little known, was also a work of no little merit. We have palm-leaf and paper manuscripts of the book in Rājasthān as well as Gujarāt[21]. Bhā-Sarvajña is represented by his *Nyāyasāra* and *Nyāyabhūṣaṇa.* The Vedāntic work, *Khaṇḍanakhaṇḍa-khādyaka* of Harṣa, probably reached Rājasthān

20. The *Naiyāyikas* regard Īśvara as creator. The Jainas disbelieve and criticize this view. The Paṭṭan *Bhaṇḍāras* have a न्यायकुसुमाञ्जलिपरिमल by Divākara. (*Catalogue of the Mss. in Paṭṭan Bhaṇḍāras, Introduction*, p. 44.)

21. *Catalogue of the Paṭṭan Bhaṇḍāra Mss.* 1. pp. 103-04. The name संकेत is given in verse 2. We have seen old paper Mss. of the book at Bikāner.

before V. 1291. Its early popularity with the Jainas probably was due not so much to their agreement with Harṣa's philosophy as to his brilliant dialectics which made short work of most systems of philosophy. It was difficult to maintain any thesis against his destructive criticism. It was in the Jaina philosopher's own interest that he should be familiar with this new weapon in the armoury of Brāhmaṇa philosophers, and turn it, whenever possible, against his own opponents.

(*d*) *Kāvyas and nāṭakas*. The *kāvyas* and *nāṭakas* studied by the Jainas of Rājasthāna can conveniently be classified under three heads : (1) Works produced by Jaina writers with a view to propagating their religious teachings, (2) Classical works of great masters like Kālidāsa, (3) Other works. We shall take them in this order.

(1) Of *Kāvyas* with a religious bias there are many, for the Jaina teachers cultivated the art of poetry not so for its own sake as to convey the message of the *Tīrthaṅkaras* to the people in a form that they could appreciate and assimilate. The versatile Haribhadra Sūri is said to have written the *Kathākośa*, the *Dhūrtākhyāna*, the *Munipaticharita*, the *Yaśodharacharita*, the *Vīrāṅgadakathā* and the *Samarāichchakahā*. But of these only two, the *Dhurtākhyāna* and the *Samarāichchakahā* have been discovered so far. The *Dhūrtākhyāna* is a good satire on popular Hinduism. The *Samarāichchakahā* is a Prakrit *gadya-kāvya* interspersed with verses. Its flowing style, easy prose, and absence of unnecessary ornamentation, coupled with an interesting narrative which drives home the Jaina lesson that a man suffers on account of his bad actions and can rise only by cultivating good virtues, has mnde it very popular with the Jaina writers of all ages and provinces.[22] It was summarised into Sanskrit by Pradyumna Sūri in V. 1324 (1267 A.D.)

Haribhadra was followed by his pupil, Dākṣiṇyāṅka Udyotana Sūri who completed his great *kathā*, *the Kuvalayamālā* at Jālor in 778 A.D., in the reign of Vatsarāja Pratihāra.[23]

22. It is highly praised for instance, by Siddharṣi Sūri, Vādideva Sūri, Lakṣmaṇagaṇi, Malayagiri and Pradyumna Sūri.

23. संवत्सरशतनवके द्विषष्टिसहितेऽतिलंघिते चास्याः ।
ज्येष्ठसितपञ्चम्यां पुनर्वसौ गुरुदिने समाप्तिरभूत् ॥

Its style is similar to that of the *Naladamayantichampū* of Trivikrama and the language used is Prākrit, though the writer has given also a few descriptions in Apabhraṁśa and Paiśāchī. This *kathā* was summarised into Sanskrit by Ratnaprabha Sūri in the thirteenth century. Of the Jaina poets earlier than himself, Dākṣinnyāka mentions Vimalāṅka, Raviṣeṇa, Devagupta, and Bhavaviraha.

Another great Jaina writer was Siddharṣi Sūri who completed his *Upamitibhavaprapañcha kathā* at Bhillamāla in V. 962. It is as much a work of philosophy as of poetry and is one of the finest allegories in any language. Written in simple and easily understandable Sanskrit (because the vain people of his time had come to think slightingly of Prakrit)[24] and with a narrative as interesting as any folk-tale, it appealed not only to scholars but also to the masses who cared probably more for the story than the allegory that underlay its structure. His *Niṣpuṇyaka* is an unimitable character. Siddharṣi's another literary creation was the *Chandrakevalicharita*. It was written in V. 974. To the same century belongs also the important Apabhraṁśa work, the *Bhaviṣayatta-kahā* of Dhanapāla. Slightly later than him was Maheśvara Sūri, who wrote his *Jñānapañchamīkahā* in Prakrit and the *Saṁyamamañjarīkāvya* in Apabhraṁśa. It is interesting to find here many old folk tales dressed out and presented in a Jaina garb.

Jaisalmer has a manuscript copy of Dhanapāla's *Tilakamañjarī*, dated V. 1130. This Dhanapāla, though originally hailing from the present Uttar Pradesh, passed most of his life at the court of the Paramāra rulers, Muñja and Bhoja of Dhārā. Some time after the Ghaznavite invasion of western India, he went to Satyapura and composed his Apabhraṁśa poem, *Satyapurīya Śrī Mahāvīra Utsāha* in praise of the Satyapura image of Mahāvīra. Earlier, probably at Dhārā, he had written the *Ṛṣabhapañchāśikā* and the *Mahāvīrastava*. Of the earlier Jaina poets referred to by him, we have already said a few words about Haribhadra Sūri. Pādalipta was the author

24. तत्रापि संस्कृतं तावद्दुर्विदग्धहृदि स्थिता ।
(उपमितिभवप्रपञ्चकथा)

of the Prākrit poem, *Taraṅgavatī*, the language of which had by Nemichandra's time become so archaic; that he had to summarise it into 1900 *gāthās* of a simpler style. I have been unable to find anything about Jīvadeva Sūri, the predecessor of Dhanapāla. Bappabhaṭṭi, the author of the *Tārāgaṇa*, a poem no longer extant, was perhaps the friend and spiritual guide of Āma (Nāgāvaloka or Nāgabhaṭa II)[25]. Mahendra Sūri was Dhanapāla's *guru*.[26]

25. See our "Studies in the प्रभावकचरित" *JA*, 1937.

26. The work of the following Jaina scholars also deserves notice : Vardhamāna Sūri (died 1021 A.D.) wrote the उपमितिभवप्रपञ्चा-समय. His disciple, Jineśvara Sūri, the founder of the Kharataragachchha, added to Jaina literature the निर्वाणलीलावती, वीरचरित्र and कथाकोष. *Nirvāṇalīlāvatī* is no longer available. But we have its summary in Sanskrit by जिनरत्नाचार्य. Jineśvara's disciple, Jinachandra, wrote the *Saṁvegaraṅgaśālā*, a manuscript of which exists at Jaisalmer. The work appears to have been very popular, for it is referred to in more than one epigraph and many books. His co-disciple जिनभद्र wrote the सुरसुन्दरी-कथा. At the suggestion of Prasannachandra, a disciple of *Navāṅgavṛttikāra* Abhayadeva, Guṇachandra composed in Prakrit a poem called *Mahāvīrachariam*. It has eight *prastāvas* and its extent is 12,000 *ślokas*. देवभद्रसूरि wrote the पार्श्वनाथचरित in V. 1168. Vardhamānāchārya composed the Prākrit *Ādināthacharita* in five *avasaras*, using Apabhraṁśa also here and there. His *Manoramācharita* was written in V. 1140. Pūrṇabhadragaṇi, a disciple of Jinapati Sūri, wrote the अतिमुक्तचरित्र. His धन्याशालिभद्र-चरित्र was written at Jaisalmer in V. 1285. Lakṣmītilaka, a disciple of the Kharatara *Achārya*, Jineśvara Sūri, finished his प्रत्येकबुद्ध-चरित in V. 1311. Then, in addition to these works of Kharatara scholars, from Vardhamāna to Lakṣmītilaka, we have at Jaisalmer many others (of the period 900-1300 A.D.), written not by *Kharataras* but followers of other *gachchhas*. Of these some were certainly studied in Rājasthān : in the case of others there is a strong probability, though absolute proof is lacking. We mention below some of them.

Śīlāchārya wrote the *Chauppanna-mahāpuruṣachariam* in V. 925. It has a *praśasti* of 48 verses presented to the Kharatara Jinabhadra which indicates its popularity among the Kharataras. *Śālibhadracharitra* (Prakrit) was copied out in V. 1222. The *Vilāsavatīkathā*, an Apabhraṁśa work by Sādhāraṇa (V. 1123) is based on the *Samarāichchakahā* of Haribhadra Sūri. Devachandra Sūri wrote the *Śāntināthacharita* in V. 1160. Its extent is 12000 *Ślokas* and the language is Prakrit. *Pṛthvīchandracharita* of Śānti Sūri was written in V. 1161. Yaśodeva Upādhyāya wrote the *Chandraprabhacharita* in V. 1178. Nine years later, came the *Narmadāsundarīkathā* of Mahendra Sūri, in V. 1216 the *Nemināthacharita* of Haribhadra Sūri, in 1216 the *Munisuvratacharita* of Padmaprabha Sūri, and in V. 1322 the *Śāntināthacharita* of Munideva.

Hemachandra's poetical works probably reached Rājasthān during his life time. They include the *Dvyāśrayamahākāvya*, *Kumārapālacharita* (Prakrit) *Triṣaṣṭiśalākāpuruṣacharita* and a number of hymns. The Sanskrit *Dvyāśraya* was commented on by Abhayatilaka (V. 1312), a pupil of the Kharatara Lakṣmītilaka, who is known to have revised his co-disciple Pūrṇakalaśa's commentary on the *Kumārapālacharita* (V. 1307). Hemachandra's one disciple, Devachandra, wrote the play, the *Chandralekhā-vijaya*, and the other, Ramachandra, wrote a large number of poems and plays.[27] To Udayasiṁha's reign belongs also the *Prabuddharauhiṇeya*, a play in six acts by another Rāmchandra, a pupil of Jayaprabha Sūri. The *Hammīramadamardana* of Jayasiṁha Sūri, a manuscript of which, dated V. 1286, has been found at Jaisalmer, has been very often referred to and utilised in this book.

(2) *Classical works*. Along with the *Kāvyas* written by Jaina authors, the Jaina community continued studying the works of great poets like Kālidāsa. Sumatigaṇi mentions his *Meghadūta*. Āsaḍa commented on it. The high regard in which the poet was held is shown also by the following verse quoted by Jinapāla [28].

कवयः कालिदासाद्याः कवयो वयमप्यमी ।
पर्वते परमाणौ च वस्तुत्वमुभयोरपि ।।

Bhāravi, the writer of the *Kirātā rjunīya* was well-known. Vinayachandra calls him *Chhatra-Bhāravi* and counts him among writers of *sadgranthas*.[29] Jaisalmer has a palm leaf manuscript of a commentary on the *Kirātārjunīya* by Prakāśavarṣa Kāśmīraka.[30] But by the twelfth century, Bhāravi's fame had been eclipsed by that of Māgha, the great Rājasthānī poet from

27. The best known of these are (1) (1) राघवाभ्युदय, (3) (4) रघुविलास, (5) कुमारविहारशतक, (6) नलविलास, (7) सत्यहरिश्चन्द्र, (8) कौमुदीमित्रानन्द, (9) मल्लिकामकरन्द, (10) रोहिणमृगाङ्क, (11) वनमाला and निर्भयभीम Of the last of these, there is a manuscriptV. 1306) written in the reign of *Mahārājakula* Udayasiṁha of Jālor. Rāmachandra's literary achievement was great enough : but even greater was his pride in it.

28. "Kalidāsa etc. are poets; so are we. The property of being material objects belongs to mountains and molecules alike." (Comment on the 5th verse of the *Charchari*).

29. *Paṭṭan Catalogue of Mss.* (G.O.S.), p. 49.

30. *Jaisalmer Catalogue of Palm-leaf Mss.* p. 55.

Bhillamāla. Jinapāla quotes the following well-known verse about Māgha[31]:—

माघेन विघ्नितोत्साहा नोत्सहन्ते पदक्रमे ।
स्मरन्ति भारवेरेव कवयः कपयो यथा ॥

Vinayachandra mentions the poet's famous designation *Ghaṇṭā-Māgha*. Pradyumnāchārya was proud of having studied the *Māgha-mahākāvya*. Jaisalmer has a copy of Bhaṭṭi's *Rāma-kāvya*. We find it quoted also in some of the books on poetics produced in Gujarāt. But much more popular than Bhaṭṭi, however, was the great stylist, Harṣa, the author of the *Naiṣa-dhīyakāvya* a copy of which was brought by the Kharatara Saṅgha of Jaisalmer in V. 1378, at the advice of Jinakuśala Sūri. Jaisalmer has also copies of a very old commentary on it, the *Sāhityavidyādharī*. The poem reached Gujarāt in Vastupāla's time, and very soon became popular among Jainas as well as non-Jainas.[32] It may have reached Rājasthān from there.

Of Prakrit poets, Vākpatirāja, the author of the *Gauḍavaho*, perhaps, attained the greatest celebrity in western India. Here is Vākpati's wife's opinion, as reported by Jinapāla:[33]

होहिंति केच्चि जे ते न याणिमो, जे गया नमो ताण ।
संपइ इह जे कविणो ते मह पइणो न सारिच्छा ॥

Jaisalmer has a palm-leaf manuscript of the *Gauḍavadhasāraṭīkā*. Copies of the work at Paṭṭan, and the story of his friendship with the Jaina scholar and teacher, Bappabhaṭṭi Sūri, in works like the *Prabhāvakacharita* also indicates his popularity in the Jaina world.[34]

Dhanapāla offers his homage among others to Vyāsa, Vālmīki, Guṇāḍhya, Pravarasena, Rājaśekhara, Rudra,

31. "With their zeal (for poesy) impeded by Māgha, poets compose not a single line. They think only of (the poet) Bhāravi, acting thus like monkeys who with their agility gone on the onset of (the cold month) of Māgha, have no desire to stir even a step. They think only of the Sun." Comment on the 4th verse of the *Charcharī*.

32. *Prabandhakośa*, p. 60 (Singhī Granthamalā) where we get the story of its being slyly copied out by Vastupāla from Harihara's manuscript.

33. "We know not the future poets; our salutations to those who are no more. But of the present poets there is none who equals my husband" (Comment on the 6th verse of the *Charcharī*).

34. See the *Bappabhaṭṭisūricharita* of the *Prabhāvakacharita*, where Vākpatirāja is depicted as a Vaiṣṇava and friend of Bappabhaṭṭasūri.

Kardamarāja, Bāṇa and Bhavabhūti. From Haribhadra we get the names of Harṣa and Subandhu. Additional names from the *Kuvalayamālā* are Sātavāhana, Śataparṇaka, and Prabhañjana. It is therefore obvious that most of the non-Jaina Sanskrit and Prakrit literature was studied by the Jaina *literati*; (a fact proved also by the facility with which they quote these authors in their books on rhetorics)[35], though possibly not to the same extent by the people in general who, as now, may have remained satisfied with elementary reading, writing and arithmetic.[36]

Jinavallabha is said to have studied eighty four dramas.[37] This obviously means that he had read most dramas, Jaina as

35. See for instance the नाट्यदर्पण of Rāmachandra and Guṇachandra which brings to light many unknown works.

36. Vyāsa and Vālmīki, the authors of the *Mahābhārata* and the *Rāmāyaṇa* are well known. Guṇāḍhya wrote the *Bṛhatakathā* and in Dhanapāla's time was regarded as a contemporary of Sātavāhana. Pravarasena is the writer of the Prakrit poem, *Setubandha* or *Rāvaṇavadha*, and Rājaśekhara, of the *Bālarāmāyaṇa*, *Bālabhārata*, *Karpūramañjarī*, the *Viddhaśālabhañjikā*, and the *Kāvyamīmāṁsā*, the last of which is known to have been utilised by Hemachandra Nemikumāra's son Vāgbhaṭa, Amarachandra and Vinayachandra. Kardamarāja is praised as the creator of 'jewel-like nice sayings', Prabhañjana may be Prābhañjana or Hanumān, the reputed author of the *Hanumannāṭaka*. Mayūra (not enumerated in the last paragraph) is mentioned by Jinapāla. Vinayachandra mentions Bhoja as a great writer. It is not unlikely that many of his works also may have reached Rājasthān, though the only one found at Jaisalmer is a *Kathā*, the शृङ्गारमञ्जरी. The Jaisalmer Catalogue lists also मधुवर्णनम् and विरहिणीप्रलापम्, the works of an otherwise unknown poet named कलि. Other poems known to us from Jaisalmer are Bilhaṇa's विक्रमाङ्कदेवचरित; वृन्दावनयमक; मेघाभ्युदय of मानाङ्क; राक्षसकाव्य; घटखर्परकाव्य; and चक्रपाणिविजय of Lakṣmīdhara.

Jinapati Sūri's rival, Pradyumnāchārya, studied the *Kādambarī*. Even his other rival, the much-ridiculed Padmaprabha, knew the work and accused Jinapati Sūri of plagiarizing it. Quotations from both the *Kādambarī* and the *Harṣacharita* abound in Jaina books on rhetorics. Subandhu is represented by a palm leaf Ms. of his वासवदत्ता, V. 1207, in the Jaina *Bhāṇḍāras* of Jaisalmer. The शृङ्गारमञ्जरी of Bhoja, listed above, is also a romance. The त्रैलोक्यमञ्जरी of Rudra, mentioned by Dhanapāla, may have been in prose. The लीलावतीकथा of कौतूहल (?), a son of भट्टभूषण and grandson of Bahalāditya, is in Prakrit verse and can according to Sri Lalchandra Bhagwandās Gāndhi, vie with the *Kādambarī* in poetic beauty. It is obvious from its palm leaf Ms. of V. 1265 that it was written in the twelfth century or even earlier.

37. Introduction to अपभ्रंशकाव्यत्रयी, p. 20.

well as non-Jaina. How comprehensive the study of some of the Jaina writers could be can be seen also from the *Nāṭya-darpaṇa* of Rāmachandra and Guṇachandra who quote from fifty-five dramas, some of them, now no longer extant.

In this age, when form predominated over sense, Murāri appears to have been specially popular. Jaisalmer has a palm-leaf manuscript of Narachandra's commentary on Murāri's *Anargharāghava*. Narachandra's *guru*, Devaprabha, wrote about it.

एकैकेन पदेन यस्य विदुषामन्तः सुधासारणि-
व्युत्पत्ति वहता परां श्रवणयोरल्पप्रबन्धस्पृहा ।
सध्रीचीरमृतस्य यस्य भणितीर्वैदग्ध्यसंवर्मिताः
श्रुत्वा हर्षजुषो विलोचनयुगे यस्याः पयोबिन्दवः ।।[38]

Murāri perhaps never received any higher praise. Another Jaina scholar, Pradyumnāchārya, when speaking of his studies of dramas, mentions *Murāri-nāṭaka* only, *i.e.*, *Anargharāghava*. Narachandra's pupil, Narendraprabha, on the other hand, exemplifies dramas by saying नाट्येषु-अभिज्ञानशाकुन्तलादिषु, showing thereby that Kālidāsa could not be forgotten even in this age of artificiality.[39]

(3) *Minor Poets.* The Rājasthānīs must have studied also the works of many other poets, now no longer extant. It was not every *kāvya* that received encouragement at the hands of Jaina teachers. They banned in temples the performance of popular plays like those dealing with the life of Rāma and Rāvaṇa, presenting only those dramas which induced people either to lead a religious life or to renounce the world.[40] This policy though not followed consistently, has led, we fear, to the extinction of many popular poems which otherwise would have been preserved in the Jaina *Bhaṇḍāras*. So all that we have now besides a few nice poems like the *Bharata-Bāhubali-ghora*, the *Gaja-sukumāra-rāsa*, *Neminātha-rāsa* and the *Bharateśvara-Bāhubali-rāsa* are a large number of short pieces, commemorating either the

38. *Catalogue of the Palm leaf Mss. in the Paṭṭana Bhaṇḍāras*, p. 301.

39. Narendraprabha also says, काव्येषु रघुवंशादिषु.

40. *Cf.* the following statement from the उपदेशरसायनरास of श्रीजिनदत्तसूरि:—

धम्मिय नाडय वर नच्चिज्जहिं, भरह-सगरनिक्खमण कहिज्जहिं ।
चक्कवट्टि-बल-रायह चरियइं, नच्चिवि अन्ति हुंति पव्वइयइं ।।३६।।
(अपभ्रंशकाव्यत्रयी), p. 47.

initiation or death of *Jaina-gurus*[41] which appeal more to the religious-minded Jaina votary than to lovers of good poetry.

(*e*) *Metrics.* On metrics the Rājasthānīs studied a number of good books. Specially popular was the *Jayadeva-chhandas*, a book in eight chapters, which is known to have been studied and taught by Jinavallabha, and is mentioned by Jinapāla in the *Kharataragachcha-paṭṭāvalī*. Jaisalmer has a manuscript not only of its text, but also a commentary on it by Harṣaṭa, son of Bhaṭṭa Mukula. The *Kaisiṭṭha* of Haribhadra was commented on by Gopāla. To V. 1192, belongs a manuscript of Jayakīrti's *Chhandonuśāsana* which is said to have been composed after consulting the works of Māṇḍavya, Piṅgala, Janāśraya, Setava, Pūjyapāda and Jayadeva. The *Chhandonuśāsana* may be presumed to have become known in Rājasthān along with his other works in the second half of the twelfth century.

(*f*) *Alaṅkāraśāstra* (Poetics). Specially popular with the Jainas was the study of Poetics. The *Gaṇadharasārdhaśatakabṛhadvṛtti* speaks of Jinavallabha's study of the *alaṅkāraśāstras* of Rudraṭa, Udbhaṭa, Daṇḍin. Vāmana and Bhāmaha. Pradyumnāchārya studied the *Kāvyaprakāṣa* of Mammaṭa. The Popularity of Rudraṭa's *Kāvyālaṅkāra* among the Jainas is shown by the commentaries of Namisādhu and Āśādhara. Udbhaṭa is represented at Jaisalmer by two manuscripts of *Udbhaṭālankāravṛtti*. Daṇḍin's *Kāvyādarśa* has a commentary, the *Hṛdayaṅgamā*, the palm-leaf manuscript of which was written in V. 1161. Vāmana, Rājaśekhara, Kuntaka, Halāyudha and Hemachandra are also represented by the manuscripts of their works at Jaisalmer.

How fond the Jainas were of *Alaṅkāras* and expert in their use can be seen from Jinapāla's *Kharataragachchhapaṭṭāvalī* and the commentary on the *Charcharī*. In the latter he extols Jinavallabha for his proficiency in *chitrakāvyas*. It is ridiculous, he says, to think highly of poets who knew only *chakra* and *muśala bandhas*. Jinavallabha was proficient in the use of *Khaḍga*, *Saptachakrikā*, *Gaja* and *Gomūtrikā-bandhas*. He could complete verses (समस्यापूर्ति) by either composing the remaining quarters or supplying the missing verbs. Nor was Jinapati Sūri's proficiency any less. If Jinavallabha pleased Naravarman of Mālwā by his *samasyāpūrti*. Jinapati gladdened the hearts of the

41. For a collection of these see the ऐतिहासिक काव्यसंग्रह edited by Sri Agarchand Nahta and Bhanwarlala Nahta.

paṇḍits in Pṛthvīrāja's court, not only by completing verses but by passing a stiff test in *Alaṅkāra-śāstra*. His description of Pṛthvirāja III's court is excellent. The verse that he presented in *chhatra-bandha* to the ruler makes good sense. He challenged Padmaprabha to vie with him in the use of Prakrit, Sanskrit, Māgadhī, Paiśāchī and Śaurasenī languages; he proved also his mastery of grammar, metrics, poetics, *rasa*, drama, logic, *jyotiṣa* (astrology and astronomy) and Jaina *siddhānta*. He asked his rival to question him about any difficult verse that needed explanation, or to put before him a verse that lacked some root or noun, a question or an answer, or something without which it could not give any sense. He could give the needed verse, even if there were no vowels or consonants; he could restore to their true order the letters of a verse that he heard once. He knew about the musical *rāgas* and could compose to order a song in any *rāga* sung before him. These achievements seem wonderful, but that a good scholar was expected to have them can be seen from the various *kaviśikṣās* of the period as well as the *Śārṅgadharapaddhati*, which is full of verses and exercises of this type. For a poet mere *pratibhā* (genius) was not enough, he was also to have *vyutpatti* and *abhyāsa*. *Abhyāsa* (practice) was to be under the direction of a poet. *Vyutpatti* resulted from the study of various arts, sciences, and scriptures.[42]

(*g*) *Grammar*. Knowledge of grammer was considered essential. An old verse quoted by Jinapāla states that one who attempts the study of the other *śāstras* without first studying grammar, verily tries to count the steps of a snake that had long ago slipped into water in the drakness of the night.[43] Buddhisāgara was the first Śvetāmbara teacher to write a comprehensive Sanskrit and Prākrit grammar, the *Pañchagranthī*.[44]

42. लोके शब्दादिशास्त्रेषु काव्यनाट्यकथासु च ।
आगमादिषु च प्रौढिव्युंत्पत्तिरिति कथ्यते ॥८॥ (अलङ्कारमहोदधि G.O.S.)

43. *Apabhraṁśakāvyatrayī*, p. 3.

44. *Catalogue of Mss. in the Jaisalmer Bhaṇḍāras*, p. 20. The reason for its composition is given thus by जिनेश्वरसूरि:—

तैरवधीरिते यत्तु प्रवृत्तिरावयोरिह ।
तत्र दुर्जनवाक्यानि प्रवृत्तेःसन्निबन्धनम् ॥
कीदृशानि दुर्जनवाक्यानींत्याह—
श्रीबुद्धिसागराचार्यैं वृत्तैर्व्याकरणं कृतम् ।
अस्माभिस्तु प्रमालक्ष्म बुद्धिमायातु साम्प्रतम् ॥

It was composed at Jālor in V. 1080, after consulting the works of Pāṇini, Chandra, Jinendra, Viśrānta, and Durga. Instead of being in the usual *sūtra* form, it was in verse, and as a grammar, thus stands in a class by itself. Kumārapāla's *guru*, Hemachandra, was another great grammarian. Pradyumnāchārya of Āśāvallī studied his *Vyākaraṇa*.[45] A copy of Hemachandra's *Laghuvṛtti*, copied as early as V. 1206, has been found at Jaisalmer.[46]

Pāṇini, Patañjali, and Bhartṛhari were known to Haribhadra Sūri as great grammarians, a fact that proves the popularity of the Pāṇinean system in the beginning of our period. This popularity continued, though in a lesser degree, after the composition of newer grammars like the *Sarasvatīkaṇṭhābharaṇa* and the *Siddha-Haima*. Jinavallabha studied eight grammatical systems,[47] of which the only one named, however, is that of Pāṇini.

(*h*) *Lexicography and other subjects.* Closely connected with grammar is lexicography.[48] Of the many lexicographical works at Jaisalmer, the *Śabdaratnapradīpa* has been mentioned more than once by Sumatigaṇi (V. 1295). It must therefore be regarded as an old lexicon. The *Apavarganāmamālā* was probably composed about 1150 A.D., as its compiler, Jinabhadra, was a contemporary of Jinavallabha and Jinadatta Sūri. Hemachandra's lexicons were well known. Of these, the *Anekārtha-saṅgraha* has a commentary by Mahendra Sūri.

The *Śārṅgadharapaddhati* has sections on *Rājanīti*, elephants, horses, military science, music, herbs and plants, omens, *svarodaya*, antidotes of poisons, *kautukas*, *bhūtavidyā*, *yoga* and *kalpasthāna*. The *Prahhāvakacharita* mentions seventy-two arts and sciences learnt by Prince Āma (Nāgāvaloka)[49]. A shorter and more authentic list is to be found in the *Upamitibhavaprapañchakathā* of Siddharṣi Sūri according to which the subjects learnt by princes Ripudāraṇa and Nandivardhana were all scripts, mathe-

45. *Kharataragachchhapaṭṭāvali* of Jinapāla.
46. *Jaina pustaka-praśastisaṅgraha* (Singhi Jaina Granthamālā), p. 105.
47. The Jaisalmer *Bhaṇḍāras* have manuscripts of कातन्त्रोत्तरम् (विद्यानन्दम्), कातन्त्रपञ्जिका of त्रिलोचनदास, कातन्त्रदुर्गपदप्रबोधम् of प्रबोधमूर्ति and कातन्त्र-विभ्रमटीका of जिनप्रभसूरि ।
48. The Jaisalmer *Bhaṇḍārs* have Mss. of शब्दरत्नप्रदीप, लिङ्गानुशासनविवरण of हेमचन्द्र, अनेकार्थकैरवकौमुदी of महेद्रसूरि, अपवर्गनाममाला of जिनभद्र, एकाक्षरनाममालिका of विश्वशम्भु, and अभिधानचिन्तामणिटीका.
49. P. 152 (Nirṇayasāgar Edition)

matics, grammar, astrology, astronomy, prosody, dancing, cutting patterns, *indrajāla*, military science, medical science, logic, and characteristics of people. [50]

Additional subjects studied by non-Jainas. The non-Jainas naturally studied a few subjects, much more than the Jainas and Buddhists. The study of the Vedas continued as before in centres like Bhīnamāla which produced the great Brāhmaṇa poet and scholar, Māgha. Even now the Śrīmālī Brāhmaṇas hold a special position in Rājasthān, not on account of their learning, but the reputation that their ancestors must have built up during our period. According to Padmanābha's opinion Bhillamāla had 45,000 Brāhmaṇas. They knew the four *Vedas*, the six *aṅgas*, the eight grammatical systems, fourteen *vidyās*, eighteen *Purāṇas*, *Āyurveda*, Bharata- (*Nāṭyaśāstra*), *jyotiṣa*, *Piṅgala* (metrics), *Bājī* (aśvaśāstra) and *nāṭaka*. In every house was a *yajñaśālā* and *agnihotra*. They knew the secrets of the *smṛtis* and performed the six *karmans*. They daily performed sacrifices, offering duly apportioned shares to the gods, beginning with Indra[51]. Alberunī knew Bhillamāla as the home of the astronomer, Brahmagupta.[52] The *Pṛthvīrājaviyaya* speaks of the *yajñas* at Ajmer, which again proves the continuity of the Vedic tradition among the Brāhmaṇas.

Similarly, in the *Pāśupata* monasteries like Harṣa and Ekaliṅga the study and practice of this *Pāśupata* doctrines must have been given the first place. As to secular subjects, they were the same for the Jainas and non-Jainas. They all loved good literature; and if the number of times, a poet is quoted be any index of his popularity among the people, the poets most studied in Śārṅgadhara's time were Kālidāsa, Māgha, Trivikrama,[53] Bhartṛhari, Jayadeva, Kṣemendra,[54] Daṇḍin and Bāṇa. Next

50. *Prastāva* 3, chapter 1; *Prastāva* 4 chapter 2. Siddharṣi's opinion on ज्योतिष and निमित्तशास्त्र is worth quoting. He writes, 'Astrology, निमित्तशास्त्र and similar other subjects, the results of which lie beyond human ken, were first taught by सर्वज्ञ. If the prediction goes wrong, it is the professor of the science who is to blame and not the science itself. People have only a limited knowledge of them. They do not know their sub-divisions.'

51. कान्हडदेप्रबन्ध (राजस्थान पुरातत्त्व मन्दिर) II, vv. 22-27.

52. Sachau, *Alberuni's India* I, 267.

53. Author of the *Naladamayantī-Champū*.

54. Author of the बृहत्कथामञ्जरी, नर्ममाला, औचित्यविचारचर्चा etc.

in order followed Dhanadeva Murāri, Rājaśekhara, Bhavabhūti, Deveśvara, Dāmodaradeva, Harihara, Harṣa, Jayamādhava, Bhallaṭa, Kṛṣṇamiśra, Bhānu, Harigaṇa, Mayūra, Rāghavachaitanya, Nārāyaṇabhaṭṭa, Lakṣmīdhara, Gauḍa Abhinanda, Chandradeva and Bhāsa. Vigraharāja's *praśasti* on the Delhi Aśokan pillar has been quoted by Śārṅgadhara, though the pillar has been wrongly described as a sacrificial post erected by Nṛga. Of women poets Śārṅgadhara notes Vijjikā, Śīlābhaṭṭārikā, Vikaṭanitambā, Phalgustanī, and Padmaśrī. If all this literature was being studied in Rājasthān, there can hardly be any doubt of the fact that Rājasthānīs then knew and studied Sanskrit more than they do at present.

Section II

(*i*) *Seats of Learning*

As feeding and teaching poor students has always been regarded as an act of great merit, there must have been a good many schools endowed by the public. The *Upamitibhavapaprañchakathā* refers to some of these.[55] Commenting on the word, *Vidyāmaṭha* of the *Dvyāśrayamahākāvya*, Abhayatilakagaṇi states, "*Vidyāmaṭha* is an institution where rich people provide food, garments, and other things to the teachers and the taught, with a view to acquiring merit."[56] Jayānaka speaks of *maṭhas* or schools in every square of Ajmer (PV, IX, 24). This indicates the popularity of such institutions in Gurjaratrā, of which western Rājasthān long remained a part, and also Sapādalakṣa almost up to the end of the period with which we are dealing. But of the great colleges established by the Chauhān rulers themselves, we hear of only one. To the *Sarsvatīmandira* founded by the illustrious Vigraharāja IV probably flocked students from all the parts of the Chauhān empire. The Jaina sources describe Jinavallabha's retreat at Chitor also as a great centre of education. Bhīnmāl and Ābū probably were respectively centres of Brahmanical and Tāntric studies. Padmanābha calls Bhīnmāl the *Brahmapurī* of the Chauhāns, the Brāhmaṇas of which were famed far and wide for their learning and performance of Vedic rites.[57] Ābū was a Śākta *pīṭha*.

55. See specially p. 624.
56. I, 7.
57. *Kānhaḍadeprabandha*, III, 22-29.

(*ii*) *System of Studies and Examinations*

From the notices that we have in the *Upamitibhavaprapañcha-kathā*, the *Kharataragachchhapaṭṭāvalī*, and the *Samarāichchakahā* we learn that on an auspicious day fixed by the astrologers, the boy was taken (generally in his eighth year) to the *kalāchārya*, *guru*, or *Upādhyāya* to be taught the various subjects we have discussed in the first section of this chapter and of which a more comprehensive list is given as an Appendix to this chapter. The teacher was given the highest respect. It was a sin to sit on his *vetrāsana*, a procedure so atrocious that it was believed to reduce the transgressor's life span and bring him obloquy everywhere.[58] The boys received individual attention, even though the classes with individual teachers were sometimes bigger than they should have been according to our modern standards. For special studies, one had to move on from one station to another, for while general studies could be carried on anywhere, expert teaching needed the attention of a specialist,[59] and not every one could claim like Jinavallabha to be an adept not only in theology and philosophy, but also *sāmudrika*, grammar, *metrics*, *sāhitya* and astrology.[60]

The present system of examinations did not exist. But the learning of scholars did not remain untested. Vigraharāja IV convened periodical assemblies of scholars and poets. Pṛthvīrāja III had *paṇḍitas* like Janārdana and Vidyāpati Gauḍa to test the scholarship of people coming to his court and deciding the points at issue between disputants. That not every one could have been, however, satisfied with their verdict, can be seen from the caustic remarks of Jayānaka in the first canto of the *Pṛthvīrājavijaya*.[61] The victor received a *jayapatra* and could be, if his followers were influential enough, carried through the city, with bands playing notes of victory and people dancing and singing. The defeated disputant, on the other hand, became subject to gibes and lampoons. The *paṇḍitasabhā*, where all sorts of "possible and impossible questions" could be asked by

58. *Upamitibhavaprapañcha-kathā*, p. 305.
59. See the *Kharataragachchhapaṭṭāvalī* for many instances of this type.
60. See the *Charcharī* of Jinadatta Sūri.
61. Verses 6-30.

the opponent as wall as the *paṇḍitas*, was thus a stiffer testing ground than our examination halls. A less informal test was the *goṣṭhī* where friends vied with each other.[62]

This old system of examination had its merits. It did not let a scholar rest on his laurels. He had to keep fresh his stock of knowledge and even increase it, for fear that he might any day be challenged to a debate by an outsider or by his own rivals from within the kingdom.[63] His study had to be intensive; he had to think deeply about questions that could be raised, and it was thus that India made some of its great advances in thought. Most of us who have studied under the old system are familiar enough with its defects also. It sometimes led to endless hair-splitting dicussion, the objective of which instead of being the advancement of truth was merely the vanquishing of the opponents; and in such a debate one naturally used *chhala* as well as *vitaṇḍā*.[64] It led also scholars sometimes to give all their time to one subject—and that sometimes not the most useful—so that one may claim to be pre-eminent in one sphere, if not more.

(*iii*) *Literacy*

The classes which had the greatest facilities for education and consequently the greatest amount of literacy were the Brāhmaṇas and Jaina *sādhus*. It was the proud boast of Ajayameru, though there may be some poetic exaggeration in it, that its streets resounded with the sound of the Vedas recited regularly in the early hours of the morning.[65] Vaiśyas, specially those converted to Jainism, produced good scholars like Yaśovīra. Jaina *sādhus*, from whichever community they may have been drawn, were generally literate, though among them also literacy differed from one community to the other, the least

62. See the *Upamitibhavaprapañchakathā*, pp. 560-1. A very good account is to be found also in Dhanapāla's *Tilakamañjarī*.

63. See the account of the disputations, Jinapati Sūri *versus* Padmaprabha and Pradyumna Suri *versus* Jinapati Sūri in the *Kharataragachchhapaṭṭāvalī*.

64. That these were well known weapons can be seen from the commentaries on the *Nyāyasūtras*.

65. *PV.*, IX, 24.

literate perhaps being those who had become owners of big religious properties and whose life consequently did not differ much from that of common people. For Kāyasthas, who had by this time grown into a caste, literacy has always been essential, and many of them figure as writers of inscriptions. The *Pāśupata* teachers, Allaṭa and Viśvarūpa, were learned, though on the basis of this scanty evidence, it would be difficult to generalise and say that most of the *Pāśupatas* were literate. In Jaina literature, it is generally the Śaiva ascetics who from the butt of ridicule. We have already spoken above of the limited amount of literacy among women and need not repeat those details.

(*iv*) *Some general remarks*

We had a few words to say about the ancient system of examinations. About the system of education in general we may remark that it generally established very cordial relations between the teacher and the taught. Teachers, even though not rich, felt compensated by the universal respect in which they were held by the rich and the poor alike, and had with the freedom given to them a great hand in shaping the lives of their pupils and wards. Even after more than a century of western education, we still hanker after a teacher of the type described in many of our sources and one who, in the words of Yuan Chwang, "forgetting fatigue expatiate(s) in the arts and sciences" and "count(s) not 1000 *li* too long a journey in the pursuit of wisdom".[66]

But of serious defects also, this system had developed many by the end of our period. On the whole it was ill-devised and unpractical. While astrology, *dhātuvāda* and *nimittaśāstra* flourished, Astronomy and Mathematics declined. Bhīnmāl which once had been the home of Brahmagupta and Māgha and probably of some more celebrities in the field of science and arts had by the time of Kānhaḍadeva become reduced to a home of *karmakāṇḍin* Brāhmaṇas. India of the Gupta Period made advances in every cultural field. By 800 A.D., this tide

66. *On Yuan Chuwang*, Vol. I, p. 161.

of Renaissance had largely spent its force and begun to recede. By 900 A.D. it was a spent force in the field of science, though in other directions some advances continued to be registered. Not merely Rājasthān but almost the whole of India knew in 1200 A.D. no more of pure science than it did nearly five centuries earlier. We were, it seems, suffering from a dose of over-complascence, with the result that Rājasthān of our period was largely unoriginal, uninventive and unprogressive, revelling either in hair-splitting discussions or composition of commentaries, and for this mental sterility, towards the latter part of our period, some part of the blame must assuredly go the educators of our period, who probably by their too much of insistence on other-worldliness, respect for tradition, self-complacency, and isolationist behaviour rendered backward a country which once had been a torch-bearer of culture and scientific progress.

APPENDIX K

Subjects of Study

The *Samarādityakathā* of Haribhadra gives the following fairly comprehensive list of subjects one had to study to be an all-round scholar :—[1]

1. *Lekha*]
2. *Gaṇita*
3. *Ālekhya*
4. *Nāṭya*
5. *Gīta*
6. *Vādita*
7. *Svaragata*
8. *Puṣkaragata*
9. *Samatāla*
10. *Dyūta*
11. *Janavāda*
12. *Horā*
13. *Kāvya*
14. *Asṭāpadam*
15. *Annavidhi*
16. *Pānavidhi*
17. *Śuyanavidhi*
18. *Āryā*
19. *Prahelikā*
20. *Māgadhikā*
21. *Gāthā*
22. *Gīti*
23. *Śloka*
24. *Madhusiktham*
25. *Gandhayukti*
26. *Ābharaṇavidhi*
27. *Taruṇipratikarma*
28. *Strīlakṣalakṣaṇa*
29. *Puruṣalakṣaṇa*
30. *Hayalakṣaṇa*
31. *Gajalakṣaṇa*
32. *Golakṣaṇa*
33. *Kukkuṭalakṣaṇa*
34. *Meṣalakṣaṇa*
35. *Chakralakṣaṇa*
36. *Chhatralakṣaṇa*
37. *Daṇḍalakṣaṇa*
38. *Asilakṣaṇa*
39. *Maṇilakṣaṇa*
40. *Kākiṇīlakṣaṇa*
41. *Charmalakṣaṇa*
42. *Chandracharita*
43. *Sūracharita*
44. *Rāhucharita*
45. *Grahacharita*
46. *Śūtrākāra*
47. *Dūtākāra*
48. *Vidyāgatam*
49. *Mantragatam*
50. *Rahasyagatam*
51. *Chāram*
52. *Pratichāram*
53. *Vyūha*
54. *Prativyūha*]
55. *Skandhāvāranyāsa*
56. *Nagarayāna*
57. *Vāstumāna*
58. *Nagaraniveśa*
59. *Vāstuniveśa*
60. *Iṣvastra*
61. *Tattvapravāda*
62. *Aśvaśikṣā*

1. The list was brought to my notice by Śrī Brij Narain Sharma, M.A., Research Scholar, Delhi University.

63. *Hastiśikṣā*
64. *Maṇiśikṣā*
65. *Dhanurveda*
66. *Hiraṇyavāda*
67. *Suvarṇavāda*
68. *Maṇivāda*
69. *Bāhuyuddha*
70. *Daṇḍayuddha*
71. *Muṣṭiyuddha*
72. *Asthiyuddha*
73. *Yuddha*
74. *Niyuddha*
75. *Yuddhaniyuddha*
76. *Sūtrakrīḍā*
77. *Vartakrīḍā*
78. *Vāhyakrīḍā*
79. *Nālikākrīḍā*
80. *Patrachchhedya*
81. *Kaṭakachchhedya*
82. *Prastarachchhedya*
83. *Sajīva-Nirjīva*
84. *Śakunaruta*

The number of subjects given here could have been easily reduced, had Haribhadra liked to group them scientifically. Siddharṣi Sūri mentions sixteen subjects and gives interesting details about political science, astrology, *nara-nārilakṣana*, *nimitta-śāstra*, and *khanyavāda*.[2] The *Prabhāvakacharīta* names the 64 *kalās*.

2. See my paper in the *Marubhāratī* on "Education as described by Siddharṣi Sūri," Vol. VII.

CHAPTER XXVI

ECONOMIC CONDITION

In the heyday of their glory, the Chauhāns ruled over almost the whole of Rājasthān, the modern centrally administered area of Delhi, and the Ambālā Division of the Punjāb. Large parts of this vast tract were, as now, covered by the inhospitable Thār Desert; others either irrigated by the rivers Yamunā, Chambal and Banās or receiving better rainfall must naturally have been more populous. There may have been also more water in the Sarasvatī basin than at present.

Towns. In the Chauhān dominions, as elsewhere in India, towns grew up round forts, courts, sacred sites, and points of strategic and commercial importance. Ajayameru, Nāḍol, Raṇthambhor, Jālor and Sāmbhar were not only capitals of important kingdoms and chiefships but also excellent places for offensive and defensive military actions. Satyapura, Kanyānayana, Bhīnmāl, Phalavardhikā, and Ābū were sacred sites, though the last one of these had also considerable strategic importance. Tabarhindah, Āsikā (Hānsī), Sunām, Sarasvatī (Sirsā), and Kohrām owed their importance to being places of defence and refuge on the route from north-western India to Ajayameru.[1] Delhi was the gateway to Madhyadeśa and Nāgapura (Nāgor) commanded the route to the riches of Sapādalakṣa and Mārwār.

Of other towns and villages whose location can reasonably be determined, we have listed more than 125 in the Appendix to this chapter. Many more perhaps lie buried under the shifting sands of the Thār Desert, many have indistinguishably changed their names, and not a few have been deserted on account of inexplicable changes in climatic conditions.[2]

1. *TF.*, p. 177.

2. The Jaisalmer area had better rainfall and more population according to all the historical and semi-historical accounts at our disposal. Various explanations have been given for a change in the climate of Sindh. They can apply equally to western Rājasthān, the neighbour of Sindh.

We do not know the exact plan on which these towns were built, though a general idea can be formed on the basis of the poetic descriptions in the *Pṛthvīrājavijaya*, the *Prabhāvakacharita*, the *Upamitibhavaprapañchakathā* and other literary works of Rājasthān and adjoining areas. The *Prabhāvakacharita* tells us that the fort of Ajmer was surrounded by a belt of thorn trees and bushes. From the *Pṛthvīrājavijaya* we learn that it was full of temples, multi-storeyed houses, step-wells, tanks and *prapās*.[3] From the *Upamitibhavaprapañchakathā* and other literary sources we find that most big towns had the following features[4] :—

(1) A *prākāra* or high wall surrounding the town which was buttressed by mounds of mud (*vapra*) on both sides.

(2) A *mahāparikhā* or moat deep and broad enough to obstruct the enemy and not unoften full of crocodiles and alligators.

(3) Deep waterless wells or pits near the *prākāra* into which the unwary enemy would fall while marching in.

(4) Two wide roads or *mahārājamārgas* which ran from one direction to the other and crossed each other at the centre of the city.

(5) Smaller roads called *rathyās* and *mahārathyās* branching off *mahārājamārgas*.

(6) Division of big towns into *pāṭakas* or wards (?) with their own *chatuṣkas* (quadrangles) and *trikas* (triangles).

(7) Markets full of commodities from various parts of the country.

(8) Magnificent temples and buildings, tanks, wells, *prapās* and parks.

None of the *kāvyas* speaks of the squalor of the towns, though this could not have been entirely absent. To the poet the town he describes is generally another Amarāvatī, the capital of Indra, whatever its actual features may have been. But Yuan Chwang who visited India in the seventh century speaks of our narrow and tortuous thoroughfares, and also of the poor fishermen, butchers, scavengers, public performers and executioners who had to live outside the city walls.[5] Ruling

3. See canto V, verses 119-190.
4. *Upamitibhavaprapañchā*, *pp*. 7, 105, 137, 312, 385. See along the *Tilakamañjarī* of Dhanapāla for the description of Ayodhyā.
5. *Buddhist Records of the Western World*, I. pp. 73-4.

chiefs lived in splendid palaces, with many courtyards.[6] The houses of the wealthy residents of a city may also have been good enough. But there is little either in literary or technical literature of the period to indicate that any one was mindful of the needs of the depressed classes.

Products. We have no direct source of information about the products of the Chauhān dominions. But from the *Āin-i-Akbarī* we learn that the *subāh* of Ajmer (which practically covered the same area as Sapādalakṣa, if the Tomara territories be excepted) produced *jawār bājra* and *moṭh* in summer.[7] The spring crop was inconsiderable. The conditions during the Chauhān rule probably were not different. In the Kurukṣetra and Delhi area there must have been besides crops of wheat, sugarcane, rice, *rājamāṣa, mudga,* and cumin.[8] From this area probably came much of the fruit consumed in the Chauhān dominions.

Of non-agricultural products, salt from the Sāmbhar lake enriched the Chauhāns of Sapādalakṣa[9] whose descendants and clansmen habitually use for their rulers the word, *Sambharī-nātha, i.e.*, the lords of Śākambharī, even during periods when Sāmbhar had passed into the hands of the Muslims. There might have been copper in the Maṇḍalgarh district of Mewāṛ and various parts of Jodhpur and Bīkāner divisions of Rājasthān where we have unmistakable signs of old workings.[10] Rājasthān produced also lead and zinc and fine building stone, of which marble, Jaisalmer stone, and red sandstone have been very extensively used from old times and produced the wonderful Dilwāra temples, the college of Vigraharāja IV at Ajmer, and numerous other splendid buildings which once studded the Chauhān dominions and still impress the spectator with their grandeur. Of pastoral products, Rājasthān produced wool, camel hair, ghee, milk and milk products. Pasturage, it seems,

6. See the *Upamitibhavaprapañchakathā*, pp. 8-9. 34-5. For earlier accounts one may consult Bāṇa's *Harṣacharita*.

7. II. p. 267.

8. *Harṣacharita*, Nirṇayasāgar edition, pp. 94-96.

9. *PV.*, IV, vv. 82-85.

10. See Moreland's *India at the death of Akbar*, p. 149; G. H. Ojha, *History of Jodhpur*, I, p. 8, and *History of Bīkaner*, I, pp. 15-16.

was in those days almost as important an industry for Sapādalakṣa, Haritānaka (Hariānā) and Kurukṣetra as agriculture.

Commerce. If we put together the information gleaned from the inscriptions of Vigraharāja II of Śākambharī, Kelhaṇa of Nāḍol, Udayasiṁha of Jālor and Mammaṭa of Hastikuṇḍī, we find that Rājasthān had a good trade in wheat, *mudga*, resin, oil, betel leaves, *kirāḍua*,[11] salt and horses, the latter of which were imported from Uttarāpatha.[12] The *Lekhapaddhati* provides evidence of some trade in slaves in the neighbouring kingdom of Gujarāt.[13] Alhaṇadeva's inscription of V. 1205 shows *Mahārājaputra* Sāhaṇapāladeva of Nāḍol granting the *kuṭumbikas* Sohiya, Asarama etc. to the god Tripuruṣadeva, along with their sons and grandsons.[14] Their condition, as pointed out by us elsewhere, is comparable to that of the Russian serfs and may have been worse even,[15] if they could be disposed of in this manner. Some idea of the trade and commerce carried within the dominions can be had also from the mention of merchants in *kāṁsya*, *kuṅkuma*, *mañjiṣtha*, betel leaves and cloth; and we read also of *vaṇajārakas*, distillers and *buṇakaras* (weavers) in our inscriptions.[16]

But for further details about the way the traders went about making money we have to consult literary works like the *Upamitibhavaprapañchakathā* which show merchants storing cereals, cotton, salt and wool, buying lac, trading in jaggery, pressing oil, manufacturing charcoal, cutting down forests, telling lies, and cheating their customers by using false weights and measures. For greater gain they sent out caravans of bullock-carts, camels, and asses, traded in ivory, alchemic preparations and other articles prohibited by the Jaina canon, and chartered boats to carry their merchandise. In some the lust for money could be

11. Spices, pulses etc.
12. See the Harṣa inscription, *EI*, II, pp. 119 ff.
13. See pp. 24-27.
14. See Appendix G (*iii*), line 20 for the inscription.
15. *Marubhāratī*, VI. Pt. 2.
16. See specially Kirāḍū inscription of Alhaṇa, *EI*, XI, pp. 43 ff, Nāḍol inscription of Rāyapāla, *ibid.*, pp. 37ff. *Bombay Gazetteer*, I, Pt. 1, Inscription No. XV, p. 485.

even so great that they descended to mean things like traffic in women and eunuchs; and even more lucrative than all these could be a sea-voyage to adjoining countries.[17] From the realistic way these voyages are described it appears that the Rājasthānīs knew not only their desert sea but also the wide open seas, with their storms and perils, crossing which one reached distant lands and made money out of articles of practically no value in their own country.[18]

Other Professions. Professional classes, other than those already noticed above, that we find mentioned in our early historical sources, epigraphic and literary, are the *bhaṭṭalokas* (soldiers), scribes, priests, teachers, astrologers, workers in stone, bards, hunters, scavengers, and butchers.[19] A much longer list is to be found in the late *Kānhaḍadeprabandha*, according to which the city of Jālor besides having the four "high castes" had 18 *varṇas*.[20] As among these so-called *varṇas* enumerated there we find shoemakers, carpenters, printers of cloths and tailors, it is obvious that they are the well-known 18 *śreṇis* of our ancient times, which included, besides these, workers in metal, ivory workers, braziers, potters, jewellers, fisher folk, caravan traders, oilmillers, rush workers and basket makers, money lenders, garland makers, flower sellers, and barbers.[21] We have already referred about to their meetings in *Deśīs* and transacting their own affairs. In the *Jātakas* robbers and freebooters also are mentioned as a *śrenis*.[22] Though they may not have been so organised in our period, highway robbery (*sāhasa*) could not have been a wholly debarred means of making money, if we might put any reliance on the following verse of the *Śārṅgadhara-paddhati*[23]:—

17. See the *Upamitibhavaprapañchakatha*, pp. 38, 427, 500, 554. For further details see my paper, "Economic conditions as depicted in the *Upamiti*," in the *Marubhāratī*, Vol VII.

18. The *Kānhaḍadeprabandha* in its description of Jālor speaks of its *vaṇiks* who traded with other countries and of its bazars where came foreign goods by land as well as water (*Khaṇḍa* IV, vv. 12-13).

19. See the Bījāpur inscription of Mammaṭa.

20. *Khaṇḍa* IV, vv. 9-20.

21. See Dr. R. C. Majumdar's *Corporate Life in Ancient India*; *Jātaka*, VI, 22. The स्कन्दपुराण also mentions 18 *Prakṛtis*.

22. Majumdār, *op. cit.*

23. verse 1446, Peterson's edition.

dhanamastīti vāṇijyaṁ kiñchidastīti karṣanam
sevā na kiñchidastīti nāhamasmīti sāhasam

Rates of Interest

We have some information about the rates of interest. A Bhīnmāl inscription of V. 1262, for instance, tells us that 40 *drammas* put in the treasury of Jagatsvāmin produced yearly 12 *drammas* as interest.[24] This gives the very high rate of 30% per annum. Another Bhīnmāl inscription, dated in the Vikrama year 1306, shows that the following articles could be had for the annual interest on 40 *drammas*:[25]

Wheat	2 *seis*	(32 *pāilīs* according to the *Gaṇitasāra*; 40 according to Dr. D. R. Bhandarkar)
Mūng	1 *maṇa*	(4 *pāilīs* according to the *Gaṇitasāra*, ; 5 according to Dr. D.R. Bhandarkar).
Chokhā (Rice)	2 *pāilīs*	
Ghee	8½ *kalaśa*	
Articles for worship	7 *drammas* in value	

According to the same record, the following could be had for the interest on 15 *drammas*:—

Wheat	25 *pāilīs*
Mung	3 *pāilīs*
Chokhā (Rice)	2 *dramnas*
Articles of worship	2 *drammas* in value

These tables put together show that the rate of interest was 33%. A Jālor inscription of V. 1323 mentions ½ *dramma* as the monthly interest on 50 *drammas*[26] In this case the rate of interest is 12%. The great discrepancy between the two rates might

24. *Bombay Gazetteer*, I, Pt. 1, Inscription No. VII, p. 474.
25. *EI*, XI, p. 56f.
26. *Jain Inscriptions*, II, No. 363.

have been partly a local matter, money being easier to obtain at the Sonigarā capital than at Bhīnmāl. Partly perhaps the rate at Bhīnmāl was put high to encourage donations. A probable reason could also be the difference in the political conditions of V. 1306 and V. 1325. Balban's activity in Mālwā about 1250 A.D. might have reacted unfavourably on the money market in the kingdom of Jālor, which had only a few years earlier experienced an invasion by Iltutmish. Seventeen years later the conditions were better. Chāchigadeva was firmly seated on the throne and Balban, busy with his own affairs, perhaps appeared to the popular mind as no great danger to the Chauhān kingdom. But the Ābū inscription of Bhaila of Gunḍoch, V. 1288, also shows the interest to have been 30%.[27] An Arāsaṇa Jaina Inscription of V. 1344 gives the same rate,[28] inclining us once again to the view that the rate of interest revealed by the Jālor inscription of V.1323 is something exceptional,[29] and that the rate of interest actually given by most bankers was not far removed from 30% per annum.

Coinage.

The chief coins known for our area are *drammas*, *viṁśopakas*, *Lohadiyās*, *rūpakas*, *raupya-tankas*, *jītals*, *dināras* and *lo*.

Drama is the Sanskritised form of the Greek word *drachma*. The silver *drammas* "bearing Ajayadeva's *mudrā*" mentioned in the Dhoḍ Inscription of V. 1228, have generally been identified with the silver *Ajayapriya-rūpakas* described in the *Pṛthvīrāja-vijaya* as the issues of Ajayadeva, the founder of Ajmer.[30]. This

27. 16 *drammas* produced 8 *viṁśopakas* per mensem, *i.e.*, 96 *viṁśopakas* per year. If a *viṁśopaka* be regarded as 1/20 of a *dramma*, the interest comes to 30%. If it be equated with *bīsā*, the interest would be 6% which is too low.

28. This inscription gives 3 *drammas* as interest per mensem, on 120 *drammas*, i.e. 30 *drammas* per cent per annum.

29. Another inscription of the same place and referring to the same temple puts the rate of interest at 10%. The Mahāvīra temple thus appears to have given a very low rate of interest to its depositors. Its credit was high and with the rich Jain community to patronise it, it had no need of bringing in fresh deposits by promising high rates of interest.

30. *PV*, V, vv. 87-88.

may be so; but it is also not unlikely that the *drammas* may have been coins of a higher denomination than the *rūpakas*, though belonging to the same series.[31] Reference has already been made to the silver *rūpakas* issued by Ajayadeva's queen Somalekhā.[32] Rapson suggested that these coins might have been issued by the queen, while she acted as a regent for her son, after Ajayadeva's death.[33] But the *Pṛthvīrājavijaya* hints at no regency. Not only does the description of the coins precede that of Arṇorāja's birth, but Arṇorāja is described also as *dorvīryasaṁhatanaya*[34] at the time of his accession. In other words he was in the prime of life at the time of his father's death or abdication.[35] We have described above the coins of Someśvara and Pṛthvīrāja III and need not repeat the description here.

Vīsalapriya drammas were current in the areas which recognised the overlordship of the Chaulukyas of Gujarāt and may be presumed to have been issued by the Vāghela ruler, Vīsaladeva (c. 1244-1262 A.D.). A *raukma* variety of these is mentioned in a Bhīnmāl inscription of V. 1345.[36] But as the *Bṛhatkalpa-bhāṣya* of Kṣemakīrti, which was composed only 13 years earlier, i.e. in V. 1332, states that "coins are of silver too, for instance the *dramma* of Bhillamāla" (*rūpamayaṁ vā nāṇakaṁ bhavati yathā Bhillamāle drammaḥ*),[37] I am not sure whether the actual reading of the Bhillamāla inscription is not *raukya*.

Another silver coin of this area was the *pāruttha dramma*. Asked by the Sultān to give 36 lacs of *drammas*, Udayasiṁha's envoy, Bāpaḍa, is reported to have said, "We do not know *drammas*. We shall give you *pād(r) uthakas*."[38] In the *Kharatara-gachchhapaṭṭāvalī* of Jinapāla, we find Naravarman of Mālwā

31. See below, p. 340.
32. See above, p. 46-47.
33. *JNSI*, XVII, Pt. 2, p. 72.
34. v. 192, vv. 90-1.
35. Almost immediately after his accession he appears to have faced a Muslim invasion and repulsed it. For its details see above.
36. *Bombay Gazetteer*, I, Pt. 1, p. 488.
37. Cited *JNSI*, XIV, p. 109.
38. *Purātanaprabandhasaṅgraha*, p. 52.

offering 300,000 *Pāruttha drammas* or alternatively three villages to Jinavallabha Sūri, and the latter accepting only 2 *pāruttha drammas* daily from the customs house of Chitore for the maintenance of the two *Kharatara* temples at Chitore.[39] The *Lekhapaddhati* mentions the *pārutthaka* silver coins minted at Bhillamāla.[40] The *Purātanaprabandhasaṅgraha* states that one *pārutthaka* equalled 8 *drammas*.[41]

Drammas are very often mentioned also without being specified as *Ajayapriya*, *Vīsalapriya* or *pāruttha*. The Harṣa Stone Inscription of Vigraharāja II (V. 1030), Alhaṇadeva's inscription of V. 1205 'Kelhaṇa's Nāḍlāi Inscription of V. 1228, Kaṭukarāja's inscription of V. 1172, and Bhīnmāl inscription of V. 1305 are only a few of the numerous records attesting to the continued use of the *drammas* in our area, almost throughout our period.[42]

Later portions of the *Kharataragachchhapaṭṭāvalī* mention *dvivallaka drammas* or coins with a mixture of two *wālas* or 6 *rattis* of base metal.[43] But as these are mostly mentioned in connection with *yātrās* in Surāṣṭra and adjoining areas, it is not certain whether they were current coins also for Rājasthān.

In the *dramma* series, we have also the *viṁśopakas*, which according to Dr. D. R. Bhandarkar was a copper piece, one twentieth in value of a *dramma*.[44] The view appears to be correct, even though an indication or two make it a bit uncertain.[45]

39. *IHQ*, XXVI, p. 224.

40. pp. 34, 43.

41. p. 53.

42. Earlier still the Ādivarāha *drammas* of Bhoja might have been used in Rājasthān. See also Allaṭa's inscription of V. 1010 for the use of *drammas* and *rūpakas* in Mewār (Ratna Chandra Agrawal, *JNSI*, XVII, p. 82)

43. *JNSI*, XVII, pt. 2, p. 73, footnote 3.

44. *Carmichael Lectures*, p. 208.

45. On the side of uncertainty is to be quoted the Dandhapur inscription of v. 1233. "If a *viṁśopaka* was," says Sri R. C. Agrawal, "1/20 of a *dramma* it (the gift of 36 *viṁśopakas*) could well have been expressed as 1 *dramma* and 16 *viṁśopakas*. But the *praśastikāra* does not do so." For the other side see the Gundoch inscription of V. 1288. The rate of interest, the usual 30%, indicates its value as 1/20 *dramma*.

Nor do we know its exact relation to another coin, the *rūpaka*, current in Rājasthān in the early tenth century A. D., and mentioned also in a number of inscriptions.[46] From the charge of one *dramma* on the sale of an elephant and 2 *rūpakas* on that of a horse in the Ahāṛ Sāraṇeśvar temple-inscription, it is, however, obvious that not only was a *rūpaka* different from a *dramma* but also a coin of lower value.[47] A coin called *lohaṭika* is mentioned in Alhaṇdeva's inscription of V. 1205.[48] *Lo* of Bhinmāl inscriptions, I think, stands for *lohaṭika*.[49]

A fairly good idea of the comparative value of some of these coins can be had on the basis of the following table from the commentary on the *Gaṇitasāra* of Śrīdhara published by Dr. B. J. Sandesara[50]: —

5 *cowries*	= 1 *pāvisā*[51]
4 *pāvīsa*	= 1 *bīsā*
5 *bīsā*	= 1 *Lohaṭika*
4 *Lohaṭika*	= 1 *rūā* (*rūpaka*)
5 *rūpaka*	= 1 *dramma*

Dr. Sandesara regards the *bīsa* of this series as *viṁśopaka* of our epigraphs. But this is rather doubtful, considering specially the facts considered in our footnotes No. 26 and 144 above. If Dr. Bhandarkar's view be correct, the value of a *viṁśopaka* should be the same as that of *lohaṭika*.

Dīnāras are mentioned in the *Upamitibhavaprapañchakathā*.[52] The gold *dīnāra* probably weighed about 3/4 *tola*.[53] We read

46. In the *Upamitibhavaprapañchakathā*, *rūpaka* appears to have been the coin most used. For epigraphic references see Allaṭa's inscription of V. 1010, Hathūṇḍī inscription of V. 1053, Nāḍol Grant of V. 1213 etc.

47. Referred to also as Allaṭa's inscription in this chapter (*IA*, XXXIX, pp. 186 ff).

48. See Appendix G. (*iii*) line 1 for the inscription.

49. *Bombay Gazetteer*, I, Pt. I, Bhīnmāl inscriptions, No. VIII and XVI.

50. *JNSI*, VIII Pt. 2, 138 ff.

51. Perhaps *pāvisā* is mentioned also in the first line of Alhaṇa's inscription of V. 1205 (?)

52. page 553.

53. Altekar, *Gupta-Vākāṭaka Age*, p. 360. But Pheru makes a *dīnāra* a gold coin of 4 *māsakas*, verse 61.

also of silver *tankas* and *jīthals* in the later portion of the *Kharataragachchhapaṭṭāvalī*, and these from the references there can be shown to have passed current not only in the areas of Rājasthān conquered by the Muslims but also in the areas that remained under the Rājpūts.[54] The standard weight of a silver *ṭanka* was 172. 8 grs.[55] A *jītal* was 1/64 of a *ṭanka*. We read also of a *hemaṭanka*.[56] According to Pheru, these gold coins were of various weights, ranging from 1 to 100 *tolās*, while the silver *ṭanka* was of 1 *tolā* only.

The value of these coins must naturally have differed according to the amount of silver, gold or any other metal they had. The ordinary *dramma*, weighing 65 grs. of silver, must have been worth 6 annas or so; and the billon *drammas* of Someśvara and Pṛthvīrāja III, weighing about 53 grs., could have been only lower in value than 6 annas. A *rūpaka* would in that case, according to the table from the *Gaṇitasāra* quoted above, be worth only 1½ annas. Coins lower in value than a *rūpaka* must have been in baser metal or with a large admixture of it. If we rely on the *Bṛhaspatismṛti*, silver has to be regarded as only three times dearer than copper. But this goes against the evidence of practically all the other *Smṛitis* and also the *Śukranītisāra*, the composition of which is not far removed from our period. According to these the ratio between the prices of silver and copper appears to have varied between 1 : 60 and 1 : 80.[57] The *lohaṭika* may have been a fair-sized copper coin, the name of which was probably derived not from *loha* or iron, a metal extremely unsuitable for purposes of currency, but from some locality like Lohaḍ. If we put the price of *lohaṭika* as 1½ pice, the *bīsā*, if a coin at all, must have been of the size of a pie. Lower transactions may have been, as during my school days in Rājasthān, carried on in *cowries*, 5 of which were called a *pāvisā*.

The assaying of coins was a common practice. A Dhoḍ in-

54. See p. 97.

55. Habibullah, *Foundation of Muslim Rule in India*, p. 264.

56. *Kharataragachchhapaṭṭāvalī*, pp. 74, 75. Its weight was probably the same as that of the silver *ṭanka*. See Habibullah, *op. cit.*

57. Bhandarkar's view based on the *Bṛhaspatismṛti* has rightly been criticised by Dr. A.S. Altekar in his paper, "Relative Prices of Metals and Coins in Ancient India", *JNSI*, II, pp. 1-14.

scription of V. 1228 speaks of 16 *drammas*, bearing the *mudrā* of Ajayadeva, being tested before their acceptance as the price of a house.[58] The *Lekhapaddhati* records very often its transactions in *triparīkṣita drammas*,[59] even though it is known from the *Dravyaparīkṣā* of Pheru that coins of the period followed a certain well-known standard. *Varṇamālikās* prepared to test the purity of silver and gold are described by Pheru.[60] According to the *Pāṭigaṇita* of Śrīdhara, these "*varṇamālikās* were prepared by affixing small pieces of gold of two *māṣakas* at one end of each needle", and the gold increased in purity with each succeeding needle, till it reached the highest standard called *solahbānī*. In Pheru's *Dravyaparīkṣā*, the best gold called *mahākanaka* is of the *barahbānī* standard.[61]

Weights and Measures. The Bījāpur Inscription of the Rāṣṭrakūṭas, Dhavala and Bālāprasāda, mentions *pala*, *karṣa*, *āḍhaka*, *droṇa* and *kalaśa*; and of these some are mentioned also in our Chauhān inscriptions, which mention, besides, *Kumāra-droṇa* and *droṇī*.[62] From the scheme of weights in the *Śārṅgadhara-saṁhitā*, given below as an appendix, it will be seen that 1 *karṣa* equalled 96 *raktikās*. In other words it was the representative of the modern *tolā*. Of *karṣas* a *pala* had four and an *āḍhaka* 256. 64 *palas* equalled an *āḍhaka*. 4 *āḍhakas* formed 1 *droṇa* or *kalaśa* and 1 *droṇī* had 4 *droṇas*. I am not sure about the meaning of a *kumāra-droṇa*. All that can be stated is that it was probably a bigger measure than a *droṇa*.[63]

Another system, which forms probably the basis of that now in use in Rājasthān, was found at Nāḍlāī and Bhīnmāl, Dr. D.R. Bhandarkar's enquiries in Goḍwād yielded the following scheme[64]:—

58. Dr. G. H. Ojha's transcript.
59. pp. 34, 43 etc.
60. Verses 31-7.
61. Verse 38.
62. See Alhana's inscription of V. 1205, Appendix G (*iii*).
63. *Ibid.*, lines 8 and 15.
64. *EI.*, XI., p. 41.

4 *pāilā* = 1 *pāilī*	4 *maṇā* = 1 *sei*
5 *pāilī* = 1 *maṇā*	2 *seī* = 1 *man*

In the *Gaṇitasāra* of Śrīdhara, however, we find the scheme given a little differently as follows[65]:—

4 *pāvala* = 1 *pālī*	12 *maṇā* = 1 *padaka*
4 *pālī* = 1 *maṇā*	4 *padaka* = 1 *hārī*
4 *maṇā* = 1 *seī*	4 *hārī* = 1 *mānī*

It is not unlikely that this might have been the actual scheme of weights for cereals in the Chauhān dominions.[66]

Of measures of length and space, we have even less of direct information, because our land-grants refer to villages, fields and shops without giving their exact dimensions. It is deemed sufficient, if the adjoining houses etc. are mentioned. A Sāṇḍerāv inscription of V. 1221 fortunately uses the word, *hael*,[67] which is generally taken to mean a piece of land that could be cultivated in a single day by a single plough. A copper plate inscription of Bhīmadeva II of Gujarāt equates nine *haels* with four *viśopakas*.[68] Sri C. D. Dalal, the editor of the *Lekhapaddhati*, conjecturally puts *viśopaka* as equal to a *bīghā*.[69] The *Gaṇitasāra*, however, gives a *halavāa* as equal to 483840 *yavas*, i.e. a length not much more than ⅓ of a *krośa*.[70]

Prices of commodities. With some idea of weights and measures, though it must be confessed to be rather hazy and incomplete, we can next proceed to discuss the prices of commodities. The fact that a house could be bought for 16 *dramma* shows sufficiently the high purchasing power of a *dramma* and the comparative cheapness of other commodities.[71] From the Bhīnmāl Inscription of Udayasiṁha, V. 1306, which we referred to while dealing with the rate of interest in the Chauhān dominions, it is obvious that for 1 *dramma*, accruing as interest, one

65. *JNSI*, VIII, pp. 138 ff.

66. Chauhān dominions were not only adjacent to Gujarāt from where we have Śrīdhara's *Gaṇitasāra*, but parts of it at times acknowledged Chalukya sovereignty. We should remember also the nearness of the *Gaṇitasāra* to the period we are dealing with.

67. *EI*, XI, p. 47.

68. *Historical Inscriptions of Gujarāt*, Pt. 2, p. 79.

69. p. 106.

70. *JNSI*, VIII, Pt. 2, pp. 138 ff.

71. See the Dhoḍ inscription of V. 1228.

could buy at Bhīnmāl either 8⅓ *pāilīs* of wheat 1 *pāilī* of *mūng*, ⅔ *pāilīs* of rice, and ⅔ *kalaśas* of *ghī* or 6-6/19 *pāilīs* of wheat, 15/19 *pāilīs* of *mūng*, 6/19 *pāilīs* of rice and 1-13/30 *kalaśas* of *ghī*. As 1 *pāilī* would according to the *Gaṇitasāra* be equal to the modern 1 standard seer and 10 *chhaṭāks*, one could easily feed a number of people with 1 *dramma*.[72] The excess of cereals and pulse under the first alternative, obviously, must be due to the excess of *ghī* in the other; and *ghī* at Bhīnmāl does not appear to have been cheap.[73] The Sāṇḍerāv Stone Inscription, V. 1221, of Kelhaṇa's reign indicates that 1 *dramma* could purchase one *hāel* of *yugandharī*, i.e., the *jawār* millet. Half a *dramma* from a customs house could suffice to celebrate an annual festival of Śrī Mahāvīradeva in the village Ghanghāṇakapadra.[74]

Some idea of prices towards the end of our period can be had also from the following table in Baranī's *Tārīkh-ī Firoz-shāhī*[75]:—

Wheat	per *man*	7½ *jītals*
Barley	,,	4 ,,
Rice, in husk	,,	5 ,,
Māsh	,,	5 ,,
Gram	,,	5 ,,
Moṭh	,,	3 ,,
Sugar	per seer	1½ ,,
Brown sugar (Gur)	,,	½ ,,
Ghī	2½ seers	1 ,,
Oil of sesamum	3 seers	1 ,,
Salt	2½ *mans*	5 ,,

As a *jītal* was nearly worth 1 pice and a *man* of Alāuddīn's was equal to 28.1 lbs., the value of money must have been much greater than it is today ; and this cheapness could not have been confined to Delhi alone.

General economic condition. We conclude the chapter with a few words about the general economic condition of the various

72. The amount comes to 16 standard *seers* and 4 *chhaṭāks* of the present day.

73. According to these tables 1 *kalaśa* of *ghī* could buy approximately 3 *pāilīs* of wheat, 2/3 *pāilīs* of *mūng* and 1/2 *pāilī* of rice.

74. Jinavijayajī, *Jaina Inscriptions*, No. 429.

75. *ED.*, III, p. 192, Alāuddīn's reign.

classes in the Chauhān dominions. The rulers of Sapādalakṣa were rich, largely on account of the revenue from the Salt Lake of Sāmbhar. The price of salt in places like Delhi was as high as 2 *jītals* per *man*. Price of barley for the same amount was 4 *jītals*.[76] The *digvijayins* Vigraharāja II, Vigraharāja IV and Pṛthvīrāja III must have enriched themselves as well as their kingdom with the booty captured during their numerous raids and conquests. Even their weak descendant, Govinda of Raṇthambhor was, after Ajmer had been well plundered by the Muslims, rich enough to present to Qutbuddīn four *kharbūzas*, the price of one of which sufficed to build a big mosque at Herāt.[77] Hammīra amassed large sums by raiding the territories of his neighbours and bringing to Raṇthambhor vast wealth which he spent in *koṭihomas* and in his fight againt the Khaljīs. But that *digvijayas* by themselves were an undependable source of revenue was proved by his last days, when he continued fighting against Alāuddīn, and with his treasury empty had to adopt many stringent and highly unpopular measures to raise money for himself and his army.

Trade, as now, was a lucrative profession, and that Rājasthānī traders remained very rich, even after some of their money had gone to the Muslim conquerors and raiders, can be seen from the large sums that they spent on religious occasions. In V. 1326, for instance, when the *Kharatara āchārya*, Jineśvara Sūri, went on a pilgrimage to Śatruñjaya, the *saṅgha* accompanying him accepted the dignities of Indra, *mantrin*, *bhāṇḍāgārika*, *pratihāra* etc. by paying the sums noted below[78]:—

Name of the tīrtha	*Money given for the dignities*
Tāraṇa	3,000 *drammas*
Vījāpura	3,000 *drammas*
Stambhanaka	3,000 *drammas*
Śatruñjaya	17,000 *drammas*
Ujjayanta	7,097 *drammas*

76. See the table from the *Tārikh-i-Firozshāhī* quoted above.
77. See above, p. 118.
78. *KP*. pp. 52-3.

Śatruñjaya temple		20,000 *drammas*
Ujjayanta temple		17,000 *drammas*
	Total	79,097 *drammas*

In normal times the agriculturist had enough to eat. The land did not suffer from over-population. So every one had land enough to cultivate and produce food, if he took to farming. But the agriculturist probably was, as now, a victim of usurers who charged high rates of interest. In periods of famine his lot was pitiable. After paying various cesses, taxes and religious tithes, he probably had not much left to face such dire calamities, the occurrence of which is a normal feature of *devamātṛka* lands.[79] On such occasions hundreds sold either themselves or their children into slavery and sometimes even committed suicide by drowning themselves in rivers to escape the pangs of hunger. In c. 1294 A.D. large numbers of people from Sapādalakṣa reached Delhi and choked the Yamunā with their dead bodies.[80] Another equally bad famine occurred in the Vikrama years 1312-1315 (1255-1258 A.D.). The *Kharataraga-chchhapaṭṭāvalī* records a third famine in V. 1377, but we are not sure whether it spread also to Rājasthān.[81] But the worst of these famines, though falling a little outside our period, was the one of V. 1392 which compelled people not merely to eat hides and carcasses of animals but also human flesh.[82] The generosity of merchant princes like Jagaḍu[83] could only partially relieve the misery brought about by these visitations. Neither Rājasthān nor any other part of India had till

79. One may read in this connection the following hyperbolic description of Ajmer which is said not to suffer from certain defects which were common to most other towns :—

Sachaurair-daṇḍaka-kṣmāpair-avarṣair-devamātṛkaiḥ /
nirdhanair-bahu-durbhikṣair-durjayaṁ tat purāntaraiḥ //
(*Pṛthvīrājavijaya*, V, 164)

Devamātṛka are the lands that have to depend on the freakish favour of monsoons.

80. *ED.*, III, p. 146.

81. p. 69.

82. *Cambridge History of India*, III, p. 152.

83. See the *Jagaḍucharita*, Canto VI.

then evolved a system of either dealing effectively with them or so building up the financial power of the peasantry that one or two bad seasons might not drive them on to the streets to starve or live on public charity.

APPENDIX L

TOWNS AND VILLAGES OF THE CHAUHAN DOMINIONS

The *Kharataragachchhapaṭṭāvalī* of Jinapāla and his successors gives the following names:—

1. Abohar.[1]
2. Babberaka.[2]
3. Bādalī.[3]
4. Bāhaḍameru.[4]
5. Baraḍiā.
6. Daridreraka.[5]
7. Ḍiṇḍiyānaka.[6]
8. Guḍahā.[7]
9. Jaisalmeru.[8]
10. Jhuñjanu.[9]
11. Karaheṭaka[10]
12. Kāsahrada.[11]
13. Khaṭṭakūpa.[12]
14. Kheṭaka.[13]
15. Koraṇṭaka.[14]
16. Kosavāṇā.[15]

1. In the Ferozepore District, Punjāb. Mentioned also by Ibn Batūta as a flourishing town in his time.

2. Mentioned also in the *Lalitavigraharāja-nāṭaka*. The *Prabandha-chintāmaṇi* calls it Bamberā. Dr. Kielhorn's identification of the town with Bagherā, 47 miles to the south-east of Ajmer, does not appear to be right. It is actually near Jasrāpur (Khetṛī, Jaipur Division, Rājasthān).

3. A village some miles to the north-west of Delhi.

4. Modern Bāṛmer in the Jodhpur Division, Rājasthān. Sometimes called Vāgbhaṭameru also.

5. Modern Dadrewā, a few miles from the Sādulpur station, Northern Railway.

6. Modern Ḍiḍwāṇā in the Jodhpur State. Mentioned also in Bhoja Pratihāra's grant of V. 900.

7. Modern Guḍḍhā near Sāmbhar.

8. Modern Jaisalmer.

9. In the Jaipur Division.

10. Modern Kareḍā in Mewār.

11. Modern Kāyadrān, 4 miles to the north of Kivarlī Station on the Western Railway, Rājasthān.

12. Modern Khāṭu, Jaipur Division.

13. Modern Kheḍ, Jodhpur Division, Rājasthān, 5 miles from Lūnī.

14. Modern Koṛṭā, 16 miles south-west of Saṇḍerāo, Jodhpur Division, Rājasthān.

15. Same as Kosāṇā of the *Rao Jetsi ro Chhanda*.

17. Lāṭahrada.[16]
18. Māṇḍavyapura.[17].
19. Marukoṭṭa.[18]
20. Merṭā.[19]
21. Nānā.[20]
22. Narabhaṭa.[21]
23. Navahara.[22]
24. Palhūpura.[23]
25. Pālī.[24]
26. Puṣkariṇī.[25]
27. Rāmaśayana.[26]
28. Ratnapura.[27]
29. Rohtak.
30. Samyānayana.[28]
31. Siriyāṇaka.[29]
32. Tilapatha.[30]
32a. Vikramapura.[31]

From the Chauhān inscriptions we can add the following:—

33. Ajayapurī.[32]
34. Badarī.[33]
35. Bhaṭuṭṭapadra.[34]
36. Bhaḍeuva.[35]
37. Bhīṭalavāṭaka.[36]
38. Bhṛgukachchha.[37]

16. For location see above.

17. Modern Maṇḍor near Jodhpur. Mentioned as early as V. 984 in Bāuka's inscription and later in the Sūndhā hill inscription.

18. Maroṭ, a little to the north-west of Sāmbhar.

19. In Jodhpur Division.

20. On the Western Railway Jodhpur Division, Rājasthān.

21. Modern Narhaḍ, Near Pilani, Jaipur Division, ājasthan. Find spot of Vigraharāja IV's inscription of V. 1218. For a description of the site read my paper on 'Narhaḍ' in the *Marubhāratī*, VI, part 3, pp. 2-15.

22. Modern Nohar, Bīkāner Division, Rājasthān.

23. Pallū, a small village now in the Bikāner Division, Rājasthān.

24. In Jodhpur Division. Had a strong fort. Mentioned also in Tāj-ul-Ma-āsīr (*ED.*, II, pp. 229-230.)

25. Modern Pokaraṇ in Jodhpur Division.

26. Modern Rāmsen in Jodhpur Division. Mentioned also in the Sūndhā inscription.

27. Modern Ratanpur in the Jodhpur Division. Mentioned also in the Sūndhā inscription.

28. Modern Siwāṇā in the Jodhpur Division.

29. Modern Sirāṇa in western Marwar.

30. Modern Tilpat.

31. Modern Bīkampur in the old Jaisalmer State.

32. Modern (Pokaran)-Phalodi in the Jodhpur Division.

33. Probably Borlī, 8 miles north of Nāḍlāī.

34. 10 miles south of Bālī, Jodhpur Division. Is now known as Bhaṭūnd.

35. Modern Baḍavā, 5 miles south-west of Lālrāi.

36. In Nāḍol territory.

37. Modern Broach in the Bombay Presidency. Was the capital of Śaṅkha and probably also of Bhartṛavaḍḍha II.

39. Būḍhapatra.[38]
40. Chhatradhārā.[39]
41. Chhechhaḍiya.[40]
42. Dārijī.[41]
43. Devasūri.[42]
44. Dhālop.[43]
45. Dhavagartā.[44]
46. Dhavalapurī.[45]
47. Ghoṇṭāvārṣikā.[46]
48. Haravandāra.[47]
49. Jayapura.[48]
50. Jhamarā.[49]
51. Kaṇasuvam.[50]
52. Kaṇhapallikā.[51]
53. Kardamakhātaka.[52]
54. Kavilāḍā.[53]
55. Kelikūpaka.[54]
56. Kirāṭakuja or Kirāṭakūpa.[55]
57. Lālrāi.[56]
58. Madaḍa.[57]
59. Maddaḍī.[58]
60. Madrapuriaka.[59]
61. Mahānāla.[60]
62. Maṅgalānaka.[61]
63. Mauvaḍī.[62]
64. Mayūrapadra.[63]
65. Medramchā.[64]

38. Modern Burtrā in the Jālor Parganā (Jodhpur Division).
39. Mentioned in the Harṣa inscription.
40. Modern Chhechhalī, about 4 miles to the north of Sevāḍī, Jodhpur State.
41. One of the Naḍḍulāi twelve.
42. Modern Desūri in Goḍvāḍ (Jodhpur Division).
43. In the Jodhpur Division.
44. Modern Dhoḍ. 7 miles from Jahazpur (Udaipur-Mewār).
45. Modern Dholpur.
46. Modern Ghotārsī, a small village in the Pratābgarh State. See the chapter on the Chauhāns of Pratābgarh.
47. One of the Naḍḍulāi 12.
48. Different from modern Jaipur. Named in the Harṣa inscription as a *viṣaya* of Spādalakṣa.
49. Modern Jhaṁvrā, a small village near Maṇḍor.
50. A village of the Naḍḍulāi 12.
51. Was in the Sarahkoṭṭa (Sargot) *viṣaya*.
52. Was in the Jayapura-*viṣaya*.
53. A village of the Naḍḍulāi twelve.
54. Was a village in Sapādalakṣa (Harṣa inscription).
55. Modern Kirāḍū near Bāḍmer (Jodhpur Division).
56. Jodhpur Division.
57. A village of the Naḍḍulāi twelve.
58. Was somewhere near modern Sevāḍī.
59. Mentioned in the Harṣa inscription.
60. Modern Menāl in Mewāṛ.
61. Modern Maṅgalāṇa 19 miles west of Maroṭ in Mārwār.
62. A village of the Naḍḍulāi twelve.
63. A village in the Khaṭṭakūpa-*viṣaya*.
64. Was a village near Sevāḍī.

66. Morākarā.[65]
67. Morākurī.[66]
68. Nāḍaḍa.[67]
69. Naḍḍūlaḍāgikā.[68]
70. Nandana.[69]
71. Nimbaḍikā.[70]
72. Pādraḍā.[71]
73. Pinchchhavallī.[72]
74. Prahlādakūpa.[73]
75. Puṣkara.[74]
76. Rāṭahrada.[75]
77. Samarapura.[76]
78. Siṁhagoṣṭha.[77]
79. Saṇapura.[78]
80. Saṇḍeraka.[79]
81. Saṅkarāṇaka.[80]
82. Sarahakoṭṭa.[81]
83. Śivā.[82]
84. Sonāṇam.[83]
85. Sujerā.[84]
86. Surāchanda.[85]
87. Tantuṭṭī.[86]

65. A village of the Naḍḍulai twelve.

66. A village in Mewāṛ granted by Someśvara to the Bijoliā Pārśvanātha temple. The name as read by Mr. A.K. Vyas now is Morājhari.

67. A village of the Naḍḍulāi twelve.

68. Modern Nāḍlāi, Jodhpur Division.

69. A village mentioned in Ojha Grant 3. Was in Nāḍol territory.

70. Modern Nīmṛā 4-- miles south of Harasnāth (Sīkar estate).

71. Was a village near Sevāḍī.

72. Mentioned in Ojha Grant 3 as a village granted to the temple of Tripuruṣa in V. 1171.

73. Modern Pallū, Bikaner Division.

74. Modern Pushkar near Ajmer.

75. Same at Lāṭahrada of the Sūndhā inscription. Was according to Naiṇsī near Sānchor.

76. Founded by Samarasiṁha of Jālor.

77. Modern Singhoṭ in Jaipur territory.

78. In the old Sirohi State. For details see Dr. G.H. Ojha's *History of Sirohī.*

79. Modern Saṇḍerā, Jodhpur Division.

80. A village in Sapādalakṣa (Harṣa inscription). Probably Sakrāi.

81. Modern Sargot near Maroṭ, Jodhpur Division.

82. Modern Sheo (Jodhpur Division).

83. A village of the Naḍḍulās 12.

84. A village of the Naḍḍulāi 12.

85. In Jodhpur Division.

86. Modern Tantoṭī of Ajmer-Merwāṛā.

88. Tūṇakūpaka.[87]
89. Valahī[88]
90. Vidyudvallī.[89]
91. Vīsalpur.[90]

The following towns may be presumed to have existed in our period on account of the antiquarian remains found in them[91]:—

92. Jahāzpur (Mewār)
93. Jāḍolī (Mewāṛ).
94. Rāyasīsar (Bikaner Division).
95. Vāsī-Varsinghsar (Bikaner Division).
96. Morkhāṇā (Bikaner Division).
97. Kaṁvalīsar (Bikaner Division).
98. Jāṅgalakūpa (Bikaner Division).
99. Bhādlā (Bikaner Division).
100. Sāraṅgasar (Bikaner Division).
101. Droṇapura (Bikaner Division).
102. Charlū (*Ibid*).
103. Reṇī (*Ibid*).
104. Lohārī. (Mewār).
105. Kīnsariyā (Jodhpur Division).
106. Revāsā (Jaipur Division).
107. Āṁvaldā (Mewār).
108. Balvan (Kotāh Division).
109. Kekind (Jaipur Division)
110. Bāmnerā (Jodhpur Division).
111. Lās (old Sirohī State).
112. Chohṭan.
113. Bīṭhū (Jodhpur Division)

Additional names supplied by the literary sources, the *Hammīramahākāvya*, the *Pṛthvīrājavijaya*, the *Kānhaḍadeprabandha* and Muslim histories are:—

114. Āmrapura.[92]
115. Bhādrājana.[93]

87. Modern Tūṇū in the Sikar estate.
88. Modern Bālī.
89. Modern Bijoliā.
90. In Jaipur Division (Rājasthān).
91. The list is largely based on the learned notes on the antiquities of Jodhpur, Bīkāner, Sirohī and Pratābgarh States in their histories by Dr. G. H. Ojha; the *Archaeological Survey Reports of the Western Circle* edited by Dr. D. R. Bhandarkar, the notes on the historical sites of Bikaner published in the *Journal of the Asiatic Society of Bengal* by Dr. Tessitori, and the *Kharataragacchhapaṭṭāvalī* of Jinapāla and his successors.
92. Modern Āmer, Jaipur Division. Mentioned in the *Hammīramahākāvya*, IV, 82.
93. *Kānhaḍadeprabandha*, IV, 107.

116. Guḍapura.[94]
117. Jagarā.[95]
118. Jhāin.[96]
119. Kailavāḍa.[97]
120. Khaṇḍilla.[98]
121. Maṇḍalgarh.[99]
122. Pūgal.[100]
123. Sirāṇa.[101]
124. Sojat.[102]
125. Toḍā.[103]

Consultation of the catalogues of old manuscripts had added the following names:—

126. Harṣapura.[104]
127. Upakeśa.[105]
128. Nagara.[106]
129. Pṛthvīpura.[107]
130. Narānayana.[108]
131. Guḍḍarayasu.[109]

The list cannot naturally claim to be exhaustive.

94. *Pṛthvīrājavijaya*. Perhaps the same as modern Guṛgāon.

95. *Hammīramahākāvya*. Was on the border of Hammīr's dominions and most probably once in the dominions of the Chauhāns.

96. Mentioned in most of the Muslim histories as a fort near Raṇthambhor. Wrongly identified with Ujjain by Dr. H.C. Ray and some other writers. The *Ain-i-Akbarī* puts it in the Sarkār of Raṇthambhor. Ujjain was a Sarkār by itself in Mālwā.

97. *Kānhaḍadeprabandha*.

98. Modern Khaṇḍelā. Mentioned both in the *Tīrthamālā* (*Paṭṭana Catalogue of Mss.*, p. 156) and the *Hammīramahākāvya*.

99. *Kānhaḍadeprabandha*.

100. In Jaisalmer State.

101. Mentioned by Naiṇsī as well as the *Kānhaḍadeprabandha* as being near Jālor.

102. *Kānhaḍadeprabandha*. Well-known town in Jodhpur Division.

103. *Ibid.*

104. Same as Harṣa of the Harṣa inscription (Sīkar principality).

105. Modern Osiā (Jodhpur Division).

106. In Jodhpur Division.

107. See the chapter on Arṇorāja.

108. Near Sāmbhar Lake.

109. *Paṭṭana Catalogue of Mss.*, p. 156.

APPENDIX M

THE SCHEME OF WEIGHTS ACCORDING TO THE ŚĀRṄGADHARA-SAṀHITĀ

30 *paramāṇus*	=	1 *trasareṇu*
5 *trasareṇus*	=	1 *marīchi*
6 *marīchis*	=	1 *rājikā*
3 *rājikās*	=	1 *sarṣapa*
8 *sarṣapas*	=	1 *yava*
4 *yavas*	=	1 *guñjā* or *raktikā*
6 *raktikās*	=	1 *māṣaka.*
4 *māṣakas*	=	1 *dharaṇa* (*ṭaṅka* or *sāṇa*)
2 *dharaṇas*	=	1 *kola* (*kṣudraka*, or *vaṭaka or draṅkṣaṇa*)
2 *kolas*	=	1 *karṣa* (*akṣa*, *pāṇimānikā* *pāṇitala*, *pīchu*, *tinduka*, *suvarṇa*, *udumbara*, *haṁsapada*, *viḍālapadaka etc.*)
2 *karṣas*	=	1 *śukti*
2 *śuktis*	=	1 *pala* (*muṣṭi*, *āmra*, *prakuñcha* or *vilva*)
2 *palas*	=	1 *prasṛti*
2 *prasṛtis*	=	1 *kuḍava* or *añjali*
2 *kuḍavas*	=	1 *śarāva* or *mānikā*
2 *śarāvas*	=	1 *prastha*
4 *prasthas*	=	1 *āḍhaka*
4 *āḍhakas*	=	1 *droṇa* (*kalaśa*, *nalva*, *umāna*, *ghaṭa*
	=	or, *rāśi*).
2 *droṇas*	=	1 *śūrpa* or *kumbha.*
2 *śūrpas*	=	1 *droṇī* (*goṇī* or *vāha*)
4 *droṇīs*	=	1 *khārī*
100 *palas*	=	1 *tulā*
2000 ,,	=	1 *bhāra.*

APPENDIX N

SOME LIGHT ON ECONOMIC CONDITION FROM THAKKURA PHERU'S WORKS

Ṭhakkura Pheru was born at Kannāṇā, a place four miles from Dādarī, composed his first book in 1290 A.D. and spent the most active part of his life at Delhi. His books, which were written with a very competent knowledge of the subjects he dealt with, throw a flood of light on the economic condition of the period. We give here a few details, reserving a fuller treatment to a paper to be published shortly.

1. Production per *bīghā* in the Delhi-Hānsī-Narhaḍ area.

Kodrava	60 mds.
Moṭh	24 ,,
Chaunlā beans	22 ,,
Black gram; *Mūng*	18 ,, each.
Rice (Kārī) (?)	18 3/4 ,, or 15¼ mds.[1]
Sesamum	16 ,,
Kāngarī (?)	20 ,,
Cotton	16 ,,
Jawār	40 ,,
Flax (?)[2]	10 ,,
Sugarcane	10 ,, (Two crops)
Wheat	45 ,,
Peas, *Masūra*, Black gram	32 ,, each.
Barley	56 ,,
Sarson, Alasī, Karaḍa	10 ,, each
Baṭulā, Arhar, Kulathī	14 mds.
Cumin, Coriander	10 ,,

1 maund here equalled 2400 *tolas*.

1. पनरह करि सवाईय (Muni Kantisagar's reading). Nahtas, however, read कूर which means rice.

2. Based on Nahta's interpretation.

2. (*a*) 50 mds. of sugarcane juice produced either 10 mds. of *guḍa* (jaggery) or 3⅓ mds. of white sugar.

   (*b*) *Til, Sarson, Karaḍ* produced respectively 9/20, 7/20 and 1/4 of the amount as oil.

3. Copper was mined at Babberā (near Khetrī, Jaipur Divison).

4. 20 *pratikākiṇīs* = 1 *kākiṇī*
   20 *kākiṇīs* = 1 *prativiṁśāṁśa*
   20 *prativiṁśāṁśās* = 1 *viṁśopaka* (visovā)
   20 *viṁśopakas* = 1 *dramma*[3]
   50 *drammas* = 1 *taṅka*

5. 24 *āṅgulas* = 1 *hasta* (cubit)
   4 *hastas* 1 *daṇḍa*
   2,000 *daṇḍas* = 1 *krośa*
   4 *krośas* = 1 *yojana*

6. 4 *karapuṭas* (*handfuls*) = 1 *pāī*
   4 *pāīs* = 1 *māṇaka*
   4 *maṇakas* = 1 *seī*
   16 *seīs* = 1 *prastha*

7. 6 *guñjās* = 1 *māṣaka*
   4 *māṣakas* = 1 *ṭaṅka*
   10 *taṅkas* = 1 *pala*
   6 *palas* = 1 *ser* (seer)
   40 seers = 1 *maṇa*

8. 16 *yavas* = 1 *māṣaka*
   4 *māṣakas* = 1 *taṅka*
   3 *taṅkas* = 1 *tolā*[4].

All this information is useful, because it refers to an area where the Chauhāns had been ruling, and the products of which could not have changed very much during the period that intervened between Pṛthvīrāja III and Pheru. We can now on the basis of Pheru's information state definitely what crops the Delhi area produced, and what the amount of produce per *bīghā* was in normal times. The table of coins also is useful, because it settles some doubts about the *kākiṇī-viṁśopaka-dramma*

3. This settles definitely the relationship between a *dramma* and *viṁśopakā*. See below also another interpretation of the Table.

4. The tables are based on the quotations from Pheru's *Gaṇitasāra* in the *Viśālabhārata*, 1947, pp. 394-5, and items 2 and 3 on Nāhtas' information.

coinage. According to the commentary on the *Gaṇitasāra*, 20 *kauḍās* equalled one *kākiṇī*. So the *pratikākiṇī* of Pheru's table should perhaps be identified with a cowrie. But as the two tables diverge very much thereafter, if we accept the interpretation leading to the table of coins given above, we should perhaps interpret the *gāthās* to mean[5] that 1 *dramma* = 20 *viṁśopakas* = 400 (20 × 20) *viśvāṁśās* or *prativiśvāṁśas* = 8000 *kākiṇīs* or *pratikākiṇīs*. In this case, too, if we do not regard the *kākiṇī* as equal to a *cowrie*, we have to assume that the price of *cowries*, 20 of which in the commentary on the *Gaṇitasāra* made a *kākiṇī*, was extremely low in the territory near Delhi. But whatever the value of a *kākiṇī* may have been, it is certain that one *viṁśopaka* was 1/20 of a *dramma*. It is interesting also to find the *dramma* connected with the *taṅka*.

5. The *gāthās* are :—

पडि काइणि तह काइणि पडि विस्संसा तह विस्संसा ।
जावय होंति विसोवा वीस उण कमेण नायव्वा ।।३।।
वीसि विसोइहि दम्मो दम्मिहि पंचासि टंकउ इक्को ।

For coinage alone read Pheru's *Dravyaparīkṣā*.

CHAPTER XXVII

THE CAUSES OF THE DOWNFALL OF THE EARLY CHAUHAN KINGDOMS

In the preceding pages we have tried to give some idea of the chief achievements of the Chauhāns, of their successes and failures and the way their people lived, thought and acted. Patriotic Hindus must have admired the Chauhāns for their long and brave stand against the Muslims. In the very beginning of their historical career, they helped the Pratihāras in stemming the onrush of the Arabs. They fought against the Ghaznavites. From the twelfth to the fourteenth century Arṇorāja, Vigraharāja IV, Pṛthvīrāja III, Vāgbhaṭa, Hammīra, Sātaladeva and Kānhaḍadeva formed the vanguard of that noble and heroic band of warriors who fought for Hindu independence and Hindu culture. That ultimately even these sturdy fighters had to succumb to the Muslim invaders calls for some explanation.

None who has gone through these pages would regard lack of valour as one of the causes of Chauhān failure. Muslim as well as Hindu historians bear incontestable testimony to the fact that the valiant Chauhāns knew well how to die and sell their lives dear. Many a time they fought on even when there was not the least chance of success,[1] because they considered it disgraceful to surrender or flee. To them nothing was more meritorious than to die fighting on the battlefield. Nor was the failure of the Chauhāns due to any lack of religious fervour. The Siwālik Pillar *praśasti* which praises Vigraharāja IV for having made Āryāvarta a real *Āryāvarta, i.e.*, an abode of the Āryas, by the repeated destruction of the *Mlechchhas*,[2] could

1. See for instance above, pp. 185-186, the last fight of Sātala.
2. आविन्ध्याद्रि-हिमाद्रेर्विरचितजयस्तीर्थयात्राप्रसङ्गा-
दुद्ग्रीवेषु प्रहर्ता नृपतिषु विनमत्कन्धरेषु प्रसन्नः ।
आर्यावर्तं यथार्थं पुनरपि कृतवान् म्लेच्छविच्छेदनाभि-
र्देवः शाकम्भरीन्द्रो जगति विजयते वीसलक्षोणिपालः ।।

not have been composed at the dictation of a ruler uninspired by the love of Hinduism and a relentless hatred of the Muslims; and the same anti-Muslim and pro-Hindu spirit pervades the drama, *Lalitavigraharāja*, wherein the hero, who is none else than Vigraharāja IV himself is represented as saying that he cared little for his life, if he could not protect the Brāhmaṇas, sacred places and the temples of Hindu gods from destruction at the hands of the *Hammīra, i.e.*, the Amīr of Ghaznā.[3] According to the *Pṛthvīrājavijaya*, the first Chauhān was born to free Puṣkara from the ill-doings of the *Mātaṅgas*.[4] Pṛthvīrāja II and Pṛthvīrāja III were regarded as incarnations of Rāma,[5] because their mission was believed to have been the destruction of the *Asuras*, meaning by this term, of course, the Muslim invaders from the north-west. Jayānaka even goes so far as to call the Muslims "demons in human form whose destruction had been vowed by Pṛthvīrāja."[6] Firishta's statement that in the second battle of Tarāīn "the Rājpūt princes, to the number of 150, had assembled in the vast camp, having sworn by the water of the Ganges, that they would conquer their enemies or die martyrs to their faith"[7] again tells the same story of the Chauhān's love of Hindu religion and determination, if necessary, to die for it. In fact, a careful perusal of the epigraphic and literary sources of the period, whether Hindu or Muslim, would belie the belief, popularly entertained, that the Muslims alone knew how to risk their lives and to make the heaviest sacrifices for their faith.

3. अकीर्तिः काप्युच्चैः सुहृदभयदानव्रतहति-
स्तथा ध्वंसस्तीर्थ-द्विज-सुमनसां वीर्यविगमः ।
ममैतेषु व्यस्तेष्वपि भृशमसह्येषु सकला-
निमानङ्गीकर्तुः कथयत विधेयं किमसुभिः ॥

4. See Brahmā's prayer to Viṣṇu, Canto I.

5. पृथ्वीराजो महाराजो रामोसौ संशयं विना
(Pṛthvīrāja II's Hānsī inscription)
श्रीराम एव पृथ्वीराजरूपो जात इति वक्ष्यति ।
(Jonarāja's comment on *PV.*, I.33)

6. Canto X, 42.

7. *TF.*, I, 175.

And equally difficult it is to agree with the dictum of those who ascribe the fall of the Chauhāns to the lack of generalship among their leaders. Arṇorāja, Vigraharāja IV and Kīrtipāla were all leaders of note, in no way inferior to their Muslim adversaries, the Yāminīs of Ghaznā and Muhammad of Ghor. Pṛthvīrāja III defeated the Muslims decisively in the first battle of Tarāīn. What his tactics might have been, if he had not been deceived by Muhammad Ghorī's promise of truce is beyond any historian's power to tell. To declare, as Sir Wolseley Haig has done, that Pṛthvīrāja III lost the battle of Tarāīn on account of being a slave to tradition is certainly going beyond the evidence at our disposal and ignoring the great advantage accruing to the Muslim forces as a result of their surprise attack, which forced the Hindus not to fight as they wished, but as well as they could, against a well-equipped army employing tactics already well-thought-out and discussed.[8] Hammīra of Raṇthambhor drove back the Muslims more than once from before the walls of his fort, and his fall, ultimately, was due more to treachery in his own ranks than to any conspicuous military skill displayed by Alāuddīn Khaljī.[9] Sātaladeva and Kānhaḍadeva resisted for years the might of Delhi. If the superior resources of a big empire, employed for years against them, along with perfidy, bribery and treachery, finally brought about their downfall, the credit for this should not go to Khaljī generalship.

We have to look elsewhere than the lack of religious fervour, lack of military skill and lack of valour for the downfall of the Chauhāns. Partly, it was due to the caste system, which whatever its services might have been towards the preservation of Hinduism, had disastrous effects in the political field. It prevented not only the amount of fusion necessary for the creation of a strong people but also kept away a large number of people from the profession of fighting. Once the fighting class (which consisted largely of Rājpūts with a small sprinkling of

8. See above, pp. 93-95, for details.
9. See above, pp. 123-125, for details.

Brāhmaṇas[10] and now and then a Vaiśya[11]) was defeated, the enemy had generally an easy walk-over. The priestly classes generally resisted only when it came to the destruction of the temples where they officiated. The traders perhaps resisted even less. All that they wanted was a settled government, and generally they were the first to come to terms with the alien government.[12] As to the depressed classes, which have always constituted a very large percentage of the Indian population, what interest could they have in the perpetuation of a political system in which they had plenty of duties but very few rights? When big kingdoms fall, one after the other, in their fight against a common enemy, obviously, it is not the political leaders alone, but the whole social system and its inadequate adjustment to changing conditions that is at fault.

In some measure the downfall must have been due also to luxury and idleness fostered by many years of continued prosperity. A ruler like Pṛthvīrāja III who could indulge in riot and revelry with the enemy just encamped opposite[13] deserved to fail against an adversary who had since his defeat in the second battle of Tarāīn "abstained from his wife's bed", "not changed the clothes of his body", and, having passed the year in grief, "sorrow and sadness", not permitted the *Amīrs* who had abandoned him in the battle to present themselves in his presence.[14] Pṛthvīrāja's brother, Harirāja, was according to the

10. Pṛthvīrāja's general, Skanda, was a Brāhmaṇa. So was also the commander of the Chaulukya forces sent against Ballala of Mālwā. The soldiers who killed Ballāla were according to the *Dvyāśraya-kāvya* of Hemachandra "bad Brāhmaṇas." Kumāra, the *purohita* of Gujarāt, is similarly said to have been a good general.

11. शस्त्राशस्त्रि युध्यमाना राजपुत्रा एव शोभन्ते न वणिजः
(खरतरगच्छपट्टावलि, *Ms.*, p. 20.)

Notable exceptions to this rule are Ambaḍa and Vastupāla.

12. See for instance the Jaina inscriptions referring themselves to the "reign" of Alp Khān (*Prāchīna-Gurjara-kāvya-saṅgraha*, Appendices VII and VIII), the *Samararāso*, and the *Nābhinandana-jinoddhāra-grantha*). Read also the present writer's paper, "New light on Alāuddīn Khaljī's achievements," *Proceedings of the Indian History* Congress, Seventeenth Session, pp. 240 ff.

13. See above, p. 94.

14. Raverty, *Tabaqāt-i-Nāsirī*, p. 467, footnote 7.

Hammīramahākāvya overpowered easily by his Muslim enemies, because towards the end of his reign he began spending most of his time in the company of the dancing girls presented to him by the ruler of Gujarāt.[15] Hammīra of Raṇthambhor allowed, to his cost, his policy to be influenced by the court-dancer, Dhārā[16]; and this general tendency towards voluptuousness and indolence finds expression in contemporary literature also,[17] though in the Rājasthān of our period it perhaps never reached the lengths it did in the Madhyadeśa.

We have to remember also that virtue carried too far turns into vice. The Chauhāns' adherence to *śāstras*, when fighting against their own countrymen, was perhaps commendable. But it was suicidal in the fight against an alien race which recognised no such rules. Similarly, though it was good to be religious, it was bad to be superstitious. A society, which turned a *Mlechchha* victor into Rudra (*Kānhaḍadeprabandha*, II, 131-4) eager to cut the heads of Kṣatriyas, and ascribed all mishaps to its own past misdeeds (*Ibid.*, I, 158-174) was bound to suffer some day for its credulity.

Equally or even more fatal to their political existence was their failure to evolve a political and military system strong enough to fight and unite India against invaders. Partly it was a fight of the elephant against the horse. The elephant was good enough under Indian conditions. It could help in breaking the gates of a fortress. It could trample under feet the slow moving force of the enemy. But it was no match for the swift Central Asian horse. The Muslim soldier shot arrows from its back-arrows which could easily pierce through the armours the Indian had. Further havoc was created by the use of naptha arrows, but this perhaps a little later. The Indians of the period 1200-1215 A.D., or so, because they could neither bring into existence a strong cavalry, with the weak horses they had nor create a mounted archer whose striking capacity equalled

15. *HM*, IV, 2-16.
16. See above.
17. See for instance the *Karpūramañjarī*, the *Laṭakamelaka* and the *Rambhāmañjarī*. My paper, "Gleanings from Sanskrit Literature, Rājaśekhara's works," *JIH*, 1939, may also be read in this connection.

that of his Asian adversary. That the Indians fully realised their essential unity is demonstrated by the existence of their most important sacred places, Rāmeśvara, Badrīnātha, Dvārakā, Jagannāthapurī respectively in the extreme south, north, west and east of India; by the repetition of a formula containing the names of the sacred rivers of both the north and the south by devout Hindus at the time of their bath every day; and also by the aspiration of the Indian *digvijayin* to rule India from the Himālayas to the southern ocean and from the western to the eastern sea.[18] But the methods that they employed to give this ambition a political and practical shape were in nine cases out of ten extremely unsatisfactory. The success of Alexander against the freedom-loving but weak republics of the Punjāb and the failure of Seleukos Nikator against Chandragupta Maurya should have shown the Indians that the interest of India could be best served by a strong central government which, while giving full freedom to municipal and rural bodies, kept severely in check fissiparous tendencies of the provinces by appointing its own governors, keeping a well-organized regular army paid direct from the State-treasury, and the use of news-writers and other agencies so well-known to us from Maurya and other records. But the Rājpūts preferred instead the traditional *digvijayin's* ideal of merely exacting tribute and leaving the administration of the acquired territories almost wholly under the control of the beaten princes. They merely asked them to keep in readiness, a number of horse and foot for the service of the suzerain,[19] and even in their own *deśa*, power largely lay with feudal lords enjoying definite rights and immunities and leading their own followers in a battle. This state of affairs, though highly extolled by some writers,[20] could hardly lead to the formation of a consolidated and strong state, powerful enough to throw back the vigorous races from the north-west, who in their fight with the Rājpūts were inspired

18. For this topic Dr. R. K. Mookerji's *Fundamental Unity of India* may be read with profit.

19. See the chapter on administration.

20. By Sri C. V. Vaidya in *History of Medieval India*, Vol. II and Dr. Ishwari Prasad who quotes Vaidya's remarks approvingly in his *Medieval India*.

by religious zeal as well as pecuniary greed. Raw levies, coming together on the spur of the moment and fighting under the leadership of their different leaders, could not be the best means of beating back a determined enemy. The Rājpūts did not lack courage. But they lacked discipline and the absolute unity of command so necessary for success in major operations[21].

Result as good as that of a strong centralised state might have been secured also, if the Rājpūts had learnt to cut down the powers of the feudal lords and feudatories, sunk their mutual differences and evolved somehow the idea of a federation. In the twelfth century this, in fact, would have been the best policy. With the Muslims knocking at the western door of India, and the three main powers of Northern India, the Chauhāns, the Chaulukyas and the Gāhaḍavālas so evenly balanced that none could secure more than a temporary advantage over the others, *digvijayas* of the old type described in the *Raghuvaṁśa*, or of any type in fact, meant not merely wastage of energy but the ruin of the country. The *digvijayins* turned these great kingdoms against one another, when a common front was needed, and allowed them to be destroyed piecemeal by the Muslims. Had the Chaulukyas and the Gāhaḍavālas come to the help of the Chauhāns immediately after the second battle of Tarāin, the fortunes of the kingdom of Sapādalakṣa could have been retrieved and the Hindus might have escaped many years of humiliation. It was the just hand of Nemesis which struck down Jayachandra in 1194 A.D. and humiliated the Chaulukyas two years later. Kelhaṇa, Hammīra and Kānhaḍadeva all fell before the relentless foe, because they forgot the axiomatic truth, "United we stand, divided we fall".

21. See above the account of the Chauhān military machine for its weak points.

CHAUHANS OF DADREWA

(*Additional Note, p.* 195)

Another feudatory Chauhān family which deserves notice, on account of its connection with the folk-god Gogājī as well as the Kyāmkhanī (Qiwām Khānī) family of Fatehpur, is that of the *maṇḍaleśvaras* of *Dadrewā* (Bīkāner Division), known to us from the *Kyām Khān Rāso* and an inscription of V. 1273.[1] From the first of these sources we learn that Gogā was the eldest son of Jevara and ruled for some years. His successor was Nāniga, who perhaps died childless. The chieftainship then probably passed on to Udayarāja, a son of Gogā's brother, Vairasī. Udayarāja's successors were Jasarāja, Kesorāja, Vijayarāja, Padmasī, Pṛthvīrāja, Lālachanda, Gopāla, and Jaitasī. It is for the last of these rulers, 'rāṇaka Jayatsīha, the son of *Maṇḍaleśvara* Gopāla', that we have an inscription of V. 1270 (1213 A.D.) at Dadrewā (*JPASB, XVI*, 257). Jayatasīha's successors were Punapāla, Rūpā, Rāvaṇa, Tihuṇapāla, and Moṭerāya. The last one of them had a son named Karama Chanda who was converted to Islām by Firūz Shāh, (1351-1388 A.D.). If we keep both these definite dates in view, Gogājī (and we may remember that there is only one Gogā in the line of Dadrewā) should be regarded as a contemporary of Mahmūd of Ghaznā, and not of Firūz Shāh, as believed by Tod and some other writers who have followed his lead. This late date is disproved also by the *Śrāvaka-vratādi-atichāra*, a Gujarātī book composed in V. 1466 1409 A.D. It requires a Jaina *Śrāvaka* not to think of worshipping Brahmā, Viṣṇu, Kṣetrapāla, Goga, Dikpālas, village gods, and *grahas* etc., merely because they fulfilled the desires of their devotees. A local god like Goga must have needed not only twenty-five years or so but centuries to be so well known, not only in his homeland of north-eastern Rājasthān but also in the distant Gujarāt, that Jaina teachers had to put his

1. Correctly read by Govind Agrawal as V. 1273 instead of 1270.

worship on a level with that of Brahmā, Viṣṇu, Śiva, and other popular gods and dub it as an *atichāra*, *i.e.*, a serious transgression of Jaina *dharma*.[2]

Further material has since writing the above been available to show that Goga was a descendant of Ghaṅga. Surjan, against whom he had to fight, came one generation earlier than him (for more details read my article in the *Śodhapatrikā*, XX, pp. 1-3).

As regards the history of the descendants of Karamachanda known to us as Kāyam Khānīs, who played an important role in the affairs of Delhi under the later Tughlaqs, Saiyyads, Lodīs and Mughals, readers may consult our introduction and critical notes appended to the *Kyām Khān Rāso*, published by the Rājasthān Purātattva Mandira, Jaipur.

2. Actually the only basis that we have for the late dating of Gogajī are the late traditional anecdotes which make him a contemporary of the Rāṭhore hero Pābūjī, who as a great grandson of Rāva Sīhoji could have flourished somewhere about 1325 A.D. It is impossible to build up serious history on the basis of such tales. To me it seems that they were concocted by a fairly late generation of the devotees of Pābūjī, who were out to prove that their hero-god was in no way inferior to the Chauhān hero, Gogojī. And if we are out to believe anecdotes, we have to believe equally the stories which make Gogojī, a contemporary of Gorakhanātha (who is generally put by historians in the beginning of the eleventh century) and of Mahmūd of Ghaznā against whom he is said to have fought with his forty-five sons and sixty nephews. How the worship of the Chauhān hero came to be so intimately connected with snake worship that Gogā came to be regarded as a snake is a subject that needs investigation.

GENEALOGICAL TABLES

(*Note*—The names in italics did not reign)

I. THE (EARLY) CHAUHĀNS OF BROACH

Maheśvardāma
|
Bhīmadāma
|
Bhartṛvaḍḍha I
|
Haradāma
|
Dhrūbhaṭa
|
Bharatṛvaḍḍha II, V. 813

II. THE (LATER) CHAUHĀNS OF BROACH

Siṁha Sindhurāja
|
Saṅgrāmasiṁha or Śaṅkha, C. V. 1279

III. THE CHAUHĀNS OF DHOLPUR

Īsuka
|
Mahisarāma = Kaṇhullā
|
Chaṇḍamahāsena, V. 895

IV. THE CHAUHĀNS OF PRATĀBGARH

Govindarāja
|
Durlabharāja
|
Indrarāja, C.V. 999

V. THE CHAUHĀNS OF RĀYABADDIYA AND CHANDAVĀRA

Bharatapāla, V. 1283
|
Abhayapāla
|
Jāhaḍa
|
Ballāla
|
Āhavamalla, V. 1313
|
Asavambhu
|
Gaṇapati
|
Sāraṅga
|
Abhayachandra
|
Rāmachandra, V. 1454
|
Pratāparudra, *yuvarāja*, V. 1449

VI. THE CHAUHĀNS OF ŚĀKAMBHARĪ

Vāsudeva, V. 608 (*PK.*)

1. Sāmanta

2. Naradeva or Nṛpa (ruled at Pūrṇatalla[1])

3. Jayarāja

4. Vigraharāja I

5. Chandrarāja I

6. Gopendrarāja or Gopendraka

7. Durlabharāja I C. V. 850.

8. Govindarāja or Gūvaka I, C. V. 786-843

9. Chandrarāja II, V. 900-925.

10. Gūvaka II (Govindarāja II), C. V. 925-950

11. Chandanarāja, V. 950-V.975.

12. Vākpatirāja I (Vappayarāja)[2] C.975-1000

1. Pūrṇatalla is generally but wrongly regarded as the name of a ruler.
2. The Prakritised form Vappayarāja is found in the Bijoliā inscription.

13. Vimdhyarāja[3] 14. Simharāja C. V. 1700. V. 1013 *Lakṣmaṇa-Vatsarāja*

15. Vigraharāja II 16. Durlabharāja II *Chandrarāja* *Govindarāja*

V. 1030 V. 1055

V 1056

17. Govindarāja III

18. Vākpatirāja II C. V. 1056-1075 19. Vīryarāma C.V.1075-1095 20. Chāmuṇḍarāja[4] C.V. 1095-1120

21. Simhaṭa[5]

22. Durlabharāja III, C.V.1120-V.1136

23. Vigraharāja III, C. V. I136-1155

24. Pṛthvīrāja VI, . 155, 1162 C.V.,

25. Ajayarāja (Ajayadeva, Salhaṇa C.V. 1162-1189

26. Arṇorāja-Ānāka-Ānalladeva c.v. 1189-1208

3. From the Bijoliā inscription.
4. Founder of the Nāḍol line.
5. Mentioned as *rāṇakavara* Simhaṭa in the Bijoliā inscription. His exact relationship with Durlabharāja III is uncertain.

27. Jagaddeva
C. V. 1208

28. Vigraharāja IV *Devadatta*[6]
C. 1208-1224

31. Someśvara[8]
V. 1226-34

29. Pṛthvīrāja II (Pṛthvībhaṭa)[7]

30. Aparagāṅgeya
or Amaragāṅgeya

32. Pṛthvīrāja III
V 1234-48.

34. Harīrāja[10]
V. 1251

33. Govindarāja IV[9]

6. Mentioned in the *Dvyāśrayamahākāvya*.
7. Came to the throne after defeating Aparagāṅgeya.
8. Put on the throne after Pṛthvīrāja II's death.
9. Founder of the Raṇthambhor line.
10. Drove away Govindarāja from Ajmer.

VII. THE CHAUHĀNS OF RAṆTHAMBHOR

- 1. Govinda (a son of Pṛthvīrāja III)
  - 2. Bālhaṇa
    - 3. Prahlād
      - 4. Vīranārāyaṇa
    - 5. Vāgbhaṭa
      - 6. Jaitrasiṁha
        - *unknown eldest brother*
        - 7. Hammīra
        - *Suratrāṇa Vīrama*

VIII. THE CHAUHĀNS OF NĀḌOL

- 1. Lakṣmaṇa
  - 2. Śobhita
    - 3. Balirāja
  - 4. Vigrahapāla
    - 5. Mahendra
      - 6. Aśvapāla
        - 7. Ahila
      - 8. Aṇahilla
        - 9. Bālaprasāda
        - 10. Jendurāja
          - 11. Pṛthvīpāla
            - 14. Ratnapāla
              - 15. Rāyapāla
                - *Rudrapāla*
                - *Amṛtapāla*
                - Sahajapāla[1]
          - 12. Jojaladeva
          - 13. Āsarāja
            - 16. Kaṭudeva
              - 17. Jayatsiṁha
            - 18. Alhaṇa
              - 19. Kelhaṇa
              - *Gajasiṁha*
              - *Kīrtipāla*[2]

1. Ruled probably as a rival of Alhaṇa, with his capital at Maṇḍor.
2. Founder of the Jālor line.

20. Jayatsīha *Āchaṇadevī* *Gīgādevī* *Śṛṅgāradevī*

21. Sāmantasiṁha

IX. THE SONIGARĀ CHAUHĀNS OF JĀLOR

1. Kīrtipāla

2. Samarasiṁha *Rūdaladevī* *Lakhaṇapāla* *Abhayapāla*

Mānavasiṁha[1] 3. Udayasiṁha *Līlādevī*

4. Chāchiga *Chāmuṇḍarāja* *Vāhaḍiasiṁha*

5. Sāmantasiṁha *Rūpādevī*

6. Kānhaḍadeva *Māladeva*

Vīrama

X. THE CHAUHĀNS OF SATYAPURA

1. Vijayasiṁha

2. Padmasiṁha

3. Śobhita

4. Sālha.

5. Vikramasiṁha 6. Hāpo or Haripāla[2]

Bhīmasiṁha 7. Saṅgrāmasiṁha

8. Pratāpasiṁha

1. Sālha's younger brother according to Naiṇsī.
2. Mentioned by Naiṇsī's *Khyāt* and the *Kharataragachchhapaṭṭāvalī*.

XI. THE DEORĀ CHAUHĀNS OF CHANDRĀVATĪ AND ĀBŪ

1. Mānavasiṁha
2. Pratāpamalla
3. Vījaḍa, Daśasyandana, Daśaratha
   - 4. Lāvaṇyakarṇa
   - 5. Luṇḍha (Lumbha, Luṇṭiga)
     - 6. Tejasiṁha.
       - 7. Kānhaḍadeva
       - 8. Sāmantasiṁha
       - 9. Raṇamalla
       - 10. Śivabhāna
       - 11. Sahasramalla; Saisamalla (Founder of Sirohī)
     - Tihuṇaka
   - *Lakṣmaṇa*
   - *Lūṇavarman*

XII. THE CHAULUKYAS OF ANAHILLAPĀṬAKA

1. Mūlarāja I
2. Chāmuṇḍarāja
   - 3. Vallabharāja
   - 4. Durlabharāja
   - *Nāgarāja*
     - 5. Bhīma I
       - *Mūlarāja*
       - *Kṣemarāja*
         - *Devaprasāda*
           - Tribhuvanapāla
       - 6. Karṇa
         - 7. Jayasiṁha Siddharāja

Mahīpāla 8. Kumārapāla *Kīrtipāla* *Premaladevī*[1]

9. Ajayapāla

10. Mūlarāja II. 11. Bhīmadeva II

XIII. THE VĀGHELAS OF GUJARĀT

Lāvaṇyaprasāda

1. Vīradhavala

2. Vīrama *Pratāpamalla* 3. Vīsala

4. Arjuna

Rāma 5. Śārṅgadeva

6. Karṇadeva

XIV. THE PARAMĀRAS OF MĀLWĀ

1. Śiyaka II, Harṣa[2]

9. Muñja 3. Sindhurāja

4. Bhoja 6. Udayāditya

5. Jayasiṁha I

7. Lakṣmadeva 8. Naravarman Jagaddeva

9. Yaśovarman

10. Jayavarman 11. Ajayavarman *Lakṣmīvarman*

12. Vindhyavarman *Harishchandra*

1. Devaladevī, a sister of Kumārapāla, supposed to have brought about a war between Kumārapāla and Arṇorāja is a fictitious character, a creation of some late chroniclers of Gujarāt.

2. The earlier names have been left out, as they do not concern Chauhān history.

13. Subhaṭavarman

14. Arjunavarman

Udayavarman   15. Devapāla

16. Jayasiṁha II Jayatugi   17. Jayavarman II

18. Jayasiṁha III

19. Arjunavarman   20. Bhoja[1]

Jayasiṁha IV

XV. THE SLAVE KINGS OF DELHI

1. Qutbuddīn Aibak

2. Ārām Shāh   *Daughter* = 3. *Iltutmish*

Nāsiruddīn Mahmūd   4. Firūz   4. Raziyā   6. Bahrām   8. Nāsiruddīn   *Daughter* =

7. Masūd   Mahmūd   9. Balban

XVI. THE KHALJĪS

Tulāk Khān

1. Jalaluddīn Firūz   *Shihābuddīn*

2. Arkalī Khān[2]   *Daughter* = 3. Alāuddīn[3]

1. Bhoja and Arjunavarman probably ruled as contemporaries in two different parts of Mālwā.
2. Arkalī Khān had some other brothers.
3. We are leaving out Alāuddīn's successors.

BIBLIOGRAPHY

1. *Inscriptions.*

The Chauhān inscriptions have mostly either been published or noticed in the *Epigraphia Indica*, the *Indian Antiquary*, the *Journal of the Asiatic Society of Bengal*, the *Annals of the Bhandarkar Oriental Research Institute*, *Zeitschrift der Deutschen Morgenlandischen Gesselschaft*, Dr. D.R. Bhandarkar's *Inscriptions of Northern India*, P.C. Nahar's *Jaina Inscription*, Muni Jinavijaya's *Prāchīnajainalekhasaṅgraha*, and the Reports of the Archaeological Survey of India, Archaeological Survey Western Circle, and the Rajputana Museum. A few unpublished inscriptions have been given at the end of part I of the book. Details are given in footnotes.

2. *Coins.*

The Chauhān coins are mainly described in the following works—

(*i*) V. A. Smith. *Catalogue of Coins in the Indian Museum*, Calcutta, Oxford, 1906.

(*ii*) Cunningham. *Coins of Mediaeval India*, London, 1894.

(*iii*) E. J. Rapson's *India's Coins* 1897.

(*iv*) E. Thomas. *The Chronicles of the Pathan Kings of Delhi*, 1871.

Monuments.

The Chief monuments of the Chauhān dominions are described in the Reports of the Archaeological Survey of India, the Archaeological Survey, Western Circle, and the Rajputana Museum; Tod's *Annals and Antiquities of Rajasthan*; Percy Brown's *Indian architecture* (*Buddhist and Hindu Periods*) and J. Fergusson's *History of Indian and Eastern Architecure.*

4. *Pro-Chauhan Historical Kāvyas*:—

(i) Jayānaka's *Pṛthvīrājavijaya* edited by G.H. Ojha and C. Guleri, Ajmer, 1941.

It is referred to in the works of Jayaratha, a Kashmīrī author of about 1200 A. D. The name *Pṛthvīrājavijaya* (Pṛthvīrāja's victory), combined with the repeated mention of Pṛthvīrāja III's mission of destroying the *Mlecchhas* (X 42) indicates that it could not have been written before his victory over the Muslims in 1191 A.D. That it could not have been composed after 1193 A.D., the year of Pṛthvīrāja's disastrous defeat at the hands of Muhammad Ghori, is shown by the absence of the slightest allusion to Pṛthvīrāja III's discomfiture; the drawing up of a conjectural horoscope for the time of Pṛthvirāja's conception in which all the planets are in the ascendant or in their own houses; and most of all, by the statements of the type that the salt of the Sāmbhar lake could not be utilised by any people excepting the descendants of Vāsudeva (IV, 97). The *Pṛthvīrāja-vijaya* is one of our most reliable sources for the history of Sapādalakṣa.

(*ii*) *Hammīramahākāvya* of Nayachandra Sūri Bombay, 1879.

Though composed nearly a hundred years after Hammīra's death, it is the best source of history for the line of Raṇthambhor. A comparison of the *Kāvya* with Muslim sources shows that Nayachandra had access to some very reliable historical records dealing with the life of Hammīra. New edition published by Rajasthan Puratattva Mandir, Jodhpur.

(*iii*) Chandraśekhara's *Surjanacharita*.

Written in Akbar's reign to commemorate the achievements of Rāo Surjan and his ancestors, it is useful as a subsidiary source book. I have used Dr. G. H. Ojha's transcript of the book. It has now been edited and published by Dr. J. B. Chaudhuri, Calcutta.[1]

(*iv*) *Kānhaḍadeprabandha of Padmanābha* edited by K. B. Vyas, Jaipur, 1953.

The *Kānhaḍadeprabandha* is a Western Rājasthānī *kāvya* dealing with the fight of Kānhaḍade and Alā-uddīn Khaljī. Being written at the court of Akhairāja, a descendant of Kānhaḍade, in the Vikrama year 1512, most probably with good traditional, and perhaps also

1. For an analysis of its contents see my paper in the *Nāgarī Prachāriṇī Patrikā* XLVI, pp. 205-223. I have used D. P. Derasari's edition, lent to me by Muni Jinavijayaji.

written material at the writer's disposal, it presents a generally reliable account of Kānhaḍade's achievements, excepting in the parts deliberately introduced either to give a romantic touch to the story or to minimise the failure of Kānhaḍade and Sātaladeva. For a critical appraisal of the book, see my paper on the subject in the *Śodhapatrikā*, Udaipur, Vol. III, Part I. New Edition published by Rajasthan Puratattva Mandir, Jodhpur.

(*v*) Gaṅgādhara Miśra's *Kosalānanda-kāvya*, Noticed *IHQ*, *VIII*, p. 620.

(*vi*) Prahlāda Dube's *Jayachandrikā*, *IHQ*, Noticed *VIII*, p. 621. Nos. v and vi are late works dealing with the history of the Chauhāns of Patnā.

(*vii*) *Hammīraputhi*

5. *Rāsos.*

(i) *Bīsalde Rāso* NPS, Banaras, 1927.

Dr. G.H. Ojha assigned the composition of the *Bīsalde Rāso* to V. 1272, *i.e.* 1215 A.D. But internal evidence proves it to be a very late work. Its language is of the sixteenth century or so, and its writer, Narapati Nālha, may as contended by Pandit Motilal Menaria be identical with the Gujarātī poet, Narapati, who wrote his poem, the *Pañchadaṇḍa* in V. 1560.[2] Bīsala, the hero of this *Rāso* has been identified by Dr. G.H. Ojha with Vigraharāja III, on the ground that their queens had identical names. Bīsala's queen was a Paramāra princess. Vigraharāja III is known to have been on very good terms with the Paramāra King, Udayāditya, whom he assisted against Karṇa of Gujarāt. Probably the proposed identification is right. But this does not render the rest of the story historical. Most of the events described in it are fictitious, and cannot form the basis of any sober history of either Vigraharāja III or Vigraharāja IV.

The earliest copy of the *Rāso* discovered so far is of V. 1633 (*Rājasthāna- Bhāratī*, Vol. III, Part 1).

2. राजस्थानी भाषा और साहित्य pp. 114. ff.

(*ii*) *Pṛthvīrāja-Rāso.*

So far I have come across four recensions of the *Rāso*. The longest of these has about 40,000 *ślokas* and has been published by the Nāgarī Prachāriṇī Sabhā, Banaras. Most of the current ideas about the unhistoric character of the *Rāso* are based on this edition. The next longest recension has about 10,000 *ślokas* and is being published with certain changes, by the Rājasthāna Viśvavidyāpīṭha, Udaipur. The third recension has about 4, 000 *ślokas*. My friend, Prof. Meenaram Ranga and I had prepared a press copy of it for the Nāgarī Prachāriṇī Sabhā, Banaras. Rangaji is no more, and I have been unable to trace the whereabouts of the copy. The shortest edition is of 1,400 *ślokas*, and has been partially edited for the *Rājasthāna Bhāratī*, Bikaner, by my friend, Prof. Narottama Dasa Swāmi.

Though there is no unanimity regarding the date and historicity of the *Rāso*, the continued discussion of more than sixty years about these makes it clear that originally the *Rāso* was a much shorter work than it is at present, and it is wrong to presume that the shorter recensions are mere abridgements of the longest.[3] On linguistic grounds also it has been proved that the Nāgarī Prachāriṇī Sabhā recension comes later than the others;[4] and even though this shortest recension also shows more evolved forms than the *Prākṛtapaiṅgalam*, there is reason to believe that the original *Rāso* was written in *Apabhraṁśa*. The verses quoted from it in the *Purātanaprabandhasaṅgraha* are in *Apabhraṁśa*, and show unmistakable signs of being extracts from some book, which I, at least, regard as the original *Rāso*. Being a popular work, which had lived on the tongues of people, it naturally underwent changes, not only in its language but also its contents. Its *Apabhraṁśa* changed—and something of this process can be known from a comparative

3. Specially readable in this connection is Dr. Mata Prasad Gupta's paper.
पृथ्वीराज रासो के तीन पाठों का आकार सम्बन्ध, अनुशीलन, वर्ष ७, अङ्क ४.

4. Read Dr. Namwar Singh's, पृथ्वीराज रासो की भाषा, pp. 2, ff.

study of its recensions—into something like the living language of the day, though not without retaining many archaic characteristics. There was along with that simplification in its contents by the reduction of four Bīsals into one and the identification of the two other Pṛthvīrājas with Pṛthvirāja III, the last Hindu emperor of Delhi. But as the actual historical figures receded into the background, their place was taken by many others, whom we cannot but regard as the creations of bardic fancy running riot. The shortest recension describes only two of Pṛthvīrāja's battles, one with Jaichand and the other with Muhammad Ghorī. The Nāgarī Prachāriṇī Sabhā recension has fifty-five battles. And similar is the case of Pṛthvirāja III's marriages.[5]

Under the circumstances, a student of history must do two things at least. He must try to get at the kernel of the story not only by means of a comparative study of the various recensions, but also by taking into account political probabilities as well as the language of the extract to a certain extent. He has to see also whether confusion is not being made worse confounded by the mistaken identity of historical persons bearing one and the same name. I have tried to attempt this difficult task in a number of essays.[6] In the body of this

5. Read Prof. Narottama Dasa Swami's introduction to the edition of the shortest recension, *Rājasthāna Bhāratī*, Vol. IV, part I, v. 5.

6. The following papers may be read :—

(*i*) The age and historicity of the *Pṛthvīrāja Rāso*, IHQ. December, 1940.

(*ii*) पृथ्वीराज रासो की एक प्राचीन प्रति और उसकी प्रामाणिकता, नागरी प्रचारिणी पत्रिका 1939

(*iii*) पृथ्वीराज रासो की कथाओं का ऐतिहासिक आधार, राजस्थानी, कलकत्ता, भाग २, अङ्क २, जनवरी 1944.

(*iv*) पृथ्वीराज रासो सम्बन्धी कुछ विचार, वीणा, April, 1944.

(*v*) The original *Pṛthvīrāja Rāso*, an Apabhraṁśa work, Rājasthāna Bhāratī, April, 1946.

(*vi*) संयोगिता, *Ibid.*, Vol. I, Part 2-3, 1946.

(*vii*) पृथ्वीराज रासो की ऐतिहासिकता पर प्रो० महमूदखाँ शीरानी के आक्षेप *Ibid.*, Vol II, Part 2, July, 1948.

(*viii*) A joint coin of Pṛthvīrāja III and Muhammad bin Sām, *JNSI*, 1954.

(*ix*) पृथ्वीराज तृतीय की जन्मतिथि, राजस्थानी, बीकानेर, अङ्क १, भाग २

thesis I have given reasons of treating the story of Saṁyogitā's marriage as historical.[7] It is likely that some of its other episodes also may be true. But as the things stand, one has to use the Rāso sparingly and with great caution, rejecting everyone of its statements which comes into conflict with the evidence of either early Chauhān inscriptions or the *Pṛthvīrāja vijaya*.

6. *Hindi and Rajasthanī poems.*

(*i*) *Hammīradeva Chaupaī* of Bhāṇḍau Vyāsa was composed in V. 1538, i.e. 1481 A.D. It gives the name of Hammīra's Queen as Hāsilade, and of his daughter as Devaladevī. Of the two traitors, Raṇamalla and Ratipāla, the latter is mentioned as Rāyapāla. The rest of the story does not differ materially from that found in the *Hammīramahākāvya* (See Sri Agar Chand Nahata's notice of the Ms. in the *Marubhāratī*, IV. Part 11. pp. 44 ff.). For a full appraisal of the poem see my Preface of 134 pages in the edition published by the Sadul Rajasthani Research Institute, Bikaner.

(*ii*) *Hammīra-rāso* of Jodharāja (V. 1885). NPS, Banaras, 1929. *Hammira-haṭha* of Chandraśekhara (V. 1902). NPS. Banaras.

(*iv*) *Hammīrarāso chhanda* of Rājarūpa (V. 1998).

(*vi*) These are rather late works dealing with the life of Hammīra. Their historical value is limited. The *chhanda* is in manuscript (Śrī Anūp Sanskrit Library, Bikaner). *Bāt Sātalde Chauhān rī.* [7a].)

(*v*) MS 15 of the Anup Sanskrit Library gives an interesting anecdote of Sātalde.

(*x*) सुरजन चरित महाकाव्य, नागरी प्रचारिणी पत्रिका

(*xi*) सम्राट् पृथ्वीराज की रानी पद्मावती, मरुभारती, भाग १, सितम्बर 1951.

(*xii*) Some New Light on Tomara History, *Proceedings of the Indian History Congress*, 1956.

(*xiii*) कन्हपट्टी कथा का मूल, मरुभारती 1959.

7. See above.

7a. For a thorough consideration of source material for Hammīra, see the preface referred to in 6(i).

7. *Some stray notices.*

(*i*) *Prākṛta-paiṅgalam*, BI, Calcutta, 1900-02, contains a few verses about Hammīra. These have been utilised in our note on Jājā, before.

(*ii*) *Śārṅgadharapaddhati* BSS, 1888, has some verses about Chauhān rulers, Vigraharāja IV, Pṛthvīrāja III, and Hammīra. Śārṅgadhara's grand father, Rāghvadeva, was one of Hammīra's court-poets. The *paddhati* is useful also for an account of the life in the Chauhān Dominions.

(*iii*) *Viruddhavidhividhvaṁsa* by Lakṣmīdhara.

Lakṣmīdhara, the author of the *Viruddhavidhividhvaṁsa*, was a grandson of Vāmana, a minister of Pṛthvīrāja III. Its colophon speaks of the author's ancestor Skanda who was a *sāndhivigrahika* of Someśvara, his son Soḍha who occupied the same position as his father, and Soḍha's sons Skanda and Vāmana who were both ministers of Pṛthvīrāja III.[8]

8. *Naiṇsī's Khyāt.*

Naiṇsī's *Khyāt*, though written somewhere in the middle of the seventeenth century, is a good source for the history of the Sonigarās, the Sānchorās, and many other Chauhān clans. I have used its manuscript from Bīkāner as well as its Hindi translation published by the Nāgarī Prachāriṇi Sabhā, Banaras.

9. *Jaina paṭṭāvalīs and colophons of manuscripts.*[9]

(*i*) The *Kharataragachchhapaṭṭāvalī* of Jinapāla etc.

It falls into three parts, the first going up to Jinavallabha Sūri drawn from traditional sources and undated, the second covering the period V. 1211-1295 which is the work of Jinapāla, and the third a continuation of the same by different hands and going up to V. 1393. Both the second and third parts are dated and extremely useful for the political and social history of our period. For a detailed notice of its contents, see my paper in

8. The MS is in the India Office Library. The colophon has been printed both in the *Rājasthānī*, I. Pt. 3 and *IHQ*, XVI, pp. 567.

9. The *Paṭṭāvalī* of Jinapāla etc. was first brought to the notice of scholars by me in *IHQ*, XI, pp. 779ff.

IHQ, 1950, pp. 223 ff. The *Paṭṭāvalī* has recently been published in the Singhi Jaina Granthamālā, Bombay.

(*ii*) *The Upakeśagachchhapaṭṭāvalī* (*finished V.* 1393).

This is still unpublished. It is reliable only for the thirteenth and fourteenth centuries, and contains valuable information about Siṁhabala, the maternal uncle of Vigraharāja IV.

(*iii*) *Jinadattasūri-stuti of Palha*, Appendix to *Apabhraṁśa-kāvyatrayī*, G. O. S. 1937.

It was copied out at Dhārā in V. 1170. It refers to Ajmer and the fort of Anala, *i.e.* Arṇorāja.

(*iv*) *Vividhatīrthakalpa of Jinaprabha Sūri* SJG, 1934.

The writer of this book was a contemporary of Muhammad bin Tughlaq. It supplies some important details about the history of the Sonigaras.

(*v*) *Aṇuratnapradīpa*[10] Ms. in Bhāratīya Vidyā Bhavan, Bombay.

The introductory portion of this book, noticed by Prof. Hiralal in the *Jaina-siddhānta-bhāskara*, VI ; pp. 160 ff. forms the basis of our account of the Chauhāns of Rāyabaddiya. Its writer Lakkana was a contemporary of the Chauhān ruler, Āhavamalla.

(*vi*) *Bāhubalicharita of Dhanapāla, Praśastisaṅgraha*, Digambara Atiśaya Kṣetra Śrī Mahāvīraji, Jaipur, pp. 188 ff. It carries the genealogy up to Ramachanda. For further details see the account of these Chauhāns in the text. The *Praśasti* in this book supplies some additional details about the Chauhāns of Chandwār.

(*vii*) Colophons of the manuscripts of the

Nirbhayabhīmavyāyoga

Āvaśyakaniryukti

Dharmaghoṣa-sūri stuti of Raviprabha Sūri

Śatakabṛhadbhāṣya of Chakreśvara Sūri

Āgamikavastuvichārasāravivaraṇa of Yaśobhadra Sūri also contain valuable historical material.[11]

Puṇyāsravakathā of Raidhū.

10. For the *Aṇuratnapradīpa* see also my paper "Chandavāra and Rāyabaddiya" published in the *Jaina-siddhānta-bhāskara*, Vol. VII, pp. 9 ff.

11. For the colophons see the *Catalogue of the Palm leaf Manuscripts in the Paṭṭan Bhaṇḍārs* (G.O.S.) and Dr. Peterson's *First Report*.

10. *Anti-Chauhan Sources*

(*i*) *Ālhākhaṇḍa.*

It deals with the exploits of the Banāfara heroes, Ālhā and Ūdal, who are depicted as *sāmantas* of Pṛthvīrāja III's rival, Paramāla, the Chandella ruler of Mahobā. Though useful as a repository of Bundela tradition it has become so far intermixed with fiction that its historical value is not great.

(*ii*) *Paramāla Rāso, NPS, Banaras.*

The book has been published by the Nāgarī Prachāriṇī Sabhā. It is a very late composition and practically useless for historical purposes.

(*iii*) *Dvyāśrayamahākāvya of Hemachandra*, Bombay, 1915.

The *kāvya* is a good source-book of Chaulukya history, and has naturally a good deal to say about the Chauhāns, some of whom were rivals of the Chaulukyas, and the others their feudatories.

(*iv*) *Kumārapālacharita of Hemachandra*, Poona, 1936.

This is a Prakrit continuation of the above book and deals with Kumārapāla Chaulukya. Arṇorāja of Śākambharī fought against him.

(*v*) An old *Kumārapālacharita* (V. 1385).

(*vi*) Somatilaka's *Kumārapāladevacharita* (V. 1422).

(*vii*) *Kumārapālapratibodhaprabandha* (V. 1495).

[(*v*)–(*vii*): Singhi Jaina Granthamālā No. 21]

(*viii*) *Kumārapālacharita* of Jayasiṁha Sūri (c. V. 1425), Bombay, 1926.

(*ix*) *Kumārapālaprabandha* of Jinamaṇḍana (V. 1492), Jāmnagar.

(*x*) *Kumārapālacharita* of Charitrasundara, *JASS*, 1917.

These lives of Kumārapāla have been used in the account of Arṇorāja and Vigraharāja IV. The first two are specially useful and much more reliable than the others.

(*xi*) *Hammīramadamardana of Jayasiṁha Sūri*, G.O.S. 1920.

This is an account of the repulse of the forces of the *Hammīra* Mīlachchhrīkāra (probably Iltutmish) by the forces of Vīradhavala Vāghela, aided by Udayasiṁha of Jālor and his allies. It is useful as a contemporary account.

(*xii*) *Pārthaparākrama* of Prahlādanadeva, G.O.S., 1917.

This drama was written by Prahlādanadeva, a younger brother of Dhāravarṣa of Ābū, who was a contemporary of Pṛthvīrāja III. Its introductory verse refers to the repulse of a night attack of Pṛthvīrāja III.

(*xiii*) *Kīrtikaumudī* of Someśvara, Bombay, 1883.

(*xiv*) *Surathotsava* of Someśvara, Bombay, 1902.

(*xv*) *Vasantavilāsa* of Bālachandra Sūri, G.O.S., 1917.

(*xvi*) *Vastupāla-Tejaḥpāla-praśasti* of Jayasiṁhạ Sūri, Appendix I to xi.

(*xvii*) *Sukṛtakīrtikallolinī* of Udayaprabha Sūri, Appendix II to xi.

xiii-xvii deal with the life of Vastupāla and history of Gujarāt. They have been found useful for the history of the Chauhāns of Bhṛgukachchha and the Chauhān ruler, Udayasiṁha of Jālor. They contain also some more material on Chauhān history.

(*xviii*) *Prabhāvakacharita* of Prabhāchandra (V. 1334), Nirṇayasagar edition, Bombay, 1909. A much better edition has been published in the SJG.

The book has a good account of Kumārapāla's campaigns into Sapādalakṣa.

(*xix*) *Prabandhachintāmaṇi* of Merutuṅga (V.1361), SJG. 1933.

This well known source-book of the history of Gujarāt supplies important details about Vigraharāja II, Arṇorāja, Pṛthvīrāja III and Śaṅkha of Bhṛgukachchha.

(*xx*) *Prabandhakośa* of Rājaśekhara (V. 1405), SJG, 1935.

Equally valuable is this Gujarāt chronicle for Kelhaṇa of Nāḍol, Udayasiṁha of Jālor, the Jaina minister Yaśovīra, Pṛthvīrāja III, Arṇorāja and Śaṅkha.

At the end of some of its *MSS* is a good genealogy of the Chauhān rulers of Sāmbhar and Raṇthambhor. One manuscript carries it up only to the reign of Jaitrasiṁha in whose reign it may therefore be assumed to have been first written. The name of Hammīra is a later addition.

(*xxi*) *Purātanaprabandhasaṅgraha*, SJG, 1936.

The *MS* on which it is largely based was copied in V. 1528. Some portions of it, however, are believed to have been compiled as early as V. 1290 (See Muni Jinavijaya's introduction to the book in the Singhī Jainagranthamālā). The *prabandhas* dealing with Pṛthvīrāja III, Lākhā of Nāḍol, Yaśovīra and Vastupāla have been utilized here.

(*xxii*) *Śaṅkha-parābhava-vyāyoga* of the Gauḍa poet Harihara.

It is a one-act play commemorating Vastupāla's victory over *Śaṅkha*, the Chauhān *maṇḍaleśvara* of Broach, and was noticed by Dr. B.J. Sandesara in the *Journal of* the Oriental *Institute*, Baroda, Vol. VII, pp. 270 ff. It has now been published.

(*xxiii*) *Lekhapaddhati*, G. O. S., 1925.

Last among the pro-Chaulukya sources, which should accurately speaking not be classed as anti-Chauhān, comes the *Lekhapaddhati*, a "compilation of models of Government documents and specimens of official and other correspondence." It throws useful light on the administrative system and life in Western Mārwār.

11. *Apabhraṁśakāvyatrayī* (G.O.S.), 1927.

This is a collection of three important works of Jinadatta Sūri, a contemporary of Arṇorāja. They give a very good exposition of the *vidhichaitya* movement.

12. *Gaṇakārikā*, G.O.S., 1921.

This is one of the oldest accounts of the *Pāśupata* system. It has been used in the chapter on Religion.

13. *Gaṇitasārā* of Śrīdhara and its Gujarati commentry.

This work brought to the notice of students of Indian numismatics by Dr. B. J. Sandesara (JNS I, VIII, pp. 141 ff) gives very useful information about the coins and weights of Western India.

14. *Works of Thakkura Pheru*

(*i*) *Yugapradhāna-chatuṣpadikā*, *MS* with Sri Agarchand Nahta.

(*ii*) *Ratnaparīkṣā*, Appendix to 14(*iii*).

(*iii*) *Vāstusāra*, edited by P. Bhagwān Das, Jaipur.

(*iv*) *Gaṇitasāra -kaumudī*, *MS* with Sri Agarchand Nahta.

(*iv*) *Dravyaparīkṣā*, *MS* with Sri Agarchand Nahta.

All these works of Pheru are highly useful, specially for the cultural portion of Chauhān history. They have now been published in the Rājasthān Purātan Granthamālā.

15. *Skanda Purāṇa.*

The Prabhāsa and Arbuda Books of this *Purāṇa* look like the composition of a resident of west India, and can, under certain limits, be used for an account of western Indian culture. Our references to it are confined to a few minor points.

16. *Muslim histories etc.*

Tāju-l Ma-āsir of Hasan Nizāmī. *ED.* II, pp.204-24.

This is a contemporary account of the years 1193-1217 A.D. It is our best source for the last years of Pṛthvīrāja III, Harirāja's attempt to revive Chauhān power, and Iltutmish's attack on Udayasiṁha.

Tārikh-i-Fakhruddīn Mubārakshāhī, Edited by E.D. Ross, London, 1927.

It is another summary but reliable and dated account of the victories of Qutbuddīn and Muhammad Ghorī. It was written in 1440, A.D.

Jami-ul-Hikāyāt of Muhammad Ūfī, *ED.* II, pp. 200 ff.

This was compiled about 1211 A.D. It gives a fairly reasonable account of Muhammad Ghori's tactics in the second battle of Tarāīn.

Tārikh-i-Wassāf

It gives a realistic account of the plight of Mālwā in the years just preceding its invasion by Alāuddīn.

Tārikh-i-Nāsirī of Minhāj-ud-dīn b. Sirāj-ud-dīn, English translation by H. G. Raverty, BI, Calcutta, 1880.

It is one of the best Muslim histories for the period up to 1260 A.D., the year in which it was completed.

Khazāin-ul-Futūh, English translation by Prof. M. Habib, Bombay, 1931. Some errors in the translation have been noted in.

Ghurratu-l Kamal *E.D. III.*

Āsikā *Ibid.*

Nuh Siphir *Ibid.*

Of these four books of Amīr Khusrau, the first, translated into English by Prof. Muhammad Habīb, has been found extremely useful for Alāuddīn's campaigns against the Chauhāns. *Nuh Siphir* can be used for cultural history. The other two (the translations of certain extracts from which have been published in the *ED.*) supplement the *Khazāinu-l Futūh* on some points.

Tārikh-i-Firuzshāhī of Baranī, *E.D.* III, 93-268.

It continues the account of the *Tabakāt-i-Nāsirī.* I have not always found him a reliable writer.

Shāhnhmā-i-Hind of Isāmī edited by Mahdi Husain Agra, 1938.

Tabakāt-i-Akbarī of Nizāmuddīn Ahmad, English translation by B. De, Calcutta, 1913-1940.

Though written as late as the reign of Akbar it gives some important details about the neo-Muslim mutiny near Jālor.

Tārikh-i-Firishta, English translation by J. Briggs, Calcutta, 1911.

It was presented to the Sultān of Bijapur in 1606 A.D. It is on certain points fuller than our earlier Muslim histories noticed above and agrees at places with Hindu sources, the *Hammīramahākāvya* and others. Some of the authorities referred to by him are now unavailable.

Āin-i-Akbarī, of Abul Fazl, English translation, BI, 1st edition.

The book gives a short and inaccurate account of the Chauhāns and Tomaras. Its geographical and statistical information has been found of great value.

Alberunī's India, English translation by E. Sachau, London. We have given in an Appendix the list of fasts and festivals from it.

References to some other Muslim sources will be found in the footnotes of the Book.

17. *Modern Works*

Of modern books and articles the following deserve being specially mentioned:—

Dashratha Sharma (Ed.)[11a] *Rājasthān through the Ages*, Vol.I.
D.R. Bhandarkar—*History of the Marwar Chāhamānas*, EI, XI, 67 ff.

,, ,, ,, — *Lectures on Ancient Indian Numismatics*

,, ,, ,, — Foreign Elements in India Population, IA, XLI, pp. 66.

F. Kielhorn — The Chāhamanas of Naddula (EI, IX).

Dr.H. C. Ray — *The Dynastic History of Northern India*, Vols, I and II, Calcutta, 1931, 1936.

H. B. Sarda — *Speeches and writings*, Ajmer, 1935.

,, ,, ,, — *Hammīra of Raṇthambhor*, Ajmer.

G. K. Forbes — *Rāsamālā*, Oxford, 1924.

V.A. Smith — *Early History of India*, 4*th* Edition, Oxford, 1924.

Dr. R. S. Tripathi — *History of Kanauj*, Banaras 1937.

Dr. R. C. Majumdar (Editor) — *History of Bengal*, Vol. I, Dacca University, 1943.

W.H. Moreland — *India at the death of Akbar*, London, 1920.

Dr. D. C. Ganguly — *History of the Paramāras*, Dacca, 1933.

11a. Practically the entire book is the work of Dr. Dasharatha Sharma. Published by the Government of Rājasthan.

Dr. G. H. Ojha — *History of Rājpūtānā*, Vol. I, Ajmer 1933.

„ „ „ — *History of Udaipur*, Vol. I, Ajmer 1928.

„ „ „ — *History of Jodhpur*, Vol. I, Ajmer, 1938.

„ „ „ — *History of Bīkāner*, Vol. I, Ajmer, 1939.

„ „ „ — *History of Sirohī*, Ajmer, 1911.

„ „ „ — *Madhyakālīna Bhāratīya Saṁskṛti*, Allahabad, 1928.

Dr. P. V. Kane — *History of Dharmaśāstra Literature*, Vols. I, II, and III, Poona.

Dr. G. H. Mees — *Dharma and society*.

R. G. Bhandarkar — *Vaiṣṇavism, Śaivism and minor religious systems*, Poona, 1928.

M.D. Desai — *Jaina sāhitya no saṁkṣipta itihāsa*, Bombay, 1933.

Dalal and Gandhi — *Catalogue of MSS at Pattan*, Vol. I (G. O. S.).

„ „ „ — *Catalogue of MSS at Jaisalmer* (G.O.S.), 1923.

Dr. A. S. Altekar — *The Rāṣṭrakūṭas and their Times*, Poona, 1934.

J. Tod — *Annals and Antiquities of Rajasthan*, O.U.P. 1920.

Elliot and Dowson — *The History of India as told by its own Historians*, Vols. I, II, and III, London, 1866-77.

E. Thomas — *The Chronicles of the Pathan Kings of Delhi*, London, 1871.

Dr. U. N. Ghoshal — *Hindu Revenue System*.

Sir W. Haig (Editor) — *Cambridge History af India*, Vol. III, Cambridge, 1928.

Dr. Mohammed Nazim — The Life and Times of *Sultān Mahmūd of Ghazna*, Cambridge, 1931.

Habibullah, A.B.H. — Foundation of Muslim Rule in India, Lahore, 1945.[12]

Dasharatha Sharma — *Lectures on Rājput History and Culture.*

18. *Periodicals.*

Of journals, besides those already mentioned in Section 1, I have found the following very useful:—

1. *Rājasthāna Bhāratī*, Bikaner.
2. *Rājasthānī*, Bikaner.
3. *Marubhāratī*, Pilāni.
4. *Śodhapatrikā*, Udaipur.
5. *Journal of the Numismatic Society of India.*
6. *Indian Historical Quarterly.*
7. *Journal of Indian History.*
8. *Varadā*, Gāngiāsar, Rājasthān.
9. *Varadā*, Bisaū, Rājasthān.
10. Rājasthānī, Calcutta.
11. *Nāgarī-Prachāriṇī-patrikā*, Banaras.
12. *Viśvambharā*, Bikaner.

12. The bibliography was compiled before 1950. But wherever any new publication has been utilised, it has been mentioned in the relevant footnote.

INDEX

* Words marked with an asterisk are to be found in footnotes.

N

O

P

Q

R

T

U

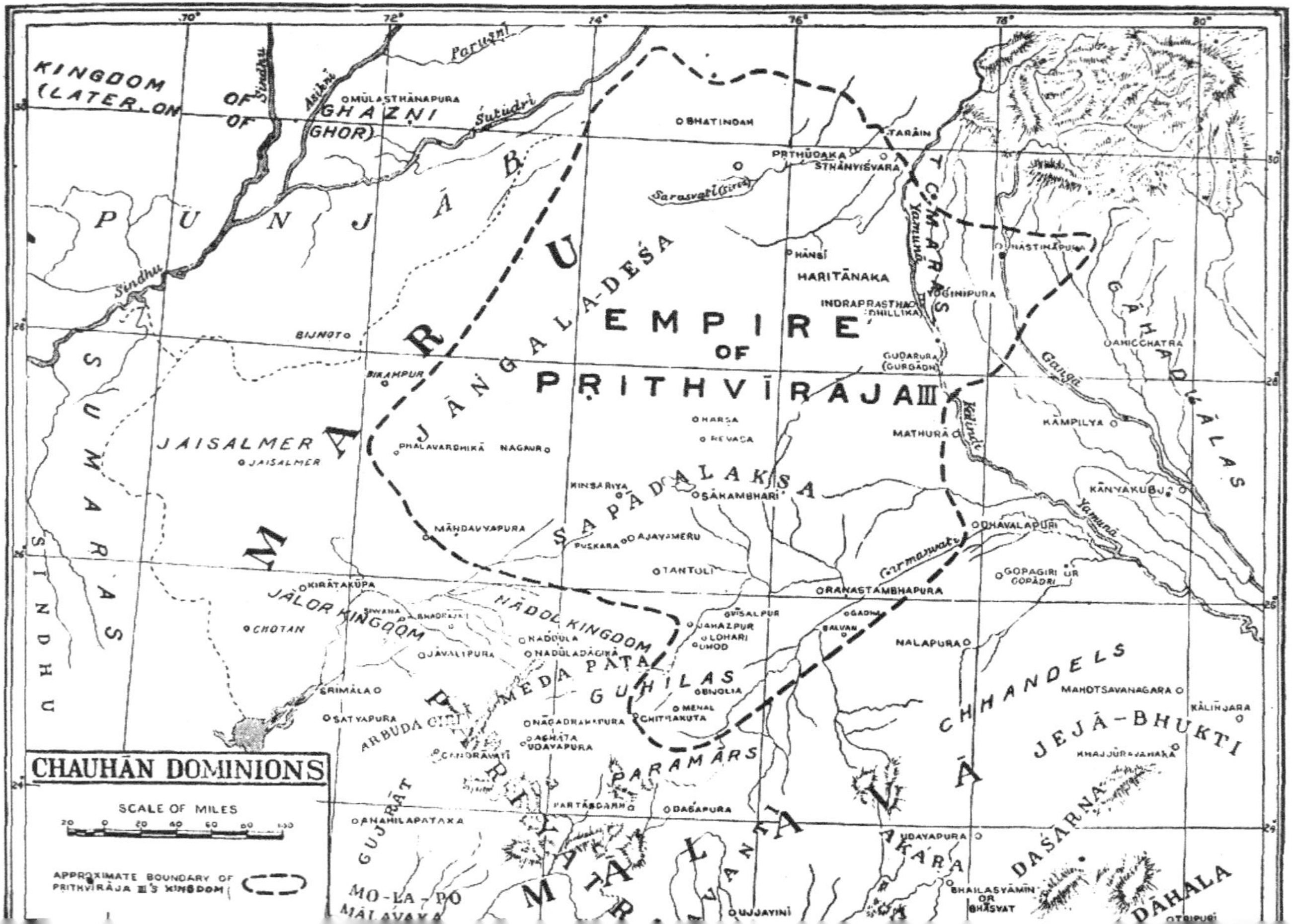
CHAUHĀN DOMINIONS
SCALE OF MILES
APPROXIMATE BOUNDARY OF PRITHVIRĀJA III'S KINGDOM
EMPIRE OF PRITHVĪRĀJA III
KINGDOM (LATER ON OF GHOR) OF GHAZNI
PUNJĀB
MARU
JĀNGALA-DEŚA
SAPĀDALAKṢA
TOMARAS
GĀHAḌAVĀLAS
CHHANDELS
JEJĀ-BHUKTI
DAŚĀRNA
DĀHALA
GUHILAS
MEDAPĀṬA
PARAMĀRS
NĀDOL KINGDOM
JĀLOR KINGDOM
SUMARAS
SINDHU
JAISALMER
GUJRĀT
MO-LA-PO MĀLAVAKA
ĀKARA
AVANTĪ
MĀLAVĀ
Sindhu
Asiknī
Paruṣṇī
Śutudri
Sarasvatī (Sirsa)
Yamunā
Gaṅgā
Kālindī
Carmaṇvatī
Mūlasthānapura
Bhatinda
Tarāin
Pṛthūdaka
Sthānvīśvara
Hānsī
Haritānaka
Indraprastha
Dhillikā
Yoginipura
Hastināpura
Ahicchatra
Gudārura (Gurgāon)
Mathurā
Kāmpilya
Kānyakubja
Dhavalapurī
Gopagiri or Gopādri
Raṇastambhapura
Nalapura
Mahotsavanagara
Kāliñjara
Khajjūravāhaka
Bijnot
Bikampur
Phalavardhikā
Nagaur
Jaisalmer
Harsa
Revāsa
Kinsariya
Śākambharī
Maṇḍavyapura
Puṣkara
Ajayameru
Tantoli
Kirātakūpa
Chotan
Siwana
Bhadrājūn
Nāḍūla
Nāḍūlaḍāgikā
Jāvālipura
Bisalpur
Jahazpur
Lohari
Uhod
Gadh
Balvan
Bijholia
Menal
Chitrakuta
Śrīmāla
Satyapura
Arbuda Giri
Nāgadrahapura
Āghāṭa
Udayapura
Candrāvatī
Partābgarh
Daśapura
Aṇahilapāṭaka
Udayapura
Bhailasvāmin or Bhāsvat
Ujjayinī
Tripurī